Working with
25
YEARS
Cambridge International Examinations

Cambridge IGCSE®

Combined and Co-ordinated
Sciences

Tom Duncan
Bryan Earl
Dave Hayward
Heather Kennett
D G Mackean
Doug Wilford

HODDER
EDUCATION
AN HACHETTE UK COMPANY

Unless otherwise acknowledged, the questions and answers that appear in this book were written by the authors. This text has not been through the Cambridge endorsement process.

® IGCSE is the registered trademark of Cambridge International Examinations.

Questions taken from Cambridge IGCSE past examination papers and the learning objectives taken from the 2019 0653 and 0654 syllabuses are reproduced by permission of Cambridge International Examinations.

Although every effort has been made to ensure that website addresses are correct at time of going to press, Hodder Education cannot be held responsible for the content of any website mentioned in this book. It is sometimes possible to find a relocated web page by typing in the address of the home page for a website in the URL window of your browser.

Hachette UK's policy is to use papers that are natural, renewable and recyclable products and made from wood grown in sustainable forests. The logging and manufacturing processes are expected to conform to the environmental regulations of the country of origin.

Orders: please contact Bookpoint Ltd, 130 Park Drive, Milton Park, Abingdon, Oxon OX14 4SE. Telephone: (44) 01235 827720. Fax: (44) 01235 400454. Email education@bookpoint.co.uk Lines are open from 9 a.m. to 5 p.m., Monday to Saturday, with a 24-hour message answering service. You can also order through our website: www.hoddereducation.com

ISBN: 9781510402461

© Tom Duncan, Bryan Earl, Dave Hayward, Heather Kennett, D G Mackean, Doug Wilford 2017

First published in 2017 by

Hodder Education,
An Hachette UK Company
Carmelite House
50 Victoria Embankment
London EC4Y 0DZ

www.hoddereducation.com

Impression number   10 9 8 7 6 5 4 3 2 1

Year   2020 2019 2018 2017

Cover photo © Life on white/Alamy Stock Photo

Illustrations by DG Mackean, Ethan Danielson, Richard Draper, Mike Humphries, Chris Etheridge, Fakenham Prepress Solutions, Wearset Ltd and Integra Software Services Pvt. Ltd

Typeset in ITC Galliard Std Roman 11/13 by Integra Software Services Pvt. Ltd., Pondicherry, India

Printed in Slovenia

A catalogue record for this title is available from the British Library.

Contents

Physics

Introduction

This textbook provides up-to-date and comprehensive coverage of the Core and Supplement/Extended curriculum for the current Cambridge International Examinations IGCSE® Combined Science 0653 and Co-ordinated Sciences (Double award) 0654 syllabuses. Your teacher will tell you which syllabus you are following, and whether you are studying the Core or Supplement/Extended curriculum.

The textbook is divided into three sections: Biology (chapters B1 to B13), Chemistry (chapters C1 to C14) and Physics (chapters P1 to P8). The chapters align with the order of the syllabuses:

Textbook chapter	Combined Science 0653 syllabus	Co-ordinated Sciences 0654 syllabus
B1 Characteristics of living organisms	B1 Characteristics of living organisms	B1 Characteristics of living organisms
B2 Cells	B2 Cells	B2 Cells
B3 Biological molecules	B3 Biological molecules	B3 Biological molecules
B4 Enzymes	B4 Enzymes	B4 Enzymes
B5 Plant nutrition	B5 Plant nutrition	B5 Plant nutrition
B6 Animal nutrition	B6 Animal nutrition	B6 Animal nutrition
B7 Transport	B7 Transport	B7 Transport
B8 Gas exchange and respiration	B8 Gas exchange and respiration	B8 Gas exchange and respiration
B9 Co-ordination and response	B9 Co-ordination and response	B9 Co-ordination and response
B10 Reproduction	B10 Reproduction	B10 Reproduction
B11 Inheritance		B11 Inheritance
B12 Organisms and their environment	B11 Organisms and their environment	B12 Organisms and their environment
B13 Human influences on ecosystems	B12 Human influences on ecosystems	B13 Human influences on ecosystems
C1 The particulate nature of matter	C1 The particulate nature of matter	C1 The particulate nature of matter
C2 Experimental techniques	C2 Experimental techniques	C2 Experimental techniques
C3 Atoms, elements and compounds	C3 Atoms, elements and compounds	C3 Atoms, elements and compounds
C4 Stoichiometry	C4 Stoichiometry	C4 Stoichiometry
C5 Electricity and chemistry	C5 Electricity and chemistry	C5 Electricity and chemistry
C6 Energy changes in chemical reactions	C6 Energy changes in chemical reactions	C6 Energy changes in chemical reactions
C7 Chemical reactions	C7 Chemical reactions	C7 Chemical reactions
C8 Acids, bases and salts	C8 Acids, bases and salts	C8 Acids, bases and salts
C9 The Periodic Table	C9 The Periodic Table	C9 The Periodic Table
C10 Metals	C10 Metals	C10 Metals
C11 Air and water	C11 Air and water	C11 Air and water
C12 Sulfur		C12 Sulfur
C13 Carbonates		C13 Carbonates
C14 Organic chemistry	C12 Organic chemistry	C14 Organic chemistry
P1 Motion	P1 Motion	P1 Motion
P2 Work, energy and power	P2 Work, energy and power	P2 Work, energy and power
P3 Thermal physics	P3 Thermal physics	P3 Thermal physics
P4 Properties of waves	P4 Properties of waves, including light and sound	P4 Properties of waves, including light and sound
P5 Electrical quantities, electricity and magnetism	P5 Electrical quantities, electricity and magnetism	P5 Electrical quantities, electricity and magnetism
P6 Electric circuits	P6 Electric circuits	P6 Electric circuits
P7 Electromagnetic effects		P7 Electromagnetic effects
P8 Atomic physics		P8 Atomic physics

How to use this book

Each chapter starts with the syllabus statements to be covered in that chapter:

B4 Enzymes

Combined	Co-ordinated
• Define *enzyme*	• Define *enzyme*
• Explain enzyme action with reference to the complementary shape of the active site of an enzyme and its substrate and the formation of a product	• Explain enzyme action with reference to the complementary shape of the active site of an enzyme and its substrate and the formation of a product
• Investigate and describe the effect of changes in temperature and pH on enzyme activity	• Investigate and describe the effect of changes in temperature and pH on enzyme activity
• Explain the effect of changes in temperature on enzyme activity, in terms of kinetic energy, shape and fit, frequency of effective collisions and denaturation	• Explain the effect of changes in temperature on enzyme activity, in terms of kinetic energy, shape and fit, frequency of effective collisions and denaturation
• Explain the effect of changes in pH on enzyme activity in terms of shape and fit and denaturation	• Explain the effect of changes in pH on enzyme activity in terms of shape and fit and denaturation

The syllabus statements are given in two lists: Combined Science (no blue bar) and Co-ordinated Sciences (blue bar). Syllabus statements highlighted in green are for the Supplement/Extended curriculum; those with no green shading are for the Core curriculum. Check with your teacher which syllabus you are studying.

This table shows which sections of the book you should study for your syllabus:

Combined Science (0653)		Co-ordinated Sciences (0654)	
Core	Supplement/Extended	Core	Supplement/Extended
Study sections with:	*Study sections with:*	*Study sections with:*	*Study sections with:*
No blue bar and no green shading	No blue bar and no green shading	No blue bar and no green shading	No blue bar and no green shading
	plus	*plus*	*plus*
	No blue bar with green shading	No blue bar with green shading	No blue bar with green shading
		plus	*plus*
		▌Blue bar and no green shading	▌Blue bar and no green shading
			plus
			▌Blue bar with green shading
			(This is all the material in the book)

To help you here are some examples from the book.

Students following the Combined Science Core syllabus should study sections with no blue bar at the side and no green shading:

> When substances such as hydrogen and magnesium combine with oxygen in this way they are said to have been **oxidised**. The process is known as **oxidation**.
>
> **Reduction** is the opposite of oxidation. In this process oxygen is removed instead of being added.

Students following the Combined Science Supplement/Extended syllabus should study sections with no blue bar at the side, both with and without green shading:

When substances such as hydrogen and magnesium combine with oxygen in this way they are said to have been **oxidised**. The process is known as **oxidation**.
  Reduction is the opposite of oxidation. In this process oxygen is removed instead of being added.

A **redox** reaction is one which involves the two processes of reduction and oxidation. For example, the oxygen has to be removed in the extraction of iron from iron(III) oxide. This can be done in a blast

Students following the Co-ordinated Sciences Core syllabus should study sections with no blue bar at the side, both with and without green shading, as well as sections with a blue bar and no green shading:

When substances such as hydrogen and magnesium combine with oxygen in this way they are said to have been **oxidised**. The process is known as **oxidation**.
  Reduction is the opposite of oxidation. In this process oxygen is removed instead of being added.

A **redox** reaction is one which involves the two processes of reduction and oxidation. For example, the oxygen has to be removed in the extraction of iron from iron(III) oxide. This can be done in a blast

Plotting compasses placed on the card settle along the field lines and show the direction of the field at different points.

Students following the Co-ordinated Sciences Supplement/Extended syllabus should study sections with no blue bar at the side, both with and without green shading, as well as sections with a blue bar both with and without green shading:

When substances such as hydrogen and magnesium combine with oxygen in this way they are said to have been **oxidised**. The process is known as **oxidation**.
  Reduction is the opposite of oxidation. In this process oxygen is removed instead of being added.

A **redox** reaction is one which involves the two processes of reduction and oxidation. For example, the oxygen has to be removed in the extraction of iron from iron(III) oxide. This can be done in a blast

Plotting compasses placed on the card settle along the field lines and show the direction of the field at different points.

When the current direction is reversed, the compasses point in the opposite direction showing that the direction of the field reverses when the current reverses.

To help draw attention to the more important scientific words, they are printed in **bold** the first time they are used:

> ● Substances that do not conduct electricity when in the molten state or in solution are called **non-electrolytes**.

Science is an experimental subject, and you are encouraged to develop your practical skills. This will enable you to achieve the following objectives. You should be able to:

1 know how to safely use techniques, apparatus and materials (including following a sequence of instructions where appropriate)
2 plan experiments and investigations
3 make and record observations, measurements and estimates
4 interpret and evaluate experimental observations and data
5 evaluate methods and suggest possible improvement.

Ideas for practical work are given in the text to help you with this aspect of the course. For biology and physics these are within the subject sections; for chemistry these appear after the section on hazard warning symbols.
 Practical work with no blue bar and no green shading is for students following the Combined Core syllabus:

Practical work

Food tests

1 Test for starch

■ Shake a little starch powder in a test-tube with some warm water to make a suspension.
■ Add 3 or 4 drops of **iodine solution**. A dark blue colour should be produced.

Students following the Combined Supplement/Extended syllabus should also study Practical work with no blue bar and green shading:

Practical work

The importance of different mineral elements

■ Place wheat seedlings in test-tubes containing water cultures as shown in Figure B5.23.
■ Cover the tubes with aluminium foil to keep out light and so stop green algae from growing in the solution.
■ Some of the solutions have one of the elements missing.
■ Leave the seedlings to grow in these solutions for a few weeks, keeping the tubes topped up with distilled water.

Students following the Co-ordinated Core syllabus should study the Practical work with no bar and the Practical work with a blue bar and no shading:

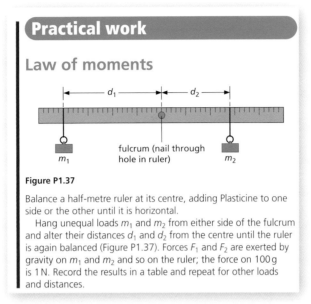

Practical work

Law of moments

Figure P1.37

Balance a half-metre ruler at its centre, adding Plasticine to one side or the other until it is horizontal.

Hang unequal loads m_1 and m_2 from either side of the fulcrum and alter their distances d_1 and d_2 from the centre until the ruler is again balanced (Figure P1.37). Forces F_1 and F_2 are exerted by gravity on m_1 and m_2 and so on the ruler; the force on 100 g is 1 N. Record the results in a table and repeat for other loads and distances.

Students following the Co-ordinated Supplement/Extended syllabus should study the Practical work with no bar and the Practical work with a blue bar with and without the green shading:

Practical work

Critical angle of glass

Place a semicircular glass block on a sheet of paper (Figure P4.23), and draw the outline LOMN where O is the centre and ON the normal at O to LOM. Direct a narrow ray (at an angle of about 30° to the normal ON) along a radius towards O. The ray is not refracted at the curved surface. Why? Note the refracted ray emerging from LOM into the air and also the weak internally reflected ray in the glass.

Slowly rotate the paper so that the angle of incidence on LOM increases until total internal reflection *just* occurs. Mark the incident ray. Measure the angle of incidence; this is the critical angle.

In the suggested practical activities, materials are used which, although familiar in many cases, are of a potentially hazardous nature. To keep you safe you must:
- follow the instructions given to you by your teacher
- wear eye protection at all times
- wear disposable gloves in certain cases when requested to do so
- work tidily at all times
- check the hazard labels of any of the substances you are using and then take appropriate care and precautions.

Questions are included to test that you have understood what you have read.

Questions for Combined Science have no blue bar; those for Supplement/Extended curriculum are highlighted in green:

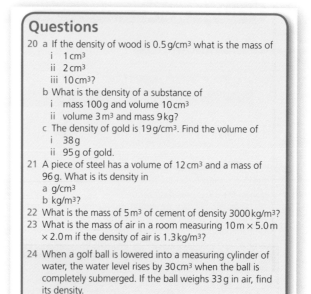

Questions

20 a If the density of wood is 0.5 g/cm³ what is the mass of
   i 1 cm³
   ii 2 cm³
   iii 10 cm³?
 b What is the density of a substance of
   i mass 100 g and volume 10 cm³
   ii volume 3 m³ and mass 9 kg?
 c The density of gold is 19 g/cm³. Find the volume of
   i 38 g
   ii 95 g of gold.
21 A piece of steel has a volume of 12 cm³ and a mass of 96 g. What is its density in
 a g/cm³
 b kg/m³?
22 What is the mass of 5 m³ of cement of density 3000 kg/m³?
23 What is the mass of air in a room measuring 10 m × 5.0 m × 2.0 m if the density of air is 1.3 kg/m³?

24 When a golf ball is lowered into a measuring cylinder of water, the water level rises by 30 cm³ when the ball is completely submerged. If the ball weighs 33 g in air, find its density.

Questions for Co-ordinated Sciences have a blue bar at the side; those for Supplement/Extended curriculum are highlighted in green:

Questions

8 Calcium oxide is a base. It combines with solid, acidic oxides in the basic oxygen furnace.
Write a chemical equation for one of these oxides reacting with the added lime.

9 'Many metals are more useful to us when mixed with some other elements.' Discuss this statement with respect to stainless steel.

If you cannot answer the question straightaway, read that section of the text again with the question in mind. Try to answer as many of the questions as you can, because asking and answering questions is at the heart of your study of science.

At the end of the book there are questions from past examination papers, so that you can practise answering these before you sit your examination.

Each chapter ends with a checklist, summarising the important points covered in that chapter:

Checklist

After studying Chapter B4 you should know and understand the following.

- Enzymes are proteins that function as biological catalysts.
- Enzyme activity is affected by pH and temperature.

- Enzymes are important in all organisms because they maintain a reaction speed needed to sustain life.
- The substance on which an enzyme acts is called the substrate. After the reaction, a product is formed.
- An enzyme and its substrate have complementary shapes.
- Enzymes are affected by pH and temperature and are denatured above 50 °C.
- Different enzymes may accelerate reactions which build up or break down molecules.

- Each enzyme acts on only one substance (breaking down), or a pair of substances (building up).
- Enzymes tend to be very specific in the reactions they catalyse, due to the complementary shape of the enzyme and its substrate.
- Changes in temperature affect the kinetic energy of enzyme molecules and their shape.
- Enzymes can be denatured by changes in temperature and pH.

Points relevant to the Co-ordinated Sciences syllabus have a blue bar at the side:

Checklist

After studying Chapter C11 you should know and understand the following.

- Acid rain is rainwater which has a pH in the range 3 to 4.8.
- Artificial fertiliser is a substance added to soil to increase the amount of elements such as nitrogen, potassium and phosphorus. This enables crops grown in the soil to grow more healthily and to produce higher yields.
- Atmosphere (air) is the mixture of gases that surrounds the Earth.
- Bulk chemicals are chemicals that, because of their large usage across a range of uses, are produced in large quantities.
- Carbon dioxide is a colourless, odourless gas, soluble in water, producing a weak acid called carbonic acid. It makes up 0.04% of air. It is produced by respiration in all living things and by the burning of fossil fuels. It is taken in by plants in photosynthesis.
- Catalyst is a substance which alters the rate of a chemical reaction without itself being chemically changed.
- Catalytic converter is a device for converting dangerous exhaust gases from cars into less harmful emissions. For example, carbon monoxide gas is converted to carbon dioxide gas.
- Chemical equilibrium is a dynamic state. The concentration of reactants and products remain constant. This is because the rate at which the forward reaction occurs is the same as that of the reverse reaction.
- Corrosion is the process that takes place when metals and alloys are chemically attacked by oxygen, water or any other substances found in their immediate environment.

- Flue gas desulfurisation (FGD) is the process by which sulfur dioxide gas is removed from the waste gases of power stations by passing them through calcium hydroxide slurry.
- Global warming is an average warming taking place due to the increasing presence of greenhouse gases such as carbon dioxide in the atmosphere.

- Greenhouse effect is the absorption of reflected infrared radiation from the Earth by gases in the atmosphere such as carbon dioxide (a greenhouse gas) leading to atmospheric or global warming.

- Haber process is the chemical process by which ammonia is made in very large quantities from nitrogen and hydrogen.
- Optimum temperature is a compromise temperature used in industry to ensure that the yield of product and the rate at which it is produced make the process as economical as possible.

- Photosynthesis is the chemical process by which green plants synthesise their carbon compounds from atmospheric carbon dioxide using light as the energy source and chlorophyll as the catalyst.
- Pollution is the modification of the environment caused by human influence. It often renders the environment harmful and unpleasant to life. Atmospheric pollution is caused by gases such as sulfur dioxide, carbon monoxide and nitrogen oxides being released into the atmosphere by a variety of industries and also by the burning of fossil fuels. Water pollution is caused by many substances, such as those found in fertilisers and in industrial effluent.
- Raw materials are basic materials from which a product is made. For example, the raw materials for the Haber process are nitrogen and hydrogen.

Note that green highlighting is used to identify Supplement/Extended material.
These checklists will be particularly helpful when you are revising the topic.

We hope you enjoy studying science, and using this textbook.
Bryan Earl, Dave Hayward, Heather Kennett, Doug Wilford

Biology

Chapters

Characteristics of living organisms

Combined	Co-ordinated
● Describe the characteristics of living organisms by defining the terms: *movement; respiration; sensitivity; growth; reproduction; excretion; nutrition*	● Describe the characteristics of living organisms by defining the terms: *movement; respiration; sensitivity; growth; reproduction; excretion; nutrition* ● Define the terms: *movement; respiration; sensitivity; growth; excretion; nutrition*

● Characteristics of living organisms

All living organisms, whether they are single-celled or multicellular, plants or animals, show the characteristics included in the definitions below: movement, respiration, sensitivity, growth, reproduction, excretion and nutrition.

You need to be able to list and describe the characteristics of living organisms:

- **Movement** is an action by an organism causing a change of position or place.
- **Respiration** describes the chemical reactions in cells that break down nutrient molecules and release energy.
- **Sensitivity** is the ability to detect and respond to changes in the environment.
- **Growth** is a permanent increase in size.
- **Reproduction** is the processes that make more of the same kind of organism.
- **Excretion** is the removal from organisms of toxic materials and substances in excess of requirements.
- **Nutrition** is the taking in of materials for energy, growth and development.

One way of remembering the list of the characteristics of living things is by using the mnemonic **MRS GREN**. The letters stand for the first letters of the characteristics.

Mnemonics work by helping to make the material you are learning more meaningful. They give a structure which is easier to recall later. This structure may be a word, or a name (such as MRS GREN) or a phrase. For example, 'Richard of York gave battle in vain' is a popular way of remembering the colours of the rainbow in the correct sequence.

Some of the characteristics of life are relatively easy to observe in living organisms or in photographs of them.

Figure B1.1 Cows and a bull in a field.

Question

1 Figure B1.1 shows a number of cows and a bull in a field. Which characteristics of life could be seen in the herd if they were observed over a period of time?

For the Co-ordinated Core syllabus you need to learn the list and descriptions of the characteristics of life that have already been given.

Question

2 Match each characteristic of living organisms to its description.

Characteristic	Description
excretion	the chemical reactions in cells that break down nutrient molecules and release energy
growth	a permanent increase in size
movement	the processes that make more of the same kind of organism
nutrition	taking in of materials for energy growth and development
reproduction	an action by an organism causing a change of position or place
respiration	the ability to detect and respond to changes in the environment
sensitivity	removal from organisms of toxic materials and substances in excess of requirements

Key definitions

If you are studying the extended syllabus you need to learn more detailed definitions of some of the characteristics of living things:

- **Movement** is an action by an organism or part of an organism causing a change of position or place.
- **Respiration** describes the chemical reactions in cells that break down nutrient molecules and release energy for metabolism.
- **Sensitivity** is the ability to detect or sense stimuli in the internal or external environment and to make appropriate responses.

- **Growth** is a permanent increase in size and dry mass by an increase in cell number or cell size or both.
- **Excretion** is the removal from organisms of the waste products of metabolism (chemical reactions in cells including respiration), toxic materials and substances in excess of requirements.
- **Nutrition** is the taking in of materials for energy, growth and development. Plants require light, carbon dioxide, water and ions. Animals need organic compounds and ions and usually need water.

Not all the characteristics can be observed by watching a living thing for a few minutes, as these are not likely to be visible or observable in a short time span. Some non-living things, such as cars, may appear to show some of the characteristics, but not all of them.

Questions

3 The photograph shows cars being driven along a road. Which characteristics of life do the cars appear to display?

Figure B1.2 Cars being driven along a road.

4 a Complete the crossword puzzle about the characteristics of life, using the clues to help you.
   b i Which characteristic of life is missing from the crossword puzzle?
      ii Write a crossword clue for this term.

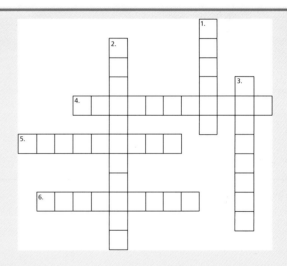

Across

4 The chemical reactions in cells that break down nutrient molecules and release energy. (11)
5 The removal from organisms of toxic materials and substances in excess of requirements. (9)
6 Taking in materials for energy, growth and development. (9)

Down

1 A permanent increase in size (6)
2 The ability to detect and respond to changes in the environment. (11)
3 An action by an organism causing a change of position or place. (8)

5 A student observed a toy train, shown below. It is powered by a solid fuel. When this burns, it heats up water, converting it to steam to turn the wheels. The light at the front of the engine switches on automatically in the dark.

The student thought that some of the processes shown by the train were similar to characteristics of life shown by living organisms.

Which characteristics of life are similar to:

a the smoke released from the chimney
b the production of heat in the boiler
c the action of the wheels
d providing the train with fuel
e the light coming on in response to darkness?

Checklist

After studying Chapter B1 you should know and understand the following.

● The seven characteristics of living things are movement, respiration, sensitivity, growth, reproduction, excretion and nutrition.
● Non-living things may appear to show some of the characteristics, but not all of them.
● You need to be able to describe each of the seven characteristics.
● You need to be able to state extended definitions of the characteristics of life.

Combined	Co-ordinated
● State that living organisms are made of cells	● State that living organisms are made of cells
● Describe and compare the structure of a plant cell with an animal cell, as seen under a light microscope, limited to cell wall, nucleus, cytoplasm, chloroplasts, vacuoles and location of the cell membrane	● Describe and compare the structure of a plant cell with an animal cell, as seen under a light microscope, limited to cell wall, nucleus, cytoplasm, chloroplasts, vacuoles and location of the cell membrane
● State the functions of the structures seen under the light microscope in the plant cell and in the animal cell	● State the functions of the structures seen under the light microscope in the plant cell and in the animal cell
● Relate the structure of the following to their functions: *ciliated cells* – movement of mucus in the trachea and bronchi; *root hair cells* – absorption; *palisade mesophyll cells* – photosynthesis; *red blood cells* – transport of oxygen; *sperm and egg cells* – reproduction	● Relate the structure of the following to their functions: *ciliated cells* – movement of mucus in the trachea and bronchi; *root hair cells* – absorption; *palisade mesophyll cells* – photosynthesis; *red blood cells* – transport of oxygen; *sperm and egg cells* – reproduction
● Calculate magnification and size of biological specimens using millimetres as units	● Calculate magnification and size of biological specimens using millimetres as units
● Define *diffusion*	● Define *diffusion*
● State that substances move into and out of cells by diffusion through the cell membrane	● Investigate the factors that influence diffusion, limited to surface area, temperature, concentration gradients and diffusion distance
● Define *osmosis*	● State that substances move into and out of cells by diffusion through the cell membrane
● State that water diffuses through partially permeable membranes by osmosis	● State that water diffuses through partially permeable membranes by osmosis
● State that water moves in and out of cells by osmosis through the cell membrane	● State that water moves in and out of cells by osmosis through the cell membrane
● Investigate and describe the effects on plant tissues of immersing them in solutions of different concentrations	● Define *osmosis*
	● Investigate and describe the effects on plant tissues of immersing them in solutions of different concentrations
	● Explain the effects on plant tissues of immersing them in solutions of different concentrations by using the terms turgid, turgor pressure, plasmolysis and flaccid
	● Explain the importance of water potential and osmosis in the uptake of water by plants
	● Explain the importance of water potential and osmosis on animal cells and tissues

● Cell structure and organisation

Cell structure

If a very thin slice of a plant stem is cut and studied under a microscope, it can be seen that the stem consists of thousands of tiny, box-like structures as in Figure B2.1 on the next page. These structures are called **cells**.

There is no such thing as a typical plant or animal cell because cells vary a great deal in their size and shape depending on their function. Nevertheless, it is possible to make a drawing like Figure B2.2 (on the next page) to show features which are present in most cells. *All cells* have a **cell membrane**, which is a thin boundary enclosing the **cytoplasm**. Most cells have a **nucleus**.

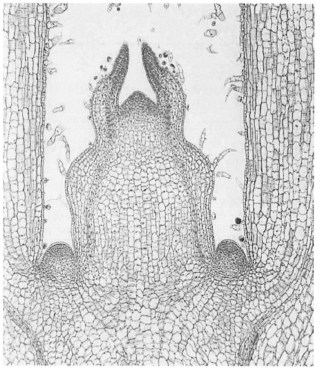

Figure B2.1 Longitudinal section through the tip of a plant shoot (×60). The slice is only one cell thick, so light can pass through it and allow the cells to be seen clearly.

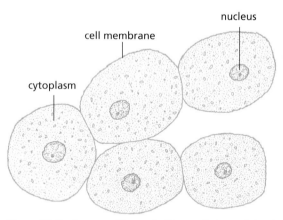

Figure B2.2 A group of liver cells. These cells have all the characteristics of animal cells.

Cytoplasm

Under the ordinary microscope (light microscope), cytoplasm looks like a thick liquid with particles in it. In plant cells it may be seen to be flowing about. The particles may be food reserves such as oil droplets or granules of starch. Other particles are structures known as **organelles**, which have particular functions in the cytoplasm. In the cytoplasm, a great many chemical reactions are taking place which keep the cell alive by providing energy and making substances that the cell needs.

The liquid part of cytoplasm is about 90% water with molecules of salts and sugars dissolved in it. Suspended in this solution there are larger molecules of fats (lipids) and proteins (see Chapter B3). Lipids and proteins may be used to build up the cell structures, such as the membranes. Some of the proteins are **enzymes** (see Chapter B4). Enzymes control the rate and type of chemical reactions which take place in the cells. Some enzymes are attached to the membrane systems of the cell, whereas others float freely in the liquid part of the cytoplasm.

Cell membrane

This is a thin layer of cytoplasm around the outside of the cell. It stops the cell contents from escaping and also controls the substances which are allowed to enter and leave the cell. In general, oxygen, food and water are allowed to enter; waste products are allowed to leave and harmful substances are kept out. In this way the cell membrane maintains the structure and chemical reactions of the cytoplasm.

Nucleus (plural: nuclei)

Most cells contain one nucleus, which is usually seen as a rounded structure enclosed in a membrane and embedded in the cytoplasm. In drawings of cells, the nucleus may be shown darker than the cytoplasm because, in prepared sections, it takes up certain stains more strongly than the cytoplasm. The function of the nucleus is to control the type and quantity of enzymes produced by the cytoplasm. In this way it regulates the chemical changes which take place in the cell. As a result, the nucleus determines what the cell will be, for example, a blood cell, a liver cell, a muscle cell or a nerve cell.

The nucleus also controls cell division. A cell without a nucleus cannot reproduce. Inside the nucleus are thread-like structures called **chromosomes**, which can be seen most easily at the time when the cell is dividing (see Chapter B11 for a fuller account of chromosomes).

Plant cells

A few generalised animal cells are represented by Figure B2.2, while Figure B2.3 on the next page, is a drawing of two palisade cells from a plant leaf. (See 'Leaf structure' in Chapter B5.)

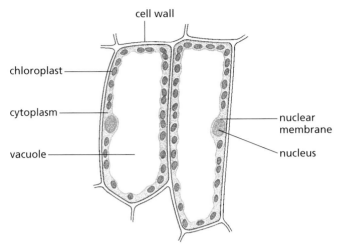

Figure B2.3 Palisade cells from a leaf.

Plant cells differ from animal cells in several ways.

1 Outside the cell membrane they all have a **cell wall** which contains cellulose and other compounds. It is non-living and allows water and dissolved substances to pass through. The cell wall is not selective like the cell membrane. (Note that plant cells *do* have a cell membrane but it is not easy to see or draw because it is pressed against the inside of the cell wall (see Figure B2.4).)

Under the microscope, plant cells are quite distinct and easy to see because of their cell walls. In Figure B2.1 it is only the cell walls (and in some cases the nuclei) which can be seen. Each plant cell has its own cell wall but the boundary between two cells side by side does not usually show up clearly. Cells next to each other therefore appear to be sharing the same cell wall.

2 Most mature plant cells have a large, fluid-filled space called a **vacuole**. The vacuole contains **cell**

sap, a watery solution of sugars, salts and sometimes pigments. This large, central vacuole pushes the cytoplasm aside so that it forms just a thin lining inside the cell wall. It is the outward pressure of the vacuole on the cytoplasm and cell wall which makes plant cells and their tissues firm (see 'Osmosis' on p.15). Animal cells may sometimes have small vacuoles in their cytoplasm but they are usually produced to do a particular job and are not permanent.

3 In the cytoplasm of plant cells are many organelles that are not present in animal cells. If they contain the green substance **chlorophyll**, the organelles are called **chloroplasts** (see Chapter B5). (Note: the term *plastid* is **not** a syllabus requirement.)

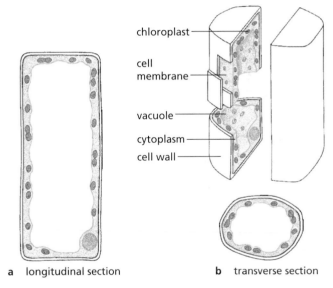

a longitudinal section b transverse section

Figure B2.4 Structure of a palisade mesophyll cell. It is important to remember that, although cells look flat in sections or in thin strips of tissue, they are in fact three-dimensional and may seem to have different shapes according to the direction in which the section is cut. If the cell is cut across it will look like **b**; if cut longitudinally it will look like **a**.

Table B2.1 Summary: the parts of a cell

	Name of part	Description	Where found	Function (supplement only)
Animal and plant cells	cytoplasm	jelly-like, with particles and organelles in	enclosed by the cell membrane	contains the cell organelles, e.g. mitochondria, nucleus site of chemical reactions
	cell membrane	a partially permeable layer that forms a boundary around the cytoplasm	around the cytoplasm	prevents cell contents from escaping controls what substances enter and leave the cell
	nucleus	a circular or oval structure containing DNA in the form of chromosomes	inside the cytoplasm	controls cell division controls cell development controls cell activities
Plant cells only	cell wall	a tough, non-living layer made of cellulose surrounding the cell membrane	around the outside of plant cells	prevents plant cells from bursting allows water and salts to pass through (freely permeable)
	vacuole	a fluid-filled space surrounded by a membrane	inside the cytoplasm of plant cells	contains salts and sugars helps to keep plant cells firm
	chloroplast	an organelle containing chlorophyll	inside the cytoplasm of some plant cells	traps light energy for photosynthesis

Practical work

Looking at cells

1 Plant cells – preparing a slide of onion epidermis cells

The onion provides a very useful source of epidermal plant tissue which is one cell thick, making it relatively easy to set up as a temporary slide. The onion is made up of fleshy leaves. On the incurve of each leaf there is an epidermal layer which can be peeled off (Figure B2.5a).

- Using forceps, peel a piece of epidermal tissue from the incurve of an onion bulb leaf.
- Place the epidermal tissue on a glass microscope slide.
- Using a scalpel, cut out a 1 cm square of tissue (discarding the rest) and arrange it in the centre of the slide.
- Add two to three drops of iodine solution. (This will stain any starch in the cells and provides a contrast between different components of the cells.)
- Using forceps, a mounted needle or a wooden splint, support a coverslip with one edge resting near to the onion tissue, at an angle of about 45° (Figure B2.5b).
- Gently lower the coverslip over the onion tissue, trying to avoid trapping any air bubbles. (Air bubbles will reflect light when viewing under the light microscope, obscuring the features you are trying to observe.)
- Leave the slide for about 5 minutes to allow the iodine stain to react with the specimen. The iodine will stain the cell nuclei pale yellow and the starch grains blue.
- Place the slide on to the microscope stage, select the lowest power objective lens and focus on the specimen. Increase the magnification using the other objective lenses. Under high power, the cells should look similar to those shown in Figure B2.6.
- Make a large drawing of **one** cell and label the following parts: cell wall, cell membrane, cytoplasm, nucleus.

An alternative tissue is rhubarb epidermis (Figure B2.5c). This can be stripped off from the surface of a stalk and treated in the same way as the onion tissue. If red epidermis from rhubarb stalk is used, you will see the red cell sap in the vacuoles.

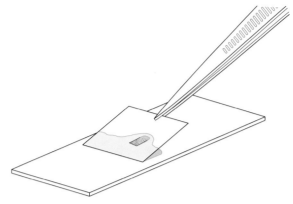

b place the epidermis on to the slide, adding 2–3 drops of iodine solution and carefully lowering a coverslip on to it

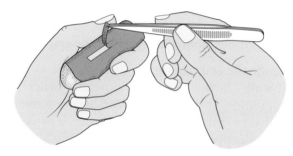

c alternatively, peel a strip of red epidermis from a piece of rhubarb skin

Figure B2.5 Looking at plant cells.

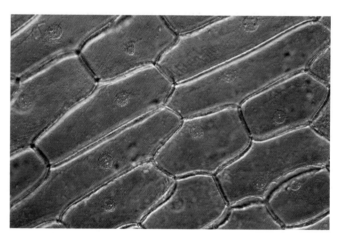

Figure B2.6 Onion epidermis cells.

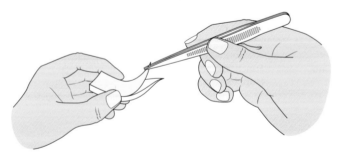

a peel the epidermis from the inside of an onion bulb leaf

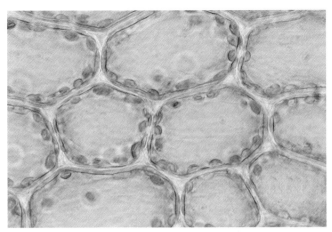

Figure B2.7 Cells in a moss leaf (×500). The vacuole occupies most of the space in each cell. The chloroplasts are confined to the layer of cytoplasm lining the cell wall.

2 Plant cells – preparing cells with chloroplasts

- Using forceps, remove a leaf from a moss plant.
- Place the leaf in the centre of a microscope slide and add one or two drops of water.
- Place a coverslip over the leaf.
- Examine the leaf cells with the high power objective of a microscope. The cells should look similar to those shown in Figure B2.7.

3 Animal cells – preparing human cheek cells

Human cheek cells are constantly being rubbed off inside the mouth as they come in contact with the tongue and food. They can therefore be collected easily for use in a temporary slide.

Note: The Department of Education and Science and, subsequently, Local Authorities, used to recommend that schools should not use the technique which involves studying the epithelial cells which appear in a smear taken from the inside of the cheek. This was because of the very small risk of transmitting the AIDS virus. However, this guidance has now changed. A document, *Safety in Science Education* (1996) by the DfEE in Britain states that official government guidance on cheek cells has been effectively reversed, indicating that the use of cotton buds is now 'permitted' together with appropriate precautions to treat contaminated items with disinfectant or by autoclaving.

- Rinse your mouth with water to remove any fragments of food.
- Take a cotton bud from a freshly opened pack. Rub the cotton bud lightly on the inside of your cheek and gums to collect some cheek cells in saliva.
- Rub the cotton bud on to the centre of a clean microscope slide, to leave a sample of saliva. Repeat if the sample is too small. Then drop the cotton bud into a container of absolute alcohol or disinfectant.
- Add two to three drops of methylene blue dye. (This will stain parts of the cheek cells to make nuclei more visible.)
- Using forceps, a mounted needle or wooden splint, support a coverslip with one edge resting near to the cheek cell sample, at an angle of about 45°. Gently lower the coverslip over the

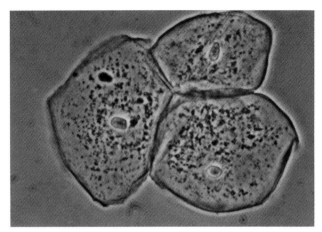

Figure B2.8 Cells from the lining epithelium of the cheek (×1500).

tissue, trying to avoid trapping any air bubbles. (Air bubbles will reflect light when viewing under the light microscope, obscuring the features you are trying to observe.)
- Leave the slide for a few minutes to allow the methylene blue stain to react with the specimen.
- Place the slide on to the microscope stage, select the lowest power objective lens and focus on the specimen. Increase the magnification using the other objective lenses. Under high power, the cells should look similar to those shown in Figure B2.8, but less magnified.
- Make a large drawing of **one** cell and label the following parts: cell membrane, cytoplasm, nucleus.
- Place your used slide in laboratory disinfectant before washing.

An alternative method of obtaining cells is to press some transparent sticky tape on to a well-washed wrist. When the tape is removed and studied under the microscope, cells with nuclei can be seen. A few drops of methylene blue solution will stain the cells and make the nuclei more distinct.

● Levels of organisation

Specialisation of cells

Most cells, when they have finished dividing and growing, become specialised. When cells are specialised:

- they do one particular job
- they develop a distinct shape
- special kinds of chemical change take place in their cytoplasm.

The changes in shape and the chemical reactions enable the cell to carry out its special function. Red blood cells and root hair cells are just two examples of specialised cells. Figure B2.9 on the next page shows a variety of specialised cells.

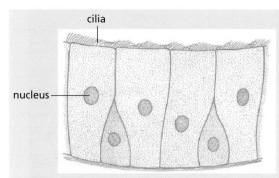

a Ciliated cells These cells form the lining of the nose and windpipe, and the tiny cytoplasmic 'hairs', called cilia, are in a continual flicking movement which creates a stream of fluid (mucus) that carries dust and bacteria through the bronchi and trachea, away from the lungs.

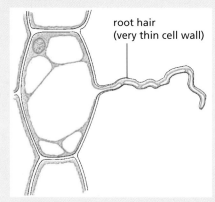

b Root hair cell These cells absorb water and mineral salts from the soil. The hair-like projection on each cell penetrates between the soil particles and offers a large absorbing surface. The cell membrane is able to control which dissolved substances enter the cell.

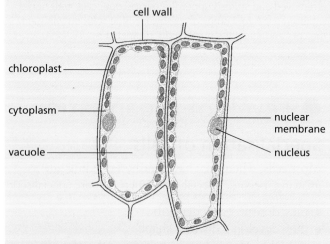

c Palisade mesophyll cells These are found underneath the upper epidermis of plant leaves. They are columnar (quite long) and packed with chloroplasts to trap light energy. Their function is to make food for the plant by photosynthesis using carbon dioxide, water and light energy.

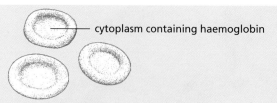

d Red blood cells These cells are distinctive because they have no nucleus when mature. They are tiny disc-like cells which contain a red pigment called haemoglobin. This readily combines with oxygen and their function is the transport of oxygen around the body.

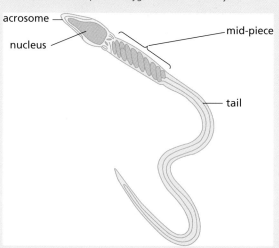

e Sperm cell Sperm cells are male sex cells. The front of the cell is oval shaped and contains a nucleus which carries genetic information. There is a tip, called an acrosome, which secretes enzymes to digest the cells around an egg and the egg membrane. Behind this is a mid-piece which is packed with mitochondria to provide energy for movement. The tail moves with a whip-like action enabling the sperm to swim. Their function is reproduction, achieved by fertilising an egg cell.

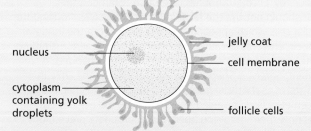

f Egg cell Egg cells (ova, singular: ovum) are larger than sperm cells and are spherical. They have a large amount of cytoplasm, containing yolk droplets made up of protein and fat. The nucleus carries genetic information. The function of the egg cell is reproduction.

Figure B2.9 Specialised cells (not to scale).

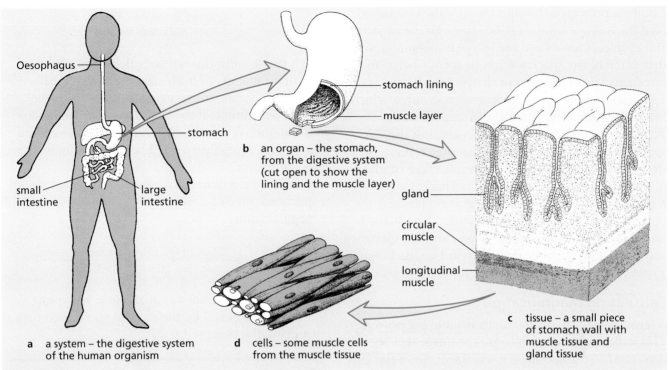

Oesophagus

stomach lining

muscle layer

stomach

b an organ – the stomach, from the digestive system (cut open to show the lining and the muscle layer)

gland

circular muscle

longitudinal muscle

small intestine

large intestine

c tissue – a small piece of stomach wall with muscle tissue and gland tissue

a a system – the digestive system of the human organism

d cells – some muscle cells from the muscle tissue

Figure B2.10 An example of how cells, tissues and organs are related.

Tissues

A **tissue**, such as bone, nerve or muscle in animals, and epidermis, xylem or pith in plants, is made up of many hundreds of cells often of a single type. The cells of each type have a similar structure and function so that the tissue itself can be said to have a particular function; for example, muscles contract to cause movement, xylem carries water in plants.

Organs

Organs consist of several tissues grouped together to make a structure with a special function. For example, the stomach is an organ which contains tissues made from epithelial cells, gland cells and muscle cells. These cells are supplied with food and oxygen brought by blood vessels. The stomach also has a nerve supply. The heart, lungs, intestines, brain and eyes are further examples of organs in animals. In flowering plants, the root, stem and leaves are

the organs. The tissues of the leaf include epidermis, palisade tissue, spongy tissue, xylem and phloem (see Chapter B5).

Organ systems

An **organ system** usually refers to a group of organs whose functions are closely related. For example, the heart and blood vessels make up the **circulatory system**; the brain, spinal cord and nerves make up the **nervous system**. In a flowering plant, the stem, leaves and buds make up a system called the **shoot**.

Organisms

An **organism** is formed by the organs and systems working together to produce an independent plant or animal.

An example in the human body of how cells, tissues and organs are related is shown in Figure B2.10.

● Size of specimens

The light microscope

Most cells cannot be seen with the naked eye. A **hand lens** has a magnification of up to ×20, but this is not sufficient to observe the detail in cells. The

light microscope (Figure B2.11 on the next page) has two convex lenses, providing magnifications of up to ×1500, although most found in school laboratories will only magnify to ×400. The eyepiece lens is usually ×10 and there is a choice of objective lenses (typically ×4, ×10 and ×40), set in a nosepiece which can be rotated. Light, provided by a mirror or a bulb, is projected through the specimen mounted on a microscope slide. It passes through the objective and eyepieces lenses and the image is magnified so that detail of the specimen can be seen. Coarse and fine focus knobs are used to sharpen the image. Specimens are mounted on microscope slides, which may be temporary or permanent preparations. Temporary slides are quick to prepare, but the specimens dry out quite rapidly, so they cannot be stored successfully. A coverslip (a thin piece of glass) is carefully laid over the specimen. This helps to keep it in place, slows down dehydration and protects the objective lens from moisture or stains. A permanent preparation usually involves dehydrating the specimen and fixing it in a special resin such as Canada Balsam. These types of slides can be kept for many years.

Calculating magnification

A lens is usually marked with its magnifying power. This indicates how much larger the image will be, compared to the specimen's actual size. So, if the lens is marked ×10, the image will be ten times greater than the specimen's real size. Since a light microscope has two lenses, the magnification of both of these lenses needs to be taken into account. For example, if the specimen is viewed using a ×10 eyepiece lens and ×40 objective lens, the total magnification will be 10 × 40 = 400.

When the image is drawn, the drawing is usually much larger than the image, so the overall magnification of the specimen is greater still.

$$\text{Magnification} = \frac{\text{observed size of the image (or drawing)}}{\text{actual size of the specimen}}$$

When performing this type of calculation, make sure that the units of both sizes are the same. If they are different, convert one to make them the same. For example, if the actual size is in millimetres and the observed size is in centimetres, convert the centimetres to millimetres. (There are 10 millimetres in a centimetre.)

You may be required to calculate the actual size of a specimen, given a drawing or photomicrograph and a magnification.

$$\text{Actual size of the specimen} = \frac{\text{observed size of the image (or drawing)}}{\text{magnification}}$$

When you state the answer, make sure you quote the units (which will be the same as those used for measuring the observed size).

Questions

1 a What structures are usually present in both animal and plant cells?
  b What structures are present in plant cells but not in animal cells?
2 What cell structure is largely responsible for controlling the entry and exit of substances into or out of the cell?
3 In what way does the red blood cell shown in Figure B2.9d differ from most other animal cells?
4 In order to see cells clearly in a section of plant tissue, which magnification would you have to use?
  A ×5
  B ×10
  C ×100
  D ×1000

● Movement in and out of cells

Cells need food materials which they can oxidise for energy or use to build up their cell structures. They also need salts and water, which play a part in chemical reactions in the cell. Finally, they need to get rid of substances such as carbon dioxide, which, if they accumulated in the cell, would upset some of the chemical reactions or even poison the cell.

Substances may pass through the cell membrane passively by diffusion.

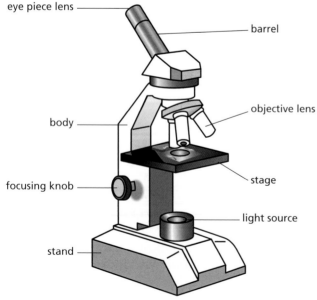

eye piece lens

barrel

objective lens

body

stage

focusing knob

light source

stand

Figure B2.11 A light microscope.

● Diffusion

> **Key definition**
>
> **Diffusion** is the net movement of particles from a region of their higher concentration to a region of their lower concentration down a concentration gradient, as a result of their random movement.

The molecules of a gas such as oxygen are moving about all the time. So are the molecules of a liquid or a substance such as sugar dissolved in water. As a result of this movement, the molecules spread themselves out evenly to fill all the available space (Figure B2.12).

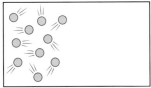

molecules moving about   become evenly distributed

Figure B2.12 Diffusion.

This process is called **diffusion**. One effect of diffusion is that the molecules of a gas, a liquid or a dissolved substance will move from a region where there are a lot of them (i.e. concentrated) to regions where there are few of them (i.e. less concentrated) until the concentration everywhere is the same. Figure B2.13a is a diagram of a cell with a high concentration of molecules (e.g. oxygen) outside and a low concentration inside. The effect of this difference in concentration is to make the molecules diffuse into the cell until the concentration inside and outside is the same, as shown in Figure B2.13b.

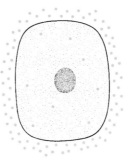
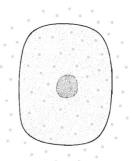

a   greater concentration outside cell   b   concentrations equal on both sides of the cell membrane

Figure B2.13 Molecules entering a cell by diffusion.

Whether this will happen or not depends on whether the cell membrane will let the molecules through. Small molecules such as water (H_2O), carbon dioxide (CO_2) and oxygen (O_2) can pass through the cell membrane fairly easily. So diffusion tends to equalise the concentration of these molecules inside and outside the cell all the time.

When a cell uses oxygen for its aerobic respiration, the concentration of oxygen inside the cell falls and so oxygen molecules diffuse into the cell until the concentration is raised again. During tissue respiration, carbon dioxide is produced and so its concentration inside the cell increases. Once again diffusion takes place, but this time the molecules move out of the cell. In this way, diffusion can explain how a cell takes in its oxygen and gets rid of its carbon dioxide.

● Rates of diffusion

Molecules and ions in liquids and gases move around randomly using **kinetic energy** (energy from movement). The speed with which a substance diffuses through a cell wall or cell membrane will depend on temperature and many other conditions including the distance it has to diffuse, the difference between its concentration inside and outside the cell, the size of its molecules or ions and the surface area across which the diffusion is occurring.

Surface area

If 100 molecules diffuse through 1 mm² of a membrane in 1 minute, it is reasonable to suppose that an area of 2 mm² will allow twice as many through in the same time. Thus the rate of diffusion into a cell will depend on the cell's surface area. The greater the surface area, the faster is the total diffusion. Cells which are involved in rapid absorption, such as those in the kidney or the intestine, often have their 'free' surface membrane formed into hundreds of tiny projections called **microvilli** (see Figure B2.14 on the next page) which increase the absorbing surface.

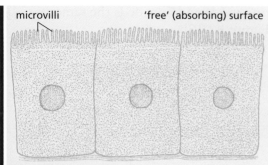

Figure B2.14 Microvilli.

The shape of a cell will also affect the surface area. For example, the cell in Figure B2.15a has a greater surface area than that in Figure B2.15b, even though they each have the same volume.

a

b

Figure B2.15 Surface area. The cells both have the same volume but the cell in **a** has a much greater surface area.

Temperature

An increase in temperature causes an increase in the kinetic energy which molecules and ions possess. This enables them to move faster, so the process of diffusion speeds up.

Concentration gradient

The bigger the difference in the concentration of a substance on either side of a membrane, the faster it will tend to diffuse. The difference is called a **concentration gradient** or **diffusion gradient** (Figure B2.16). If a substance on one side of a membrane is steadily removed, the diffusion gradient is maintained. When oxygen molecules enter a red blood cell they combine with a chemical (haemoglobin) which takes them out of solution. Thus the concentration of free oxygen molecules inside the cell is kept very low and the diffusion gradient for oxygen is maintained.

molecules will move from the densely packed area

Figure B2.16 Concentration gradient.

Distance

Cell membranes are all about the same thickness (approximately $0.007\,\mu m$) but plant cell walls vary in

their thickness and permeability. Generally speaking, the thicker the wall, the slower the rate of diffusion. When oxygen diffuses from the alveoli of the lungs into red blood cells, it has to travel through the cell membranes of the alveoli, the blood capillaries and the red blood cells in addition to the cytoplasm of each cell. This increased distance slows down the diffusion rate.

Practical work

Experiments on diffusion

1 Diffusion and surface area

- Use a block of starch agar or gelatine at least 3 cm thick. Using a ruler and a sharp knife, measure and cut four cubes from the jelly with sides of 3.0 cm, 2.0 cm, 1.0 cm and 0.5 cm.
- Place the cubes into a beaker of methylene blue dye or potassium permanganate solution.
- After 15 minutes, remove the cubes with forceps and place them on to a white tile.
- Cut each of the cubes in half and measure the depth to which the dye has diffused.
- Calculate the surface area and volume of each cube and construct a table of your data. Remember to state the units in the heading for each column.

Question
Imagine that these cubes were animals, with the jelly representing living cells and the dye representing oxygen. Which of the 'animals' would be able to survive by relying on diffusion through their surface to provide them with oxygen?

2 Diffusion and temperature

- Set up two beakers with equal volumes of hot water and iced water.
- Add a few grains of potassium permanganate to each beaker and observe how rapidly the dissolved dye spreads through each column of water. An alternative is to use tea bags.

Question
Give an explanation for the results you observed.

3 Diffusion and concentration gradients and distance

- Push squares of wetted red litmus paper with a glass rod or wire into a wide glass tube which is at least 30 cm long and corked at one end, so that they stick to the side and are evenly spaced out, as shown in Figure B2.17. (It is a good strategy to mark 2 cm intervals along the outside of the tube, starting at 10 cm from one end, with a permanent marker or white correction fluid before inserting the litmus paper.)

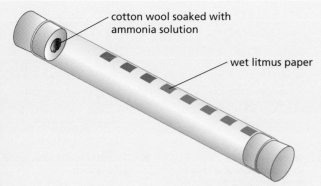

Figure B2.17 Experiment to measure the rate of diffusion of ammonia in air.

- Close the open end of the tube with a cork carrying a plug of cotton wool saturated with a strong solution of ammonia. Start a stop watch.
- Observe and record the time when each square of litmus starts to turn blue in order to determine the rate at which the alkaline ammonia vapour diffuses along the tube.
- Repeat the experiment using a dilute solution of ammonia.
- Plot both sets of results on a graph, labelling each plot line.

Questions

1 Which ammonia solution diffused faster? Can you explain why?
2 Study your graph. What happened to the rate of diffusion as the ammonia travelled further along the tube? Can you explain why?

4 Diffusion and particle size

- Take a 15 cm length of dialysis tubing which has been soaked in water and tie a knot tightly at one end.
- Use a dropping pipette to partly fill the tubing with a mixture of 1% starch solution and 1% glucose solution.
- Rinse the tubing and test-tube under the tap to remove all traces of starch and glucose solution from the outside of the dialysis tubing.
- Put the tubing in a boiling tube and hold it in place with an elastic band as shown in Figure B2.18.
- Fill the boiling tube with water and leave for 30 minutes.

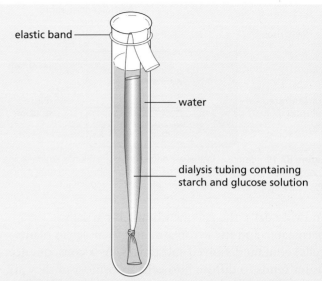

Figure B2.18 Demonstrating the partial permeability of dialysis tubing.

- Use separate teat pipettes to remove samples of liquid from the dialysis tubing and the boiling tube. Test both samples with iodine solution and Benedict's reagent.

Result

The liquid inside the dialysis tubing goes blue with iodine solution and may give a positive Benedict's test, but the sample from the boiling tube only gives a positive Benedict's test.

Interpretation

The blue colour is characteristic of the reaction which takes place between starch and iodine, and is used as a test for starch. A positive Benedict's test gives a colour change from blue to cloudy green, yellow or brick red (see Chapter B3). The results show that glucose molecules have passed through the dialysis tubing into the water but the starch molecules have not moved out of the dialysis tubing. This is what we would expect if the dialysis tubing was partially permeable on the basis of its pore size. Starch molecules are very large (see Chapter B3) and probably cannot get through the pores. Glucose molecules are much smaller and can, therefore, get through.

● Osmosis

If a dilute solution is separated from a concentrated solution by a **partially permeable** membrane, water diffuses across the membrane from the dilute to the concentrated solution. This is known as **osmosis** and is shown in Figure B2.19 on the next page.

A partially permeable membrane is porous but allows water to pass through more rapidly than dissolved substances.

Since a dilute solution contains, in effect, more water molecules than a concentrated solution, there is a diffusion gradient which favours the passage of water from the dilute solution to the concentrated solution.

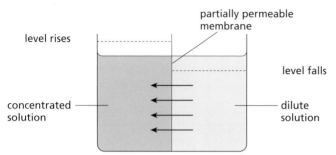

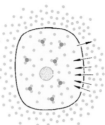

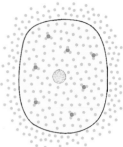

Figure B2.19 Osmosis. Water will diffuse from the dilute solution to the concentrated solution through the partially permeable membrane. As a result, the liquid level will rise on the left and fall on the right.

In living cells, the cell membrane is partially permeable and the cytoplasm and vacuole (in plant cells) contain dissolved substances. As a consequence, water tends to diffuse into cells by osmosis if they are surrounded by a weak solution, e.g. fresh water. If the cells are surrounded by a stronger solution, e.g. sea water, the cells may lose water by osmosis. These effects are described more fully later.

Animal cells

In Figure B2.20 an animal cell is shown very simply. The coloured circles represent molecules in the cytoplasm. They may be sugar, salt or protein molecules. The blue circles represent water molecules.

The cell is shown surrounded by pure water. Nothing is dissolved in the water; it has 100% concentration of water molecules. So the concentration of free water molecules outside the cell is greater than that inside and, therefore, water will diffuse into the cell by osmosis.

The membrane allows water to go through either way. So in our example, water can move into or out of the cell.

The cell membrane is partially permeable to most of the substances dissolved in the cytoplasm. So although the concentration of these substances inside may be high, they cannot diffuse freely out of the cell.

The water molecules move into and out of the cell, but because there are more of them on the outside, they will move in faster than they move out. The liquid outside the cell does not have to be 100% pure water. As long as the concentration of water outside is higher than that inside, water will diffuse in by osmosis.

Water entering the cell will make it swell up and, unless the extra water is expelled in some way, the cell will burst.

a There is a higher concentration of free water molecules outside the cell than inside, so water diffuses into the cell.

b The extra water makes the cell swell up.

Figure B2.20 Osmosis in an animal cell.

Conversely, if the cells are surrounded by a solution which is more concentrated than the cytoplasm, water will pass out of the cell by osmosis and the cell will shrink. Excessive uptake or loss of water by osmosis may damage cells.

Plant cells

The cytoplasm of a plant cell and the cell sap in its vacuole contain salts, sugars and proteins which effectively reduce the concentration of free water molecules inside the cell. The cell wall is freely permeable to water and dissolved substances but the cell membrane of the cytoplasm is partially permeable. If a plant cell is surrounded by water or a solution more dilute than its contents, water will pass into the vacuole by osmosis. The vacuole will expand and press outwards on the cytoplasm and cell wall. The cell wall of a mature plant cell cannot be stretched, so there comes a time when the inflow of water is resisted by the inelastic cell wall, as shown in Figure B2.21.

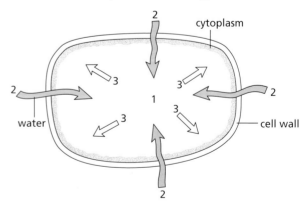

1 since there is effectively a lower concentration of water in the cell sap
2 water diffuses into the vacuole
3 and makes it push out against the cell wall

Figure B2.21 Osmosis in a plant cell.

This has a similar effect to inflating a soft bicycle tyre. The tyre represents the firm cell wall, the floppy inner tube is like the cytoplasm and the air inside corresponds to the vacuole. If enough air is pumped in, it pushes the inner tube against the tyre and makes the tyre hard.

When plant cells have absorbed a maximum amount of water by osmosis, they become very rigid, due to the pressure of water pressing outwards on the cell wall. The end result is that the stems and leaves are supported. If the cells lose water there is no longer any water pressure pressing outwards against the cell walls and the stems and leaves are no longer supported. At this point, the plant becomes limp and wilts (see Figure B2.22).

a   plant wilting   **b**   plant recovered after watering
Figure B2.22   Wilting.

Practical work

Experiments on osmosis

Some of the experiments use 'Visking' dialysis tubing. It is made from cellulose and is partially permeable, allowing water molecules to diffuse through freely, but restricting the passage of dissolved substances to varying extents.

1 Osmosis and water flow

- Take a 20 cm length of dialysis tubing which has been soaked in water and tie a knot tightly at one end.
- Place 3 cm³ of a strong sugar solution in the tubing using a plastic syringe and add a little coloured dye.
- Fit the tubing over the end of a length of capillary tubing and hold it in place with an elastic band. Push the capillary tubing into the dialysis tubing until the sugar solution enters the capillary.
- Now clamp the capillary tubing so that the dialysis tubing is totally immersed in a beaker of water, as shown in Figure B2.23.
- Watch the level of liquid in the capillary tubing over the next 10–15 minutes.

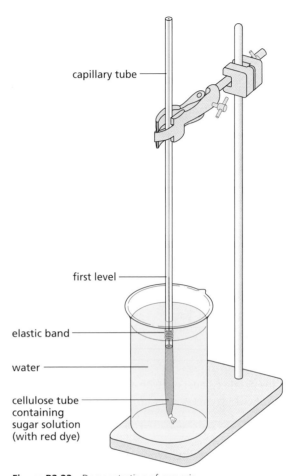

Figure B2.23   Demonstration of osmosis.

Result
The level of liquid in the capillary tube rises.

Interpretation
Water must be passing into the sugar solution from the beaker. This is what you would expect when a concentrated solution is separated from water by a partially permeable membrane.

A process similar to this might be partially responsible for moving water from the roots to the stem of a plant.

2 The effects of water and sugar solution on potato tissue

- Push a No.4 or No.5 cork borer into a large potato.
  Caution: Do not hold the potato in your hand but use a board as in Figure B2.24a on the next page.
- Push the potato tissue out of the cork borer using a pencil as in Figure B2.24b. Prepare a number of potato cylinders in this way and choose the two longest. (They should be at least 50 mm long.) Cut these two accurately to the same length, e.g. 50, 60 or 70 mm. Measure carefully.
- Label two test-tubes A and B and place a potato cylinder in each. Cover the potato tissue in tube A with water; cover the tissue in B with a 20% sugar solution.
- Leave the tubes for 24 hours.
- After this time, remove the cylinder from tube A and measure its length. Notice also whether it is firm or flabby. Repeat this for the potato in tube B, but rinse it in water before measuring it.

a place the potato on a board

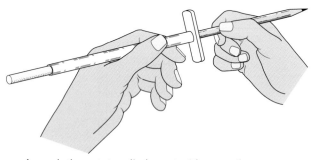

b push the potato cylinder out with a pencil

Figure B2.24 Obtaining cylinders of potato tissue.

Result

The cylinder from tube A should have gained a millimetre or two and feel firm. The cylinder from tube B should be a millimetre or two shorter and feel flabby.

Interpretation

The cells of the potato in tube A have absorbed water by osmosis, causing an increase in the length of the potato cylinder.

In tube B, the sugar solution is stronger than the cell sap of the potato cells, so these cells have lost water by osmosis, resulting in the potato cylinder becoming flabby and shorter.

An alternative to measuring the potato cores is to weigh them before and after the 24 hours' immersion in water or sugar solution. The core in tube A should gain weight and that in tube B should lose weight. It is important to blot the cores dry with a paper towel before weighing them.

Whichever method is used, it is a good idea to pool the results of the whole class since the changes may be quite small. A gain in length of 1 or 2 mm might be due to an error in measurement, but if most of the class record an increase in length, then experimental error is unlikely to be the cause.

Key definition

Osmosis is the net movement of water molecules from a region of higher water potential (a dilute solution) to a region of lower water potential (a concentrated solution) through a partially permeable membrane.

How osmosis works

When a substance such as sugar dissolves in water, the sugar molecules attract some of the water molecules and stop them moving freely. This, in effect, reduces the concentration of water molecules. In Figure B2.25 the sugar molecules on the right have 'captured' half the water molecules. There are more free water molecules on the left of the membrane than on the right, so water will diffuse more rapidly from left to right across the membrane than from right to left.

The partially permeable membrane does not act like a sieve in this case. The sugar molecules can diffuse from right to left but, because they are bigger and surrounded by a cloud of water molecules, they diffuse more slowly than the water, as shown in Figure B2.26.

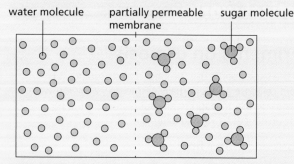

Figure B2.25 The diffusion gradient for water. There are more free water molecules on the left, so more will diffuse from left to right than in the other direction. Sugar molecules will diffuse more slowly from right to left.

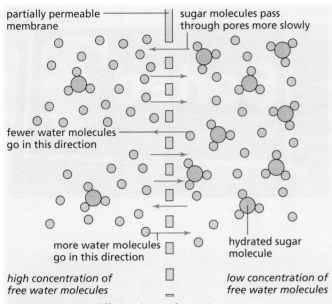

partially permeable membrane

sugar molecules pass through pores more slowly

fewer water molecules go in this direction

more water molecules go in this direction

hydrated sugar molecule

high concentration of free water molecules

low concentration of free water molecules

Figure B2.26   The diffusion theory of osmosis.

Water potential

The **water potential** of a solution is a measure of whether it is likely to lose or gain water molecules from another solution. A dilute solution, with its high proportion of free water molecules, is said to have a higher water potential than a concentrated solution, because water will flow from the dilute to the concentrated solution (from a high potential to a low potential). Pure water has the highest possible water potential because water molecules will flow from it to any other aqueous solution, no matter how dilute. When adjacent cells contain sap with different water potentials, a water potential gradient is created. Water will move from a cell with a higher water potential (a more dilute solution) to a cell with a lower water potential (a more concentrated solution). This is thought to be one way in which water moves from root hair cells through to the xylem of a plant root (see Figure B7.9 on p. 78).

The importance of water potential and osmosis in the uptake of water by plants

A plant cell with the vacuole pushing out on the cell wall is said to be **turgid** and the vacuole is exerting **turgor pressure** on the inelastic cell wall.

If all the cells in a leaf and stem are turgid, the stem will be firm and upright and the leaves held out straight. If the vacuoles lose water for any reason, the cells will lose their turgor and become **flaccid**. (See Experiment 2 'Plasmolysis' on p. 21.) If a plant has flaccid cells, the leaves will be limp and the stem will droop. A plant which loses water to this extent is said to be 'wilting' (see Figure B2.22).

Root hair cells are in contact with water trapped between soil particles. When the water potential of the cell sap is lower than that of the soil water, the water will enter the cells by osmosis providing the plant with the water it needs. (This process is described in more detail in 'Water uptake' in Chapter B7.)

When a farmer applies chemical fertilisers to the soil, the fertilisers dissolve in the soil water. Too much fertiliser can lower the osmotic potential of the soil water. This can draw water out of the plant root hair cells by osmosis, leading to wilting and death of crop plants.

Irrigation of crops can have a similar effect. Irrigation which provides just enough water for the plant can lead to a build-up of salts in the soil. The salts will eventually cause the soil water to have a lower water potential than the plant root cells. Crops can then no longer be grown on the land, because they wilt and die because of water loss by osmosis. Much agricultural land in hot countries has become unusable due to the side-effects of irrigation (Figure B2.27).

Some countries apply salt to roads in the winter to prevent the formation of ice (Figure B2.28 on the next page). However, vehicle wheels splash the salt on to plants at the side of the road. The build-up of salts in the roadside soil can kill plants living there, due to water loss from the roots by osmosis.

Figure B2.27   An irrigation furrow.

Figure B2.28 Salt gritter at work to prevent ice formation on a road.

Figure B2.29 Poster campaign featuring Leah Betts to raise awareness of the dangers of taking the drug ecstasy.

The importance of water potential and osmosis in animal cells and tissues

It is vital that the fluid which bathes cells in animals, such as the fluid surrounding cells or blood plasma, has the same water potential as the cell contents. This prevents any net flow of water into or out of the cells. If the bathing fluid has a higher water potential (a weaker concentration) than the cells, water will move into the cells by osmosis causing them to swell up. As animal cells have no cell wall and the membrane has little strength, water would continue to enter and the cells will eventually burst (a process called **haemolysis** in red blood cells).

When surgeons carry out operations on a patient's internal organs, they sometimes need to rinse a wound. Pure water cannot be used as this would enter any cells it came into contact with and cause them to burst. A saline solution, with the same water potential as fluid surrounding cells, has to be used.

In England in 1995, a teenager called Leah Betts (Figure B2.29) collapsed after taking an Ecstasy tablet. One of the side-effects of taking Ecstasy is that the brain thinks the body is dehydrating so the person becomes very thirsty. Leah drank far too much water: over 7 litres (12 pints) in 90 minutes. Her kidneys could not cope and the extra water in her system diluted her blood. Her brain cells took in water by osmosis, causing them to swell up and burst. She died hours later.

During physical activity, the body may sweat in order to maintain a steady temperature. If liquids are not drunk to compensate for water loss through sweating, the body can become dehydrated. Loss of water from the blood results in the plasma becoming more concentrated (its water potential decreases). Water is then drawn out of the red blood cells by osmosis. The cells become **plasmolysed**. Their surface area is reduced, causing them to be less effective in carrying oxygen. The shape of the cells is known as being **crenated** (see Figure B2.30).

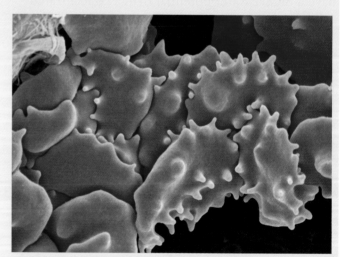

Figure B2.30 Plasmolysed red blood cells.

People doing sport sometimes use sports drinks (Figure B2.31) which are **isotonic** (they have the same water potential as body fluids). The drinks contain water, salts and glucose and are designed to replace lost water and salts, as well as providing energy, without creating osmotic problems to body cells. However, use of such drinks when not exercising vigorously can lead to weight gain in the same way as the prolonged use of any sugar-rich drink.

Figure B2.31   People may use isotonic sports drinks.

Practical work

Further experiments on osmosis

1 Osmosis and turgor

- Take a 20 cm length of dialysis tubing which has been soaked in water and tie a knot tightly at one end.
- Place 3 cm³ of a strong sugar solution in the tubing using a plastic syringe (Figure B2.32a) and then knot the open end of the tube (Figure B2.32b). The partly-filled tube should be quite floppy (Figure B2.32c).
- Place the tubing in a test-tube of water for 30–45 minutes.
- After this time, remove the dialysis tubing from the water and note any changes in how it looks or feels.

Result
The tubing will become firm, distended by the solution inside.

Interpretation
The dialysis tubing is partially permeable and the solution inside has fewer free water molecules than outside. Water has, therefore, diffused in and increased the volume and the pressure of the solution inside.

This is a crude model of what is thought to happen to a plant cell when it becomes turgid. The sugar solution represents the cell sap and the dialysis tubing represents the cell membrane and cell wall combined.

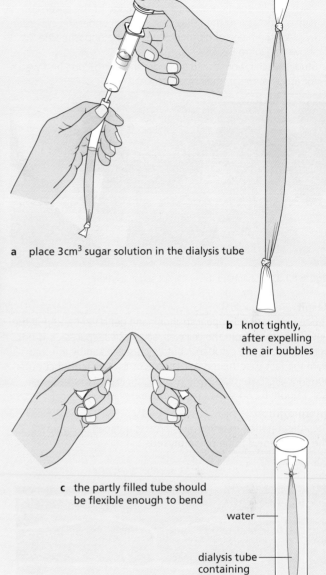

a   place 3 cm³ sugar solution in the dialysis tube

b   knot tightly, after expelling the air bubbles

c   the partly filled tube should be flexible enough to bend

water

dialysis tube containing sugar solution

Figure B2.32   Experiment to illustrate turgor in a plant cell.

2 Plasmolysis

- Peel a small piece of epidermis (the outer layer of cells) from a red area of a rhubarb stalk (see Figure B2.5c on p. 8).
- Place the epidermis on a slide with a drop of water and cover with a coverslip (see Figure B2.5b).
- Put the slide on a microscope stage and find a small group of cells.

- Place a 30% solution of sugar at one edge of the coverslip with a pipette and then draw the solution under the coverslip by placing a piece of blotting paper on the opposite side, as shown in Figure B2.33.
- Study the cells you identified under the microscope and watch for any changes in their appearance.

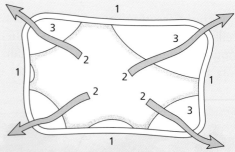

1 the solution outside the cell is more concentrated than the cell sap
2 water diffuses out of the vacuole
3 the vacuole shrinks, pulling the cytoplasm away from the cell wall, leaving the cell flaccid

Figure B2.35 Plasmolysis.

The plasmolysis can be reversed by drawing water under the coverslip in the same way that you drew the sugar solution under. It may need two or three lots of water to flush out all the sugar. If you watch a group of cells, you should see their vacuoles expanding to fill the cells once again.

Rhubarb is used for this experiment because the coloured cell sap shows up. If rhubarb is not available, the epidermis from a red onion scale can be used.

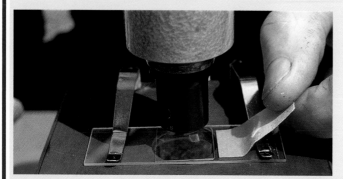

Figure B2.33 Changing the water for sugar solution.

Result

The red cell sap will appear to shrink and get darker and pull the cytoplasm away from the cell wall leaving clear spaces. (It is not possible to see the cytoplasm but its presence can be inferred from the fact that the red cell sap seems to have a distinct outer boundary in those places where it has separated from the cell wall.) Figure B2.34 shows the turgid and plasmolysed cells.

Interpretation

The interpretation in terms of osmosis is outlined in Figure B2.35. The cells are said to be **plasmolysed**.

3 The effects of varying the concentration of sucrose solution on potato tissue

- Push a No.4 or No.5 cork borer into a large potato.
  Caution: Do not hold the potato in your hand, but use a board as in Figure B2.24a on p.18.

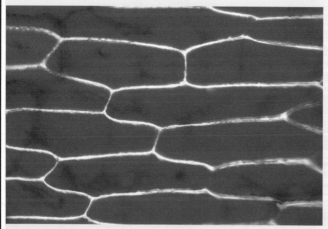

a Turgid cells (×100). The cells are in a strip of epidermis from a rhubarb stalk. The cytoplasm is pressed against the inside of the cell wall by the vacuole.

Figure B2.34 Demonstration of plasmolysis in rhubarb cells.

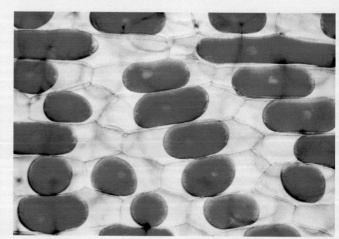

b Plasmolysed cells (×100). The same cells as they appear after treatment with sugar solution. The vacuole has lost water by osmosis, shrunk and pulled the cytoplasm away from the cell wall.

- Push the potato tissue out of the cork borer using a pencil as in Figure B2.24b. Prepare six potato cylinders in this way and cut them all to the same length. (They should be at least 50 mm long.) Measure them carefully.
- Label six test-tubes with the concentration of sucrose solution in them (e.g. $0.0\,mol/dm^3$, $0.2\,mol/dm^3$, $0.4\,mol/dm^3$, $0.6\,mol/dm^3$, $0.8\,mol/dm^3$ and $1.0\,mol/dm^3$) and place them in a test-tube rack.
- Add the same volume of the correct sucrose solution to each test-tube.
- Weigh a cylinder of potato, record its mass and place it in the first test-tube. Repeat until all the test-tubes have been set up.
- Leave the tubes for at least 30 minutes.
- After this time, remove the potato cylinder from the first tube, surface dry the potato and re-weigh it. Notice also whether it is firm or flabby. Repeat this for the other potato cylinders.
- Calculate the change in mass and the percentage change in mass for each cylinder.

$$\text{Percentage change in mass} = \frac{\text{change in mass}}{\text{mass at start}} \times 100$$

- Plot the results on a graph with sucrose concentration on the horizontal axis and percentage change in mass on the vertical axis.
  Note: there will be negative as well as positive percentage changes in mass, so your graph axes will have to allow for this.

Result

The cylinders in the weaker sucrose solutions will have gained mass and feel firm. One of the cylinders may have shown no change in mass. The cylinders in the more concentrated sucrose solutions will have lost mass and feel limp.

Interpretation

If the cells of the potato have absorbed water by osmosis, there will be an increase in the mass of the potato cylinder. This happens when the external solution has a higher water potential than that inside the potato cells. (The sucrose solution is less concentrated than the contents of the potato cells.) Water molecules move into each cell through the cell membrane. The water molecules move from a higher water potential to a lower water potential. The cells become turgid, so the cylinder feels firm.

If the cells of the potato have lost water by osmosis, there will be a decrease in mass of the potato cylinder. This happens when the external solution has a lower water potential than that inside the potato cells. (The sucrose solution is more concentrated than the contents of the potato cells.) Water molecules move out of each cell through the cell membrane. The water molecules move from a higher water potential to a lower water potential. The cells become plasmolysed or flaccid, so the cylinder feels flabby.

Question

Study your graph. Can you predict the sucrose concentration which would be equivalent to the concentration of the cell sap in the potato cells?

Questions

5 A 10% solution of copper sulfate is separated by a partially permeable membrane from a 5% solution of copper sulfate. Will water diffuse from the 10% solution to the 5% solution or from the 5% solution to the 10% solution? Explain your answer.

6 If a fresh beetroot is cut up, the pieces washed in water and then left for an hour in a beaker of water, little or no red pigment escapes from the cells into the water. If the beetroot is boiled first, the pigment does escape into the water. Bearing in mind the properties of a living cell membrane, offer an explanation for this difference.

7 In Experiment 1 (Figure B2.23), what do you think would happen in these cases?
  a A much stronger sugar solution was placed in the cellulose tube.

  b The beaker contained a weak sugar solution instead of water.
  c The sugar solution was in the beaker and the water was in the cellulose tube.

8 In Experiment 1, the column of liquid accumulating in the capillary tube exerts an ever-increasing pressure on the solution in the dialysis tubing. Bearing this in mind and assuming a very long capillary, at what stage would you expect the net flow of water from the beaker into the dialysis tubing to cease?

9 When doing experiments with animal tissues they are usually bathed in Ringer's solution, which has a concentration similar to that of blood or fluid surrounding cells. Why do you think this is necessary?

Checklist

After studying Chapter B2 you should know and understand the following.

- Living organisms are made up of cells.
- All cells contain cytoplasm enclosed in a cell membrane.
- The membrane controls what substances enter and leave the cell.
- Most cells have a nucleus, which contains DNA, and controls cell division and the cell's activities.
- Many chemical reactions take place in the cytoplasm to keep the cell alive.
- Plant cells have a cellulose cell wall, a large central vacuole and some have chloroplasts, to trap light energy for photosynthesis. The cell wall is permeable and prevents the cell from bursting. The vacuole contains salts and sugars and helps to keep the cell firm.
- The magnification of a specimen can be calculated if the actual size and the size of the image are known.
- Diffusion is the result of particles moving about.
- Particles diffuse from a region where they are very concentrated to a region where they are less concentrated, down a concentration gradient, as a result of their random movement.
- Substances may move into and out of cells by diffusion through the cell membrane.

- Osmosis is the diffusion of water through a partially permeable membrane. Water can move in and out of cells by osmosis.
- Cells take up water from dilute solutions but lose water to concentrated solutions because of osmosis.

- Cells are often specialised in their shapes and activities to carry out particular jobs.
- Large numbers of similar cells packed together form a tissue.
- Different tissues arranged together form organs.
- A group of related organs makes up a system.
- Ciliated cells, root hair cells, palisade mesophyll cells, red blood cells and sperm and egg cells have special structures which are related to their functions.
- Osmosis is the diffusion of water from a region of higher water potential (dilute solution) to a region of lower water potential (concentrated solution), through a partially permeable membrane.
- Factors affecting diffusion include surface area, temperature, concentration gradients and diffusion distance.
- Understand the terms turgid, turgor pressure, plasmolysis and flaccid.
- Understand the importance of water potential and osmosis on animal and plant cells, including the role of turgor pressure in cells to provide support in plants.

Biological molecules

<table>
<tr><td>

Combined

- List the chemical elements that make up: *carbohydrates; fats; proteins*
- State that large molecules are made from smaller molecules, limited to: *starch and glycogen from glucose; proteins from amino acids; fats and oils from fatty acids and glycerol*
- Describe the use of: *iodine solution to test for starch; Benedict's solution to test for reducing sugars; biuret test for proteins; ethanol emulsion test for fats and oils*
- State that water is important as a solvent

</td><td>

Co-ordinated

- List the chemical elements that make up: *carbohydrates; fats; proteins*
- State that large molecules are made from smaller molecules, limited to: *starch and glycogen from glucose; proteins from amino acids; fats and oils from fatty acids and glycerol*
- Describe the use of: *iodine solution to test for starch; Benedict's solution to test for reducing sugars; biuret test for proteins; ethanol emulsion test for fats and oils*
- State that water is important as a solvent

</td></tr>
</table>

● Biological molecules

Carbon is an element present in all biological molecules. Carbon atoms can join together to form chains or ring structures, so biological molecules can be very large (macromolecules), often constructed of repeating sub-units (monomers). Other elements always present are oxygen and hydrogen. Nitrogen is sometimes present. When macromolecules are made of long chains of monomers held together by chemical bonds, they are known as **polymers** (poly means 'many'). Examples are polysaccharides (chains of single sugar units such as glucose) and proteins (chains of amino acids). Molecules constructed of lots of small units often have different properties from their sub-units, making them suitable for specific functions in living things. For example, glucose is very soluble and has no strength, but cellulose (a macromolecule made of glucose units) is insoluble and very tough – ideal for the formation of cell walls around plant cells.

Cells need chemical substances to make new cytoplasm and to produce energy. Therefore the organism must take in food to supply the cells with these substances. Of course, it is not quite as simple as this; most cells have specialised functions (Chapter B2) and so have differing needs. However, all cells need water, oxygen, salts and food substances and all cells consist of water, proteins, lipids, carbohydrates, salts and vitamins or their derivatives.

Carbohydrates

These may be simple, soluble sugars or complex materials like starch and cellulose, but all carbohydrates contain carbon, hydrogen and oxygen only. A commonly occurring simple sugar is **glucose**, which has the chemical formula $C_6H_{12}O_6$ (Figure B3.1).

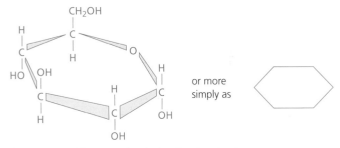

Figure B3.1 Glucose molecule showing ring structure.

When many glucose molecules are joined together, the carbohydrate is a large molecule. **Glycogen** (Figure B3.2) is a polysaccharide which forms a food storage substance in many animal cells. The **starch** molecule is made up of hundreds of glucose molecules joined together to form long chains. Starch is an important storage substance in plant cells.

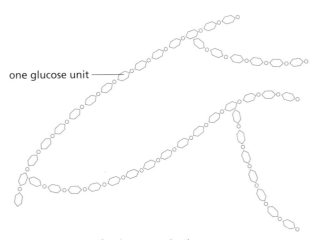

Figure B3.2 Part of a glycogen molecule.

Fats

Fats are a solid form of a group of molecules called **lipids**. When lipids are liquid they are known as oils. Fats and oils are formed from carbon, hydrogen and oxygen only. A molecule of fat (or oil) is made up of three molecules of an organic acid, called a **fatty acid**, combined with one molecule of **glycerol**.

$$\text{glycerol} \begin{cases} H_2\!-\!C\!-\!O\!-\! & \text{fatty acid} \\ H\!-\!C\!-\!O\!-\! & \text{fatty acid} \\ H_2\!-\!C\!-\!O\!-\! & \text{fatty acid} \end{cases}$$

Drawn simply, fat molecules can be represented as in Figure B3.3.

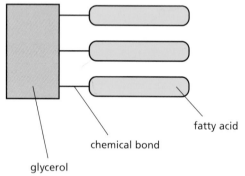

fatty acid

chemical bond

glycerol

Figure B3.3   Fat molecule.

Proteins

Some proteins contribute to the structures of the cell, e.g. to the cell membranes, the mitochondria, ribosomes and chromosomes. These proteins are called **structural proteins**.

There is another group of proteins called **enzymes**. Enzymes are present in the membrane systems, in the mitochondria, in special vacuoles and in the fluid part of the cytoplasm. Enzymes control the chemical reactions that keep the cell alive (see Chapter B4).

Although there are many different types of protein, all contain carbon, hydrogen, oxygen and nitrogen, and many contain sulfur. Their molecules are made up of long chains of simpler chemicals called **amino acids** (Figure B3.4).

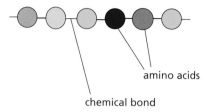

amino acids

chemical bond

Figure B3.4   Protein molecule (part of).

Water

Most cells contain about 75% water and will die if their water content falls much below this. Water is a good solvent and many substances move about the cells in a watery solution.

Table B3.1 Summary of the main biological molecules

Nutrient	Elements present	Examples	Sub-units
carbohydrate	carbon, hydrogen, oxygen	starch, glycogen	glucose
fat/oil (oils are liquid at room temperature, but fats are solid)	carbon, hydrogen, oxygen (but lower oxygen content than carbohydrates	vegetable oils (e.g. olive oil), animal fats (e.g. cod liver oil, waxes)	fatty acids and glycerol
protein	carbon, hydrogen, oxygen, nitrogen, sometimes sulfur or phosphorus	enzymes, muscle, haemoglobin, cell membranes	amino acids (about 20 different forms)

Practical work

Food tests

1 Test for starch

■ Shake a little starch powder in a test-tube with some warm water to make a suspension.
■ Add 3 or 4 drops of **iodine solution**. A dark blue colour should be produced.

Note: it is also possible to use iodine solution to test for starch in leaves, but a different procedure is used (see Chapter B5).

2 Test for reducing sugar

■ Heat a little glucose solution with an equal volume of **Benedict's solution** in a test-tube. The heating is done by placing the test-tube in a beaker of boiling water (see Figure B3.5), or warming it gently over a blue Bunsen flame. However, if this second technique is used, the test-tube should be moved constantly in and out of the Bunsen flame to prevent the liquid boiling and shooting out of the tube. The solution will change from clear blue to cloudy green, then yellow and finally to a red precipitate (deposit) of copper(I) oxide.

3 Test for protein (Biuret test)

■ To a 1% solution of albumen (the protein of egg-white) add 5 cm³ dilute sodium hydroxide (**Caution**: this solution is caustic), followed by 5 cm³ 1% copper sulfate solution. A purple colour indicates protein. If the copper sulfate is run into the food solution without mixing, a violet halo appears where the two liquids come into contact.

4 Test for fat

■ Shake two drops of cooking oil with about 5 cm³ ethanol in a dry test-tube until the fat dissolves.
■ Pour this solution into a test-tube containing a few cm³ water. A milky white emulsion will form. This shows that the solution contained some fat or oil.

Application of the food tests

The tests can be used on samples of food such as milk, potato, raisins, onion, beans, egg-yolk or peanuts to find out what food materials are present. The solid samples are crushed in a mortar and shaken with warm water to extract the soluble products. Separate samples of the watery mixture of crushed food are tested for starch, glucose or protein as described above. To test for fats, the food must first be crushed in ethanol, not water, and then filtered. The clear filtrate is poured into water to see if it goes cloudy, indicating the presence of fats.

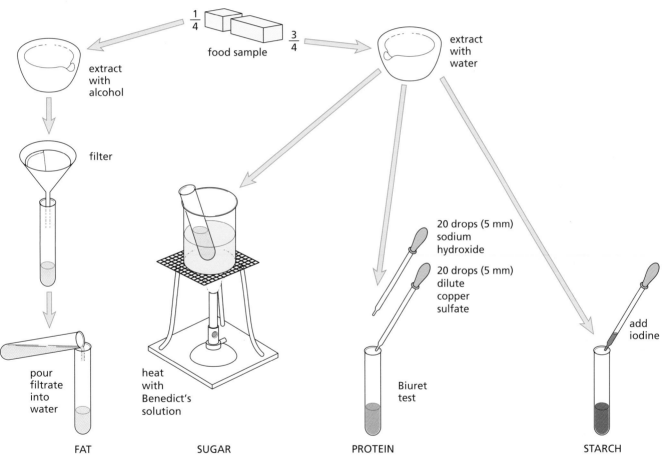

Figure B3.5 Experiment to test foods for different nutrients.

Question

1 a What do the chemical structures of carbohydrates and fats have in common?
  b How do their chemical structures differ?
  c Suggest why there are many more different proteins than there are carbohydrates.

Checklist

After studying Chapter B3 you should know and understand the following.

● Living matter is made up of a number of important types of molecules, including proteins, lipids and carbohydrates.
● All three types of molecule contain carbon, hydrogen and oxygen atoms; proteins also contain nitrogen and sometimes phosphorus or sulfur.
● Carbohydrates are made from single units, often glucose.
● Carbohydrates are used as an energy source; glycogen and starch make good storage molecules.
● Proteins are built up from amino acids joined together by chemical bonds.
● Lipids include fats, fatty acids and oils.
● Fats are made from fatty acids and glycerol.
● Food tests are used to identify the main biological molecules.
● Water is important in living things as a solvent.

B4 Enzymes

> **Key definition**
> An **enzyme** is a protein that functions as a biological catalyst.

Enzymes are proteins that act as **catalysts**. They are made in all living cells. Enzymes, like catalysts, can be used over and over again because they are not used up during the reaction and only a small amount is needed to speed the reaction up (Figure B4.1).

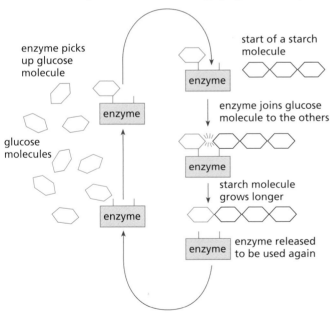

Figure B4.1 Building up a starch molecule.

● Enzyme action

How an enzyme molecule might work to join two other molecules together and so form a more complicated substance (the product) is shown in Figure B4.2 on the next page.

An example of an enzyme-controlled reaction such as this is the joining up of two glucose molecules to make a larger molecule called maltose. You can see that the enzyme and substrate molecules have **complementary** shapes (like adjacent pieces of a jigsaw) so they fit together. Other substrate molecules would not fit into this enzyme as they would have the 'wrong' shape. For example, the substrate molecule in Figure B4.2b would not fit the enzyme molecule in Figure B4.2a. The product (substance AB in Figure B4.2a) is released by the enzyme molecule and the enzyme is then free to repeat the reaction with more substrate molecules. Molecules of the two substances might have combined without the enzyme being present, but they would have done so very slowly (it could take hours or days to happen without the enzyme). By bringing the substances close together, the enzyme molecule makes the reaction take place much more rapidly. The process can be extremely fast: it has been found that catalase, a very common enzyme found in most cells, can break down 40 000 molecules of hydrogen peroxide every second! A complete chemical reaction takes only a few seconds when the right enzyme is present.

As well as enzymes being responsible for joining two substrate molecules together, such as two glucose molecules to form maltose, they can also create long chains. For example, hundreds of glucose molecules can be joined together, end to end, to form a long molecule of starch to be stored in the cytoplasm of a plant cell. The glucose molecules can also be built up into a molecule of cellulose to be added to the cell wall. Protein molecules are built up by enzymes, which join together tens or hundreds of amino acid molecules. These proteins are added to the cell membrane, to the cytoplasm or to the nucleus of the cell. They may also become the proteins that act as enzymes.

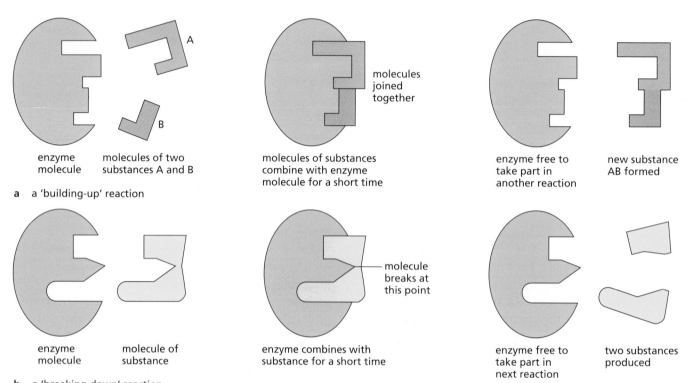

a   a 'building-up' reaction

b   a 'breaking-down' reaction

Figure B4.2   Possible explanation of enzyme action.

Enzymes and temperature

Figure B4.3 shows the effect of temperature on an enzyme-controlled reaction.

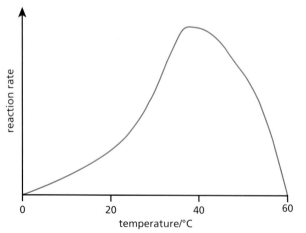

Figure B4.3   Graph showing the effect of temperature on the rate of an enzyme-controlled reaction.

A rise in temperature increases the rate of most chemical reactions; a fall in temperature slows them down. However, above 50 °C the enzymes stop working.

Figure B4.2 shows how the shape of an enzyme molecule could be very important if it has to fit the substances on which it acts. Above 50 °C the shapes of enzymes are permanently changed and the enzymes can no longer combine with the substances.

This is one of the reasons why organisms may be killed by prolonged exposure to high temperatures. The enzymes in their cells are denatured and the chemical reactions proceed too slowly to maintain life.

One way to test whether a substance is an enzyme is to heat it to boiling point. If it can still carry out its reactions after this, it cannot be an enzyme. This technique is used as a 'control' (see 'Aerobic respiration' in Chapter B8) in enzyme experiments.

Enzymes and pH

Acid or alkaline conditions alter the chemical properties of proteins, including enzymes. Most enzymes work best at a particular level of acidity or alkalinity (pH), as shown in Figure B4.4.

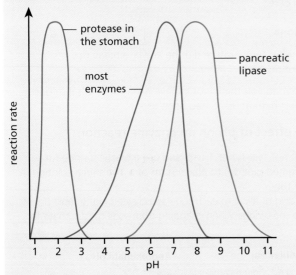

Figure B4.4 The effect of pH on digestive enzymes.

The protein-digesting enzyme in your stomach, for example, works well at an acidity of pH 2. At this pH, the enzyme amylase, from your saliva, cannot work at all. Inside the cells, most enzymes will work best in neutral conditions (pH 7). The pH or temperature at which an enzyme works best is often called its **optimum** pH or temperature. Conditions in the duodenum are slightly alkaline: the optimum pH for pancreatic lipase is pH 8.

Enzymes and temperature

Generally, a rise of 10 °C will double the rate of an enzyme-controlled reaction in a cell, up to an optimum temperature of around 37 °C (body temperature). This is because the enzyme and substrate molecules are constantly moving, using kinetic energy. The reaction only occurs when the enzyme and substrate molecules come into contact with each other. As the temperature is increased, the molecules gain more kinetic energy, so they move faster and there is a greater chance of collisions happening. Therefore the rate of reaction increases. Above the optimum temperature the reaction will slow down. This is because enzyme

molecules are proteins. Protein molecules start to lose their shape at higher temperatures, so the active site becomes deformed. Substrate molecules cannot fit together with the enzyme, stopping the reaction. Not all the enzyme molecules are affected straight away, so the reaction does not suddenly stop – it is a gradual process as the temperature increases above 37 °C. Denaturation is a permanent change in the shape of the enzyme molecule. Once it has happened the enzyme will not work any more, even if the temperature is reduced below 37 °C. An example of a protein denaturing is the cooking of egg-white (made of the protein albumin). Raw egg-white is liquid, transparent and colourless. As it is heated, it turns solid and becomes opaque and white. It cannot be changed back to its original state or appearance.

Enzymes and pH

Although changes in pH affect the activity of enzymes, these effects are usually reversible, i.e. an enzyme that is inactivated by a low pH will resume its normal activity when its optimum pH is restored.

Extremes of pH may denature some enzymes irreversibly. This is because the active site of the enzyme molecule can become deformed (as it does when exposed to high temperatures). As a result, the enzyme and substrate molecules no longer have complementary shapes and so will not fit together.

Practical work

Tests for proteins, fats and carbohydrates are described in Chapter B3.

1 The effect of temperature on an enzyme reaction
Amylase is an enzyme that breaks down starch to a sugar (maltose).

- Draw up 5 cm³ of 5% amylase solution in a plastic syringe (or graduated pipette) and place 1 cm³ in each of three test-tubes labelled A, B and C.
- Rinse the syringe thoroughly and use it to place 5 cm³ of a 1% starch solution in each of three test-tubes labelled 1, 2 and 3.
- To each of tubes 1 to 3, add six drops only of dilute iodine solution using a dropping pipette.

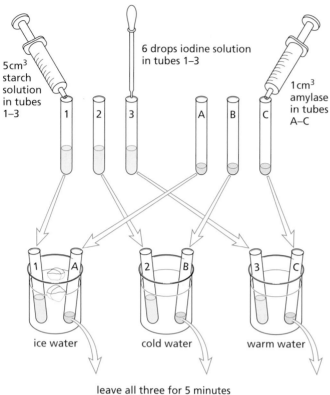

note the time and add the amylase to the starch solution

Figure B4.5 Experiment to investigate the effect of temperature on an enzyme reaction.

- Prepare three water baths by half filling beakers or jars with:
  a ice and water, adding ice during the experiment to keep the temperature at about 10 °C
  b water from the cold tap at about 20 °C
  c warm water at about 35 °C by mixing hot and cold water.
- Place tubes 1 and A in the cold water bath, tubes 2 and B in the water at room temperature, and tubes 3 and C in the warm water.
- Leave them for 5 minutes to reach the temperature of the water (Figure B4.5).

- After 5 minutes, take the temperature of each water bath, then pour the amylase from tube A into the starch solution in tube 1 and return tube 1 to the water bath.
- Repeat this with tubes 2 and B, and 3 and C.
- As the amylase breaks down the starch, it will cause the blue colour to disappear. Make a note of how long this takes in each case.

Questions

1 At what temperature did the amylase break down starch most rapidly?

2 What do you think would have been the result if a fourth water bath at 90 °C had been used?

2 The effect of pH on an enzyme reaction

- Label five test-tubes 1 to 5 and use a plastic syringe (or graduated pipette) to place 5 cm³ of a 1% starch solution in each tube.
- Add acid or alkali to each tube as indicated in the table below. Rinse the syringe when changing from sodium carbonate to acid.

Tube	Chemical	Approximate pH	
1	1 cm³ sodium carbonate solution (0.05 mol/dm³)	9	(alkaline)
2	0.5 cm³ sodium carbonate solution (0.05 mol/dm³)	7–8	(slightly alkaline)
3	nothing	6–7	(neutral)
4	2 cm³ ethanoic (acetic) acid (0.1 mol/dm³)	6	(slightly acid)
5	4 cm³ ethanoic (acetic) acid (0.1 mol/dm³)	3	(acid)

- Place several rows of iodine solution drops in a cavity tile.
- Draw up 5 cm³ of 5% amylase solution in a clean syringe and place 1 cm³ in each tube. Shake the tubes and note the time (Figure B4.6).
- Use a clean dropping pipette to remove a small sample from each tube in turn and let one drop fall on to one of the iodine drops in the cavity tile. Rinse the pipette in a beaker of water between each sample. Keep on sampling in this way.
- When any of the samples fails to give a blue colour, this means that the starch in that tube has been completely broken down to sugar by the amylase. Note the time when this happens for each tube and stop taking samples from that tube. Do not continue sampling for more than about 15 minutes, but put a drop from each tube on to a piece of pH paper and compare the colour produced with a colour chart of pH values.

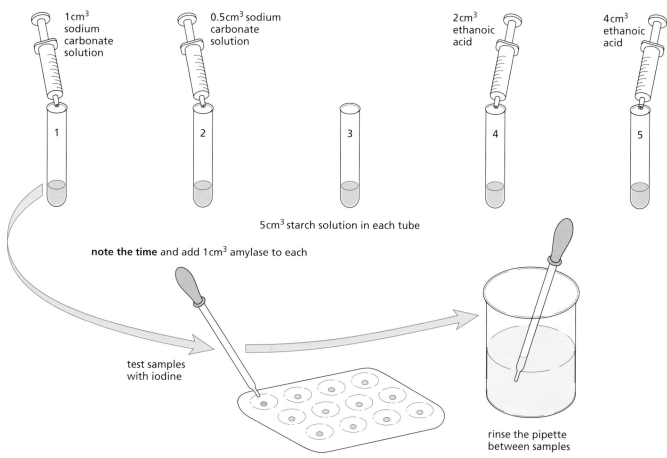

Figure B4.6 Experiment to investigate the effect of pH on an enzyme reaction.

Questions

1 At what pH did the enzyme, amylase, work most rapidly?
2 Is this its optimum pH?

3 Explain why you might have expected the result that you got.
4 Your stomach pH is about 2. Would you expect starch digestion to take place in the stomach?

Questions

1 How would you expect the rate of an enzyme-controlled reaction to change if the temperature was raised:
a from 20 °C to 30 °C
b from 35 °C to 55 °C?
Explain your answers.

2 In what ways does protease show the characteristics of an enzyme?

Checklist

After studying Chapter B4 you should know and understand the following.

- Enzymes are proteins that function as biological catalysts.
- Enzyme activity is affected by pH and temperature.

- Enzymes are important in all organisms because they maintain a reaction speed needed to sustain life.
- The substance on which an enzyme acts is called the substrate. After the reaction, a product is formed.
- An enzyme and its substrate have complementary shapes.
- Enzymes are affected by pH and temperature and are denatured above 50 °C.
- Different enzymes may accelerate reactions which build up or break down molecules.

- Each enzyme acts on only one substance (breaking down), or a pair of substances (building up).
- Enzymes tend to be very specific in the reactions they catalyse, due to the complementary shape of the enzyme and its substrate.
- Changes in temperature affect the kinetic energy of enzyme molecules and their shape.
- Enzymes can be denatured by changes in temperature and pH.

B5 Plant nutrition

<table>
<tr><td>

Combined

- Define *photosynthesis*

- State the word equation for photosynthesis:
  carbon dioxide + water → glucose + oxygen
  in the presence of light and chlorophyll

- State the balanced equation for photosynthesis

$$6CO_2 + 6H_2O \xrightarrow[\text{chlorophyll}]{\text{light}} C_6H_{12}O_6 + 6O_2$$

- Explain that chlorophyll transfers light energy into chemical energy in molecules, for the synthesis of carbohydrates

- Outline the subsequent use and storage of the carbohydrates made in photosynthesis

- Investigate the necessity for chlorophyll, light and carbon dioxide for photosynthesis, using appropriate controls

- Identify chloroplasts, cuticle, guard cells and stomata, upper and lower epidermis, palisade mesophyll, spongy mesophyll, vascular bundles, xylem and phloem in leaves of a dicotyledonous plant

- Describe the significance of the features of a leaf in terms of functions, to include: palisade mesophyll and distribution of chloroplasts – photosynthesis; stomata, spongy mesophyll cells and guard cells – gas exchange; xylem for transport and support; phloem for transport

- Investigate and describe the effect of varying light intensity and temperature on the rate of photosynthesis (e.g. in submerged aquatic plants)

- Describe the importance of: nitrate ions for making amino acids; magnesium ions for making chlorophyll

- Explain the effects of nitrate ion and magnesium ion deficiency on plant growth

</td><td>

Co-ordinated

- Define *photosynthesis*

- State the word equation for photosynthesis:
  carbon dioxide + water → glucose + oxygen,
  in the presence of light and chlorophyll

- State the balanced equation for photosynthesis in symbols

$$6CO_2 + 6H_2O \xrightarrow[\text{chlorophyll}]{\text{light}} C_6H_{12}O_6 + 6O_2$$

- Explain that chlorophyll transfers light energy into chemical energy in molecules, for the synthesis of carbohydrates

- Outline the subsequent use and storage of the carbohydrates made in photosynthesis

- Investigate the necessity for chlorophyll, light and carbon dioxide for photosynthesis, using appropriate controls

- Investigate and describe the effect of varying light intensity and temperature on the rate of photosynthesis (e.g. in submerged aquatic plants)

- Identify chloroplasts, cuticle, guard cells and stomata, upper and lower epidermis, palisade mesophyll, spongy mesophyll, vascular bundles, xylem and phloem in leaves of a dicotyledonous plant

- Describe the significance of the features of a leaf in terms of functions, to include: palisade mesophyll and distribution of chloroplasts – photosynthesis; stomata, spongy mesophyll cells and guard cells – gas exchange; xylem for transport and support; phloem for transport

- Describe the importance of: nitrate ions for making amino acids; magnesium ions for making chlorophyll

- Explain the effects of nitrate ion and magnesium ion deficiency on plant growth

</td></tr>
</table>

● Photosynthesis

> **Key definition**
> **Photosynthesis** is the process by which plants manufacture carbohydrates from raw materials using energy from light.

All living organisms need food. They need it as a source of raw materials to build new cells and tissues as they grow. They also need food as a source of energy. Food is a kind of 'fuel' that drives essential living processes and brings about chemical changes (see 'Diet' in Chapter B6 and 'Aerobic respiration' in Chapter B8).

Animals take in food, digest it and use the digested products to build their tissues or to produce energy.

Plants also need energy and raw materials but, apart from a few insect-eating species, plants do not appear to take in food. The most likely source of their raw materials would appear to be the soil. However, experiments show that the weight gained by a growing plant is far greater than the weight lost by the soil it is growing in. So there must be additional sources of raw materials.

Jean-Baptiste van Helmont was a Dutch scientist working in the 17th century. At that time very little was known about the process of photosynthesis. He carried out an experiment using a willow shoot. He planted the shoot in a container with 90.8 kg of dry soil and placed a metal grill over the soil to prevent any accidental gain or loss of mass. He left the shoot for 5 years in an open yard, providing it with only rainwater and distilled water for growth. After 5 years he reweighed the tree and the soil (see Figure B5.1) and came to the conclusion that the increase in mass of the tree (74.7 kg) was due entirely to the water it had received. However, he was unaware that plants also take in mineral salts and carbon dioxide, or that they use light as a source of energy.

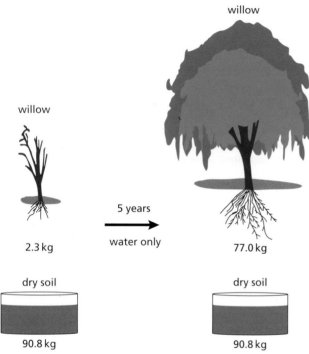

Figure B5.1 Van Helmont's experiment.

A **hypothesis** to explain the source of food in a plant is that it *makes it* from air, water and soil salts. Carbohydrates (Chapter B3) contain the elements carbon, hydrogen and oxygen, as in glucose ($C_6H_{12}O_6$). The carbon and oxygen could be supplied by carbon dioxide (CO_2) from the air, and the hydrogen could come from the water (H_2O) in the soil. The nitrogen and sulfur needed for making proteins (Chapter B3) could come from nitrates and sulfates in the soil.

This building-up of complex food molecules from simpler substances is called **synthesis** and it needs enzymes and energy to make it happen. The enzymes are present in the plant's cells and the energy for the first stages in the synthesis comes from sunlight. The process is, therefore, called **photosynthesis** ('photo' means 'light'). There is

evidence to suggest that the green substance, **chlorophyll**, in the chloroplasts of plant cells, plays a part in photosynthesis. Chlorophyll absorbs sunlight and makes the energy from sunlight available for chemical reactions. Thus, in effect, the function of chlorophyll is to convert light energy to chemical energy.

A chemical equation for photosynthesis would be

$$\text{carbon dioxide} + \text{water} \xrightarrow[\text{chlorophyll}]{\text{light energy}} \text{glucose} + \text{oxygen}$$

In order to keep the equation simple, glucose is shown as the food compound produced. In reality, the glucose is rapidly converted to sucrose for transport around the plant, then stored as starch or converted into other molecules.

Practical work

Experiments to investigate photosynthesis

A hypothesis is an attempt to explain certain observations. In this case the hypothesis is that plants make their food by photosynthesis. The equation shown above is one way of stating the hypothesis and is used here to show how it might be tested.

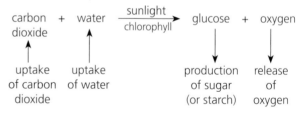

If photosynthesis is occurring in a plant, then the leaves should be producing sugars. In many leaves, as fast as sugar is produced it is turned into starch. Since it is easier to test for starch than for sugar, we regard the production of starch in a leaf as evidence that photosynthesis has taken place.

The first three experiments described below are designed to see if the leaf can make starch without chlorophyll, sunlight or carbon dioxide, in turn. If the photosynthesis hypothesis is sound, then the lack of any one of these three conditions should stop photosynthesis, and so stop the production of starch. But, if starch production continues, then the hypothesis is no good and must be altered or rejected.

In designing the experiments, it is very important to make sure that only *one* variable is altered. If, for example, the method of keeping light from a leaf also cuts off its carbon dioxide supply, it would be impossible to decide whether it was the lack of light or lack of carbon dioxide that stopped the production of starch. To make sure that the experimental design has not altered more than one variable, a **control** is set up in each case. This is an identical situation, except that the condition missing from the experiment, e.g. light, carbon dioxide or chlorophyll, is present in the control (see 'Aerobic respiration' in Chapter B8).

Destarching a plant

If the production of starch is your evidence that photosynthesis is taking place, then you must make sure that the leaf does not contain any starch at the beginning of the experiment. This is done by **destarching** the leaves. It is not possible to remove the starch chemically, without damaging the leaves, so a plant is destarched simply by leaving it in darkness for 2 or 3 days. Potted plants are destarched by leaving them in a dark cupboard for a few days. In the darkness, any starch in the leaves will be changed to sugar and carried away from the leaves to other parts of the plant. For plants in the open, the experiment is set up on the day before the test. During the night, most of the starch will be removed from the leaves. Better still, wrap the leaves in aluminium foil for 2 days while they are still on the plant. Then test one of the leaves to see that no starch is present.

Testing a leaf for starch

Iodine solution (yellow/brown) and starch (white) form a deep blue colour when they mix. The test for starch, therefore, is to add iodine solution to a leaf to see if it goes blue. However, a living leaf is impermeable to iodine and the chlorophyll in the leaf masks any colour change. So, the leaf has to be treated as follows:

- Heat some water to boiling point in a beaker and then **turn off the Bunsen flame**.
- Use forceps to dip a leaf in the hot water for about 30 seconds. This kills the cytoplasm, denatures the enzymes and makes the leaf more permeable to iodine solution.
- **Caution**: make sure the Bunsen flame is extinguished before starting the next part of the procedure, as ethanol is flammable.

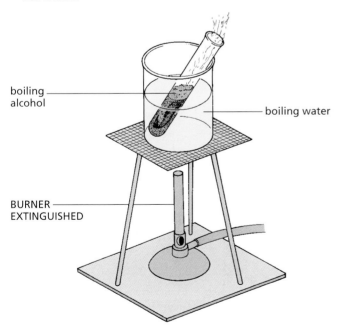

boiling alcohol

boiling water

BURNER EXTINGUISHED

Figure B5.2   Experiment to remove chlorophyll from a leaf.

- Push the leaf to the bottom of a test-tube and cover it with ethanol (alcohol). Place the tube in the hot water (Figure B5.2). The alcohol will boil and dissolve out most of the chlorophyll. This makes colour changes with iodine easier to see.
- Pour the green alcohol into a spare beaker, remove the leaf and dip it once more into the hot water to soften it.
- Spread the decolourised leaf flat on a white tile and drop iodine solution on to it. The parts containing starch will turn blue; parts without starch will stain brown or yellow with iodine.

a   variegated leaf   b   after testing for starch

Figure B5.3   Experiment to show that chlorophyll is necessary.

1 Is chlorophyll necessary for photosynthesis?

It is not possible to remove chlorophyll from a leaf without killing it, and so a variegated leaf, which has chlorophyll only in patches, is used. A leaf of this kind is shown in Figure B5.3a. The white part of the leaf serves as the experiment, because it lacks chlorophyll, while the green part with chlorophyll is the control. After being destarched, the leaf – still on the plant – is exposed to daylight for a few hours. Remove a leaf from the plant; draw it carefully to show where the chlorophyll is (i.e. the green parts) and test it for starch as described above.

Result

Only the parts that were previously green turn blue with iodine. The parts that were white stain brown (Figure B5.3b).

Interpretation

Since starch is present only in the parts that originally contained chlorophyll, it seems reasonable to suppose that chlorophyll is needed for photosynthesis.

It must be remembered, however, that there are other possible interpretations that this experiment has not ruled out; for example, starch could be made in the green parts and sugar in the white parts. Such alternative explanations could be tested by further experiments.

2 Is light necessary for photosynthesis?

- Cut a simple shape from a piece of aluminium foil to make a stencil and attach it to a destarched leaf (Figure B5.4a on the next page).
- After 4 to 6 hours of daylight, remove the leaf and test it for starch.

Result

Only the areas which had received light go blue with iodine (Figure B5.4b).

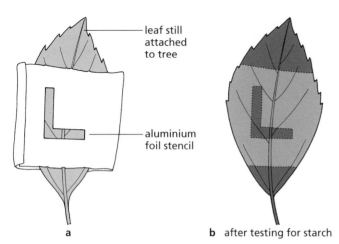

Figure B5.4 Experiment to show that light is necessary.

Interpretation

As starch has not formed in the areas that received no light, it seems that light is needed for starch formation and thus for photosynthesis.

You could argue that the aluminium foil had stopped carbon dioxide from entering the leaf and that it was shortage of carbon dioxide rather than absence of light which prevented photosynthesis taking place. A further control could be designed, using transparent material instead of aluminium foil for the stencil.

3 Is carbon dioxide needed for photosynthesis?

- Water two destarched potted plants and enclose their shoots in polythene bags.
- In one pot place a dish of soda-lime to absorb the carbon dioxide from the air (the experiment). In the other place a dish of sodium hydrogencarbonate solution to produce carbon dioxide (the control), as shown in Figure B5.5.
- Place both plants in the light for several hours and then test a leaf from each for starch.

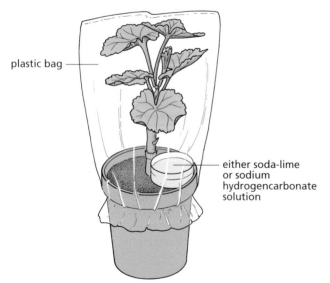

Figure B5.5 Experiment to show that carbon dioxide is necessary.

Result

The leaf that had no carbon dioxide does not turn blue. The one from the polythene bag containing carbon dioxide does turn blue.

Interpretation

The fact that starch was made in the leaves that had carbon dioxide, but not in the leaves that had no carbon dioxide, suggests that this gas must be necessary for photosynthesis. The control rules out the possibility that high humidity or high temperature in the plastic bag prevents normal photosynthesis.

4 Is oxygen produced during photosynthesis?

- Place a short-stemmed funnel over some Canadian pondweed in a beaker of water.
- Fill a test-tube with water and place it upside-down over the funnel stem (Figure B5.6). (The funnel is raised above the bottom of the beaker to allow the water to circulate.)
- Place the apparatus in sunlight. Bubbles of gas should appear from the cut stems and collect in the test-tube.
- Set up a control in a similar way but place it in a dark cupboard.
- When sufficient gas has collected from the plant in the light, remove the test-tube and insert a glowing splint.

Result

The glowing splint bursts into flames.

Interpretation

The relighting of a glowing splint does not prove that the gas collected in the test-tube is *pure* oxygen, but it does show that it contains extra oxygen and this must have come from the plant. The oxygen is given off only in the light.

Note that water contains dissolved oxygen, carbon dioxide and nitrogen. These gases may diffuse in or out of the bubbles as they pass through the water and collect in the test-tube. The composition of the gas in the test-tube may not be the same as that in the bubbles leaving the plant.

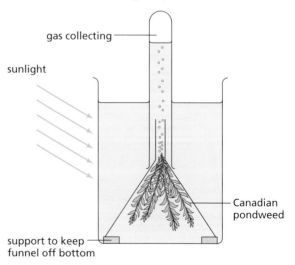

Figure B5.6 Experiment to show that oxygen is produced.

Controls

When setting up an experiment and a control, which of the two procedures constitutes the 'control' depends on the way the prediction is worded. For example, if the prediction is that 'in the absence of light, the pondweed will not produce oxygen', then the 'control' is the plant in the light. If the prediction is that 'the pondweed in the light will produce oxygen', then the 'control' is the plant in darkness. As far as the results and interpretation are concerned, it does not matter which is the 'control' and which is the 'experiment'.

The results of the four experiments support the hypothesis of photosynthesis as stated at the beginning of this chapter and as represented by the equation. Starch formation (our evidence for photosynthesis) does not take place in the absence of light, chlorophyll or carbon dioxide, and oxygen production occurs only in the light.

If starch or oxygen production had occurred in the absence of any one of these conditions, we should have to change our hypothesis about the way plants obtain their food. Bear in mind, however, that although our results support the photosynthesis theory, they do not prove it. For example, it is now known that many stages in the production of sugar and starch from carbon dioxide do not need light (the 'light-independent' reaction).

5 What is the effect of changing light intensity on the rate of photosynthesis? (Method 1)

In this investigation, the rate of production of bubbles by a pond plant is used to calculate the rate of photosynthesis.

- Prepare a beaker of water or a boiling tube, into which a spatula end of sodium hydrogencarbonate has been stirred (this dissolves rapidly and saturates the water with carbon dioxide, so CO_2 is not a limiting factor).
- Collect a fresh piece of Canadian pondweed and cut one end of the stem, using a scalpel blade.
- Attach a piece of modelling clay or paperclip to the stem and put it into the beaker (or boiling tube).
- Set up a light source 10 cm away from the beaker and switch on the lamp (Figure B5.7). Bubbles should start appearing from the cut end of the plant stem. Count the number of bubbles over a fixed time e.g. 1 minute and record the result. Repeat the count.
- Now move the light source so that it is 20 cm from the beaker. Switch on the lamp and leave it for a few minutes, to allow the plant to adjust to the new light intensity. Count the bubbles as before and record the results.
- Repeat the procedure so that the numbers of bubbles for at least five different distances have been recorded. Also, try switching off the bench lamp and observe any change in the production of bubbles.
- There is a relationship between the distance of the lamp from the plant and the light intensity received by the plant. Light intensity = $\frac{1}{D^2}$ where D = distance.

- Convert the distances to light intensity, then plot a graph of light intensity/arbitrary units (*x*-axis) against rate of photosynthesis/bubbles per minute (*y*-axis).

Note: in this investigation another variable, which could affect the rate of photosynthesis, is the heat given off from the bulb. To improve the method, another beaker of water could be placed between the bulb and the plant to act as a heat filter while allowing the plant to receive the light.

- If the bubbles appear too rapidly to count, try tapping a pen or pencil on a sheet of paper at the same rate as the bubbles appear and get your partner to slide the paper slowly along for 15 seconds. Then count the dots (Figure B5.8).

Result
The rate of bubbling should decrease as the lamp is moved further away from the plant. When the light is switched off, the bubbling should stop.

Interpretation
Assuming that the bubbles contain oxygen produced by photosynthesis, as the light intensity is increased the rate of photosynthesis (as indicated by the rate of oxygen bubble production) increases. This is because the plant uses the light energy to photosynthesise and oxygen is produced as a waste product. The oxygen escapes from the plant through the cut stem. We are assuming also that the bubbles do not change in size during the experiment. A fast stream of small bubbles might represent the same volume of gas as a slow stream of large bubbles.

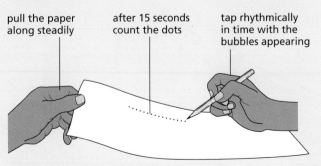

pull the paper along steadily

after 15 seconds count the dots

tap rhythmically in time with the bubbles appearing

Figure B5.8 Estimating the rate of bubble production.

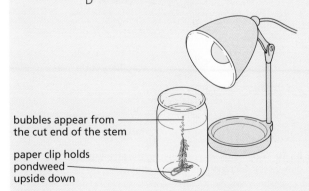

bubbles appear from the cut end of the stem

paper clip holds pondweed upside down

Figure B5.7 Experiment to investigate light intensity and oxygen production.

6 What is the effect of changing light intensity on the rate of photosynthesis? (Method 2)

This alternative investigation uses leaf discs from land plants (Figure B5.9).

- Use a cork borer or paper hole punch to cut out discs from a fresh, healthy leaf such as spinach, avoiding any veins (Figure B5.9a). The leaves contain air spaces. These cause the leaf discs to float when they are placed in water.
- At the start of the experiment, the air needs to be removed from the discs. To do this place about 10 discs into a large (10 cm³) syringe and tap it so the discs fall to the bottom (opposite the plunger end).
- Place one finger over the hole at the end of the syringe barrel. Fill the barrel with water, then replace the plunger.
- Turn the syringe so the needle end is facing up and release your finger.
- Gently push the plunger into the barrel of the syringe to force out any air from above the water (Figure B5.9b).
- Now replace your finger over the syringe hole and withdraw the plunger to create a vacuum.
- Keep the plunger withdrawn for about 10 seconds. This sucks out all the air from the leaf discs. They should then sink to the bottom (Figure B5.9c). Release the plunger.
- Repeat the procedure if the discs do not all sink.
- Remove the discs from the syringe and place them in a beaker, containing water, with a spatula of sodium hydrogencarbonate dissolved in it (Figure B5.9d).
- Start a stopwatch and record the time taken for each of the discs to float to the surface. Ignore those that did not sink. Calculate an average time for the discs to float.
- Repeat the method, varying the light intensity the discs are exposed to in the beaker (see Experiment 5 for varying the light intensity produced by a bench lamp).

Result
The greater the light intensity, the quicker the leaf discs float to the surface.

Interpretation
As the leaf discs photosynthesise they produce oxygen, which is released into the air spaces in the disc. The oxygen makes the discs more buoyant, so as the oxygen accumulates, they float to the surface of the water. As light intensity increases, the rate of photosynthesis increases.

7 What is the effect of changing carbon dioxide concentration on the rate of photosynthesis?

Sodium hydrogencarbonate releases carbon dioxide when dissolved in water. Use the apparatus shown in Figure B5.10.

- To set this up, remove the plunger from the 20 cm³ syringe and place two or three pieces of pondweed (*Elodea*), with freshly cut stems facing upwards, into the syringe barrel. Hold a finger over the end of the capillary tube and fill the syringe with distilled water.
- Replace the plunger, turn the apparatus upside down and push the plunger to the 20 cm³ mark, making sure that no air is trapped.
- Arrange the apparatus as shown in Figure B5.10 and move the syringe barrel until the meniscus is near the top of the graduations on the ruler. The bulb should be a fixed distance from the syringe, e.g. 10 cm.
- Switch on the lamp and measure the distance the meniscus moves over 3 minutes. Repeat this several times, then calculate an average.

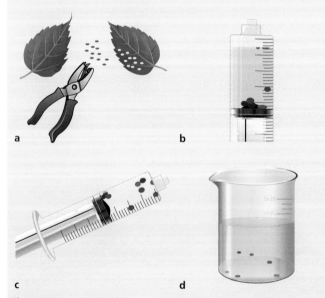

a   b   c   d

Figure B5.9 Using leaf discs to investigate the effect of light intensity on photosynthesis.

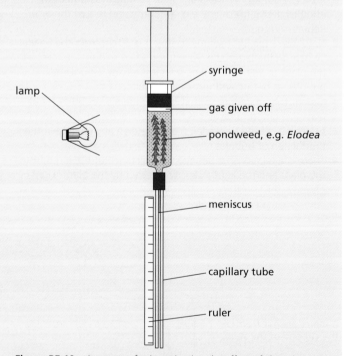

lamp

syringe

gas given off

pondweed, e.g. *Elodea*

meniscus

capillary tube

ruler

Figure B5.10 Apparatus for investigating the effect of changing carbon dioxide concentration on the rate of photosynthesis.

- Repeat the procedure using the following concentrations of sodium hydrogencarbonate solution: 0.010, 0.0125, 0.0250, 0.0500 and 0.1000 mol/dm³.
- Plot a graph of the concentration of sodium hydrogencarbonate solution (*x*-axis) against the mean distance travelled by the meniscus (*y*-axis).

Result

The higher the concentration of sodium hydrogencarbonate solution, the greater the distance moved by the meniscus.

Interpretation

As the concentration of available carbon dioxide is increased, the distance travelled by the meniscus also increases. The movement of the meniscus is caused by oxygen production by the pondweed due to photosynthesis. So an increase in carbon dioxide increases the rate of photosynthesis.

8 What is the effect of changing temperature on the rate of photosynthesis?

Use the methods described in Experiments 5 or 6, but vary the temperature of the water instead of the light intensity.

Questions

1 Which of the following are needed for starch production in a leaf?
  carbon dioxide, oxygen, nitrates, water, chlorophyll, soil, light
2 In Experiment 1 (concerning the need for chlorophyll), why was it not necessary to set up a separate control experiment?
3 What is meant by 'destarching' a leaf? Why is it necessary to destarch leaves before setting up some of the photosynthesis experiments?
4 In Experiment 3 (concerning the need for carbon dioxide), what were the functions of:
  a the soda-lime
  b the sodium hydrogencarbonate
  c the polythene bag?
5 a Why do you think pondweed, rather than a land plant, is used for Experiment 4 (concerning production of oxygen)?
  b In what way might this choice make the results less useful?
6 A green plant makes sugar from carbon dioxide and water. Why is it not suitable to carry out an experiment to see if depriving a plant of water stops photosynthesis?
7 Does the method of destarching a plant take for granted the results of Experiment 2? Explain your answer.

The process of photosynthesis

You need to be able to state the balanced chemical equation for photosynthesis.

$$6CO_2 + 6H_2O \xrightarrow[\text{chlorophyll}]{\text{light energy}} C_6H_{12}O_6 + 6O_2$$

Although the details of photosynthesis vary in different plants, the hypothesis as stated in this chapter has stood up to many years of experimental testing and is universally accepted. The next section describes how photosynthesis takes place in a plant.

The process takes place mainly in the cells of the leaves (Figure B5.11) and is summarised in Figure B5.12 on the next page. In land plants, water is absorbed from the soil by the roots and carried in the water vessels of the veins, up the stem to the leaf. Carbon dioxide is absorbed from the air through the stomata (pores in the leaf, see 'Leaf structure' later in this chapter). In the leaf cells, the carbon dioxide and water are combined to make sugar. The energy for this reaction comes from sunlight that has been absorbed by the green pigment **chlorophyll**. The chlorophyll is present in the chloroplasts of the leaf cells and it is inside the **chloroplasts** that the reaction takes place. Chloroplasts (Figure B5.12d) are small, green structures present in the cytoplasm of the leaf cells. Chlorophyll is the substance that gives leaves and stems their green colour. It is able to absorb energy from light and use it to split water molecules into hydrogen and oxygen. The oxygen escapes from the leaf and the hydrogen molecules are added to carbon dioxide molecules to form sugar. In this way the light energy has been transferred into the chemical energy of carbohydrates as they are synthesised.

Figure B5.11 All the reactions involved in producing food take place in the leaves. Notice how little the leaves overlap.

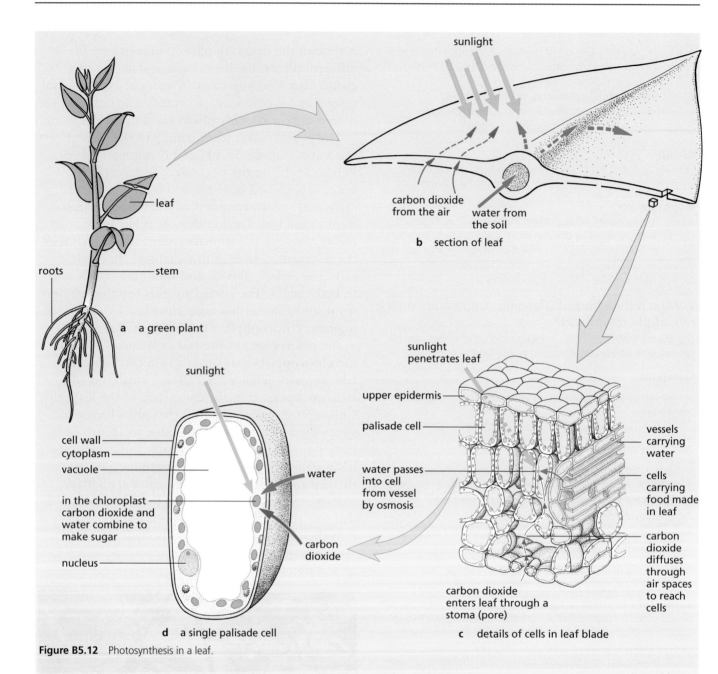

Figure B5.12 Photosynthesis in a leaf.

Labels within figure:

- leaf
- roots
- stem
- **a** a green plant
- sunlight
- carbon dioxide from the air
- water from the soil
- **b** section of leaf
- sunlight penetrates leaf
- upper epidermis
- palisade cell
- water passes into cell from vessel by osmosis
- vessels carrying water
- cells carrying food made in leaf
- carbon dioxide diffuses through air spaces to reach cells
- carbon dioxide enters leaf through a stoma (pore)
- **c** details of cells in leaf blade
- sunlight
- cell wall
- cytoplasm
- vacuole
- in the chloroplast carbon dioxide and water combine to make sugar
- nucleus
- water
- carbon dioxide
- **d** a single palisade cell

The plant's use of photosynthetic products

The glucose molecules produced by photosynthesis are quickly built up into starch molecules and added to the growing starch granules in the chloroplast. If the glucose concentration was allowed to increase in the mesophyll cells of the leaf, it could disturb the osmotic balance between the cells (see 'Osmosis' in Chapter B2). Starch is a relatively insoluble compound and so does not alter the osmotic potential of the cell contents.

The starch, however, is steadily broken down to sucrose (Chapter B3) and this soluble sugar is transported out of the cell into the food-carrying cells (see Chapter B7) of the leaf veins. These veins will distribute the sucrose to all parts of the plant that do not photosynthesise, e.g. the growing buds, the ripening fruits, the roots and the underground storage organs.

The cells in these regions will use the sucrose in a variety of ways (Figure B5.13).

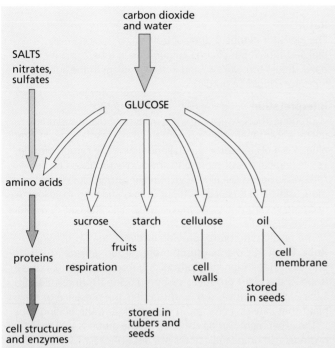

Figure B5.13 Green plants can make all the materials they need from carbon dioxide, water and salts.

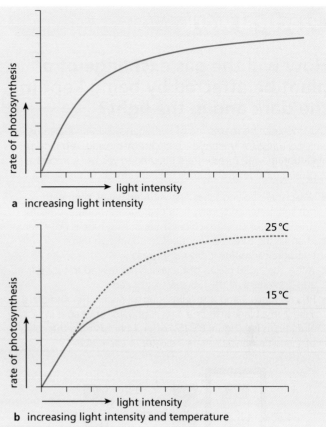

Figure B5.14 Limiting factors in photosynthesis.

Respiration

The sugar can be used to provide energy. It is oxidised by respiration (Chapter B8) to carbon dioxide and water, and the energy released is used to drive other chemical reactions such as the building-up of proteins described below.

Storage

Sugar that is not needed for respiration is turned into starch and stored. Some plants store it as starch grains in the cells of their stems or roots. Other plants, such as the potato or parsnip, have special storage organs (tubers) for holding the reserves of starch (see 'Asexual reproduction' in Chapter B10). Sugar may be stored in the fruits of some plants; grapes, for example, contain a large amount of glucose.

Effects of external factors on rate of photosynthesis

The rate of photosynthesis will depend on the light intensity. The brighter the light, the faster will water molecules be split in the chloroplasts. The reaction will be affected by temperature. A rise in temperature will increase the rate at which carbon dioxide is combined with hydrogen to make carbohydrate.

Practical work

How will the gas exchange of a plant be affected by being kept in the dark and in the light?

This investigation makes use of hydrogencarbonate indicator, which is a test for the presence of carbon dioxide. A build-up of carbon dioxide turns it from pink/red to yellow. A decrease in carbon dioxide levels causes the indicator to turn purple.

- Wash three boiling tubes first with tap water, then with distilled water and finally with hydrogencarbonate indicator (the indicator changes colour if the boiling tube is not clean).
- Then fill the three boiling tubes to about two thirds full with hydrogencarbonate indicator solution.
- Add equal-sized pieces of Canadian pondweed to tubes 1 and 2 and seal all the tubes with stoppers.
- Expose tubes 1 and 3 to light using a bench lamp and place tube 2 in a black box, or a dark cupboard, or wrap it in aluminium foil (Figure B5.15). After 24 hours note the colour of the hydrogencarbonate indicator in each tube.

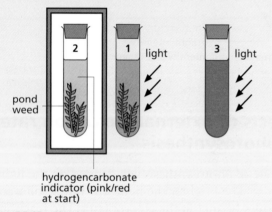

pond weed

hydrogencarbonate indicator (pink/red at start)

Figure B5.15 Experiment to compare gas exchange in plants kept in the dark and in the light.

Result

The indicator in tube 3 (the control) which was originally pink/red should not change colour; that in tube 2 (plant in the dark) should turn yellow; and in tube 1 (plant in the light) the indicator should be purple.

Interpretation

Hydrogencarbonate indicator is a mixture of dilute sodium hydrogencarbonate solution with the dyes cresol red and thymol blue. It is a pH indicator in equilibrium with the carbon dioxide, i.e. its original colour represents the acidity produced by the carbon dioxide in the air. An increase in carbon dioxide makes it more acidic and it changes colour from orange/red to yellow. A decrease in carbon dioxide makes it less acid and causes a colour change to purple.

The results, therefore, provide evidence that in the light (tube 1) aquatic plants use up more carbon dioxide in photosynthesis than they produce in respiration. In darkness (tube 2) the plant produces carbon dioxide (from respiration). Tube 3 is the control, showing that it is the presence of the plant that causes a change in the solution in the boiling tube.

The experiment can be criticised on the grounds that the hydrogencarbonate indicator is not a specific test for carbon dioxide but will respond to any change in acidity or alkalinity. In tube 1 there would be the same change in colour if the leaf produced an alkaline gas such as ammonia, and in tube 2 any acid gas produced by the leaf would turn the indicator yellow. However, knowledge of the metabolism of the leaf suggests that these are less likely events than changes in the carbon dioxide concentration.

● Leaf structure

The relationship between a leaf and the rest of the plant is described in Chapter B7.

A typical leaf of a broad-leaved plant is shown in Figure B5.16a. (Figure B5.16b shows a transverse section through the leaf.) It is attached to the stem by a **leaf stalk**, which continues into the leaf as a **midrib**. Branching from the midrib is a network of veins that deliver water and salts to the leaf cells and carry away the food made by them.

As well as carrying food and water, the network of veins forms a kind of skeleton that supports the softer tissues of the leaf blade.

The **leaf blade** (or **lamina**) is broad. A vertical section through a small part of a leaf blade is shown in Figure B5.16c and Figure B5.17 (on p.46) is a photograph of a leaf section under the microscope.

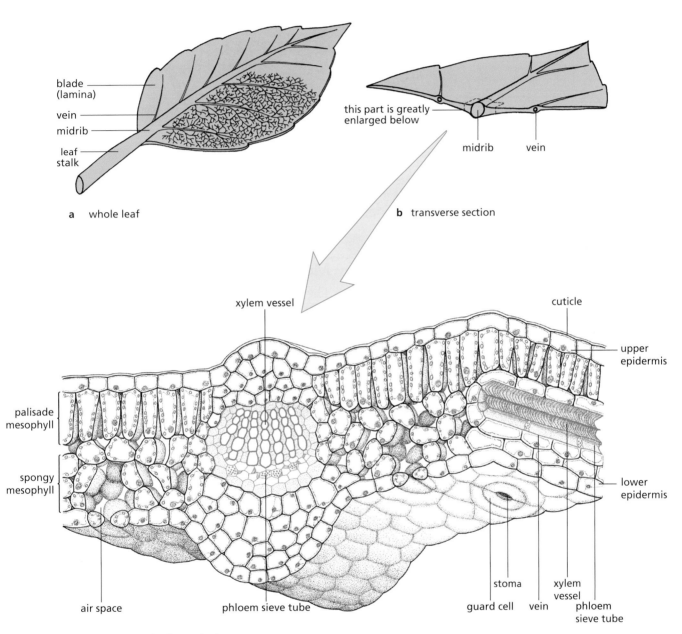

blade
(lamina)

vein

midrib

leaf
stalk

a   whole leaf

this part is greatly
enlarged below

midrib   vein

b   transverse section

xylem vessel

cuticle

upper
epidermis

palisade
mesophyll

spongy
mesophyll

lower
epidermis

air space

phloem sieve tube

stoma

guard cell   vein

xylem
vessel

phloem
sieve tube

c   arrangement of cells in a leaf

Figure B5.16   Leaf structure.

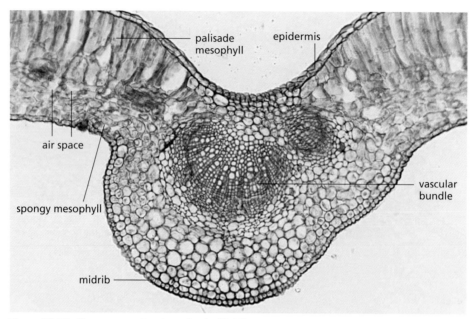

Figure B5.17 Transverse section through a leaf (×30).

Epidermis

The epidermis is a single layer of cells on the upper and lower surfaces of the leaf. There is a thin waxy layer called the **cuticle** over the epidermis.

Stomata

In the leaf epidermis there are structures called **stomata** (singular = stoma). A stoma consists of a pair of **guard cells** (Figure B5.18) surrounding an opening or stomatal pore. In most dicotyledons (i.e. the broad-leaved plants), the stomata occur only in the lower epidermis. In monocotyledons (i.e. narrow-leaved plants such as grasses) the stomata are equally distributed on both sides of the leaf.

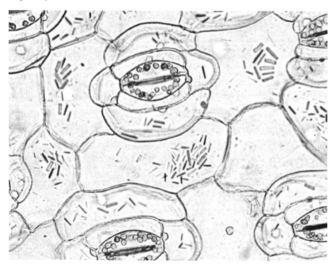

Figure B5.18 Stomata in the lower epidermis of a leaf (×350).

Mesophyll

The tissue between the upper and lower epidermis is called **mesophyll** (Figure B5.16). It consists of two zones: the upper **palisade mesophyll** and the lower **spongy mesophyll** (Figure B5.21 on p.49). The palisade cells are usually long and contain many **chloroplasts**. Chloroplasts are green organelles, due to the presence of the pigment chlorophyll, found in the cytoplasm of the photosynthesising cells. The spongy mesophyll cells vary in shape and fit loosely together, leaving many air spaces between them. They also contain chloroplasts.

Veins (vascular bundles)

The main **vein** of the leaf is called the midrib. Other veins branch off from this and form a network throughout the leaf. Vascular bundles consist of two different types of tissues, called **xylem** and **phloem**. The xylem vessels are long thin tubes with no cell contents when mature. They have thickened cell walls, impregnated with a material called **lignin**, which can form distinct patterns in the vessel walls, e.g. spirals (see Chapter B7). Xylem carries water and salts to cells in the leaf. The phloem is in the form of sieve tubes. The ends of each elongated cell are perforated to form sieve plates and the cells retain their contents. Phloem transports food substances such as sugars away from the leaf to other parts of the plant.

Table B5.1 Summary of parts of a leaf

Part of leaf	Details
cuticle	Made of wax, waterproofing the leaf. It is secreted by cells of the upper epidermis.
upper epidermis	These cells are thin and transparent to allow light to pass through. No chloroplasts are present. They act as a barrier to disease organisms.
palisade mesophyll	The main region for photosynthesis. Cells are columnar (quite long) and packed with chloroplasts to trap light energy. They receive carbon dioxide by diffusion from air spaces in the spongy mesophyll.
spongy mesophyll	These cells are more spherical and loosely packed. They contain chloroplasts, but not as many as in palisade cells. Air spaces between cells allow gaseous exchange – carbon dioxide to the cells, oxygen from the cells during photosynthesis.
vascular bundle	This is a leaf vein, made up of xylem and phloem. Xylem vessels bring water and minerals to the leaf. Phloem vessels transport sugars and amino acids away (this is called translocation).
lower epidermis	This acts as a protective layer. Stomata are present to regulate the loss of water vapour (this is called transpiration). It is the site of gaseous exchange into and out of the leaf.
stomata	Each stoma is surrounded by a pair of guard cells. These can control whether the stoma is open or closed. Water vapour passes out during transpiration. Carbon dioxide diffuses in and oxygen diffuses out during photosynthesis.

Functions of parts of the leaf

Epidermis

The epidermis helps to keep the leaf's shape. The closely fitting cells (Figure B5.16c) reduce evaporation from the leaf and prevent bacteria and fungi from getting in. The cuticle is a waxy layer lying over the epidermis, which helps to reduce water loss. It is produced by the epidermal cells.

Stomata

Changes in the turgor (see 'Osmosis' in Chapter B2) and shape of the guard cells can open or close the stomatal pore. In very general terms, stomata are open during the hours of daylight but closed during the evening and most of the night (Figure B5.19). This pattern, however, varies greatly with the plant species. A satisfactory explanation of stomatal rhythm has not been worked out, but when the stomata are open (i.e. mostly during daylight), they allow carbon dioxide to diffuse into the leaf where it is used for photosynthesis.

If the stomata close, the carbon dioxide supply to the leaf cells is virtually cut off and photosynthesis stops. However, in many species, the stomata are closed during the hours of darkness, when photosynthesis is not taking place anyway.

It seems, therefore, that stomata allow carbon dioxide into the leaf when photosynthesis is taking place and prevent excessive loss of water vapour (see 'Transpiration' in Chapter B7) when photosynthesis stops, but the story is likely to be more complicated than this.

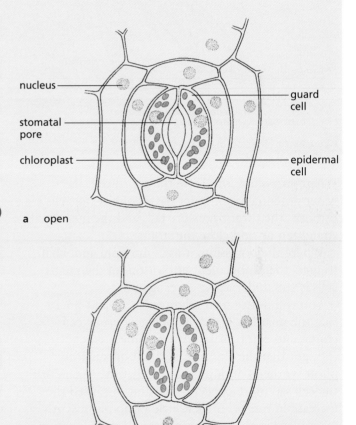

a   open

b   closed

Figure B5.19   Stoma.

The detailed mechanism by which stomata open and close is not fully understood, but it is known that in the light, the potassium concentration in the guard cell vacuoles increases. This lowers the water potential (see 'Osmosis' in Chapter B2) of the cell sap and water enters the guard cells by osmosis from their neighbouring epidermal cells. This inflow of water raises the turgor pressure inside the guard cells.

The cell wall next to the stomatal pore is thicker than elsewhere in the cell and is less able to stretch (Figure B5.20). So, although the increased turgor tends to expand the whole guard cell, the thick inner wall cannot expand. This causes the guard cells to curve in such a way that the stomatal pore between them is opened.

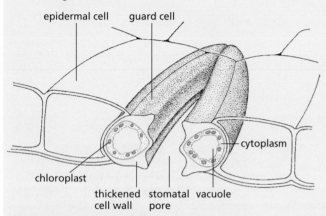

Figure B5.20 Structure of guard cells.

When potassium ions leave the guard cell, the water potential rises, water passes out of the cells by osmosis, the turgor pressure falls and the guard cells straighten up and close the stoma.

Where the potassium ions come from and what triggers their movement into or out of the guard cells is still under active investigation.

You will notice from Figures B5.18 and B5.19 that the guard cells are the only epidermal cells containing chloroplasts. At one time it was thought that the chloroplasts built up sugar by photosynthesis during daylight, that the sugars made the cell sap more concentrated and so caused the increase in turgor. In fact, little or no photosynthesis takes place in these chloroplasts and their function has not been explained, though it is known that starch accumulates in them during the hours of darkness. In some species of plants, the guard cells have no chloroplasts.

Mesophyll
The function of the palisade cells and – to a lesser extent – of the spongy mesophyll cells is to make food by photosynthesis. Their chloroplasts absorb sunlight and use its energy to join carbon dioxide

and water molecules to make sugar molecules as described earlier in this chapter.

In daylight, when photosynthesis is rapid, the mesophyll cells are using up carbon dioxide. As a result, the concentration of carbon dioxide in the air spaces falls to a low level and more carbon dioxide diffuses in (Chapter B2) from the outside air, through the stomata (Figure B5.21). This diffusion continues through the air spaces, up to the cells which are using carbon dioxide. These cells are also producing oxygen as a by-product of photosynthesis. When the concentration of oxygen in the air spaces rises, it diffuses out through the stomata.

Vascular bundles
The water needed for making sugar by photosynthesis is brought to the mesophyll cells by the veins. The mesophyll cells take in the water by osmosis (Chapter B2) because the concentration of free water molecules in a leaf cell, which contains sugars, will be less than the concentration of water in the water vessels of a vein. The branching network of leaf veins means that no cell is very far from a water supply.

The sugars made in the mesophyll cells are passed to the phloem cells (Chapter B7) of the veins, and these cells carry the sugars away from the leaf into the stem.

The ways in which a leaf is thought to be well adapted to its function of photosynthesis are listed in the next paragraph.

Adaptation of leaves for photosynthesis

When biologists say that something is **adapted**, they mean that its structure is well suited to its function. The detailed structure of the leaf is described in the first section of this chapter and although there are wide variations in leaf shape, the following general statements apply to a great many leaves, and are illustrated in Figures B5.16b and c.

- Their broad, flat shape offers a large surface area for absorption of sunlight and carbon dioxide.
- Most leaves are thin and the carbon dioxide only has to diffuse across short distances to reach the inner cells.

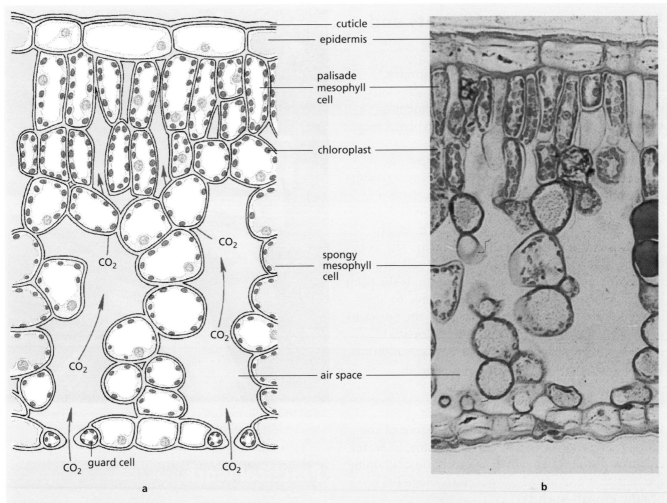

Figure B5.21 Vertical section through a leaf blade (×300).

- The large spaces between cells inside the leaf provide an easy passage through which carbon dioxide can diffuse.
- There are many stomata (pores) in the lower surface of the leaf. These allow the exchange of carbon dioxide and oxygen with the air outside.
- There are more chloroplasts in the upper (palisade) cells than in the lower (spongy mesophyll) cells. The palisade cells, being on the upper surface, will receive most sunlight and this will reach the chloroplasts without being absorbed by too many cell walls.
- The branching network of veins provides a good water supply to the photosynthesising cells. No cell is very far from a water-conducting vessel in one of these veins.

Although photosynthesis takes place mainly in the leaves, any part of the plant that contains chlorophyll will photosynthesise. Many plants have green stems in which photosynthesis takes place.

● Mineral requirements

Plants need a source of nitrate ions (NO_3^-) for making amino acids (Chapter B3). Amino acids are important because they are joined together to make proteins, needed to form the enzymes and cytoplasm of the cell. Nitrates are absorbed from the soil by the roots.

Magnesium ions (Mg^{2+}) are needed to form chlorophyll, the photosynthetic pigment in chloroplasts. This metallic element is also obtained in salts from the soil (see the salts listed under 'Water cultures' on p.50).

Sources of mineral elements and effects of their deficiency

The substances mentioned previously (nitrates, magnesium) are often referred to as 'mineral salts' or 'mineral elements'. If any mineral element is lacking, or deficient, in the soil then the plants may show visible deficiency symptoms.

Many slow-growing wild plants will show no deficiency symptoms even on poor soils. Fast-growing crop plants, on the other hand, will show distinct deficiency symptoms though these will vary according to the species of plant. If nitrate ions are in short supply, the plant will show stunted growth. The stem becomes weak. The lower leaves become yellow and die, while the upper leaves turn pale green. If the plant is deficient in magnesium, it will not be able to make magnesium. The leaves turn yellow from the bottom of the stem upwards (a process called **chlorosis**). Farmers and gardeners can recognise these symptoms and take steps to replace the missing minerals.

Water cultures

It is possible to demonstrate the importance of the various mineral elements by growing plants in **water cultures**. A full water culture is a solution containing the salts that provide all the necessary elements for healthy growth, such as:

- potassium nitrate for potassium and nitrogen
- magnesium sulfate for magnesium and sulfur
- potassium phosphate for potassium and phosphorus
- calcium nitrate for calcium and nitrogen.

From these elements, plus the carbon dioxide, water and sunlight needed for photosynthesis, a green plant can make all the substances it needs for a healthy existence.

Some branches of horticulture, e.g. growing of glasshouse crops, make use of water cultures on a large scale. Sage plants may be grown with their roots in flat polythene tubes. The appropriate water culture solution is pumped along these tubes (Figure B5.22). This method has the advantage that the yield is increased and the need to sterilise the soil each year, to destroy pests, is eliminated. This kind of technique is sometimes described as **hydroponics** or soil-less culture.

Figure B5.22   Soil-less culture. The sage plants are growing in a nutrient solution circulated through troughs of polythene.

Practical work

The importance of different mineral elements

- Place wheat seedlings in test-tubes containing water cultures as shown in Figure B5.23.
- Cover the tubes with aluminium foil to keep out light and so stop green algae from growing in the solution.
- Some of the solutions have one of the elements missing.
- Leave the seedlings to grow in these solutions for a few weeks, keeping the tubes topped up with distilled water.

Result

The kind of result that might be expected from wheat seedlings is shown in Figure B5.24. Generally, the plants in a complete culture will be tall and sturdy, with large, dark green leaves. The plants lacking nitrogen will usually be stunted and have small, pale leaves. In the absence of magnesium, chlorophyll cannot be made, and these plants will be small with yellow leaves.

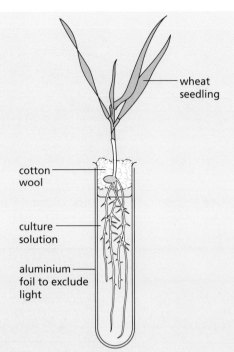

Figure B5.23   Apparatus for a water culture to investigate plant mineral requirements.

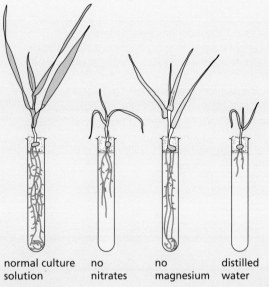

normal culture solution   no nitrates   no magnesium   distilled water

Figure B5.24   Result of water culture experiment.

Interpretation
The healthy plant in the full culture is the control and shows that this method of raising plants does not affect them. The other, less healthy plants show that a full range of mineral elements is necessary for normal growth.

Quantitative results
Although the effects of mineral deficiency can usually be seen simply by looking at the wheat seedlings, it is better if actual measurements are made.

The height of the shoot, or the total length of all the leaves on one plant, can be measured. The total root length can also be measured, though this is difficult if root growth is profuse.

Alternatively, the **dry weight** of the shoots and roots can be measured. In this case, it is best to pool the results of several experiments. All the shoots from the complete culture are placed in a labelled container; all those from the 'no nitrate' culture solution are placed in another container; and so on for all the plants from the different solutions. The shoots are then dried at 110 °C for 24 hours and weighed. The same procedure can be carried out for the roots.

You would expect the roots and shoots from the complete culture to weigh more than those from the nutrient-deficient cultures.

Questions

1 a What substances must a plant take in, in order to carry on photosynthesis?
   b Where does it get each of these substances from?

2 Look at Figure B5.21a. Identify the palisade cells, the spongy mesophyll cells and the cells of the epidermis. In which of these would you expect photosynthesis to occur:
   a most rapidly
   b least rapidly
   c not at all?
   Explain your answers.

3 Look at Figure B5.20. Why do you think that photosynthesis does not take place in the cells of the epidermis?

4 During bright sunlight, what gases are:
   a passing out of the leaf through the stomata
   b entering the leaf through the stomata?

5 a What substances does a green plant need to take in, to make:
     i sugar   ii proteins?
   b What must be present in the cells to make reactions i and ii work?

6 What gases would you expect a leaf to be (i) taking in and (ii) giving out:
   a in bright sunlight   b in darkness?

7 Measurements on a leaf show that it is giving out carbon dioxide and taking in oxygen. Does this prove that photosynthesis is *not* going on in the leaf? Explain your answer.

8 What salts would you put in a water culture which is to contain *no* nitrogen?

9 How can a floating pond plant, such as duckweed, survive without having its roots in soil?

10 In the water culture experiment, why should a lack of nitrate cause reduced growth?

11 Figure B5.25 shows the increased yield of winter wheat in response to adding more nitrogenous fertiliser.
   a If the applied nitrogen is doubled from 50 to 100 kg per hectare, how much extra wheat does the farmer get?
   b If the applied nitrogen is doubled from 100 to 200 kg per hectare, how much extra wheat is obtained?
   c What sort of calculations will a farmer need to make before deciding to increase the applied nitrogen from 150 to 200 kg per hectare?

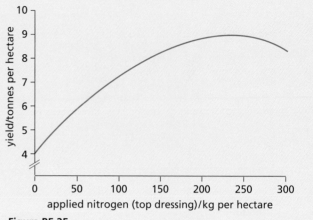

Figure B5.25

Checklist

After studying Chapter B5 you should know and understand the following.

- Photosynthesis is the way plants make their food.
- They combine carbon dioxide and water to make sugar.
- To do this, they need energy from sunlight, which is absorbed by chlorophyll.
- Chlorophyll converts light energy to chemical energy.
- The equation to represent photosynthesis is

$$\text{carbon dioxide} + \text{water} \xrightarrow[\text{chlorophyll}]{\text{light energy}} \text{glucose} + \text{oxygen}$$

- In daylight, a plant will be taking in carbon dioxide and giving out oxygen.
- Experiments to test photosynthesis are designed to exclude light, or carbon dioxide, or chlorophyll, to see if the plant can still produce starch.
- A starch test can be carried out to test if photosynthesis has occurred in a leaf.
- Leaves have a structure which adapts them for photosynthesis.
- Plants need a supply of nitrate ions to make amino acids and magnesium ions to make chlorophyll.

- The balanced chemical equation for photosynthesis is

$$6CO_2 + 6H_2O \xrightarrow[\text{absorbed by chlorophyll}]{\text{energy from sunlight}} C_6H_{12}O_6 + 6O_2$$

- Chlorophyll is needed to transfer light energy into chemical energy in carbohydrate molecules.
- From the sugar made by photosynthesis, a plant can make all the other substances it needs, provided it has a supply of mineral salts like nitrates.
- The rate of photosynthesis may be restricted by light intensity and temperature.
- Plant leaves are adapted for the process of photosynthesis by being broad and thin, with many chloroplasts in their cells. Some parts of the leaf are involved with gas exchange. Xylem is present for transport and support. Phloem is involved with the transport of photosynthetic products.
- Nitrate ions are needed to make proteins; magnesium ions are needed to make chlorophyll. If supplies of these are deficient, plant growth is affected.

Animal nutrition

Combined	Co-ordinated
Combined	**Co-ordinated**

Combined

- State what is meant by the term *balanced diet* for humans

- Explain how age, gender and activity affect the dietary needs of humans including during pregnancy and whilst breast-feeding

- List the principal sources of, and describe the dietary importance of: carbohydrates; fats; proteins; vitamins, limited to C and D; mineral salts, limited to calcium and iron; fibre (roughage); water

- Describe the effects of malnutrition in relation to starvation, constipation, coronary heart disease, obesity and scurvy

- Explain the causes and effects of vitamin D and iron deficiencies

- Define *ingestion*

- Define *digestion*

- Define *mechanical digestion*

- Define *chemical digestion*

- Define *absorption*

- Define *egestion*

- Identify the main regions of the alimentary canal and associated organs, limited to mouth, salivary glands, oesophagus, stomach, small intestine, pancreas, liver, gall bladder, large intestine and anus

- Describe the functions of the regions of the alimentary canal listed above, in relation to ingestion, digestion, absorption and egestion of food

- State the significance of chemical digestion in the alimentary canal in producing small, soluble molecules that can be absorbed

- State the functions of enzymes as follows: amylase breaks down starch to simpler sugars; protease breaks down protein to amino acids; lipase breaks down fats to fatty acids and glycerol

- State where, in the alimentary canal, amylase, protease and lipase are secreted

- State the functions of the hydrochloric acid in gastric juice, limited to killing bacteria in food and giving an acid pH for enzymes

Co-ordinated

- State what is meant by the term *balanced diet* for humans

- Explain how age, gender and activity affect the dietary needs of humans including during pregnancy and whilst breast-feeding

- List the principal sources of, and describe the dietary importance of: *carbohydrates; fats; proteins; vitamins, limited to C and D; mineral salts, limited to calcium and iron; fibre (roughage); water*

- Describe the effects of malnutrition in relation to starvation, constipation, coronary heart disease, obesity and scurvy

- Explain the causes and effects of vitamin D and iron deficiencies

- Explain the causes and effects of protein–energy malnutrition, e.g. kwashiorkor and marasmus

- Define *ingestion*

- Define *digestion*

- Define *mechanical digestion*

- Define *chemical digestion*

- Define *absorption*

- Define *assimilation*

- Define *egestion*

- Identify the main regions of the alimentary canal and associated organs, including mouth, salivary glands, oesophagus, stomach, small intestine, pancreas, liver, gall bladder, large intestine and anus

- Describe the functions of the regions of the alimentary canal listed above, in relation to ingestion, digestion, absorption, assimilation and egestion of food

- Identify the types of human teeth (incisors, canines, premolars and molars)

- Describe the structure of human teeth, limited to enamel, dentine, pulp, nerves and cement, as well as the gums

- Describe the functions of the types of human teeth in mechanical digestion of food

- Describe the proper care of teeth in terms of diet and regular brushing

- State the causes of dental decay in terms of a coating of bacteria and food on teeth, the bacteria respiring sugars in the food, producing acid which dissolves the enamel and dentine

The need for food

All living organisms need food. An important difference between plants and animals is that green plants can make food in their leaves but animals have to take it in 'ready-made' by eating plants or the bodies of other animals. In all plants and animals, food is used as follows:

For growth

It provides the substances needed for making new cells and tissues.

As a source of energy

Energy is required for the chemical reactions that take place in living organisms to keep them alive. When food is broken down during respiration (see Chapter B8), the energy from the food is used for chemical reactions such as building complex molecules (Chapter B3). In animals the energy is also used for activities such as movement, the heart beat and nerve impulses. Mammals and birds use energy to maintain their body temperature.

For replacement of worn and damaged tissues

The substances provided by food are needed to replace the millions of our red blood cells that break down each day, to replace the skin that is worn away and to repair wounds.

● Diet

Balanced diets

A **balanced diet** must contain enough carbohydrates and fats to meet our energy needs. It must also contain enough protein of the right kind to provide the essential amino acids to make new cells and tissues for growth or repair. The diet must also contain vitamins and mineral salts, plant fibre and water. The composition of four food samples is shown in Figure B6.1.

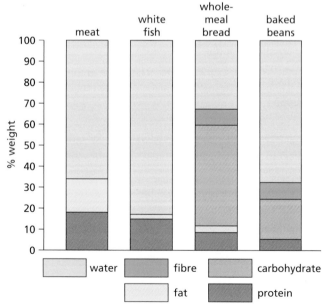

Figure B6.1 An analysis of four food samples.

Note: The percentage of water includes any salts and vitamins. There are wide variations in the composition of any given food sample according to its source and the method of preservation and cooking. 'White fish' (e.g. cod, haddock, plaice) contains only 0.5% fat whereas herring and mackerel contain up to 14%. White bread contains only 2–3% fibre. Frying the food greatly adds to its fat content.

Energy requirements

Energy can be obtained from carbohydrates, fats and proteins. The cheapest energy-giving food is usually carbohydrate; the greatest amount of energy is available in fats; proteins give about the same energy as carbohydrates but are expensive. Whatever mixture of carbohydrate, fat and protein makes up the diet, the total energy must be sufficient:

- to keep our internal body processes working (e.g. heart beating, breathing action)
- to keep up our body temperature
- to meet the needs of work and other activities.

Females tend to have lower energy requirements than males. Two reasons for this are that females have, on average, a lower body mass than males, which has a lower demand on energy intake, and there are also different physical demands made on boys and girls. However, an active female may well have a higher energy requirement than an inactive male of the same age.

As children grow, the energy requirement increases because of the energy demands of the growth process and the extra energy associated with maintaining their body temperature. However, metabolism, and therefore energy demands, tends to slow down with age once we become adults due to a progressive loss of muscle tissue.

Special needs
Pregnancy

A pregnant woman who is already receiving an adequate diet needs no extra food. Her body's metabolism will adapt to the demands of the growing baby although the demand for energy and protein does increase. If, however, her diet is deficient in protein, calcium, iron, vitamin D or folic acid, she will need to increase her intake of these substances to meet the needs of the baby. The baby needs protein for making its tissues, calcium and vitamin D are needed for bone development, and iron is used to make the haemoglobin in its blood.

Lactation

'Lactation' means the production of breast milk for feeding the baby. The production of milk, rich in proteins and minerals, makes a large demand on the mother's resources. If her diet is already adequate, her metabolism will adjust to these demands. Otherwise, she may need to increase her intake of proteins, vitamins and calcium to produce milk of adequate quality and quantity.

Malnutrition

Malnutrition is often taken to mean simply not getting enough food, but it has a much wider meaning than this, including getting too much food or the wrong sort of food.

If the total intake of food is not sufficient to meet the body's need for energy, the body tissues themselves are broken down to provide the energy to stay alive. This leads to loss of weight, muscle wastage, weakness and ultimately **starvation**. Extreme slimming diets, such as those that avoid carbohydrate foods, can result in the disease anorexia nervosa.

Coronary heart disease can occur when the diet contains too much fat (see 'Heart' in Chapter B7). Deposits of a fatty substance build up in the arteries, reducing the diameter of these blood vessels, including the coronary artery. Blood clots are then more likely to form. Blood supply to the heart can be reduced resulting in **angina** (chest pains when exercising or climbing stairs, for example) and eventually a coronary **heart attack**.

If food intake is drastically inadequate, it is likely that the diet will also be deficient in proteins, minerals and vitamins so that deficiency diseases such as anaemia, rickets and scurvy also make an appearance. **Scurvy** is caused by a lack of vitamin C (ascorbic acid) in the diet. Vitamin C is present in citrus fruit such as lemons, blackcurrants, tomatoes, fresh green vegetables and potatoes. It is not unusual for people in developed countries who rely on processed food such as tinned products, rather than eating fresh produce, to suffer from scurvy. Symptoms of scurvy include bleeding under the skin, swollen and bleeding gums and poor healing of wounds. The victims of malnutrition due to food deficiencies such as those mentioned above will also have reduced resistance to infectious diseases such as malaria or measles. Thus, the symptoms of malnutrition are usually the outcome of a variety of causes, but all resulting from an inadequate diet.

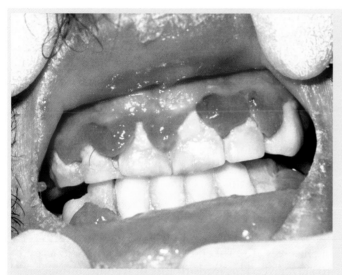

Figure B6.2 Symptoms of scurvy.

Many of the processed foods in Western diets contain too little fibre. White bread, for example, has had the fibre (bran) removed. A lack of fibre can result in **constipation** see 'Classes of food' below. Unprocessed foods, such as unskinned potatoes, vegetables and fruit, contain plenty of fibre. Food rich in fibre is usually bulky and makes you feel 'full up' so that you are unlikely to overeat. Fibre enables the process of peristalsis to move food through the gut more efficiently and may also protect the intestine from cancer and other disorders. Fibre helps prevent constipation.

Overweight and obesity

These are different degrees of the same disorder. If you take in more food than your body needs for energy, growth and replacement, the excess is converted to fat and stored in fat deposits under the skin or in the abdomen.

Obese people are more likely to suffer from high blood pressure, coronary heart disease (see the previous section on malnutrition) and diabetes. Having extra weight to carry also makes you reluctant to take exercise. By measuring a person's height and body mass, it is possible to use a chart to predict whether or not they have an ideal body mass (Figure B6.3).

Why some people should be prone to obesity is unclear. There may be a genetic predisposition, in which the brain centre that responds to food intake may not signal when sufficient food has been taken in; in some cases it may be the outcome of an infectious disease. Whatever the cause, the remedy is to reduce food intake to a level that matches but does not exceed the body's needs. Taking exercise helps, but it takes a great deal of exercise to 'burn off' even a small amount of surplus fat.

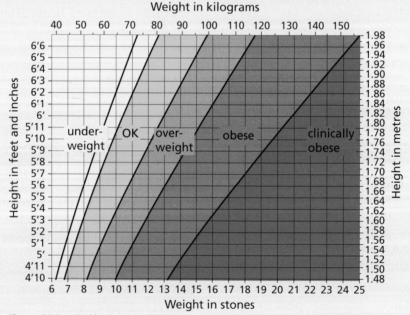

Figure B6.3 Ideal body mass chart.

Classes of food

There are three classes of food: carbohydrates, proteins and fats. The chemical structure of these substances is described in Chapter B3. In addition to proteins, carbohydrates and fats, the diet must include salts, vitamins, water and vegetable fibre (roughage). These substances are present in a balanced diet and do not normally have to be taken in separately. A summary of the three classes of food and their sources is shown in Table B6.1.

Table B6.1 Summary of the main nutrients

Nutrient	Elements present	Examples	Sub-units
carbohydrate	carbon, hydrogen, oxygen	starch, glycogen, cellulose, sucrose	glucose
fat/oil (oils are liquid at room temperature, but fats are solid)	carbon, hydrogen, oxygen (but lower oxygen content than carbohydrates)	vegetable oils, e.g. olive oil; animal fats, e.g. cod liver oil, waxes	fatty acids and glycerol
protein	carbon, hydrogen, oxygen, nitrogen, sometimes sulfur or phosphorus	enzymes, muscle, haemoglobin, cell membranes	amino acids (about 20 different forms)

Carbohydrates

Sugar and **starch** are important carbohydrates in our diet. Starch is abundant in potatoes, bread, maize, rice and other cereals. Sugar appears in our diet mainly as **sucrose** (table sugar) which is added to drinks and many prepared foods such as jam, biscuits and cakes. Glucose and fructose are sugars that occur naturally in many fruits and some vegetables.

Although all foods provide us with energy, carbohydrates are the cheapest and most readily available source of energy. They contain the elements carbon, hydrogen and oxygen (e.g. glucose is $C_6H_{12}O_6$). When carbohydrates are oxidised to provide energy by respiration they are broken down to carbon dioxide and water (Chapter B8). One gram of carbohydrate can provide, on average, 16 kilojoules (kJ) of energy.

If we eat more carbohydrates than we need for our energy requirements, the excess is converted in the liver to either glycogen or fat. The glycogen is stored in the liver and muscles; the fat is stored in fat

deposits in the abdomen, round the kidneys or under the skin (Figure B6.4).

The **cellulose** in the cell walls of all plant tissues is a carbohydrate. We probably derive relatively little nourishment from cellulose but it is important in the diet as **fibre**, which helps to maintain a healthy digestive system.

Fats

Animal fats are found in meat, milk, cheese, butter and egg-yolk. Plant fats occur as oils in fruits (e.g. palm oil) and seeds (e.g. sunflower seed oil), and are used for cooking and making margarine. Fats and oils are sometimes collectively called **lipids**.

Lipids are used in the cells of the body to form part of the cell membrane and other membrane systems. Lipids can also be oxidised in respiration, to carbon dioxide and water. When used to provide energy in this way, 1 g fat gives 37 kJ of energy. This is more than twice as much energy as can be obtained from the same weight of carbohydrate or protein.

Fats can be stored in the body, so providing a means of long-term storage of energy in fat deposits. The fatty tissue, **adipose tissue**, under the skin forms a layer that, if its blood supply is restricted, can reduce heat losses from the body.

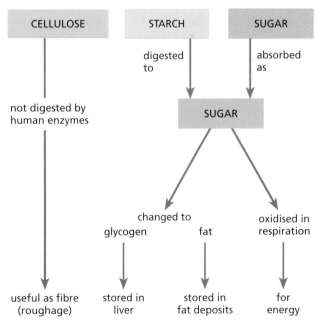

Figure B6.4 Digestion and use of carbohydrate.

Proteins

Lean meat, fish, eggs, milk and cheese are important sources of animal protein. All plants contain some protein, but soybeans, seeds such as pumpkin, and nuts are the best sources (see Table B6.2).

Table B6.2 Comparing the protein content of foods (source: USDA database)

Food	Protein content/g per 100 g
soybeans	35
pumpkin seeds	30
beef, lean	27
peanuts	26
fish, e.g. salmon	25
cheese, e.g. cheddar	25
bacon	20
Tofu	18
beef sausage	18
chicken breast	17
Quorn sausage	14
eggs	13
wheat flour	13
yoghurt	4

Proteins, when digested, provide the chemical substances needed to build cells and tissues, e.g. skin, muscle, blood and bones. Neither carbohydrates nor fats can do this so it is essential to include some proteins in the diet.

Protein molecules consist of long chains of **amino acids** (see Chapter B3). When proteins are digested, the molecules are broken up into the constituent amino acids. The amino acids are absorbed into the bloodstream and used to build up different proteins. These proteins form part of the cytoplasm and enzymes of cells and tissues.

The amino acids that are not used for making new tissues cannot be stored, but the liver removes their amino ($-NH_2$) groups and changes the residue to glycogen. The glycogen can be stored or oxidised to provide energy (Chapter B8). One gram of protein can provide 17 kJ of energy.

Chemically, proteins differ from both carbohydrates and fats because they contain nitrogen and sometimes sulfur as well as carbon, hydrogen and oxygen.

Vitamins

All proteins are similar to each other in their chemical structure, as are all carbohydrates. Vitamins, on the other hand, are a group of organic substances quite unrelated to each other in their chemical structure.

The features shared by all vitamins are:

- they are not digested or broken down for energy
- mostly, they are not built into the body structures
- they are essential in small quantities for health
- they are needed for chemical reactions in the cells, working in association with enzymes.

Plants can make these vitamins in their leaves, but animals have to obtain many of them ready-made either from plants or from other animals.

If any one of the vitamins is missing or deficient in the diet, a vitamin-deficiency disease may develop. Such a disease can be cured, at least in the early stages, simply by adding the vitamin to the diet.

Fifteen or more vitamins have been identified and they are sometimes grouped into two classes: water-soluble and fat-soluble. The fat-soluble vitamins are found mostly in animal fats or vegetable oils, which is one reason why our diet should include some of these fats. The water-soluble vitamins are present in green leaves, fruits and cereal grains.

See Table B6.3 for details of vitamins C and D.

Table B6.3 Vitamins

Name and source of vitamin	Importance of vitamin	Diseases and symptoms caused by lack of vitamin	Notes
vitamin C (ascorbic acid); water-soluble: oranges, lemons, grapefruit, tomatoes, fresh green vegetables, potatoes	prevents scurvy	Fibres in connective tissue of skin and blood vessels do not form properly, leading to bleeding under the skin, particularly at the joints, swollen, bleeding gums and poor healing of wounds. These are all symptoms of scurvy (Figure B6.2).	Possibly acts as a catalyst in cell respiration. Scurvy is only likely to occur when fresh food is not available. Cows' milk and milk powders contain little ascorbic acid so babies may need additional sources. Cannot be stored in the body; daily intake needed.
vitamin D (calciferol); fat-soluble: butter, milk, cheese, egg-yolk, liver, fish-liver oil	prevents rickets	Calcium is not deposited properly in the bones, causing **rickets** in young children. The bones remain soft and are deformed by the child's weight (Figure B6.5 on p.60). Deficiency in adults causes **osteo-malacia**; fractures are likely.	Vitamin D helps the absorption of calcium from the intestine and the deposition of calcium salts in the bones. Natural fats in the skin are converted to a form of vitamin D by sunlight.

Salts

These are sometimes called 'mineral salts' or just 'minerals'. Proteins, carbohydrates and fats provide the body with carbon, hydrogen, oxygen, nitrogen, sulfur and phosphorus but there are several more elements that the body needs and which occur as salts in the food we eat.

Iron

Red blood cells contain the pigment haemoglobin (see 'Blood' in Chapter B7). Part of the haemoglobin molecule contains iron and this plays an important role in carrying oxygen around the body. Millions of red cells break down each day and their iron is stored by the liver and used to make more haemoglobin. However, some iron is lost and needs to be replaced through dietary intake.

Red meat, especially liver and kidney, is the richest source of iron in the diet, but eggs, groundnuts, wholegrains such as brown rice, spinach and other green vegetables are also important sources.

If the diet is deficient in iron, a person may suffer from some form of **anaemia**. Insufficient haemoglobin is made and the oxygen-carrying capacity of the blood is reduced.

Calcium

Calcium, in the form of calcium phosphate, is deposited in the bones and the teeth and makes them hard. It is present in blood plasma and plays an essential part in normal blood clotting (see 'Blood' in Chapter B7). Calcium is also needed for the chemical changes that make muscles contract and for the transmission of nerve impulses.

The richest sources of calcium are milk (liquid, skimmed or dried) and cheese, but calcium is present in most foods in small quantities and also in 'hard' water.

Many calcium salts are not soluble in water and may pass through the alimentary canal without being absorbed. Simply increasing the calcium in the diet may not have much effect unless the calcium is in the right form, the diet is balanced and the intestine is healthy. Vitamin D and bile salts are needed for efficient absorption of calcium.

Dietary fibre (roughage)

When we eat vegetables and other fresh plant material, we take in a large quantity of plant cells. The cell walls of plants consist mainly of cellulose, but we do not have enzymes for digesting this substance. The result is that the plant cell walls reach the large intestine (colon) without being digested. This undigested part of the diet is called fibre or roughage. The colon contains many bacteria that can digest some of the substances in the plant cell walls to form fatty acids (Chapter B3). Vegetable fibre, therefore, may supply some useful food material, but it has other important functions.

Most vegetables and whole cereal grains contain fibre, but white flour and white bread do not contain much. Good sources of dietary fibre are vegetables, fruit and wholemeal bread.

Water

About 70% of most tissue consists of water; it is an essential part of cytoplasm. The body fluids, blood, lymph and tissue fluid (Chapter B7) are composed mainly of water.

Digested food, salts and vitamins are carried around the body as a watery solution in the blood (Chapter B7) and excretory products such as excess salt and urea are removed from the body in solution by the kidneys. Water thus acts as a solvent and as a transport medium for these substances.

Digestion is a process that uses water in a chemical reaction to break down insoluble substances to soluble ones. These products then pass, in solution, into the bloodstream. In all cells there are many reactions in which water plays an essential part as a reactant and a solvent.

Since we lose water by evaporation, sweating, urinating and breathing, we have to make good this loss by taking in water with the diet.

Causes and effects of mineral and vitamin deficiencies

Iron

Iron is present in red meat, eggs, nuts, brown rice, shellfish, soybean flour, dried fruit such as apricots, spinach and other dark-green leafy vegetables.

Lack of iron in the diet can lead to iron-deficiency anaemia, which is a decrease in the number of red blood cells. Red blood cells, when mature, have no nucleus and this limits their life to about 3 months, after which they are broken down in the liver and replaced. Most of the iron is recycled, but some is lost as a chemical called bilirubin in the faeces and needs to be replaced. Adults need to take in about 15 mg each day. Without sufficient iron, your body is unable to produce enough haemoglobin, the protein in red blood cells responsible for transporting oxygen to respiring tissues. Iron is also needed by the muscles and for enzyme systems in all the body cells. The symptoms of anaemia are feeling weak, tired and irritable.

Vitamin D

Vitamin D is the only vitamin that the body can manufacture, when the skin is exposed to sunlight. However, for 6 months of the year (October to April), much of western Europe does not receive enough UV rays in sunlight to make vitamin D in the skin. So, many people living there are at risk of not getting enough vitamin D unless they get it in their diet. Also, people who have darker skin, such as people of African, African-Caribbean and South Asian origin, are at risk because their skin reduces UV light absorption.

Foods that provide vitamin D include oily fish such as sardines and mackerel, fish liver oil, butter, milk, cheese and egg-yolk. In addition, many manufactured food products contain vitamin D supplements.

Vitamin D helps in the absorption of calcium and phosphorus through the gut wall. Bone is made of the mineral calcium phosphate. A lack of the vitamin therefore results in poor calcium and phosphorus deposition in bones, leading to softening. The weight of the body can deform bones in the legs, causing the condition called rickets in children (Figure B6.5). Adults deficient in vitamin D can suffer from **osteo-malacia**; they are very vulnerable to fracturing bones if they fall.

Kwashiorkor

Kwashiorkor (roughly = 'deposed child') is an example of protein–energy malnutrition (PEM)

Figure B6.5 A child with rickets.

in the developing world. When a mother has her second baby, the first baby is weaned on to a starchy diet of yam, cassava or sweet potato, all of which have inadequate protein. The first baby then develops symptoms of kwashiorkor (dry skin, pot-belly, changes to hair colour, weakness and irritability). Protein deficiency is not the only cause of kwashiorkor. Infection, plant toxins, digestive failure or even psychological effects may be involved. The good news, however, is that it can often be cured or prevented by an intake of protein in the form of dried skimmed milk.

Marasmus

The term 'marasmus' is derived from a Greek word, meaning decay. It is an acute form of malnutrition. The condition is due to a very poor diet with inadequate carbohydrate intake as well as a lack of protein. The incidence of marasmus increases in babies until they reach the age of 12 months. Sufferers are extremely emaciated with reduced fat and muscle tissue. Their skin is thin and hangs in folds. Marasmus is distinguished from kwashiorkor because kwashiorkor is due to lack of protein intake, while energy intake is adequate. Treatment involves provision of an energy-rich, balanced diet, but the complications of the disorder, which may include infections and dehydration, also need attention to increase chances of survival and recovery.

Practical work

Energy from food

- Set up the apparatus as shown in Figure B6.6.
- Use a measuring cylinder to place 20 cm³ cold water in the boiling tube.
- With a thermometer, find the temperature of the water and make a note of it.
- Weigh a peanut (or other piece of dried food), secure it onto a mounted needle and heat it with the Bunsen flame until it begins to burn.

Caution: make sure that no students have nut allergies.
- As soon as it starts burning, hold the nut under the boiling tube so that the flames heat the water.
- If the flame goes out, do not apply the Bunsen burner to the food while it is under the boiling tube, but return the nut to the Bunsen flame to start the nut burning again and replace it beneath the boiling tube as soon as the nut catches alight.
- When the nut has finished burning and cannot be ignited again, gently stir the water in the boiling tube with the thermometer and record its new temperature.

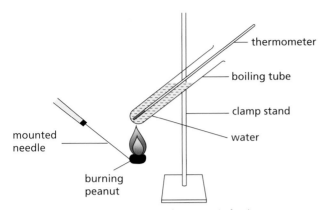

Figure B6.6 Experiment to show the energy in food.

■ Calculate the rise in temperature by subtracting the first from the second temperature.
■ Work out the quantity of energy transferred to the water from the burning peanut as follows:

4.2 J raise 1 g water by 1 °C
20 cm³ cold water weighs 20 g

The energy (in joules) released by the burning nut
= rise in temperature × mass of water × 4.2

Note: The value 4.2 in the equation is used to convert the answer from calories to joules, as the calorie is an obsolete unit.

■ To calculate the energy from 1 g of nut, divide your answer by the mass of nut you used. This gives a value in J/g.
■ The experiment can now be repeated using different sizes of nut, or different varieties of nut, or other types of food. Remember to replace the warm water in the boiling tube with 20 cm³ cold water each time.
■ The experiment is quite inaccurate: compare the value you obtained with an official value (2385 kJ per 100 g). There are plenty of websites with this sort of information if you use different nuts or other food. To make the comparison you may need to convert your energy value from joules to kilojoules (divide by 1000) and to 100 g of the food (multiply by 100).
■ Try to list some of the faults in the design of the experiment to account for the difference you find. Where do you think some of the heat is going? Can you suggest ways of reducing this loss to make the results more accurate?

Questions

1 What sources of protein-rich foods are available to a vegetarian who:
  a will eat animal products but not meat itself
  b will eat only plants and their products?
2 Why must all diets contain some protein?
3 Could you survive on a diet that contained no carbohydrate? Justify your answer.
4 How do proteins differ from fats (lipids) in:
  a their chemical composition (Chapter B3)
  b their energy value
  c their role in the body?
5 Some examples of the food that would give a balanced diet are shown in Figure B6.7. Consider the picture and say what class of food or item of diet is mainly present. For example, the meat is mainly protein but will also contain some iron.
6 What is the value of leafy vegetables, such as cabbage and lettuce, in the diet?
7 Why is a diet consisting mainly of one type of food, e.g. rice or potatoes, likely to be unsatisfactory even if it is sufficient to meet our energy needs?

8 A zoologist is trying to find out whether rabbits need vitamin C in their diet. Assuming that a sufficiently large number of rabbits is used and adequate controls are applied, the best design of experiment would be to give the rabbits:
  a an artificial diet of pure protein, carbohydrate, fats, minerals and vitamins but lacking vitamin C
  b an artificial diet as above but with extra vitamin C
  c a natural diet of grass, carrots, etc. but with added vitamin C
  d natural food but of one kind only, e.g. exclusively grass or exclusively carrots?
Justify your choice and say why you excluded the other alternatives.

Figure B6.7 Examples of types of food in a balanced diet.

● Alimentary canal

Key definitions
Ingestion is the taking of substances such as food and drink into the body through the mouth.
Digestion is the breakdown of large, insoluble food molecules into small, water-soluble molecules using mechanical and chemical processes.
Absorption is the movement of small food molecules and ions through the wall of the intestine into the blood.
Egestion is the passing out of food that has not been digested or absorbed, as faeces, through the anus.

Feeding involves taking food into the mouth, chewing it and swallowing it down into the stomach. This satisfies our hunger, but for food to be of any use to the whole body it has first to be **digested**. This means that the solid food is dissolved and the molecules reduced in size. The soluble products then have to be **absorbed** into the bloodstream and carried by the blood all around the body. In this way, the blood delivers dissolved food to the living cells in all parts of the body such as the muscles, brain, heart and kidneys. This section describes how the food is digested and absorbed. Chapter B7 describes how the blood carries it around the body.

Regions of the alimentary canal and their functions

The **alimentary canal** is a tube running through the body. Food is digested in the alimentary canal. The soluble products are absorbed and the indigestible residues expelled (egested). A simplified diagram of an alimentary canal is shown in Figure B6.8.

The inside of the alimentary canal is lined with layers of cells forming what is called an **epithelium**. New cells in the epithelium are being produced all the time to replace the cells worn away by the movement of the food. There are also cells in the lining that produce **mucus**. Mucus is a slimy liquid that lubricates the lining of the canal and protects it from wear and tear. Mucus may also protect the lining from attack by the **digestive enzymes** which are released into the alimentary canal.

Some of the digestive enzymes are produced by cells in the lining of the alimentary canal, as in the stomach lining. Others are produced by **glands** that are outside the alimentary canal but pour their enzymes through tubes (called **ducts**) into the alimentary canal (Figure B6.9). The **salivary glands** and the **pancreas** (see Figure B6.10) are examples of such digestive glands.

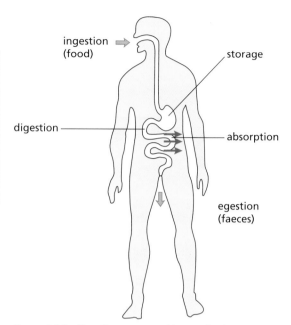

Figure B6.8   The alimentary canal (generalised).

The alimentary canal has a great many blood vessels in its walls, close to the lining. These bring oxygen needed by the cells and take away the carbon dioxide they produce. They also absorb the digested food from the alimentary canal.

There are five main processes occurring in the alimentary canal that are associated with digestion.

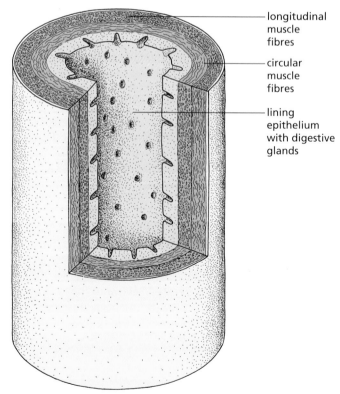

Figure B6.9   The general structure of the alimentary canal.

These are **ingestion**, digestion, absorption, assimilation and digestion. Figure B6.8 shows where four of these processes occur. Assimilation can happen in any cells of the body which use the digested food molecules. The functions of the main parts of the alimentary canal are given in Table B6.4.

Table B6.4   Functions of main parts of the alimentary canal

Region of alimentary canal	Function
mouth	**ingestion** of food; **mechanical digestion** by teeth; **chemical digestion** of starch by amylase; formation of a bolus for swallowing
salivary glands	saliva contains amylase for **chemical digestion** of starch in food; also liquid to lubricate food and make small pieces stick together
oesophagus (gullet)	transfers food from the mouth to the stomach, by peristalsis
stomach	produces gastric juice containing pepsin, for **chemical digestion** of protein; also hydrochloric acid to kill bacteria; peristalsis churns food up into a liquid
duodenum	first part of the small intestine; receives pancreatic juice for **chemical digestion** of proteins, fats and starch as well as neutralising the acid from the stomach; receives bile to emulsify fats (a form of **physical digestion**)
ileum	second part of the small intestine; enzymes in the epithelial lining carry out **chemical digestion** of maltose and peptides; very long and has villi (see Figures B6.18 and B6.19) to increase surface area for **absorption** of digested food molecules
pancreas	secretes pancreatic juice into the duodenum via pancreatic duct (see Figure B6.17) for **chemical digestion** of proteins, fats and starch
liver	makes bile, containing salts to emulsify fats (**physical digestion**); **assimilation** of digested food such as glucose; **deamination** of excess amino acids
gall bladder	stores bile, made in the liver, to be secreted into the duodenum via the bile duct (see Figure B6.17)
colon	first part of the large intestine; **absorption** of water from undigested food; **absorption** of bile salts to pass back to the liver
rectum	second part of the large intestine; stores faeces
anus	**egestion** of faeces

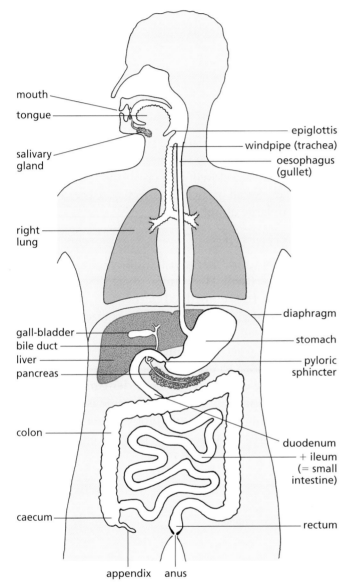

Figure B6.10   The alimentary canal.

Labels: mouth, tongue, salivary gland, right lung, gall-bladder, bile duct, liver, pancreas, colon, caecum, appendix, anus, epiglottis, windpipe (trachea), oesophagus (gullet), diaphragm, stomach, pyloric sphincter, duodenum + ileum (= small intestine), rectum

Key definitions
Mechanical digestion is the breakdown of food into smaller pieces without chemical change to the food molecules.
Chemical digestion is the breakdown of large insoluble molecules into small soluble molecules.

Key definition
Mechanical digestion is the breakdown of food into smaller pieces without any chemical change taking place. It mainly occurs in the mouth by means of the teeth, through a process called mastication.

● Mechanical digestion

The process of mechanical digestion mainly occurs in the mouth by means of the teeth, through a process called mastication.

Humans are omnivores (organisms that eat animal and plant material). Broadly, we have the same types of teeth as carnivores, but human teeth are not used for catching, holding, killing or tearing up prey, and we cannot cope with bones. Thus, although we have incisors, canines, premolars and molars, they do not show such big variations in size and shape as, for example, a wolf's. Figure B6.11 shows the position of teeth in the upper jaw and Figure B6.12 shows how they appear in both jaws when seen from the side.

Table B6.5 gives a summary of the types of human teeth and their functions.

Our top incisors pass in front of our bottom incisors and cut pieces off the food, such as when biting into an apple or taking a bite out of a piece of toast.

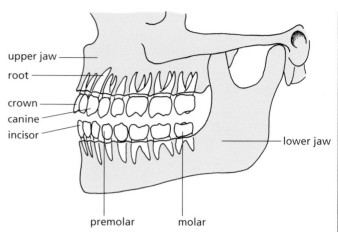

Figure B6.12   Human jaws and teeth.

Our premolars and molars are similar in shape and function. Their knobbly surfaces, called cusps, meet when the jaws are closed, and crush the food into small pieces. Small particles of food are easier to digest than large chunks.

Tooth structure

The part of a tooth that is visible above the gum line is called the **crown**. The **gum** is tissue that overlays the jaws. The rest, embedded in the jaw bone, is called the **root** (Figure B6.13). The surface of the crown is covered by a very hard layer of **enamel**. This layer is replaced by **cement** in the root, which enables the tooth to grip to its bony socket in the jaw. Below the enamel is a layer of **dentine**. Dentine is softer than enamel. Inside the dentine is a **pulp cavity**, containing nerves and blood vessels. These enter the tooth through a small hole at the base of the root.

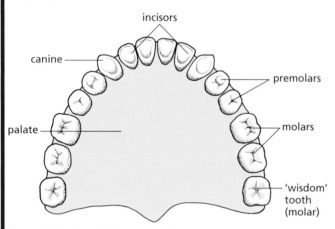

Figure B6.11   Teeth in human upper jaw.

Our canines are more pointed than the incisors but are not much larger. They function like extra incisors.

Table B6.5   Summary of types of human teeth and their functions

Type	Incisor	Canine	Premolar	Molar
Diagram				
Position in mouth	front	either side of incisors	behind canines	back
Description	chisel-shaped (sharp edge)	slightly more pointed than incisors	have two points (cusps); have one or two roots	have four or five cusps; have two or three roots
Function	biting off pieces of food	similar function to incisors	tearing and grinding food	chewing and grinding food

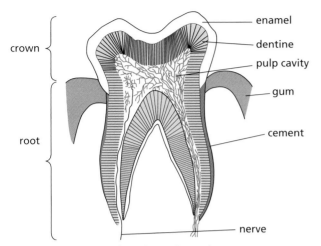

Figure B6.13 Section through a molar tooth.

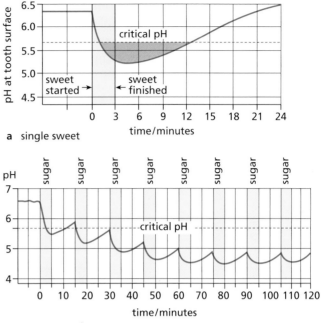

Figure B6.14 pH in the mouth when sweets are sucked.

Dental decay (dental caries)

Decay begins when small holes (cavities) appear in the enamel. The cavities are caused by bacteria on the tooth surface. The bacteria feed on the sugars deposited on the teeth, respiring them and producing acid, which dissolves the calcium salts in the tooth enamel. The enamel is dissolved away in patches, exposing the dentine to the acids. Dentine is softer than enamel and dissolves more quickly so cavities are formed. The cavities reduce the distance between the outside of the tooth and the nerve endings. The acids produced by the bacteria irritate the nerve endings and cause toothache. If the cavity is not cleaned and filled by a dentist, the bacteria will get into the pulp cavity and cause a painful abscess at the root. Often, the only way to treat this is to have the tooth pulled out.

Western diets contain a good deal of refined sugar and many children suck sweets between one meal and the next. The high level of dental decay in Western society is thought to be caused mainly by keeping sugar in the mouth for long periods of time.

Figure B6.14 shows the effect on pH in the mouth when sweets are sucked over time. The critical pH is the acidity below which tooth enamel starts to be damaged by the acid.

The best way to prevent tooth decay, therefore, is to avoid eating sugar at frequent intervals either in the form of sweets or in sweet drinks such as orange squash or soft (fizzy) drinks.

It is advisable also to visit the dentist every 6 months or so for a 'check-up' so that any **caries** or gum disease can be treated at an early stage.

Brushing the teeth is very important in the prevention of gum disease. It may not be so effective in preventing caries, although the use of fluoride toothpaste does help to reduce the bacterial population on the teeth and to increase their resistance to decay. The use of dental floss and interdental brushes reduces the incidence of gum disease because these help to remove food trapped between the teeth.

● Chemical digestion

Digestion

Digestion is the breakdown of large, insoluble food molecules into small, water-soluble molecules using mechanical and chemical processes.

In the alimentary canal, chemical digestion results in the production of small, soluble molecules. These can be absorbed through the gut wall.

Digestion is mainly a chemical process and consists of breaking down large molecules to small molecules. The large molecules are usually not soluble in water, while the smaller ones are. The small molecules can be absorbed through the epithelium of the alimentary canal, through the walls of the blood vessels and into the blood.

Some food can be absorbed without digestion. The **glucose** in fruit juice, for example, could pass through the walls of the alimentary canal and enter the blood vessels without further change. Most food, however, is solid and cannot get into blood vessels. Digestion is the process by which solid food is dissolved to make a solution.

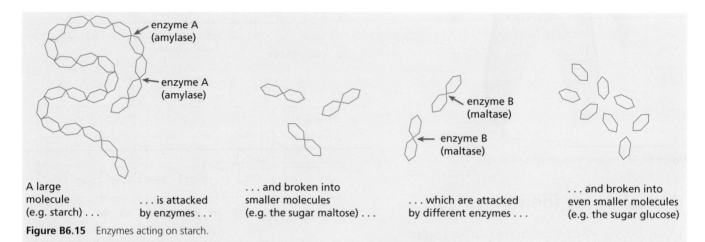

A large molecule (e.g. starch) . . .   . . . is attacked by enzymes . . .   . . . and broken into smaller molecules (e.g. the sugar maltose) . . .   . . . which are attacked by different enzymes . . .   . . . and broken into even smaller molecules (e.g. the sugar glucose)

Figure B6.15 Enzymes acting on starch.

The chemicals that dissolve the food are **enzymes**, described in Chapter B4. A protein might take 50 years to dissolve if just placed in water but is completely digested by enzymes in a few hours. All the solid starch in foods such as bread and potatoes is digested to glucose, which is soluble in water. The solid proteins in meat, eggs and beans are digested to soluble substances called amino acids. Fats are digested to two soluble products called **glycerol** and **fatty acids** (see Chapter B3). Figure B6.15 shows the effect of enzymes acting on starch.

The mouth

The act of taking food into the mouth is called **ingestion**. In the mouth, the food is chewed and mixed with **saliva**. The chewing breaks the food into pieces that can be swallowed and it also increases the surface area for the enzymes to work on later. Saliva is a digestive juice produced by three pairs of glands whose ducts lead into the mouth. It helps to lubricate the food and make the small pieces stick together. Saliva contains one enzyme, **salivary amylase** (sometimes called **ptyalin**), which acts on cooked starch and begins to break it down into maltose.

The stomach

The stomach has elastic walls, which stretch as the food collects in it. The **pyloric sphincter** is a circular band of muscle at the lower end of the stomach that stops solid pieces of food from passing through. The main function of the stomach is to store the food from a meal, turn it into a liquid and release it in small quantities at a time to the rest of the alimentary canal. An example of mechanical digestion is the peristaltic action of muscles in the wall of the stomach. These muscles alternately contract and relax, churning and squeezing the food in the stomach and mixing it with gastric juice, turning the mixture into a creamy liquid called **chyme**. This action gives the food a greater surface area so that it can be digested more efficiently.

Glands in the lining of the stomach (Figure B6.16) produce **gastric juice** containing a **protease** enzyme. It helps in the process of breaking down large protein molecules into small, soluble amino acids. The stomach lining also produces hydrochloric acid, which makes a weak solution in the gastric juice. This acid provides the best degree of acidity for stomach protease to work in (Chapter B3) and kills many of the bacteria taken in with the food.

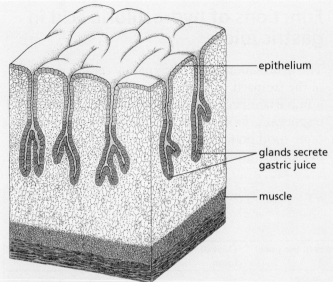

Figure B6.16 Diagram of section through stomach wall.

The small intestine

A digestive juice from the pancreas (**pancreatic juice**) and bile from the liver are poured into the duodenum to act on food there. The pancreas is a digestive gland lying below the stomach (Figure B6.17). It makes a number of enzymes, which act on all classes of food. **Protease** breaks down proteins into amino acids. **Pancreatic amylase** attacks starch and converts it to maltose. **Lipase** digests fats (lipids) to fatty acids and glycerol.

Bile

Bile is a green, watery fluid made in the liver, stored in the gall-bladder and delivered to the duodenum by the bile duct (Figure B6.17). It contains no enzymes, but its green colour is caused by bile pigments, which are formed from the breakdown of haemoglobin in the liver. Bile also contains bile salts, which act on fats rather like a detergent. The bile salts **emulsify** the fats. That is, they break them up into small droplets with a large surface area, which are more efficiently digested by lipase.

Bile is slightly alkaline as it contains sodium hydrogencarbonate and, along with pancreatic juice, has the function of neutralising the acidic mixture of food and gastric juices as it enters the duodenum. This is important because enzymes secreted into the duodenum need alkaline conditions to work at their optimum rate.

Pancreatic juice contains sodium hydrogencarbonate, which partly neutralises the acidic liquid from the stomach. This is necessary because the enzymes of the pancreas do not work well in acid conditions.

All the digestible material is thus changed to soluble compounds, which can pass through the lining of the intestine and into the bloodstream. The final products of digestion are:

Food		Final products
starch	$\rightarrow$	glucose (a simple sugar)
proteins	$\rightarrow$	amino acids
fats (lipids)	$\rightarrow$	fatty acids and glycerol

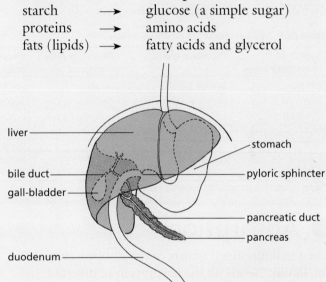

Figure B6.17 Relationship between stomach, liver and pancreas.

Digestion of protein

There are several proteases which break down proteins. One protease is **pepsin**, which is secreted in the stomach. Pepsin acts on proteins and breaks them down into soluble compounds called peptides. These are shorter chains of amino acids than proteins. Another protease is called **trypsin**. Trypsin is secreted by the pancreas in an inactive form which is changed to an active enzyme in the duodenum. It has a similar role to pepsin, breaking down proteins to peptides.

The small intestine also produces digestive enzymes, but these are held in the epithelial cells of the villi. They complete the breakdown of sugars and peptides, before they pass through the cells on their way to the bloodstream. For example, **peptidase** breaks down polypeptides and peptides into amino acids.

Digestion of starch

Starch is digested in two places in the alimentary canal: by salivary amylase in the mouth and by pancreatic amylase in the duodenum. Amylase works best in a neutral or slightly alkaline pH and converts large, insoluble starch molecules into smaller, soluble maltose molecules. Maltose is a disaccharide sugar and is still too big to be absorbed through the wall of the intestine. Maltose is broken down to glucose by the enzyme **maltase**, which is present in the membranes of the epithelial cells of the villi.

Functions of hydrochloric acid in gastric juice

The hydrochloric acid, secreted by cells in the wall of the stomach, creates a very acid pH of 2. This pH is important because it denatures enzymes in harmful organisms in food, such as bacteria (which may otherwise cause food poisoning) and it provides the optimum pH for the protein-digesting enzyme pepsin to work.

Table B6.6 Principal substances produced by digestion

Region of alimentary canal	Digestive gland	Digestive juice produced	Enzymes in the juice/cells	Class of food acted upon	Substances produced
mouth	salivary glands	saliva	salivary amylase	starch	maltose
stomach	glands in stomach lining	gastric juice	pepsin	proteins	peptides
duodenum	pancreas	pancreatic juice	proteases, such as trypsin amylase lipase	proteins and peptides starch fats	peptides and amino acids maltose fatty acids and glycerol
ileum	epithelial cells	(none)	maltase peptidase	maltose peptides	glucose amino acids

(**Note**: details of peptidase and peptides are **not** a syllabus requirement)

● Absorption

The small intestine consists of the duodenum and the **ileum**. Nearly all the absorption of digested food takes place in the ileum, along with most of the water. Small molecules of the digested food such as glucose and amino acids pass into the bloodstream, while fatty acids and glycerol pass into the **lacteals** (Figure B6.19) connected to the **lymphatic system**, which eventually passes them into the bloodstream.

The ileum is efficient in the absorption of digested food for the following reasons:

● It is fairly long and presents a large absorbing surface to the digested food.
● Its internal surface is greatly increased by circular folds (Figure B6.18) bearing thousands of tiny projections called **villi** (singular = villus) (Figures B6.19 and B6.20). These villi are about 0.5 mm long and may be finger-like or flattened in shape.
● The lining epithelium is very thin and the fluids can pass rapidly through it. The outer membrane of each epithelial cell has **microvilli**, which increase by 20 times the exposed surface of the cell.
● There is a dense network of blood capillaries (tiny blood vessels, see 'Transport in animals' in Chapter B7) in each villus (Figure B6.19).

The small molecules of digested food, for example glucose and amino acids, pass into the epithelial cells and then through the wall of the capillaries in the villus and into the bloodstream. They are then carried away in the capillaries, which join up to form veins. These veins unite to form one large vein, which carries all the blood from the intestines to the liver, which may store or alter any of the digestion products. When these products are released from the liver, they enter the general blood circulation.

Some of the fatty acids and glycerol from the digestion of fats enter the blood capillaries of the villi. However, a large proportion of the fatty acids and glycerol may be combined to form fats again in the intestinal epithelium. These fats then pass into the lacteals (Figure B6.19). The fluid in the lacteals flows into the lymphatic system, which forms a network all over the body and eventually empties its contents into the bloodstream (see 'Transport in animals' in Chapter B7).

Water-soluble vitamins may diffuse into the epithelium but fat-soluble vitamins are carried in the microscopic fat droplets that enter the cells. The ions of mineral salts are probably absorbed by active transport. Calcium ions need vitamin D for their effective absorption.

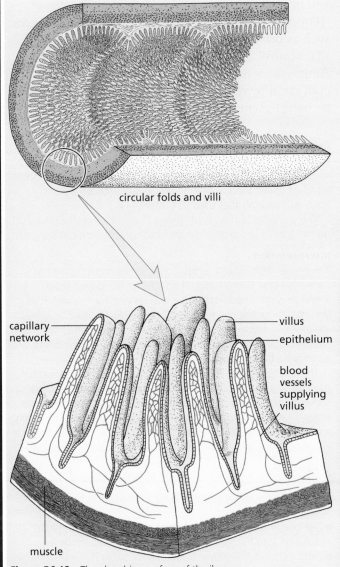

capillary network
villus
epithelium
blood vessels supplying villus
muscle

circular folds and villi

Figure B6.18 The absorbing surface of the ileum.

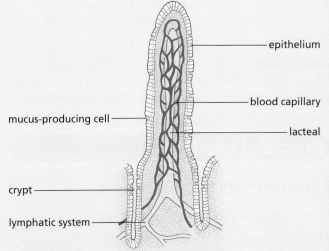

epithelium
blood capillary
lacteal
mucus-producing cell
crypt
lymphatic system

Figure B6.19 Structure of a single villus.

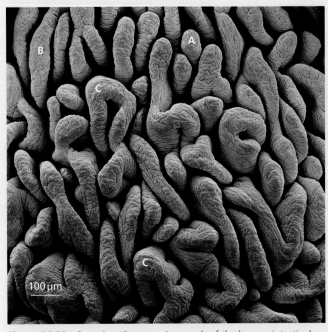

Figure B6.20 Scanning electron micrograph of the human intestinal lining (×60). The villi are about 0.5 mm long. In the duodenum they are mostly leaf-like (C), but further towards the ileum they become narrower (B), and in the ileum they are mostly finger-like (A). This micrograph is of a region in the duodenum.

Assimilation

Key definition
Assimilation is the movement of digested food molecules into the cells of the body where they are used, becoming part of the cells

The products of digestion are carried around the body in the blood. From the blood, cells absorb and use glucose, fats and amino acids. This uptake and use of food is called **assimilation**.

Glucose
During respiration in the cells, glucose is oxidised to carbon dioxide and water (see 'Aerobic respiration' in Chapter B8). This reaction provides energy to drive the many chemical processes in the cells, which result in, for example, the building-up of proteins, contraction of muscles or electrical changes in nerves.

Fats
These are built into cell membranes and other cell structures. Fats also form an important source of energy for cell metabolism. Fatty acids produced from stored fats or taken in with the food, are oxidised in the cells to carbon dioxide and water.

This releases energy for processes such as muscle contraction. Fats can provide twice as much energy as sugars.

Amino acids

These are absorbed by the cells and built up, with the aid of enzymes, into proteins. Some of the proteins will become plasma proteins in the blood (see 'Blood' in Chapter B7). Others may form structures such as cell membranes or they may become enzymes that control the chemical activity within the cell. Amino acids not needed for making cell proteins are converted by the liver into glycogen, which can then be used for energy.

Practical work

Experiments on digestion

1 The action of salivary amylase on starch

- Rinse the mouth with water to remove traces of food.
- Collect saliva* in two test-tubes, labelled A and B, to a depth of about 15 mm (see Figure B6.21).
- Heat the saliva in tube B over a small flame, or in a water bath of boiling water, until it boils for about 30 seconds and then cool the tube under the tap.
- Add about 2 cm³ of a 2% starch solution to each tube; shake each tube and leave them for 5 minutes.
- Share the contents of tube A between two clean test-tubes.
- To one of these add some iodine solution. To the other add some Benedict's solution and heat in a water bath as described in Chapter B3.
- Test the contents of tube B in exactly the same way.

Results

The contents of tube A fail to give a blue colour with iodine, showing that the starch has gone. The other half of the contents, however, gives a red or orange precipitate with Benedict's solution, showing that sugar is present.

The contents of tube B still give a blue colour with iodine but do not form a red precipitate on heating with Benedict's solution.

Interpretation

The results with tube A suggest that something in saliva has converted starch into sugar. The fact that the boiled saliva in tube B fails to do this suggests that it was an enzyme in saliva that brought about the change (see Chapter B6), because enzymes are proteins and are destroyed by boiling. If the boiled saliva had changed starch to sugar, it would have ruled out the possibility of an enzyme being responsible.

This interpretation assumes that it is something in saliva that changes starch into sugar. However, the results could equally well support the claim that starch can turn unboiled saliva into sugar. Our knowledge of (1) the chemical composition of starch and saliva and (2) the effect of heat on enzymes, makes the first interpretation more plausible.

2 Modelling the action of amylase on starch

- Collect a 15 cm length of Visking tubing which has been softened in water.
- Tie one end tightly. Use a syringe to introduce 2% starch solution into the Visking tubing, to about two thirds full.
- Add 2 cm³ of 5% amylase solution (or saliva if it is permissible).
- Pinch the top of the Visking tubing to keep it closed, before carefully mixing its contents by squeezing the tubing.
- Rinse the outside of the Visking tubing thoroughly with tap water, then place it in a boiling tube, trapping the top of the tubing with an elastic band (see Figure B6.22).
- Add enough distilled water to cover the Visking tubing.
- Test a small sample of the distilled water and the contents of the Visking tubing for starch and reducing sugar, using iodine solution and Benedict's solution (see page 58 for methods).
- Place the boiling tube in a beaker of water or a water bath at 37 °C.
- After 20 minutes, use clean teat pipettes to remove a sample of the water surrounding the Visking tubing and from inside the Visking tubing.
- Test some of each sample for starch, using iodine solution, and for reducing sugar, using Benedict's solution (see Chapter B3 for methods). Also test some of the original starch solution for reducing sugar, to make sure it is not contaminated with glucose.

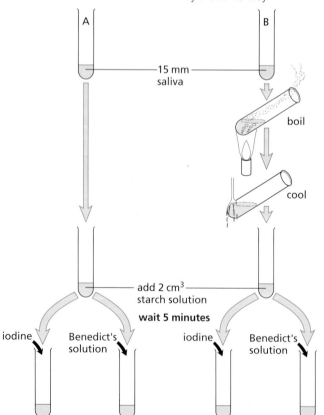

Figure B6.21 Experiment to show the action of salivary amylase on starch.

*If there is some objection to using your own saliva, use a 5% solution of commercially prepared amylase instead.

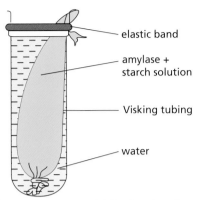

Figure B6.22   Experiment to model the digestion of starch.

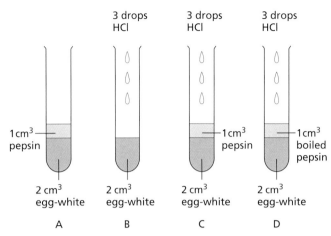

Figure B6.23   Experiment to show the action of pepsin on egg-white.

Result

At the start of the investigation the distilled water tests negative for starch (stays brown) and reducing sugar (stays turquoise). The contents of the Visking tubing are positive for starch (blue-black), but negative for reducing sugars (stays turquoise).

After 20 minutes, the contents of the Visking tubing are yellow/brown with iodine solution, but turn orange or brick red with Benedict's solution. The water sample stays yellow/brown with iodine solution, but turns orange or brick red with Benedict's solution.

Interpretation

The amylase digests the starch in the Visking tubing, producing reducing sugar. The complete digestion of starch results in a negative colour change with iodine solution. The presence of reducing sugar (maltose or glucose) causes the Benedict's solution to turn orange or brick red. The reducing sugar molecules can diffuse through the Visking tubing into the surrounding water, so the water gives a positive result with Benedict's solution. Starch is a large molecule, so it cannot diffuse through the tubing: the water gives a negative result with iodine solution.

This model can be used to represent digestion in the gut. The starch solution and amylase are the contents of the mouth or duodenum. The Visking tubing represents the duodenum wall and the distilled water represents the bloodstream, into which the products of digestion are absorbed.

3 The action of pepsin on egg-white protein

A cloudy suspension of egg-white is prepared by stirring the white of one egg into 500 cm³ tap water, heating it to boiling point and filtering it through glass wool to remove the larger particles.

■ Label four test-tubes A, B, C and D and place 2 cm³ egg-white suspension in each of them. Then add pepsin solution

and/or dilute hydrochloric acid (HCl) to the tubes as follows (Figure B6.23):

   A   egg-white suspension + 1 cm³ pepsin solution (1%)
   B   egg-white suspension + 3 drops dilute HCl
   C   egg-white suspension + 1 cm³ pepsin + 3 drops HCl
   D   egg-white suspension + 1 cm³ boiled pepsin + 3 drops HCl

■ Place all four tubes in a beaker of warm water at 35 °C for 10–15 minutes.

Result

The contents of tube C go clear. The rest remain cloudy.

Interpretation

The change from a cloudy suspension to a clear solution shows that the solid particles of egg protein have been digested to soluble products. The failure of the other three tubes to give clear solutions shows that:

■ pepsin will only work in acid solutions
■ it is the pepsin and not the hydrochloric acid that does the digestion
■ pepsin is an enzyme, because its activity is destroyed by boiling.

4 The action of lipase

■ Place 5 cm³ milk and 7 cm³ dilute (0.05 mol dm⁻³) sodium carbonate solution into each of three test-tubes labelled 1 to 3 (Figure B6.24 on the next page).
■ Add six drops of phenolphthalein to each to turn the contents pink.
■ Add 1 cm³ of 3% bile salts solution to tubes 2 and 3.
■ Add 1 cm³ of 5% lipase solution to tubes 1 and 3, and an equal volume of boiled lipase to tube 2.

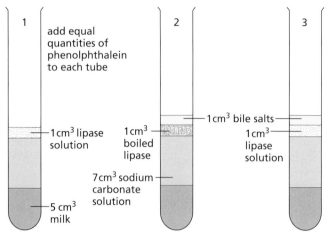

Figure B6.24   Experiment to show the action of lipase.

Result

In 10 minutes or less, the colour of the liquids in tubes 1 and 3 will change to white, with tube 3 changing first. The liquid in tube 2 will remain pink.

Interpretation

Lipase is an enzyme that digests fats to fatty acids and glycerol. When lipase acts on milk fats, the fatty acids that have been produced react with the alkaline sodium carbonate and make the solution more acid. In acid conditions the pH indicator, phenolphthalein, changes from pink to colourless. The presence of bile salts in tube 3 seems to speed up the reaction, although bile salts with the denatured enzyme in tube 2 cannot bring about the change on their own.

For experiments investigating the effect of temperature and pH on enzyme action see Chapter B4.

Questions

1   In Experiment 2, why does some reducing sugar remain inside the Visking tubing?
2   In Experiment 3, why does the change from cloudy to clear suggest that digestion has occurred?
3   How would you modify Experiment 3 if you wanted to find the optimum temperature for the action of pepsin on egg-white?
4   Experiment 3 is really two experiments combined because there are two variables.
    a   Identify the variables.
    b   Which of the tubes could be the control?
5   It was suggested that an alternative interpretation of the result in Experiment 1 might be that starch has turned saliva into sugar. From what you know about starch, saliva and the design of the experiment, explain why this is a less acceptable interpretation.

Questions

9   Name three functions of the alimentary canal shown in Figure B6.8.
10 Into what parts of the alimentary canal do the following pour their digestive juices?
    a   the pancreas
    b   the salivary glands
11 a   Why is it necessary for our food to be digested?
    b   Why do plants not need a digestive system? (See 'Photosynthesis' in Chapter B5.)
12 In which parts of the alimentary canal are the following digested?
    a   starch
    b   protein
13 What process, described in Chapter B2, enables
    a   reducing sugar in the small intestine to be absorbed by the bloodstream
    b   water in the small and large intestine to be absorbed into the bloodstream?
14 What characteristics of the small intestine enable it to absorb digested food efficiently?
15 State briefly what happens to a protein molecule in food, from the time it is swallowed, to the time its products are built up into the cytoplasm of a muscle cell.

Checklist

After studying Chapter B6 you should know and understand the following.
- A balanced diet must contain proteins, carbohydrates, fats, minerals, vitamins, fibre and water, in the correct proportions.
- Examples of good food sources for the components of a balanced diet.
- Fats, carbohydrates and proteins provide energy.
- Proteins provide amino acids for the growth and replacement of the tissues.
- Mineral salts like calcium and iron are needed in tissues such as bone and blood.
- Vegetable fibre helps to maintain a healthy intestine.
- Vitamins are essential in small quantities for chemical reactions in cells.
- Shortage of vitamin C causes scurvy; inadequate vitamin D causes rickets.

- Dietary needs are affected by the age, gender and activity of humans.
- Growing children and pregnant women have special dietary needs.
- Malnutrition is the result of taking in food which does not match the energy needs of the body, or is lacking in proteins, vitamins or minerals.
- The effects of malnutrition include starvation, coronary heart disease, constipation and scurvy.
- Western diets often contain too much sugar and fat and too little fibre.
- Obesity results from taking in more food than the body needs for energy, growth or replacement.
- Malnutrition includes kwashiorkor and marasmus.

- Regions of the alimentary canal include the mouth, salivary glands, oesophagus, stomach, small intestine, pancreas, liver, gall bladder, large intestine and anus.
- Each of these regions has a specific function, related to the ingestion, digestion, absorption or egestion of food.

- Assimilation is the movement of digested food molecules into the cells of the body where they are used, becoming part of the cells.
- Mechanical digestion breaks down food into smaller pieces, without any chemical change of the food molecules. Chemical digestion is the process which changes large, insoluble food molecules into small, soluble molecules.

- Mechanical digestion involves teeth, which can become decayed if not cared for properly.
- The causes of tooth decay

- Digestion takes place in the alimentary canal.
- Chemical digestion is important in producing small, soluble molecules which can be absorbed.
- The changes are brought about by chemicals called digestive enzymes.

- Enzymes include amylase, protease and lipase. These are secreted in specific sites in the alimentary canal.
- The stomach produces gastric juice, which contains hydrochloric acid as well as pepsin.
- The role of bile in emulsifying fats.
- The ileum absorbs amino acids, glucose and fats.
- The small intestine and the colon both absorb water.
- These are carried in the bloodstream first to the liver and then to all parts of the body.
- Undigested food is egested through the anus as faeces.
- Internal folds, villi and microvilli greatly increase the absorbing surface of the small intestine.
- The villi have a special structure to enable efficient absorption of digested food.

B7 Transport

Combined

- State the functions of xylem and phloem
- Identify the position of xylem as seen in sections of roots, stems and leaves, limited to non-woody dicotyledonous plants
- Identify root hair cells, as seen under the light microscope, and state their functions
- Explain that the large surface area of root hairs increases the rate of the absorption of water
- State the pathway taken by water through root, stem and leaf as root hair cell, root cortex cells, xylem and mesophyll cells
- Investigate, using a suitable stain, the pathway of water through the above-ground parts of a plant
- State that water is transported from the roots to leaves through the xylem vessels
- Define *transpiration* as loss of water vapour from plant leaves
- Investigate and describe the effects of variation of temperature and humidity on transpiration rate
- Explain the effects of variation of temperature, and humidity on transpiration rate
- Describe the circulatory system as a system of blood vessels with a pump and valves to ensure one-way flow of blood
- Describe the double circulation in terms of circulation to the lungs and circulation to the body tissues in mammals
- Explain the advantages of a double circulation
- Name and identify the structures of the mammalian heart, limited to the muscular wall, the septum, the left and right ventricles and atria, one-way valves and coronary arteries
- State that blood is pumped away from the heart into arteries and returns to the heart in veins
- Describe the functioning of the heart in terms of the contraction of muscles of the atria and ventricles and the action of the valves
- Name the main blood vessels to and from the: heart, limited to vena cava, aorta, pulmonary artery and pulmonary vein; lungs, limited to the pulmonary artery and pulmonary vein
- Explain the effect of physical activity on the heart rate
- Describe coronary heart disease in terms of the blockage of coronary arteries and state the possible risk factors as diet, stress, smoking, genetic predisposition, age and gender
- Investigate and state the effect of physical activity on pulse rate
- Describe the structure and functions of arteries, veins and capillaries
- Explain how the structures of arteries, veins and capillaries are adapted for their function
- List the components of blood as red blood cells, white blood cells, platelets and plasma
- Identify red and white blood cells, as seen under the light microscope, on prepared slides and in diagrams and photomicrographs
- State the functions of the following components of blood: red blood cells; white blood cells; platelets; plasma

Co-ordinated

- State the functions of xylem and phloem
- Identify the position of xylem as seen in sections of roots, stems and leaves, limited to non-woody dicotyledonous plant
- Identify root hair cells, as seen under the light microscope, and state their functions
- Explain that the large surface area of root hairs increases the rate of the absorption of water and ions
- State the pathway taken by water through root, stem and leaf as root hair, root cortex cells, xylem, mesophyll cells
- Investigate, using a suitable stain, the pathway of water through the above-ground parts of a plant
- State that water is transported from the roots to leaves through the xylem vessels
- Define *transpiration* as loss of water vapour from plant leaves
- Explain the mechanism by which water moves upwards in the xylem in terms of a transpiration pull, helping to create a water potential gradient that draws up a column of water molecules, held together by cohesion
- Investigate and describe the effects of variation of temperature and humidity on transpiration rate
- Explain the effects of variation of temperature and humidity on transpiration rate
- Define *translocation* in terms of the movement of sucrose and amino acids in phloem
- Describe the circulatory system as a system of blood vessels with a pump and valves to ensure one-way flow of blood
- Describe the double circulation in terms of circulation to the lungs and circulation to the body tissues in mammals
- Explain the advantages of a double circulation
- Name and identify the structures of the mammalian heart, limited to the muscular wall, the septum, the left and right ventricles and atria, one-way valves and coronary arteries
- State that blood is pumped away from the heart into arteries and returns to the heart in veins
- Name the main blood vessels to and from the: heart, limited to vena cava, aorta, pulmonary artery and pulmonary vein; lungs, limited to the pulmonary artery and pulmonary vein; kidney, limited to the renal artery and renal vein
- Describe the functioning of the heart in terms of the contraction of muscles of the atria and ventricles and the action of the valves
- Explain the effect of physical activity on the heart rate
- Describe coronary heart disease in terms of the blockage of coronary arteries and state the possible risk factors as diet, stress, smoking, genetic predisposition, age and gender
- Investigate and state the effect of physical activity on pulse rate
- Explain how the structures of arteries, veins and capillaries are adapted for their function

● Transport in plants

Plant structure and function

Leaf

The structure of a leaf has already been described in Chapter B5. Xylem and phloem appear in the midrib of the leaf, as well as in the leaf veins. These features are identified in Chapter B5, Figures B5.16 and B5.17 (pp.45 and 46).

Stem

Figure B7.1 shows a stem cut across (transversely) and down its length (longitudinally) to show its internal structure.

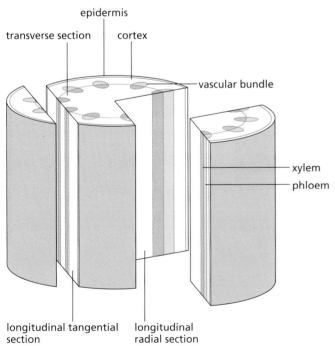

Figure B7.1 Structure of a plant stem.

Epidermis

Like the leaf epidermis, this is a single layer of cells that helps to keep the shape of the stem and cuts down the loss of water vapour.

Vascular bundles

These are made up of groups of specialised cells that conduct water, dissolved salts and food up or down the stem. The vascular bundles in the roots, stem, leaf stalks and leaf veins all connect up to form a transport system throughout the entire plant (Figure B7.2). The two main tissues in the vascular bundles are called **xylem** and **phloem** (Figure B7.3 and B7.4 on the next page). Food substances travel in the phloem; water and salts travel mainly in the xylem. The cells in each tissue form elongated tubes called **vessels** (in the xylem) or **sieve tubes** (in the phloem) and they are surrounded and supported by other cells.

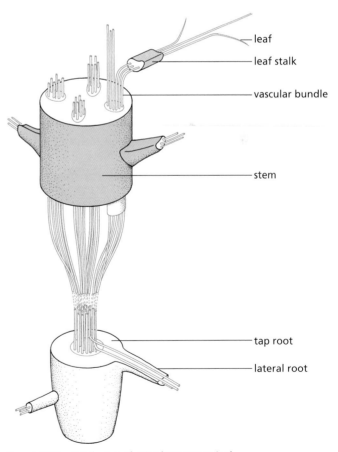

Figure B7.2 Distribution of veins from root to leaf.

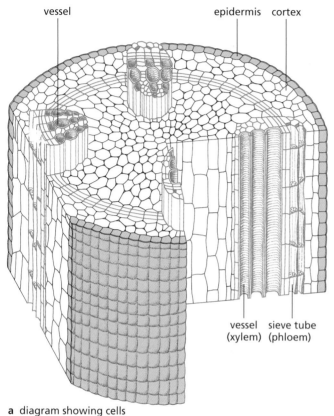

vessel   epidermis   cortex

vessel   sieve tube
(xylem)   (phloem)

a diagram showing cells

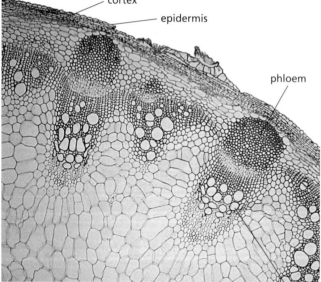

cortex

epidermis

phloem

b transverse section through sunflower stem (x40)   xylem

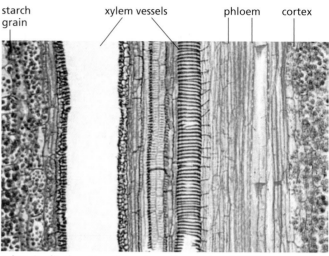

starch grain   xylem vessels   phloem   cortex

c longitudinal section through sunflower stem (x200)

Figure B7.3   Structure of plant stem.

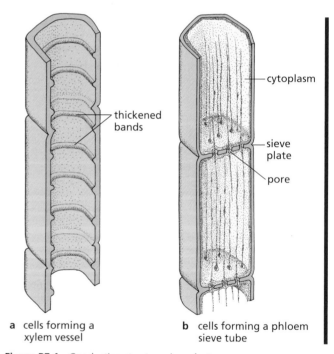

thickened bands

cytoplasm

sieve plate

pore

a cells forming a xylem vessel

b cells forming a phloem sieve tube

Figure B7.4   Conducting structures in a plant.

Cortex

The tissue between the vascular bundles and the epidermis is called the **cortex**. Its cells often store starch. In green stems, the outer cortex cells contain chloroplasts and make food by photosynthesis.

Root

The internal structure of a typical root is shown in Figure B7.6. The vascular bundle is in the centre of the root (Figure B7.5), unlike the stem where the bundles form a cylinder in the cortex.

The xylem carries water and salts from the root to the stem. The phloem brings food from the stem to the root, to provide the root cells with substances for their energy and growth.

Root hairs

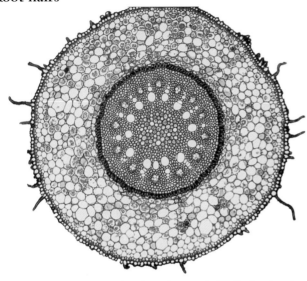

Figure B7.5 Transverse section through a root (×40). Notice that the vascular tissue is in the centre. Some root hairs can be seen in the outer layer of cells.

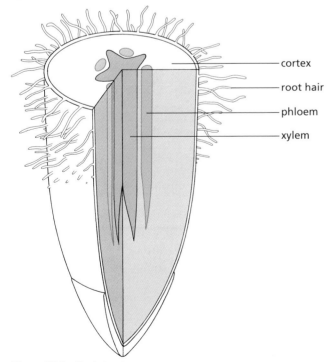

Figure B7.6 Root structure.

Figure B7.7 Root hairs (×5) as they appear on a root grown in moist air.

In a region above the root tip, where the root has just stopped growing, the cells of the outer layer produce tiny, tube-like outgrowths called **root hairs** (Figure B7.9 on the next page). These can just be seen as a white furry layer on the roots of seedlings grown in moist air (Figure B7.7). In the soil, the root hairs grow between the soil particles and stick closely to them. The root hairs take up water from the soil by osmosis.

Water uptake

Pathway taken by water

The water tension developed in the vessels by a rapidly transpiring plant (see next section) is thought to be sufficient to draw water through the root from the soil. The water enters the root hair cells and is then passed on to cells in the root cortex. It enters the xylem vessels to be transported up the stem and into the leaves, arriving at the leaf mesophyll cells.

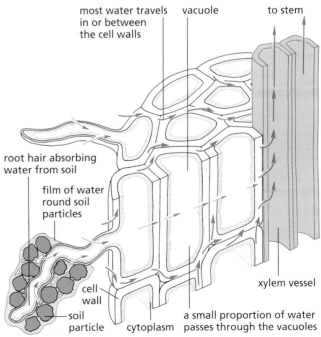

Figure B7.8 The probable pathways of water through a root.

Practical work

Transport in the vascular bundles

- Place the shoots of several leafy plants in a solution of 1% methylene blue. 'Busy Lizzie' (*Impatiens*) or celery stalks with leaves are usually effective.
- Leave the shoots in the light for up to 24 hours.

Result
If some of the stems are cut across, the dye will be seen in the vascular bundles. In some cases the blue dye will also appear in the leaf veins.

Interpretation
These results show that the dye and, therefore, probably also the water, travel up the stem in the vascular bundles. Closer study would show that they travel in the xylem vessels.

Transport of water in the xylem

- Cut three leafy shoots from a deciduous tree or shrub. Each shoot should have about the same number of leaves.
- On one twig remove a ring of bark about 5 mm wide, about 100 mm up from the cut base.
- With the second shoot, smear a layer of Vaseline over the cut base so that it blocks the vessels. The third twig is a control.
- Place all three twigs in a jar with a little water. The water level must be below the region from which you removed the ring of bark.
- Leave the twigs where they can receive direct sunlight.

Result
After an hour or two, you will probably find that the twig with blocked vessels shows signs of wilting. The other two twigs should still have firm leaves.

Interpretation
Removal of the bark (including the phloem) has not prevented water from reaching the leaves, but blocking the xylem vessels has. The vessels of the xylem, therefore, offer the most likely route for water passing up the stem.

As Figures B7.5 and B7.6 illustrate, the large number of tiny root hairs greatly increases the absorbing surface of a root system. The surface area of the root system of a mature rye plant has been estimated at about 200 m². The additional surface provided by the root hairs was calculated to be 400 m². The water in the surrounding soil is absorbed by osmosis (see Chapter B2). The precise pathway taken by the water is the subject of some debate, but the path of least resistance seems to be in or between the cell walls rather than through the cells.

When water loss through transpiration is slow, e.g. at night-time or just before bud burst in a deciduous tree, then osmosis may play a more important part in the uptake of water than water tension developed in the vessels. In Figure B7.8, showing a root hair in the soil, the cytoplasm of the root hair is partially permeable to water. The soil water is more dilute than the cell sap and so water passes by osmosis from the soil into the cell sap of the root hair cell. This flow of water into the root hair cell raises the cell's turgor pressure. So water is forced out through the cell wall into the next cell and so on, right through the cortex of the root to the xylem vessels (Figure B7.9).

One problem for this explanation is that it has not been possible to demonstrate that there is an osmotic gradient across the root cortex that could produce this flow of water from cell to cell. Nevertheless, root pressure developed probably by osmosis does force water up the root system and into the stem.

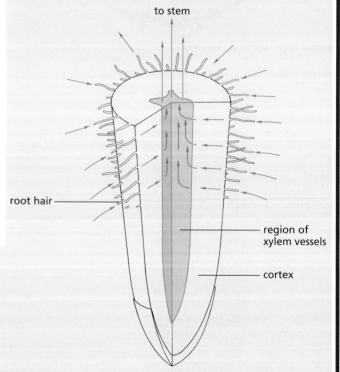

Figure B7.9 Diagrammatic section of root to show passage of water from the soil.

Key definition
Transpiration is the loss of water vapour from plant leaves by evaporation of water at the surfaces of the mesophyll cells followed by the diffusion of water vapour through the stomata.

Transpiration

The main force that draws water from the soil and through the plant is caused by a process called **transpiration**. Water evaporates from the leaves and causes a kind of 'suction', which pulls water up the stem (Figure B7.10). The water travels up the xylem vessels in the vascular bundles (see Figure B7.2) and this flow of water is called the **transpiration stream**.

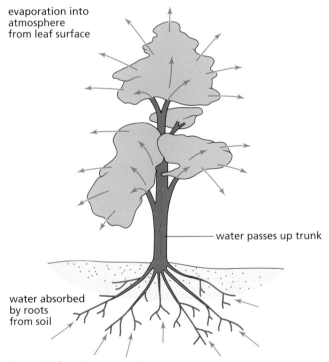

Figure B7.10 The transpiration stream.

Figure B7.11 Californian redwoods. Some of these trees are over 100 metres tall. Transpiration from their leaves pulls hundreds of litres of water up the trunk.

Practical work

To demonstrate water loss by a plant

The apparatus shown in Figure B7.12 on the next page is called a weight **potometer**. A well-watered potted plant is prepared by surrounding the pot with a plastic bag, sealed around the stem of the plant with an elastic band or string. The plant is then placed on a top-pan balance and its mass is recorded. After a measured time period, e.g. 24 hours, the plant is re-weighed and the difference in mass calculated. Knowing the time which has elapsed, the rate of mass loss per hour can be calculated. The process can be repeated, exposing the plant to different environmental conditions, such as higher temperature, wind speed, humidity or light intensity.

Results
The plant loses mass over the measured time period. Increases in temperature, wind speed and light intensity result in larger rates of loss of mass. An increase in humidity would be expected to reduce the rate of loss of mass.

Interpretation
As the roots and soil surrounding the plant have been sealed in a plastic bag, it can be assumed that any mass lost must be due to the evaporation of water vapour from the stem or leaves (transpiration). Increases in temperature, wind speed and light intensity all cause the rate of transpiration to get higher, so the rate of loss of mass from the plant increases. An increase in humidity reduces transpiration, so the rate of loss of mass slows down.

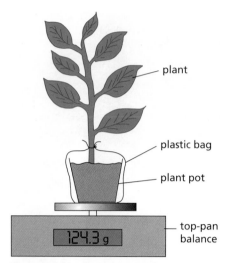

Figure B7.12 A weight potometer.

Rates of water uptake in different conditions

The apparatus shown in Figure B7.13 is called a potometer. It is designed to measure the rate of uptake of water in a cut shoot.

- Fill the syringe with water and attach it to the side arm of the 3-way tap.
- Turn the tap downwards (i) and press the syringe until water comes out of the rubber tubing at the top.
- Collect a leafy shoot and push its stem into the rubber tubing as far as possible. Set up the apparatus in a part of the laboratory that is not receiving direct sunlight.
- Turn the tap up (ii) and press the syringe until water comes out of the bottom of the capillary tube. Turn the tap horizontally (iii).
- As the shoot transpires, it will draw water from the capillary tube and the level can be seen to rise. Record the distance moved by the water column in 30 seconds or a minute.
- Turn the tap up and send the water column back to the bottom of the capillary. Turn the tap horizontally and make another measurement of the rate of uptake. In this way obtain the average of three readings.
- The conditions can now be changed in one of the following ways:
  1 Move the apparatus into sunlight or under a fluorescent lamp.
  2 Blow air past the shoot with an electric fan or merely fan it with an exercise book.
  3 Cover the shoot with a plastic bag.
- After each change of conditions, take three more readings of the rate of uptake and notice whether they represent an increase or a decrease in the rate of transpiration.

Results

1 An increase in light intensity should make the stomata open and allow more rapid transpiration.
2 Moving air should increase the rate of evaporation and, therefore, the rate of uptake.
3 The plastic bag will cause a rise in humidity round the leaves and suppress transpiration.

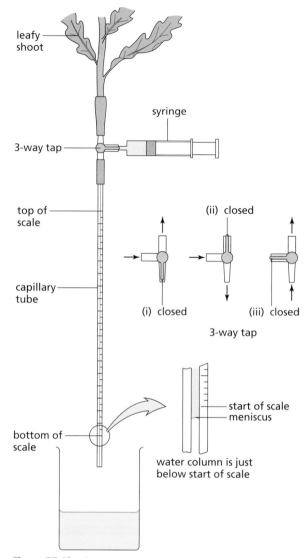

Figure B7.13 A potometer.

Interpretation

Ideally, you should change only one condition at a time. If you took the experiment outside, you would be changing the light intensity, the temperature and the air movement. When the rate of uptake increased, you would not know which of these three changes was mainly responsible.

To obtain reliable results, you should really keep taking readings until three of them are nearly the same. A change in conditions may take 10 or 15 minutes before it produces a new, steady rate of uptake. In practice, you may not have time to do this, but even your first three readings should indicate a trend towards increased or decreased uptake.

Note: a simpler version of potometer can be used effectively. This does not include the syringe or scaled capillary tubing shown in Figure B7.13.

- The plant stem can be attached directly to a length of capillary tubing with a short section of rubber tubing. This is best carried out in a bowl of water.
- While still in the water, squeeze the rubber tubing to force out any air bubbles.

- Remove the potometer from the water and rub a piece of filter paper against the end of the capillary tubing to introduce an air bubble. The capillary tubing does not need to have a scale: a ruler can be clamped next to the tubing.
- Record the distance moved by the bubble over a measured period of time. Then place the end of the capillary tubing in a beaker of water and squeeze out the air bubble.
- Introduce a new air bubble as previously described and take further readings.

Limitations of the potometer

Although we use the potometer to compare rates of transpiration, it is really the rates of uptake that we are observing. Not all the water taken up will be transpired; some will be used in photosynthesis; some may be absorbed by cells and stored there. However, these quantities are very small compared with the volume of water transpired and they can be disregarded.

The rate of uptake of a cut shoot may not reflect the rate in the intact plant. If the root system were present, it might offer resistance to the flow of water or it could be helping the flow by means of its root pressure.

To find which surface of a leaf loses more water vapour

- Cut four leaves of about the same size from a plant (do not use an evergreen plant). Protect the bench with newspaper and then treat the leaves a–d as follows:
  a Smear a thin layer of Vaseline (petroleum jelly) on the lower surface.
  b Smear Vaseline on the upper surface.
  c Smear Vaseline on both surfaces.
  d Leave both surfaces free of Vaseline.
- Place a little Vaseline on the cut end of the leaf stalk and then suspend the four leaves from a retort stand with cotton threads for several days.

Result

All the leaves will have shrivelled and curled up to some extent but the ones that lost most water will be the most shrivelled (Figure B7.14).

| a lower surface | b upper surface | c both surfaces | d neither surface |

Figure B7.14 The results of evaporation from leaves subjected to different treatments.

Interpretation

The Vaseline prevents evaporation. The untreated leaf and the leaf with its upper surface sealed show the greatest degree of shrivelling, so it is from the lower surface that leaves lose most water by evaporation.

More accurate results may be obtained by weighing the leaves at the start and the end of the experiment. It is best to group the leaves from the whole class into their respective batches and weigh each batch. Ideally, the weight loss should be expressed as a percentage of the initial weight.

More rapid results can be obtained by sticking small squares of blue cobalt chloride paper to the upper and lower surface of the same leaf using transparent adhesive tape (Figure B7.15). Cobalt chloride paper changes from blue to pink as it takes up moisture. By comparing the time taken for each square to go pink, the relative rates of evaporation from each surface can be compared.

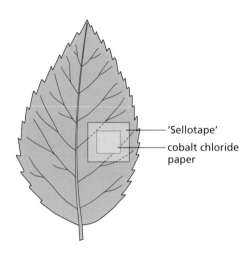

'Sellotape'

cobalt chloride paper

Figure B7.15 To find which surface of a leaf loses more water vapour.

The results of either experiment can be correlated with the numbers of stomata on the upper and lower epidermis. This can be done by painting clear nail varnish or 'Germoline New-skin' over each surface and allowing it to dry. The varnish is then peeled off and examined under the microscope. The outlines of the guard cells can be seen and counted.

Rate of transpiration

Transpiration is the evaporation of water from the leaves, so any change that increases or reduces evaporation will have the same effect on transpiration.

Humidity

If the air is very humid, i.e. contains a great deal of water vapour, it can accept very little more from the plants and so transpiration slows down. In dry air, the diffusion of water vapour from the leaf to the atmosphere will be rapid.

Temperature

Warm air can hold more water vapour than cold air. Thus evaporation or transpiration will take place more rapidly into warm air.

Translocation

> **Key definition**
> **Translocation** is the movement of sucrose and amino acids in the phloem, from regions of production (the 'source') to regions of storage or to regions where they are used in respiration or growth (the 'sink').

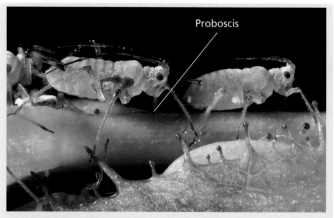

Proboscis

Figure B7.16   Aphids feeding on a rose plant.

The xylem sap is always a very dilute solution, but the phloem sap may contain up to 25% of dissolved solids, the bulk of which consists of sucrose and amino acids. There is a good deal of evidence to support the view that sucrose, amino acids and many other substances are transported in the phloem. This is called **translocation**.

The movement of water and salts in the xylem is always upwards, from soil to leaf, but in the phloem the solutes may be travelling up or down the stem. The carbohydrates made in the leaf during photosynthesis are converted to sucrose and carried out of the leaf (the source) to the stem. From here, the sucrose may pass upwards to growing buds and fruits or downwards to the roots and storage organs (sink). All parts of a plant that cannot photosynthesise will need a supply of nutrients brought by the phloem. It is quite possible for substances to be travelling upwards and downwards at the same time in the phloem.

Some insects feed using syringe-like mouthparts, piercing the stems of plants to extract liquid from the phloem vessels. Figure B7.16 shows aphids feeding on a rose plant. The pressure of sucrose solution in the phloem can be so great that it is forced through the gut of the aphid and droplets of the sticky liquid exude from its anus.

Some parts of a plant can act as a source and a sink at different times during the life of a plant. For example, while a bud containing new leaves is forming it would require nutrients and therefore act as a sink. However, once the bud has burst and the leaves are photosynthesising, the region would act as a source, sending newly synthesised sugars and amino acids to other parts of the plant. Similarly, the new tuber of a potato plant would act as a sink while it was growing, storing sugars as starch. (Starch is a good storage molecule because it is insoluble and quite compact.) However, once the buds on the tubers start to grow, the stored starch is converted to sucrose, a soluble nutrient, which will be passed to these buds from the tuber. So the tuber becomes the source. The shoots will eventually become sources, once they break through the soil and produce new leaves that can photosynthesise. Bulbs, such as those of the daffodil and snowdrop (see 'Asexual reproduction' in Chapter B10), act in the same way, although they tend to store sugars as well as starch.

There is no doubt that substances travel in the sieve tubes of the phloem, but the mechanism by which they are moved is not fully understood. We do know that translocation depends on living processes because anything that inhibits cell metabolism, e.g. poisons or high temperatures, also arrests translocation.

Questions

1   What are the functions of the xylem and phloem?
2   If you were given a cylindrical structure cut from part of a plant, how could you tell whether it was a piece of stem or a piece of root:
  a   with the naked eye
  b   with the aid of a microscope or hand lens?

3   Describe the path taken by a water molecule from the soil until it reaches a mesophyll cell of a leaf to be made into sugar.
4   Why do you think that, in a deciduous tree in spring, transpiration is negligible before bud burst?
5   What kind of climate and weather conditions do you think will cause a high rate of transpiration?

● Transport in animals

The blood, pumped by the heart, travels all around the body in blood vessels. It leaves the heart in arteries and returns in veins. Valves, present in the heart and veins, ensure a one-way flow for the blood. As blood enters an organ, the arteries divide into smaller arterioles, which supply capillaries. In these vessels the blood moves much more slowly, allowing the exchange of materials such as oxygen and glucose, carbon dioxide and other wastes. Blood leaving an organ is collected in venules, which transfer it on to larger veins.

Double circulation of mammals

The route of the circulation of blood in a mammal is shown in Figure B7.17.

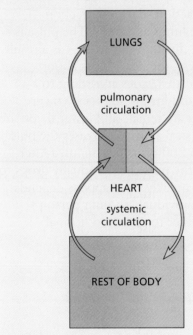

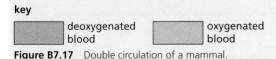

key

| | deoxygenated blood | | oxygenated blood |

Figure B7.17   Double circulation of a mammal.

The blood passes twice through the heart during one complete circuit: once on its way to the body and again on its way to the lungs. The circulation through the lungs is called the **pulmonary circulation**; the circulation around the rest of the body is called the **systemic circulation**.

On average, a red blood cell would go around the whole circulation in 45 seconds. A more detailed diagram of the circulation is shown in Figure B7.30 on p.89.

A **double circulation** has the advantage of maintaining a high blood pressure to all the major organs of the body. The right side of the heart collects blood from the body, builds up the blood pressure and sends it to the lungs to be oxygenated, but the pressure drops during the process. The left side of the heart receives oxygenated blood from the lungs, builds up the blood pressure again and pumps the oxygenated blood to the body.

Heart

The heart pumps blood through the circulatory system to all the major organs of the body. The appearance of the heart from the outside is shown in Figure B7.18. Figure B7.19 shows the left side cut open, while Figure B7.20 (on the next page) is a diagram of a vertical section to show its internal structure. Since the heart is seen as if in a dissection of a person facing you, the left side is drawn on the right.

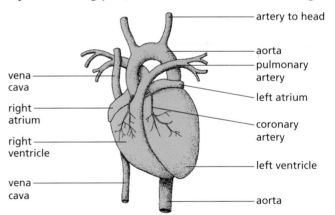

Figure B7.18   External view of the heart.

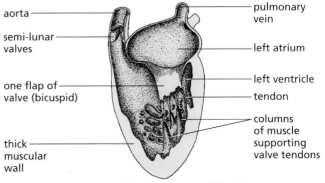

Figure B7.19   Diagram of the heart cut open (left side).

If you study Figure B7.20 you will see that there are four chambers. The upper, thin-walled chambers are the **atria** (singular = atrium) and each of these opens into a thick-walled chamber, the **ventricle**, below.

Blood enters the atria from large veins. The **pulmonary vein** brings oxygenated blood from the lungs into the left atrium. The **vena cava** brings deoxygenated blood from the body tissues into the right atrium. The blood passes from each atrium to its corresponding ventricle, and the ventricle pumps it out into the arteries. The left chambers are separated from the right chambers by a wall of muscle called a **septum**.

The artery carrying oxygenated blood to the body from the left ventricle is the **aorta**. The **pulmonary artery** carries deoxygenated blood from the right ventricle to the lungs.

In pumping the blood, the muscle in the walls of the atria and ventricles contracts and relaxes (Figure B7.20). The walls of the atria contract first and force blood into the two ventricles. Then the ventricles contract and send blood into the arteries. Valves prevent blood flowing backwards during or after heart contractions.

The heart muscle is supplied with food and oxygen by the **coronary arteries** (Figure B7.19).

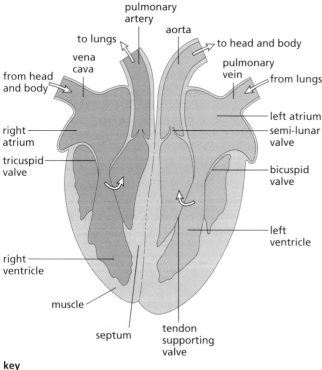

key

deoxygenated blood   oxygenated blood

Figure B7.20   Diagram of the heart, vertical section.

There are a number of ways by which the activity of the heart can be monitored. These include measuring pulse rate, listening to heart sounds and the use of electrocardiograms (ECGs).

Pulse rate

The ripple of pressure that passes down an artery as a result of the heart beat can be felt as a **'pulse'** when the artery is near the surface of the body. You can feel the pulse in your radial artery by pressing the fingertips of one hand on the wrist of the other (Figure B7.21). It is important that the thumb is *not* used because it has its own pulse. There is also a detectable pulse in the carotid artery in the neck. Digital pulse rate monitors are also available. These can be applied to a finger, wrist or earlobe depending on the type and provide a very accurate reading.

The effect of physical activity on the pulse rate

A heartbeat is a contraction. Each contraction squeezes blood to the lungs and body. The pulse is a pressure wave passing through the arteries as a result of the heartbeat. At rest, the heart beats about 70 times a minute, but this varies according to a person's age, gender and fitness: higher if you are younger, higher if you are female and lower if you are fit. An increase in physical activity increases the pulse rate, which can rise to 200 beats per minute. After exercise has stopped, the pulse rate gradually drops to its resting state. How quickly this happens depends on the fitness of the individual (an unfit person's pulse rate will take longer to return to normal).

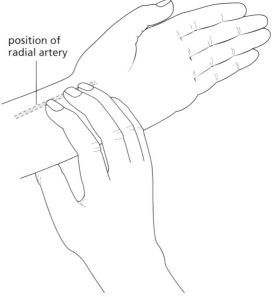

Figure B7.21   Taking the pulse.

Coronary heart disease

In the lining of the large and medium arteries, deposits of a fatty substance, called **atheroma**, are laid down in patches. This happens to everyone and the patches get more numerous and extensive with age, but until one of them actually blocks an important artery the effects are not noticed. It is not known how or why the deposits form. Some doctors think that fatty substances in the blood pass into the lining. Others believe that small blood clots form on damaged areas of the lining and are covered over by the atheroma patches. The patches may join up to form a continuous layer, which reduces the internal diameter of the vessel (Figure B7.22).

The surface of a patch of atheroma sometimes becomes rough and causes fibrinogen in the plasma to deposit fibrin on it, causing a blood clot (a **thrombus**) to form. If the blood clot blocks the coronary artery (Figure B7.23), which supplies the muscles of the ventricles with blood, it starves the muscles of oxygenated blood and the heart may stop beating. This is a severe heart attack from **coronary thrombosis**. A thrombus might form anywhere in the arterial system, but its effects in the coronary artery and in parts of the brain (strokes) are the most drastic.

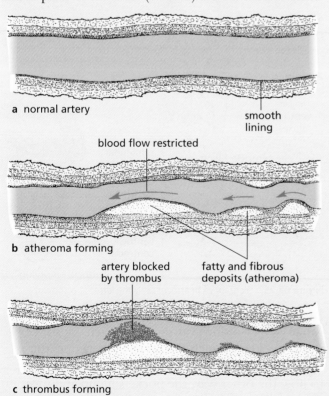

a normal artery
smooth lining

blood flow restricted

b atheroma forming

artery blocked by thrombus
fatty and fibrous deposits (atheroma)

c thrombus forming

Figure B7.22 Atheroma and thrombus formation.

In the early stages of coronary heart disease, the atheroma may partially block the coronary artery and reduce the blood supply to the heart (Figure B7.24 on the next page). This can lead to **angina**, i.e. a pain in the chest that occurs during exercise or exertion. This is a warning to the person that he or she is at risk and should take precautions to avoid a heart attack.

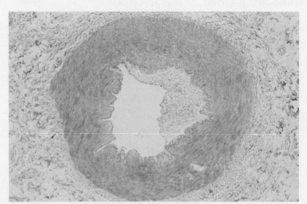

Figure B7.23 Atheroma partially blocking the coronary artery.

Possible causes of coronary heart disease

Atheroma and thrombus formation are the immediate causes of a heart attack but the long-term causes that give rise to these conditions are not well understood.

There is an inherited tendency towards the disease but incidences of the disease have increased very significantly in affluent countries in recent years. This makes us think that some features of 'Western' diets or lifestyles might be causing it. The main risk factors are thought to be an unbalanced diet with too much fat, stress, smoking, genetic disposition, age, gender and lack of exercise.

Diet

The atheroma deposits contain **cholesterol**, which is present, combined with lipids and proteins, in the blood. Cholesterol plays an essential part in our physiology, but it is known that people with high levels of blood cholesterol are more likely to suffer from heart attacks than people with low cholesterol levels.

Blood cholesterol can be influenced, to some extent, by the amount and type of fat in the diet. Many doctors and dieticians believe that animal fats (milk, cream, butter, cheese, egg-yolk, fatty meat) are more likely to raise the blood cholesterol than are the vegetable oils, which contain a high proportion of unsaturated fatty acids (see 'Diet' in Chapter B6).

An unbalanced diet with too many calories can lead to obesity. Being overweight puts extra strain on the heart and makes it more difficult for the person to exercise.

Stress

Emotional stress often leads to raised blood pressure. High blood pressure may increase the rate at which atheroma are formed in the arteries.

Smoking

Statistical studies suggest that smokers are two to three times more likely to die from a heart attack than are non-smokers of a similar age (Figure B7.24). The carbon monoxide and other chemicals in cigarette smoke may damage the lining of the arteries, allowing atheroma to form, but there is very little direct evidence for this.

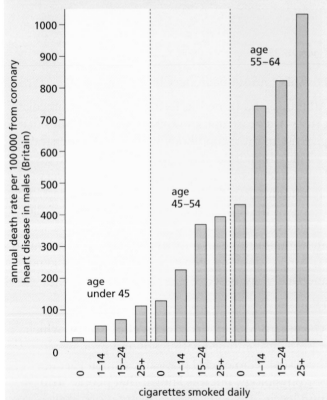

Figure B7.24 Smoking and heart disease. Obviously, as you get older you are more likely to die from a heart attack, but notice that, in any age group, the more you smoke the higher your chances of dying from heart disease.

Genetic predisposition

Coronary heart disease appears to be passed from one generation to the next in some families. This is not something we have any control over, but we can be aware of this risk and reduce some of the other risk factors to compensate.

Age and gender

As we get older our risk of suffering from coronary heart disease increases. Males are more at risk of a heart attack than females: it may be that males tend to have less healthy lifestyles than females.

Lack of exercise

Heart muscle loses its tone and becomes less efficient at pumping blood when exercise is not taken. A sluggish blood flow, resulting from lack of exercise, may allow atheroma to form in the arterial lining but, once again, the direct evidence for this is slim.

Control of blood flow through the heart

The blood is stopped from flowing backwards by four sets of valves (Figure B7.25). Valves that separate each atrium from the ventricle below it are known as **atrioventricular valves**. Between the right atrium and the right ventricle is the **tricuspid** (= three flaps) valve. Between the left atrium and left ventricle is the **bicuspid** (= two flaps) valve. The flaps of these valves are shaped rather like parachutes, with 'strings' called **tendons** or **cords** to prevent them from being turned inside out.

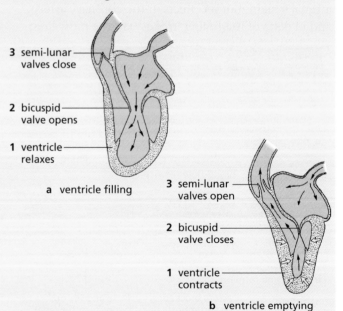

Figure B7.25 Diagram of heartbeat (only the left side is shown).

In the pulmonary artery and aorta are the **semi-lunar** (= half-moon) valves. These each consist of three 'pockets', which are pushed flat against the artery walls when blood flows one way. If blood tries to flow the other way, the pockets fill up and meet in the middle to stop the flow of blood (Figure B7.26).

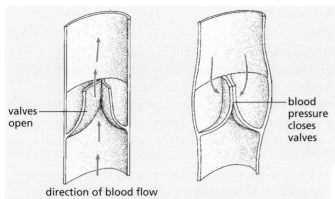

valves open

blood pressure closes valves

direction of blood flow

Figure B7.26   Action of the semi-lunar valves.

When the ventricles contract, blood pressure closes the bicuspid and tricuspid valves and these prevent blood returning to the atria. When the ventricles relax, the blood pressure in the arteries closes the semi-lunar valves, preventing the return of blood to the ventricles.

From the description above, it may seem that the ventricles are filled with blood as a result of the contraction of the atria. However, the atria have much thinner muscle walls than the ventricles. In fact, when the ventricles relax, their internal volume increases and they draw in blood from the pulmonary vein or vena cava through the relaxed atria. Atrial contraction then forces the final amount of blood into the ventricles just before ventricular contraction.

The left ventricle (sometimes referred to as the 'large left ventricle') has a wall made of cardiac muscle that is about three times thicker than the wall of the right ventricle. This is because the right ventricle only needs to create enough pressure to pump blood to one organ, the lungs, which are next to the heart. However, the left ventricle has to pump blood to all the major organs of the body, as shown in Figure B7.30 on p.89. It should be noted that the left and right ventricles pump the same volume of blood: the left ventricle does *not* have a thicker wall to pump *more* blood!

Physical activity and heart rate

During periods of physical activity, active parts of the body (mainly skeletal muscle) respire faster, demanding more oxygen and glucose. Increased respiration also produces more carbon dioxide, which needs to be removed. Blood carries the oxygen and glucose, so the heart rate needs to increase to satisfy demand. If the muscle does not get enough oxygen, it will start to respire anaerobically, producing lactic acid (lactate). Lactic acid build-up causes muscle fatigue, leading to cramp. An 'oxygen debt' is created, which needs to be repaid after exercise by continued rapid breathing and higher than normal heart rate (see 'Anaerobic respiration' in Chapter B8).

Practical work

Heart dissection

- Obtain an intact heart (sheep or goat for example) from a butcher's shop or abattoir.
- Rinse it under a tap to remove excess blood.
- Observe the surface of the heart, identifying the main visible features (shown in Figure B7.18). The blood vessels may have been cut off, but it is possible to identify where these would have been attached later in the dissection.
- Gently squeeze the ventricles. They can be distinguished because the wall of the right ventricle is much thinner than that of the left ventricle.
- Using a pair of sharp scissors or a scalpel, make an incision from the base of the left ventricle, up through the left atrium.
- Using a pair of forceps, remove any blood clots lying in the exposed chambers.
- Identify the main features as shown in Figure B7.19.
- If you have not cut open the aorta, gently push the handle of a blunt seeker or an old pencil, behind the bicuspid valve. It should find its way into the aorta. Note how thick the wall of this blood vessel is.
- Compare the semi-lunar valves in the base of the aorta with the bicuspid valve between the atrium and ventricle. Note that the latter has tendons to prevent it turning inside-out.
- Now repeat the procedure on the right side of the heart to expose the right atrium and ventricle.
- Pushing the handle of the seeker behind the tricuspid valve should allow it to enter the pulmonary artery. Cut open the artery to expose semi-lunar valves. Note the relative thinness of the wall, compared to that of the aorta.
- Also compare the thickness of the left ventricle wall to that of the right ventricle.

Investigating the effect of exercise on pulse rate

- Find your pulse in your wrist or neck – see Figure B7.21.
- Count the number of beats in 15 seconds, then multiply the result by four to provide a pulse rate in beats per minute. This is your resting pulse rate.
- Repeat the process two more times and then calculate an average resting pulse rate.

- Carry out 2 minutes of exercise, e.g. running on the spot, then sit down and immediately start a stopwatch and measure your pulse rate over 15 seconds as before.
- Allow the stopwatch to keep timing. Measure your pulse rate every minute for 10 minutes.
- Convert all the readings to beats per minute. Plot a graph of pulse rate after exercise against time, with the first reading being 0 minutes.
- Finally, draw a line across the graph representing your average resting pulse rate.

Result
The pulse rate immediately after exercise should be much higher than the average resting pulse rate. With time the pulse rate gradually falls back to the average resting pulse rate.

Interpretation
During exercise the muscles need more oxygen and glucose for aerobic respiration to provide the energy needed for the increased movement. The heart rate increases to provide these materials. After exercise, demand for oxygen and glucose decreases, so the pulse rate gradually returns to normal.

Blood vessels
Arteries
These are fairly wide vessels (Figure B7.27) which carry blood from the heart to the limbs and organs of the body (Figure B7.30 on the next page). The blood in the arteries, except for the pulmonary arteries, is oxygenated.

Arteries have elastic tissue and muscle fibres in their thick walls. The arteries divide into smaller vessels called **arterioles**.

The arterioles divide repeatedly to form a branching network of microscopic vessels passing between the cells of every living tissue. These final branches are called **capillaries**.

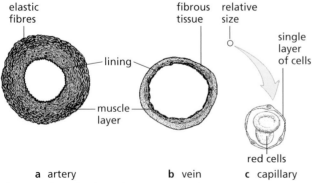

a artery   **b** vein   **c** capillary

Figure B7.27 Blood vessels, transverse section.

Capillaries
These are tiny vessels, often as little as 0.001 mm in diameter and with walls only one cell thick (Figures B7.27c and B7.28). Although the blood as a whole cannot escape from the capillary, the thin capillary walls allow some liquid to pass through, i.e. they are permeable. Blood pressure in the capillaries forces part of the plasma out through the walls.

The capillary network is so dense that no living cell is far from a supply of oxygen and food. The capillaries join up into larger vessels, called **venules**, which then combine to form **veins**.

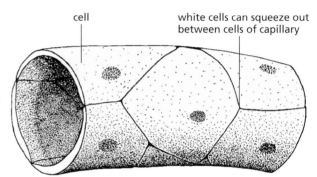

Figure B7.28 Diagram of blood capillary.

Veins
Veins return blood from the tissues to the heart (Figure B7.30). The blood pressure in them is steady and is less than that in the arteries. They are wider and their walls are thinner, less elastic and less muscular than those of the arteries (Figures B7.29b and B7.30). They also have valves in them similar to the semi-lunar valves (Figure B7.28).

The blood in most veins is deoxygenated and contains less food but more carbon dioxide than the blood in most arteries. This is because respiring cells

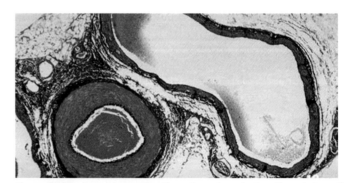

Figure B7.29 Transverse section through a vein and artery. The vein is on the right, the artery on the left. Notice that the wall of the artery is much thicker than that of the vein. The material filling the artery is formed from coagulated red blood cells. These are also visible in two regions of the vein.

have used the oxygen and food and produced carbon dioxide. The pulmonary veins, which return blood from the lungs to the heart, are an exception. They contain oxygenated blood and a reduced level of carbon dioxide.

The main blood vessels associated with the heart, lungs and kidneys are shown in Figure B7.30. The right side of the heart is supplied by the vena cava (the main vein of the body) and sends blood to the lungs along the pulmonary artery. The left side of the heart receives blood from the lungs in the pulmonary vein and sends it to the body in the aorta, the main artery (see Chapter B8). In reality there are two pulmonary arteries and two pulmonary veins, because there are two lungs. There are also two vena cavae: one returns blood from the lower body; the other from the upper body.

Each kidney receives blood from a renal artery. Once the blood has been filtered it is returned to the vena cava through a renal vein.

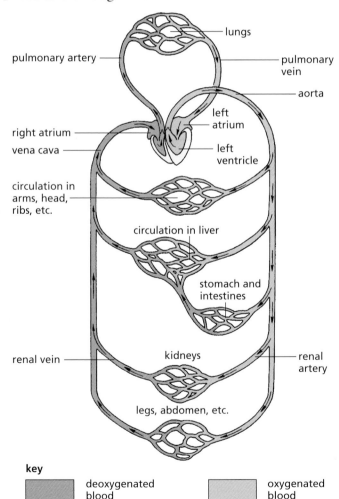

key

□ deoxygenated blood   □ oxygenated blood

Figure B7.30 Diagram of human circulation.

Table B7.1 compares the structure of arteries, veins and capillaries and provides an explanation of how their structures are related to their functions.

Table B7.1 Comparing arteries, veins and capillaries

Blood vessel	Structure	Explanation of how structure is related to function
artery	thick, tough wall with muscles, elastic fibres and fibrous tissue	Carries blood at high pressure – prevents bursting and maintains pressure wave. The large arteries, near the heart, have a greater proportion of elastic tissue, which allows these vessels to stand up to the surges of high pressure caused by the heartbeat.
	lumen quite narrow, but increases as a pulse of blood passes through	This helps to maintain blood pressure.
	valves absent	High pressure prevents blood flowing backwards.
vein	thin wall – mainly fibrous tissue, with little muscle or elastic fibres	Carries blood at low pressure.
	lumen large	To reduce resistance to blood flow
	valves present	To prevent backflow of blood. Contraction of body muscles, particularly in the limbs, compresses the thin-walled veins. The valves in the veins prevent the blood flowing backwards when the vessels are compressed in this way. This assists the return of venous blood to the heart.
capillary	permeable wall, one cell thick, with no muscle or elastic tissue	This allows diffusion of materials between the capillary and surrounding tissues.
	lumen approximately one red blood cell wide	White blood cells can squeeze between cells of the wall. Blood cells pass through slowly to allow diffusion of materials.
	valves absent	Blood is still under pressure.

Blood

Blood consists of red cells, white cells and platelets floating in a liquid called plasma. There are between 5 and 6 litres of blood in the body of an adult, and each cubic centimetre contains about 5 billion red cells.

Red cells

These are tiny, disc-like cells (Figures B7.31a and B7.33) which do not have nuclei. They are made of spongy cytoplasm enclosed in an elastic cell membrane. In their cytoplasm is the red pigment haemoglobin, a protein combined with iron. Haemoglobin combines with oxygen in places where there is a high concentration of oxygen, to form **oxyhaemoglobin**. Oxyhaemoglobin is an unstable compound. It breaks down and releases its oxygen in places where the oxygen concentration is low (Figure B7.32). This makes haemoglobin very useful in carrying oxygen from the lungs to the tissues.

Blood that contains mainly oxyhaemoglobin is said to be **oxygenated**. Blood with little oxyhaemoglobin is **deoxygenated**.

Each red cell lives for about 4 months, after which it breaks down. The red haemoglobin changes to a yellow pigment, bilirubin, which is excreted in the bile. The iron from the haemoglobin is stored in the liver. About 200 000 million red cells wear out and are replaced each day. This is about 1% of the total. Red cells are made by the red bone marrow of certain bones in the skeleton – in the ribs, vertebrae and breastbone for example.

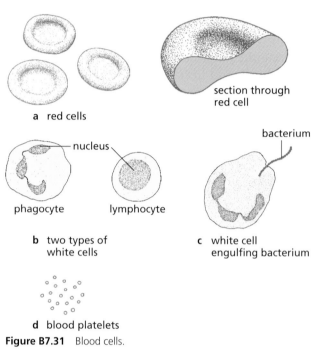

a red cells

b two types of white cells

c white cell engulfing bacterium

d blood platelets

Figure B7.31 Blood cells.

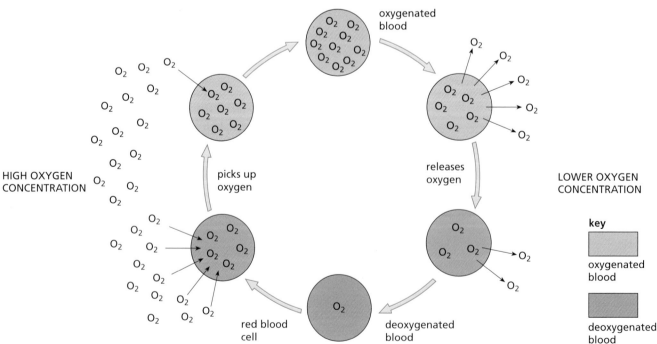

Figure B7.32 The function of the red cells.

White cells

There are several different kinds of white cell (Figures B7.31b and B7.33). Most are larger than the red cells and they all have a nucleus. There is one white cell to every 600 red cells and they are made in the same bone marrow that makes red cells. Many of them undergo a process of maturation and development in the thymus gland, lymph nodes or spleen. White blood cells are involved with phagocytosis and antibody production.

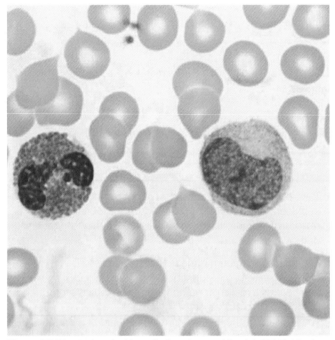

Figure B7.33   Red and white cells from human blood (×2500). The large nucleus can be seen clearly in the white cells.

Platelets

These are pieces of special blood cells budded off in the red bone marrow. They help to clot the blood at wounds and so stop the bleeding.

Plasma

The liquid part of the blood is called plasma. It is water with a large number of substances dissolved in it. The ions of sodium, potassium, calcium, chloride and hydrogen carbonate, for example, are present. Proteins such as fibrinogen, albumin and globulins make up an important part of the plasma. Fibrinogen is needed for clotting (see below), and the globulin proteins include antibodies, which combat bacteria and other foreign matter. The plasma will also contain varying amounts of food substances such as amino acids, glucose and lipids (fats). There may also be hormones (Chapter B9) present, depending on the activities taking place in the body. The excretory product, urea, is dissolved in the plasma, along with carbon dioxide.

The liver and kidneys keep the composition of the plasma more or less constant, but the amount of digested food, salts and water will vary within narrow limits according to food intake and body activities.

Table B7.2 summarises the role of transport by the blood system

Table B7.2   Transport by the blood system

Substance	From	To
oxygen	lungs	whole body
carbon dioxide	whole body	lungs
urea	liver	kidneys
hormones	glands	target organs
digested food	intestine	whole body
heat	abdomen and muscles	whole body

Questions

6 Starting from the left atrium, put the following in the correct order for circulation of the blood:
left atrium, vena cava, aorta, lungs, pulmonary artery, right atrium, pulmonary vein, right ventricle, left ventricle
7 How do veins differ from arteries in:
   a their function
   b their structure?
8 How do capillaries differ from other blood vessels in:
   a their structure
   b their function?
9 In what ways are white cells different from red cells in their function?
10 Which parts of the heart:
   a pump blood into the arteries
   b stop blood flowing the wrong way?
11 Put the following in the correct order:
   A blood enters arteries
   B ventricles contract
   C atria contract
   D ventricles relax
   E blood enters ventricles
   F semi-lunar valves close
   G tri- and bicuspid valves close.

12 Why do you think that:
  a the walls of the ventricles are more muscular than the walls of the atria
  b the muscle of the left ventricle is thicker than that of the right ventricle?
  (Hint: look back at Figure B7.30.)
13 Why is a person whose heart valves are damaged by disease unable to take part in active sport?
14 a What positive steps could you take, and
  b what things should you avoid, to reduce your risk of coronary heart disease in later life?
15 Figure B7.34 shows the relative increase in the rates of four body processes in response to vigorous exercise.
  a How are the changes related physiologically to one another?
  b What other physiological changes are likely to occur during exercise?
  c Why do you think that the increase in blood flow in muscle is less than the total increase in the blood flow?

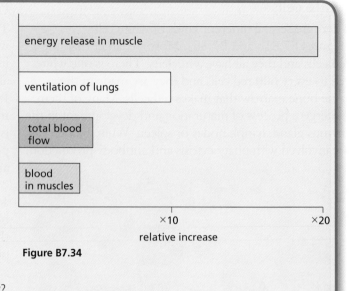

Figure B7.34

Checklist

After studying Chapter B7 you should know and understand the following.
● The xylem vessels transport water.
● The phloem transports food that has been made in the leaves, or that has been stored.
● The root hair cells are the main route by which water enter the plant.
● The pathway taken by water is through the root hairs, root cortex cells, xylem and mesophyll cells.
● The pathway taken by water can be identified using a stain.
● The xylem vessels transport water from the roots to the leaves.
● Transpiration is the loss of water vapour from the plant leaves by evaporation of water followed by diffusion of water vapour through the stomata.
● The rate of transpiration is increased by high temperature and low humidity.

● The root hair cells are adapted by being elongated to increase their surface area, making very close contact with soil particles.
● Transpiration produces the force (the transpiration pull) which draws water up the stem.
● Root pressure forces water up the stem as a result of osmosis in the roots.
● The large surface area provided by root hairs increases the rate of absorption of water by osmosis.
● When the temperature increases, molecules of water vapour gain kinetic energy to diffuse faster from the leaf, so the rate of transpiration increases.
● When the humidity decreases, molecules of water vapour inside the air spaces of the leaf are at a higher concentration than those surrounding the leaf, so the rate of transpiration increases.

● Translocation is the movement of sucrose and amino acids in phloem from the regions of production (source) to regions of storage, or to where they are used in respiration or growth (sink).

● The circulatory system is made up of blood vessels with a heart and valves to ensure one-way flow of blood.
● The heart is a muscular pump with valves, which sends blood round the circulatory system.
● The left side of the heart pumps oxygenated blood round the body.
● The right side of the heart pumps deoxygenated blood to the lungs.
● The left and right sides of the heart are divided by a septum, keeping oxygenated and deoxygenated blood separate.
● The atria are thin walled and receive blood from veins.
● The ventricles have thick muscular walls to pump blood through arteries.
● Arteries carry blood from the heart to the tissues.
● Veins return blood to the heart from the tissues.
● Coronary arteries supply the heart muscle with oxygen and glucose.
● Capillaries form a network of tiny vessels in all tissues. Their thin walls allow dissolved food and oxygen to pass from the blood into the tissues, and carbon dioxide and other waste substances to pass back into the blood.
● The main blood vessels to and from the heart are: vena cava, pulmonary veins, pulmonary arteries and aorta.
● The lungs are supplied by the pulmonary arteries and veins.
● Blood consists of red cells, white cells and platelets suspended in plasma.
● The red cells carry oxygen. The white cells attack bacteria by phagocytosis and production of antibodies. Platelets are needed to clot blood.

- Plasma transports blood cells, ions, soluble nutrients e.g. glucose, hormones and carbon dioxide.
- The kidneys are supplied by the renal arteries and veins.

- Mammals have a double circulation, which involves circulation to the lungs and circulation to the body tissues.
- The double circulation helps to maintain blood pressure, making circulation efficient.
- The heart contains atrioventricular and semi-lunar valves, preventing backflow of blood.
- Blockage of the coronary arteries in the heart leads to a heart attack.

- Smoking, fatty diets, stress, lack of exercise, genetic disposition and age may contribute to heart disease.
- Physical activity results in the heart rate increasing to supply active tissues e.g. muscle with more oxygen and glucose for respiration.
- Arteries have tough walls containing muscle so they can carry blood at high pressure and maintain a pressure wave.
- Veins carry blood at low pressure so they have thin walls, and valves to prevent backflow of blood.
- Capillaries have thin walls to allow dissolved food and oxygen to pass from the blood into the tissues, and carbon dioxide and other waste substances to pass back into the blood.

B8 Gas exchange and respiration

Combined

- Name and identify the lungs, diaphragm, ribs, intercostal muscles, larynx, trachea, bronchi, bronchioles, alveoli and associated capillaries

- List the features of gas exchange surfaces in animals, limited to large surface area, thin surface, good blood supply and good ventilation with air

- State the differences in composition between inspired and expired air, limited to oxygen, carbon dioxide and water vapour

- Explain the differences in composition between inspired and expired air

- Use limewater as a test for carbon dioxide to investigate the differences in composition between inspired and expired air
- Investigate and describe the effects of physical activity on rate and depth of breathing

- Explain the effects of physical activity on rate and depth of breathing in terms of the increased carbon dioxide concentration in the blood, causing an increased rate of breathing
- Explain the role of goblet cells, mucus and ciliated cells in protecting the gas exchange system from pathogens and particles
- State that tobacco smoking can cause chronic obstructive pulmonary disease (COPD), lung cancer and coronary heart disease
- Describe the effects on the gas exchange system of tobacco smoke and its major toxic components, limited to carbon monoxide, nicotine and tar
- Define *aerobic respiration* as the chemical reactions in cells that use oxygen to break down nutrient molecules to release energy

- State the uses of energy in the body of humans limited to: muscle contraction, protein synthesis, growth and the maintenance of a constant body temperature
- State the word equation for aerobic respiration as glucose + oxygen → carbon dioxide + water

- State the balanced chemical equation for aerobic respiration as $C_6H_{12}O_6 + 6O_2 \rightarrow 6CO_2 + 6H_2O$

Co-ordinated

- Name and identify the lungs, diaphragm, ribs, intercostal muscles, larynx, trachea, bronchi, bronchioles, alveoli and associated capillaries

- List the features of gas exchange surfaces in humans, limited to large surface area, thin surface, good blood supply and good ventilation with air

- State the differences in composition between inspired and expired air, limited to oxygen, carbon dioxide and water vapour

- Explain the differences in composition between inspired and expired air

- Use limewater as a test for carbon dioxide to investigate the differences in composition between inspired and expired air
- Investigate and describe the effects of physical activity on rate and depth of breathing

- Explain the effects of physical activity on rate and depth of breathing in terms of the increased carbon dioxide concentration in the blood, causing an increased rate of breathing
- Explain the role of goblet cells, mucus and ciliated cells in protecting the gas exchange system from pathogens and particles
- State that tobacco smoking can cause chronic obstructive pulmonary disease (COPD), lung cancer and coronary heart disease
- Describe the effects on the gas exchange system of tobacco smoke and its major toxic components, limited to carbon monoxide, nicotine and tar
- Define *aerobic respiration* as the chemical reactions in cells that use oxygen to break down nutrient molecules to release energy

- State the uses of energy in the body of humans limited to: muscle contraction, protein synthesis, cell division, growth and the maintenance of a constant body temperature
- State the word equation for aerobic respiration as glucose + oxygen → carbon dioxide + water

- State the balanced chemical equation for aerobic respiration as $C_6H_{12}O_6 + 6O_2 \rightarrow 6CO_2 + 6H_2O$
- Define *anaerobic respiration* as the chemical reactions in cells that break down nutrient molecules to release energy without using oxygen
- State the word equation for anaerobic respiration in muscles during vigorous exercise (glucose → lactic acid)
- State that lactic acid builds up in muscles and blood during vigorous exercise causing an oxygen debt
- State the word equation for anaerobic respiration in the microorganism yeast (glucose → alcohol + carbon dioxide)
- Describe the role of anaerobic respiration in yeast during bread-making
- State that anaerobic respiration releases much less energy per glucose molecule than aerobic respiration

● Gas exchange in humans

All the processes carried out by the body, such as movement, growth and reproduction, require energy. In animals, this energy can be obtained only from the food they eat. Before the energy can be used by the cells of the body, it must be set free from the chemicals of the food by a process called 'respiration'. Aerobic respiration needs a supply of oxygen and produces carbon dioxide as a waste product. All cells, therefore, must be supplied with oxygen and must be able to get rid of carbon dioxide.

In humans and other mammals, the oxygen is obtained from the air by means of the lungs. In the lungs, the oxygen dissolves in the blood and is carried to the tissues by the circulatory system (Chapter B7).

Characteristics of respiratory surfaces

The exchange of oxygen and carbon dioxide across a respiratory surface, as in the lungs, depends on the diffusion of these two gases. Diffusion occurs more rapidly if:

- there is a large surface area exposed to the gas
- the distance across which diffusion has to take place is small
- there is a good blood supply, and
- there is a big difference in the concentrations of the gas at two points brought about by **ventilation**.

Large surface area

The presence of millions of alveoli in the lungs provides a very large surface for gaseous exchange. The many branching filaments in a fish's gills have the same effect.

Thin epithelium

There is only a two-cell layer, at the most, separating the air in the alveoli from the blood in the capillaries (Figure B8.1). One layer is the alveolus wall; the other is the capillary wall. Thus, the distance for diffusion is very short.

Good blood supply

The alveoli are surrounded by networks of blood capillaries. The continual removal of oxygen by the blood in the capillaries lining the alveoli keeps its concentration low. In this way, a steep diffusion gradient is maintained, which favours the rapid diffusion of oxygen from the air passages to the alveolar lining.

The continual delivery of carbon dioxide from the blood into the alveoli, and its removal from the air passages by ventilation, similarly maintains a diffusion gradient that promotes the diffusion of carbon dioxide from the alveolar lining into the bronchioles.

Ventilation

Ventilation of the lungs helps to maintain a steep diffusion gradient (see 'Diffusion' in Chapter B2) between the air at the end of the air passages and the alveolar air. The concentration of the oxygen in the air at the end of the air passages is high, because the air is constantly replaced by the breathing actions.

The respiratory surfaces of land-dwelling mammals are invariably moist. Oxygen has to dissolve in the thin film of moisture before passing across the epithelium.

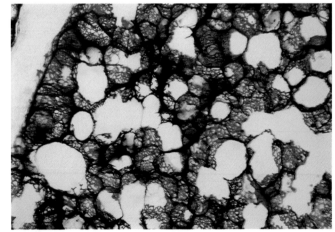

Figure B8.1   Small piece of lung tissue (×40). The capillaries have been injected with red and blue dye. The networks surrounding the alveoli can be seen.

Lung structure

The lungs are enclosed in the thorax (chest region) (see Figures B6.10 (p.63) and B8.2). They have a spongy texture and can be expanded and compressed by movements of the thorax in such a way that air is sucked in and blown out. The lungs are joined to the back of the mouth by the windpipe or **trachea** (Figure B8.3). The trachea divides into two smaller tubes, called **bronchi** (singular = bronchus), which enter the lungs and divide into even smaller branches. When these branches are only about 0.2 mm in diameter, they are called **bronchioles** (Figure B8.4a). These fine branches end in a mass of little, thin-walled, pouch-like air sacs called **alveoli** (Figures B8.4b, c and B8.5).

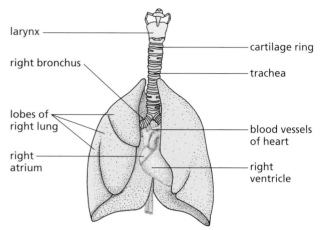

Figure B8.3 Diagram of lungs, showing position of heart.

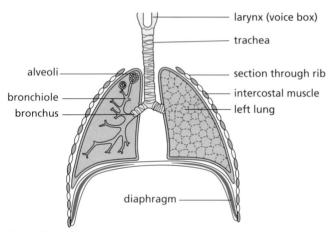

Figure B8.2 Section through the thorax.

Gaseous exchange

Ventilation refers to the movement of air into and out of the lungs. Gaseous exchange refers to the exchange of oxygen and carbon dioxide, which takes place between the air and the blood vessels in the lungs (Figure B8.5).

The 1.5 litres of residual air in the alveoli is not exchanged during ventilation and oxygen has to reach the capillaries by the slower process of diffusion. Figure B8.5 shows how oxygen reaches the red blood cells and how carbon dioxide escapes from the blood.

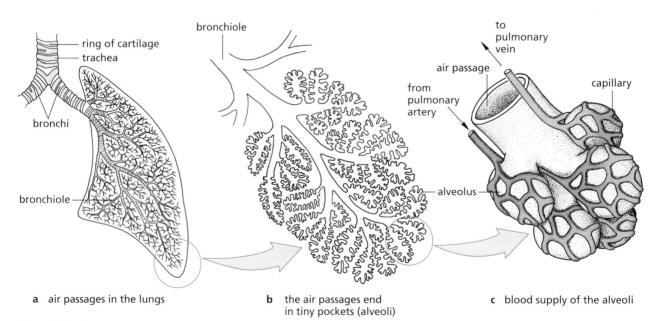

a air passages in the lungs

b the air passages end in tiny pockets (alveoli)

c blood supply of the alveoli

Figure B8.4 Lung structure.

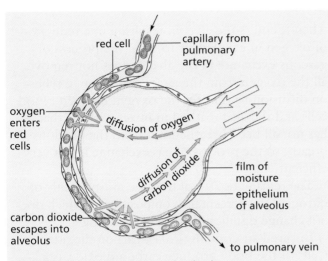

Figure B8.5 Gaseous exchange in the alveolus.

The oxygen combines with the haemoglobin in the red blood cells, forming **oxyhaemoglobin** (see 'Blood' in Chapter B7). The carbon dioxide in the plasma is released when the hydrogencarbonate ions (HCO^{3-}) break down to CO_2 and H_2O.

The capillaries carrying oxygenated blood from the alveoli join up to form the pulmonary vein (see Figure B7.30, p. 89), which returns blood to the left atrium of the heart. From here it enters the left ventricle and is pumped all around the body, so supplying the tissues with oxygen.

Table B8.1 shows changes in the composition of air as it is breathed in and out.

Table B8.1 Changes in the composition of breathed air

	Inhaled/%	Exhaled/%
oxygen	21	16
carbon dioxide	0.04	4
water vapour	variable	saturated

Sometimes the word **respiration** or **respiratory** is used in connection with breathing. The lungs, trachea and bronchi are called the **respiratory system**; a person's rate of breathing may be called his or her **respiration rate**. This use of the word should not be confused with the biological meaning of respiration, namely the release of energy in cells. This chemical process is sometimes called **tissue respiration** or **internal respiration** to distinguish it from breathing.

Practical work

Oxygen in exhaled air

- Place a large screw-top jar on its side in a bowl of water (Figure B8.6a).
- Put a rubber tube in the mouth of the jar and then turn the jar upside-down, still full of water and with the rubber tube still in it.
- Start breathing out and when you feel your lungs must be about half empty, breathe the last part of the air down the rubber tubing so that the air collects in the upturned jar and fills it (Figure B8.6b).
- Put the screw top back on the jar under water, remove the jar from the bowl and place it upright on the bench.
- Light the candle on the special wire holder (Figure B8.6c), remove the lid of the jar, lower the burning candle into the jar and count the number of seconds the candle stays alight.
- Now take a fresh jar, with ordinary air, and see how long the candle stays alight in this.

Results
The candle will burn for about 15–20 seconds in a large jar of ordinary air. In exhaled air it will go out in about 5 seconds.

Interpretation
Burning needs oxygen. When the oxygen is used up, the flame goes out. It looks as if exhaled air contains much less oxygen than atmospheric air.

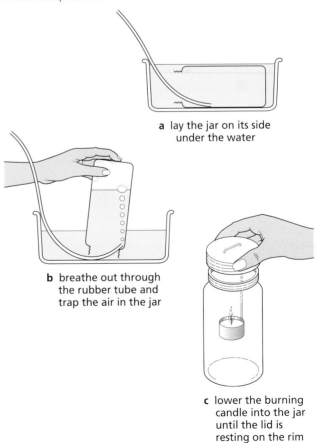

a lay the jar on its side under the water

b breathe out through the rubber tube and trap the air in the jar

c lower the burning candle into the jar until the lid is resting on the rim

Figure B8.6 Experiment to test exhaled air for oxygen.

Carbon dioxide in exhaled air

- Prepare two large test-tubes, A and B, as shown in Figure B8.7, each containing a little clear limewater.
- Put the mouthpiece in your mouth and breathe in and out *gently* through it for about 15 seconds. Notice which tube is bubbling when you breathe out and which one bubbles when you breathe in.

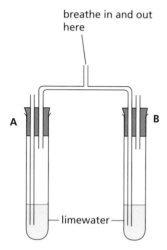

breathe in and out here

A   B

limewater

Figure B8.7 Experiment to compare the carbon dioxide content of inhaled and exhaled air.

If after 15 seconds there is no difference in the appearance of the limewater in the two tubes, continue breathing through them for another 15 seconds.

Results
The limewater in tube B goes milky. The limewater in tube A stays clear.

Interpretation
Carbon dioxide turns limewater milky. Exhaled air passes through tube B. Inhaled air passes through tube A. Exhaled air must, therefore, contain more carbon dioxide than inhaled air.

Note 1: if the breathing process is carried out for too long, the limewater that had turned milky will revert to being colourless. This is because the calcium carbonate formed (milky precipitate) reacts in water with carbon dioxide to form calcium hydrogencarbonate, which is soluble and colourless.

Note 2: Hydrogencarbonate indicator is an alternative to limewater. It changes from red to yellow when carbon dioxide is bubbled through it.

Differences in composition of inspired and expired air

Air in the atmosphere (which is breathed in) contains about 21% oxygen (see Table B8.1). Some of this is absorbed into the bloodstream when it enters the alveoli, resulting in a reduction of oxygen in exhaled air to 16% (the process of gaseous exchange in the alveoli does not remove all the oxygen from the air). Gas exchange relies on diffusion to transfer the oxygen into red blood cells and the air breathed in mixes with air that has not all been breathed out from the previous breath, so the process of gas exchange is not very efficient.

The remaining 79% of the air consists mainly of nitrogen, the percentage composition of which does not change significantly during breathing.

Inspired air contains 0.04% carbon dioxide. Cells of the body produce carbon dioxide as a waste product during aerobic respiration. The bloodstream carries carbon dioxide to the lungs for excretion. It diffuses across the walls of the alveoli to be expired. The percentage breathed out is 4%, 100 times greater than the percentage breathed in.

The lining of the alveoli is coated with a film of moisture in which the oxygen dissolves. Some of this moisture evaporates into the alveoli and saturates the air with water vapour. The air you breathe out, therefore, always contains a great deal more water vapour than the air you breathe in. The presence of water vapour in expired air is easily demonstrated by breathing onto a cold mirror: condensation quickly builds up on the glass surface. The exhaled air is warmer as well, so in cold and temperate climates you lose heat to the atmosphere by breathing.

Practical work

Investigating the effect of exercise on rate and depth of breathing

This investigation makes use of an instrument called a spirometer. It may be one as illustrated in Figure B8.8, or a digital version, connected to a computer. A traditional spirometer has a hinged chamber, which rises and falls as a person breathes through the mouthpiece. The chamber is filled with medical oxygen from a cylinder. There is a filter containing soda lime, which removes any carbon dioxide in the user's breath, so that it is not re-breathed. The hinged chamber has a pen attached (shown in red in Figure B8.8), which rests against the paper-covered drum of a kymograph. This can be set to revolve at a fixed rate so that the trace produced by the user progresses across the paper.

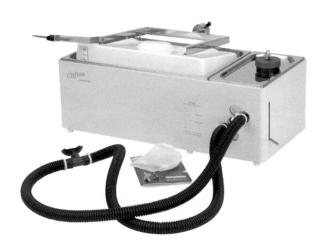

Figure B8.8 A spirometer. This instrument measures the volume of air breathed in and out of the lungs and can be used to measure oxygen consumption.

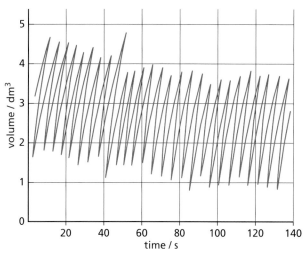

Figure B8.9 Spirometer trace taken during exercise.

- A volunteer is asked to breathe in and out through the mouthpiece and the kymograph is set to revolve slowly. This will generate a trace, which will provide information about the volunteer's tidal volume and breathing rate (each peak on the trace represents one breath and the depth between a peak and trough can be used to calculate the tidal volume).
- Next, the volunteer is asked to take a deep breath with the mouthpiece removed, then breathe out through the mouthpiece for one long continuous breath. The depth between the peak and trough produced can be used to calculate the vital capacity.
- Finally, the volunteer is asked insert the mouthpiece, then run on the spot or pedal an exercise bicycle, while breathing through the spirometer. The trace produced (Figure B8.9) can be used to compare the breathing rate and depth during exercise with that at rest. A study of the trace would also show a drop in the trace with time. This can be used to calculate the volume of oxygen consumed over time.

Results

Tidal volume is about 500 cm^3, but tends to appear higher if the person is nervous or influenced by the trace being created.

Vital capacity can be between 2.5 and 5.0 litres, depending on the sex, physical size and fitness of the person.

The breathing rate at rest is around 12 breaths per minute. During exercise this increases and may reach 20 or more breaths per minute.

Note: this experiment makes use of medical oxygen. This has a high purity and is toxic if inhaled for a prolonged period of time. If the volunteer starts to feel dizzy while using the spirometer, he or she should remove the mouthpiece immediately and rest.

Breathing rate and exercise

The increased rate and depth of breathing during exercise allows more oxygen to dissolve in the blood and supply the active muscles. The extra carbon dioxide that the muscles put into the blood is detected by the brain, which instructs the intercostal muscles and diaphragm muscles to contract and relax more rapidly, increasing the breathing rate. Carbon dioxide will be removed by the faster, deeper breathing.

The relationship between physical activity and the rate and depth of breathing

It has already been stated that the rate and depth of breathing increase during exercise. In order for the limbs to move faster, aerobic respiration in the skeletal muscles increases. Carbon dioxide is a waste product of aerobic respiration. As a result, CO_2 builds up in the muscle cells and diffuses into the plasma in the bloodstream more rapidly. The brain detects increases in carbon dioxide concentration in the blood and stimulates the breathing mechanism to speed up, increasing the rate of expiration of the gas. An increase in the breathing rate also has the advantage of making more oxygen available to the more rapidly respiring muscle cells.

Protection of the gas exchange system from pathogens and particles

Pathogens are disease-causing organisms. Pathogens, such as bacteria, and dust particles are present in the air we breathe in and are potentially dangerous if not actively removed. There are two types of cells that provide mechanisms to help achieve this.

Goblet cells are found in the epithelial lining of the trachea, bronchi and some bronchioles of the respiratory tract (Figure B8.10). Their role is to secrete **mucus**. The mucus forms a thin film over the internal lining. This sticky liquid traps pathogens and small particles, preventing them from entering the alveoli where they could cause infection or physical damage.

Ciliated cells are also present in the epithelial lining of the respiratory tract (Figure B8.10). They are in a continually flicking motion to move the mucus, secreted by the goblet cells, upwards and away from the lungs. When the mucus reaches the top of the trachea, it passes down the gullet during normal swallowing.

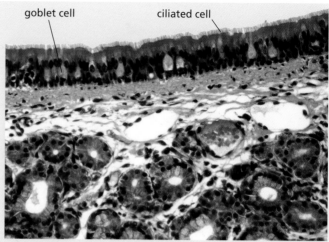

Figure B8.10   Goblet cells and ciliated cells in the trachea.

Smoking

The short-term effects of smoking cause the bronchioles to constrict and the cilia lining the air passages to stop beating. The smoke also makes the lining produce more mucus. **Nicotine**, the addictive component of tobacco smoke, produces an increase in the rate of the heartbeat and a rise in blood pressure. It may, in some cases, cause an erratic and irregular heart beat. Tar in cigarette smoke is thought to be the main cause of lung cancer in smokers. **Carbon monoxide** permanently binds with haemoglobin in red blood cells, reducing the smoker's ability to provide oxygen to respiring cells. This results in a smoker getting out of breath more easily and it reduces physical fitness.

The long-term effects of smoking may take many years to develop but they are severe, disabling and often lethal.

Lung cancer

Cancer is a term used for diseases in which cells become abnormal and divide out-of-control. They can then move around the body and invade other tissues. A chemical that causes cancer is known as a **carcinogen**. Carcinogens present in cigarette smoke, such as tar, increase the risk of lung cells becoming cancerous. Tumours develop. These are balls of abnormal cells, which do not allow gaseous exchange like normal lung cells.

Many studies have now demonstrated how cigarette smoke damages lung cells, confirming that smoking does cause cancer. The higher the number of cigarettes smoked, the greater the risk of lung cancer.

Chronic obstructive pulmonary disease (COPD)

This term covers a number of lung diseases, which include chronic bronchitis, emphysema and chronic obstructive airways disease. A person suffering from COPD will experience difficulties with breathing, mainly because of narrowing of the airways (bronchi and bronchioles). Symptoms of COPD include breathlessness when active, frequent chest infections and a persistent cough with phlegm (sticky mucus).

Heart disease

Coronary heart disease is the leading cause of death in most developed countries. It results from a blockage of coronary arteries by fatty deposits. This reduces the supply of oxygenated blood to the heart muscle and sooner or later leads to heart failure (see Chapter B7). High blood pressure, diets with too much animal fat and lack of exercise are also thought to be causes of heart attack, but about a quarter of all deaths due to coronary heart disease are thought to be caused by smoking (see Figure B7.24 p. 86).

The nicotine and carbon monoxide from cigarette smoke increase the tendency for the blood to clot and so block the coronary arteries, already partly blocked by fatty deposits. The carbon monoxide increases the rate at which the fatty material is deposited in the arteries.

Question

1 Place the following structures in the order in which air will reach them when breathing in: bronchus, trachea, nasal cavity, alveolus.

● Respiration

Most of the processes taking place in cells need energy to make them happen. Examples of energy-consuming processes in living organisms are:

- the contraction of muscle cells – to create movement of the organism, or peristalsis to move food along the alimentary canal, or contraction of the uterus wall during childbirth
- building up proteins from amino acids
- the process of cell division to create more cells, or replace damaged or worn out cells, or to make reproductive cells
- growth of an organism through the formation of new cells or a permanent increase in cell size
- the conduction of electrical impulses by nerve cells
- maintaining a constant body temperature in homoiothermic (warm-blooded) animals ('Homeostasis' in Chapter B9) to ensure that vital chemical reactions continue at a predictable rate and do not slow down or speed up as the surrounding temperature varies.

This energy comes from the food that cells take in. The food mainly used for energy in cells is glucose.

The process by which energy is produced from food, in the presence of oxygen, is called **aerobic respiration**. It can be summed up by the word equation

$$\text{glucose} + \text{oxygen} \xrightarrow{\text{enzymes}} \text{carbon dioxide} + \text{water}$$

Respiration is a chemical process that takes place in cells and involves the action of enzymes. It must not be confused with the process of breathing, which is also sometimes called 'respiration'.

● Aerobic respiration

Key definition
Aerobic respiration is the term for the chemical reactions in cells that use oxygen to break down nutrient molecules to release energy.

The word **aerobic** means that oxygen is needed for this chemical reaction. The food molecules are combined with oxygen. The process is called **oxidation** and the food is said to be **oxidised**. All food molecules contain carbon, hydrogen and oxygen atoms. The process of oxidation converts the carbon to carbon dioxide (CO_2) and the hydrogen to water (H_2O) and, at the same time, sets free energy, which the cell can use to drive other reactions.

The balanced chemical equation for aerobic respiration is

$$C_6H_{12}O_6 + 6O_2 \longrightarrow 6CO_2 + 6H_2O + 2830\,kJ$$

$$\text{glucose} \quad \text{oxygen} \quad \text{carbon} \quad \text{water} \quad \text{energy}$$
$$\text{dioxide}$$

● Anaerobic respiration

Key definition
Anaerobic respiration is the term for the chemical reactions in cells that break down nutrient molecules to release energy without using oxygen.

The word **anaerobic** means 'in the absence of oxygen'. In this process, energy is still released from food by breaking it down chemically but the reactions do not use oxygen though they do often produce carbon dioxide. A common example is the action of yeast on sugar solution to produce alcohol. The sugar is not completely oxidised to carbon dioxide and water but converted to carbon dioxide and alcohol. This process is called **fermentation** and is shown by the following equation:

$$\text{glucose} \xrightarrow{\text{enzymes}} \text{alcohol} + \text{carbon dioxide} + 118\,kJ$$
$$\text{energy}$$

The processes of brewing and bread-making rely on anaerobic respiration by yeast. As with aerobic respiration, the reaction takes place in small steps and needs several different enzymes. The yeast uses the energy for its growth and living activities, but you can see from the equation that less energy is produced by anaerobic respiration than in aerobic respiration. This is because the alcohol still contains a great deal of energy that the yeast is unable to use.

Anaerobic respiration also occurs in muscles during vigorous exercise, because oxygen cannot be delivered fast enough to satisfy the needs of the respiring muscle cells. The products are different to those produced by anaerobic respiration in yeast. The process is shown by the following equation:

glucose ⟶ lactic acid

The lactic acid builds up in the muscles and causes muscle fatigue (cramp).

Anaerobic respiration is much less efficient than aerobic respiration because it releases much less energy per glucose molecule broken down (respired).

During vigorous exercise, **lactic acid** may build up in a muscle. In this case it is removed in the bloodstream. The blood needs to move more quickly during and after exercise to maintain this lactic acid removal process, so the heart rate is rapid. On reaching the liver, some of the lactic acid is oxidised to carbon dioxide and water, using up oxygen in the process. After exercise has stopped, a high level of oxygen consumption may persist until the excess of lactic acid has been oxidised. This is characterised by deeper breathing (an athlete pants for breath). The build-up of lactic acid that is oxidised later is said to create an **oxygen debt**.

Accumulation of lactic acid in the muscles results in muscular fatigue, leading to cramp.

Questions

2 a If, in one word, you had to say what respiration was about, which word would you choose from this list: breathing, energy, oxygen, cells, food?
  b In which parts of a living organism does respiration take place?

3 What are the main differences between aerobic and anaerobic respiration?
4 What is the difference between aerobic and anaerobic respiration in the amount of energy released from one molecule of glucose?
5 Why do you think your breathing rate and heart rate stay high for some time after completing a spell of vigorous exercise?

Checklist

After studying Chapter B8 you should know and understand the following.
- The ribs, rib muscles and diaphragm make the lungs expand and contract. This causes inhaling and exhaling.
- Air is drawn into the lungs through the trachea, bronchi and bronchioles.
- Inspired air contains a higher percentage of oxygen and a lower percentage of carbon dioxide and (usually) water vapour than exhaled air.
- Limewater is used as a test for the presence of carbon dioxide. It turns milky.
- During exercise, the rate and depth of breathing increase.
- Alveoli in the lungs are very numerous, provide a large surface area, have a thin, moist surface and are well-ventilated for efficient gas exchange.
- Alveoli have a good blood supply.
- Exchange of oxygen and carbon dioxide in the alveoli takes place by diffusion.

- The blood in the capillaries picks up oxygen from the air in the alveoli and gives out carbon dioxide. This is called gaseous exchange.
- The oxygen is carried round the body by the blood and used by the cells for their respiration.
- During exercise, the rate and depth of breathing increase. This supplies extra oxygen to the muscles and removes their excess carbon dioxide.
- During physical activity increases in levels of carbon dioxide in the blood are detected in the brain, causing an increased rate of breathing.
- Goblet cells make mucus to trap pathogen and particles to protect the gas exchange system.
- Ciliated cells move mucus away from the alveoli.
- Tobacco smoke can cause COPD, lung cancer and coronary heart disease.
- Tobacco smoke affects the gaseous exchange system because it contains toxic components, including carbon monoxide, nicotine and tar.

- The uses of energy in the body of humans include muscle contraction, protein synthesis, growth and the maintenance of a constant body temperature,
- The word equation for aerobic respiration is

  glucose + oxygen → carbon dioxide + water

- Aerobic respiration is the chemical reactions in that use oxygen to break down nutrient molecules cells to release energy.
- The balanced chemical equation for aerobic respiration is

  $C_6H_{12}O_6 + 6O_2 \rightarrow 6CO_2 + 6H_2O$

- Anaerobic respiration is the chemical reactions in that use oxygen to break down nutrient molecules cells to release energy without using oxygen.
- The word equation for anaerobic respiration in muscles during vigorous exercise is

  glucose → lactic acid

- Lactic acid builds up in muscles due to anaerobic respiration, causing an oxygen debt.
- The word equation for anaerobic respiration in the microorganism yeast during vigorous exercise is

  glucose → alcohol + carbon dioxide

- Yeast is used in bread making because the carbon dioxide produced as it respires anaerobically makes the bread rise.
- Aerobic respiration releases much more energy per glucose molecule than anaerobic respiration.

B9 Co-ordination and response

Combined

- Define a *hormone*
- Describe adrenaline as the hormone secreted in 'fight or flight' situations and its effects, limited to increased breathing and pulse rate and widened pupils
- Give examples of situations in which adrenaline secretion increases

- Discuss the role of the hormone adrenaline in the chemical control of metabolic activity, including increasing the blood glucose concentration and pulse rate
- Compare nervous and hormonal control system in terms of speed and longevity of action

- Define *gravitropism*
- Define *phototropism*

- Explain phototropism and gravitropism of a shoot as examples of the chemical control of plant growth

- Investigate gravitropism and phototropism in shoots and roots

- Explain the role of auxin in controlling shoot growth, limited to: auxin made in shoot tip (only); auxin spreads through the plant from the shoot tip; auxin is unequally distributed in response to light and gravity; auxin stimulates cell elongation

Co-ordinated

- Describe a nerve impulse as an electrical signal that passes along nerve cells called neurones
- Describe the human nervous system in terms of: the central nervous system consisting of brain and spinal cord; the peripheral nervous system; coordination and regulation of body functions

- Distinguish between voluntary and involuntary actions

- Identify motor (effector), relay (connector) and sensory neurones from diagrams
- Describe a simple reflex arc in terms of receptor, sensory neurone, relay neurone, motor neurones and effector
- Describe a reflex action as a means of automatically and rapidly integrating and coordinating stimuli with the responses of effectors (muscles and glands)

- Identify the structures of the eye, limited to cornea, iris, pupil, lens, retina, optic nerve, ciliary muscles, suspensory ligaments and blind spot
- Describe the function of each part of the eye, limited to: cornea – refracts light; iris – controls how much light enters pupil; lens – focuses light onto retina; retina – contains light receptors, some sensitive to light of different colours; optic nerve – carries impulses to the brain
- Explain the pupil reflex in terms of light intensity and antagonistic action of circular and radial muscles in the iris
- Explain accommodation to view near and distant objects in terms of the contraction and relaxation of the ciliary muscles, tension in the suspensory ligaments, shape of the lens and refraction of light

- Define a *hormone*
- Describe adrenaline as the hormone secreted in 'fight or flight' situations and its effects, limited to increased breathing and pulse rate and widened pupils
- Give examples of situations in which adrenaline secretion increases

- Discuss the role of the hormone adrenaline in the chemical control of metabolic activity, including increasing the blood glucose concentration and pulse rate
- Compare nervous and hormonal control system in terms of speed and longevity of action

- Define *homeostasis*

- Explain that homeostasis is the control of internal conditions within set limits
- Explain the concept of control by negative feedback
- Describe the control of the glucose content of the blood by the liver and the roles of insulin and glucagon from the pancreas

- Name and identify on a diagram of the skin: hairs, hair erector muscles, sweat glands, receptors, sensory neurones, blood vessels and fatty tissue
- Describe the maintenance of a constant internal body temperature in humans in terms of vasodilation and vasoconstriction of arterioles supplying the skin surface capillaries

Co-ordinated (continued...)

- Describe the maintenance of a constant internal body temperature in humans in terms of insulation, sweating, shivering and the role of the brain (limited to blood temperature receptors and co-ordination)
- Describe the control of the glucose content of the blood by the liver and the roles of insulin and glucagon from the pancreas
- Describe the maintenance of a constant internal body temperature in humans in terms of vasodilation and vasoconstriction of arterioles supplying skin surface capillaries

- Define *gravitropism*
- Define *phototropism*
- Explain phototropism and gravitropism of a shoot as examples of the chemical control of plant growth
- Investigate gravitropism and phototropism in shoots and roots
- Explain the role of auxin in controlling shoot growth, limited to: auxin made in shoot tip (only); auxin spreads through the plant from the shoot tip; auxin is unequally distributed in response to light and gravity; auxin stimulates cell elongation

Co-ordination is the way all the organs and systems of the body are made to work efficiently together (Figure B9.1). If, for example, the leg muscles are being used for running, they will need extra supplies of glucose and oxygen. To meet this demand, the lungs breathe faster and deeper to obtain the extra oxygen and the heart pumps more rapidly to get the oxygen and glucose to the muscles more quickly.

The brain detects changes in the oxygen and carbon dioxide content of the blood and sends nervous impulses to the diaphragm, intercostal muscles and heart. In this example, the co-ordination of the systems is brought about by the **nervous system**.

The extra supplies of glucose needed for running come from the liver. Glycogen in the liver is changed to glucose, which is released into the bloodstream (see 'Homeostasis' on p.113). The conversion of glycogen to glucose is stimulated by, among other things, a chemical called adrenaline. Co-ordination by chemicals is brought about by the **endocrine system**.

The nervous system works by sending electrical impulses along nerves. The endocrine system depends on the release of chemicals, called **hormones**, from **endocrine glands**. Hormones are carried by the bloodstream. For example, insulin is carried from the pancreas to the liver by the circulatory system.

● Nervous control in humans

The human nervous system is shown in Figure B9.2 on the next page. The brain and spinal cord together form the **central nervous system**. Nerves carry electrical impulses from the central nervous system to all parts of the body, making muscles contract or glands produce enzymes or hormones. Electrical impulses are electrical signals that pass along nerve cells (neurones).

Glands and muscles are called **effectors** because they go into action when they receive nerve impulses or hormones. The biceps muscle is an effector that flexes the arm; the salivary gland (see 'Alimentary canal' in Chapter B6) is an effector that produces saliva when it receives a nerve impulse from the brain.

Figure B9.1 Co-ordination. The badminton player's brain is receiving sensory impulses from his eyes, ears (sound and balance) and muscle stretch receptors. Using this information, the brain co-ordinates the muscles of his limbs so that even while running or leaping he can control his stroke.

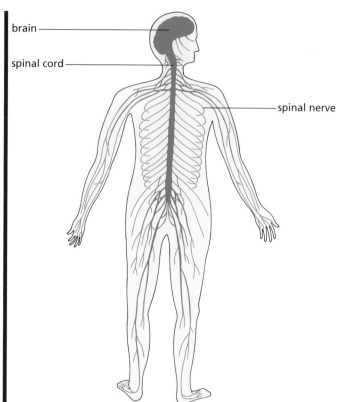

Figure B9.2 The human nervous system.

The nerves also carry impulses back to the central nervous system from receptors in the sense organs of the body. These impulses from the eyes, ears, skin, etc. make us aware of changes in our surroundings or in ourselves. Nerve impulses from the sense organs to the central nervous system are called **sensory impulses**; those from the central nervous system to the effectors, resulting in action, are called **motor impulses**.

The nerves that connect the body to the central nervous system make up the **peripheral** nervous system.

Nerve cells (neurones)

The central nervous system and the peripheral nerves are made up of nerve cells, called **neurones**. Three types of neurone are shown in Figure B9.3. **Motor neurones** carry impulses from the central nervous system to muscles and glands. **Sensory neurones** carry impulses from the sense organs to the central nervous system. **Relay neurones** (also called multi-polar or connector neurones) are neither sensory nor motor but make connections to other neurones inside the central nervous system.

Each neurone has a **cell body** consisting of a nucleus surrounded by a little cytoplasm. Branching fibres, called **dendrites**, from the cell body make

contact with other neurones. A long filament of cytoplasm, surrounded by an insulating sheath, runs from the cell body of the neurone. This filament is called a **nerve fibre** (Figure B9.3a and b). The cell bodies of the neurones are mostly located in the brain or in the spinal cord and it is the nerve fibres that run in the nerves. A **nerve** is easily visible, white, tough and stringy and consists of hundreds of microscopic nerve fibres bundled together (Figure B9.4). Most nerves will contain a mixture of sensory and motor fibres. So a nerve can carry many different impulses. These impulses will travel in one direction in sensory fibres and in the opposite direction in motor fibres.

Some of the nerve fibres are very long. The nerve fibres to the foot have their cell bodies in the spinal cord and the fibres run inside the nerves, without a break, to the skin of the toes or the muscles of the foot. A single nerve cell may have a fibre 1 metre long.

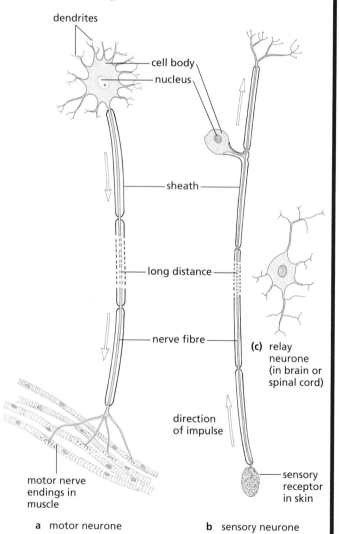

Figure B9.3 Nerve cells (neurones).

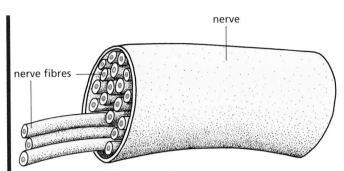

Figure B9.4 Nerve fibres grouped into a nerve.

The nerve impulse

The nerve fibres do not carry sensations like pain or cold. These sensations are felt only when a nerve impulse reaches the brain. The impulse itself is a series of electrical pulses that travel down the fibre. Each pulse lasts about 0.001 s and travels at speeds of up to 100 m/s. All nerve impulses are similar; there is no difference between nerve impulses from the eyes, ears or hands.

We are able to tell where the sensory impulses have come from and what caused them only because the impulses are sent to different parts of the brain. The nerves from the eye go to the part of the brain concerned with sight. So when impulses are received in this area, the brain recognises that they have come from the eyes and we 'see' something.

The reflex arc

One of the simplest situations where impulses cross synapses to produce action is in the reflex arc. A **reflex action** is an automatic response to a **stimulus**. (A stimulus is a change in the external or internal environment of an organism.) It provides a means of rapidly integrating and co-ordinating a stimulus with the response of an effector (a muscle or a gland) without the need for thought or a decision. When a particle of dust touches the cornea of the eye, you will blink; you cannot prevent yourself from blinking. A particle of food touching the lining of the windpipe will set off a coughing reflex that cannot be suppressed. When a bright light shines in the eye, the pupil contracts. You cannot stop this reflex and you are not even aware that it is happening.

The nervous pathway for such reflexes is called a **reflex arc**. In Figure B9.5 the nervous pathway for a well-known reflex called the 'knee-jerk' reflex is shown.

One leg is crossed over the other and the muscles are totally relaxed. If the tendon just below the kneecap of the upper leg is tapped sharply, a reflex arc makes the thigh muscle contract and the lower part of the leg swings forward.

The pathway of this reflex arc is traced in Figure B9.6. Hitting the tendon stretches the muscle and stimulates a stretch receptor. The receptor sends off impulses in a sensory fibre. These sensory impulses travel in the nerve to the spinal cord.

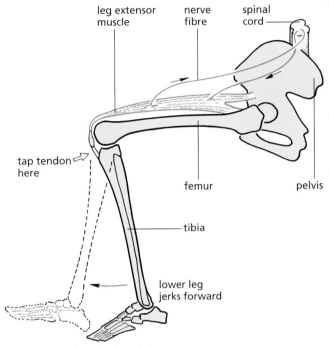

Figure B9.5 The reflex knee jerk.

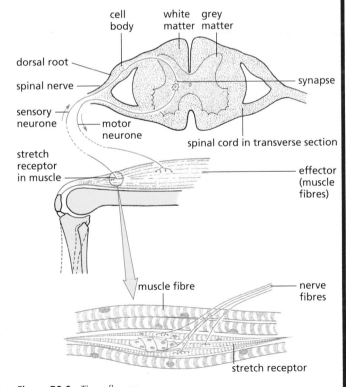

Figure B9.6 The reflex arc.

In the central region of the spinal cord, the sensory fibre passes the impulse across a synapse to a motor neurone, which conducts the impulse down the fibre, back to the thigh muscle (the effector). The arrival of the impulses at the muscle makes it contract and jerk the lower part of the limb forward. You are aware that this is happening (which means that sensory impulses must be reaching the brain), but there is nothing you can do to stop it.

The sequence of events in a simple reflex arc is shown below.

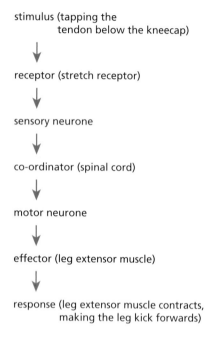

stimulus (tapping the tendon below the kneecap)

↓

receptor (stretch receptor)

↓

sensory neurone

↓

co-ordinator (spinal cord)

↓

motor neurone

↓

effector (leg extensor muscle)

↓

response (leg extensor muscle contracts, making the leg kick forwards)

Voluntary and involuntary actions

Voluntary actions

A **voluntary action** starts in the brain. It may be the result of external events, such as seeing a book on the floor, but any resulting action, such as picking up the book, is entirely voluntary. Unlike a reflex action it does not happen automatically; you can decide whether or not you carry out the action.

The brain sends motor impulses down the spinal cord in the nerve fibres. These make synapses with motor fibres, which enter spinal nerves and make connections to the sets of muscles needed to produce effective action. Many sets of muscles in the arms, legs and trunk would be brought into play in order to stoop and pick up the book, and impulses passing between the eyes, brain and arm would direct the hand to the right place and 'tell' the fingers when to close on the book.

One of the main functions of the brain is to co-ordinate these actions so that they happen in the right sequence and at the right time and place.

Involuntary actions

The reflex closure of the iris (see 'Sense organs' later in this chapter) protects the retina from bright light; the withdrawal reflex removes the hand from a dangerously hot object; the coughing reflex dislodges a foreign particle from the windpipe. Thus, these reflexes have a protective function and all are **involuntary actions**.

There are many other reflexes going on inside our bodies. We are usually unaware of these, but they maintain our blood pressure, breathing rate, heartbeat, etc. and so maintain the body processes.

Questions

1 Put the following in the correct order for a simple reflex arc:
 A impulse travels in motor fibre
 B impulse travels in sensory fibre
 C effector organ stimulated
 D receptor organ stimulated
 E impulse crosses synapse.

2 Discuss whether coughing is a voluntary or a reflex action.

The eye

Note: details of conjunctiva, humours, choroid and sclera are **not** a syllabus requirement, but are included here to put parts seen in a diagram of the eye in context.

The structure of the eye is shown in Figures B9.7 and B9.8. The **sclera** is the tough, white outer coating. The front part of the sclera is clear and allows light to enter the eye. This part is called the **cornea**. The **conjunctiva** is a thin epithelium, which lines the inside of the eyelids and the front of the sclera and is continuous with the epithelium of the cornea.

The eye contains a clear liquid whose outward pressure on the sclera keeps the spherical shape of the eyeball. The liquid behind the lens is jelly-like and called **vitreous humour**. The **aqueous humour** in front of the lens is watery.

The **lens** is a transparent structure, held in place by a ring of fibres called the **suspensory ligament**. Unlike the lens of a camera or a telescope, the eye lens is flexible and can change its shape. In front of the lens is a disc of tissue called the **iris**. It is the iris we refer to when we describe the colour of the eye as brown or blue. The iris controls how much light enters the **pupil**, which is a hole in the centre of the iris. The pupil lets in light to the rest of the eye.

The pupil looks black because all the light entering the eye is absorbed by the black pigment in the **choroid**. The choroid layer, which contains many blood vessels, lies between the retina and the sclera. In the front of the eyeball, it forms the iris and the **ciliary body**. The ciliary body produces aqueous humour.

The internal lining at the back of the eye is the **retina** and it consists of many thousands of cells that respond to light. When light falls on these cells, they send off nervous impulses, which travel in nerve fibres, through the **optic nerve**, to the brain and so give rise to the sensation of sight. The part of the retina lying directly in front of the optic nerve contains no light-sensitive cells. This region is called the **blind spot**.

Table B9.1 gives the functions of the parts of the eye required for the syllabus.

Table B9.1 Functions of parts of the eye

Part	Function
cornea	a transparent, curved layer at the front of the eye that refracts the light entering and helps to focus it
iris	a coloured ring of circular and radial muscle that controls the size of the pupil
lens	a transparent, convex, flexible, jelly-like structure that refracts light to focus it onto the retina
retina	a light-sensitive layer made up of rods, which detect light of low intensity, and cones, which detect different colours
optic nerve	transmits electrical impulses from the retina to the brain

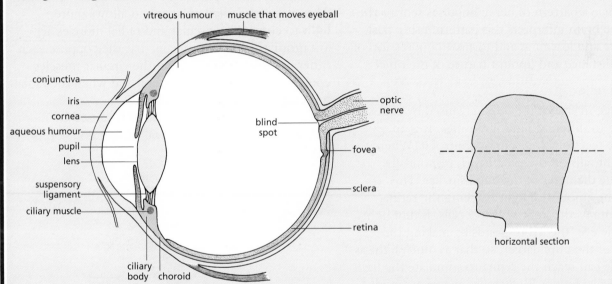

Figure B9.7 Horizontal section through left eye.

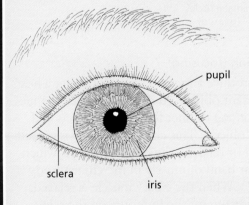

Figure B9.8 Appearance of right eye from the front.

Vision

Light from an object produces a focused **image** on the retina (like a 'picture' on a cinema screen) (Figure B9.9 on the next page). The curved surfaces of the cornea and lens both refract ('bend') the light rays that enter the eye, in such a way that each 'point of light' from the object forms a 'point of light' on the retina. These points of light will form an image, upside-down and smaller than the object.

The cornea and the aqueous and vitreous humours are mainly responsible for the refraction of light. The lens makes the final adjustments to the focus (Figure B9.9b).

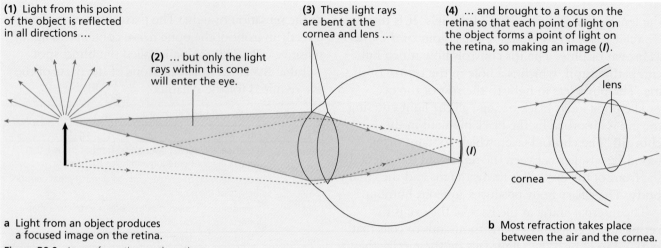

(1) Light from this point of the object is reflected in all directions ...

(2) ... but only the light rays within this cone will enter the eye.

(3) These light rays are bent at the cornea and lens ...

(4) ... and brought to a focus on the retina so that each point of light on the object forms a point of light on the retina, so making an image (*I*).

a Light from an object produces a focused image on the retina.

b Most refraction takes place between the air and the cornea.

Figure B9.9   Image formation on the retina.

The pattern of sensory cells stimulated by the image will produce a pattern of nerve impulses sent to the brain. The brain interprets this pattern, using past experience and learning, and forms an impression of the size, distance and upright nature of the object.

The pupil reflex

The change in size of the pupil is caused by exposure of the eye to different light intensities. It is an automatic reaction: you cannot control it. When bright light falls on the eye, the iris responds by making the diameter of the pupil smaller. This restricts the amount of light reaching the retina, which contains the light-sensitive cells. If dim light falls on the eye, the iris responds by making the diameter of the pupil larger, so that as much light as is available can reach the retina to stimulate the light-sensitive cells. Figure B9.8 shows an eye exposed to bright light: the pupil is small. It would become much larger if the light intensity was reduced.

Control of light intensity

This section gives more detail about the roles of the iris and pupil in controlling light intensity falling on the retina, needed if you are following the extended syllabus.

The amount of light entering the eye is controlled by altering the size of the pupil (Figure B9.10). If the light intensity is high, it causes a contraction in a ring of muscle fibres (**circular muscle**) in the iris. This reduces the size of the pupil and cuts down the intensity of light entering the eye. High-intensity light can damage the retina, so this reaction has a protective function.

In low light intensities, the circular muscle of the iris relaxes and **radial muscle** fibres (which are arranged like the spokes of a bicycle wheel) contract. This makes the pupil enlarge and allows more light to enter. The circular and radial muscles act **antagonistically**. This means that they oppose each other in their actions – when the circular muscles contract they constrict the pupil and when the radial muscles contract the pupil dilates.

The change in size of the pupil is caused by an automatic reflex action; you cannot control it consciously.

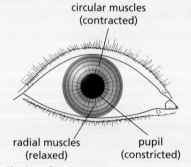

circular muscles (contracted)

radial muscles (relaxed)

pupil (constricted)

Figure B9.10   The iris reflex.

Accommodation (focusing)

The eye can produce a focused image of either a near object or a distant object. To do this the lens changes its shape, becoming thinner for distant objects and fatter for near objects. This change in shape is caused by contracting or relaxing the **ciliary muscle**, which forms a circular band of muscle in the **ciliary body** (Figure B9.11). When the ciliary muscle is relaxed, the outward pressure of the humours on the sclera pulls on the suspensory ligament and stretches the lens to its thin shape. The eye is now accommodated (i.e. focused) for distant objects (Figures B9.11a and B9.12a). To focus a near object, the ciliary muscle contracts to a smaller circle and this takes the tension out of the suspensory ligament (Figures B9.11b and B9.12b). The lens is elastic and flexible and so is able

to change to its fatter shape. This shape is better at bending the light rays from a close object.

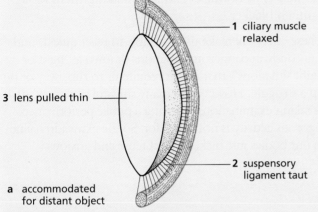

1 ciliary muscle relaxed

3 lens pulled thin

2 suspensory ligament taut

a accommodated for distant object

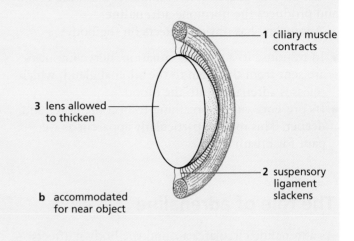

1 ciliary muscle contracts

3 lens allowed to thicken

2 suspensory ligament slackens

b accommodated for near object

Figure B9.11 How accommodation is brought about.

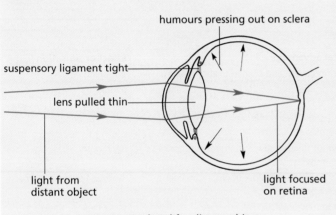

humours pressing out on sclera

suspensory ligament tight

lens pulled thin

light from distant object

light focused on retina

a accommodated for distant object

ciliary muscle contracts

lens gets thicker

light from near object

tension in suspensory ligament relaxed

light focused on retina

b accommodated for near object

Figure B9.12 Accommodation.

Questions

3 Construct a crossword using a grid with a minimum of 10 × 10 squares. Insert names associated with parts of the eye. Write a clue for each part used, based on either a description or function of the part.

4 A student looking at a distant object suddenly focuses on another object close to her. Describe the process of accommodation that enables her to focus on the object close to her.

● Hormones in humans

Key definition
A **hormone** is a chemical substance, produced by a gland and carried by the blood, which alters the activity of one or more specific target organs.

Co-ordination in humans is brought about by the nervous system and the **endocrine system**. The endocrine system depends on chemicals, called **hormones**, which are released from special glands, called **endocrine glands**, into the bloodstream. The hormones circulate around the body in the blood and eventually reach certain organs, called **target organs**. Hormones speed up, slow down or alter the activity of those organs.

Adrenal glands

These glands are attached to the back of the abdominal cavity, one above each kidney. One part of the adrenal gland receives impulses from the brain and produces the hormone **adrenaline**.

Adrenaline has obvious effects on the body:

- In response to a stressful situation, nerve impulses are sent from the brain to the adrenal gland, which releases adrenaline into the blood.
- Its presence causes breathing to become faster and deeper. This may be particularly apparent as we pant for breath.
- The heart beats faster, resulting in an increase in pulse rate. This increase in heart rate can be quite alarming, making us feel as if our heart is going to burst out of our chest.
- The pupils of our eyes dilate, making them look much blacker.

These effects all make us more able to react quickly and vigorously in dangerous situations (known as 'fight or flight situations') that might require us to run away or put up a struggle. However, in many stressful situations, such as taking examinations or giving a public performance, vigorous activity is not called for. So the extra adrenaline in our bodies just makes us feel tense and anxious.

The role of adrenaline

As adrenaline circulates around the body it affects a number of organs, as shown in Table B9.2.

Table B9.2 Responses to adrenaline

Target organ	Effects of adrenaline	Biological advantage	Effect or sensation
heart	beats faster	sends more glucose and oxygen to the muscles	thumping heart
breathing centre of the brain	faster and deeper breathing	increased oxygenation of the blood; rapid removal of carbon dioxide	panting
arterioles of the skin	constricts them (see 'Homeostasis')	less blood going to the skin means more is available to the muscles	person goes paler
arterioles of the digestive system	constricts them	less blood for the digestive system allows more to reach the muscles	dry mouth
muscles of alimentary canal	relax	peristalsis and digestion slow down; more energy available for action	'hollow' feeling in stomach
muscles of body	tenses them	ready for immediate action	tense feeling; shivering
liver	conversion of glycogen to glucose	more glucose available in blood for energy production, to allow metabolic activity to increase	no sensation
fat deposits	conversion of fats to fatty acids	fatty acids available in blood for muscle contraction	

You will recognise the sensations described in column four of Table B9.2 as characteristic of fear and anxiety.

Adrenaline is quickly converted by the liver to a less active compound, which is excreted by the kidneys. All hormones are similarly altered and excreted, some within minutes, others within days. Thus their effects are not long-lasting. The long-term hormones, such as thyroxine, are secreted continuously to maintain a steady level.

There are a number of differences between co-ordination by the nervous system and co-ordination by the endocrine system. Table B9.3 compares control by these two systems.

Question

5   Study Table B9.3 and give one example for each point of comparison.

Table B9.3 Endocrine and nervous control compared

Endocrine	Nervous
transmission of chemicals	transmission of electrical impulses
transmission via blood	transmission in nerves
slow transmission	rapid transmission
hormones dispersed throughout body	impulse sent directly to target organ
long-term effects	short-lived effects

Homeostasis

> **Key definition**
> **Homeostasis** is the maintenance of a constant internal environment.

Homeostasis literally means 'staying similar'. It refers to the fact that internal conditions in the body, such as temperature, composition and concentration of fluids, e.g. in the fluid surrounding tissues, are controlled within narrow limits to prevent any big changes.

The skin and temperature control

Skin structure

Figure B9.13 shows a section through skin. The thickness of the epidermis and the abundance of hairs vary in different parts of the body (Figure B9.14 on the next page).

The dermis contains connective tissue with hair follicles, sebaceous glands, sweat glands, blood vessels and nerve endings. There is usually a layer of adipose tissue (a fat deposit) beneath the dermis.

Skin function

The functions of the skin include protection, sensitivity and temperature regulation.

Protection

The outermost layer of dead cells of the epidermis helps to reduce water loss and provides a barrier against bacteria. The pigment cells protect the skin from damage by the ultraviolet rays in sunlight. In white-skinned people, more melanin is produced in response to exposure to sunlight, giving rise to a tan.

Sensitivity

Scattered throughout the skin are large numbers of tiny sense receptors, which give rise to sensations of touch, pressure, heat, cold and pain. These make us aware of changes in our surroundings and enable us to take action to avoid damage, to recognise objects by touch and to manipulate objects with our hands.

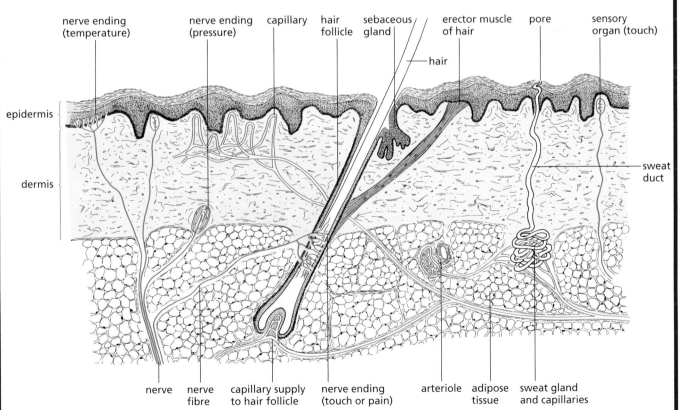

Figure B9.13   Generalised section through the skin.

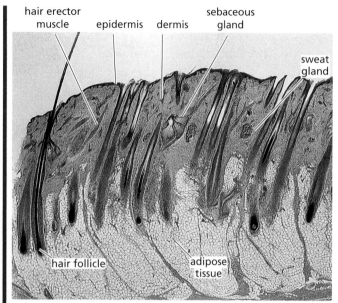

hair erector muscle · epidermis · dermis · sebaceous gland · sweat gland · hair follicle · adipose tissue

Figure B9.14 Section through hairy skin (×20).

Temperature regulation

The skin helps to keep the body temperature more or less constant. This is done by adjusting the flow of blood near the skin surface and by sweating. These processes are described more fully below.

Temperature control

Normal human body temperature varies between 35.8 °C and 37.7 °C. Temperatures below 34 °C or above 40 °C, if maintained for long, are considered dangerous. Different body regions, e.g. the hands, feet, head or internal organs, will be at different temperatures, but the **core** temperature, as measured with a thermometer under the tongue, will vary by only 1 or 2 degrees.

Heat is lost from the body surface by conduction, convection, radiation and evaporation. The amount of heat lost is reduced to an extent due to the insulating properties of adipose (fatty) tissue in the dermis. Some mammals living in extreme conditions, such as whales and seals, make much greater use of this: they have thick layers of blubber to reduce heat loss more effectively. Just how much insulation the blubber gives depends on the amount of water in the tissue: a smaller proportion of water and more fat provide better insulating properties.

Heat is gained, internally, from the process of respiration (Chapter B8) in the tissues and, externally, from the surroundings or from the Sun.

The two processes of heat gain and heat loss are normally in balance but any imbalance is corrected by a number of methods, including those described below.

Overheating
- More blood flows near the surface of the skin, allowing more heat to be exchanged with the surroundings.
- **Sweating** – the sweat glands secrete sweat on to the skin surface. When this layer of liquid evaporates, it takes heat (latent heat) from the body and cools it down (Figure B9.15).

Overcooling
- Less blood flows near the surface of the skin, reducing the amount of heat lost to the surroundings.
- Sweat production stops – thus the heat lost by evaporation is reduced.
- **Shivering** – uncontrollable bursts of rapid muscular contraction in the limbs release heat as a result of respiration in the muscles.

In these ways, the body temperature remains at about 37 °C. We also control our temperature by adding or removing clothing or deliberately taking exercise.

Whether we feel hot or cold depends on the sensory nerve endings in the skin, which respond to heat loss or gain. You cannot consciously detect changes in your core temperature. The brain plays a direct role in detecting any changes from normal by monitoring the temperature of the blood. A region called the **hypothalamus** contains a thermoregulatory centre in which temperature receptors detect temperature changes in the blood and co-ordinate a response to them. Temperature receptors are also present in the skin. They send information to the brain about temperature changes.

Figure B9.15 Sweating. During vigorous activity the sweat evaporates from the skin and helps to cool the body. When the activity stops, continued evaporation of sweat may overcool the body unless it is towelled off.

Homeostasis and negative feedback

Temperature regulation is an example of homeostasis. Maintenance of a constant body temperature ensures that vital chemical reactions continue at a predictable rate and do not speed up or slow down when the surrounding temperature changes.

In the hypothalamus of the brain there is a thermoregulatory centre. This centre monitors the temperature of the blood passing through it and also receives sensory nerve impulses from temperature receptors in the skin. A rise in body temperature is detected by the thermoregulatory centre and it sends nerve impulses to the skin, which result in vasodilation and sweating. Similarly, a fall in body temperature will be detected and will promote impulses that produce vasoconstriction and shivering.

This system of control is called **negative feedback**. The outgoing impulses counteract the effects that produced the incoming impulses. For example, a rise in temperature triggers responses that counteract the rise.

Regulation of blood sugar

If the level of sugar in the blood falls, the islets release a hormone called **glucagon** into the bloodstream. Glucagon acts on the cells in the liver and causes them to convert some of their stored glycogen into glucose and so restore the blood sugar level.

Insulin has the opposite effect to glucagon. If the concentration of blood sugar increases (e.g. after a meal rich in carbohydrate), insulin is released from the islet cells. When the insulin reaches the liver it stimulates the liver cells to take up glucose from the blood and store it as glycogen.

Insulin has many other effects; it increases the uptake of glucose in all cells for use in respiration; it promotes the conversion of carbohydrates to fats and slows down the conversion of protein to carbohydrate.

All these changes have the effect of regulating the level of glucose in the blood to within narrow limits – a very important example of homeostasis.

blood glucose
levels too high

glucose $\xrightarrow{\text{insulin}}$ glycogen

$\xleftarrow{\text{glucagon}}$

blood glucose
levels too low

Temperature control

In addition to the methods already described, the skin has another very important mechanism for maintaining a constant body temperature. This involves arterioles in the dermis of the skin, which can widen or narrow to allow more or less blood to flow near the skin surface through the blood capillaries. Further details of this process, involving the use of shunt vessels, are given in Chapter B7.

Vasodilation – the widening of the arterioles in the dermis allows more warm blood to flow through blood capillaries near the skin surface and so lose more heat (Figure B9.16a).

Vasoconstriction – narrowing (constriction) of the arterioles in the skin reduces the amount of warm blood flowing through blood capillaries near the surface (Figure B9.16b).

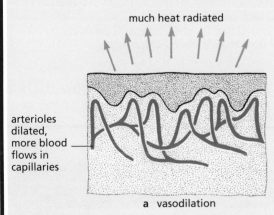

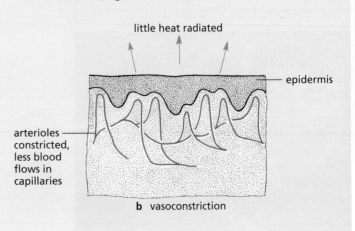

Figure B9.16 Vasodilation and vasoconstriction.

Questions

6 What conscious actions do we take to reduce the heat lost from the body?

7 a What sort of chemical reaction in active muscle will produce heat?
   b How does this heat get to other parts of the body?

8 Draw up a balance sheet to show all the possible ways the human body can gain or lose heat. Make two columns, with 'Gains' on the left and 'Losses' on the right.

9 a Which structures in the skin of humans help to reduce heat loss?
   b What changes take place in the skin of humans to reduce heat loss?

● Tropic responses

Sensitivity is the ability of living organisms to respond to stimuli. Although plants do not respond by moving their whole bodies, parts of them do respond to stimuli. Some of these responses are described as tropic responses or **tropisms**.

> **Key definitions**
> **Gravitropism** is a response in which parts of a plant grow towards or away from gravity.
> **Phototropism** is a response in which parts of a plant grow towards or away from the direction from which light is coming.

Tropisms

Tropisms are growth movements related to directional stimuli, e.g. a shoot will grow towards a source of light but away from the direction of gravity. Growth movements of this kind are usually in response to the *direction* of light or gravity. Responses to light are called **phototropisms**; responses to gravity are **gravitropisms** (or **geotropisms**).

If the plant organ responds by growing towards the stimulus, the response is said to be 'positive'. If the response is growth away from the stimulus it is said to be 'negative'. For example, if a plant is placed horizontally, its stem will change its direction and grow upwards, away from gravity (Figure B9.17).

Figure B9.17 Negative gravitropism. The tomato plant has been left on its side for 24 hours.

The shoot is **negatively gravitropic**. The roots, however, will change their direction of growth to grow vertically downwards towards the pull of gravity (Experiment 1). Roots, therefore, are **positively gravitropic**.

Phototropism and gravitropism are best illustrated by some simple controlled experiments. Seedlings are good material for experiments on sensitivity because their growing roots (radicles) and shoots respond readily to the stimuli of light and gravity.

Practical work

Experiments on tropisms

1 Gravitropism in pea radicles

- Soak about 20 peas in water for a day and then let them germinate in a vertical roll of moist blotting-paper.
- After 3 days, choose 12 seedlings with straight radicles and pin six of these to the turntable of a clinostat so that the radicles are horizontal.
- Pin another six seedlings to a cork that will fit in a wide-mouthed jar. Leave the jar on its side.
- A **clinostat** is a clockwork or electric turntable, which rotates the seedlings slowly about four times an hour. Although gravity is pulling sideways on their roots, it will pull equally on all sides as they rotate.
- Place the jar and the clinostat in the same conditions of lighting or leave them in darkness for 2 days.

Result

The radicles in the clinostat will continue to grow horizontally but those in the jar will have changed their direction of growth, to grow vertically downwards (Figure B9.18).

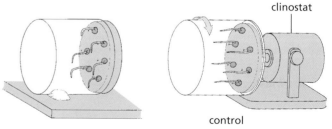

Figure B9.18 Results of an experiment to show gravitropism in roots.

Interpretation

The stationary radicles have responded to the stimulus of one-sided gravity by growing towards it. The radicles are positively gravitropic.

The radicles in the clinostat are the controls. Rotation of the clinostat has allowed gravity to act on all sides equally and there is no one-sided stimulus, even though the radicles were horizontal.

2 Phototropism in shoots

■ Select two potted seedlings, e.g. sunflower or runner bean, of similar size and water them both.

■ Place one of them under a cardboard box with a window cut in one side so that light reaches the shoot from one direction only (Figure B9.19).

■ Place the other plant in an identical situation but on a clinostat. This will rotate the plant about four times per hour and expose each side of the shoot equally to the source of light. This is the control.

Result

After 1 or 2 days, the two plants are removed from the boxes and compared. It will be found that the stem of the plant with one-sided illumination has changed its direction of growth and is growing towards the light (Figure B9.20). The control shoot has continued to grow vertically.

Interpretation

The results suggest that the young shoot has responded to one-sided lighting by growing towards the light. The shoot is said to be positively phototropic because it grows towards the direction of the stimulus.

However, the results of an experiment with a single plant cannot be used to draw conclusions that apply to green plants as a whole. The experiment described here is more of an illustration than a critical investigation. To investigate phototropisms thoroughly, a large number of plants from a wide variety of species would have to be used.

Figure B9.20 Positive phototropism. The sunflower seedlings have received one-sided lighting for a day.

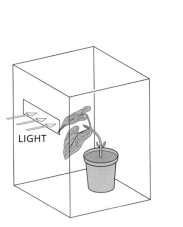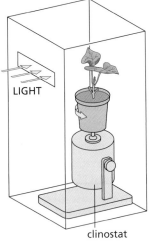

LIGHT

LIGHT

clinostat

control

Figure B9.19 Experiment to show phototropism in a shoot.

Plant growth substances and tropisms

Control of growth

In animals and plants, the growth rate and extent of growth are controlled by chemicals: **hormones** in animals and **growth substances** in plants. Additionally, growth may be limited in animals by the availability of food, and in plants by light, water and minerals.

There are many different growth substances ('plant hormones') in plants. They are similar in some ways to animal hormones because they are produced in specific regions of the plant and transported to 'target' organs such as roots, shoots and buds. However, the sites of production are not specialised organs, as in animals, but regions of actively dividing cells such as the tips of shoots and roots. Also, plant growth substances are not transported in vessels.

The responses made by shoots and roots to light and gravity are influenced by growth substances.

Growth substances also control seed germination, bud burst, leaf fall, initiation of lateral roots and many other processes.

It has already been explained that growth substances, e.g. auxin, are produced by the tips of roots and shoots and can stimulate or, in some cases,

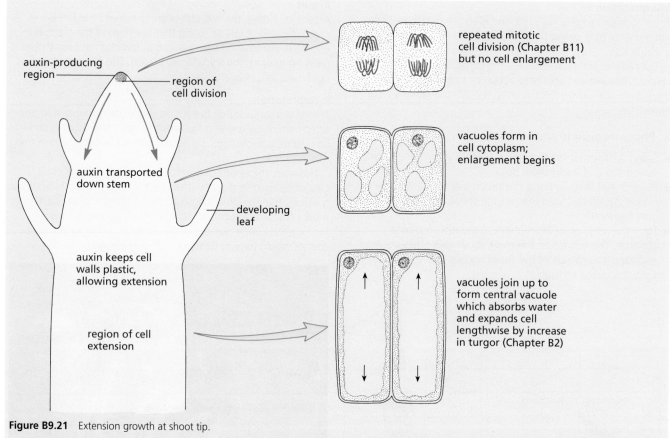

auxin-producing region

region of cell division

repeated mitotic cell division (Chapter B11) but no cell enlargement

auxin transported down stem

developing leaf

vacuoles form in cell cytoplasm; enlargement begins

auxin keeps cell walls plastic, allowing extension

region of cell extension

vacuoles join up to form central vacuole which absorbs water and expands cell lengthwise by increase in turgor (Chapter B2)

Figure B9.21 Extension growth at shoot tip.

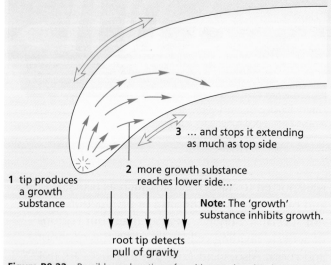

3 ... and stops it extending as much as top side

1 tip produces a growth substance

2 more growth substance reaches lower side...

Note: The 'growth' substance inhibits growth.

root tip detects pull of gravity

Figure B9.22 Possible explanation of positive gravitropism in roots.

inhibit extension growth (Figure B9.21). Tropic responses could be explained if the one-sided stimuli produced a corresponding one-sided distribution of growth substance.

In the case of positive gravitropism in roots there is evidence that, in a horizontal root, more growth substance accumulates on the lower side.

In this case the growth substance is presumed to inhibit extension growth, so that the root tip curves downwards (Figure B9.22).

In the case of phototropism, it is generally accepted that the distribution of growth substance causes reduced extension on the illuminated side and/or increased extension on the non-illuminated side.

Summary of control of shoot growth by auxin

When a shoot is exposed to light from one side, auxins that have been produced by the tip move towards the shaded side of the shoot (or the auxins are destroyed on the light side, causing an unequal distribution). Cells on the shaded side are stimulated to absorb *more* water than those on the light side, so the unequal growth causes the stem to bend towards the light. Growth of a shoot towards light is called **positive phototropism**.

If a shoot is placed horizontally in the absence of light, auxins accumulate on the lower side of the shoot, due to gravity. This makes the cells on the lower side grow *faster* than those on the upper side, so the shoot bends upwards. This is called **negative gravitropism**.

The opposite applies to roots because root cell elongation appears to be slowed down by exposure to auxin.

Questions

10 a To what directional stimuli do:
   i   roots respond
   ii shoots respond?
   b Name the plant organs which are
   i   positively phototropic
   ii positively gravitropic
   iii negatively gravitropic.
11 Why is it incorrect to say:
   a 'Plants grow towards the light.'
   b 'If a root is placed horizontally, it will bend towards gravity'?
12 Look at Figure B9.17. What will the shoot look like in 24 hours after the pot has been stood upright again? (Just draw the outline of the stem.)
13 In Figure B9.23 the two sets of pea seedlings were sown at the same time, but the pot on the left was kept under a lightproof box. From the evidence in the picture:

a what effects does light appear to have on growing seedlings
b how might this explain positive phototropism?

Figure B9.23 Effect of light on shoots.

Checklist

After studying Chapter B9 you should know and understand the following.

Nervous control in humans
- A nerve impulse is an electrical signal that passes along nerve cells called neurones.
- The central nervous system consists of the brain and the spinal cord.
- The peripheral nervous system consists of the nerves.
- Motor, relay and sensory neurones are distinctive cells which can be distinguished by their features.
- A reflex is an automatic nervous reaction that cannot be consciously controlled.
- A reflex arc is the nervous pathway which carries the impulses causing a reflex action.
- The simplest reflex involves a sensory nerve cell and a motor nerve cell, connected by synapses in the spinal cord.

- Voluntary actions start in the brain, while involuntary actions are automatic.

Sense organs
- Sense organs are groups of receptor cells responding to specific stimuli: light, sound, touch, temperature and chemicals.
- Describe the structure of the eye.
- Describe the function of the parts of the eye.
- Describe the pupil reflex.
- Explain the pupil reflex.
- Explain accommodation to view near and distant objects.
- Describe the roles of parts of the eye in accommodation.

Hormones in humans
- A hormone is a chemical substance, produced by a gland, carried by the blood, which alters the activity of one or more specific target organs.

- The pancreas is an endocrine gland which releases adrenalin into the blood system.
- Adrenaline causes an increased breathing and pulse rate and widened pupils.
- It is secreted in 'fight or flight' situations.

- Adrenaline has a role in the chemical control of metabolic activity, including increasing the blood glucose concentration and pulse rate.
- The nervous system is much faster and its action tends to be shorter than hormonal control systems.

Homeostasis
- Homeostasis is the maintenance of a constant internal environment.
- The skin contains hairs, hair erector muscles, sweat glands, receptors, sensory neurones, blood vessels and fatty tissue.
- If the body temperature rises too much, the skin cools it down by sweating and vasodilation.
- If the body loses too much heat, vasoconstriction and shivering help to keep it warm.
- Body temperature is also maintains through insulation of the skin.
- The brain has a role in maintaining body temperature.

- Homeostasis is the control of internal conditions within set limits.
- Negative feedback provides a means of control: if level of substances in the body change, the change is monitored and a response to adjust levels to normal is brought about.
- Glucose concentration in the blood is controlled using insulin and glucagon.
- Vasodilation and vasoconstriction of arterioles in the skin are mechanisms to control body temperature.

Tropic responses
- A response related to the direction of the stimulus is a tropism.
- The roots and shoots of plants may respond to the stimuli of light or gravity.
- Gravitropism is a response in which parts of a plant grows towards or away from gravity.
- Phototropism is a response in which parts of a plant grow towards or away from the direction from which light is coming.
- Growth towards the direction of the stimulus is called 'positive'; growth away from the stimulus is called 'negative'.

- Tropic responses bring shoots and roots into the most favourable positions for their life-supporting functions.
- Describe investigations into gravitropism and phototropism in shoots and roots.

- Explain phototropism and gravitropism of a shoot as examples of the chemical control of plant growth by auxin.
- Auxin is only made in the shoot tip and moves through the plant, dissolved in water.
- Auxin is unequally distributed in response to light and gravity.
- Auxin stimulates cell elongation.

B10 Reproduction

Combined

- Define *asexual reproduction*
- Identify examples of asexual reproduction from information provided
- Define *sexual reproduction*
- Identify and draw, using a hand lens if necessary, the sepals, petals, stamens, filaments and anthers, carpels, style, stigma, ovary and ovules, of an insect-pollinated flower

- Use a hand lens to identify and describe the anthers and stigmas of a wind-pollinated flower

- State the functions of the sepals, petals, anthers, stigmas and ovaries

- Distinguish between the pollen grains of insect-pollinated and wind-pollinated flowers

- Define *pollination*
- Name the agents of pollination
- State that fertilisation occurs when a pollen nucleus fuses with a nucleus in an ovule

- Describe the structural adaptations of insect-pollinated and wind-pollinated flowers

- Investigate and state the environmental conditions that affect germination of seeds: limited to the requirement for water, oxygen and a suitable temperature
- Identify and name on diagrams of the male reproductive system: the testes, scrotum, sperm ducts, prostate gland, urethra and penis
- State the function of the parts of the male reproductive system limited to: testes; scrotum; sperm ducts; prostate gland; urethra; penis
- Identify and name on diagrams of the female reproductive system: the ovaries, oviducts, uterus, cervix and vagina
- State the function of the parts of the female reproductive system limited to: ovaries; oviducts; uterus; cervix; vagina
- Describe fertilisation as the fusion of the nuclei from a male gamete (sperm) and a female gamete (egg cell/ovum)

- Compare male and female gametes in terms of size, structure, motility and numbers

- State the adaptive features of sperm, limited to flagellum and the presence of enzymes

- State the adaptive features of egg cells, limited to energy stores and a jelly coating that changes after fertilisation

- Describe the menstrual cycle in terms of changes in the ovaries and in the lining of the uterus (knowledge of sex hormones not required)

Co-ordinated

- Define asexual reproduction

- Discuss the advantages and disadvantages of asexual reproduction to a population of a species in the wild

- Identify examples of asexual reproduction from information provided
- Define sexual reproduction

- State that the nuclei of gametes are haploid and that the nucleus of a zygote is diploid

- Discuss the advantages and disadvantages of sexual reproduction to a population of a species in the wild

- Identify and draw, using a hand lens if necessary, the sepals, petals, stamens, filaments and anthers, carpels, style, stigma, ovary and ovules, of an insect-pollinated flower

- Use a hand lens to identify and describe the anthers and stigmas of a wind-pollinated flower

- State the functions of the sepals, petals, anthers, stigmas and ovaries

- Distinguish between the pollen grains of insect-pollinated and wind-pollinated flowers

- Define pollination as the transfer of pollen grains from the anther to the stigma
- Name the agents of pollination
- State that fertilisation occurs when a pollen nucleus fuses with a nucleus in an ovule

- Describe the structural adaptations of insect-pollinated and wind-pollinated flower

- Investigate and state the environmental conditions that affect germination of seeds, limited to the requirement for water, oxygen and a suitable temperature
- Identify and name on diagrams of the male reproductive system: the testes, scrotum, sperm ducts, prostate gland, urethra and penis
- State the function of the parts of the male reproductive system limited to: testes; scrotum; sperm ducts; prostate gland; urethra; penis
- Identify and name on diagrams of the female reproductive system: the ovaries, oviducts, uterus, cervix and vagina
- State the function of the parts of the female reproductive system limited to: ovaries; oviducts; uterus; cervix; vagina
- Describe fertilisation as the fusion of the nuclei from a male gamete (sperm) and a female gamete (egg cell/ovum)

Combined (continued...)

- State that in early development, the zygote forms an embryo which is a ball of cells that implants into the wall of the uterus

- State the functions of the umbilical cord, placenta, amniotic sac and amniotic fluid

- Describe the function of the placenta and umbilical cord in relation to exchange of dissolved nutrients, gases and excretory products and providing a barrier to toxins (structural details are not required)

- State that human immunodeficiency virus (HIV) infection may lead to acquired immune deficiency syndrome (AIDS)
- Describe the methods of transmission of HIV
- Explain how the spread of sexually transmitted infections (STIs) is controlled

Co-ordinated (continued...)

- Compare male and female gametes in terms of size, structure, numbers and mobility

- State the adaptive features of sperm, limited to flagellum and the presence of enzymes

- State the adaptive features of egg cells, limited to energy stores and a jelly coating that changes after fertilisation

- Describe the menstrual cycle in terms of changes in the uterus and ovaries (knowledge of sex hormones not required)
- State that in early development, the zygote forms an embryo which is a ball of cells that implants into the wall of the uterus

- State the functions of the umbilical cord, placenta, amniotic sac and amniotic fluid

- Describe the function of the placenta and umbilical cord in relation to exchange of dissolved nutrients, gases and excretory products and providing a barrier to toxins (structural details are not required)

- State that human immunodeficiency virus (HIV) infection may lead to acquired immune deficiency syndrome (AIDS)
- Describe the methods of transmission of HIV
- Explain how the spread of sexually transmitted infections (STIs) is controlled

● Asexual reproduction

Key definition
Asexual reproduction is the process resulting in the production of genetically identical offspring from one parent.

Asexual means 'without sex' and this method of reproduction does not involve gametes (sex cells). In some single-celled organisms or in bacteria, the cell simply divides into two and each new cell becomes an independent organism.

In more complex organisms, part of the body may grow and develop into a separate individual. For example, a small piece of stem planted in the soil may form roots and grow into a complete plant.

Bacteria reproduce by cell division or **fission**. Any bacterial cell can divide into two and each daughter cell becomes an independent bacterium. In some cases, this cell division can take place every 20 minutes so that, in a very short time, a large colony of bacteria can be produced. This is one reason why a small

number of bacteria can seriously contaminate our food products. This kind of reproduction, without the formation of gametes (sex cells), is called **asexual reproduction**.

Asexual reproduction in flowering plants (vegetative propagation)

Although all flowering plants reproduce sexually (that is why they have flowers), many of them also have asexual methods.

Several of these asexual methods (also called '**vegetative propagation**') are described below. When vegetative propagation takes place naturally, it usually results from the growth of a lateral bud on a stem which is close to, or under, the soil. Instead of just making a branch, the bud produces a complete plant with roots, stem and leaves. When the old stem dies, the new plant is independent of the parent that produced it.

An unusual method of vegetative propagation is shown by *Bryophyllum* (Figure B10.1).

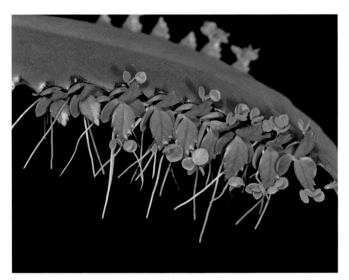

Figure B10.1 *Bryophyllum*. The plantlets are produced from the leaf margin. When they fall to the soil below, they grow into independent plants.

Stolons and rhizomes

The flowering shoots of plants such as the strawberry and the creeping buttercup are very short and, for the most part, below ground. The stems of shoots such as these are called **rootstocks**. The rootstocks bear leaves and flowers. After the main shoot has flowered, the lateral buds produce long shoots, which grow horizontally over the ground (Figure B10.2). These shoots are called **stolons** (or 'runners'), and have only small, scale-leaves at their nodes and very long internodes. At each node there is a bud that can produce not only a shoot, but roots as well. Thus a complete plant may develop and take root at the node, nourished for a time by food sent from the parent plant through the stolon. Eventually, the stolon dries up and withers, leaving an independent daughter plant growing a short distance away from the parent. In this way a strawberry plant can produce many daughter plants by vegetative propagation in addition to producing seeds.

In many plants, horizontal shoots arise from lateral buds near the stem base, and grow under the ground. Such underground horizontal stems are called **rhizomes**. At the nodes of the rhizome are buds, which may develop to produce shoots above the ground. The shoots become independent plants when the connecting rhizome dies.

Many grasses propagate by rhizomes; the couch grass (Figure B10.3 on the next page) is a good example. Even a small piece of rhizome, provided it has a bud, can produce a new plant.

In the bracken, the entire stem is horizontal and below ground. The bracken fronds you see in summer are produced from lateral buds on a rhizome many centimetres below the soil.

Bulbs and corms

Bulbs such as those of the daffodil and snowdrop are very short shoots. The stem is only a few millimetres long and the leaves which encircle the stem are thick and fleshy with stored food.

In spring, the stored food is used by a rapidly growing terminal bud, which produces a flowering stalk and a small number of leaves. During the growing season, food made in the leaves is sent to the leaf bases and stored. The leaf bases swell and form a new bulb ready for growth in the following year.

Vegetative reproduction occurs when some of the food is sent to a lateral bud as well as to the leaf bases. The lateral bud grows inside the parent bulb and, next year, will produce an independent plant (Figure B10.4 on the next page).

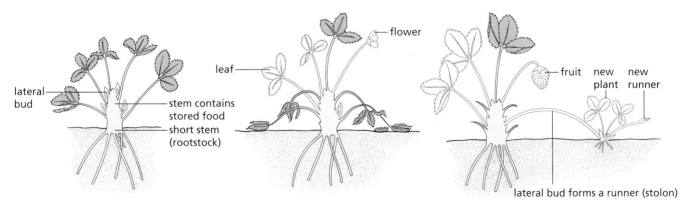

Figure B10.2 Strawberry runner developing from rootstock.

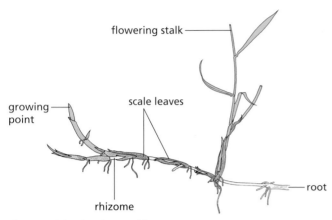

Figure B10.3 Couch grass rhizome.

The **corms** of crocuses and anemones have life cycles similar to those of bulbs but it is the stem, rather than the leaf bases, which swells with stored food. Vegetative reproduction takes place when a lateral bud on the short, fat stem grows into an independent plant. In many cases the organs associated with asexual reproduction also serve as food stores. Food in the storage organs enables very rapid growth in the spring. A great many of the spring and early summer plants have bulbs, corms, rhizomes or tubers: daffodil, snowdrop and bluebell, crocus and cuckoo pint, iris and lily-of-the-valley and lesser celandine.

Potatoes are **stem tubers**. Lateral buds at the base of the potato shoot produce underground shoots (rhizomes). These rhizomes swell up with stored starch and form tubers (Figure B10.5a). Because the tubers are stems, they have buds. If the tubers are left in the ground or transplanted, the buds will produce shoots, using food stored in the tuber (Figure B10.5b). In this way, the potato plant can propagate vegetatively.

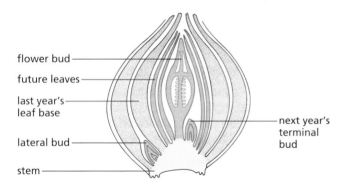

a at beginning of season

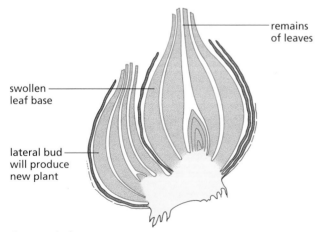

b at end of season

Figure B10.4 Daffodil bulb; vegetative reproduction.

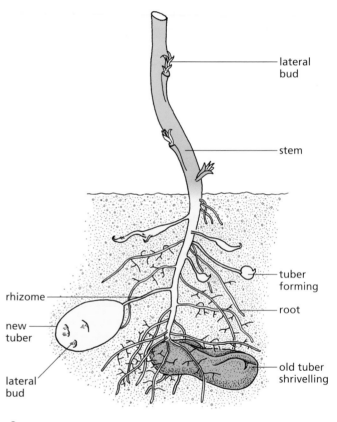

a

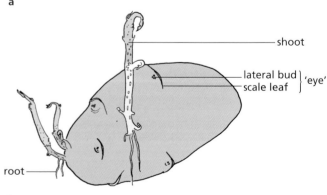

b

Figure B10.5 Stem tubers growing on a potato plant and a potato tuber sprouting.

Asexual reproduction in animals

Some species of invertebrate animals are able to reproduce asexually.

Hydra is a small animal, 5–10 mm long, which lives in ponds attached to pondweed. It traps small animals with its tentacles, swallows and digests them. *Hydra* reproduces sexually by releasing its male and female gametes into the water but it also has an asexual method, which is shown in Figure B10.6.

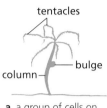

a a group of cells on the column start dividing rapidly and produce a bulge

b the bulge develops tentacles

c the daughter *Hydra* pulls itself off the parent

d the daughter becomes an independent animal

Figure B10.6 Asexual reproduction in *Hydra*.

e *Hydra* with bud

The advantages and disadvantages of asexual reproduction

The advantages and disadvantages of asexual reproduction discussed below are in the context of flowering plants. However, the points made are equally applicable to most forms of asexual reproduction.

In asexual reproduction no gametes are involved and all the new plants are produced by cell division ('Mitosis', Chapter B11) from only one parent. Consequently they are genetically identical; there is no variation. A population of genetically identical individuals produced from a single parent is called a clone. This has the advantage of preserving the 'good' characteristics of a successful species from generation to generation. The disadvantage is that there is no variability for natural selection (Chapter B11) to act on in the process of gradual change.

Dispersal
A plant that reproduces vegetatively will already be growing in a favourable situation, so all the offspring will find themselves in a suitable environment. However, there is no vegetative dispersal mechanism and the plants will grow in dense colonies, competing with each other for water and minerals. The dense colonies, on the other hand, leave little room for competitors of other species.

As mentioned before, most plants that reproduce vegetatively also produce flowers and seeds. In this way they are able to colonise more distant habitats.

Food storage
The store of food in tubers, tap roots, bulbs, etc. enables the plants to grow rapidly as soon as conditions become favourable. Early growth enables the plant to flower and produce seeds before competition with other plants (for water, mineral salts and light) reaches its maximum. This must be particularly important in woods where, in summer, the leaf canopy prevents much light from reaching the ground and the tree roots tend to drain the soil of moisture over a wide area.

Table B10.1 Summary: advantages and disadvantages of asexual reproduction

Advantages	Disadvantages
No mate is needed. No gametes are needed. All the good characteristics of the parent are passed on to the offspring. Where there is no dispersal (e.g. with potato tubers), offspring will grow in the same favourable environment as the parent. Plants that reproduce asexually usually store large amounts of food that allow rapid growth when conditions are suitable.	There is little variation created, so adaptation to a changing environment is unlikely. If the parent has no resistance to a particular disease, none of the offspring will have resistance. Lack of dispersal (e.g. with potato tubers) can lead to competition for nutrients, water and light.

● Sexual reproduction

Key definitions
Sexual reproduction is a process involving the fusion of the nuclei of two gametes (sex cells) to form a zygote and the production of offspring that are genetically different from each other.

The following statements apply equally to plants and animals. **Sexual reproduction** involves the production of sex cells. These sex cells are called **gametes** and they are made in reproductive organs. In sexual reproduction, the male and female gametes come together and **fuse**, that is, their cytoplasm and nuclei join together to form a single cell called a **zygote**. The zygote then grows into a new individual (see Figure B10.17, p.132).

In flowering plants the male gametes are found in pollen grains and the female gametes, called **egg cells**, are present in **ovules**. In animals, male gametes are sperm and female gametes are eggs. Details of **fertilisation** are given later in this chapter.

In both plants and animals, the male gamete is microscopic and mobile (i.e. can move from one place to another). The sperm swim to the ovum; the pollen cell moves down the pollen tube (Figure B10.7). The female gametes are always larger than the male gametes and are not mobile. Pollination in seed-bearing plants and mating in most animals bring the male and female gametes close together.

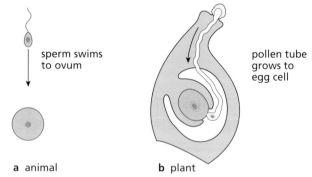

sperm swims to ovum

pollen tube grows to egg cell

a animal   b plant

Figure B10.7 The male gamete is small and mobile; the female gamete is larger.

Chromosome numbers

In normal body cells (somatic cells) the chromosomes are present in the nucleus in pairs. Humans, for example, have 46 chromosomes: 23 pairs. Maize (sweetcorn) has 10 pairs. This is known as the **diploid** number. When gametes are formed, the number of chromosomes in the nucleus of each sex cell is halved. This is the **haploid** number. During fertilisation, when the nuclei of the sex cells fuse, a zygote is formed. It gains the chromosomes from both gametes, so it is a diploid cell (see Chapter B11).

The advantages and disadvantages of sexual reproduction

In plants, the gametes may come from the same plant or from different plants of the same species. In either case, the production and subsequent fusion of gametes produce a good deal of variation among the offspring (see Chapter B11). This may result from new combinations of characteristics, e.g. petal colour of one parent combined with fruit size of the other. It may also be the result of spontaneous changes in the gametes when they are produced.

Variation can have its disadvantages: some combinations will produce less successful individuals. On the other hand, there are likely to be some more successful combinations that have greater survival value or produce individuals which can thrive in new or changing environments.

In a population of plants that have been produced sexually, there is a chance that at least some of the offspring will have resistance to disease. These plants will survive and produce further offspring with disease resistance.

The seeds produced as a result of sexual reproduction will be scattered over a relatively wide range. Some will land in unsuitable environments, perhaps lacking light or water. These seeds will fail to germinate. Nevertheless, most methods of seed dispersal result in some of the seeds establishing populations in new habitats.

The seeds produced by sexual reproduction all contain some stored food but it is quickly used up during germination, which produces only a miniature plant. It takes a long time for a seedling to become established and eventually produce seeds of its own.

Sexual reproduction is exploited in agriculture and horticulture to produce new varieties of animals and plants by cross-breeding.

Table B10.2 Summary: advantages and disadvantages of sexual reproduction

Advantages	Disadvantages
There is variation in the offspring, so adaptation to a changing or new environment is likely, enabling survival of the species. New varieties can be created, which may have resistance to disease. In plants, seeds are produced, which allow dispersal away from the parent plant, reducing competition.	Two parents are usually needed (though not always – some plants can self-pollinate). Growth of a new plant to maturity from a seed is slow.

Questions

1 a Name one organism that reproduces asexually.
  b Describe how the process results on offspring.
  c Identify one advantage and one disadvantage of the process to the species.

2 a Define the term *asexual reproduction*.
  b State three ways in which the process of sexual reproduction is different from asexual reproduction.

● Sexual reproduction in plants

Flowers are reproductive structures; they contain the reproductive organs of the plant. The male organs are the **stamens**, which produce pollen. The female organs are the **carpels**. After fertilisation, part of the carpel becomes the fruit of the plant and contains the seeds. In the flowers of most plants there are both stamens and carpels. These flowers are, therefore, both male and female, a condition known as **bisexual** or **hermaphrodite**.

Some species of plants have unisexual flowers, i.e. any one flower will contain either stamens or carpels but not both. Sometimes both male and female flowers are present on the same plant, e.g. the hazel, which has male and female catkins on the same tree. In the willow tree, on the other hand, the male and female catkins are on different trees.

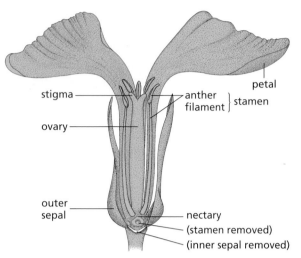

Figure B10.8 Wallflower; structure of flower (one sepal, two petals and stamen removed).

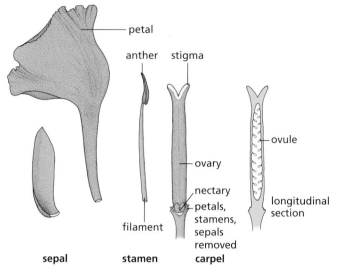

Figure B10.9 Floral parts of wallflower.

The male gamete is a cell in the pollen grain. The female gamete is an egg cell in the ovule. The process that brings the male gamete within reach of the female gamete (i.e. from stamen to stigma) is called **pollination**. The pollen grain grows a microscopic tube, which carries the male gamete the last few millimetres to reach the female gamete for fertilisation. The zygote then grows to form the seed. These processes are all described in more detail later in this chapter.

Flower structure

The basic structure of a flower is shown in Figures B10.8 and B10.11.

Petals

Petals are usually brightly coloured and sometimes scented. They are arranged in a circle (Figure B10.8) or a cylinder. Most flowers have from four to ten petals. Sometimes they are joined together to form a tube (Figures B10.15 and B10.16, pp.130 and 131) and the individual petals can no longer be distinguished. The colour and scent of the petals attract insects to the flower; the insects may bring about pollination.

The flowers of grasses and many trees do not have petals but small, leaf-like structures that enclose the reproductive organs (Figures B10.13 and B10.16 on p.131).

Figure B10.10 Daffodil flower cut in half. The inner petals form a tube. Three stamens are visible round the long style and the ovary contains many ovules.

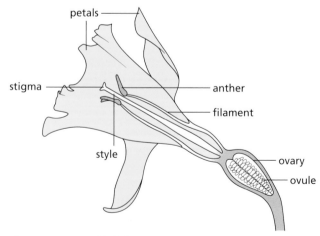

Figure B10.11 Daffodil flower. Outline drawing of Figure B10.10. In daffodils, lilies, tulips, etc. (monocots) there is no distinction between sepals and petals.

Sepals

Outside the petals is a ring of **sepals**. They are often green and much smaller than the petals. They may protect the flower when it is in the bud.

Stamens

The stamens are the male reproductive organs of a flower. Each stamen has a stalk called the **filament**, with an **anther** on the end. Flowers such as the buttercup and blackberry have many stamens; others such as the tulip have a small number, often the same as, or double, the number of petals or sepals. Each anther consists of four **pollen sacs** in which the pollen grains are produced by cell division. When the anthers are ripe, the pollen sacs split open and release their pollen (see Figure B10.13).

Pollen

Insect-pollinated flowers tend to produce smaller amounts of pollen grains (Figure B10.12a), which are often round and sticky, or covered in tiny spikes to attach to the furry bodies of insects.

Wind-pollinated flowers tend to produce larger amounts of smooth, light pollen grains (Figure B10.12b), which are easily carried by the wind. Large amounts are needed because much of the pollen is lost: there is a low chance of it reaching another flower of the same species.

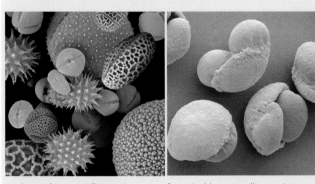

a insect-borne pollen grains   **b** wind-borne pollen grains

Figure B10.12   Pollen grains.

Carpels

These are the female reproductive organs. Flowers such as the buttercup and blackberry have a large number of carpels while others, such as the lupin, have a single carpel. Each carpel consists of an **ovary**, bearing a **style** and a **stigma**.

Inside the ovary there are one or more ovules. Each blackberry ovary contains one ovule but the wallflower ovary contains several. The ovule will become a **seed**, and the whole ovary will become a **fruit**. (In biology, a fruit is the fertilised ovary of a flower, not necessarily something to eat.)

The style and stigma project from the top of the ovary. The stigma has a sticky surface and pollen grains will stick to it during pollination. The style may be quite short (e.g. wallflower, Figure B10.8) or very long (e.g. daffodil, Figures B10.10 and B10.11).

Pollination

> **Key definition**
> **Pollination** is the transfer of pollen grains from the anther to the stigma.

The transfer of pollen from the anthers to the stigma is called **pollination**. The anthers split open, exposing the microscopic pollen grains (Figure B10.13). The pollen grains are then carried away on the bodies of insects, or simply blown by the wind, and may land on the stigma of another flower.

Something that helps pollination in this way is known as an **agent of pollination**.

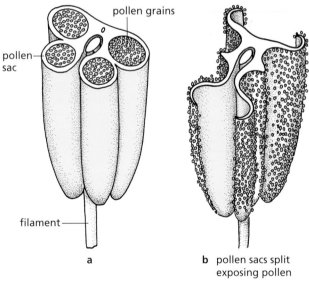

pollen grains

pollen sac

filament

a

b pollen sacs split exposing pollen

Figure B10.13   Structure of an anther (top cut off).

Insect pollination

Lupin flowers have no nectar. The bees that visit them come to collect pollen, which they take back to the hive for food. Other members of the lupin family (Leguminosae, e.g. clover) do produce nectar.

The weight of the bee, when it lands on the flower's wings, pushes down these two petals and the petals of the keel. The pollen from the anthers has collected in the tip of the keel and, as the petals are pressed down, the stigma and long stamens push the pollen out from the keel on to the underside of the bee (Figure B10.14). The bee, with pollen grains sticking to its body, then flies to another flower. If this flower is older than the first one, it will already have lost its pollen. When the bee's weight pushes the keel down, only the stigma comes out and touches the insect's body, picking up pollen grains on its sticky surface.

Lupin and wallflower are examples of **insect-pollinated flowers**.

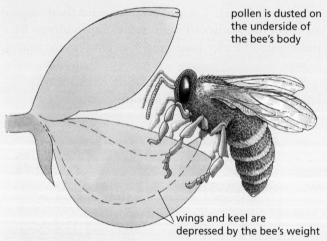

pollen is dusted on the underside of the bee's body

wings and keel are depressed by the bee's weight

Figure B10.14   Pollination of the lupin.

Wind pollination

Grasses, cereals and many trees are pollinated not by insects but by wind currents. The flowers are often quite small with inconspicuous, green, leaf-like bracts, rather than petals. They produce no nectar. The anthers and stigma are not enclosed by the bracts but are exposed to the air. The pollen grains, being light and smooth, may be carried long distances by the moving air and some of them will be trapped on the stigmas of other flowers.

In the grasses, at first, the feathery stigmas protrude from the flower, and pollen grains floating in the air are trapped by them. Later, the anthers hang outside the flower (Figures B10.15 and B10.16), the

Figure B10.15   Grass flowers. Note that the anthers hang freely outside the bracts.

pollen sacs split and the wind blows the pollen away. This sequence varies between species.

If the branches of a birch or hazel tree with ripe male catkins, or the flowers of the ornamental pampas grass, are shaken, a shower of pollen can easily be seen.

Adaptation

Insect-pollinated flowers are considered to be adapted in various ways to their method of pollination. The term '**adaptation**' implies that, in the course of evolution, the structure and physiology of a flower have been modified in ways that improve the chances of successful pollination by insects.

Most insect-pollinated flowers have brightly coloured petals and scent, which attract a variety of insects. Some flowers produce nectar, which is also attractive to many insects. The dark lines ('honey guides') on petals are believed to help direct the insects to the nectar source and thus bring them into contact with the stamens and stigma.

These features are adaptations to insect pollination in general, but are not necessarily associated with any particular insect species. The various petal colours and the nectaries of the wallflower attract a variety of insects. Many flowers, however, have modifications that adapt them to pollination by only one type or species of insect. Flowers such as the honeysuckle, with narrow, deep petal tubes, are likely to be pollinated only by moths or butterflies, whose long 'tongues' can reach down the tube to the nectar.

Tube-like flowers such as foxgloves need to be visited by fairly large insects to effect pollination. The petal tube is often lined with dense hairs, which impede small insects that would take the nectar without pollinating the flower. A large bumble-bee, however, pushing into the petal tube, is forced to rub against the anthers and stigma.

Many tropical and sub-tropical flowers are adapted to pollination by birds, or even by mammals such as bats and mice.

Wind-pollinated flowers are adapted to their method of pollination by producing large quantities of light pollen, and having anthers and stigmas that project outside the flower (Figures B10.15 and B10.16).

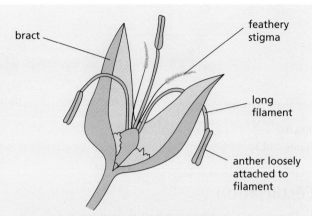

Figure B10.16   Wind-pollinated grass flower.

Many grasses have anthers that are not rigidly attached to the filaments and can be shaken by the wind. The stigmas of grasses are feathery, providing a large surface area, and act as a net that traps passing pollen grains.

Table B10.3 compares the features of wind- and insect-pollinated flowers.

Table B10.3 Features of wind- and insect-pollinated flowers

Feature	Insect-pollinated	Wind-pollinated
petals	present – often large, coloured and scented, with guidelines to guide insects into the flower	absent, or small, green and inconspicuous
nectar	produced by nectaries, to attract insects	absent
stamen	present inside the flower	long filaments, allowing the anthers to hang freely outside the flower so the pollen is exposed to the wind
stigmas	small surface area; inside the flower	large and feathery; hanging outside the flower to catch pollen carried by the wind
pollen	smaller amounts; grains are often round and sticky or covered in spikes to attach to the furry bodies of insects	larger amounts of smooth and light pollen grains, which are easily carried by the wind
bracts (modified leaves)	absent	sometimes present

Practical work

The growth of pollen tubes

Method A

■ Make a solution of 15 g sucrose and 0.1 g sodium borate in 100 cm³ water.
■ Put a drop of this solution on a cavity slide and scatter some pollen grains on the drop. This can be done by scraping an anther (which must already have opened to expose the pollen) with a mounted needle, or simply by touching the anther on the liquid drop.
■ Cover the drop with a coverslip and examine the slide under the microscope at intervals of about 15 minutes. In some cases, pollen tubes may be seen growing from the grains.
■ Suitable plants include lily, narcissus, tulip, bluebell, lupin, wallflower, sweet pea or deadnettle, but a 15% sucrose

solution may not be equally suitable for all of them. It may be necessary to experiment with solutions ranging from 5 to 20%.

Method B

■ Cut the stigma from a mature flower, e.g. honeysuckle, crocus, evening primrose or chickweed, and place it on a slide in a drop of 0.5% methylene blue.
■ Squash the stigma under a coverslip (if the stigma is large, it may be safer to squash it between two slides), and leave it for 5 minutes.
■ Put a drop of water on one side of the slide, just touching the edge of the coverslip, and draw it under the coverslip by holding a piece of filter paper against the opposite edge. This will remove excess stain.
■ If the squash preparation is now examined under the microscope, pollen tubes may be seen growing between the spread-out cells of the stigma.

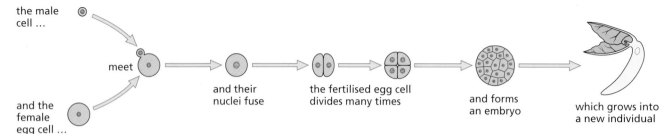

Figure B10.17   Fertilisation. The male and female gametes fuse to form a zygote, which grows into a new individual.

Fertilisation

Pollination is complete when pollen from an anther has landed on a stigma. If the flower is to produce seeds, pollination has to be followed by a process called **fertilisation**. In all living organisms, fertilisation happens when a male sex cell and a female sex cell meet and join together (they are said to fuse together). The cell that is formed by this fusion is called a **zygote** and develops into an embryo of an animal or a plant (Figure B10.17). The sex cells of all living organisms are called **gametes**.

In flowering plants, the male gamete is in the pollen grain; the female gamete, called the egg cell, is in the ovule. For fertilisation to occur, the nucleus of the male cell from the pollen grain has to reach the female nucleus of the egg cell in the ovule, and fuse with it.

Practical work

Experiments on the conditions for germination

The environmental conditions that might be expected to affect germination are temperature, light intensity and the availability of water and air. The relative importance of some of these conditions can be tested by the experiments that follow.

1 The need for water

- Label three containers A, B and C and put dry cotton wool in the bottom of each.
- Place equal numbers of soaked seeds in all three.
- Leave A quite dry; add water to B to make the cotton wool moist; add water to C until all the seeds are completely covered (Figure B10.18).
- Put lids on the containers and leave them all at room temperature for a week.

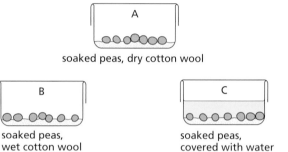

Figure B10.18   Experiment to show the need for water in germination.

Result

The seeds in B will germinate normally. Those in A will not germinate. The seeds in C may have started to germinate but will probably not be as advanced as those in B and may have died and started to decay.

Interpretation

Although water is necessary for germination, too much of it may prevent germination by cutting down the oxygen supply to the seed.

2 Temperature and germination

- Soak some maize grains for a day and then roll them up in three strips of moist blotting paper as shown in Figure B10.19.
- Put the rolls into plastic bags. Place one in a refrigerator (about 4 °C), leave one upright in the room (about 20 °C) and put the third in a warm place such as over a radiator or, better, in an incubator set to 30 °C.
- Because the seeds in the refrigerator will be in darkness, the other seeds must also be enclosed in a box or a cupboard, to exclude light. Otherwise it could be objected that it was lack of light rather than low temperature that affected germination.
- After a week, examine the seedlings and measure the length of the roots and shoots.

Result

The seedlings kept at 30 °C will be more advanced than those at room temperature. The grains in the refrigerator may not have started to germinate at all.

Interpretation

Seeds will not germinate below a certain temperature. The higher the temperature, the faster the germination, at least up to 35–40 °C.

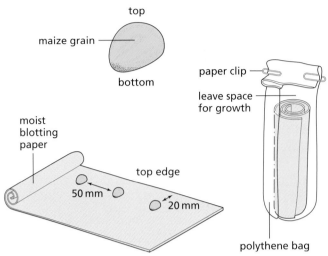

Figure B10.19 Experiment to show the influence of temperature on germination. Roll the seeds in moist blotting-paper and stand the rolls upright in plastic bags.

Questions

3 Working from outside to inside, list the parts of a bisexual flower.
4 What features of flowers might attract insects?
5 Which part of a flower becomes:
 a the seed
 b the fruit?
6 Put the following events in the correct order for pollination in a lupin plant:
 A Bee gets dusted with pollen.
 B Pollen is deposited on stigma.
 C Bee visits older flower.
 D Bee visits young flower.
 E Anthers split open.
7 List all the possible purposes for which a growing seedling might use the food stored in its cotyledons.
8 In not more than two sentences, distinguish between the terms *pollination* and *fertilisation*.

Controlling the variables

These experiments on germination illustrate one of the problems of designing biological experiments. You have to decide what conditions (the '**variables**') could influence the results and then try to change only one condition at a time. The dangers are that: (1) some of the variables might not be controllable, (2) controlling some of the variables might also affect the condition you want to investigate, and (3) there might be a number of important variables you have not thought of.

1 In your germination experiments, you were unable to control the quality of the seeds, but had to assume that the differences between them would be small. If some of the seeds were dead or diseased, they would not germinate in any conditions and this could distort the results. This is one reason for using as large a sample as possible in the experiments.
2 You had to ensure that, when temperature was the variable, the exclusion of light from the seeds in the refrigerator was not an additional variable. This was done by putting all the seeds in darkness.
3 A variable you might not have considered could be the way the seeds were handled. Some seeds can be induced to germinate more successfully by scratching or chipping the testa.

● Sexual reproduction in humans

Reproduction is the process of producing new individuals. In human reproduction the two sexes, male and female, each produce special types of reproductive cells, called gametes. The male gametes are the **sperm** (or **spermatozoa**) and the female gametes are the **ova** (singular = ovum) or eggs (Figure B10.20 on the next page).

To produce a new individual, a sperm has to reach an ovum and join with it (fuse with it). The sperm nucleus then passes into the ovum and the two nuclei also fuse. This is fertilisation. The cell formed after the fertilisation of an ovum by a sperm is called a zygote. A zygote will grow by cell division to produce first an **embryo** and then a fully formed animal (Figure B10.21 on the next page).

To bring the sperm close enough to the ova for fertilisation to take place, there is an act of mating or **copulation**. In mammals this act results in sperm from the male animal being injected into the female. The sperm swim inside the female's reproductive system and fertilise any eggs that are present. The zygote then grows into an embryo inside the body of the female.

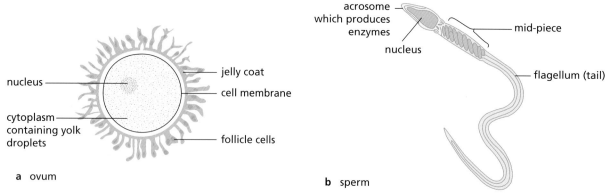

Figure B10.20 Human gametes.

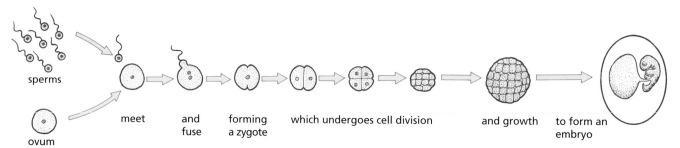

Figure B10.21 Fertilisation and development.

Comparing male and female gametes

Figure B10.20b shows a sperm cell in detail. Sperm are much smaller than eggs and are produced in much larger numbers (over 300 million in a single ejaculation). The tip of the cell carries an acrosome, which secretes enzymes capable of digesting a path into an egg cell, through the jelly coat, so the sperm nucleus can fuse with the egg nucleus. The cytoplasm of the mid-piece of the sperm contains many mitochondria. They carry out respiration, providing energy to make the tail (flagellum) move and propel the sperm forward.

The egg cell (see Figure B10.20a) is much larger than a sperm cell and only one egg is released each month while the woman is fertile. It is surrounded by a jelly coat, which protects the contents of the cell and prevents more than one sperm from entering and fertilising the egg. The egg cell contains a large amount of cytoplasm, which is rich in fats and proteins. The fats act as energy stores. Proteins are available for growth if the egg is fertilised.

The human reproductive system

Male

Table B10.4 summarises the functions of parts of the male reproductive system. Sperm are produced in the male reproductive organs (Figures B10.22 and B10.23), called the **testes** (singular = testis). These lie outside the abdominal cavity in a special sac called the **scrotum**. In this position they are kept at a temperature slightly below the rest of the body. This is the best temperature for sperm production.

The testes consist of a mass of sperm-producing tubes (Figure B10.23). These tubes join to form ducts leading to the epididymis, a coiled tube about 6 metres long on the outside of each testis. The epididymis, in turn, leads into a muscular **sperm duct**.

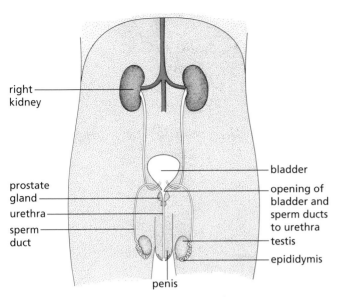

Figure B10.22 The male reproductive organs; front view.

The two sperm ducts, one from each testis, open into the top of the urethra just after it leaves the bladder. At this point, the urethra is surrounded by the **prostate gland**.

The urethra passes through the **penis** and may conduct either urine or sperm at different times. The penis consists of connective tissue with many blood spaces in it. This is called **erectile tissue**.

Table B10.4 Functions of parts of the male reproductive system

Part	Function
penis	can become firm, to insert into the vagina of the female during sexual intercourse in order to transfer sperm
prostate gland	adds fluid and nutrients to sperm to form semen
scrotum	a sac that holds the testes outside the body, keeping them cooler than body temperature
sperm duct	muscular tube that links the testis to the urethra to allow the passage of semen containing sperm
testis	male gonad that produces sperm
urethra	passes semen containing sperm through the penis; also carries urine from the bladder

Female

Table B10.5 summarises the functions of parts of the female reproductive system. The eggs are produced from the female reproductive organs called **ovaries**. These are two whitish oval bodies, 3–4 cm long. They lie in the lower half of the abdomen, one on each side of the **uterus** (Figure B10.24 and Figure B10.25 on the next page) Close to each ovary is the expanded, funnel-shaped opening of the **oviduct**, the tube down which the ova pass when released from the ovary. The oviduct is sometimes called the **Fallopian tube**.

The oviducts are narrow tubes that open into a wider tube, the uterus or womb, lower down in the abdomen. When there is no embryo developing in it, the uterus is only about 80 mm long. It leads to the outside through a muscular tube, the **vagina**. The **cervix** is a ring of muscle closing the lower end of the uterus where it joins the vagina. The urethra, from the bladder, opens into the **vulva** just in front of the vagina.

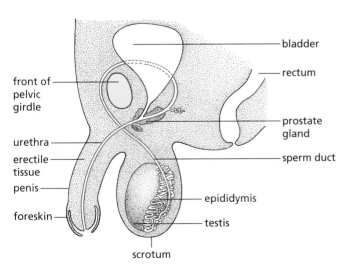

Figure B10.23 The male reproductive organs; side view.

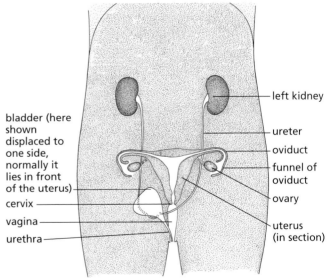

Figure B10.24 The female reproductive organs; front view.

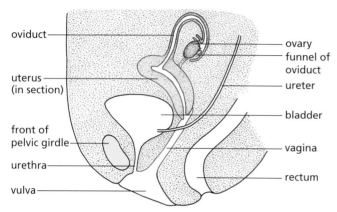

Figure B10.25 The female reproductive organs; side view.

Table B10.5 Functions of parts of the female reproductive system

Part	Function
cervix	a ring of muscle, separating the vagina from the uterus
ovary	contains follicles in which ova (eggs) are produced
oviduct	carries an ovum to the uterus, with propulsion provided by tiny cilia in the wall; also the site of fertilisation
uterus	where the fetus develops
vagina	receives the male penis during sexual intercourse; sperm are deposited here

The menstrual cycle

The ovaries release an ovum about every 4 weeks. In preparation for this the lining of the uterus wall thickens, so that an embryo can embed itself if the released ovum is fertilised. If no implantation occurs, the uterus lining breaks down. The cells, along with blood are passed out of the vagina. This is called a **menstrual period**. The appearance of the first menstrual period is one of the signs of puberty in girls. After menstruation, the uterus lining starts to re-form and another ovum starts to mature.

Pregnancy and development

The fertilised ovum (zygote) first divides into two cells. Each of these divides again, so producing four cells. The cells continue to divide in this way to produce a solid ball of cells (Figure B10.26), an early stage in the development of the embryo. This early embryo travels down the oviduct to the uterus. Here it sinks into the lining of the uterus, a process called **implantation** (Figure B10.28a). The embryo continues to grow and produces new cells that form tissues and organs (Figure B10.27). After 8 weeks, when all the organs are formed, the embryo is called a **fetus**. One of the first organs to form is the heart, which pumps blood around the body of the embryo.

As the embryo grows, the uterus enlarges to contain it.

Inside the uterus the embryo becomes enclosed in a fluid-filled sac called the **amnion** or water sac, which protects it from damage and prevents unequal pressures from acting on it (Figure B10.28b and c). The fluid is called **amniotic fluid**. The oxygen and food needed to keep the embryo alive and growing are obtained from the mother's blood by means of a structure called the **placenta**.

Placenta

Soon after the ball of cells reaches the uterus, some of the cells, instead of forming the organs of the embryo, grow into a disc-like structure, the placenta (Figure B10.28c). The placenta becomes closely attached to the lining of the uterus and is attached to the embryo by a tube called the **umbilical cord** (Figure B10.28c). The nervous system (brain, spinal cord and sense organs) start to develop very quickly. After a few weeks, the embryo's heart has developed and is circulating blood through the umbilical cord and placenta as well as through its own tissues (Figure B10.27b).

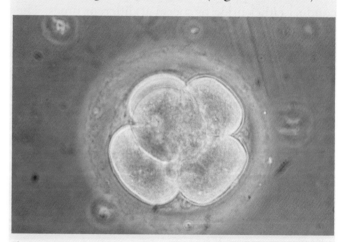

Figure B10.26 Human embryo at the 8-cell stage (×230) with five of the cells clearly visible. The embryo is surrounded by the zona pellucida.

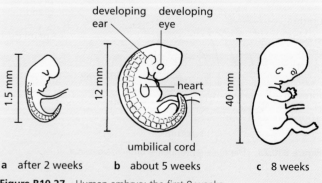

a after 2 weeks   b about 5 weeks   c 8 weeks

Figure B10.27 Human embryo: the first 8 weeks.

Oxygen and nutrients such as glucose and amino acids pass across the placenta to the embryo's bloodstream. Carbon dioxide passes from the embryo's blood to that of the mother. Blood entering the placenta from the mother does not mix with the embryo's blood.

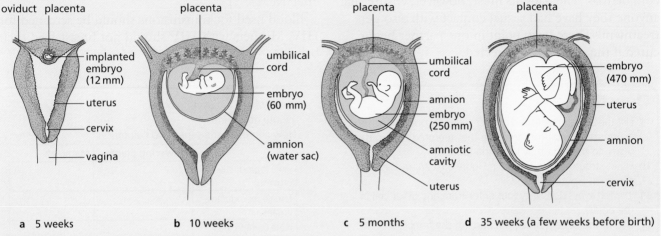

a   5 weeks   **b   10 weeks**   **c   5 months**   **d   35 weeks (a few weeks before birth)**

Figure B10.28   Growth and development in the uterus (not to scale).

● Sexually transmitted infections (STIs)

A **sexually transmitted infection** is an infection that is transmitted via body fluids through sexual contact.

AIDS and HIV

The initials of AIDS stand for **acquired immune deficiency syndrome**. (A 'syndrome' is a pattern of symptoms associated with a particular disease.) The virus that causes AIDS is the **human immunodeficiency virus** (**HIV**).

After a person has been infected, years may pass before symptoms develop. So people may carry the virus yet not show any symptoms. They can still infect other people, however. It is not known for certain what proportion of HIV carriers will eventually develop AIDS: perhaps 30–50%, or more.

HIV is transmitted by direct infection of the blood. Drug users who share needles contaminated with infected blood run a high risk of the disease. It can also be transmitted sexually, both between men and women and, especially, between homosexual men who practise anal intercourse. Prostitutes, who have many sexual partners, are at risk of being infected if they have sex without using condoms and are, therefore, a potential source of HIV to others.

Haemophiliacs have also fallen victim to AIDS. Haemophiliacs have to inject themselves with a blood product that contains a clotting factor. Before the risks were recognised, infected carriers sometimes donated blood, which was used to produce the clotting factor.

Babies born to HIV carriers may become infected with HIV, either in the uterus or during birth or from the mother's milk. The rate of infection varies from about 40% in parts of Africa to 14% in Europe. If the mother is given drug therapy during labour and the baby within 3 days, this method of transmission is reduced.

There is no evidence to suggest that the disease can be passed on by droplets, by saliva or by normal everyday contact.

Controlling the spread of STIs

The best way to avoid sexually transmitted infections is to avoid having sexual intercourse with an infected person. However, the symptoms of the disease are often not obvious and it is difficult to recognise an infected individual. So the disease is avoided by not having sexual intercourse with a person who *might* have the disease.

The risk of catching a sexually transmitted disease can be greatly reduced if the man uses a condom or if a woman uses a femidom. These act as barriers to bacteria or viruses.

If a person suspects that he or she has caught a sexually transmitted disease, treatment must be sought at once. Information about treatment can be obtained by phoning one of the numbers listed under 'Venereal Disease' or 'Health Information Service' in the telephone directory. Treatment is always confidential. The patients must, however, ensure that anyone they have had sexual contact with also gets treatment. There is no point in one partner being cured if the other is still infected.

STIs which are caused by a bacterium, such as syphilis and gonorrhoea, can be treated with antibiotics if the symptoms are recognised early enough. However, HIV is viral so antibiotics are not effective.

Blood used for transfusions should be screened for HIV. Mothers with HIV should not breast-feed their babies.

Questions

9 List the structures, in the correct order, through which the sperm must pass from the time they are produced in the testis, to the time they leave the urethra.
10 What structures are shown in Figure B10.24, but are not shown in Figure B10.23?
11 In what ways does a zygote differ from any other cell in the body?
12 List, in the correct order, the parts of the female reproductive system through which sperm must pass before reaching and fertilising an ovum.
13 State exactly what happens at the moment of fertilisation.
14 Draw up a table with three columns as shown below. In the first column write:
male reproductive organs
female reproductive organs
male gamete
female gamete

place where fertilisation occurs
zygote grows into
Now complete the other two columns.

	Flowering plants	Mammals
male reproductive organs		
female reproductive organs		
male gamete, etc.		

15 How do sperm differ from ova in their structure (see Figure B10.21)?
16 In what ways will the composition of the blood in the umbilical vein differ from that in the umbilical artery?
17 An embryo is surrounded with fluid, its lungs are filled with fluid and it cannot breathe. Why doesn't it suffocate?

Checklist

After studying Chapter B10 you should know and understand the following.

Asexual and sexual reproduction

● Asexual reproduction is the process resulting in the production of genetically identical offspring from one parent.
● Asexual reproduction occurs without gametes or fertilisation.
● Fungi can reproduce asexually by single-celled spores.
● Many flowering plants reproduce asexually by vegetative propagation.

● Asexual reproduction keeps the characteristics of the organism the same from one generation to the next, but does not result in variation, to cope with environmental change.

● Sexual reproduction is the process involving the fusion of the nuclei of two gametes (sex cells) to form a zygote and the production of offspring that are genetically different from each other.

● The nuclei of the gametes are haploid, while the nucleus of a zygote is diploid.
● There are advantages and disadvantages of sexual reproduction to a species.

Sexual reproduction in plants

● Flowers contain the reproductive organs of plants.
● The stamens are the male organs. They produce pollen grains which contain the male gamete.
● The carpels are the female organs. They produce ovules which contain the female gamete and will form the seeds.
● The flowers of most plant species contain male and female organs. A few species have unisexual flowers.
● Brightly coloured petals attract insects, which pollinate the flower.
● Pollination is the transfer of pollen from the anthers of one flower to the stigma of the same or another plant.
● Pollination may be done by insects or by the wind.
● Flowers which are pollinated by insects are usually brightly coloured and have nectar.
● Fertilisation occurs when a pollen tube grows from a pollen grain into the ovary and up to an ovule. The pollen nucleus passes down the tube and fuses with the ovule nucleus.
● Temperature and the amount of water and oxygen available have an effect on germination.

● Flowers which are pollinated by the wind are usually small and green. Their stigmas and anthers hang outside the flower where they are exposed to air movements.

- The pollen grains of insect-pollinated flowers are usually light and smooth, while those of wind-pollinated flowers are usually round and sticky, or covered in spikes.
- Flowers which are pollinated by insects are usually large and brightly coloured.
- Their stigmas and anthers are found inside the flower.

Sexual reproduction in humans

- The male reproductive system includes the testes, scrotum, sperm ducts, prostate glands, urethra and penis and each part has a specific function.
- The female reproductive system includes the ovaries, oviducts, uterus, cervix and vagina and each part has a specific function.
- Fertilisation happens when a sperm enters an ovum and the sperm and egg nuclei join up (fuse).

- Eggs and sperm are different in size, structure, mobility and numbers produced.
- Sperm and eggs have special features to adapt them for their functions.

- In the menstrual cycle, each month the uterus lining thickens up in readiness to receive the fertilised ovum. If an ovum is not fertilised, the lining and some blood is lost through the vagina. This is menstruation.

- The fertilised ovum (zygote) divides into many cells and becomes embedded in the lining of the uterus. Here it grows into an embryo.
- The embryo gets its food and oxygen from its mother.
- The placenta and umbilical cord are involved in exchange of materials between the mother and fetus. Some toxins and viruses can also be passed across and affect the fetus.
- The amniotic sac surrounds the fetus and prevents the entry of bacteria.
- The sac contains amniotic fluid. The fluid supports the fetus, protecting it from physical damage. It absorbs excretory materials released by the fetus.

- A sexually transmitted infection is an infection transmitted via bodily fluids through sexual contact.
- HIV is an example of an STI and HIV infection may lead to AIDS.
- HIV can be transmitted in a number of ways.
- The spread of HIV can be controlled.

Co-ordinated

- Define *inheritance*
- Define *chromosome*
- Define *gene*
- Define *allele*
- Describe the inheritance of sex in humans with reference to XX and XY chromosomes
- Define a *haploid nucleus*
- Define a *diploid nucleus*
- State that in a diploid cell, chromosomes are arranged in pairs and in a human diploid cell there are 23 pairs
- Define *mitosis*
- State that the exact duplication of chromosomes occurs before mitosis
- State the role of mitosis in growth, repair of damaged tissues, replacement of cells and asexual reproduction
- Define *meiosis*
- State that *meiosis* is involved in the production of gametes
- Define *genotype*
- Define *phenotype*
- Define *homozygous*
- State that two identical homozygous individuals that breed together will be pure-breeding
- Define *heterozygous*
- State that a heterozygous individual will not be pure-breeding
- Define *dominant*
- Define *recessive*
- Use genetic diagrams to predict the results of monohybrid crosses and calculate phenotypic ratios, limited to 1:1 and 3:1 ratios
- Use Punnett squares in crosses which result in more than one genotype to work out and show the possible different genotypes
- Interpret pedigree diagrams for the inheritance of a given characteristic
- Define *variation*

- Distinguish between phenotypic variation and genetic variation
- State that phenotypic variation is caused by both genetic and environmental factors
- State that continuous variation results in a range of phenotypes between two extremes, e.g. height in humans
- State that discontinuous variation is mostly caused by genes alone, e.g. A, B, AB and O blood groups in humans
- State that discontinuous variation results in a limited number of phenotypes with no intermediates, e.g. tongue rolling
- Record and present the results of investigations into continuous and discontinuous variation
- Define *mutation*
- State that ionising radiation and some chemicals increase the rate of mutation
- Describe natural selection with reference to: variation within populations; production of many offspring; competition for resources; struggle for survival; reproduction by individuals that are better adapted to the environment than others; passing on of their alleles to the next generation
- Describe evolution as the change in adaptive features of a population over time as the result of natural selection
- Define the process of *adaptation*
- Describe the development of strains of antibiotic resistant bacteria as an example of evolution by natural selection
- Describe selective breeding with reference to: selection by humans of individuals with desirable features; crossing these individuals to produce the next generation; selection of offspring showing the desirable features
- State the differences between natural and artificial selection
- Outline how selective breeding by artificial selection is carried out over many generations to improve crop plants and domesticated animals

● Inheritance

Key definition

Inheritance is the transmission of genetic information from generation to generation.

We often talk about people **inheriting** certain characteristics: 'Nathan has inherited his father's curly hair', or 'Fatima has inherited her mother's brown eyes'. We expect tall parents to have tall children. The inheritance of such characteristics is called **heredity** and the branch of biology that studies how heredity works is called **genetics**.

● Chromosomes and genes

Key definitions

A **chromosome** is a thread of DNA, carrying genetic information in the form of genes.
A **gene** is a length of DNA that codes for a protein.
An **allele** is a version of a gene.

Inside a nucleus are thread-like structures called **chromosomes** which can be seen most clearly at the time when the cell is dividing. Each chromosome has certain characteristics when ready to divide: there are two **chromatids**, joined at one point called

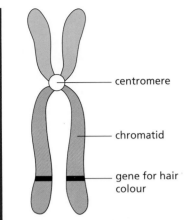

Figure B11.1 Structure of a chromosome.

a **centromere** (Figure B11.1). Each chromatid is a string of **genes**, coding for the person's characteristics. The other chromatid carries the same genes in the same order.

The genes that occupy corresponding positions on homologous chromosomes and control the same characteristic are called **allelomorphic genes**, or **alleles**. The word 'allelomorph' means 'alternative form'. For example, there are two alternative forms of a gene for eye colour. One allele produces brown eyes and one allele produces blue eyes.

The inheritance of sex

Whether you are a male or female depends on the pair of chromosomes called the 'sex chromosomes'. In females, the two sex chromosomes, called the X chromosomes, are the same size as each other. In males, the two sex chromosomes are of different sizes. One corresponds to the female sex chromosomes and is called the X chromosome. The other is smaller and is called the Y chromosome. So the female cells contain **XX** and male cells contain **XY**.

A process takes place in the female's ovaries and the male's testes which makes gametes (sex cells). These contain half the normal number of chromosomes. During the process in the female's ovaries, each ovum receives one of the chromosomes, so all the ova are the same for this. The process in the male's testes results in 50% of the sperms getting an X chromosome and 50% getting a Y chromosome (Figure B11.2). If an X sperm fertilises the ovum, the zygote will be XX and will grow into a girl. If a Y sperm fertilises the ovum, the zygote will be XY and will grow into a boy. There is an equal chance of an X or a Y sperm fertilising an ovum, so the numbers of girl and boy babies are more or less the same.

Figure B11.3 on the next page shows how sex is inherited.

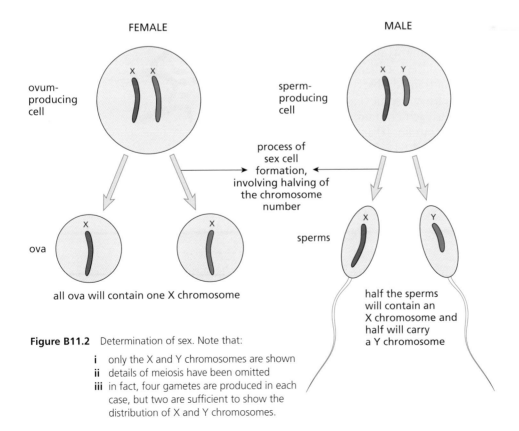

Figure B11.2 Determination of sex. Note that:

i only the X and Y chromosomes are shown
ii details of meiosis have been omitted
iii in fact, four gametes are produced in each case, but two are sufficient to show the distribution of X and Y chromosomes.

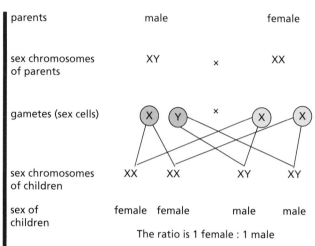

parents	male		female

sex chromosomes
of parents   XY   ×   XX

gametes (sex cells)

sex chromosomes
of children   XX   XX   XY   XY

sex of
children   female female   male   male

The ratio is 1 female : 1 male

Figure B11.3   Determination of sex.

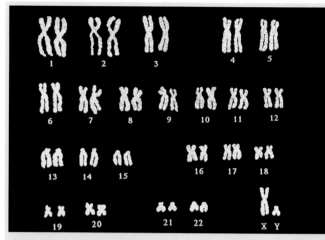

Figure B11.4   Human karyotype.

Number of chromosomes

> **Key definitions**
> A **haploid nucleus** is a nucleus containing a single set of
>   unpaired chromosomes present, for example, in sperm
>   and egg cells.
> A **diploid nucleus** is a nucleus containing two sets of
>   chromosomes present, for example, in body cells.

Figure B11.4 is a karyotype of a human body
cell because there are 23 pairs of chromosomes
present (they come from a **diploid** cell). Because
the chromosomes are in pairs, the diploid number is
always an even number. The karyotype of a sperm cell
would show 23 single chromosomes (they come from
a **haploid** cell). The sex chromosome would be either
X or Y. The chromosomes have different shapes and
sizes and can be recognised by a trained observer.

There is a fixed number of chromosomes in
each species. Human body cells each contain
46 chromosomes, mouse cells contain 40 and
garden pea cells 14 (see also Figure B11.5).

The number of chromosomes in a species
is the same in all of its body cells. There are
46 chromosomes in each of your liver cells, in
every nerve cell, skin cell and so on.

kangaroo (12)

human (46)

domestic fowl (36)

fruit fly (8)

Figure B11.5   Chromosomes of different species. Note that the
chromosomes are always in pairs.

Questions

1   A married couple has four girl children but no boys. This
    does not mean that the husband produces only X sperms.
    Explain why not.

2   Which sex chromosome determines the sex of a baby?
    Explain your answer.

3   How many chromosomes would there be in the nucleus of:
    a   a human muscle cell
    b   a mouse kidney cell
    c   a human skin cell that has just been produced by mitosis
    d   a kangaroo sperm cell?

4   What is the diploid number in humans?

5   Which of the following cells would be haploid and which
    diploid: white blood cell, male cell in pollen grain, guard
    cell, root hair, ovum, sperm, skin cell, egg cell in ovule?

6   How many chromosomes would be present in:
    a   a mouse sperm cell
    b   a mouse ovum?

● Mitosis

Key definitions
Mitosis is nuclear division giving rise to genetically
identical cells.

The process of **mitosis** is important in growth.
We all started off as a single cell (a zygote). That
cell divided into two cells, then four and so on, to
create the organism we are now, made up of millions
of cells. Cells have a finite life: they wear out or
become damaged, so they need to be replaced
constantly. The processes of **growth**, **repair** and
replacement of cells all rely on mitosis. Organisms
that reproduce asexually (see Chapter B10) also use
mitosis to create more cells.

The process of cell division in an animal cell is shown
in Figure B11.6. The events in a plant cells are shown
in Figure B11.7. Because of the cell wall, the cytoplasm
cannot simply pinch off in the middle, and a new cell
wall has to be laid down between the daughter cells.
Also, a new vacuole has to form. Organelles such as
chloroplasts are able to divide and are shared more or
less equally between the daughter cells at cell division.

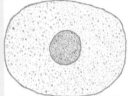 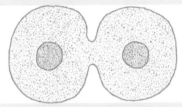 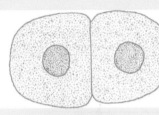

a Animal cell about to divide.

b The nucleus divides first.

c The daughter nuclei separate and the cytoplasm pinches off between the nuclei.

d Two cells are formed – one may keep the ability to divide, and the other may become specialised.

Figure B11.6   Cell division in an animal cell.

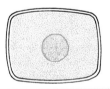 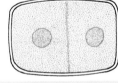 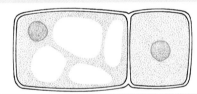 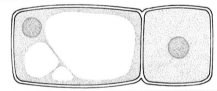

a A plant cell about to divide has a large nucleus and no vacuole.

b The nucleus divides first. A new cell wall develops and separates the two cells.

c The cytoplasm adds layers of cellulose on each side of the new cell wall. Vacuoles form in the cytoplasm of one cell.

d The vacuoles join up to form one vacuole. This takes in water and makes the cell bigger. The other cell will divide again.

Figure B11.7   Cell division in a plant cell.

The process of mitosis

To understand how the 'instructions' are passed
from cell to cell, we need to look in more detail at
what happens when the zygote divides and produces
an organism consisting of thousands of cells. This
type of cell division is called mitosis. It takes place
not only in a zygote but in all growing tissues.

When a cell is not dividing, there is very little detailed
structure to be seen in the nucleus even if it is treated
with special dyes called stains. Just before cell division,
however, a number of long, thread-like structures
appear in the nucleus and show up very clearly when
the nucleus is stained (Figures B11.8 and B11.9 on
the next page). These thread-like structures are called
chromosomes. Although they are present in the nucleus
all the time, they show up clearly only at cell division
because at this time they get shorter and thicker.

Each chromosome duplicates itself and is seen
to be made up of two parallel strands, called
chromatids (Figure B11.1). When the nucleus
divides into two, one chromatid from each
chromosome goes into each daughter nucleus.
The chromatids in each nucleus now become
chromosomes and later they will make copies
of themselves ready for the next cell division.
The process of copying is called **replication**
because each chromosome makes a replica (an exact

copy) of itself. As Figure B11.8 is a simplified diagram of mitosis, only two chromosomes are shown, but there are always more than this. Human cells contain 46 chromosomes.

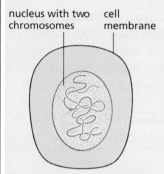

a Just before the cell divides, chromosomes appear in the nucleus.

b The chromosomes get shorter and thicker.

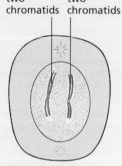

c Each chromosome is now seen to consist of two chromatids.

d The nuclear membrane disappears and the chromatids are pulled apart to opposite ends of the cell.

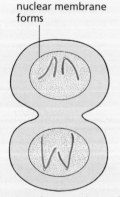

e A nuclear membrane forms round each set of chromatids, and the cell starts to divide.

f Cell division completed, giving two 'daughter' cells, each containing the same number of chromosomes as the parent cell.

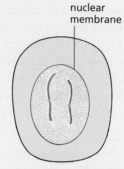

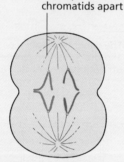

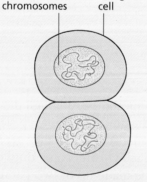

Figure B11.8 Mitosis. Only two chromosomes are shown. Three of the stages described here are shown in Figure B11.9. Details of the stages are not required.

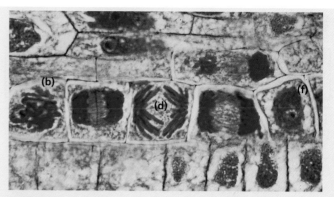

Figure B11.9 Mitosis in a root tip (×500). The letters refer to the stages described in Figure B11.8. (The tissue has been squashed to separate the cells.)

● Meiosis

> **Key definition**
> **Meiosis** is reduction division in which the chromosome number is halved from diploid to haploid, resulting in genetically different cells.

The process of **meiosis** takes place in the **gonads** of animals (e.g. the testes and ovaries of mammals, and the anthers and ovules of flowering plants). The cells formed are **gametes** (sperm and egg cells in mammals; egg cells and pollen grain nuclei in flowering plants). Gametes are different from other cells because they have half the normal number of chromosomes (they are **haploid**).

Gamete production and chromosomes

The genes on the chromosomes carry the instructions that turn a single-cell zygote into a bird or a rabbit or an oak tree. The zygote is formed at fertilisation, when a male gamete fuses with a female gamete. Each gamete brings a set of chromosomes to the zygote. The gametes, therefore, must each contain only half the diploid number of chromosomes, otherwise the chromosome number would double each time an organism reproduced sexually. Each human sperm cell contains 23 chromosomes and each human ovum has 23 chromosomes. When the sperm and ovum fuse at fertilisation (Chapter B10), the diploid number of 46 (23 + 23) chromosomes is produced (Figure B11.10).

The process of cell division that gives rise to gametes is different from mitosis because it results in the cells containing only half the diploid number of chromosomes. This number is called the haploid number and the process of cell division that gives rise to gametes is called **meiosis**.

Meiosis takes place only in reproductive organs.

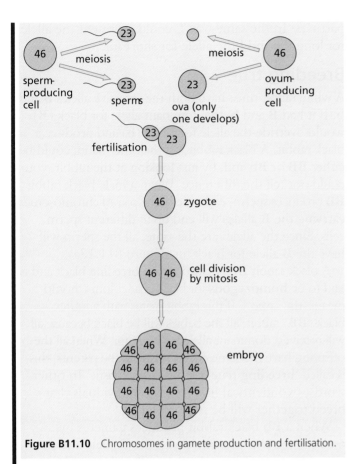

Figure B11.10 Chromosomes in gamete production and fertilisation.

Question

7 In which human tissues would you expect mitosis to be going on, in:
   a a 5-year-old child
   b an adult?

⬤ Monohybrid inheritance

Key definitions
Genotype is the genetic make-up of an organism in terms of the alleles present.
Phenotype is the observable features of an organism.
Homozygous means having two identical alleles of a particular gene.
Heterozygous means having two different alleles of a particular gene.
Dominant means an allele that is expressed if it is present.
Recessive means an allele that is only expressed when there is no dominant allele of the gene present.

Patterns of inheritance

A knowledge of mitosis and meiosis allows us to explain, at least to some extent, how heredity works. The allele in a mother's body cells that causes her to have brown eyes may be present on one of the chromosomes in each ovum she produces. If the father's sperm cell contains an allele for brown eyes on the corresponding chromosome, the zygote will receive an allele for brown eyes from each parent. These alleles will be reproduced by mitosis in all the embryo's body cells and when the embryo's eyes develop, the alleles will make the cells of the iris produce brown pigment (melanin) and the child will have brown eyes. In a similar way, the child may receive alleles for curly hair.

Figure B11.11 shows this happening, but it does not, of course, show all the other chromosomes with thousands of genes for producing the enzymes, making different types of cell and all the other processes that control the development of the organism.

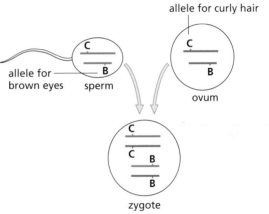

Figure B11.11 Fertilisation. Fertilisation restores the diploid number of chromosomes and combines the alleles from the mother and father.

Monohybrid inheritance

Because it is impossible to follow the inheritance of the thousands of characteristics controlled by genes, it is usual to start with the study of a single gene that controls one characteristic. We have used eye colour as an example so far. Probably more than one allele pair is involved, but the simplified example will serve our purpose. It has already been explained how an allele for brown eyes from each parent results in the child having brown eyes. Suppose, however, that the mother has blue eyes and the father brown eyes. The child might receive an allele for blue eyes from its mother and an allele for brown eyes from its father (Figure B11.12).

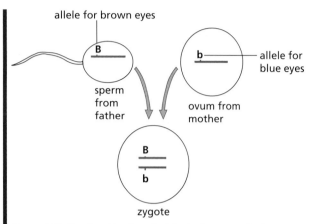

Figure B11.12 Combination of alleles in the zygote (only one chromosome is shown). The zygote has both alleles for eye colour; the child will have brown eyes.

If this happens, the child will have brown eyes. The allele for brown eyes is said to be **dominant** to the allele for blue eyes. Although the allele for blue eyes is present in all the child's cells, it is not expressed. It is said to be **recessive** to brown.

Eye colour is a useful 'model' for explaining inheritance but it is not wholly reliable because 'blue' eyes vary in colour and sometimes contain small amounts of brown pigment.

This example illustrates the following important points:

- There is a pair of alleles for each characteristic, one allele from each parent.
- Although the allele pairs control the same characteristic, e.g. eye colour, they may have different effects. One tries to produce blue eyes, the other tries to produce brown eyes.
- Often one allele is dominant over the other.
- The alleles of each pair are on corresponding chromosomes and occupy corresponding positions. For example, in Figure B11.11 the alleles for eye colour are shown in the corresponding position on the two short chromosomes and the alleles for hair curliness are in corresponding positions on the two long chromosomes. In diagrams and explanations of heredity:
  - alleles are represented by letters
  - alleles controlling the same characteristic are given the same letter
  - the dominant allele is given the capital letter.

For example, in rabbits, the dominant allele for black fur is labelled **B**. The recessive allele for white fur is labelled **b** to show that it corresponds to **B** for black fur. If it were labelled **w**, we would not see any connection between **B** and **w**. **B** and **b** are obvious partners. In the same way **L** could represent the allele for long fur and **l** the allele for short fur.

Breeding true

A white rabbit must have both the recessive alleles **b** and **b**. If it had **B** and **b**, the dominant allele for black (**B**) would override the allele for white (**b**) and produce a black rabbit. A black rabbit, on the other hand, could be either **BB** or **Bb** and, by just looking at the rabbit, you could not tell the difference. When a male black rabbit **BB** produces sperm, each one of the pair of chromosomes carrying the **B** alleles will end up in different sperm cells. Since the alleles are the same, all the sperm will have the **B** allele for black fur (Figure B11.13a).

A black rabbit **BB** is called a pure-breeding black and is said to be **homozygous** for black coat colour ('homo-' means 'the same'). If this rabbit mates with another black (**BB**) rabbit, all the babies will be black because all will receive a dominant allele for black fur. When all the offspring have the same characteristic as the parents, this is called '**breeding true**' for this characteristic. In other words, two identical homozygous individuals that breed together will be pure-breeding.

When a **Bb** black rabbit produces gametes by meiosis, the chromosomes with the **B** allele and the chromosomes with the **b** allele will end up in different gametes. So 50% of the sperm cells will carry **B** alleles and 50% will carry **b** alleles (Figure B11.13b). Similarly, in the female, 50% of the ova will have a **B** allele and 50% will have a **b** allele. So, a heterozygous individual will not be pure breeding. If a **b** sperm fertilises a **b** ovum, the offspring, with two **b** alleles (**bb**), will be white. The black **Bb** rabbits are not true-breeding because they may produce some white babies as well as black ones. The **Bb** rabbits are called **heterozygous** ('hetero-' means 'different').

The black **BB** rabbits are homozygous dominant. The white **bb** rabbits are homozygous recessive.

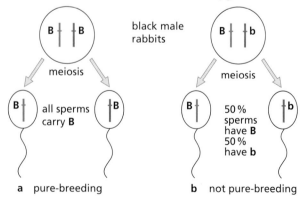

Figure B11.13 Pure breeding.

Genotype and phenotype

The two kinds of black rabbit **BB** and **Bb** are said to have the same **phenotype**. This is because their coat colours look exactly the same. However, because they have different allele pairs for coat colour they are said to have different **genotypes**, i.e. different combinations of alleles. One genotype is **BB** and the other is **Bb**.

You and your brother might both be brown-eyed phenotypes but your genotype could be **BB** and his could be **Bb**. You would be homozygous dominant for brown eyes; he would be heterozygous for eye colour.

The three to one ratio

The result of a mating between a true-breeding (homozygous) black mouse (**BB**) and a true-breeding (homozygous) brown mouse (**bb**) is shown in Figure B11.14a. The illustration is greatly simplified because it shows only one pair of the 20 pairs of mouse chromosomes and only one pair of alleles on the chromosomes.

Because black is dominant to brown, all the offspring from this mating will be black phenotypes, because they all receive the dominant allele for black fur from the father. Their genotypes, however, will be **Bb** because they all receive the recessive **b** allele from the mother. They are heterozygous for coat colour. The offspring resulting from this first mating are called the **F₁ generation**.

Figure B11.14b (on the next page) shows what happens when these heterozygous, F₁ black mice are mated together to produce what is called the F₂ generation. Each sperm or ovum produced by meiosis can contain only one of the alleles for coat colour, either **B** or **b**. So there are two kinds of sperm cell, one kind with the **B** allele and one kind with the **b** allele. There are also two kinds of ovum, with either **B** or **b** alleles. When fertilisation occurs, there is no way of telling whether a **b** or a **B** sperm will fertilise a **B** or a **b** ovum, so we have to look at all the possible combinations as follows:

- A **b** sperm fertilises a **B** ovum. Result: **bB** zygote.
- A **b** sperm fertilises a **b** ovum. Result: **bb** zygote.
- A **B** sperm fertilises a **B** ovum. Result: **BB** zygote.
- A **B** sperm fertilises a **b** ovum. Result: **Bb** zygote.

There is no difference between **bB** and **Bb**, so there are three possible genotypes in the offspring – **BB**, **Bb** and **bb**. There are only two phenotypes – black (**BB** or **Bb**) and brown (**bb**). So, according to the laws of chance, we would expect three black baby mice and one brown. Mice usually have more than four offspring

and what we really expect is that the **ratio** (proportion) of black to brown will be close to 3:1.

If the mouse had 13 babies, you might expect nine black and four brown, or eight black and five brown. Even if she had 16 babies you would not expect to find exactly 12 black and four brown because whether a **B** or **b** sperm fertilises a **B** or **b** ovum is a matter of chance. If you spun ten coins, you would not expect to get exactly five heads and five tails. You would not be surprised at six heads and four tails or even seven heads and three tails. In the same way, we would not be surprised at 14 black and two brown mice in a litter of 16.

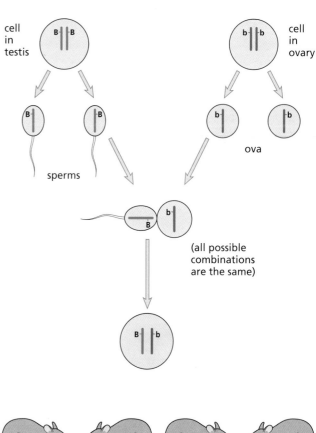

a all the F₁ generation are heterozygous black

Figure B11.14 Inheritance of coat colour in mice.

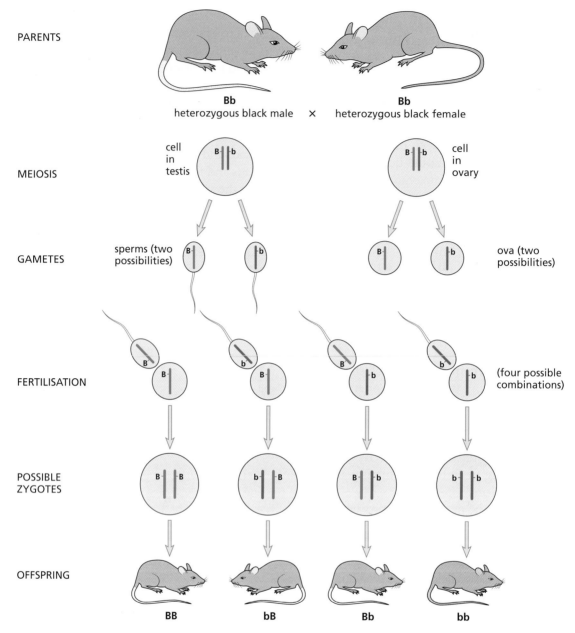

PARENTS

Bb
heterozygous black male × **Bb**
heterozygous black female

MEIOSIS

cell in testis

cell in ovary

GAMETES

sperms (two possibilities)

ova (two possibilities)

FERTILISATION

(four possible combinations)

POSSIBLE ZYGOTES

OFFSPRING

BB   bB   Bb   bb

b the probable ratio of coat colours in the F₂ generation is 3 black : 1 brown

Figure B11.14 Inheritance of coat colour in mice *(continued)*.

Figure B11.15 F₂ hybrids in maize. In the two left-hand cobs, the grain colour phenotypes appear in a 3:1 ratio (try counting single rows in the lighter cob). What was the colour of the parental grains for each of these cobs?

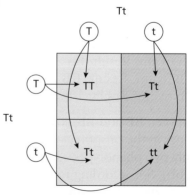

Tt

T   t

Tt

T   → TT   Tt

t   → Tt   tt

Figure B11.16 Using a Punnett square to predict the outcomes of a genetic cross.

To decide whether there really is a 3:1 ratio, we need a lot of results. These may come either from breeding the same pair of mice together for a year or so to produce many litters, or from mating 20 black and 20 brown mice, crossing the offspring and adding up the number of black and brown babies in the F₂ families (see also Figure B11.15).

When working out the results of a genetic cross, it is useful to display the outcomes in a '**Punnett square**' (Figure B11.16). This a box divided into four compartments. The two boxes along the top are labelled with the genotypes of the gametes of one parent. The genotypes are circled to show they are gametes. The parent's genotype is written above the gametes. The boxes down the left-hand side are labelled with the genotypes of the gametes of the other parent. The parent's genotype is written to the left. The genotypes of the offspring can then be predicted by completing the four boxes, as shown. In this example, two heterozygous tall organisms (**Tt**) are the parents. The genotypes of the offspring are **TT**, **Tt**, **Tt** and **tt**. We know that the allele **T** is dominant because the parents are tall, although they carry both tall and dwarf alleles. So, the phenotypes of the offspring will be three tall to one dwarf.

The one to one ratio

This is achieved when a heterozygous organism such as a black mouse (**Bb**) is crossed with an organism which is homozygous recessive (**bb**). Figure B11.17 shows what happens. Half the gametes from a black heterozygous mouse would carry the B allele and half would have the b allele. The **bb** mouse will produce gametes with only the recessive **b** allele. Half the offspring from the cross will, on average, be brown homozygotes, **bb**, and half will be black heterozygotes, **Bb**.

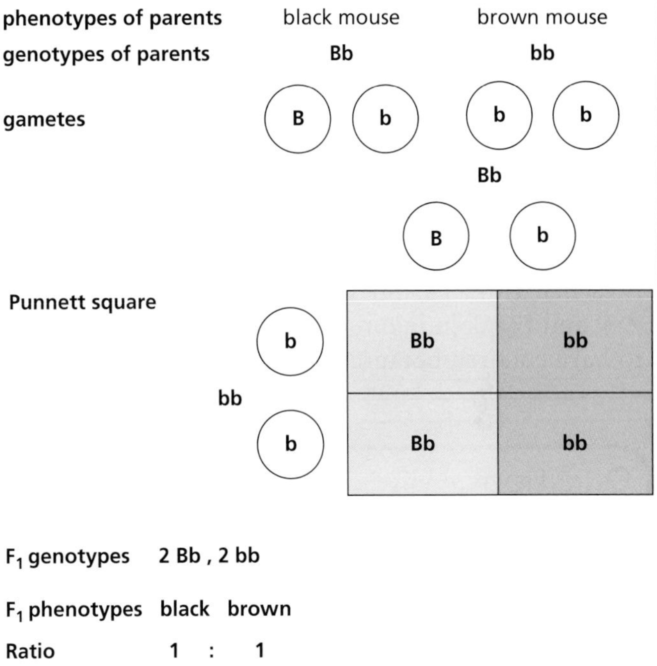

Figure B11.17 Crossing a heterozygous organism with a homozygous recessive organism.

Pedigree diagrams and inheritance

The term **pedigree** often refers to the pure breeding nature of animals, but is also used to describe human inheritance. Pedigree diagrams are similar to family trees and can be used to demonstrate how genetic diseases can be inherited. They include symbols to indicate whether individuals are male or female and what their genotype is for a particular genetic characteristic.

One genetic disease is called cystic fibrosis. The symptom of cystic fibrosis is the production of very sticky mucus in the lungs. This makes gas exchange more difficult and traps microbes so the cystic fibrosis sufferer gets respiratory diseases more frequently. Sticky mucus can also block ducts responsible for transferring enzymes into the small intestine and can block reproductive ducts, resulting in lower fertility or sterility. Cystic fibrosis sufferers tend to have a much shorter life span than normal, although treatment of the disease is becoming more effective and average life expectancies are improving.

A sufferer of cystic fibrosis has received two recessive alleles (**cc**); one from each parent. A carrier of the disease has one normal allele and one recessive allele (**Cc**). This condition is not uncommon: 1 in 25 people of European descent is a carrier. A normal person has two normal alleles (**CC**).

A normal man (**CC**) who has children with a normal woman (**CC**) will produce 100% normal children (all **CC**).

If one parent is a carrier for cystic fibrosis (**Cc**) and the other parent is normal (**CC**), 50% of their children are likely to be carriers (**Cc**) and 50% will be normal (**CC**).

However, if both parents are carriers, then the likely ratio of offspring is one normal (**CC**): two carriers (**Cc**): one cystic fibrosis sufferer (**cc**). So there is a 1 in 4 chance of a child born to these parents having cystic fibrosis.

The pedigree diagram (Figure B11.18 on the next page) shows the inheritance of cystic fibrosis in a family. Parents Alfred and Mildred are married and both are cystic fibrosis carriers. However, because carriers have no symptoms of the disease, they may be unaware that they have defective alleles for cystic fibrosis. They go on to have four children. Three of these children eventually get married and have children of their own. One child, Helen, suffers from cystic fibrosis. The pedigree diagram shows that she does not get married and has no children.

It is possible for individuals in a family with a history of cystic fibrosis to have genetic counselling. In this process, carriers and sufferers would be given an explanation of the risk of having children with cystic fibrosis. Genetic screening can be carried out on developing embryos to identify their genotype. A carrier with a partner who is also a carrier (such as Zoe and Frank in Figure B11.18) may choose not to have children because of the 1 in 4 chance of the

inheritance of cystic fibrosis. Alternatives may be to foster or adopt children instead.

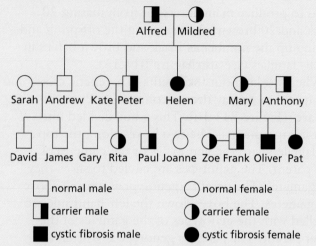

Figure B11.18 Pedigree diagram to show the inheritance of cystic fibrosis in a family.

Questions

8   Some plants occur in one of two sizes, tall or dwarf. This characteristic is controlled by one pair of genes. Tallness is dominant to shortness. Choose suitable letters for the gene pair.

9   Why are there two types of gene controlling one characteristic? Do the two types affect the characteristic in the same way as each other?

10 The allele for red hair is recessive to the allele for black hair. What colour hair will a person have if he inherits an allele for red hair from his mother and an allele for black hair from his father?

11 Use the words 'homozygous', 'heterozygous', 'dominant' and 'recessive' (where suitable) to describe the following allele combinations: **Aa**, **AA**, **aa**.

12 Two black guinea-pigs are mated together on several occasions and their offspring are invariably black. However, when their black offspring are mated with white guinea-

pigs, half of the matings result in all black litters and the other half produce litters containing equal numbers of black and white babies. From these results, deduce the genotypes of the parents and explain the results of the various matings, assuming that colour in this case is determined by a single pair of alleles. Use punnett squares to illustrate your answer.

13 Figure B11.18 is a pedigree diagram to show the inheritance in a family of a disease called cystic fibrosis.
    Using the letters **C** (dominant allele) and **c** (recessive allele):
    a Identify the genotypes of
       i   Alfred
       ii   Helen
       iii   Sarah
       iv   Zoe.
    b Explain how Joanne can be born as a normal female when both her parents are carriers of the disease. Identify Joanne in a Punnett square to support your answer.

● Variation

Key definition
Variation is the differences between individuals of the same species.

The term '**variation**' refers to observable differences within a species. All domestic cats belong to the same species, i.e. they can all interbreed, but there are many variations of size, coat colour, eye colour, fur length, etc. Those variations that can be

inherited are determined by genes. They are **genetic variations**. **Phenotypic variations** may be brought about by genes, but can also be caused by the environment, or a combination of both genes and the environment.

So, there are variations that are not heritable, but determined by factors in the environment. A kitten that gets insufficient food will not grow to the same size as its litter mates. A cat with a skin disease may have bald patches in its coat. These conditions are not heritable. They are caused by environmental effects.

Similarly, a fair-skinned person may be able to change the colour of his or her skin by exposing it to the Sun, so getting a tan. The tan is an **acquired characteristic**. You cannot inherit a suntan. Black skin, on the other hand, is an **inherited characteristic**.

Many features in plants and animals are a mixture of acquired and inherited characteristics (Figure B11.19). For example, some fair-skinned people never go brown in the Sun, they only become sunburned. They have not inherited the genes for producing the extra brown pigment in their skin. A fair-skinned person with the genes for producing pigment will only go brown if he or she exposes themselves to sunlight. So the tan is a result of both inherited and acquired characteristics.

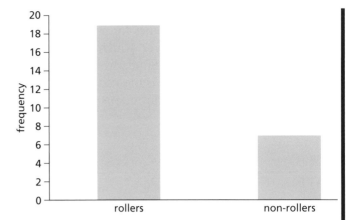

Figure B11.20 Discontinuous variation. Tongue rollers and non-rollers in a class.

north side, upper branches   south side, upper branches

north side, lower branches   south side, lower branches

Figure B11.19 Acquired characteristics. These apples have all been picked from different parts of the same tree. All the apples have similar genotypes, so the differences in size must have been caused by environmental effects.

Discontinuous variation

In **discontinuous variation**, the variations take the form of distinct, alternative phenotypes with no intermediates (Figures B11.20 and B11.21). The mice in Figure B11.14 are either black or brown; there are no intermediates. You are either male or female. Apart from a small number of abnormalities, sex is inherited in a discontinuous way. Some people can roll their tongue into a tube. Others are unable to do it. They are known as non-tongue rollers. Again, there are no intermediates (Figure B11.20).

Discontinuous variation cannot usually be altered by the environment. You cannot change your eye colour by altering your diet. A genetic dwarf cannot grow taller by eating more food. You cannot learn how to roll your tongue.

Discontinuous variation is under the control of a single pair of alleles or a small number of genes. An example is human blood groups (Figure B11.21).

A person is one of four blood groups: A, B, AB or O. There are no groups in between.

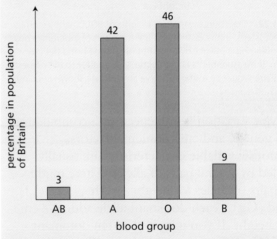

Figure B11.21 Discontinuous variation. Frequencies of ABO blood groups in Britain. The figures could not be adjusted to fit a smooth curve because there are no intermediates.

Continuous variation

An example of **continuous variation** is height. There are no distinct categories of height; people are not either tall or short. There are all possible intermediates between very short and very tall (Figure B11.22 on the next page).

There are many characteristics that are difficult to classify as either wholly continuous or discontinuous variations. Human eye colour has already been mentioned. People can be classified roughly as having blue eyes or brown eyes, but there are also categories described as grey, hazel or green. It is likely that there are a small number of genes for eye colour and a dominant gene for brown eyes, which overrides all the others when it is present. Similarly, red hair is a discontinuous variation but it is masked by genes for other colours and there is a continuous range of hair colour from blond to black.

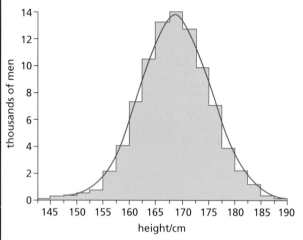

Figure B11.22 Continuous variation. Heights of 90 000 army recruits. The apparent 'steps' in the distribution are the result of arbitrarily chosen categories, differing in height by 1 cm. But heights do not differ by exactly 1 cm. If measurements could be made accurately to the nearest millimetre there would be a smooth curve like the one shown in colour.

Phenotypic variation is influenced by a combination of both genetic and environmental factors. Continuously variable characteristics are usually controlled by several pairs of alleles. There might be five pairs of alleles for height – (**Hh**), (**Tt**), (**Ll**), (**Ee**) and (**Gg**) – each dominant allele adding 4 cm to your height. If you inherited all ten dominant genes (**HH, TT**, etc.) you could be 40 cm taller than a person who inherited all ten recessive genes (**hh, tt**, etc.).

The actual number of genes that control height, intelligence, and even the colour of hair and skin, is not known.

Continuously variable characteristics are greatly influenced by the environment. A person may inherit genes for tallness and yet not get enough food to grow tall. A plant may have the genes for large fruits but not get enough water, minerals or sunlight to produce large fruits. Continuous variations in human populations, such as height, physique and intelligence, are always the result of interaction between the genotype and the environment.

● Recording and presenting the results of investigations

When carrying out any investigation it is very important to record the results as you collect them. The recording is usually presented in the form of a table, which may have the data in columns or rows. It is often best to plan the headings for a table before starting the investigation, remembering to include a description of what the data represents (the physical quantity) and also the units used in the measurement, if appropriate. For example, initial data collected to produce a graph of the heights of students in your class could be recorded using the table headings:

Name of student	Height/cm

The outline of the table should be drawn using a ruler. The number of rows would depend on the number of students in the class. Note that the units (in this case cm) are only written in the heading, not the body of the table.

Once all the data has been collected and recorded, a second table would be useful, containing a tally of groups of heights:

Height/cm	Tally	Total number of students
145–149		
150–154		
155–159		
160–164		
etc.		

Note that none of the ranges in the groups of heights overlaps with the next one, to prevent one student's data being tallied twice. This processed data can then be used to plot a graph, similar to the one shown in Figure B11.22. This is a histogram – each of the blocks touches the next and all the blocks have the same width. The numerical characteristic, in this case height, is the independent variable and is displayed in the horizontal axis and the frequency (the dependent variable) is displayed on the vertical axis. The graph should have a title that describes what it represents.

Data collected for discontinuous variation, such as blood groups or tongue rolling, is categoric rather than numerical. There are distinct categories. The data would be displayed in a bar chart, as shown in Figures B11.20 and B11.21. The horizontal axis is a list of the categories, and the blocks are of equal width. There is an equal space between each block.

Mutations

> **Key definition**
> A **mutation** is a change in a gene or chromosome.

Many of the coat variations seen in cats may have arisen, in the first place, as **mutations** in a wild stock of cats. A recent variant produced by a mutation is the 'rex' variety, in which the coat has curly hairs.

Many of our high-yielding crop plants have arisen as a result of mutations in which the whole chromosome set has been doubled.

Exposure to **mutagens**, namely certain chemicals and radiation, is known to increase the rate of mutation. Some of the substances in tobacco smoke, such as tar, are mutagens, which can cause cancer.

Ionising radiation from X-rays and radioactive compounds, and ultraviolet radiation from sunlight, can both increase the mutation rate. It is uncertain whether there is a minimum dose of radiation below which there is negligible risk. It is possible that repeated exposure to low doses of radiation is as harmful as one exposure to a high dose. It has become clear in recent years that, in light-skinned people, unprotected exposure to ultraviolet radiation from the Sun can cause a form of skin cancer.

Generally speaking, however, exposure to natural and medical sources of radiation carries less risk than smoking cigarettes or driving a car, but it is sensible to keep exposure to a minimum.

A mutation may occur in a gene or a chromosome. In a gene mutation it may be that one or more genes are not replicated correctly. A chromosome mutation may result from damage to or loss of part of a chromosome during mitosis or meiosis, or even the gain of an extra chromosome, as in Down's syndrome.

An abrupt change in a gene or chromosome is likely to result in a defective enzyme and will usually disrupt the complex reactions in the cells. Most mutations, therefore, are harmful to the organism.

Surprisingly, only about 3% of human DNA consists of genes. The rest consists of repeated sequences of nucleotides that do not code for proteins. This is sometimes called '**junk DNA**', but that term only means that we do not know its function. If mutations occur in these non-coding sequences they are unlikely to have any effect on the organism and are, therefore, described as 'neutral'.

Rarely, a gene or chromosome mutation produces a beneficial effect and this may contribute to the success of the organism (see 'Selection' later in this chapter).

If a mutation occurs in a gamete, it will affect all the cells of the individual that develops from the zygote. Thus the whole organism will be affected. If the mutation occurs in a somatic cell (body cell), it will affect only those cells produced, by mitosis, from the affected cell.

Thus, a mutation in a gamete may result in a genetic disorder, e.g. haemophilia or cystic fibrosis. Mutations in somatic cells may give rise to cancers by promoting uncontrolled cell division in the affected tissue. For example, skin cancer results from uncontrolled cell division in the basal layer of the skin.

A mutation may be as small as the change within a single gene or as large as the breakage, loss or gain of a chromosome.

Selection

Natural selection

Theories of evolution have been put forward in various forms for hundreds of years. In 1858, Charles Darwin and Alfred Russel Wallace published a theory of evolution by natural selection, which is still an acceptable theory today.

The theory of evolution by natural selection is as follows:

- Individuals within a species are all slightly different from each other (Figure B11.23 on the next page). These differences are called variations.
- If the climate or food supply changes, individuals possessing some of these variations may be better able to survive than others. For example, a variety of animal that could eat the leaves of shrubs as well as grass would be more likely to survive a drought than one that fed only on grass.
- If one variety lives longer than others, it is also likely to leave behind more offspring. A mouse that lives for 12 months may have ten litters of five

Figure B11.23 Variation. The garden tiger moths in this picture are all from the same family. There is a lot of variation in the pattern on the wings.

babies (50 in all). A mouse that lives for 6 months may have only five litters of five babies (25 in all).
- If some of the offspring inherit alleles responsible for the variation that helped the parent survive better, they too will live longer and have more offspring.
- In time, this particular variety will outnumber and finally replace the original variety.

This is sometimes called 'the survival of the fittest'. However, 'fitness', in this case, does not mean good health but implies that the organism is well fitted to the conditions in which it lives.

Thomas Malthus, in 1798, suggested that the increase in the size of the human population would outstrip the rate of food production. He predicted that the number of people would eventually be regulated by famine, disease and war. When Darwin read the Malthus essay, he applied its principles to other populations of living organisms.

He observed that animals and plants produce vastly more offspring than can possibly survive to maturity and he reasoned that, therefore, there must be a 'struggle for survival'.

For example, if a pair of rabbits had eight offspring that grew up and formed four pairs, eventually having eight offspring per pair, in four generations the number of rabbits stemming from the original pair would be 512 (i.e. $2 \rightarrow 8 \rightarrow 32 \rightarrow 128 \rightarrow 512$). The population of rabbits, however, remains more or less constant. Many of the offspring in each generation must, therefore, have failed to survive to reproductive age.

Competition and selection

There will be **competition** between members of the rabbit population for food, burrows and mates. If food is scarce, space is short and the number of potential mates limited, then only the healthiest, most vigorous, most fertile and otherwise well-adapted rabbits will survive and breed.

The competition does not necessarily involve direct conflict. The best adapted rabbits may be able to run faster from predators, digest their food more efficiently, have larger litters or grow coats that camouflage them better or more effectively reduce heat losses. These rabbits will survive longer and leave more offspring. If the offspring inherit the advantageous characteristics of their parents, they may give rise to a new race of faster, different coloured, thicker furred and more fertile rabbits, which gradually replace the original, less well-adapted varieties. The new variations are said to have **survival value**.

This is natural selection; the better adapted varieties are 'selected' by the pressures of the environment (**selection pressures**).

For natural selection to be effective, the variations have to be heritable. Variations that are not heritable are of no value in natural selection. Training may give athletes more efficient muscles, but this characteristic will not be passed on to their children.

The peppered moth

A possible example of natural selection is provided by a species of moth called the peppered moth, found in Great Britain. The common form is speckled but there is also a variety that is black. The black variety was rare in 1850, but by 1895 in the Manchester area of England its numbers had risen to 98% of the population of peppered moths. Observation showed that the light variety was concealed better than the dark variety when they rested on tree-trunks covered with lichens (Figure B11.24). In the Manchester area of England, pollution had caused the death

a   b   c   d

Figure B11.24   Selection for varieties of the peppered moth.

of the lichens and the darkening of the tree-trunks with soot. In this industrial area the dark variety was the better camouflaged (hidden) of the two and was not picked off so often by birds. So the dark variety survived better, left more offspring and nearly replaced the light form.

The selection pressure, in this case, was presumed to be mainly predation by birds. The adaptive variation that produced the selective advantage was the dark colour.

Although this is an attractive and plausible hypothesis of how natural selection could occur, some of the evidence does not support the hypothesis or has been called into question.

For example, the moths settle most frequently on the underside of branches rather than conspicuously on tree trunks, as in Figure B11.24. Also, in several unpolluted areas the dark form is quite abundant, for example 80% in East Anglia in England. Research is continuing in order to test the hypothesis.

Adaptation

> **Key definition**
> **Adaptation** is the process, resulting from natural selection, by which populations become more suited to their environment over many generations.

When biologists say that a plant or animal is *adapted* to its habitat they usually mean that, in the course of evolution, changes have occurred in the organism, which make it more successful in exploiting its habitat, e.g. animals finding and digesting food, selecting nest sites or hiding places, or plants exploiting limited mineral resources or tolerating salinity or drought. It is tempting to assume that because we find a plant or animal in a particular habitat it must be adapted to its habitat. There is some logic in this; if an organism was not adapted to its habitat, presumably it would be eliminated by natural selection. However, it is best to look for positive evidence of **adaptation**.

Sometimes, just by looking at an organism and comparing it with related species, it is possible to make reasoned guesses about adaptation. For example, there seems little doubt that the long, hair-fringed hind legs

of a water beetle are adaptations to locomotion in water when compared with the corresponding legs of a land-living relative (Figure B11.25).

Similarly, in Figure B11.26 (on the next page) it seems reasonable to suppose that, compared with the generalised mammalian limb, the forelimbs of whales are adapted for locomotion in water.

By studying animals which live in extreme habitats, it is possible to suggest ways in which they might be adapted to these habitats especially if the observations are supported by physiological evidence.

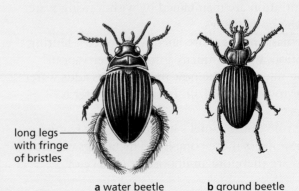

long legs with fringe of bristles

a water beetle   b ground beetle

Figure B11.25   Adaptation to locomotion in water and on land.

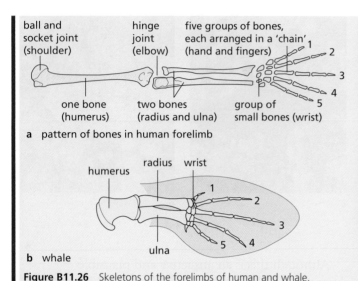

a   pattern of bones in human forelimb

b   whale

Figure B11.26   Skeletons of the forelimbs of human and whale.

Figure B11.27   Protection against wind-blown sand. The nostrils are slit-like and can be closed. The long eyelashes protect the eyes.

The camel

Camels are adapted to survive in a hot, dry and sandy environment. Adaptive physical features are closable nostrils and long eyelashes, which help keep out wind-blown sand (Figure B11.27). Their feet are broad and splay out under pressure, so reducing the tendency to sink into the sand. Thick fur insulates the body against heat gain in the intense sunlight.

Physiologically, a camel is able to survive without water for 6–8 days. Its stomach has a large water-holding capacity, though it drinks to replace water lost by evaporation rather than in anticipation of water deprivation.

The body temperature of a 'thirsty' camel rises to as much as 40 °C during the day and falls to about 35 °C at night. The elevated daytime temperature reduces the heat gradient between the body and the surroundings, so less heat is absorbed. A camel is able to tolerate water loss equivalent to 25% of its body weight, compared with humans for whom a 12% loss may be fatal. The blood volume and concentration are maintained by withdrawing water from the body tissues.

The nasal passages are lined with mucus. During exhalation, the dry mucus absorbs water vapour. During inhalation the now moist mucus adds water vapour to the inhaled air. In this way, water is conserved.

The role of the camel's humps in water conservation is more complex. The humps contain fat and are therefore an important reserve of energy-giving food. However, when the fat is metabolised during respiration, carbon dioxide and water (metabolic water) are produced. The water enters the blood circulation and would normally be lost by evaporation from the lungs, but the water-conserving nasal mucus will trap at least a proportion of it.

The polar bear

Polar bears live in the Arctic, spending much of their time on snow and ice. Several physical features contribute to their adaptation to this cold environment.

It is a very large bear (Figure B11.28), which means that the ratio of its surface area to its volume is relatively small. The relatively small surface area means that the polar bear loses proportionately less heat than its more southerly relatives. Also its ears are small, another feature that reduces heat loss (Figure B11.29).

It has a thick coat with long, loosely packed coarse hairs (guard hairs) and a denser layer of shorter woolly hairs forming an insulating layer. The long hairs are oily and water-repellent and enable the bear to shake off water when it emerges from a spell of swimming.

The principal thermal insulation comes from a 10 cm layer of fat (blubber) beneath the skin. The thermal conductivity of fat is little different from any other tissue but it has a limited blood supply. This means that very little warm blood circulates close to the skin surface.

Figure B11.28 The polar bear and the sun bear (from SE Asia). The smaller surface area/volume ratio in the polar bear helps conserve heat.

Figure B11.29 The heavy coat and small ears also help the polar bear to reduce heat losses.

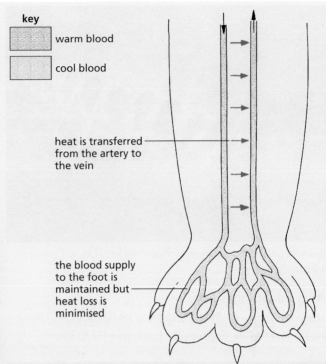

key

▢ warm blood

▢ cool blood

heat is transferred from the artery to the vein

the blood supply to the foot is maintained but heat loss is minimised

Figure B11.30 The heat-exchange mechanism in the polar bear's limb.

The hollow hairs of the white fur are thought to transmit the Sun's heat to the black skin below. Black is an efficient colour for absorbing heat. The white colour is also probably an effective camouflage when hunting its prey, mainly seals.

A specific adaptation to walking on snow and ice is the heat-exchange arrangement in the limbs. The arteries supplying the feet run very close to the veins returning blood to the heart. Heat from the arteries is transferred to the veins before the blood reaches the feet (Figure B11.30). So, little heat is lost from the feet but their temperature is maintained above freezing point, preventing frost-bite.

Polar bears breed in winter when temperatures fall well below zero. However, the pregnant female excavates a den in the snow in which to give birth and rear her two cubs. In this way the cubs are protected from the extreme cold.

The female remains in the den for about 140 days, suckling her young on the rich milk, which is formed from her fat reserves.

Venus flytrap

Many plants show adaptions as well as animals. Insectivorous plants such as the Venus flytrap (Figure B11.31 on the next page) live in habitats where there is often a shortage of nitrates for growth. They have developed pairs of leaves with tooth-like edges. The leaves have sensitive hairs on their surface. When an insect walks inside the leaves, the hairs are triggered, causing the leaves to close very rapidly – trapping the animal. The leaves then secrete protease enzymes, which digest the insect's protein and produce soluble amino acids. These are absorbed by the leaf and used to build new proteins. It is unusual for a photosynthetic plant to show such rapid movement or to gain nourishment other than by photosynthesis.

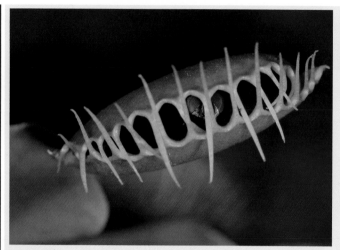

Figure B11.31 Venus flytrap with trapped insect, which will eventually be digested.

Other adaptations

Adaptive features of the long-eared bat and the hare are illustrated in Figures B11.32 and B11.33.

Figure B11.32 Long-eared bat. The bat gives out high-pitched sounds, which are reflected back from its prey and from obstacles, to its ears and sensitive patches on its face. By timing these echoes the bat can judge its distance from the obstacle or prey. This allows it to fly and feed in the dark. Its body is covered in fur for insulation. Its forearms are covered by a membrane of skin to form a wing. The fingers are very long to stretch out the membrane to increase the surface area of the wing.

Figure B11.33 Hare. This animal is a herbivore and is hunted by predators such as foxes. Its fur is a good insulator and its colour provides excellent camouflage. The long ears help to pick up and locate sound vibrations. The eyes at the side of the head give the hare good all-round vision. The hind legs are very long to enable the animal to run away from predators and its kick is a good defence mechanism. Some species of hare change the colour of their fur in winter from brown to white to provide better camouflage in snow.

Evolution

> **Key definition**
> **Evolution** can be described as the change in adaptive features of a population over time as the result of natural selection.

Most biologists believe that natural selection, among other processes, contributes to the **evolution** of new species and that the great variety of living organisms on the Earth is the product of millions of years of evolution involving natural selection.

Antibiotic-resistant bacteria

Antibiotics are drugs used to treat infections caused by bacteria. Bacterial cells reproduce very rapidly, perhaps as often as once every 20 minutes. Thus a mutation, even if it occurs only rarely, is likely to appear in a large population of bacteria. If a population of bacteria containing one or two drug-resistant mutants is subjected to that particular drug, the non-resistant bacteria will be killed but the drug-resistant mutants survive (Figure B11.34). Mutant genes are inherited in the same way as normal genes, so when the surviving mutant bacteria reproduce, all their offspring will be resistant to the drug.

If a course of antibiotics is not completed, some of the bacteria it is being used to destroy will not be killed, but will have been exposed to the drug. Some of the survivors may be drug-resistant mutants. When they reproduce, all their offspring will have the drug resistance, so the antibiotic will become less effective (Figure B11.34).

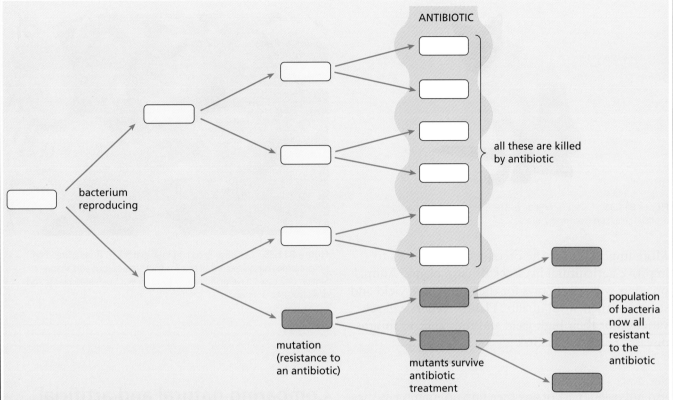

Figure B11.34 Mutation in bacteria can lead to drug resistance.

One type of bacteria that has developed resistance to a number of widely used antibiotics is called MRSA (methicillin-resistant *Staphylococcus aureus*). These types of bacteria are sometime referred to as 'superbugs' because they are so difficult to treat. *Staphylococcus aureus* is very common and is found living harmlessly on the skin, the nose and throat, sometimes causing mild infections. It becomes dangerous if there is a break in the skin, allowing it to infect internal organs and causing blood poisoning. This can happen in hospitals with infection during operations, especially if hygiene precautions are not adequate.

Doctors now have to be much more cautious about prescribing antibiotics, to reduce the risk of resistant strains developing. Patients need to be aware of the importance of completing a course of antibiotics, again to reduce the risk of development of resistant strains.

Selective breeding

The process of selective breeding involves humans selecting individuals with desirable features. These individuals are then cross-bred to produce the next generation. Offspring with the most desirable features are chosen to continue the breeding programme and the process is repeated over a number of generations.

Human communities practise this form of selection when they breed plants and animals for specific characteristics. The many varieties of cat that you see today have been produced by selecting individuals with pointed ears, particular fur colour or length, or even no tail, etc. One of the kittens in a litter might vary from the others by having distinctly pointed ears. This individual, when mature, is allowed to breed. From the offspring, another very pointed-eared variant is selected for the next breeding stock, and so on, until the desired or 'fashionable' ear shape is established in a true-breeding population (Figure B11.35 on the next page).

Figure B11.35 Selective breeding. The Siamese cat, produced by artificial selection over many years.

Figure B11.36 Selective breeding in tomatoes. Different breeding programmes have selected genes for fruit size, colour and shape. Similar processes have given rise to most of our cultivated plants and domesticated animals.

More important are the breeding programmes to improve agricultural livestock or crop plants. Animal-breeders will select cows for their high milk yield and sheep for their wool quality. Plant-breeders will select varieties for their high yield and resistance to fungus diseases (Figure B11.36).

An important part of any breeding programme is the selection of the desired varieties. The largest fruit on a tomato plant might be picked and its seeds planted next year. In the next generation, once again only seeds from the largest tomatoes are planted. Eventually it is possible to produce a true-breeding variety of tomato plant that forms large fruits. Figure B11.36 shows the result of such selective breeding. The same technique can be used for selecting other desirable qualities, such as flavour and disease resistance.

Similar principles can be applied to farm animals. Desirable characteristics, such as high milk yield and resistance to disease, may be combined. Stock-breeders will select calves from cows that give large quantities of milk. These calves will be used as breeding stock to build a herd of high yielders. A characteristic such as milk yield is probably under the control of many genes. At each stage of selective breeding the farmer, in effect, is keeping the beneficial genes and discarding the less useful genes from his or her animals.

Selective breeding in farm stock can be slow and expensive because the animals often have small numbers of offspring and breed only once a year.

Comparing natural and artificial selection

Natural selection occurs in groups of living organisms through the passing on of genes to the next generation by the best adapted organisms, without human interference. Those with genes that provide an advantage, to cope with changes in environmental conditions for example, are more likely to survive, while others die before they can breed and pass on their genes. However, variation within the population remains.

Artificial selection is used by humans to produce varieties of animals and plants that have an increased economic importance. It is considered a safe way of developing new strains of organisms, compared with genetic engineering, and is a much faster process than natural selection. However, artificial selection removes variation from a population, leaving it susceptible to disease and unable to cope with changes in environmental conditions. Potentially, therefore, artificial selection puts a species at risk of extinction.

a   b   c   d   e

Figure B11.37 The genetics of bread wheat. A primitive wheat (a) was crossed with a wild grass (b) to produce a better-yielding hybrid wheat (c). The hybrid wheat (c) was crossed with another wild grass (d) to produce one of the varieties of wheat (e) which is used for making flour and bread.

In **agriculture** and **horticulture**, asexual reproduction (vegetative propagation) is exploited to preserve desirable qualities in crops: the good characteristics of the parent are passed on to all the offspring. With a flower such as a daffodil, the bulbs produced can be guaranteed to produce the same shape and colour of flower from one generation to the next. In some cases, such as tissue culture, the young plants grown can be transported much more cheaply than, for example, potato tubers as the latter are much heavier and more bulky. Growth of new plants by asexual reproduction tends to be a quick process.

In natural conditions in the wild it might be a disadvantage to have no variation in a species. If the climate or other conditions change and a vegetatively produced plant has no resistance to a particular disease, the whole population could be wiped out.

Checklist

After studying Chapter B11 you should know and understand the following.

Chromosomes and genes

- Inheritance is the transmission of genetic information from generation to generation.
- A chromosome is a thread-like structure of DNA, carrying genetic information in the form of genes.
- A gene is a length of DNA that codes for a protein.
- An allele is a version of a gene.
- Sex, in mammals, is determined by the X and Y chromosomes. Males are XY; females are XX.

- A haploid nucleus is a nucleus containing a single set of unpaired chromosomes e.g. in gametes.
- A diploid nucleus is a nucleus containing two sets of chromosomes e.g. in body cells.
- In a diploid cell, the chromosomes are in pairs; in a human diploid cell there are 23 pairs.

Cell division

- Mitosis is nuclear division giving rise to genetically identical cells.
- Before mitosis, the exact duplication of chromosomes occurs.
- Mitosis is important in growth, repair of damaged tissues, replacement of cells and in asexual reproduction.

Questions

14 Study the following photographs and captions, then make a list of the adaptations of each animal.
  a long-eared bat (Figure B11.32)
  b hare (Figure B11.33)
  c polar bear (Figure B11.29) (See also details in the text.)

15 Suggest some good characteristics that an animal-breeder might try to combine in sheep by mating different varieties together.

16 A variety of barley has a good ear of seed but has a long stalk and is easily blown over. Another variety has a short, sturdy stalk but a poor ear of seed.
  a Suggest a breeding programme to obtain and select a new variety that combines both of the useful characteristics.
  b Choose letters to represent the genes and show the genotypes of the parent plants and their offspring.

- Meiosis is reduction division in which the chromosome number is halved from diploid to haploid resulting in genetically different cells.
- Meiosis is involved in the production of gametes.

Monohybrid inheritance

- The genotype of an organism is its genetic make-up in terms of the alleles present.
- The phenotype of an organism is its observable features.
- Homozygous means having two identical alleles of a particular gene.
- Two identical homozygous individuals that breed together will be pure-breeding.
- Heterozygous means having two different alleles of a particular gene.
- A heterozygous individual will not be pure-breeding.
- A dominant allele is one that is that is expressed if it is present.
- A recessive allele is one that is only expressed when there is no dominant allele of the gene present.
- Genetic diagrams are used to predict the results of monohybrid crosses and calculate phenotypic ratios.
- Punnett squares can be used in crosses to work out and show the possible different genotypes.

- Pedigree diagrams can be used to interpret the inheritance of particular characteristics.

Variation

- Variation is the differences between individuals of the same species.
- The difference between phenotypic and genetic variation.
- Continuous variation results in a range of phenotypes between two extremes, e.g. height in humans.

- Discontinuous variation results in a limited number of phenotypes with no intermediates, e.g. tongue rolling.
- Phenotypic variations are usually caused by both genetic and environmental factors.
- Discontinuous variation is mostly caused by genes alone e.g. A, B, AB and O blood groups in humans.
- A mutation is a change in a gene or a chromosome.
- Increases in the rate of mutation can be caused by ionising radiation and some chemicals.

- Some members of a species may have variations which enable them to compete more effectively.
- Within a population there will be competition for resources.
- There will be a struggle for survival.
- Those variants that are better adapted to the environment will live longer and leave more offspring.
- These variants pass on their alleles to the next generation.

- Evolution is the change in adaptive features of a population over time as the result of natural selection.
- Adaptation is a process, resulting from natural selection, by which populations become more suited to their environment over many generations.
- The development of strains of antibiotic resistant bacteria is an example of evolution by natural selection.

- Selective breeding is used to improve commercially useful plants and animals.
- Humans select individuals with desirable features.
- These individuals are crossed to produce the next generation.
- Humans select offspring with the desirable features.

- There are a number of differences between natural and artificial selection.
- Selective breeding by artificial selection is carried out over many generations to improve crop plants and domesticated animals.

Combined	Co-ordinated
• State that the Sun is the principal source of energy input to biological systems	• State that the Sun is the principal source of energy input to biological systems
• Define the terms: *food chain*; *food web*; *producer*; *consumer*; *herbivore*; *carnivore*; *decomposer*	• Define the terms: *food chain*; *food web*; *producer*; *consumer*; *herbivore*; *carnivore*; *decomposer*
• Define the terms: *ecosystem*; *trophic level*	• Define the terms: *ecosystem*; *trophic level*
• Describe how energy is transferred between trophic levels	• Describe how energy is transferred between trophic levels
• Explain why food chains usually have fewer than five trophic levels	• Explain why food chains usually have fewer than five trophic levels
• Construct simple food chains	• Construct simple food chains
• Interpret food chains and food webs in terms of identifying producers and consumers	• Interpret food chains and food webs in terms of identifying producers and consumers
• State that consumers may be classed as primary, secondary and tertiary according to their position in a food chain	• State that consumers may be classed as primary, secondary and tertiary according to their position in a food chain
• Identify producers, primary consumers, secondary consumers, tertiary consumers and quaternary consumers as the trophic levels in food webs and food chains	• Identify producers, primary consumers, secondary consumers, tertiary consumers and quaternary consumers as the trophic levels in food webs and food chains

● Energy flow

Nearly all living things depend on the Sun to provide energy. This is harnessed by photosynthesising plants and the energy is then passed through food chains.

Dependence on sunlight

With the exception of atomic energy and tidal power, all the energy released on Earth is derived from sunlight. The energy released by animals comes, ultimately, from plants that they or their prey eat and the plants depend on sunlight for making their food. Photosynthesis is a process in which light energy is trapped by plants and converted into chemical energy (stored in molecules such as carbohydrates, fats and proteins). Since all animals depend, in the end, on plants for their food, they therefore depend indirectly on sunlight. A few examples of our own dependence on photosynthesis are given below.

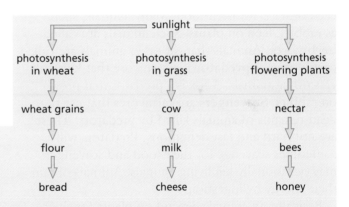

Nearly all the energy released on the Earth can be traced back to sunlight. Coal comes from tree-like plants, buried millions of years ago. These plants absorbed sunlight for their photosynthesis when they were alive. Petroleum was formed, also millions of years ago, probably from the partly decayed bodies of microscopic algae that lived in the sea. These, too, had absorbed sunlight for photosynthesis.

● Food chains and food webs

Key definitions
A **food chain** shows the transfer of energy from one organism to the next, beginning with a producer.
A **food web** is a network of interconnected food chains.
A **producer** is an organism that makes its own organic nutrients, usually using energy from sunlight, through photosynthesis.
A **consumer** is an organism that gets its energy from feeding on other organisms.
A **herbivore** is an animal that gets its energy by eating plants.
A **carnivore** is an animal that gets its energy by eating other animals.

'Interdependence' means the way in which living organisms depend on each other in order to remain alive, grow and reproduce. For example, bees depend for their food on pollen and nectar from flowers. Flowers depend on bees for pollination (Chapter B10). Bees and flowers are, therefore, interdependent.

Food chains

One important way in which organisms depend on each other is for their food. Many animals, such as rabbits, feed on plants. Such animals are called **herbivores**. Animals that eat other animals are called **carnivores**. A **predator** is a carnivore that kills and eats other animals. A fox is a predator that preys on rabbits. **Scavengers** are carnivores that eat the dead remains of animals killed by predators. These are not hard and fast definitions. Predators will sometimes scavenge for their food and scavengers may occasionally kill living animals. Animals obtain their energy by ingestion.

Basically, all animals depend on plants for their food. Foxes may eat rabbits, but rabbits feed on grass. A hawk eats a lizard, the lizard has just eaten a grasshopper but the grasshopper was feeding on a grass blade. This relationship is called a **food chain** (Figure B12.1).

The organisms at the beginning of a food chain are usually very numerous while the animals at the end of the chain are often large and few in number.

Figure B12.1 A food chain. The caterpillar eats the leaf; the blue tit eats the caterpillar but may fall prey to the kestrel.

The food chains in Figure B12.2 show this relationship. There will be millions of microscopic, single-celled algae in a pond (Figure B12.3a). These will be eaten by the larger but less numerous water fleas and other crustacea (Figure B12.3b), which in turn will become the food of small fish such as minnow. The hundreds of small fish may be able to provide enough food for only four or five large carnivores, like perch.

The organisms at the beginning of the food chains in Figure B12.2 are plants. Plants produce food from carbon dioxide, water and salts (see 'Photosynthesis', Chapter B5), and are, therefore, called **producers**. The animals that eat the plants are called **primary consumers**, e.g. grasshoppers. Animals that prey on the plant-eaters are called **secondary consumers**, e.g. shrews, and these may be eaten by **tertiary consumers**, e.g. weasels or kestrels.

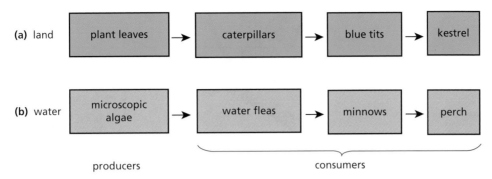

Figure B12.2 Examples of food chains.

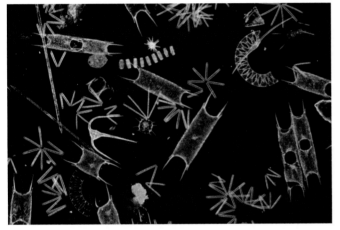

a phytoplankton (×100) these microscopic algae form the basis of a
food pyramid in the water

b zooplankton (×20) these crustacea will eat microscopic algae

Figure B12.3 Plankton. The microscopic organisms that live in the surface waters of the sea or fresh water are called, collectively, plankton. The single-celled algae are the phytoplankton. They are surrounded by water, salts and dissolved carbon dioxide. Their chloroplasts absorb sunlight and use its energy for making food by photosynthesis. Phytoplankton is eaten by small animals in the zooplankton, mainly crustacea. Small fish will eat the crustacea.

When constructing a food chain, always start with the name of the producer, usually a type of plant. It is not necessary to include an illustration. The instruction used in exam questions 'Draw a food chain' should not be taken literally. It just means that the food chain should be completed using arrows to link the names of the organisms involved. There should then be an arrow, pointing right towards a named herbivore (the animal which eats the plant). This is linked by another arrow to a named carnivore (the animal which eats the herbivore). There may be higher carnivores involved, also linked by arrows.

Food webs

Food chains are not really as straightforward as described above, because most animals eat more than one type of food. A fox, for example, does not feed entirely on rabbits but takes beetles, rats and voles in its diet. To show these relationships more accurately,

a **food web** can be drawn up (Figure B12.4 on the next page).

The food webs for land, sea and fresh water, or for ponds, rivers and streams, will all be different. Food webs will also change with the seasons when the food supply changes.

If some event interferes with a food web, all the organisms in it are affected in some way. For example, if the rabbits in Figure B12.4 were to die out, the foxes, owls and stoats would eat more beetles and rats. Something like this happened in 1954 when the disease myxomatosis wiped out nearly all the rabbits in England. Foxes ate more voles, beetles and blackberries, and attacks on lambs and chickens increased. Even the vegetation was affected because the tree seedlings that the rabbits used to nibble on were able to grow. As a result, woody scrubland started to develop on what had been grassy downs. A similar effect is shown in Figure B12.5 on the next page.

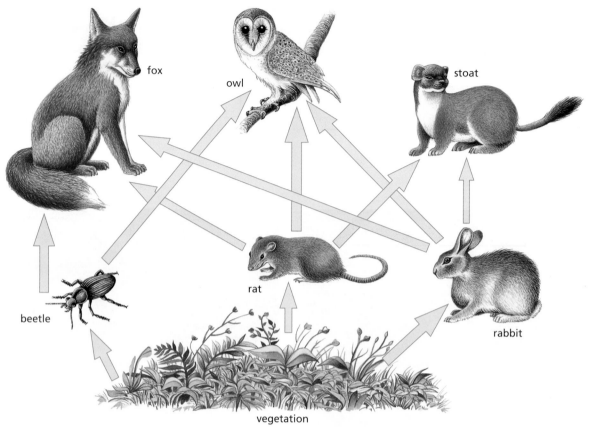

Figure B12.4 A food web.

a   sheep have eaten any seedlings that grew under the trees
Figure B12.5   Effect of grazing.

b   ten years later, the fence has kept the sheep off and the tree seedlings have grown

● Energy transfer

Study Figure B12.1. When an herbivorous animal eats a plant (the caterpillar feeding on a leaf), the chemical energy stored in that plant leaf is transferred to the herbivore. Similarly, when a carnivore (the blue tit) eats the herbivore, the carnivore gains the energy stored in the herbivore. If the carnivore is eaten by another carnivore (the kestrel), the energy is transferred again.

Use of sunlight

To try to estimate just how much life the Earth can support it is necessary to examine how efficiently the Sun's energy is used. The amount of energy from the Sun reaching the Earth's surface in 1 year ranges from 2 million to 8 million kilojoules per m² ($2-8 \times 10^9$ J/m²/yr) depending on the latitude. When this energy falls onto grassland, about 20% is reflected by the vegetation, 39% is used in evaporating water from the leaves (transpiration), 40% warms up the plants, the soil and the air, leaving only about 1% to be used in photosynthesis for making new organic matter in the leaves of the plants (Figure B12.6).

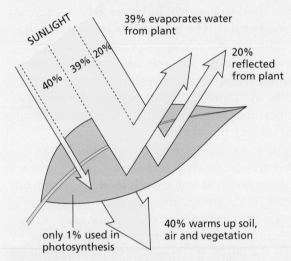

39% evaporates water from plant

SUNLIGHT

40% 39% 20%

20% reflected from plant

only 1% used in photosynthesis

40% warms up soil, air and vegetation

Figure B12.6 Absorption of Sun's energy by plants.

This figure of 1% will vary with the type of vegetation being considered and with climatic factors, such as availability of water and the soil temperature. Sugar-cane grown in ideal conditions can convert 3% of the Sun's energy into photosynthetic products; sugar-beet at the height of its growth has nearly a 9% efficiency. Tropical forests and swamps are far more productive than grassland but it is difficult, and, in some cases undesirable, to harvest and utilise their products.

In order to allow crop plants to approach their maximum efficiency they must be provided with sufficient water and mineral salts. This can be achieved by irrigation and the application of fertiliser.

Energy transfer between organisms

Having considered the energy conversion from sunlight to plant products, the next step is to study the efficiency of transmission of energy from plant products to primary consumers. On land, primary consumers eat only a small proportion of the available vegetation. In a deciduous forest only about 2% is eaten; in grazing land, 40% of the grass may be eaten by cows. In open water, however, where the producers are microscopic plants (phytoplankton, see Figure B12.3a) and are swallowed whole by the primary consumers in the zooplankton (see Figure B12.3b), 90% or more may be eaten. In the land communities, the parts of the vegetation not eaten by the primary consumers will eventually die and be used as a source of energy by the decomposers.

A cow is a primary consumer; over 60% of the grass it eats passes through its alimentary canal (Chapter B6) without being digested. Another 30% is used in the cow's respiration to provide energy for its movement and other life processes. Less than 10% of the plant material is converted into new animal tissue to contribute to growth (Figure B12.7). This figure will vary with the diet and the age of the animal. In a fully grown animal all the digested food will be used for energy and replacement and none will contribute to growth. Economically it is desirable to harvest the primary consumers before their rate of growth starts to fall off.

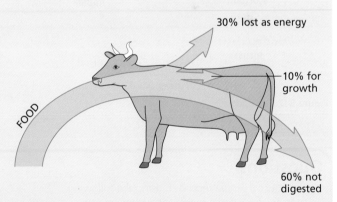

30% lost as energy

10% for growth

FOOD

60% not digested

Figure B12.7 Energy transfer from plants to animals.

The transfer of energy from primary to secondary consumers is probably more efficient, since a greater proportion of the animal food is digested and absorbed than is the case with plant material.

Key definitions
The **trophic level** of an organism is its position in a food
chain or food web.

Figure B12.8 A food chain containing five trophic levels.

Trophic levels in food chains and food webs

Food chains are lists of organisms that show the
feeding relationship between them, as in the example
in Figure B12.8.

The arrows used to link each organism to the next
represent the transfer of energy. The feeding level is
known as the **trophic level**.

Food webs are more realistic than food chains
because they show the range of organisms that the
consumers rely on for food. For example, in Figure
B12.9, the leopard feeds on baboons and impala.

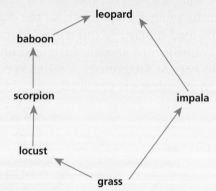

Figure B12.9 A food web.

The producer is grass. Locusts and impala are
primary consumers (herbivores) and the baboon is a
tertiary consumer (carnivore). The leopard is acting
as a secondary and quaternary consumer, depending
on what it is feeding on.

In the food web shown in Figure B12.4, there are
eight food chains. The producer is the vegetation.
The beetle, rat and rabbit are primary consumers
(herbivores) and the fox, owl and stoat are tertiary
consumers (carnivores). In reality, this food web
would be even more complex because the primary
consumers may select particular species of vegetation
to feed on and avoid others.

It is very unusual for food chains to have more
than five trophic levels because, on average, about
90% of the energy is lost at each level. Consequently,
very little of the energy entering the chain through
the producer is available to the top consumer. The
food chain below shows how the energy reduces
through the chain. It is based on grass obtaining
100 units of energy.

grass	→	locust	→	lizard	→	snake	→	mongoose
100 units		10 units		1 unit		0.1 unit		0.01 unit

Questions

1 Construct a simple food web using the following:
   sparrow, fox, wheat seeds, cat, kestrel, mouse.
2 Construct a simple food chain involving the following
   organisms:
   blackbird, earthworm, grass, hawk.
   On your food chain, identify the producer and the levels of
   the consumers.
3 An electric motor, a car engine and a race horse can all
   produce energy.
   a Show how this energy could come, originally, from sunlight.
   b What forms of energy on the Earth are *not* derived from
     sunlight?

4 Outline the events that might happen to a carbon atom
   in a molecule of carbon dioxide, which entered the
   stoma in the leaf of a potato plant and became part of a
   starch molecule in a potato tuber, which was then eaten
   by a man. Finally the carbon atom is breathed out again
   in a molecule of carbon dioxide.

Checklist

After studying Chapter B12 you should know and understand the following.

Organisms and their environment

- The Sun is the principal source of energy input to biological systems.
- A food chain shows the transfer of energy from one organism to the next, beginning with a producer.
- A food web is a network of interconnected food chains.
- Producers are organisms that make their own organic nutrients, usually using energy from sunlight, through photosynthesis.
- Consumers are organisms that get their energy from feeding on other organisms.
- A herbivore is an animal that gets its energy by eating plants.
- A carnivore is an animal that gets its energy by eating other animals.
- A decomposer is an organism that gets its energy from dead or waste organic material.

- An ecosystem is a unit containing all of the organisms and their environment, interacting together, in a given area.
- A trophic level is the position of an organism in a food chain or food web.

- Energy from the sun flows through living organisms.
- Energy is transferred between trophic levels through feeding.
- First, light energy is converted into chemical energy in photosynthetic organisms. Then they are eaten by herbivores. Carnivores eat herbivores.
- As organisms die, the energy is transferred to the environment.
- The transfer of energy from one trophic level to another is inefficient.
- Only about 1% of the Sun's energy which reaches the Earth is trapped by plants during photosynthesis.
- At each step in a food chain, only a small proportion of the food is used for growth. The rest is used for energy to keep the organism alive.
- Food chains usually have less than five trophic levels because, on average, 90% of the energy is lost at each level.

- All animals depend, ultimately, on plants for their source of food.
- Plants are the producers in a food chain or food web; animals may be primary, secondary or tertiary consumers.

- Plants are the producers in a food chain or food web; animals may be primary, secondary, tertiary or quaternary consumers. These represent trophic levels.

B13 Human influences on ecosystems

Combined

- Describe the carbon cycle, limited to photosynthesis, respiration, feeding, decomposition, fossilisation and combustion
- Discuss the effects of the combustion of fossil fuels and the cutting down of forests on the oxygen and carbon dioxide concentrations in the atmosphere
- List the undesirable effects of deforestation as an example of habitat destruction, to include extinction, loss of soil, flooding and increase of carbon dioxide in the atmosphere
- Explain the process of eutrophication of water in terms of: increased availability of nitrate and other ions; increased growth of producers; increased decomposition after death of producers; increased aerobic respiration by decomposers; reduction in dissolved oxygen; death of organisms requiring dissolved oxygen in water

Co-ordinated

- Describe the carbon cycle, limited to photosynthesis, respiration, feeding, decomposition, fossilisation and combustion
- Discuss the effects of the combustion of fossil fuels and the cutting down of forests on the oxygen and carbon dioxide concentrations in the atmosphere
- List the undesirable effects of deforestation as an example of habitat destruction, to include extinction, loss of soil, flooding and increase of carbon dioxide in the atmosphere
- Explain the undesirable effects of deforestation on the environment
- State the sources and effects of pollution of water (rivers, lakes and the sea) by chemical waste, discarded rubbish, untreated sewage and fertilisers
- Explain the process of eutrophication of water in terms of: increased availability of nitrate and other ions; increased growth of producers; increased decomposition after death of producers; increased aerobic respiration by decomposers; reduction in dissolved oxygen; death of organisms requiring dissolved oxygen in water

● The carbon cycle

Carbon is an element that occurs in all the compounds which make up living organisms. Plants get their carbon from carbon dioxide in the atmosphere and animals get their carbon from plants. The carbon cycle, therefore, is mainly concerned with what happens to carbon dioxide (Figure B13.1).

Removal of carbon dioxide from the atmosphere

Photosynthesis

Green plants remove carbon dioxide from the atmosphere as a result of their photosynthesis. The carbon from the carbon dioxide is built first into a carbohydrate such as sugar. Some of this is changed into starch or the cellulose of cell walls, and the proteins, pigments and other compounds of a plant. When the plants are eaten by animals, the organic plant material is digested, absorbed and built into the compounds making up the animals' tissues. Thus the carbon atoms from the plant become part of the animal.

Fossilisation

Any environment that prevents rapid decay may produce **fossils**. The carbon in the dead organisms

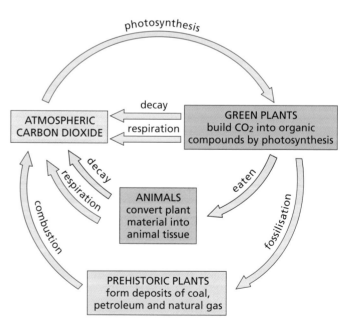

Figure B13.1 The carbon cycle.

becomes trapped and compressed and can remain there for millions of years. The carbon may form **fossil fuels** such as coal, oil and natural gas. Some animals make shells or exoskeletons containing carbon and these can become fossils.

Addition of carbon dioxide to the atmosphere

Respiration

Plants and animals obtain energy by oxidising carbohydrates in their cells to carbon dioxide and water (Chapter B8). The carbon dioxide and water are excreted so the carbon dioxide returns once again to the atmosphere.

Decomposition

A crucial factor in carbon recycling is the process of decomposition, or decay. If it were not for decay, essential materials would not be released from dead organisms. When an organism dies, the enzymes in its cells, freed from normal controls, start to digest its own tissues (auto-digestion). Soon, scavengers appear on the scene and eat much of the remains; blowfly larvae devour carcases, earthworms consume dead leaves.

Finally the decomposers, fungi and bacteria (collectively called **micro-organisms**), arrive and invade the remaining tissues (Figure B13.2). These saprophytes secrete extracellular enzymes (Chapter B4) into the tissues and reabsorb the liquid products of digestion. When the micro-organisms themselves die, auto-digestion takes place, releasing the products such as nitrates, sulfates, phosphates, etc. into the soil or the surrounding water to be taken up again by the producers in the ecosystem.

The speed of decay depends on the abundance of micro-organisms, temperature, the presence of water and, in many cases, oxygen. High temperatures speed up decay because they speed up respiration of the micro-organisms. Water is necessary for all living processes and oxygen is needed for aerobic respiration of the bacteria and fungi. Decay can take place in

Figure B13.2 Mould fungus growing on over-ripe oranges.

anaerobic conditions but it is slow and incomplete, as in the waterlogged conditions of peat bogs.

Combustion (burning)

When carbon-containing fuels such as wood, coal, petroleum and natural gas are burned, the carbon is oxidised to carbon dioxide ($C + O_2 \rightarrow CO_2$). The hydrocarbon fuels, such as coal and petroleum, come from ancient plants, which have only partly decomposed over the millions of years since they were buried.

So, an atom of carbon which today is in a molecule of carbon dioxide in the air may tomorrow be in a molecule of cellulose in the cell wall of a blade of grass. When the grass is eaten by a cow, the carbon atom may become part of a glucose molecule in the cow's bloodstream. When the glucose molecule is used for respiration, the carbon atom will be breathed out into the air once again as carbon dioxide.

The same kind of cycling applies to nearly all the elements of the Earth. No new matter is created, but it is repeatedly rearranged. A great proportion of the atoms of which you are composed will, at one time, have been part of other organisms.

The effects of the combustion of fossil fuels

If you look back at the carbon cycle, you will see that the natural processes of photosynthesis, respiration and decomposition would be expected to keep the CO_2 concentration at a steady level. However, since the Industrial Revolution, we have been burning the fossil fuels such as coal and petroleum and releasing extra CO_2 into the atmosphere. As a result, the concentration of CO_2 has increased from 0.029% to 0.035% since 1860. It is likely to go on increasing as we burn more and more fossil fuel.

Although it is not possible to prove beyond all reasonable doubt that production of CO_2 and other 'greenhouse gases' is causing a rise in the Earth's temperature, i.e. global warming, the majority of scientists and climatologists agree that it is happening now and will get worse unless we take drastic action to reduce the output of these gases.

Another factor contributing to the increase in atmospheric CO_2 is **deforestation**. Trees are responsible for removing gaseous CO_2 and trapping the carbon in organic molecules (carbohydrates, proteins and fats – see Chapter B3). When they are cut down the amount of photosynthesis globally is reduced. Often deforestation is achieved by a process called 'slash and burn', where the felled trees are burned to provide land for agriculture and this releases even more atmospheric CO_2.

● Deforestation

The removal of large numbers of trees results in habitat destruction on a massive scale.

- Animals living in the forest lose their homes and sources of food; species of plant become extinct as the land is used for other purposes such as agriculture, mining, housing and roads.

- Soil erosion is more likely to happen as there are no roots to hold the soil in place. The soil can end up in rivers and lakes, destroying habitats there.
- Flooding becomes more frequent as there is no soil to absorb and hold rainwater. Plant roots rot and animals drown, destroying food chains and webs.
- Carbon dioxide builds up in the atmosphere as there are fewer trees to photosynthesise, increasing global warming. Climate change affects habitats.

Figure B13.3   Cutting a road through a tropical rainforest. The road not only destroys the natural vegetation, it also opens up the forest to further exploitation.

Figure B13.4   Soil erosion. Removal of forest trees from steeply sloping ground has allowed the rain to wash away the topsoil.

The undesirable effects of deforestation on the environment

Forests have a profound effect on climate, water supply and soil maintenance. They have been described as environmental buffers. For example, they intercept heavy rainfall and release the water steadily and slowly to the soil beneath and to the streams and rivers that start in or flow through them. The tree roots hold the soil in place.

At present, we are destroying forests, particularly tropical forests, at a rapid rate (1) for their timber, (2) to make way for agriculture, roads (Figure B13.3) and settlements, and (3) for firewood. The Food and Agriculture Organisation, run by the United Nations, reported that the overall tropical deforestation rates in the decade up to 2010 were 8.5% higher than during the 1990s. At the current rate of destruction, it is estimated that all tropical rainforests will have disappeared in the next 75 years.

Removal of forests allows soil erosion, silting up of lakes and rivers, floods and the loss for ever of thousands of species of animals and plants.

Trees can grow on hillsides even when the soil layer is quite thin. When the trees are cut down and the soil is ploughed, there is less protection from the wind and rain. Heavy rainfall washes the soil off the hillsides into the rivers. The hillsides are left bare and useless and the rivers become choked up with mud and silt, which can cause floods (Figures B13.4 and B13.5). For example, Argentina spends 10 million dollars a year on dredging silt from the River Plate estuary to keep the port of Buenos Aires open to shipping. It has been found that 80% of this sediment comes from a deforested and overgrazed region 1800 km upstream, which represents only 4% of the river's total catchment area. Similar sedimentation has halved the lives of reservoirs, hydroelectric schemes and irrigation programmes. The disastrous floods in India and Bangladesh in recent years may be attributed largely to deforestation.

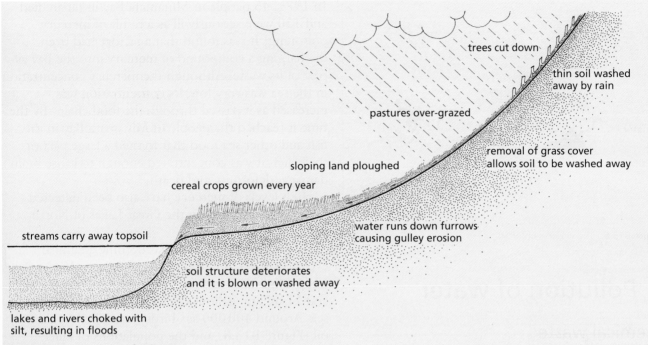

Figure B13.5 The causes of soil erosion.

The soil of tropical forests is usually very poor in nutrients. Most of the organic matter is in the leafy canopy of the tree tops. For a year or two after felling and burning, the forest soil yields good crops but the nutrients are soon depleted and the soil eroded. The agricultural benefit from cutting down forests is very short-lived, and the forest does not recover even if the impoverished land is abandoned.

Forests and climate

About half the rain that falls in tropical forests comes from the transpiration of the trees themselves. The clouds that form from this transpired water help to reflect sunlight and so keep the region relatively cool and humid. When areas of forest are cleared, this source of rain is removed, cloud cover is reduced and the local climate changes quite dramatically. The temperature range from day to night is more extreme and the rainfall diminishes.

In North Eastern Brazil, for example, an area which was once rainforest is now an arid wasteland. If more than 60% of a forest is cleared, it may cause irreversible changes in the climate of the whole region. This could turn the region into an unproductive desert.

Removal of trees on such a large scale also reduces the amount of carbon dioxide removed from the atmosphere in the process of photosynthesis. Most scientists agree that the build-up of CO_2 in the atmosphere contributes to global warming.

Forests and biodiversity

One of the most characteristic features of tropical rainforests is the enormous diversity of species they contain. In Britain, a forest or wood may consist of only one or two species of tree such as oak, ash, beech or pine. In tropical forests there are many more species and they are widely dispersed throughout the habitat. It follows that there is also a wide diversity of animals that live in such habitats. In fact, it has been estimated that half of the world's 10 million species live in tropical forests.

Destruction of tropical forest, therefore, destroys a large number of different species, driving many of them to the verge of extinction, and also drives out the indigenous populations of humans. In addition, we may be depriving ourselves of many valuable sources of chemical compounds that the plants and animals produce. The US National Cancer Institute has identified 3000 plants having products active against cancer cells and 70% of them come from rainforests (Figure B13.6 on the next page).

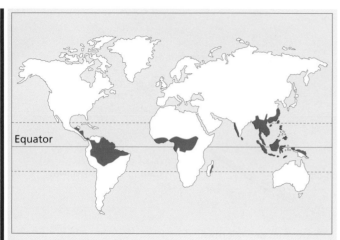

Figure B13.6 The world's rainforests.

● Pollution of water

Chemical waste

Many industrial processes produce poisonous waste products. Electroplating, for example, produces waste containing copper and cyanide. If these chemicals are released into rivers they poison the animals and plants and could poison humans who drink the water. It is estimated that the River Trent receives 850 tonnes of zinc, 4000 tonnes of nickel and 300 tonnes of copper each year from industrial processes.

Any factory getting rid of its effluent into water systems risks damaging the environment (Figure B13.7). Some detergents contain a lot of phosphate. This is not removed by sewage treatment and is discharged into rivers. The large amount of phosphate encourages growth of microscopic plants (algae).

Figure B13.7 River pollution. The river is badly polluted by the effluent from a paper mill.

In 1971, 45 people in Minamata Bay in Japan died and 120 were seriously ill as a result of mercury poisoning. It was found that a factory had been discharging a compound of mercury into the bay as part of its waste. Although the mercury concentration in the sea was very low, its concentration was increased as it passed through the food chain. By the time it reached the people of Minamata Bay in the fish and other sea food that formed a large part of their diet, it was concentrated enough to cause brain damage, deformity and death.

High levels of mercury have also been detected in the Baltic Sea and in the Great Lakes of North America.

Oil pollution of the sea has become a familiar event. In 1989, a tanker called the *Exxon Valdez* ran on to Bligh Reef in Prince William Sound, Alaska, and 11 million gallons of crude oil spilled into the sea. Around 400 000 sea birds were killed by the oil (Figure B13.8) and the populations of killer whales, sea otters and harbour seals among others, were badly affected. The hot water high-pressure hosing techniques and chemicals used to clean up the shoreline killed many more birds and sea creatures living on the coast. Since 1989, there have continued to be major spillages of crude oil from tankers and off-shore oil wells.

Figure B13.8 Oil pollution. Oiled sea birds like this long-tailed duck cannot fly to reach their feeding grounds. They also poison themselves by trying to clean the oil from their feathers.

Discarded rubbish

The development of towns and cities, and the crowding of growing populations into them, leads to problems of waste disposal. The domestic waste from a town of several thousand people can cause disease and pollution in the absence of effective means of disposal. Much ends up in landfill sites, taking up valuable space, polluting the ground and attracting vermin and insects, which can spread disease. Most consumable items come in packaging, which, if not recycled, ends up in landfill sites or is burned, causing air pollution. Discarded rubbish that ends up in the sea can cause severe problems for marine animals.

Sewage

Diseases like typhoid and cholera are caused by certain bacteria when they get into the human intestine. The faeces passed by people suffering from these diseases will contain the harmful bacteria. If the bacteria get into drinking water they may spread the disease to hundreds of other people. For this reason, among others, untreated sewage must not be emptied into rivers. It is treated at the sewage works so that all the solids are removed. The human waste is broken down by bacteria and made harmless (free from harmful bacteria and poisonous chemicals), but the breakdown products include phosphates and nitrates. When the water from the sewage treatment is discharged into rivers it contains large quantities of phosphate and nitrate, which allow the microscopic plant life to grow very rapidly (Figure B13.9).

Figure B13.9 Growth of algae in a lake. Abundant nitrate and phosphate from treated sewage and from farmland make this growth possible.

Fertilisers

When nitrates and phosphates from farmland and sewage escape into water they cause excessive growth of microscopic green plants. This may result in a serious oxygen shortage in the water, resulting in the death of aquatic animals – a process called **eutrophication**.

Eutrophication

Nitrates and phosphates are present from a number of sources, including untreated sewage, detergents from manufacturing and washing processes, arable farming and factory farming.

If these nitrates or phosphates enter a water system, they become available for algae (aquatic plants) to absorb. The plants need these nutrients to grow. More nutrients result in faster growth (Figure B13.9). As the plants die, some through lack of light because of overcrowding, aerobic bacteria decompose them and respire, taking oxygen out of the water. As oxygen levels drop, animals such as fish cannot breathe, so they die and the whole ecosystem is destroyed (Figure B13.10).

Figure B13.10 Fish killed by pollution. The water may look clear but is so short of oxygen that the fish have died from suffocation.

Figure B13.11 shows this sequence of events as a flow chart.

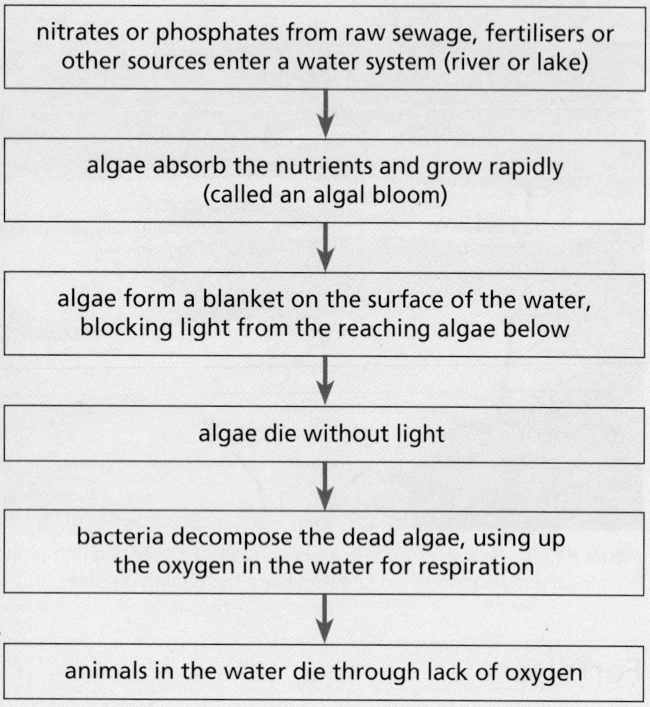

nitrates or phosphates from raw sewage, fertilisers or other sources enter a water system (river or lake)

↓

algae absorb the nutrients and grow rapidly (called an algal bloom)

↓

algae form a blanket on the surface of the water, blocking light from the reaching algae below

↓

algae die without light

↓

bacteria decompose the dead algae, using up the oxygen in the water for respiration

↓

animals in the water die through lack of oxygen

Figure B13.11   The sequence of events leading to eutrophication.

Questions

1   Write three chemical equations:
   a   to illustrate that respiration produces carbon dioxide (see Chapter B8)
   b   to show that burning produces carbon dioxide
   c   to show that photosynthesis uses up carbon dioxide (see Chapter B5).

2   What kinds of human activity can lead to the extinction of a species?

3   a   What pressures lead to destruction of tropical forest?
   b   Give three important reasons for trying to preserve tropical forests.

4   What is the possible connection between:
   a   cutting down trees on hillsides and flooding in the valleys, and
   b   clear-felling (logging) in tropical forests and local climate change?

Checklist

After studying Chapter B13 you should know and understand the following.

● The materials which make up living organisms are constantly recycled.
● Plants take up carbon dioxide during photosynthesis; all living organisms give out carbon dioxide during respiration; the burning of carbon-containing fuels produces carbon dioxide.
● The uptake of carbon dioxide by plants balances the production of carbon dioxide from respiration and combustion.
● The combustion of fossil fuels and the cutting down of forests increases the carbon dioxide concentrations in the atmosphere.
● Deforestation is an example of habitat destruction: it can lead to extinction, soil erosion, flooding and carbon dioxide build-up in the atmosphere.
● The conversion of tropical forest to agricultural land usually results in failure because forest soils are poor in nutrients.
● Deforestation has many undesirable effects on the environment.
● We pollute our rivers, lakes and the sea with chemical, discarded rubbish, untreated sewage and fertilisers.
● The process of eutrophication of water involves:
● increased availability of nitrate and other ions
● increased growth of producers
● increased decomposition after death of the producers
● increased aerobic respiration by bacteria, resulting in a reduction in dissolved oxygen
● the death of organisms requiring dissolved oxygen in water.

Chemistry

C1 — The particulate nature of matter

Combined	Co-ordinated
• State the distinguishing properties of solids, liquids and gases	• State the distinguishing properties of solids, liquids and gases
• Describe the structure of solids, liquids and gases in terms of particle separation, arrangement and types of motion	• Describe the structure of solids, liquids and gases in terms of particle separation, arrangement and types of motion
• Describe the changes of state in terms of melting, boiling, evaporation, freezing and condensation	• Describe changes of state in terms of melting, boiling, evaporation, freezing and condensation
• Explain changes of state in terms of particle theory and the energy changes involved	• Demonstrate understanding of the terms *atom*, *molecule* and *ion*
• Describe qualitatively the pressure and temperature of a gas in terms of the motion of its particles	• Explain changes of state in terms of particle theory and the energy changes involved
• Demonstrate understanding of the terms *atom*, *molecule* and *ion*	• Describe and explain diffusion in terms of the movement of particles (atoms, molecules or ions)
	• Describe and explain dependence of rate of diffusion on molecular mass

Chemistry is about what **matter** is like and how it behaves, and our explanations and predictions of its behaviour. What is matter? This word is used to cover all the substances and materials from which the physical universe is composed. There are many millions of different substances known, and all of them can be categorised as solids, liquids or gases (Figure C1.1). These are what we call the **three states of matter**.

b liquid

a solid

Figure C1.1 Water in three different states.

c gas

● Solids, liquids and gases

A **solid**, at a given temperature, has a definite volume and shape which may be affected by changes in temperature. Solids usually increase slightly in size when heated (**expansion**) (Figure C1.2) and usually decrease in size if cooled (**contraction**).

A **liquid**, at a given temperature, has a fixed volume and will take up the shape of any container into which it is poured. Like a solid, a liquid's volume is slightly affected by changes in temperature.

A **gas**, at a given temperature, has neither a definite shape nor a definite volume. It will take up the shape of any container into which it is placed and will spread out evenly within it. Unlike those of solids and liquids, the volumes of gases are affected quite markedly by changes in temperature.

Liquids and gases, unlike solids, are relatively **compressible**. This means that their volume can be reduced by the application of pressure. Gases are much more compressible than liquids.

Figure C1.2 Without expansion gaps between the rails, the track would buckle in hot weather.

● The kinetic theory of matter

The **kinetic theory** helps to explain the way in which matter behaves. The evidence is consistent with the idea that all matter is made up of tiny **particles**. This theory explains the physical properties of matter in terms of the movement of its constituent particles.

The main points of the theory are:

● All matter is made up of tiny, moving particles, invisible to the naked eye. Different substances have different types of particles (atoms, molecules or ions) which have different sizes.
● The particles move all the time. The higher the temperature, the faster they move on average.
● Heavier particles move more slowly than lighter ones at a given temperature.

The kinetic theory can be used as a scientific model to explain how the arrangement of particles relates to the properties of the three states of matter.

Explaining the states of matter

In a solid the particles attract one another. There are attractive forces between the particles which hold them close together. The particles have little freedom of movement and can only vibrate about a fixed position. They are arranged in a regular manner, which explains why many solids form crystals.

It is possible to model such crystals by using spheres to represent the particles (Figure C1.3a). If the spheres are built up in a regular way then the shape compares very closely with that of a part of a chrome alum crystal (Figure C1.3b).

a a model of a chrome alum crystal **b** an actual chrome alum crystal
Figure C1.3

In a liquid the particles are still close together but they move around in a random way and often collide with one another. The forces of attraction between the particles in a liquid are weaker than those in a solid. Particles in the liquid form of a substance have more energy on average than the particles in the solid form of the same substance.

In a gas the particles are relatively far apart. They are free to move anywhere within the container in which they are held. They move randomly at very high velocities, much more rapidly than those in a liquid. They collide with each other, but less often than in a liquid, and they also collide with the walls of the container. They exert virtually no forces of attraction on each other because they are relatively far apart. Such forces, however, are very significant. If they did not exist we could not have solids or liquids (see Changes of state).

The pressure inside a balloon is caused by the gas particles striking the inside surface of the balloon. There is increased pressure inside the balloon at higher temperatures as the gas particles have more energy and therefore move around faster, striking the inside surface of the balloon more frequently. Since the balloon is an elastic envelope, the increased pressure causes the skin to stretch and the volume to increase.

The arrangement of particles in solids, liquids and gases is shown in Figure C1.4.

solid
particles only vibrate about fixed positions. Regular structure

liquid
particles have some freedom and can move around each other. Collide often

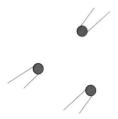

gas
particles move freely and at random in all the space available; they collide less often than in liquid also

Figure C1.4 The arrangement of particles in solids, liquids and gases.

Questions

1 When a metal such as copper is heated it expands. Explain what happens to the metal particles as the solid metal expands.
2 a Draw diagrams to show the arrangement of particles in:
   i solid lead
   ii molten lead
   iii gaseous lead.
 b Explain how the particles move in these three states of matter.
 c Explain, using the kinetic theory, what happens to the particles in oxygen as it is cooled down.

● Changes of state

The kinetic theory model can be used to explain how a substance changes from one state to another. If a solid is heated the particles vibrate faster as they gain energy. This makes them 'push' their neighbouring particles further away from themselves. This causes an increase in the volume of the solid, and the solid expands. Expansion has taken place.

Eventually, the heat energy causes the forces of attraction to weaken. The regular pattern of the structure breaks down. The particles can now move around each other. The solid has melted. The temperature at which this takes place is called the **melting point** of the substance. The temperature of a pure melting solid will not rise until it has all melted. When the substance has become a liquid there are still very significant forces of attraction between the particles, which is why it is a liquid and not a gas.

Solids which have high melting points have stronger forces of attraction between their particles than those which have low melting points. A list of some substances with their corresponding melting and boiling points is shown in Table C1.1.

Table C1.1

Substance	Melting point/°C	Boiling point/°C
Aluminium	661	2467
Ethanol	−117	79
Magnesium oxide	827	3627
Mercury	−30	357
Methane	−182	−164
Oxygen	−218	−183
Sodium chloride	801	1413
Sulfur	113	445
Water	0	100

If the liquid is heated the particles will move around even faster as their average energy increases. Some particles at the surface of the liquid have enough energy to overcome the forces of attraction between themselves and the other particles in the liquid and they escape to form a gas. The liquid begins to **evaporate** as a gas is formed.

Eventually, a temperature is reached at which the particles are trying to escape from the liquid so quickly that bubbles of gas actually start to form inside the bulk of the liquid. This temperature is called the **boiling point** of the substance. At the boiling point the pressure of the gas created above the liquid equals that in the air – **atmospheric pressure**.

Liquids with high boiling points have stronger forces between their particles than liquids with low boiling points.

When a gas is cooled the average energy of the particles decreases and the particles move closer together. The forces of attraction between the particles now become significant and cause the gas to **condense** into a liquid. When a liquid is cooled it **freezes** to form a solid. In each of these changes energy is given out.

Changes of state are summarised in Figure C1.5 and are examples of **physical changes**. Whenever a physical change of state occurs, the temperature remains constant during the change (see Heating and cooling curves). During a physical change no new substance is formed.

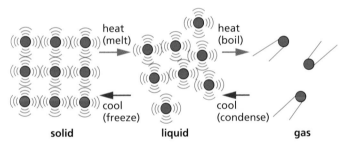

Figure C1.5 Summary of the changes of state.

Heating and cooling curves

The graph shown in Figure C1.6 was drawn by plotting the temperature of water as it was heated steadily from –15 °C to 110 °C. You can see from the curve that changes of state have taken place. When the temperature was first measured only ice was present. After a short time the curve flattens, showing that even though heat energy is being put in, the temperature remains constant.

In ice the particles of water are close together and are attracted to one another. For ice to melt the particles must obtain sufficient energy to overcome the forces of attraction between the water particles to allow relative movement to take place. This is where the heat energy is going.

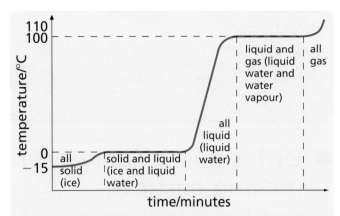

Figure C1.6 Graph of temperature against time for the change from ice at –15 °C to water to steam.

The temperature will begin to rise again only after all the ice has melted. Generally, the heating curve for a pure solid always stops rising at its melting point and gives rise to a sharp melting point. A sharp melting point indicates a pure sample. The addition or presence of impurities lowers the melting point. You can try to find the melting point of a substance using the apparatus shown in Figure C1.7.

In the same way, if you want to boil a liquid such as water you have to give it some extra energy. This can be seen on the graph (Figure C1.6) where the curve levels out at 100 °C – the boiling point of water.

Solids and liquids can be identified from their characteristic melting and boiling points.

The reverse processes of condensing and freezing occur on cooling. This time, however, energy is given out when the gas condenses to the liquid and the liquid freezes to give the solid.

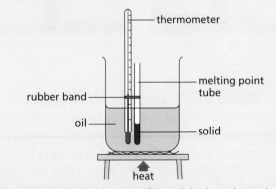

Figure C1.7 Apparatus shown here if heated slowly can be used to find the melting point of a substance such as the solid in the melting point tube.

● Diffusion – evidence for moving particles

When you walk past a cosmetics counter in a department store you can usually smell the perfumes. For this to happen gas particles must be leaving open perfume bottles and be spreading out through the air in the store. This spreading out of a gas is called **diffusion** and it takes place in a haphazard and random way.

All gases diffuse to fill the space available. In Figure C1.8, after a day the brown–red fumes of gaseous bromine have spread evenly throughout both gas jars from the liquid present in the lower gas jar.

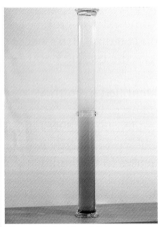

Figure C1.8 After 24 hours the bromine fumes have diffused throughout both gas jars.

Gases diffuse at different rates. If one piece of cotton wool is soaked in concentrated ammonia solution and another is soaked in concentrated hydrochloric acid and these are put at opposite ends of a dry glass tube, then after a few minutes a white cloud of ammonium chloride appears

(Figure C1.9). This shows the position at which the two gases meet and react. The white cloud forms in the position shown because the ammonia particles are lighter and have a smaller relative formula mass (Chapter C4, p.221) than the hydrogen chloride particles (released from the hydrochloric acid) and so move faster.

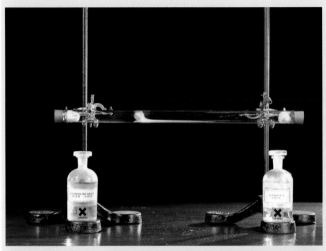

Figure C1.9 Hydrochloric acid (left) and ammonia (right) diffuse at different rates.

Diffusion also takes place in liquids (Figure C1.10) but it is a much slower process than in gases. This is because the particles of a liquid move much more slowly.

When diffusion takes place between a liquid and a gas it is known as **intimate mixing**. The kinetic theory can be used to explain this process. It states that collisions are taking place randomly between particles in a liquid or a gas and that there is sufficient space between the particles of one substance for the particles of the other substance to move into.

a   b

Figure C1.10 Diffusion within nickel(II) sulfate solution can take days to reach the stage shown on the right.

Questions

5 When a jar of coffee is opened, people in all parts of the room soon notice the smell. Use the kinetic theory to explain how this happens.

6 Describe, with the aid of diagrams, the diffusion of copper(II) sulfate solution.

7 Explain why diffusion is faster in gases than in liquids.

● Atoms, molecules and ions

In 1803, John Dalton (Figure C1.11) suggested that each element was composed of its own kind of particles, which he called **atoms**. Atoms are much too small to be seen. We now know that about 20×10^6 of them would stretch over a length of only 1 cm.

Figure C1.11 John Dalton (1766–1844).

Atoms – the smallest particles

Everything is made up of billions of atoms. The atoms of all elements are extremely small; in fact they are too small to be seen. The smallest atom known is hydrogen, with each atom being represented as a sphere having a diameter of 0.000 000 07 mm (or 7×10^{-8} mm) (Table C1.2). Atoms of different elements have different diameters as well as different masses. How many atoms of hydrogen would have to be placed side by side along the edge of your ruler to fill just one of the 1 mm divisions?

Table C1.2 Sizes of atoms

Atom	Diameter of atom/mm
Hydrogen	7×10^{-8}
Oxygen	12×10^{-8}
Sulfur	20.8×10^{-8}

Molecules

The atoms of some elements are joined together in small groups. These small groups of atoms are called **molecules**. For example, the atoms of the elements hydrogen, oxygen, nitrogen, fluorine, chlorine (Figure C1.12 on the next page),

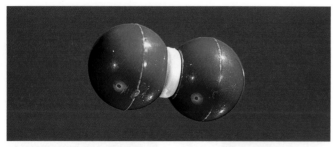

Figure C1.12 A chlorine molecule.

bromine and iodine are each joined in pairs and they are known as **diatomic** molecules. In the case of phosphorus and sulfur the atoms are joined in larger numbers, four and eight respectively (P_4, S_8).

Molecules are not always formed by atoms of the same type joining together. For example, water exists as molecules containing oxygen and hydrogen atoms.

Ions

An ion is another type of small particle. Unlike atoms and molecules, however, ions have either a positive or a negative electrical charge. These opposite electrical charges cause the ions to attract one another strongly to form hard solids with high melting and boiling points.

Checklist

After studying Chapter C1 you should know and understand the following.

- Atmospheric pressure is the pressure exerted by the atmosphere on the surface of the Earth due to the weight of the air.
- Boiling point is the temperature at which the pressure of the gas created above a liquid equals atmospheric pressure.
- Condensation is the change of a vapour or a gas into a liquid. This process is accompanied by the evolution of heat.
- Diffusion is the process by which different substances mix as a result of the random motions of their particles.
- Evaporation is a process occurring at the surface of a liquid involving the change of state of a liquid into a vapour at a temperature below the boiling point.
- Kinetic theory is a theory which accounts for the bulk properties of matter in terms of the constituent particles.
- Matter is anything which occupies space and has a mass.
- Melting point is the temperature at which a solid begins to liquefy. Pure substances have a sharp melting point.
- Solids, liquids and gases are the three states of matter to which all substances belong.

Questions

8 Are the following composed of atoms, molecules or ions?
   a carbon, C
   b water H_2O
   c sodium chloride Na^+Cl^-
   d carbon dioxide, CO_2
   e iron, Fe
9 How would you use chemical shorthand to write a representation of the molecules of iodine and fluorine?

C2 Experimental techniques

Combined	Co-ordinated
• Name and suggest appropriate apparatus for the measurement of time, temperature, mass and volume, including burettes, pipettes and measuring cylinders • Interpret simple chromatograms • Interpret simple chromatograms, including the use of R_f values • Describe and explain methods of separation and purification by the use of a suitable solvent, filtration, crystallisation, distillation, fractional distillation, paper chromatography • Suggest suitable separation and purification techniques, given information about the substances involved	• Name and suggest appropriate apparatus for the measurement of time, temperature, mass and volume including burettes, pipettes and measuring cylinders • Demonstrate knowledge and understanding of paper chromatography • Interpret simple chromatograms • Interpret simple chromatograms, including the use of R_f values • Understand the importance of purity in substances for use in everyday life, e.g. in the manufacture of compounds to use in drugs and food additives • Recognise that mixtures melt and boil over a range of temperatures • Identify substances and assess their purity from melting point and boiling point information • Describe and explain methods of separation and purification by the use of a suitable solvent, filtration, crystallisation, distillation, fractional distillation, paper chromatography • Suggest suitable separation and purification techniques, given information about the substances involved

● Accuracy in experimental work in the laboratory

Scientists find out about the nature of materials by carrying out experiments in a laboratory. Many of these experiments require apparatus that you have used in your study of chemistry to date. Certainly a knowledge and understanding of the use of this scientific apparatus is required for successful experimentation and investigations that you may carry out in your further study of chemistry. Much of the work involves **accurate** measurements with particular pieces of apparatus in particular experiments, many of which are shown in the section below.

Apparatus used for measurement in chemistry

Measurement of time

Experiments involving rates of reaction will require the use of an accurate stopwatch – one that measures to a hundredth of a second. The units of time are hours (h), minutes (min) and seconds (s).

Figure C2.1 This stopwatch can be used to measure the time passed in a chemical reaction.

Measurement of temperature

The most commonly used thermometers in a laboratory are alcohol-in-glass. However, mercury

Figure C2.2 A thermometer can be used to measure temperature.

in-glass thermometers can be used but should be handled with great care. The mercury inside them is poisonous and should not be handled if a thermometer breaks. The units of temperature are those of the Celsius scale. This scale is based on the temperature at which water freezes and boils, that is:

- the freezing point of water is 0 °C whilst
- the boiling point of water is 100 °C.

For accuracy the thermometer should be capable of being read to a tenth of a degree Celsius. The usual thermometer used is that shown in the photograph that measures accurately between –10° and 110 °C (Figure C2.2). When reading the thermometer always ensure that your eye is at the same level as the liquid meniscus in the thermometer to ensure there are no parallax effects. The meniscus is the way that the liquid curves at the edges of the capillary in which the liquid is held in the thermometer.

Measurement of mass

There are many different electronic balances which can be used. The important detail with any of them is that they are accurate to one hundredth of a gram.

Figure C2.3 An electronic balance can be used to measure the mass of reagents.

The units for measuring mass are grams (g) and kilograms (kg).

$$1 \, kg = 1000 \, g$$

When using an electronic balance you should wait until the reading is steady before taking it.

Measurement of volume

Different experiments involving liquids will require one or other or all the various measuring apparatus for volume. The volume of a liquid is a measure of the amount of space that it takes up. The units of volume are litres (l) and cubic centimetres (cm³).

$$1 \, litre = 1000 \, cm^3$$

However, some of the manufacturers of apparatus used for measuring volume use millilitres (ml). This is not a problem, however, since $1 \, cm^3 = 1 \, ml$.

When reading the volume using one of the pieces of apparatus (Figure C2.4) it is important to ensure that the apparatus is vertical and that your eye is level with the top of the meniscus of the liquid being measured.

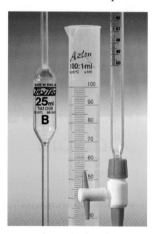

Figure C2.4 The apparatus shown in the photograph is generally used in different experiments to measure volume accurately.

Questions

1 What measuring device would you use to obtain values for:
   a the volume of liquid in a coffee mug
   b the mass of an apple
   c the temperature of a cup of tea
   d the time taken to run up 20 stairs
   e the time taken by an apple to fall through one metre?

2 Complete the table below by stating the typical accuracy of each of the measuring devices listed.

Device	Accuracy
stopwatch	
digital timer	
digital balance	
liquid in glass thermometer	
100 ml measuring cylinder	

Criteria for purity

Drugs are manufactured to a very high degree of purity (Figure C2.5). To ensure that the highest possible purity is obtained, the drugs are dissolved in a suitable solvent and subjected to fractional crystallisation.

It is illegal to put anything harmful into food. Also, government legislation requires that a lot of testing takes place before a new pharmaceutical is marketed.

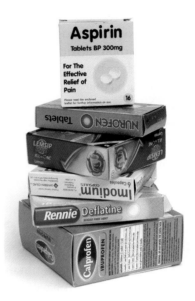

Figure C2.6 These pharmaceuticals must have been through a lot of testing before they can be sold in a chemist's shop.

Figure C2.5 Drugs are manufactured to a high degree of purity by fractional crystallisation.

Question

3 Describe how you would use chromatography to show whether blue ink contains a single pure dye or a mixture of dyes.

Throughout the chemical, pharmaceutical and food industries it is essential that the substances used are pure. Any impurities may interfere chemically, physically or biologically with the behaviour of the product. The purity of a substance can be gauged by:

- its melting point – if it is a pure solid it will have a sharp melting point. If an impurity is present then melting takes place over a range of temperatures.
- its boiling point – if it is a pure liquid the temperature will remain steady at its boiling point. If the substance is impure then the mixture will boil over a temperature range.

- chromatography – if it is a pure substance it will produce only one well-defined spot on a chromatogram. If impurities are present then several spots will be seen on the chromatogram (see Figure C2.8 on the next page).

- Solubility – if it is a pure substance then all of the substance will dissolve in a suitable solvent at a given temperature. Any undissolved solid would be impurity and would need to be filtered off.

● Mixtures

Many everyday things are not pure substances, they are mixtures. A mixture contains more than one substance (elements and/or compounds). An example of a common mixture is sea water (Figure C2.7).

Figure C2.7 Sea water is a common mixture.

Other mixtures include the air, which is a mixture of elements such as oxygen, nitrogen and neon and compounds such as carbon dioxide (see Chapter C11, p.295), and alloys such as brass, which is a mixture of copper and zinc (for a further discussion of alloys see Chapter C10, p.289).

a chromatographic separation of black ink

> ## Question
> 4 What criteria can be used to test the purity of a substance?

● Separating mixtures

Many mixtures contain useful substances mixed with unwanted material. In order to obtain these useful substances, chemists often have to separate them from the impurities. Chemists have developed many different methods of separation, particularly for separating compounds from complex mixtures. Which separation method they use depends on what is in the mixture and the properties of the substances present. It also depends on whether the substances to be separated are solids, liquids or gases.

Separating solid/solid mixtures

Chromatography

What happens if you have to separate two or more solids that are soluble? This type of problem is encountered when you have mixtures of coloured materials such as inks and dyes. A technique called **chromatography** is widely used to separate these materials so that they can be identified.

There are several types of chromatography; however, they all follow the same basic principles. The simplest kind is paper chromatography. To separate the different-coloured dyes in a sample of black ink, a spot of the ink is put on to a piece of chromatography paper. This paper is then set in a suitable solvent as shown in Figure C2.8.

As the solvent moves up the paper, the dyes are carried with it and begin to separate. They separate because the substances have different solubilities in the solvent and are absorbed to different degrees by the chromatography paper. As a result, they are separated gradually as the solvent moves up the paper. The **chromatogram** in Figure C2.8b shows how the ink contains three dyes, P, Q and R.

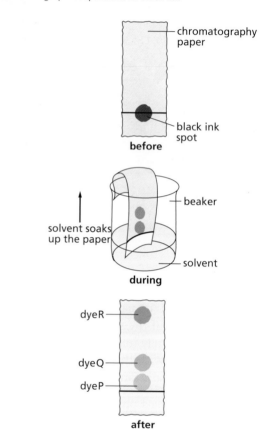

b the black ink separates into three dyes: P, Q and R

Figure C2.8

Numerical measurements (retardation factors) known as R_f **values** can be obtained from chromatograms. An R_f value is defined as the ratio of the distance travelled by the solute (for example P, Q or R) to the distance travelled by the solvent.

Separating solid/liquid mixtures

If a solid substance is added to a liquid it may **dissolve** to form a **solution**. In this case the solid is said to be **soluble** and is called the **solute**. The liquid it has dissolved in is called the **solvent**. An example of this type of process is when sugar is added to tea or coffee. What other examples can you think of where this type of process takes place?

Sometimes the solid does not dissolve in the liquid. This solid is said to be **insoluble**. For example, tea leaves themselves do not dissolve in boiling water when tea is made from them, although the soluble materials from which tea is made are seen to dissolve from them.

Filtration

When a cup of tea is poured through a tea strainer you are carrying out a **filtering** process. **Filtration** is a common separation technique used in chemistry laboratories throughout the world. It is used when a solid needs to be separated from a liquid. For example, sand can be separated from a mixture with water by filtering through filter paper as shown in Figure C2.9.

The filter paper contains holes that, although too small to be seen, are large enough to allow the molecules of water through but not the sand particles. It acts like a sieve. The sand gets trapped in the filter paper and the water passes through it. The sand is called the **residue** and the water is called the **filtrate**.

Crystallisation

In many parts of the world, salt is obtained from sea water on a vast scale. This is done by using the heat of the sun to evaporate the water to leave a saturated solution of salt known as brine. A **saturated solution** is defined as one that contains as much solute as can be dissolved at a particular temperature. When the solution is saturated the salt begins to **crystallise**, and it is removed using large scoops (Figure C2.10).

Figure C2.10 Salt is obtained in north-eastern Brazil by evaporation of sea water.

Simple distillation

If we want to obtain the solvent from a solution, then the process of **distillation** can be carried out. The apparatus used in this process is shown in Figure C2.11 on the next page.

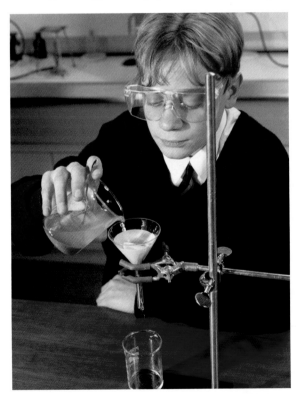

Figure C2.9 It is important when filtering not to overfill the filter paper.

Figure C2.12 This plant produces large quantities of drinking water in Saudi Arabia.

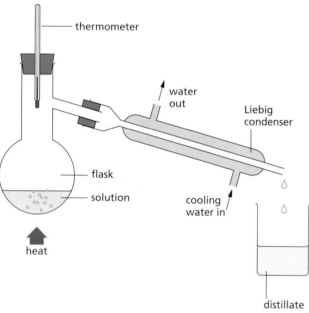

Figure C2.11 Water can be obtained from salt water by distillation.

Water can be obtained from salt water using this method. The solution is heated in the flask until it boils. The steam rises into the Liebig condenser, where it condenses back into water. The salt is left behind in the flask. In hot and arid countries such as Saudi Arabia this sort of technique is used on a much larger scale to obtain pure water for drinking (Figure C2.12). This process is carried out in a desalination plant.

Separating liquid/liquid mixtures

Liquids that mix with each other can be separated by **fractional distillation**. The apparatus used for this process is shown in the photo and diagram in Figure C2.13, and could be used to separate a mixture of ethanol and water.

Fractional distillation relies upon the liquids having different boiling points. When an ethanol and water mixture is heated the vapours of ethanol and water boil off at different temperatures and can be condensed and collected separately.

Ethanol boils at 78 °C whereas water boils at 100 °C. When the mixture is heated the vapour produced is mainly ethanol with some steam. Because water has the higher boiling point of the two, it condenses out from the mixture with ethanol. This is what takes place in the fractionating column. The water condenses and drips back into the flask while the ethanol vapour moves up the column and into the condenser, where it condenses into liquid ethanol and is collected in the receiving flask as the distillate. When all the ethanol has distilled over, the temperature reading on the thermometer rises steadily to 100 °C, showing that the steam is now entering the condenser. At this point the receiver can be changed and the condensing water can now be collected.

Questions

5 What is the difference between simple distillation and fractional distillation?
6 Devise a method for obtaining salt (sodium chloride) from sea water in the school laboratory.
7 Which method would you use to separate:
   a coffee grains from coffee solution
   b petrol (b.pt. 30 °C) from a crude oil
   c pieces of steel from engine oil
   d oxygen (b.pt. −183 °C) from liquid air?

Checklist

After studying Chapter C2 you should know and understand the following.

- The accuracy of each measurement in experimental work depends on the quality of the measuring apparatus (e.g. the thermometer or electronic balance) and on the skill of the scientists taking the measurement.
- Chromatography is a technique employed for the separation of mixtures of dissolved substances.
- Crystallisation is the process of forming crystals from a liquid.
- Distillate is the condensed vapour produced from a mixture of liquids on distillation.
- Distillation is the process of boiling a liquid and then condensing the vapour produced back into a liquid. It is used to purify liquids and to separate mixtures of liquids.
- Evaporation occurs when a solution is heated the solvent evaporates and leaves the solute behind.
- Filtrate is the liquid which passes through the filter paper during filtration.
- Filtration is the process of separating a solid from a liquid using a fine filter paper which does not allow the solid to pass through.
- Fractional distillation is a distillation technique used to separate a mixture of liquids that have different boiling points.
- If the solute does not dissolve in the solvent it is said to be insoluble.
- A mixture is a system of two or more substances that can be separated by physical means.
- The residue is the solid left behind in the filter paper after filtration has taken place.
- The R_f value is the ratio of the distance travelled by the solute to the distance travelled by the solvent in chromatography.
- A saturated solution is a solution which contains as much dissolved solute as it can at a particular temperature.
- If the solute dissolves in the solvent it is said to be soluble.
- Solute is the substance that dissolves (disappears) in(to) the solvent.
- Solution is the liquid formed when a substance (solute) disappears (dissolves) into another substance (solvent).
- Solvent is the liquid that the solute has dissolved in.

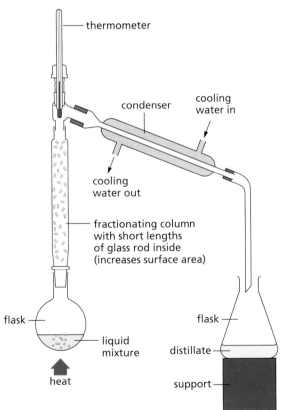

Figure C2.13 Typical fractional distillation apparatus.

Labels on figure: thermometer; condenser; cooling water in; cooling water out; fractionating column with short lengths of glass rod inside (increases surface area); flask; liquid mixture; heat; flask; distillate; support

C3 Atoms, elements and compounds

Combined

- Identify physical and chemical changes, and understand the differences between them
- Describe the differences between elements, mixtures and compounds, and between metals and non-metals
- Define the terms solvent, solute, solution and concentration
- Describe the structure of an atom in terms of a central nucleus, containing protons and neutrons, and 'shells' of electrons
- Describe the build-up of electrons in 'shells' and understand the significance of the noble gas electronic structures and of the outer electrons (the ideas of the distribution of electrons in s and p orbitals and in d block elements are not required)
- State the charges and approximate relative masses of protons, neutrons and electrons
- Define and use *proton number* (atomic number) as the number of protons in the nucleus of an atom
- Define and use *nucleon number* (mass number) as the total number of protons and neutrons in the nucleus of an atom
- Use proton number and the simple structure of atoms to explain the basis of the Periodic Table, with special reference to the elements of proton number 1 to 20
- Describe the formation of ions by electron loss or gain
- Use dot-and-cross diagrams to describe the formation of ionic bonds between Group I and Group VII
- Describe the formation of ionic bonds between metallic and non-metallic elements, to include the strong attraction between ions because of their opposite electrical charges
- Describe the lattice structure of ionic compounds as a regular arrangement of alternating positive and negative ions, exemplified by the sodium chloride structure
- State that non-metallic elements form simple molecules with covalent bonds between atoms
- Describe the formation of single covalent bonds in H_2, Cl_2, H_2O, CH_2, NH_3 and HCl as the sharing of pairs of electrons leading to the noble gas configuration, including the use of dot-and-cross diagrams
- Use and draw dot-and-cross diagrams to represent the bonding in the more complex covalent molecules such as N_2, C_2H_4, CH_3OH and CO_2
- Describe the differences in volatility, solubility and electrical conductivity between ionic and covalent compounds
- Explain the differences in melting point and boiling point of ionic and covalent compounds in terms of attractive forces

Co-ordinated

- Identify physical and chemical changes, and understand the differences between them
- Understand that some chemical reactions can be reversed by changing the reaction conditions (limited to the effects of heat and water on hydrated and anhydrous copper(II) sulfate and cobalt(II) chloride – concept of equilibrium is not required)
- Describe the differences between elements, mixtures and compounds, and between metals and non-metals
- Define the terms solvent, solute, solution and concentration
- Describe the structure of an atom in terms of a central nucleus, containing protons and neutrons, and 'shells' of electrons
- Describe the build-up of electrons in 'shells' and understand the significance of the noble gas electronic structures and of outer electrons (the ideas of the distribution of electrons in s and p orbitals and in d block elements are not required)
- State the charges and approximate relative masses of protons, neutrons and electrons
- Define and use *proton number* (atomic number) as the number of protons in the nucleus of an atom
- Define and use *nucleon number* (mass number) as the total number of protons and neutrons in the nucleus of an atom
- Use proton number and the simple structure of atoms to explain the basis of the Periodic Table, with special reference to the elements of proton number 1 to 20
- Define *isotopes* as atoms of the same element which have the same proton number but a different nucleon number
- Understand that isotopes have the same properties because they have the same number of electrons in their outer shell
- Describe the formation of ions by electron loss or gain
- Use dot-and-cross diagrams to describe the formation of ionic bonds between Group I and Group VII
- Describe the formation of ionic bonds between metallic and non-metallic elements, to include the strong attraction between ions because of their opposite electrical charges
- Describe the lattice structure of ionic compounds as a regular arrangement of alternating positive and negative ions, exemplified by the sodium chloride structure
- State that non-metallic elements form simple molecules with covalent bonds between atoms
- Describe the formation of single covalent bonds in H_2, Cl_2, H_2O, CH_4, NH_3 and HCl as the sharing of pairs of electrons leading to the noble gas configuration, including the use of dot-and-cross diagrams
- Describe the differences in volatility, solubility and electrical conductivity between ionic and covalent compounds

Physical and chemical changes

In Chapter C1 (p.181) we noted that when a substance changes its physical state from, say, a solid to a liquid then this is called a **physical change**. A good example of this process takes place when water, as ice, melts to form liquid water. In these changes no new substances are produced.

Figure C3.1 Magnesium burns brightly in oxygen to produce magnesium oxide.

When a new substance is formed during a chemical reaction, a **chemical change** has taken place.

magnesium + oxygen → magnesium oxide

$$2Mg(s) + O_2(g) \rightarrow 2MgO(s)$$

However, chemical changes do not just happen with reactions in test tubes. All living things need chemical changes to stay alive. For example we eat lots of food (Figure C3.2) so that we can stay healthy. The food has to be digested and this involves chemical changes.

Figure C3.2 This child is getting energy from the chemical changes that take place in her body from eating the apple.

Reversible reactions

Many of these chemical reactions cannot be reversed easily. However, there are some that can be reversed easily. For example, when metal hydrates such as copper(II) sulfate pentahydrate ($CuSO_4.5H_2O$) are heated the water of crystallisation is driven away. Anhydrous copper(II) sulfate remains. Also in this case a colour change takes place from blue to white.

copper(II) sulfate pentahydrate → anhydrous copper(II) sulfate + water

$$CuSO_4.5H_2O(s) \rightarrow CuSO_4(s) + 5H_2O(g)$$
(blue)   (white)

When water is added to anhydrous copper(II) sulfate the reverse process occurs. It turns blue and the pentahydrate is produced. This is an extremely exothermic process.

$$CuSO_4(s) + 5H_2O(g) \rightarrow CuSO_4.5H_2O(s)$$
(white)   (blue)

These processes give a simple example of a reversible reaction:

$$CuSO_4(s) + 5H_2O(l) \rightarrow CuSO_4.5H_2O(s)$$

● Elements

Robert Boyle used the name element for any substance that cannot be broken down further, into a simpler substance. This definition can be extended to include the fact that each element is made up of only one kind of atom. The word atom comes from the Greek word *atomos* meaning 'unsplittable'.

For example, aluminium is an element which is made up of only aluminium atoms. It is not possible to obtain a simpler substance chemically from the aluminium atoms. You can only make more complicated substances from it, such as aluminium oxide, aluminium nitrate or aluminium sulfate.

There are 118 elements which have now been identified. Twenty-five of these do not occur in nature and have been made artificially by scientists. They include elements such as curium and unnilpentium. Ninety-one of the elements occur naturally and range from some very reactive gases, such as fluorine and chlorine, to gold and platinum, which are unreactive elements.

All elements can be classified according to their various properties. A simple way to do this is to classify them as **metals** or **non-metals** (Figures C3.3 and C3.4). Table C3.1 shows the physical data for some common metallic and non-metallic elements.

You will notice that many metals have high densities, high melting points and high boiling points, and that most non-metals have low densities, low melting points and low boiling points. Table C3.2 summarises the different properties of metals and non-metals.

A discussion of the chemical properties of metals is given in Chapters C9 and C10. The chemical properties of certain non-metals are discussed in Chapters C9, C11 and C12.

Table C3.1 Physical data for some metallic and non-metallic elements at room temperature and pressure

Element	Metal or non-metal	Density/ g/cm³	Melting point/°C	Boiling point/°C
Aluminium	Metal	2.70	660	2580
Copper	Metal	8.92	1083	2567
Gold	Metal	19.29	1065	2807
Iron	Metal	7.87	1535	2750
Lead	Metal	11.34	328	1740
Magnesium	Metal	1.74	649	1107
Nickel	Metal	8.90	1453	2732
Silver	Metal	10.50	962	2212
Zinc	Metal	7.14	420	907
Carbon	Non-metal	2.25	Sublimes at 3642	
Hydrogen	Non-metal	0.07[a]	−259	−253
Nitrogen	Non-metal	0.88[b]	−210	−196
Oxygen	Non-metal	1.15[c]	−218	−183
Sulfur	Non-metal	2.07	113	445

Source: Earl B., Wilford L.D.R. Chemistry data book. Nelson Blackie, 1991 [a] At −254°C [b] At −197°C [c] At −184°C.

a gold is very decorative
Figure C3.3 Some metals.

b aluminium has many uses in the aerospace industry

c these coins contain nickel

Table C3.2 How the properties of metals and non-metals compare

Property	Metal	Non-metal
Physical state at room temperature	Usually solid (occasionally liquid)	Solid, liquid or gas
Malleability	Good	Poor – usually soft or brittle
Ductility	Good	
Appearance (solids)	Shiny (lustrous)	Dull
Melting point	Usually high	Usually low
Boiling point	Usually high	Usually low
Density	Usually high	Usually low
Conductivity (thermal and electrical)	Good	Very poor

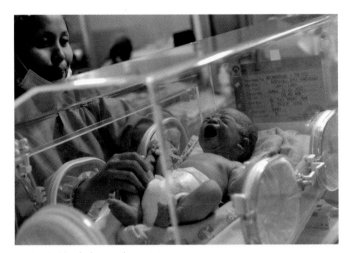

a a premature baby needs oxygen

b artists often use charcoal (carbon) to produce an initial sketch

c neon is used in advertising signs

Figure C3.4 Some non-metals.

● Compounds

Compounds are pure substances which are formed when two or more elements chemically combine together. Water is a simple compound formed from the elements hydrogen and oxygen (Figure C3.5). This combining of the elements can be represented by a word equation:

hydrogen + oxygen → water

| hydrogen a pure element | oxygen a pure element | hydrogen and oxygen mixed together | water a pure compound formed from hydrogen burning in oxygen |

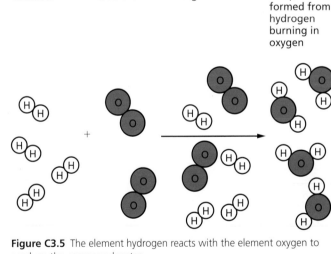

Figure C3.5 The element hydrogen reacts with the element oxygen to produce the compound water.

Water molecules contain two atoms of hydrogen and one atom of oxygen, and hence water has the **chemical formula** H_2O. Elements other than hydrogen will also react with oxygen to form compounds called oxides. For example, magnesium reacts violently with oxygen gas to form the white powder magnesium oxide (Figure C3.1). This reaction is accompanied by a release of energy as new chemical bonds are formed.

What is the difference between mixtures and compounds?

There are differences between compounds and mixtures. This can be shown by considering the reaction between iron filings and sulfur. A mixture of iron filings and sulfur looks different from the individual elements (Figure C3.6). This mixture has the properties of both iron and sulfur; for example, a magnet can be used to separate the iron filings from the sulfur (Figure C3.7).

Substances in a mixture have not undergone a chemical reaction and it is possible to separate them provided that there is a suitable difference in their physical properties. If the mixture of iron and sulfur is heated a chemical reaction occurs and a new substance is formed called iron(II) sulfide (Figure C3.6). The word equation for this reaction is:

$$\text{iron} + \text{sulfur} \xrightarrow{\text{heat}} \text{iron(II) sulfide}$$

Figure C3.6 The elements sulfur and iron at the top of the photograph, and (below) black iron(II) sulfide on the left and a mixture of the two elements on the right.

Figure C3.7 A magnet will separate the iron from the mixture.

During the reaction heat energy is given out as new chemical bonds are formed. This is called an **exothermic** reaction and accompanies a chemical change (Chapter C6, p.243). The iron(II) sulfide formed has totally different properties to the mixture of iron and sulfur (Table C3.3). Iron(II) sulfide, for example, would not be attracted towards a magnet.

Table C3.3 The iron(II) sulfide formed has totally different properties from the mixture of iron and sulfur

Substance	Appearance	Effect of a magnet	Effect of dilute hydrochloric acid
Iron	Dark grey powder	Attracted to it	Very little action when cold. When warm, a gas is produced with a lot of bubbling (effervescence)
Sulfur	Yellow powder	None	No effect when hot or cold
Iron/sulfur mixture	Dirty yellow powder	Iron powder attracted to it	Iron powder reacts as above
Iron(II) sulfide	Black solid	No effect	A foul-smelling gas is produced with some effervescence

Table C3.4 The major differences between mixtures and compounds

Mixture	Compound
It contains two or more substances	It is a single substance
The composition can vary	The composition is always the same
No chemical change takes place when a mixture is formed	When the new substance is formed it involves chemical change
The properties are those of the individual elements/compounds	The properties are very different to those of the component elements
The components may be separated quite easily by physical means	The components can only be separated by one or more chemical reactions

In iron(II) sulfide, FeS, one atom of iron has combined with one atom of sulfur. No such ratio exists in a mixture of iron and sulfur, because the atoms have not chemically combined. Table C3.4 summarises how mixtures and compounds compare.

Questions

3 Make a list of some other common mixtures, stating what they are mixtures of.
4 Make a list of some other common compounds, stating the elements they contain and giving the chemical formulae for them.

● Solutions

Some people cannot swallow tablets. To make medicines easier to swallow, many manufacturers now produce tablets which can be **dissolved** in water, such as the **soluble** aspirin shown in Figure C3.8.

Figure C3.8 The soluble aspirin dissolves in the water

When stirred in water the tablet dissolves, leaving no trace of solid. The solid aspirin has dissolved in the water to form a **solution**. The solid chemicals in the tablets are the **solute** and the water is the **solvent**. The solute dissolves in the solvent to form a solution. The process of dissolving involves the separation of the added solute particles as the liquid particles move about and collide with them (Figures C3.9 and C3.10).

a Initially, the aspirin particles hold one another together. Then the water particles begin to pull the particles in the aspirin tablet apart.

b Soon the aspirin particles are scattered in a random way through the water solvent. We now have a solution. The aspirin has dissolved in the water to form an aspirin solution.

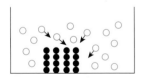

Figure C3.9 Particles in an aspirin tablet surrounded by water molecules.

Figure C3.10 A solution of aspirin in water.

If more aspirin tablets were dissolved in the solution then the solution would become more concentrated. There would be more particles of aspirin present in the same volume of water.

This concentration effect can be seen quite clearly if we use copper(II) sulfate solution. There is less copper(II) sulfate in the solution present in Figure C3.11a (it's a dilute solution) compared with that shown in Figure C3.11b (it's more concentrated).

Figure C3.11 a Left beaker containing dilute copper(II) sulfate solution; **b** right beaker containing more concentrated solution of copper(II) sulfate solution.

Other solvents

Water is not the only solvent which can be used to dissolve substances. There are many solutions which we use every day which use other solvents (Figure C3.12).

Figure C3.12 a Correction fluid is a solution of a plastic dissolved in a non-toxic, non-volatile hydrocarbon. **b** Aftershave lotion is a solution of perfume dissolved in ethanol.

● Atomic structure

We have already seen in Chapter C1 that everything you see around you is made out of tiny particles called atoms (Figure C3.13 on the next page). When John Dalton developed his atomic theory, about 200 years ago (1807/1808), he stated that the atoms of any one element were identical and that each atom was 'indivisible'. Scientists in those days believed that atoms were solid particles like marbles.

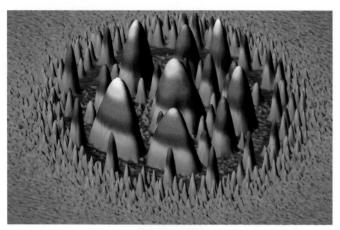

Figure C3.13 A micrograph of atoms.

However, in the last hundred years or so it has been proved by great scientists, such as Niels Bohr, Albert Einstein, Henry Moseley, Joseph Thomson, Ernest Rutherford and James Chadwick, that atoms are in fact made up of even smaller 'sub-atomic' particles. The most important of these are **electrons**, **protons** and **neutrons**, although 70 sub-atomic particles have now been discovered.

● Inside atoms

The three sub-atomic particles are found in distinct and separate regions. The protons and neutrons are found in the centre of the atom, which is called the **nucleus**. The neutrons have no charge and protons are positively charged. The nucleus occupies only a very small volume of the atom but is very dense.

The rest of the atom surrounding the nucleus is where electrons are most likely to be found. The electrons are negatively charged and move around very quickly in **electron shells** or **energy levels**. The electrons are held within the atom by an **electrostatic force of attraction** between themselves and the positive charge of protons in the nucleus (Figure C3.14).

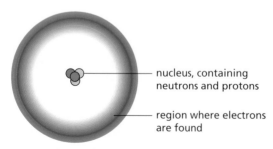

nucleus, containing neutrons and protons

region where electrons are found

Figure C3.14 Diagram of an atom.

About 1837 electrons are equal in mass to the mass of one proton or one neutron. A summary of each type of particle, its mass and relative charge is shown in Table C3.5. You will notice that the masses of all these particles are measured in **atomic mass units (amu)**. This is because they are so light that their masses cannot be measured usefully in grams.

Table C3.5 Characteristics of a proton, a neutron and an electron

Particle	Symbol	Relative mass/amu	Relative charge
Proton	p	1	+1
Neutron	n	1	0
Electron	e	1/1837	−1

Although atoms contain electrically charged particles, the atoms themselves are electrically neutral (they have no overall electric charge). This is because atoms contain equal numbers of electrons and protons. For example, the diagram in Figure C3.15 represents the atom of the non-metallic element helium. The atom of helium possesses two protons, two neutrons and two electrons. The electrical charge of the protons in the nucleus is, therefore, balanced by the opposite charge of the two electrons.

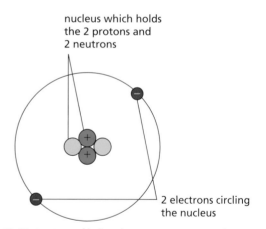

nucleus which holds the 2 protons and 2 neutrons

2 electrons circling the nucleus

Figure C3.15 An atom of helium has two protons, two electrons and two neutrons.

Proton number and nucleon number

The number of protons in the nucleus of an atom is called the **proton number** (or atomic number) and is given the symbol Z. Hence in the diagram shown in Figure C3.15, the helium atom has a proton number of 2, since it has two protons in its nucleus. Each element has its own proton number and no two different elements have the same proton number. For example, a different element, lithium, has a proton number of 3, since it has three protons in its nucleus.

Neutrons and protons have a similar mass. Electrons possess very little mass. So the mass of any atom depends on the number of protons and neutrons in its nucleus. The total number of protons and neutrons found in the nucleus of an atom is called the **nucleon number** (or mass number) and is given the symbol A.

$$\underset{(A)}{\text{nucleon number}} = \underset{(Z)}{\text{proton number}} + \underset{\text{neutrons}}{\text{number of}}$$

Hence, in the example shown in Figure C3.15 the helium atom has a nucleon number of 4, since it has two protons and two neutrons in its nucleus. If we consider the metallic element lithium, it has three protons and four neutrons in its nucleus. It therefore has a nucleon number of 7.

The proton number and nucleon number of an element are usually written in the following shorthand way:

$$\text{nucleon number } (A) \searrow {}_{2}^{4}\text{He} \leftarrow \text{symbol of the element}$$
$$\text{proton number } (Z) \nearrow$$

The number of neutrons present can be calculated by rearranging the relationship between the proton number, nucleon number and number of neutrons to give:

$$\underset{\text{neutrons}}{\text{number of}} = \underset{(A)}{\text{nucleon number}} - \underset{(Z)}{\text{proton number}}$$

For example, the number of neutrons in one atom of ${}_{12}^{24}\text{Mg}$ is:

$$\underset{(A)}{24} - \underset{(Z)}{12} = 12$$

and the number of neutrons in one atom of ${}_{82}^{207}\text{Pb}$ is:

$$\underset{(A)}{207} - \underset{(Z)}{82} = 125$$

Table C3.6 shows the number of protons, neutrons and electrons in the atoms of some common elements.

Isotopes

Not all of the atoms in a sample of chlorine, for example, will be identical. Some atoms of the same element can contain different numbers of neutrons and so have different nucleon numbers. Atoms of the same element which have the same proton number but different neutron numbers are called **isotopes**. The two isotopes of chlorine are shown in Figure C3.16 on the next page.

Table C3.6 Number of protons, neutrons and electrons in some elements

Element	Symbol	Proton number	Number of electrons	Number of protons	Number of neutrons	Nucleon number
Hydrogen	H	1	1	1	0	1
Helium	He	2	2	2	2	4
Carbon	C	6	6	6	6	12
Nitrogen	N	7	7	7	7	14
Oxygen	O	8	8	8	8	16
Fluorine	F	9	9	9	10	19
Neon	Ne	10	10	10	10	20
Sodium	Na	11	11	11	12	23
Magnesium	Mg	12	12	12	12	24
Sulfur	S	16	16	16	16	32
Potassium	K	19	19	19	20	39
Calcium	Ca	20	20	20	20	40
Iron	Fe	26	26	26	30	56
Zinc	Zn	30	30	30	35	65

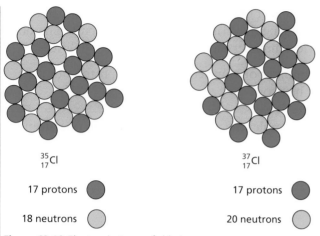

Figure C3.16 The two isotopes of chlorine.

Generally, isotopes behave in the same way during chemical reactions because they have the same number of electrons on their outer shell (see p.201).

The only effect of the extra neutron is to alter the mass of the atom and properties which depend on it, such as density. Some other examples of atoms with isotopes are shown in Table C3.7.

There are two types of isotopes: those which are stable and those which are unstable. The isotopes which are unstable, as a result of the extra neutrons in their nuclei, are **radioactive** and are called **radioisotopes**. For example, uranium-235, which is used as a source of power in nuclear reactors, and cobalt-60, which is used in radiotherapy treatment (Figure C3.17), are both radioisotopes.

Table C3.7 Some atoms and their isotopes

Element	Symbol	Particles present
Hydrogen	$^{1}_{1}H$	1 e, 1 p, 0 n
(Deuterium)	$^{2}_{1}H$	1 e, 1 p, 1 n
(Tritium)	$^{3}_{1}H$	1 e, 1 p, 2 n
Carbon	$^{12}_{6}C$	6 e, 6 p, 6 n
	$^{13}_{6}C$	6 e, 6 p, 7 n
	$^{14}_{6}C$	6 e, 6 p, 8 n
Oxygen	$^{16}_{8}O$	8 e, 8 p, 8 n
	$^{17}_{8}O$	8 e, 8 p, 9 n
	$^{18}_{8}O$	8 e, 8 p, 10 n
Strontium	$^{86}_{38}Sr$	38 e, 38 p, 48 n
	$^{88}_{38}Sr$	38 e, 38 p, 50 n
	$^{90}_{38}Sr$	38 e, 38 p, 52 n
Uranium	$^{235}_{92}U$	92 e, 92 p, 143 n
	$^{238}_{92}U$	92 e, 92 p, 146 n

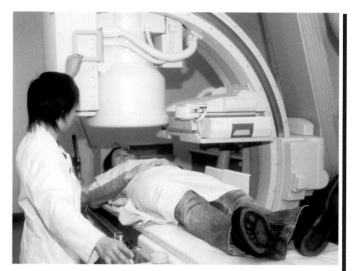

Figure C3.17 Cobalt-60 is used in radiotherapy treatment.

Questions

5 Calculate the number of neutrons in the following atoms:
   a $^{27}_{13}Al$ b $^{31}_{15}P$ c $^{262}_{107}Uus$ d $^{190}_{76}Os$

6 a Define the terms: proton, neutron and electron.
   b An atom X has a proton number of 19 and relative atomic mass of 39.
     i   How many electrons, protons and neutrons are there in an atom of X?
     ii How many electrons will there be in the outer energy level (shell) of an atom of X?
     iii What is the electronic configuration of X?

7 $^{60}_{31}Ga$ and $^{71}_{31}Ga$ are isotopes of gallium. With reference to this example, explain what you understand by the term isotope.

● The arrangement of electrons in atoms

The nucleus of an atom contains the heavier sub-atomic particles – the protons and the neutrons. The electrons, the lightest of the sub-atomic particles, move around the nucleus at great distances from the nucleus relative to their size. They move very fast in electron energy levels very much as the planets orbit the Sun.

It is not possible to give the exact position of an electron in an energy level. However, we can state that electrons can only occupy certain, definite energy levels and that they cannot exist between them. Each of the electron energy levels can hold only a certain number of electrons.

- First energy level holds up to two electrons.
- Second energy level holds up to eight electrons.
- Third energy level holds up to 18 electrons.

There are further energy levels which contain increasing numbers of electrons.

The third energy level can be occupied by a maximum of 18 electrons. However, when eight electrons have occupied this level a certain stability is given to the atom and the next two electrons go into the fourth energy level, and then the remaining ten electrons complete the third energy level.

The electrons fill the energy levels starting from the energy level nearest to the nucleus, which has the lowest energy. When this is full (with two electrons) the next electron goes into the second energy level. When this energy level is full with eight electrons, then the electrons begin to fill the third and fourth energy levels as stated above.

For example, a $^{16}_{8}O$ atom has a proton number of 8 and therefore has eight electrons. Two of the eight electrons enter the first energy level, leaving six to occupy the second energy level, as shown in Figure C3.18. The electron configuration for oxygen can be written in a shorthand way as 2,6.

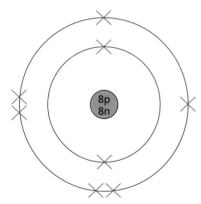

Figure C3.18 Arrangement of electrons in an oxygen atom.

There are 118 elements, and Table C3.8 on the next page shows the way in which the electrons are arranged in the first 20 of these elements. The way in which the electrons are distributed is called the **electronic structure** (or electron configuration). Figure C3.19 shows the electronic structure of a selection of atoms.

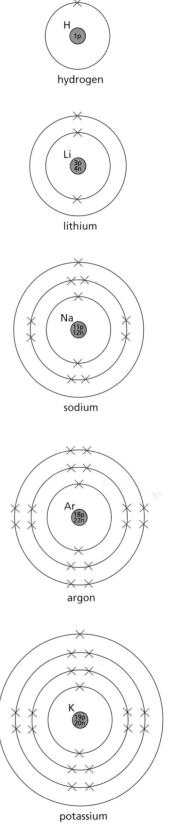

Figure C3.19 Electron arrangements of hydrogen, lithium, sodium, argon and potassium.

Table C3.8 Electronic structure of the first 20 elements

Element	Symbol	Proton number	Number of electrons	Electron structure
Hydrogen	H	1	1	1
Helium	He	2	2	2
Lithium	Li	3	3	2,1
Beryllium	Be	4	4	2,2
Boron	B	5	5	2,3
Carbon	C	6	6	2,4
Nitrogen	N	7	7	2,5
Oxygen	O	8	8	2,6
Fluorine	F	9	9	2,7
Neon	Ne	10	10	2,8
Sodium	Na	11	11	2,8,1
Magnesium	Mg	12	12	2,8,2
Aluminium	Al	13	13	2,8,3
Silicon	Si	14	14	2,8,4
Phosphorus	P	15	15	2,8,5
Sulfur	S	16	16	2,8,6
Chlorine	Cl	17	17	2,8,7
Argon	Ar	18	18	2,8,8
Potassium	K	19	19	2,8,8,1
Calcium	Ca	20	20	2,8,8,2

You will notice from Table C3.8 that the elements helium, neon and argon have completely full outer shells. In Chapter C9 you will see that these elements are known as the noble or inert gases and that they are generally very stable and unreactive (p.274–275). This is linked to the full outer shells that they possess. It would seem that when elements react to form compounds they do so to achieve full electron energy levels. This idea forms the basis of the electronic theory of chemical bonding.

● Electronic structure and the Periodic Table

The number of electrons in the outer energy level was discussed above. It can be seen that it corresponds with the number of the group in the Periodic Table in which the element is found. For example, the elements shown in Table C3.9 have one electron in their outer energy level and they are all found in Group I. The elements in Group 0, however, are an exception to this rule, as they have two or eight electrons in their outer energy level.

The outer electrons are mainly responsible for the chemical properties of any element, and, therefore, elements in the same group have similar chemical properties (Tables C.3.9, C.3.10 and C3.11).

Table C3.9 Electronic structure of the first three elements of Group I

Element	Symbol	Proton number	Electronic structure
Lithium	Li	3	2,1
Sodium	Na	11	2,8,1
Potassium	K	19	2,8,8,1

Table C3.10 Electronic structure of the first three elements of Group II

Element	Symbol	Proton number	Electronic structure
Beryllium	Be	4	2,2
Magnesium	Mg	12	2,8,2
Calcium	Ca	20	2,8,8,2

Table C3.11 Electronic structure of the first three elements in Group VII

Element	Symbol	Proton number	Electronic structure
Fluorine	F	9	2,7
Chlorine	Cl	17	2,8,7
Bromine	Br	35	2,8,18,7

The metallic character of the elements in a group increases as you move down the group. This is because electrons become easier to lose as the outer shell electrons become further from the nucleus. There is less attraction between the nucleus and the outer shell electrons because of the increased distance between them.

Questions

8 How many electrons may be accommodated in the first three energy levels?

9 What is the same about the electron structures of:
   a lithium, sodium and potassium
   b beryllium, magnesium and calcium?

● Ions and ionic bonding

Ions

An ion is an electrically charged particle. When an atom loses one or more electrons it becomes a positively charged ion. For example, during the chemical reactions of potassium, each atom loses an electron to form a positive ion, K^+.

$$_{19}K^+ \quad \begin{array}{l} 19 \text{ protons} \quad = 19+ \\ 18 \text{ electrons} \quad = 18- \\ \hline \text{Overall charge} = 1+ \end{array}$$

When an atom gains one or more electrons it becomes a negatively charged ion. For example, during some of the chemical reactions of oxygen it gains two electrons to form a negative ion, O^{2-}.

$$_8O^{2-} \quad \begin{array}{l} 8 \text{ protons} \quad = 8+ \\ 10 \text{ electrons} \quad = 10- \\ \hline \text{Overall charge} = 2- \end{array}$$

Table C3.12 shows some common ions. You will notice from Table C3.12 that:

- some ions contain more than one type of atom, for example NO_3^-
- an ion may possess more than one unit of charge (either negative or positive), for example Al^{3+}, O^{2-} or SO_4^{2-}.

Table C3.12 Some common ions

Name	Formula
Lithium ion	Li^+
Sodium ion	Na^+
Potassium ion	K^+
Magnesium ion	Mg^{2+}
Calcium ion	Ca^{2+}
Aluminium ion	Al^{3+}
Zinc ion	Zn^{2+}
Ammonium ion	NH_4^+
Fluoride ion	F^-
Chloride ion	Cl^-
Bromide ion	Br^-
Hydroxide ion	OH^-
Oxide ion	O^{2-}
Sulfide ion	S^{2-}
Carbonate ion	CO_3^{2-}
Nitrate ion	NO_3^-
Sulfate ion	SO_4^{2-}

Ionic bonding

Ionic bonds are usually found in compounds that contain metals combined with non-metals. When this type of bond is formed, electrons are transferred from the metal atoms to the non-metal atoms during the chemical reaction. In doing this, the atoms become more stable by getting full outer energy levels. For example, consider what happens when sodium and chlorine react together and combine to make sodium chloride (Figure C3.20).

sodium + chlorine → sodium chloride

Figure C3.20 The properties of salt are very different from those of the sodium and chlorine it was made from. To get your salt you would not eat sodium or inhale chlorine!

Sodium has just one electron in its outer energy level ($_{11}Na$ 2,8,1). Chlorine has seven electrons in its outer energy level ($_{17}Cl$ 2,8,7). When these two elements react, the outer electron of each sodium atom is transferred to the outer energy level of a chlorine atom (Figure C3.21 on the next page).

In this way both the atoms obtain full outer energy levels and become 'like' the nearest noble gas. The sodium atom has become a sodium ion and the process is known as **ionisation**. This sodium ion has an electron configuration like neon.

sodium atom → sodium ion + electron
$$Na(g) \quad \rightarrow \quad Na^+(g) \quad + \quad e^-$$

The chlorine atom has become a chloride ion with an electron configuration like argon.

chlorine atom + electron → chloride ion
$$Cl(g) \quad + \quad e^- \quad \rightarrow \quad Cl^-(g)$$

Only the outer electrons are important in bonding, so we can simplify the diagrams by missing out the inner energy levels (Figure C3.22 on the next page).

The charges on the sodium and chloride ions are equal but opposite. They balance each other and the resulting formula for sodium chloride is NaCl. These oppositely charged ions attract each other and are pulled, or **bonded**, to one another by strong electrostatic forces.

This type of bonding is called **ionic bonding**. The alternative name, **electrovalent bonding**, is derived from the fact that there are electrical charges on the atoms involved in the bonding.

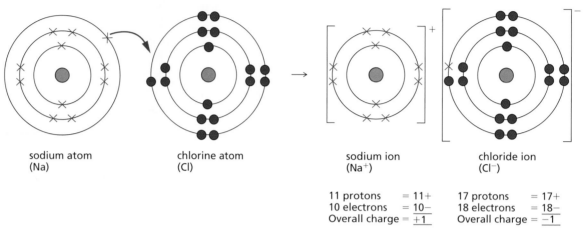

11 protons	= 11+	17 protons	= 17+
10 electrons	= 10−	18 electrons	= 18−
Overall charge	= +1	Overall charge	= −1

Figure C3.21 Ionic bonding in sodium chloride.

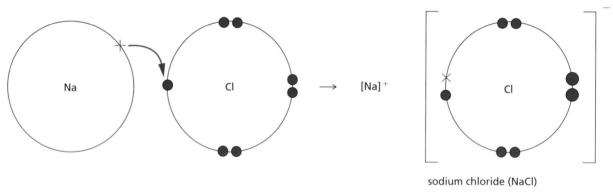

Figure C3.22 Simplified diagram of ionic bonding in sodium chloride.

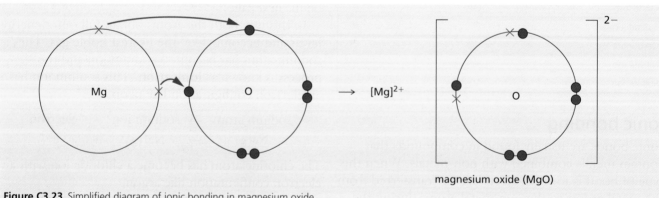

Figure C3.23 Simplified diagram of ionic bonding in magnesium oxide.

Figure C3.23 shows the electron transfers that take place between a magnesium atom and an oxygen atom during the formation of magnesium oxide.

Magnesium obtains a full outer energy level by losing two electrons. These are transferred to the oxygen atom. In magnesium oxide, the Mg^{2+} and

O^{2-} are oppositely charged and are attracted to one another. The formula for magnesium oxide is MgO.

Figure C3.24 shows the electron transfers that take place during the formation of calcium chloride. When these two elements react, the calcium atom gives each of the two chlorine atoms one electron. In this case, a compound is formed containing two chloride ions (Cl^-) for each calcium ion (Ca^{2+}). The chemical formula is $CaCl_2$.

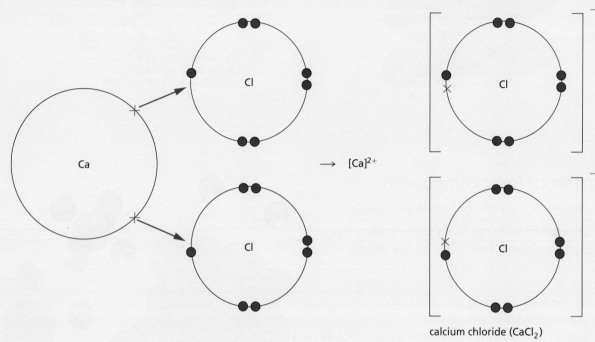

Figure C3.24 The transfer of electrons that takes place during the formation of calcium chloride.

Ionic structures

Scientists, using a technique called X-ray diffraction, have obtained photographs that indicate the way in which the ions are arranged in crystals of ionic substance such as sodium chloride. Figure C3.25 shows the structure of sodium chloride as determined by the X-ray diffraction technique.

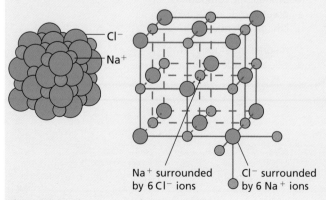

Figure C3.25 The structure of sodium chloride.

Ionic structures are solids at room temperature and have high melting and boiling points. The ions are packed together in a regular arrangement called a **lattice**. Within the lattice, oppositely charged ions attract one another strongly.

Figure C3.25 shows only a tiny part of a small crystal of sodium chloride. Many millions of sodium ions and chloride ions would be arranged in this way in a crystal of sodium chloride to make up the giant ionic structure. Each sodium ion in the lattice is surrounded by six chloride ions, and each chloride ion is surrounded by six sodium ions.

Not all ionic substances form the same structures. Caesium chloride (CsCl), for example, forms a different structure due to the larger size of the caesium ion compared with that of the sodium ion. This gives rise to the structure shown in Figure C3.26 on the next page, which is called a body-centred cubic structure. Each caesium ion is surrounded by eight chloride ions and, in turn, each chloride ion is surrounded by eight caesium ions.

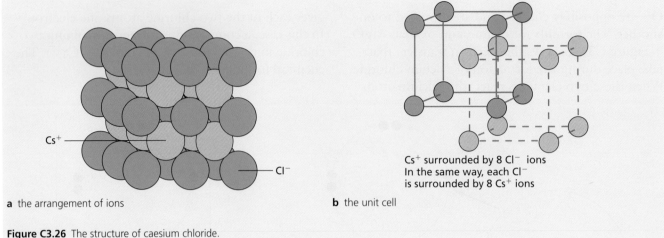

a the arrangement of ions

b the unit cell

Cs^+ surrounded by 8 Cl^- ions
In the same way, each Cl^-
is surrounded by 8 Cs^+ ions

Figure C3.26 The structure of caesium chloride.

Properties of ionic compounds

Ionic compounds have the following properties.

- They are usually solids at room temperature, with high melting points. This is due to the strong electrostatic forces holding the crystal lattice together. A lot of energy is therefore needed to separate the ions and melt the substance.
- They are usually hard substances.
- They usually cannot conduct electricity when solid, because the ions are not free to move.
- They mainly dissolve in water. This is because water molecules are able to bond with both the positive and the negative ions, which breaks up the lattice and keeps the ions apart. Figure C3.27 shows the interaction between water molecules (the solvent) and sodium and chloride ions from sodium chloride (the solute).
- They usually conduct electricity when in the molten state or in aqueous solution. The forces of attraction between the ions are weakened and the ions are free to move to the appropriate electrode. This allows an electric current to be passed through the molten compound (see Chapter C5, pp.230–231).

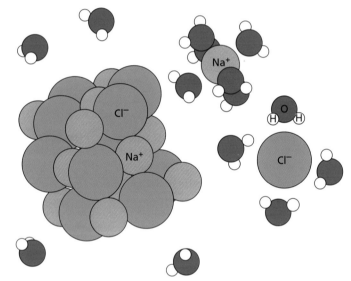

Figure C3.27 Salt (an ionic compound) dissolving in water.

Question

10 Draw diagrams to represent the bonding in each of the following ionic compounds:
  a potassium fluoride (KF)
  b lithium chloride (LiCl)
  c magnesium fluoride (MgF$_2$)
  d calcium oxide (CaO).

● Covalent bonding

Another way in which atoms can gain the stability of the noble gas electron configuration is by sharing the electrons in their outer energy levels. This occurs between non-metal atoms, and the bond formed is called a **covalent bond**. The simplest example of this type of bonding can be seen by considering the hydrogen molecule, H_2.

Each hydrogen atom in the molecule has one electron. In order to obtain a full outer energy level and gain the electron configuration of the noble gas helium, each of the hydrogen atoms must have two electrons. To do this, the two hydrogen atoms allow their outer energy levels to overlap (Figure C3.28a). A molecule of hydrogen is formed, with two hydrogen atoms sharing a pair of electrons (Figure C3.28a, b, c). This shared pair of electrons is known as a single covalent bond and is represented by a single line as in hydrogen:

$$H\text{—}H$$

A similar example exists in the diatomic halogen molecule chlorine, Cl_2 (Figure C3.29).

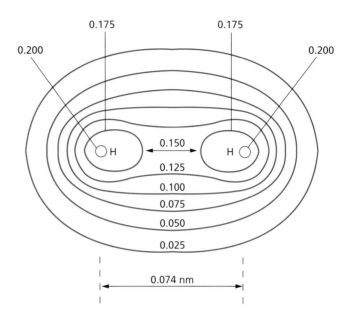

electron densities in electrons per cubic atomic unit of length

c Electron density map of a hydrogen molecule
Figure C3.28

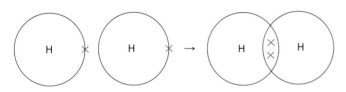

2 hydrogen atoms · hydrogen molecule (H_2)

a The electron sharing to form the single covalent bond in H_2 molecules

b Model of hydrogen molecule

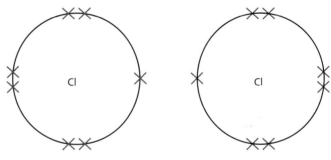

2 chlorine atoms

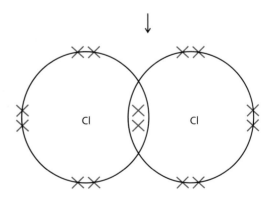

chlorine molecule (Cl_2)

Figure C3.29 The electron sharing to form the single covalent bond in Cl_2 molecules (sharing outer electron shells only).

Other covalent compounds

Methane (natural gas), CH₄, is a gas whose molecules contain atoms of carbon and hydrogen. The electron structures are:

$$_6C\ 2,4 \qquad _1H\ 1$$

The carbon atom needs four more electrons to attain the electron configuration of the noble gas neon. Each hydrogen atom needs only one electron to form the electron configuration of helium. Figure C3.30 shows how the atoms gain these electron configurations by the sharing of electrons. You will note that only the outer electron energy levels are shown. Figure C3.31 shows the shape of the methane molecule.

Ammonia, NH₃, is a gas containing the elements nitrogen and hydrogen. It is used in large amounts to make fertilisers. The electron configurations of the two elements are:

$$_7N\ 2,5 \qquad _1H\ 1$$

The nitrogen atom needs three more electrons to obtain the noble gas structure of neon. Each hydrogen requires only one electron to form the noble gas structure of helium. The nitrogen and

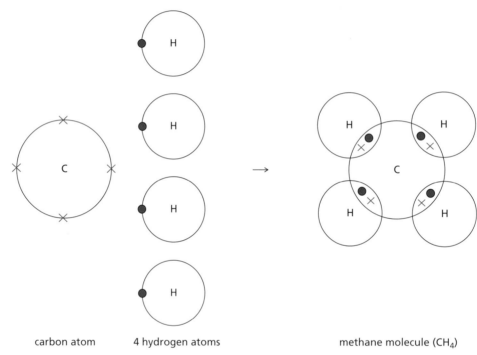

carbon atom   4 hydrogen atoms

methane molecule (CH₄)

Figure C3.30 Formation of methane.

the methane molecule is tetrahedral

a Methane molecule.

Figure C3.31

b Model of the methane molecule. The tetrahedral shape is caused by the repulsion of the C–H bonding pairs of electrons.

hydrogen atoms share electrons, forming three single covalent bonds (Figure C3.32). Unlike methane the shape of an ammonia molecule is pyramidal (Figure C3.33).

Water, H₂O, is a liquid containing the elements hydrogen and oxygen. The electronic structures of the two elements are:

$$_8O\ 2,6 \qquad _1H\ 1$$

The oxygen atom needs two electrons to gain the electron configuration of neon. Each hydrogen requires one more electron to gain the electron configuration of helium. Again, the oxygen and hydrogen atoms share electrons, forming a water molecule with two single covalent bonds as shown in Figure C3.34 on the next page. A water molecule is V-shaped (Figure C3.35 on the next page).

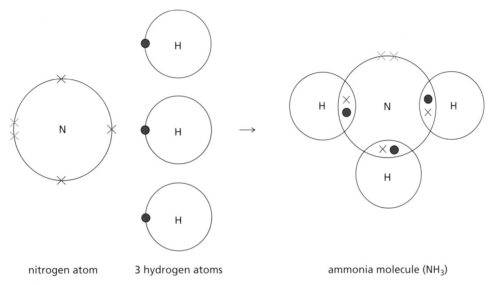

nitrogen atom　　3 hydrogen atoms　　　　ammonia molecule (NH₃)

Figure C3.32 Formation of ammonia.

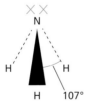

a Ammonia molecule

Figure C3.33

b Model of the ammonia molecule. The pyramidal shape is caused by the repulsion between the bonding pairs of electrons as well as the lone pair (or non-bonding pair) of electrons.

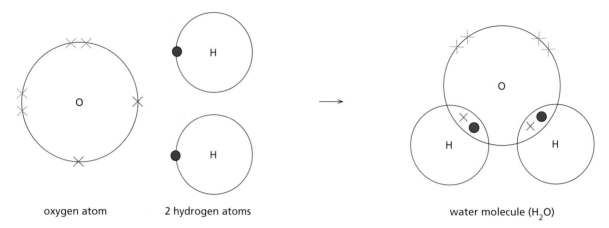

oxygen atom   2 hydrogen atoms   water molecule (H₂O)

Figure C3.34 Formation of water.

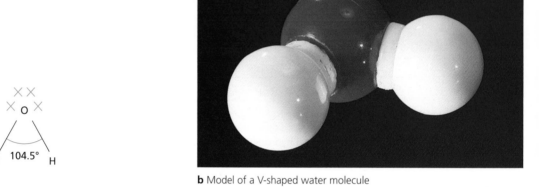

a Water molecule

Figure C3.35

b Model of a V-shaped water molecule

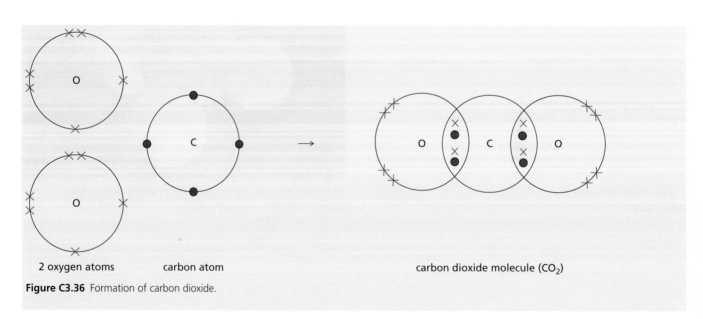

2 oxygen atoms   carbon atom   carbon dioxide molecule (CO₂)

Figure C3.36 Formation of carbon dioxide.

$$O=C=O$$

a carbon dioxide molecule, note the double covalent bond is represented by a double line

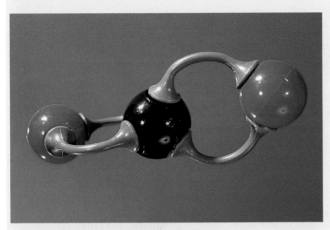

b model of the linear carbon dioxide molecule

Figure C3.37

Carbon dioxide, CO_2, is a gaseous compound found in the air. It contains the elements carbon and oxygen. The electronic structures of the two elements are:

$$_6C\ 2,4 \qquad _8O\ 2,6$$

In this case each carbon atom needs to share four electrons to gain the electron configuration of neon. Each oxygen needs to share two electrons to gain the electron configuration of neon. This is achieved by forming two **double covalent bonds** in which two pairs of electrons are shared in each case, as shown in Figure C3.36. Carbon dioxide is a linear molecule (Figure C3.37).

$$N\equiv N$$

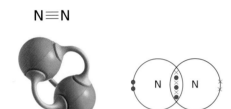

Figure C3.38 Nitrogen.

Nitrogen, N_2, is a gaseous element found in the air and it contains two atoms of nitrogen. The electronic structures of the nitrogen atoms is:

$$_6N\ 2,5$$

In this case each nitrogen atom needs to share three of its electrons to gain the electron configuration of neon. This is achieved by forming a triple covalent bond in which three pairs of electrons are shared in each case, as shown in Figure C3.38.

Ethene, C_2H_4, is a gaseous compound used in the manufacture of polyethene. It contains the elements carbon and hydrogen. The electronic structures of the two elements present are:

$$_6C\ 2,4 \qquad _1H\ 1$$

In this case each carbon atom needs to share its four electrons to gain the electron configuration of neon. Each hydrogen atom needs only one electron to gain the electron configuration of helium. This is achieved

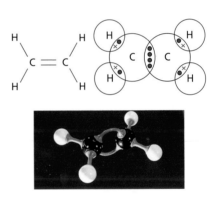

Figure C3.39 Ethene.

by forming a double covalent bond between the two carbon atoms as well two single covalent bonds between each carbon atom and two hydrogen atoms (Figure C3.39).

Methanol, CH_3OH, is a volatile liquid compound used in the manufacture of biodiesel. It contains the elements carbon, oxygen and hydrogen. The electronic structures of the three elements are:

$$_6C\ 2,4 \qquad _8O\ 2,6 \qquad _1H\ 1$$

In this case each carbon atom needs to share four electrons to gain the electron configuration of neon. Each oxygen needs to share two electrons to gain the electron configuration of neon. Each hydrogen

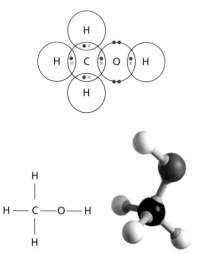

Figure C3.40 Methanol.

atom needs to share one electron to gain the electron configuration of helium. This is achieved by forming three carbon–hydrogen, one carbon–oxygen and one oxygen–hydrogen single covalent bonds as shown in Figure C3.40.

Questions

11 Draw diagrams to represent the bonding in each of the following covalent compounds:
   a tetrachloromethane (CCl_4)   **d** hydrogen chloride (HCl)
   b oxygen gas (O_2)   **e** ethane (C_2H_6)
   c hydrogen sulfide (H_2S)
12 The diagram shows the arrangement of the outer electrons only in a molecule of ethanoic acid.

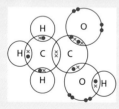

   a Name the different elements found in this compound.
   b What is the total number of atoms present in this molecule?
   c Between which two atoms is there a double covalent bond?
   d How many single covalent bonds does each carbon atom have?
   e Write a paragraph explaining the sorts of properties you would expect this substance to have.

Properties of covalent compounds

Covalent compounds have the following properties.

- As simple molecular substances, they are usually gases, liquids or solids with low melting and boiling points. The melting points are low because of the weak intermolecular forces of attraction which exist between simple molecules. These are weaker compared to the

strong covalent bonds. Giant molecular substances have higher melting points, because the whole structure is held together by strong covalent bonds.

It should be noted that in ionic compounds the interionic forces are much stronger than the intermolecular forces in simple covalent substances and so the melting and boiling points are generally higher.

- Generally, they do not conduct electricity when molten or dissolved in water. This is because they do not contain ions. However, some molecules actually react with water to form ions. For example, hydrogen chloride gas produces aqueous hydrogen ions and chloride ions when it dissolves in water:

$$HCl(g) \xrightarrow{\text{water}} H^+(aq) + Cl^-(aq)$$

- Generally, they do not dissolve in water. However, water is an excellent solvent and can interact with and dissolve some covalent molecules better than others. Covalent substances are generally soluble in organic solvents. For a further discussion of solubility of substances in organic solvents see Chapter C14.

Allotropy

When an element can exist in more than one physical form in the same state it is said to exhibit **allotropy** (or polymorphism). Each of the different physical forms is called an **allotrope**. Allotropy is actually quite a common feature of the elements the Periodic Table chapter C9, p.268. Some examples of elements which show allotropy are sulfur, tin, iron and carbon.

Allotropes of carbon

Carbon is a non-metallic element which exists in more than one solid structural form. Its allotropes are called **graphite** and **diamond**. Each of the allotropes has a different structure (Figures C3.42 and C3.43) and so the allotropes exhibit different physical properties (Table C3.13). The different physical properties that they exhibit lead to the allotropes being used in different ways (Table C3.14 and Figure C3.41).

Table C3.13 Physical properties of graphite and diamond

Property	Graphite	Diamond
Appearance	A dark grey, shiny solid	A colourless transparent crystal which sparkles in light
Electrical conductivity	Conducts electricity	Does not conduct electricity
Hardness	A soft material with a slippery feel	A very hard substance
Density/g/cm³	2.25	3.51

Figure C3.41 Uses of graphite (as a pencil 'lead' and in a squash racket) and diamond (as a toothed saw to cut marble and on a dentist's drill).

Table C3.14 Uses of graphite and diamond

Graphite	Diamond
Pencils	Jewellery
Electrodes	Glass cutters
Lubricant	Diamond-studded saws
	Drill bits
	Polishers

Graphite

Figure C3.42a (on the next page) shows the structure of graphite. This is a layer structure. Within each layer each carbon atom is bonded to three others by strong covalent bonds. Each layer is therefore like a giant molecule. Between these layers there are weak forces of attraction (van der Waals' forces) and so the layers will pass over each other easily.

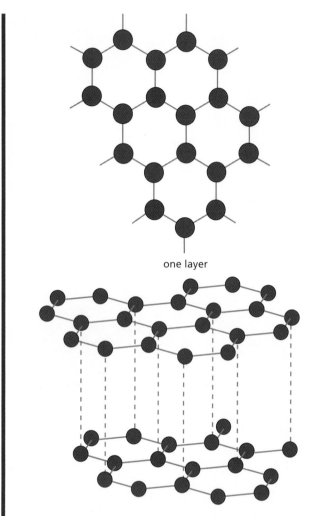

one layer

showing how the layers fit together

a a portion of the graphite structure

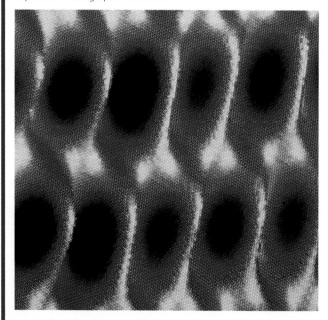

b piece of graphite as imaged through a scanning tunnelling microscope

Figure C3.42

With only three covalent bonds formed between carbon atoms within the layers, an unbonded electron is present on each carbon atom. These 'spare' (or **delocalised**) electrons form electron clouds between the layers and it is because of these spare electrons that graphite conducts electricity.

Diamond

In diamond the carbon atoms form a tetrahedral arrangement (Figure C3.43a (top)). This bonding scheme gives rise to a very rigid, three-dimensional structure and accounts for the extreme hardness of the substance. All the outer energy level electrons of the carbon atoms are used to form covalent bonds, so there are no electrons available to enable diamond to conduct electricity.

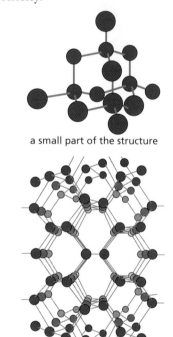

a small part of the structure

a view of a much larger part of the structure

a the structure of diamond

b the Regent Diamond has been worn by Queen Elizabeth II

Figure C3.43

In diamond the carbon atoms form a tetrahedral arrangement similar to that found in silicon(IV) oxide. This bonding scheme gives rise to a very rigid, three-dimensional structure and accounts for the extreme hardness of the substances silicon(IV) oxide and diamond. All the outer energy level electrons of the carbon atoms are used to form covalent bonds, so there are no electrons available to enable diamond to conduct electricity.

It is possible to manufacture the different allotropes of carbon. Diamond is made by heating graphite to about 300 °C at very high pressures. Diamond made by this method is known as industrial diamond. Graphite can be made by heating a mixture of coke and sand at a very high temperature in an electric arc furnace for about 24 hours.

Silicon(IV) oxide

Silicon is also a Group 4 non-metal element but with an electronic structure of 2,8,4. Crystalline silicon has the same structure as diamond. To change it into a similar macromolecular structure shown by silicon(IV) oxide, all you need to do is to modify the silicon structure by including some oxygen atoms. You will notice that each silicon atom is bridged to its neighbours by an oxygen atom forming the macromolecular structure shown in Figure C3.44. As before, the structure shown is just a tiny part of a giant structure extending into three dimensions. Again the structure of this substance gives rise to its properties. Since the structure is like that of diamond you might expect them to be similar. However, silicon(IV) oxide is not as hard as diamond, which is the hardest naturally occurring substance.

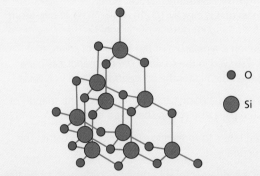

a the silicon(IV) oxide structure in quartz

b quartz is a hard solid at room temperature, it has a melting point of 1610 °C and a boiling point of 2230 °C

Figure C3.44

Questions

13 Explain why graphite conducts electricity while diamond does not.

14 From your knowledge of the structure of silicon dioxide and diamond predict the following properties of silicon dioxide: hardness, melting and boiling point, electrical conductivity and solubility.

Checklist

After studying Chapter C3 you should know and understand the following.

- Allotropy is the existence of an element in two or more different forms in the same physical state.
- Atomic mass unit is exactly 1/12th of the mass of one atom of the most abundant isotope of carbon-12.

- Concentration is a measure of the amount of solute that has been dissolved in the solvent. The more that has been dissolved then the higher the concentration and vice versa.

- Covalent bond is a chemical bond formed by the sharing of one or more pairs of electrons between two atoms.

- Delocalised refers to spreading out of electrons within the metal structure.

- Electron is a fundamental sub-atomic particle with a negative charge present in all atoms within energy levels around the nucleus.
- Electron energy levels (shells) are the allowed energies of electrons in atoms.
- Electronic structure (configuration) is a shorthand method of describing the arrangement of electrons within the energy levels of an atom.
- Electrostatic force of attraction is a strong force of attraction between opposite charges.

- Giant ionic structure is a lattice held together by the electrostatic forces of attraction between ions.

- Giant molecular or macromolecular substance is a substance containing thousands of atoms per molecule.

- Ion is an atom or group of atoms which has either lost one or more electrons, making it positively charged, or gained one or more electrons, making it negatively charged.
- Ionic (electrovalent) bond is a strong electrostatic force of attraction between oppositely charged ions.
- Ionisation is the process whereby an atom gains or loses an electron(s) to become an ion.
- Isotopes are atoms of the same element which possess different numbers of neutrons. They differ in nucleon number (mass number).

- Lattice is a regular three-dimensional arrangement of atoms/ions in a crystalline solid.

- Neutron is a fundamental, uncharged sub-atomic particle present in the nuclei of atoms.
- Nucleon number (mass number) Symbol A, is the total number of protons and neutrons found in the nucleus of an atom.
- Nucleus is found at the centre of the atom, and contains the protons and neutrons.
- Proton is a fundamental sub-atomic particle which has a positive charge equal in magnitude to that of an electron. Protons occur in all nuclei.
- Proton number (atomic number) Symbol Z, is the number of protons in the nucleus of an atom. The number of electrons present in an atom. It gives the order of the element within the Periodic Table.
- Radioactivity is a property of unstable isotopes. They disintegrate spontaneously to give off one or more types of radiation.
- Radioisotope is a radioactive isotope.

(C4) Stoichiometry

Combined	Co-ordinated
• Use the symbols of the elements and write the formulae of simple compounds • Deduce the formula of a simple compound from the relative numbers of atoms present • Deduce the formula of a simple compound from a model or a diagrammatic representation • Determine the formula of an ionic compound from the charges on the ions present • Construct and use word equations • Interpret and balance simple symbol equations • Construct and use symbol equations, with state symbols, including ionic equations	• Use the symbols of the elements and write the formulae of simple compounds • Deduce the formula of a simple compound from the relative numbers of atoms present • Deduce the formula of a simple compound from a model or a diagrammatic representation • Determine the formula of an ionic compound from the charges on the ions present • Construct and use word equations • Interpret and balance simple symbol equations • Construct and use symbol equations, with state symbols, including ionic equations • Deduce the balanced equation for a chemical reaction, given relevant information • Define *relative atomic mass*, A_r, as the average mass of naturally occurring atoms of an element on a scale where the $_{12}C$ atom has a mass of exactly 12 units • Define *relative molecular mass*, M_r, as the sum of the relative atomic masses (*relative formula mass* or M_r will be used for ionic compounds) • Define the *mole* in terms of a specific number of particles called Avogadro's constant • Use the molar gas volume, taken as 24 dm^3 at room temperature and pressure • Calculate stoichiometric reacting masses, volumes of gases and solutions, and concentrations of solutions expressed in g/dm^3 and mol/dm^3 (Calculations involving the idea of limiting reactants may be set.)

Chemical symbols and formulae

Symbols

Chemists use shorthand symbols to label the elements and their atoms. The symbol consists of one, two or three letters, the first of which must be a capital. Where several elements have the same initial letter, a second letter of the name or subsequent letter is added. For example, **C** is used for **carbon**, **Ca** for **calcium** and **Cl** for **chlorine**. Some symbols seem to have no relationship to the name of the element, for example **Na** for **sodium** and **Pb** for **lead**. These symbols come from their Latin names, natrium for sodium and plumbum for lead. A list of some common

elements and their symbols is given in Table C4.1 on the next page.

Chemical formulae

The formula of a compound is made up from the symbols of the elements present and numbers to show the ratio in which the different atoms are present. Carbon dioxide has the formula CO_2. This tells you that it contains one carbon atom for every two oxygen atoms. The 2 in the formula tells you that there are two oxygen atoms present in each molecule of carbon dioxide. For further discussion see p.210.

Table C4.2 (on the next page) shows the names and formulae of some common compounds which you will meet in your study of chemistry.

Table C4.1 Some common elements and their symbols, the Latin names of some of the elements are given in brackets

Element	Symbol	Physical state at room temperature and pressure
Aluminium	Al	Solid
Argon	Ar	Gas
Barium	Ba	Solid
Boron	B	Solid
Bromine	Br	Liquid
Calcium	Ca	Solid
Carbon	C	Solid
Chlorine	Cl	Gas
Chromium	Cr	Solid
Copper (Cuprum)	Cu	Solid
Fluorine	F	Gas
Germanium	Ge	Solid
Gold (Aurum)	Au	Solid
Helium	He	Gas
Hydrogen	H	Gas
Iodine	I	Solid
Iron (Ferrum)	Fe	Solid
Lead (Plumbum)	Pb	Solid
Magnesium	Mg	Solid
Mercury (Hydragyrum)	Hg	Liquid
Neon	Ne	Gas
Nitrogen	N	Gas
Oxygen	O	Gas
Phosphorus	P	Solid
Potassium (Kalium)	K	Solid
Silicon	Si	Solid
Silver (Argentum)	Ag	Solid
Sodium (Natrium)	Na	Solid
Sulfur	S	Solid
Tin (Stannum)	Sn	Solid
Zinc	Zn	Solid

Table C4.2 Names and formulae of some common compounds

Compound	Formula
Ammonia	NH_3
Calcium hydroxide	$Ca(OH)_2$
Carbon dioxide	CO_2
Copper sulfate	$CuSO_4$
Ethanol (alcohol)	C_2H_5OH
Glucose	$C_6H_{12}O_6$
Hydrochloric acid	HCl
Nitric acid	HNO_3
Sodium carbonate	Na_2CO_3
Sodium hydroxide	NaOH
Sulfuric acid	H_2SO_4

Petrol is a mixture of many different chemicals designed to burn effectively in the car engine to provide power to drive the car forward. One of the chemicals in petrol is heptane. Heptane is a molecule made from 7 carbon atoms and 16 hydrogen atoms bonded together. Knowing the relative number of each type of atom in a molecule allows us to write down its molecular formula. Heptane has the molecular formula C_7H_{16}.

The molecular formula can also be obtained from a structural or displayed formula. The molecule ethyl ethanoate can be shown as the structural formula below.

$$CH_3 - \overset{\overset{\textstyle O}{\|}}{C} - O - CH_2CH_3$$

The molecular formula of ethyl ethanoate is found by simply counting the number of each type of atom in the molecule. The molecular formula of ethyl ethanoate is $C_4H_8O_2$.

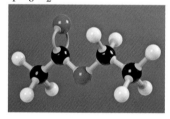

Another way of showing the molecule ethyl ethanoate is as a model. Here the carbon atoms are shown by the black spheres, the hydrogen atoms as white spheres and oxygen atoms as red spheres.

Questions

1 Write down the molecular formulae of the compounds with the following numbers and types of atom.
   a Ethanoic acid; two carbon atoms, four hydrogen atoms and two oxygen atoms.
   b Methyl ethanoate; three carbon atoms, six hydrogen atoms and two oxygen atoms.
2 Write down the molecular formulae of these molecules.

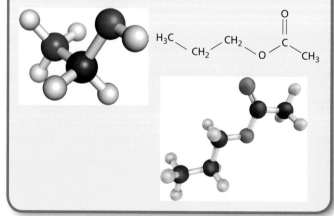

Formulae of ionic substances

On p.203 we saw that ionic compounds contain positive and negative ions, whose charges balance. For example, sodium chloride contains one Na^+ ion for every Cl^- ion, giving rise to the formula NaCl. This method can be used to write down formulae which show the ratio of the number of ions present in any ionic compound.

The formula of magnesium chloride is $MgCl_2$. This formula is arrived at by each Mg^{2+} ion combining with two Cl^- ions, and once again the charges balance. The size of the charge on an ion is a measure of its **valency** or **combining power**. Na^+ has a valency of 1, but Mg^{2+} has a valency of 2. Na^+ can bond (combine) with only one Cl^- ion, whereas Mg^{2+} can bond with two Cl^- ions.

Some elements, such as copper and iron, possess two ions with different valencies. Copper can form the Cu^+ ion and the Cu^{2+} ion, with valencies 1 and 2 respectively. Therefore it can form two different compounds with chlorine, CuCl and $CuCl_2$. We can also distinguish the difference by using Roman numerals in their names: CuCl is copper(I) chloride

and $CuCl_2$ is copper(II) chloride. Similarly, iron forms the Fe^{2+} and Fe^{3+} ions and so can also form two different compounds with, for example, chlorine: $FeCl_2$ (iron(II) chloride) and $FeCl_3$ (iron(III) chloride).

Table C4.3 shows the valencies of a series of ions you will normally meet in your study of chemistry.

You will notice that Table C4.3 includes groups of atoms which have net charges. For example, the nitrate ion is a single unit composed of one nitrogen atom and three oxygen atoms and has one single negative charge. The formula, therefore, of magnesium nitrate would be $Mg(NO_3)_2$. You will notice that the NO_3 has been placed in brackets with a $_2$ outside the bracket. This indicates that there are two nitrate ions present for every magnesium ion. The ratio of the atoms present is therefore:

$$Mg\,(N\,O_3)_2$$
$$1Mg:2N:6O$$

The charge on the element ion is often referred to as its **oxidation state**.

Table C4.3 Valencies (and oxidation states) of some elements (ions) and groups of atoms

	Valency (oxidation state)					
	1		**2**		**3**	
Metals	Lithium	(Li^+)	Magnesium	(Mg^{2+})	Aluminium	(Al^{3+})
	Sodium	(Na^+)	Calcium	(Ca^{2+})	Iron(III)	(Fe^{3+})
	Potassium	(K^+)	Copper(II)	(Cu^{2+})		
	Silver	(Ag^+)	Zinc	(Zn^{2+})		
	Copper(I)	(Cu^+)	Iron(II)	(Fe^{2+})		
			Lead	(Pb^{2+})		
			Barium	(Ba^{2+})		
Non-metals	Fluoride	(F^-)	Oxide	(O^{2-})		
	Chloride	(Cl^-)	Sulfide	(S^{2-})		
	Bromide	(Br^-)				
	Hydrogen	(H^+)				
Groups of atoms	Hydroxide	(OH^-)	Carbonate	(CO_3^{2-})	Phosphate	(PO_4^{3-})
	Nitrate	(NO_3^-)	Sulfate	(SO_4^{2-})		
	Ammonium	(NH_4^+)	Dichromate(VI)	$(Cr_2O_7^{2-})$		
	Hydrogencarbonate	(HCO_3^-)				
	Manganate(VII)	(MnO_4^-)				

The 'cross-over' method

A simple method to work out the formula of compounds is called the 'cross-over' method. In this method it is only necessary to 'swap' the valencies of the elements or groups of atoms (or radicals) concerned. This is easily done by 'crossing over' their valencies, by placing the valency of the first element after the symbol of the second and placing the valency of the second element or radical after the symbol of the first.

For example, in aluminium sulfide the valencies of the elements are:

$$Al = 3 \quad and \quad S = 2$$

Hence the chemical formula is Al_2S_3.
Similarly, in sodium sulfate the valencies are:

$$Na = 1 \quad and \quad SO_4 = 2$$

Hence the chemical formula is Na_2SO_4.

Questions

3 Using the information in Table C4.3, write the formulae for:
  a copper(I) oxide   d lead bromide
  b zinc phosphate   e potassium manganate(VII)
  c iron(III) chloride   f sodium dichromate(VI).
4 Using the formulae in your answer to question 3, write down the ratio of atoms present for each of the compounds.

● Chemical equations

Word equations

A word equation describes, in words, a chemical reaction. The reactants are named on the left-hand side of the arrow, which represents the reaction occurring, and the products appear on the right-hand side. The word equation for the reaction between zinc and hydrochloric acid to produce zinc chloride and hydrogen gas is:

zinc + hydrochloric acid → zinc chloride + hydrogen
reactants   **products**

Word equations are a useful way of representing chemical reactions but a better and more useful method is to produce a **balanced chemical equation**. This type of equation gives the formulae of the reactants and the products as well as showing the relative numbers of each particle involved.

Balanced equations often include the physical state symbols:

(s) = solid, (l) = liquid, (g) = gas, (aq) = aqueous solution

The word equation to represent the reaction between iron and sulfur is:

iron + sulfur $\xrightarrow{heat}$ iron(II) sulfide

When we replace the words with symbols for the reactants and the products and include their physical state symbols, we obtain:

$$Fe(s) + S(s) \xrightarrow{heat} FeS(s)$$

Since there is the same number of each type of atom on both sides of the equation this is a **balanced** chemical equation.

In the case of magnesium reacting with oxygen, the word equation was:

magnesium + oxygen $\xrightarrow{heat}$ magnesium oxide

When we replace the words with symbols for the reactants and the products and include their physical state symbols, it is important to remember that oxygen is a diatomic molecule:

$$Mg(s) + O_2(g) \xrightarrow{heat} MgO(s)$$

In the equation there are two oxygen atoms on the left-hand side (O_2) but only one on the right (MgO). We cannot change the formula of magnesium oxide, so to produce the necessary two oxygen atoms on the right-hand side we will need 2MgO – this means $2 \times$ MgO. The equation now becomes:

$$Mg(s) + O_2(g) \xrightarrow{heat} 2MgO(s)$$

There are now two atoms of magnesium on the right-hand side and only one on the left. By placing a 2 in front of the magnesium, we obtain the following balanced chemical equation:

$$2Mg(s) + O_2(g) \xrightarrow{heat} 2MgO(s)$$

This balanced chemical equation now shows us that two atoms of magnesium react with one molecule of oxygen gas when heated to produce two units of magnesium oxide.

Ionic equations

An ionic equation differs from a chemical equation in that it shows only the chemical species which take part in the chemical reaction. For example, when sodium chloride solution and silver nitrate solution react together the products are solid silver chloride and sodium nitrate solution.

The chemical equation for the reaction is:

$$NaCl(aq) + AgNO_3(aq) \rightarrow AgCl(s) + NaNO_3(aq)$$

The ions which are present in aqueous solution act independently of one another. In this reaction the sodium ions and nitrate ions start off as ions in solution and end the reaction unchanged. These ions are called spectator ions and they do not appear in the ionic equation. Without the spectator ions the ionic equation for the reaction is:

$$Ag^+(aq) + Cl^-(aq) \rightarrow AgCl(s)$$

An ionic equation has not only to balance in terms the number of each type of atom on each side of the equation but also each side of the equation must have the same overall charge.

Question

5 Write the word and balanced chemical equations for the reactions which take place between:
a calcium and oxygen   b copper and oxygen.

● Relative atomic mass

There are at present 118 different elements known. The atoms of these elements differ in mass because of the different numbers of protons, neutrons and electrons they contain. The actual mass of one atom is very small. For example, the mass of a single atom of sulfur is around:

0.000 000 000 000 000 000 000 000 053 16 g

This small quantity is not easy to work with so a scale called the **relative atomic mass** scale is used. In this scale an atom of carbon is given a relative

atomic mass, A_r, of 12.00. All other atoms of the other elements are given a relative atomic mass compared to that of carbon.

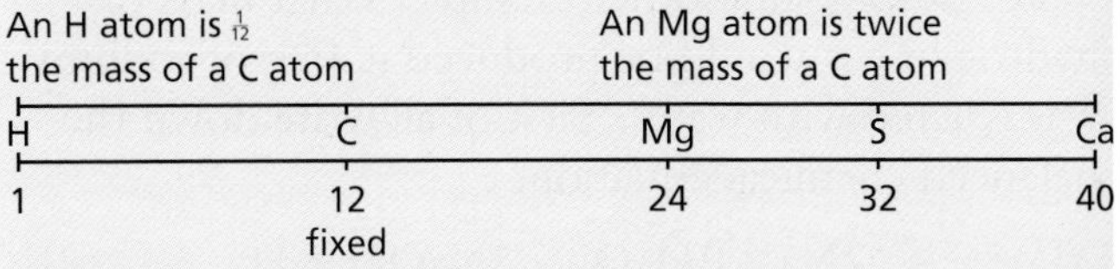

An H atom is ½ the mass of a C atom. An Mg atom is twice the mass of a C atom.

H	C	Mg	S	Ca
1	12 fixed	24	32	40

Figure C4.1 The relative atomic masses of the elements H, C, Mg, S and Ca.

● Reacting masses

Chemists often need to be able to show the relative masses of the atoms involved in a chemical process. For example, what mass of carbon dioxide would be produced if 6 g of carbon was completely combusted?

$$C + O_2 \rightarrow CO_2$$

Instead of using the actual masses of atoms we use the relative atomic mass to help us answer this type of question.

In the example above we can work out the **relative formula mass (RFM)** of molecules such as O_2 and CO_2 using the relative atomic masses of the atoms they are made from. The RFM is the sum of the relative atomic masses of all those elements shown in the formula of the substance.

O_2 has a relative formula mass of $2 \times 16 = 32$
CO_2 has a relative formula mass of $12 + (2 \times 16) = 44$

So we can now use the equation to answer the question asked earlier.

$$\begin{array}{ccc} C & + O_2 & \rightarrow CO_2 \\ 12 & 32 & 44 \end{array}$$

Converting these relative masses to actual masses by adding mass units, g, would give:

$$\begin{array}{ccc} C & + O_2 & \rightarrow CO_2 \\ 12 & 32 & 44 \\ 12\,g & 32\,g & 44\,g \end{array}$$

The above calculation shows that if 12 g of carbon were burned completely then 44 g of carbon dioxide gas would be formed. So 6 g of carbon burning would result in the formation of 22 g of carbon dioxide gas.

Let us look at another example. What mass of hydrogen gas would be produced if 46 g of sodium was reacted with water? First of all write down the balanced chemical equation:

$$2Na + 2H_2O \rightarrow 2NaOH + H_2$$

Next find the relative atomic mass of sodium from the Periodic Table and work out the relative formula masses of water, sodium hydroxide and hydrogen gas.
Relative atomic mass of sodium is 23.
Relative formula mass of water, H_2O, is $(2 \times 1) + 16 = 18$
Relative formula mass of sodium hydroxide is $23 + 16 + 1 = 40$
Relative formula mass of hydrogen gas, H_2, is $2 \times 1 = 2$
Now you can write these masses under the balanced chemical equation taking into account the numbers used to balance the equation.

$2Na$	$+$	$2H_2O$	$\rightarrow$	$2NaOH$	$+$	H_2
$2 \times 23 = 46$		$2 \times 18 = 36$		$2 \times 40 = 80$		2

These relative masses can now be converted into actual or reacting masses by putting in mass units, for example, grams.

$2Na$	$+$	$2H_2O$	$\rightarrow$	$2NaOH$	$+$	H_2
$2 \times 23 = 46$		$2 \times 18 = 36$		$2 \times 40 = 80$		2
46 g		36 g		80 g		2 g

So the answer to the question of what mass of hydrogen would be produced if 46 g of sodium was reacted with water is 2 g.

Questions

6 What mass of carbon dioxide gas would be produced if 10 g of calcium carbonate reacted with an excess of hydrochloric acid?
7 What mass of sulfur dioxide would be produced if 64 tonnes of sulfur was completely reacted with oxygen gas?

The mole

Chemists often need to know how much of a substance has been formed or used up during a chemical reaction (Figure C4.2). This is particularly important in the chemical industry, where the substances being reacted (the **reactants**) and the substances being produced (the **products**) are worth thousands of pounds. Waste costs money!

To solve this problem they need a way of counting atoms, ions or molecules. Atoms, ions and molecules are very tiny particles and it is impossible to measure out a dozen or even a hundred of them. Instead, chemists weigh out a very large number of particles.

This number is 6×10^{23} atoms, ions or molecules and is called **Avogadro's constant** after the famous Italian scientist Amedeo Avogadro (1776–1856). An amount of substance containing 6×10^{23} particles is called a **mole** (often abbreviated to mol). So, a mole of the element magnesium is 6×10^{23} atoms of magnesium and a mole of the element carbon is 6×10^{23} atoms of carbon (Figure C4.3).

Figure C4.2 The chemists at paint manufacturers need to know how much pigment is going to be produced.

222

a A mole of magnesium

b A mole of carbon

Figure C4.3

● Calculating moles

We can compare the masses of all the other atoms with the mass of carbon atoms. This is the basis of the **relative atomic mass scale**. Chemists have found by experiment that if you take the relative atomic mass of an element in grams, it always contains 6×10^{23} or one mole of its atoms.

Moles and elements

For example, the relative atomic mass (A_r) of iron is 56, so one mole of iron is 56 g. Therefore, 56 g of iron contains 6×10^{23} atoms.

The A_r for aluminium is 27. In 27 g of aluminium it is found that there are 6×10^{23} atoms. Therefore, 27 g of aluminium is one mole of aluminium atoms.

The mass of a substance present in any number of moles can be calculated using the relationship:

$$\frac{\text{mass}}{\text{(in grams)}} = \frac{\text{number}}{\text{of moles}} \times \frac{\text{mass of 1 mole}}{\text{of the element}}$$

Example 1

Calculate the mass of **a** 2 moles and **b** 0.25 mole of iron. (A_r: Fe = 56)

a mass of 2 moles of iron
= number of moles × relative atomic mass (A_r)
= 2 × 56
= 112 g

b mass of 0.25 mole of iron
= number of moles × relative atomic mass (A_r)
= 0.25 × 56
= 14 g

If we know the mass of the element then it is possible to calculate the number of moles of that element using:

$$\text{number of moles} = \frac{\text{mass of the element}}{\text{mass of 1 mole of that element}}$$

Example 2

Calculate the number of moles of aluminium present in **a** 108 g and **b** 13.5 g of the element. (A_r: Al = 27)

a number of moles of aluminium

$$= \frac{\text{mass of aluminium}}{\text{mass of 1 mole of aluminium}}$$

$$= \frac{108}{27}$$

= 4 moles

b number of moles of aluminium

$$= \frac{\text{mass of aluminium}}{\text{mass of 1 mole of aluminium}}$$

$$= \frac{13.5}{27}$$

= 0.5 mole

Moles and compounds

The idea of the mole has been used so far only with elements and atoms. However, it can also be used with compounds (Figure C4.4 on the next page).

What is the mass of 1 mole of water (H_2O) molecules? (A_r: H = 1; O = 16)

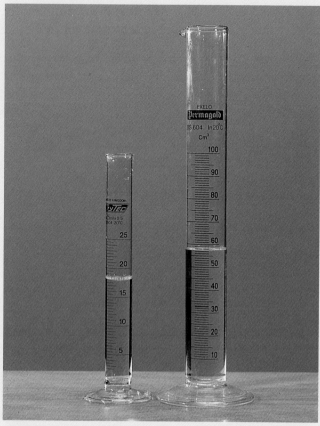

Figure C4.4 One mole of water (H₂O) (left) and one mole of ethanol (C₂H₅OH) (right) in separate measuring cylinders.

From the formula of water, H_2O, you will see that 1 mole of water molecules contains 2 moles of hydrogen (H) atoms and 1 mole of oxygen (O) atoms. The mass of 1 mole of water molecules is therefore:

$(2 \times 1) + (1 \times 16) = 18\,g$

The mass of 1 mole of a compound is called its molar mass. If you write the molar mass of a compound without any units then it is the relative formula mass, often called the **relative molecular mass** (M_r). So the relative formula mass of water is 18.

Now follow these examples to help you learn and understand more about moles and compounds.

Example 1

What is **a** the mass of 1 mole and **b** the relative formula mass (RFM) of ethanol, C_2H_5OH? (A_r: H = 1; C = 12; O = 16)

a One mole of C_2H_5OH contains 2 moles of carbon atoms, 6 moles of hydrogen atoms and 1 mole of oxygen atoms. Therefore:

mass of 1 mole of ethanol
$= (2 \times 12) + (6 \times 1) + (1 \times 16)$
$= 46\,g$

b The RFM of ethanol is 46.

Example 2

What is **a** the mass of 1 mole and **b** the RFM of nitrogen gas, N_2? (A_r: N = 14)

a Nitrogen is a diatomic gas. Each nitrogen molecule contains two atoms of nitrogen. Therefore:

mass of 1 mole of N_2
$= 2 \times 14$
$= 28\,g$

b The RFM of N_2 is 28.

The mass of a compound found in any number of moles can be calculated using the relationship:

mass of compound = number of moles of the compound × mass of 1 mole of the compound

Example 3

Calculate the mass of **a** 3 moles and **b** 0.2 moles of carbon dioxide gas, CO_2. (A_r: C = 12; O = 16)

a One mole of CO_2 contains 1 mole of carbon atoms and 2 moles of oxygen atoms. Therefore:

mass of 1 mole of CO_2
$= (1 \times 12) + (2 \times 16)$
$= 44\,g$

mass of 3 moles of CO_2
= number of moles × mass of 1 mole of CO_2
$= 3 \times 44$
$= 132\,g$

b mass of 0.2 mole of CO_2
= number of moles × mass of 1 mole of CO_2
$= 0.2 \times 44$
$= 8.8\,g$

If we know the mass of the compound then we can calculate the number of moles of the compound using the relationship:

$$\text{number of moles} = \frac{\text{mass of compound}}{\text{mass of 1 mole of the compound}}$$

Example 4

Calculate the number of moles of magnesium oxide, MgO, in **a** 80 g and **b** 10 g of the compound. (A_r: O = 16; Mg = 24)

a One mole of MgO contains 1 mole of magnesium atoms and 1 mole of oxygen atoms. Therefore:

mass of 1 mole of MgO
= (1 × 24) + (1 × 16)
= 40 g

number of moles of MgO in 80 g

$$= \frac{\text{mass of MgO}}{\text{mass of 1 mole of MgO}}$$

$$= \frac{80}{40}$$

= 2 moles

b number of moles of MgO in 10 g

$$= \frac{\text{mass of MgO}}{\text{mass of 1 mole of MgO}}$$

$$= \frac{10}{40}$$

= 0.25 moles

Moles and gases

Many substances exist as gases. If we want to find the number of moles of a gas we can do this by measuring the volume rather than the mass.

Chemists have shown by experiment that:

One mole of any gas occupies a volume of approximately 24 dm³ (24 litres) at room temperature and pressure (rtp). This quantity is also known as the molar gas volume, V_m.

Therefore, it is relatively easy to convert volumes of gases into moles and moles of gases into volumes using the following relationship:

$$\text{number of moles} = \frac{\text{volume of the gas (in dm}^3 \text{ at rtp)}}{24 \text{ dm}^3}$$
$$\text{of a gas}$$

or

$$\text{volume of} = \text{number of moles} \times 24 \text{ dm}^3$$
$$\text{a gas} \qquad \text{of gas} \qquad \text{(in dm}^3 \text{ at rtp)}$$

Example 1

Calculate the number of moles of ammonia gas, NH_3, in a volume of 72 dm³ of the gas measured at rtp.

$$\text{number of moles} = \frac{\text{volume of ammonia in dm}^3}{24 \text{ dm}^3}$$
$$\text{of ammonia}$$

$$= \frac{72}{24}$$

= 3 moles

Example 2

Calculate the volume of carbon dioxide gas, CO_2, occupied by **a** 5 moles and **b** 0.5 mole of the gas measured at rtp.

a volume of CO_2
= number of moles of CO_2 × 24 dm³
= 5 × 24
= 120 dm³

b volume of CO_2
= number of moles of CO_2 × 24 dm³
= 0.5 × 24
= 12 dm³

The volume occupied by one mole of any gas must contain 6 × 10²³ molecules. Therefore, it follows that equal volumes of all gases measured at the same temperature and pressure must contain the same number of molecules. This idea was also first put forward by Amedeo Avogadro and is called **Avogadro's Law**.

Moles and solutions

Chemists often need to know the concentration of a solution. Sometimes it is measured in grams per cubic decimetre (g/dm³) but more often concentration is measured in **moles per cubic decimetre (mol/dm³)**. When 1 mole of a substance is dissolved in water and the solution is made up to 1 dm³ (1000 cm³), a **1 molar (1 mol/dm³)** solution is produced. Chemists do not always need to make up such large volumes of solution. A simple method of calculating the concentration is by using the relationship:

$$\text{concentration (in mol/dm}^3) = \frac{\text{number of moles}}{\text{volume (in dm}^3)}$$

Example 1

Calculate the concentration (in mol/dm³) of a solution of sodium hydroxide, NaOH, which was made by dissolving 10 g of solid sodium hydroxide in water and making up to 250 cm³. (A_r: H = 1; O = 16; Na = 23)

1 mole of NaOH contains 1 mole of sodium, 1 mole of oxygen and 1 mole of hydrogen. Therefore:

mass of 1 mole of NaOH
$= (1 \times 23) + (1 \times 16) + (1 \times 1)$
$= 40\,g$

number of moles of NaOH in 10 g
$= \dfrac{\text{mass of NaOH}}{\text{mass of 1 mole of NaOH}}$
$= \dfrac{10}{40}$
$= 0.25$ moles

$(250\,cm^3 = \dfrac{250}{1000}\,dm^3 = 0.25\,dm^3)$

concentration of the NaOH solution
$= \dfrac{\text{number of moles of NaOH}}{\text{volume of solution (dm}^3)}$
$= \dfrac{0.25}{0.25}$
$= 1\,mol/dm^3$

Sometimes chemists need to know the mass of a substance that has to be dissolved to prepare a known volume of solution at a given concentration. A simple method of calculating the number of moles and so the mass of substance needed is by using the relationship:

number of = concentration × volume in solution
moles   (in mol/dm³)   (in dm³)

Example 2

Calculate the mass of potassium hydroxide, KOH, that needs to be used to prepare 500 cm³ of a 2 mol/dm³ solution in water. (A_r: H = 1; O = 16; K = 39)

number of moles of KOH

= concentration of solution × volume of solution
      (mol/dm³)   (dm³)

$= 2 \times \dfrac{500}{1000}$
$= 1$ mole

1 mole of KOH contains 1 mole of potassium, 1 mole of oxygen and 1 mole of hydrogen. Therefore:

mass of 1 mole of KOH
$= (1 \times 39) + (1 \times 16) + (1 \times 1)$
$= 56\,g$

Therefore:

mass of KOH in 1 mole
= number of moles × mass of 1 mole
$= 1 \times 56$
$= 56\,g$

Questions

Use the values of A_r which follow to answer the questions below.
H = 1; C = 12; N = 14; O = 16; Ne = 20; Na = 23; Mg = 24; S = 32; K = 39; Fe = 56; Cu = 63.5; Zn = 65.
One mole of any gas at rtp occupies 24 dm³.

8 Calculate the number of moles in:
   a 2 g of neon atoms
   b 4 g of magnesium atoms
   c 24 g of carbon atoms.
9 Calculate the mass of:
   a 0.1 mole of oxygen molecules
   b 5 moles of sulfur atoms
   c 0.25 mole of sodium atoms.
10 Calculate the number of moles in:
   a 9.8 g of sulfuric acid (H_2SO_4)
   b 40 g of sodium hydroxide (NaOH)
   c 720 g of iron(II) oxide (FeO).
11 Calculate the mass of:
   a 2 moles of zinc oxide (ZnO)
   b 0.25 mole of hydrogen sulfide (H_2S)
   c 0.35 mole of copper(II) sulfate ($CuSO_4$).
12 Calculate the number of moles at rtp in:
   a 2 dm³ of carbon dioxide (CO_2)
   b 240 dm³ of sulfur dioxide (SO_2)
   c 20 cm³ of carbon monoxide (CO).
13 Calculate the volume of:
   a 0.3 mole of hydrogen chloride (HCl)
   b 4.4 g of carbon dioxide
   c 34 g of ammonia (NH_3).
14 Calculate the concentration of solutions containing:
   a 0.2 mole of sodium hydroxide dissolved in water and made up to 100 cm³
   b 9.8 g of sulfuric acid dissolved in water and made up to 500 cm³.
15 Calculate the mass of:
   a copper(II) sulfate ($CuSO_4$) which needs to be used to prepare 500 cm³ of a 0.1 mol/dm³ solution
   b potassium nitrate (KNO_3) which needs to be used to prepare 200 cm³ of a 2 mol/dm³ solution.

● Moles and chemical equations

When we write a balanced chemical equation we are indicating the numbers of moles of reactants and products involved in the chemical reaction. Consider the reaction between magnesium and oxygen.

magnesium + oxygen → magnesium oxide
$2Mg(s)$ + $O_2(g)$ → $2MgO(s)$

This shows that 2 moles of magnesium react with 1 mole of oxygen to give 2 moles of magnesium oxide.

Using the ideas of moles and masses we can use this information to calculate the quantities of the different chemicals involved.

$$2Mg(s) + O_2(g) \rightarrow 2MgO(s)$$
$$2 \text{ moles} \quad 1 \text{ mole} \quad 2 \text{ moles}$$
$$2 \times 24 \quad 1 \times (16 \times 2) \quad 2 \times (24 + 16)$$
$$= 48\,g \quad = 32\,g \quad = 80\,g$$

You will notice that the total mass of reactants is equal to the total mass of product. This is true for any chemical reaction and it is known as the **Law of conservation of mass**. This law was understood by the Greeks but was first clearly formulated by Antoine Lavoisier in 1774. Chemists can use this idea to calculate masses of products formed and reactants used in chemical processes before they are carried out.

Example 1 – using a solid

Lime (calcium oxide, CaO) is used in the manufacture of mortar. It is manufactured in large quantities in Europe (see Figure C4.5) by heating limestone (calcium carbonate, $CaCO_3$).

The equation for the process is:

$$CaCO_3(s) \rightarrow CaO(s) + CO_2(g)$$
$$1 \text{ mole} \quad 1 \text{ mole} \quad 1 \text{ mole}$$
$$(40 + 12 + (3 \times 16)) \quad 40 + 16 \quad 12 + (2 \times 16)$$
$$= 100\,g \quad = 56\,g \quad = 44\,g$$

Calculate the amount of lime produced when 10 tonnes of limestone are heated (Figure C4.6). (A_r: C = 12; O = 16; Ca = 40)

1 tonne (t) = 1000 kg
1 kg = 1000 g

From this relationship between grams and tonnes we can replace the masses in grams by masses in tonnes.

Figure C4.5 A rotary kiln for burning (calcining) limestone into lime, located in Moha, Belgium.

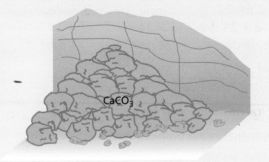

10 tonnes of limestone

heat

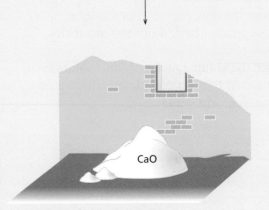

CaO

? tonnes of lime

Figure C4.6 How much lime is produced?

$$CaCO_3(s) \rightarrow CaO(s) + CO_2(g)$$

Hence
100 t	56 t	44 t
10 t	5.6 t	4.4 t

The equation now shows that 100 t of limestone will produce 56 t of lime. Therefore, 10 t of limestone will produce 5.6 t of lime.

Example 2 – using a gas

Many chemical processes involve gases. The volume of a gas is measured more easily than its mass. This example shows how chemists work out the volumes of gaseous reactants and products needed using Avogadro's Law and the idea of moles.

Some rockets use hydrogen gas as a fuel. When hydrogen burns in oxygen it forms water vapour. Calculate the volumes of **a** $O_2(g)$ used and **b** water, $H_2O(g)$, produced if 960 dm³ of hydrogen gas, $H_2(g)$, were burned in oxygen. (A_r: H = 1; O = 16) Assume 1 mole of any gas occupies a volume of 24 dm³.

$$2H_2(g) + O_2(g) \rightarrow 2H_2O(g)$$

2 moles	1 mole	2 moles
2 × 24	1 × 24	2 × 24
= 48 dm³	= 24 dm³	= 48 dm³

Therefore:

(× 2)	96 dm³	48 dm³	96 dm³
(× 10)	960 dm³	480 dm³	960 dm³

When 960 dm³ of hydrogen are burned in oxygen:

a 480 dm³ of oxygen are required and
b 960 dm³ of $H_2O(g)$ are produced.

Example 3 – using a solution

Chemists usually carry out reactions using solutions. If they know the concentration of the solution(s) they are using they can find out the quantities reacting.

Calculate the volume of 1 mol/dm³ solution of H_2SO_4 required to react completely with 6 g of magnesium. (A_r: Mg = 24)

number of moles of magnesium

$$= \frac{\text{mass of magnesium}}{\text{mass of 1 mole of magnesium}}$$

$$= \frac{6}{24}$$

$$= 0.25 \text{ moles}$$

$$Mg(s) + H_2SO_4(aq) \rightarrow MgSO_4(aq) + H_2(g)$$

1 mole	1 mole	1 mole	1 mole
0.25 mol	0.25 mol	0.25 mol	0.25 mol

So 0.25 mol of $H_2SO_4(aq)$ is required. Using:

volume of $H_2SO_4(aq)$ (dm³)

$$= \frac{\text{moles of } H_2SO_4}{\text{concentration of } H_2SO_4 \text{ (mol/dm}^3\text{)}}$$

$$= \frac{0.25}{1}$$

$$= 0.25 \text{ dm}^3 \text{ or } 250 \text{ cm}^3$$

Example 4 – using a solution

What is the concentration of sodium hydroxide solution used in the following neutralisation reaction? 40 cm³ of 0.2 mol/dm³ solution of hydrochloric acid just neutralised 20 cm³ of sodium hydroxide solution.

number of moles of HCl used
= concentration (mol/dm³) × volume (dm³)
= 0.2 × 0.04
= 0.008 moles

$$HCl(aq) + NaOH(aq) \rightarrow NaCl(aq) + H_2O(l)$$

1 mole	1 mole	1 mole	1 mole
0.008 mol	0.008 mol	0.008 mol	0.008 mol

You will see that 0.008 mole of NaOH was present. The concentration of the $NaOH(aq)$ is given by:

concentration of NaOH (mol/dm³)

$$= \frac{\text{number of moles of NaOH}}{\text{volume of NaOH (dm}^3\text{)}}$$

(volume of NaOH in dm³ $= \frac{20}{1000} = 0.02$)

$$= \frac{0.008}{0.02}$$

$$= 0.4 \text{ mol/dm}^3$$

Limiting reactant

A chemical reaction stops when one of the reactants has been completely used up. This reactant is known as the limiting reactant. It is this amount of this reactant which was used up in the reaction which determines the amount of the products which are made. It is, therefore, important that the limiting reactant is determined before trying to determine how much of a product is made during at reaction.

For example, when 2.4 g of magnesium reacts with 50 cm^3 of 2 mol/dm^3 hydrochloric acid what volume of hydrogen gas will be produced?

The chemical equation for this reaction is:

$Mg(s) + 2HCl(aq) \rightarrow MgCl_2(aq) + H_2(g)$

Moles of magnesium reacting = 2.4/24
= 0.1 moles

Moles of hydrochloric acid reacting = 2 × 50/1000
= 0.1 moles

So, we can see that the reaction starts with the same amount of magnesium and hydrochloric acid. From the balanced chemical equation, you can see there is a 1:2 mole ratio between magnesium and hydrochloric acid, so 0.1 moles of magnesium will react with 0.2 moles of hydrochloric acid. Since we have only used 0.1 moles of hydrochloric acid this will all be used up in the reaction. The hydrochloric acid is the limiting reactant. The magnesium is in excess, 0.05 moles of it will be left at the end of the reaction.

So when we determine the volume of hydrogen gas produced it is the amount of hydrochloric acid that we must use in the calculation.

There is a 2:1 mole ratio between hydrochloric acid and hydrogen so 0.1 moles of hydrochloric acid will give 0.05 moles of hydrogen gas.

Volume of hydrogen gas = 0.05 × 24 = 1.2 dm^3.

Questions

16 This question concerns the reaction of copper(ii) carbonate with dilute hydrochloric acid. The equation for the reaction is:
$CuCO_3(s) + 2HCl(aq) \rightarrow CuCl_2(aq) + CO_2(aq) + H_2O(l)$
Calculate the mass of copper(ii) carbonate used to produce 60 cm^3 of carbon dioxide. One mole of a gas occupies 24 dm^3 at room temperature and pressure (rtp).)

17 0.048 g of magnesium was reacted with excess dilute hydrochloric acid at room temperature and pressure. The hydrogen gas given off was collected.

a Write a word and balanced symbol equation for the reaction taking place.
b Draw a diagram of an apparatus which could be used to carry out this experiment and collect the hydrogen gas.
c How many moles of magnesium were used?
d Using the equation you have written in your answer to **a**, calculate the number of moles of hydrogen and hence the volume of this gas produced.
e Calculate the volume of a solution containing 0.1 mol/dm^3 hydrochloric acid which would be needed to react exactly with 0.048 g of magnesium.

Checklist

After studying Chapter C4 you should know and understand the following.

- Avogadro's Law states that equal volumes of all gases measured under the same conditions of temperature and pressure contain equal numbers of molecules.
- To calculate moles of compounds
mass of compound (in grams) =
   number of moles × mass of 1 mole of compound
number of moles = $\dfrac{\text{mass of compound}}{\text{mass of 1 mole of compound}}$
- To calculate moles of elements
mass of compound (in grams) =
   number of moles × mass of 1 mole of compound
number of moles = $\dfrac{\text{mass of the element}}{\text{mass of 1 mole of that element}}$
- To calculate moles of gases
1 mole of any gas occupies 24 dm^3 (litres) at room temperature and pressure (rtp).
number of moles of gas = $\dfrac{\text{volume of the gas (in dm}^3\text{ at rtp)}}{24\,\text{dm}^3}$

- To calculate moles of solutions
concentration of a solution (in mol/dm^3) = number of moles of solute volume (in dm^3)
number of moles = concentration (mol/dm^3) × volume of solution (in dm^3)
- One mole is the amount of substance which contains 6×10^{23} atoms, ions or molecules. This number is called Avogadro's constant.
- Atoms – 1 mole of atoms has a mass equal to the relative atomic mass (A_r) in grams.
- Molecules – 1 mole of molecules has a mass equal to the relative molecular mass (M_r) in grams.
- Molecular formula shows the actual number of atoms of each element present in one molecule.
- Relative formula mass (RFM) is the sum of the relative atomic masses of all those elements shown in the formula of the substance. This is often referred to as the relative molecular mass (M_r).

Electricity and chemistry

C5

<table>
<tr><th>Combined</th><th>Co-ordinated</th></tr>
<tr><td>

- Define *electrolysis* as the breakdown of an ionic compound when molten or in aqueous solution by the passage of electricity
- Use the terms *inert electrode, electrolyte, anode* and *cathode*
- Describe electrolysis in terms of the ions present and the reactions at the electrodes, in terms of gain of electrons by cations and loss of electrons by anions to form atoms
- Describe the electrode products and the observations made, using inert electrodes (platinum or carbon), in the electrolysis of: molten lead(ɪɪ) bromide; concentrated aqueous sodium chloride; dilute sulfuric acid
- Predict the products of the electrolysis of a specified molten binary compound

</td><td>

- Define *electrolysis* as the breakdown of an ionic compound when molten or in aqueous solution by the passage of electricity
- Use the terms *inert electrode, electrolyte, anode* and *cathode*
- Describe electrolysis in terms of the ions present and the reactions at the electrodes, in terms of gain of electrons by cations and loss of electrons by anions to form atoms
- Describe the electrode products, using inert electrodes (platinum or carbon), in the electrolysis of: molten lead(ɪɪ) bromide; concentrated aqueous sodium chloride; *dilute sulfuric acid*
- State the general principle that metals or hydrogen are formed at the negative electrode (cathode), and that non-metals (other than hydrogen) are formed at the positive electrode (anode)
- Relate the products of electrolysis to the electrolyte and electrodes used, exemplified by the specific examples in the Core together with aqueous copper(ɪɪ) sulfate using carbon electrodes and using copper electrodes (as used in the refining of copper)
- Construct simple ionic half-equations for the formation of elements at the cathode

- Describe electroplating with copper
- Predict the products of the electrolysis of a specified molten binary compound
- Describe, in outline, the chemistry of the manufacture of: aluminium from pure aluminium oxide in molten cryolite; chlorine, hydrogen and sodium hydroxide from concentrated aqueous sodium chloride
(Starting materials and essential conditions should be given but not technical details or diagrams.)

</td></tr>
</table>

What do all the items in the photographs shown in Figure C5.1 have in common? They all involve electricity through a process known as **electrolysis**. Electrolysis is the breakdown of an ionic compound, molten or in solution, by the passage of electricity through it. The substance which is decomposed is called the **electrolyte** (Figure C5.2). An electrolyte is a substance that conducts electricity when in the molten state or in solution.

The electricity is carried through the electrolyte by **ions**. In the molten state and in solution the ions are free to move to the appropriate electrodes due to weakened forces of attraction between them.

- Substances that do not conduct electricity when in the molten state or in solution are called **non-electrolytes**.

- Substances that conduct electricity **to a small extent** in the molten state or in solution are called **weak electrolytes**.

The electric current enters and leaves the electrolyte through **electrodes**, which are usually made of unreactive metals such as platinum or of the non-metal carbon (graphite). These are said to be **inert** electrodes because they do not react with the products of electrolysis. The names given to the two electrodes are **cathode**, the negative electrode which attracts **cations** (positively charged ions), and **anode**, the positive electrode which attracts **anions** (negatively charged ions).

a This watch has a thin coating of gold over steel; the thin coating is produced by electrolysis

b This picture frame has been silver plated using an electroplating process involving electrolysis

Figure C5.1

c Aluminium is produced by electrolysis

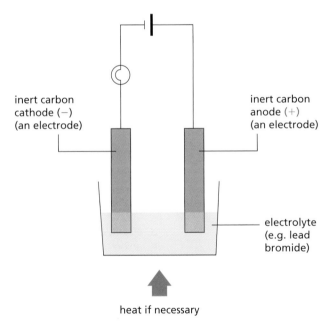

Figure C5.2 The important terms used in electrolysis.

inert carbon cathode (−) (an electrode)

inert carbon anode (+) (an electrode)

electrolyte (e.g. lead bromide)

heat if necessary

The transfer of charge during electrolysis is by:
- the movement of electrons in the metallic or graphite electrodes
- the removal or addition of electrons from the external circuit at the electrodes
- the movement of ions in the electrolyte.

Note that the conduction which takes place in the electrodes is due to the movement of delocalised electrons (pp.214 and 278) whereas in the electrolyte, as stated earlier, the charge carriers are ions.

Electrolysis is very important in industry. To help you to understand what is happening in the process shown in the photographs, we will first consider the electrolysis of lead(II) bromide.

● Electrolysis of lead(II) bromide

Consider Figure C5.3 on the next page, which shows solid lead(II) bromide ($PbBr_2$) in a crucible with two carbon electrodes in contact with it. When the electrodes are first connected, the bulb does not light, because the solid compound does not allow electricity to pass through it. However, when the compound is heated until it is molten, the bulb does light. The lead(II) bromide is now behaving as an electrolyte. When this happens an orange-red vapour is seen at the anode and lead metal is produced at the cathode.

The break-up (decomposition) of lead(II) bromide into its constituent elements by the passage of an electric current is called **electrolysis**.

$$\text{molten lead(II) bromide} \rightarrow \text{bromine} + \text{lead}$$
$$PbBr_2(l) \rightarrow Br_2(g) + Pb(l)$$

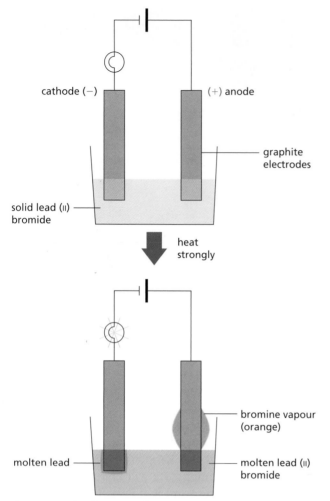

Figure C5.3 The electrolysis of molten lead(II) bromide.

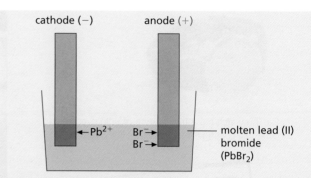

Figure C5.4 The lead ions (Pb^{2+}) are attracted to the cathode and the bromide ions (Br^-) are attracted to the anode.

This process of gaining electrons is called **reduction**.

To form bromine molecules each bromide ion must first of all move to the anode and lose its extra negative charge at the anode and so form a neutral bromine atom:

$$bromide\ ion \rightarrow bromine\ atom + electron$$
$$Br^-(l) \quad \rightarrow \quad Br \quad + \quad e^-$$

Two bromine atoms then combine to form a bromine molecule:

$$bromine\ atoms \rightarrow bromine\ molecule$$
$$2Br \quad \rightarrow \quad Br_2(g)$$

This process of losing electrons is called **oxidation**.

For lead metal to be formed, or deposited, at the cathode, the lead ions must be attracted to and move towards the electrode (Figure C5.4). To produce lead metal atoms these lead ions must each collect two electrons at the cathode:

$$lead\ ion + electrons \rightarrow lead\ atom$$
$$Pb^{2+}(l) \quad + \quad 2e^- \quad \rightarrow \quad Pb(l)$$

Questions

1 Explain the meaning of each of the following terms. Use a suitable example, in each case, to help with your explanation:
   a anode   d electrolyte
   b cathode   e anion
   c electrolysis   f cation.
2 Predict the products of the electrolysis of:
   a potassium chloride
   b lead oxide.

● Extraction of aluminium oxide

Aluminium is the most abundant metallic element in the Earth's crust. It makes up 8% of the crust and is found mainly as bauxite (which is mainly aluminium oxide) (Figure C5.5), as well as in the minerals cryolite and mica, and also in clay. It is a reactive metal (see Chapter C10, p.279) and is difficult to extract from its ore. Reactive metals hold on tightly to the element(s) they have combined with and, today, many, including aluminium, are therefore extracted from their ores by electrolysis.

Uses of aluminium are many and varied:

Alloy or metal element	Use
alloy	in aircraft construction and bicycle parts
element	metal cans, cooking foils, car body parts, saucepans, electricity cables

The process of extraction is often called the Hall–Héroult process after the two people who developed it. The process involves the electrolysis of aluminium oxide (alumina) in the following stages.

- Bauxite, an impure form of aluminium oxide, is treated with sodium hydroxide to obtain pure aluminium oxide by removing impurities such as iron(III) oxide and sand. This improves the conductivity of the molten aluminium oxide.

- The purified aluminium oxide is dissolved in molten cryolite (Na_3AlF_6) in an electrolysis cell. Cryolite is used to reduce the working temperature of the Hall–Héroult cell from 2017 °C (the melting point of pure aluminium oxide) to between 800 and 1000 °C. Therefore, the cryolite provides a considerable saving in the energy requirements of the process. In recent years, it has become necessary to manufacture the cryolite since the naturally occurring mineral is in very short supply.

Figure C5.5 Bauxite mining.

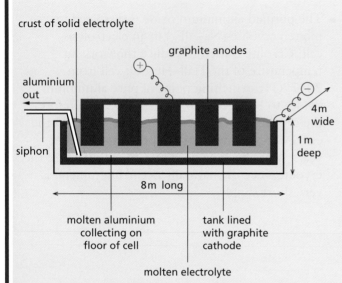

Figure C5.6 The Hall–Héroult cell is used in industry to extract aluminium by electrolysis.

• The molten mixture is then electrolysed in a cell similar to that shown in Figure C5.6.

The anodes of this process are blocks of graphite which are lowered into the molten mixture from above. The cathode is the graphite lining of the steel vessel containing the cell.

Aluminium oxide is an ionic compound. When it is melted the ions become mobile, as the strong electrostatic forces of attraction between them are broken by the input of heat energy. During electrolysis the negatively charged oxide ions are attracted to the anode (the positive electrode), where they lose electrons (oxidation).

$$\text{oxide ions} \rightarrow \text{oxygen molecules} + \text{electrons}$$
$$2O^{2-}(l) \rightarrow O_2(g) + 4e^-$$

The positive aluminium ions are attracted to the cathode (the negative electrode). They gain electrons to form molten aluminium metal (reduction).

$$\text{aluminium ions} + \text{electrons} \rightarrow \text{aluminium metal}$$
$$Al^{3+}(l) + 3e^- \rightarrow Al(l)$$

A handy way of remembering it is **OIL RIG** (**O**xidation **I**s **L**oss, **R**eduction **I**s **G**ain of electrons).

The overall reaction which takes place in the cell is:

$$\text{aluminium oxide} \xrightarrow{\text{electrolysis}} \text{aluminium} + \text{oxygen}$$
$$2Al_2O_3(l) \longrightarrow 4Al(l) \quad 3O_2(g)$$

The molten aluminium collects at the bottom of the cell and it is siphoned out at regular intervals. No

problems arise with other metals being deposited, since the cryolite is largely 'unaffected' by the flow of electricity. Problems do arise, however, with the graphite anodes. At the working temperature of the cell, the oxygen liberated reacts with the graphite anodes, producing carbon dioxide.

$$\text{carbon} + \text{oxygen} \rightarrow \text{carbon dioxide}$$
$$C(s) + O_2(g) \rightarrow CO_2(g)$$

The anodes burn away and have to be replaced on a regular basis.

The electrolysis of aluminium oxide is a continuous process in which vast amounts of electricity are used. In order to make the process an economic one, a cheap form of electricity is required. Hydroelectric power (HEP) is usually used for this process. The plant shown in Figure C5.7 uses an HEP scheme to provide some of the electrical energy required for this process. Further details about HEP are given in Chapter P2, p.367.

Figure C5.7 An aluminium smelting plant.

Questions
3 Produce a flow chart to summarise the processes involved in the extraction of aluminium metal from bauxite.
4 Explain why the mixture of gases formed at the anode contains oxygen, carbon dioxide and traces of fluorine.

● Electrolysis of aqueous solutions

Other industrial processes involve the electrolysis of aqueous solutions. To help you to understand what is happening in these processes, we will first consider the electrolysis of water.

Pure water is a very poor conductor of electricity because there are so few ions in it. However, it can be made to decompose if an electric current is passed through it in a Hofmann voltameter, shown below in Figure C5.8.

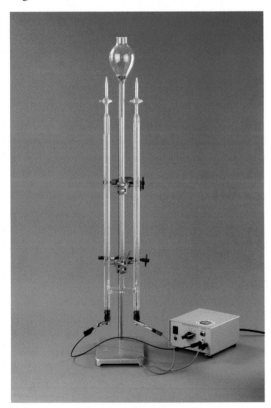

Figure C5.8 A Hofmann voltameter.

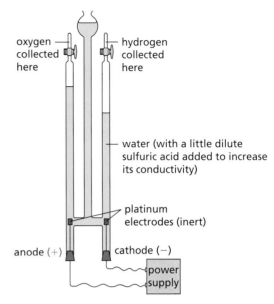

Figure C5.9 A Hofmann voltameter used to electrolyse water.

To enable water to conduct electricity better because it only contain a few H^+ and OH^- ions, some dilute sulfuric acid (or sodium hydroxide solution) is added. When the power is turned on and an electric current flows through this solution, gases can be seen to be produced at the two electrodes and they are collected in the side arms of the apparatus. After about 20 minutes, roughly twice as much gas is produced at the cathode as at the anode.

The gas collected at the cathode burns with a squeaky pop, showing it to be hydrogen gas. For hydrogen to be collected in this way, the positively charged hydrogen ions must have moved to the cathode.

$$\text{hydrogen ions} + \text{electrons} \rightarrow \text{hydrogen molecules}$$
$$4H^+(aq) + 4e^- \rightarrow 2H_2(g)$$

The $OH^-(aq)$ ions are attracted to the anode and lose electrons. Water and oxygen are formed. The oxygen collects at the anode. It relights a glowing splint, showing it to be oxygen.

This gas is produced in the following way.

$$\begin{matrix}\text{hydroxide} & \rightarrow & \text{water} & + & \text{oxygen} & + & \text{electrons} \\ \text{ions} & & \text{molecules} & & \text{molecules} & & \\ 4OH^-(aq) & \rightarrow & 2H_2O(l) & + & O_2(g) & + & 4e^- \end{matrix}$$

This experiment was first carried out by Sir Humphry Davy. It confirmed that the formula for water was H_2O.

It should be noted that in the electrolysis of dilute sulfuric acid, platinum (an inert electrode) may be replaced by carbon (graphite). The only difference to occur is that as well as oxygen being produced at the anode, a little carbon dioxide will also be formed.

Question

5

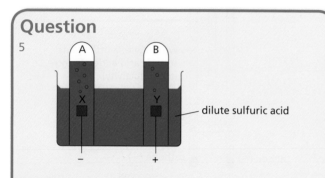

dilute sulfuric acid

This is a diagram of an experiment in which electricity was passed through a mixture of distilled water containing a little dilute sulfuric acid.

a   Name the gas that collects at **A**.
b   Name the gas that collects at **B**.
c   If 100 cm³ of gas collects in **A** how much would there be in **B**?
d   Name the metal usually used for **X** and **Y**.
e   **X** is called the _____ .
f   **Y** is called the _____ .
g   Write down the formulae of the three ions present in the solution.
h   Write down the equations for the reactions that take place at both **X** and **Y** (or describe the changes that take place if you cannot write the equations).

The electrolysis of aqueous sodium chloride

Figure C5.10 The PVC pipes, hydrochloric acid and fertiliser are made from substances obtained by the electrolysis of saturated salt solution.

Everything in Figure C5.10 is made using substances obtained from salt. Salt is one of the most important raw materials. Salt is found in the sea and also in underground deposits left by ancient seas.

Sodium chloride is an ionic compound of sodium and chlorine. If we wish to obtain the constituent elements from sodium chloride then we can electrolyse either the molten sodium chloride or aqueous sodium chloride.

The chlor-alkali industry

The electrolysis of saturated sodium chloride solution (brine) is the basis of a major industry. In countries where rock salt (sodium chloride) is found underground it is mined. In other countries it can be obtained by evaporation of sea water in large shallow lakes. Three very important substances are produced in this electrolysis process – chlorine, sodium hydroxide and hydrogen. The electrolytic process is a very expensive one, requiring vast amounts of electricity. The process is economical only because all three products have a large number of uses (Figure C5.11).

There are two well-established methods for electrolysing brine, the **diaphragm cell** and the **mercury cell**. However, recent developments in electrolysis technology, by chemical engineers, have produced the **membrane cell** (Figure C5.12 on p.238). This method is now preferred to the other two because it produces a purer product, it causes less pollution and it is cheaper to run.

The brine is first purified to remove calcium, strontium and magnesium compounds by a process of ion exchange.

The membrane cell is used continuously, with fresh brine flowing into the cell as the process breaks up the brine. The cell has been designed to ensure that the products do not mix. The ions in this concentrated sodium chloride solution are:

from the water: $H^+(aq)$ $OH^-(aq)$
from the sodium chloride: $Na^+(aq)$ $Cl^-(aq)$

When the current flows, the chloride ions, $Cl^-(aq)$, are attracted to the anode. Chlorine gas is produced by the electrode process.

$$\text{chloride ions} \xrightarrow{\text{oxidation}} \text{chlorine molecules + electrons}$$
$$2Cl^-(aq) \longrightarrow Cl_2(g) + 2e^-$$

This leaves a high concentration of sodium ions, $Na^+(aq)$, around the anode.

The hydrogen ions, $H^+(aq)$, are attracted to the cathode and hydrogen gas is produced.

hydrogen ions + electrons $\xrightarrow{\text{reduction}}$ hydrogen molecules

$$2H^+(aq) \quad + \quad 2e^- \quad \longrightarrow \quad H_2(g)$$

This leaves a high concentration of hydroxide ions, $OH^-(aq)$, around the cathode. The sodium ions, $Na^+(aq)$, are drawn through the membrane, where they combine with the $OH^-(aq)$ to form sodium hydroxide, NaOH, solution. The annual production worldwide is now in excess of 60 million tonnes.

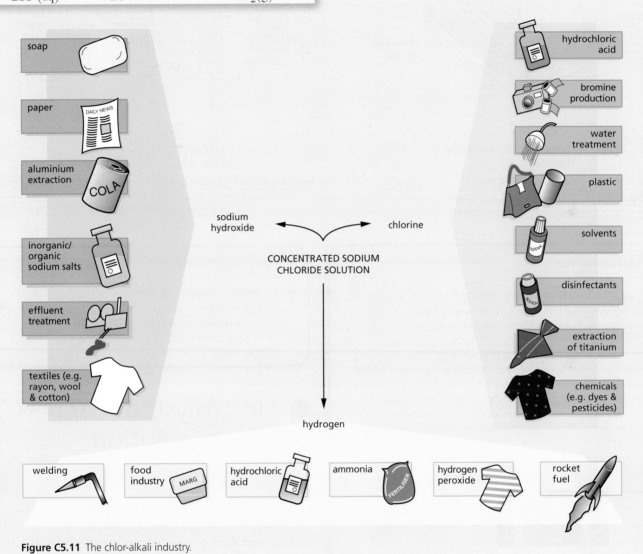

Figure C5.11 The chlor-alkali industry.

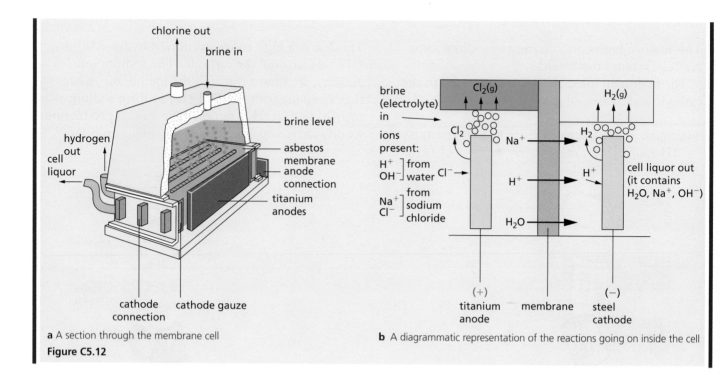

a A section through the membrane cell

Figure C5.12

b A diagrammatic representation of the reactions going on inside the cell

Questions

6 Account for the following observations which were made when concentrated sodium chloride solution, to which a little universal indicator had been added, was electrolysed in the laboratory in a Hofmann voltameter.
  a The universal indicator initially turns red in the region of the anode, but as the electrolysis proceeds it loses its colour.
  b The universal indicator turns blue in the region of the cathode.

7 The apparatus shown in the diagram below was used to investigate the gases produced when a concentrated solution of potassium chloride was electrolysed.

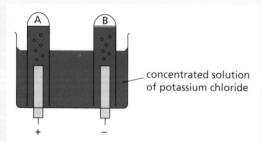

concentrated solution of potassium chloride

  a Name a non-metal suitable for use as electrodes.
  b Name the gas collected in **A** and the gas collected in **B**.
  c Describe how you would test the gases collected.
  d The volume of gas collected in **B** was slightly less than that collected in **A**. The teacher said the volumes should have been equal but gave a simple explanation of the 'missing' gas in **B**. What was the explanation? (Assume that the apparatus was working perfectly).

  e Write down the equations which describe the production of the gases at the electrodes in **A** and **B**.
  f i If the concentrated solution of potassium chloride was now replaced by dilute sodium hydroxide what gases would be produced at **A** and **B**?
    ii In what ratio would you expect these gases to be produced?

● Electrolysis of copper(II) sulfate solution

Copper(II) sulfate solution ($CuSO_4(aq)$) may be electrolysed using inert graphite electrodes in a cell similar to that shown in Figure 5.13. When the solution is electrolysed, oxygen gas and copper metal are formed at the anode and cathode respectively. Four ions are present in solution:

from the water: $H^+(aq)$ $OH^-(aq)$
from the copper(II) sulfate: $Cu^{2+}(aq)$ $SO_4{}^{2-}(aq)$

$H^+(aq)$ and $Cu^{2+}(aq)$ ions are both attracted to the cathode, the Cu^{2+} ions accepting electrons more readily than the H^+ ions (preferential discharge). Copper metal is therefore deposited at the cathode (Figure C5.14).

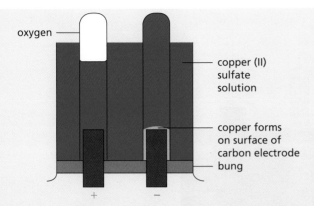

oxygen

copper (II) sulfate solution

copper forms on surface of carbon electrode

bung

+ −

Figure C5.13 The electrolysis of copper(II) sulfate solution using inert electrodes.

$$\text{copper ions} + \text{electrons} \rightarrow \text{copper atoms}$$
$$Cu^{2+}(aq) + 2e^- \rightarrow Cu(s)$$

$OH^-(aq)$ and $SO_4^{2-}(aq)$ ions are both attracted to the anode. The OH^- ions release electrons more easily than the SO_4^{2-} ions, so oxygen gas and water are produced at the anode (Figure C5.14).

$$\text{hydroxide ions} \rightarrow \text{oxygen} + \text{water} + \text{electrons}$$
$$4OH^-(aq) \rightarrow O_2(g) + 2H_2O(l) + 4e^-$$

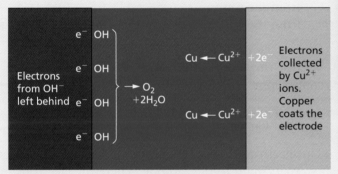

Electrons from OH^- left behind

e^- OH
e^- OH
e^- OH
e^- OH

$\rightarrow O_2$ $+2H_2O$

$Cu \leftarrow Cu^{2+}$ $+2e^-$
$Cu \leftarrow Cu^{2+}$ $+2e^-$

Electrons collected by Cu^{2+} ions. Copper coats the electrode

Figure C5.14 Oxygen is given off at the anode and copper is deposited at the cathode.

Purification of copper

Because copper is a very good conductor of electricity, it is used for electrical wiring and cables (Figure C5.15). Pure copper is also used in the manufacture of cooking utensils owing to its high thermal conductivity, a property of its metallic structure (Chapter C10, p.278).

However, even small amounts of impurities cut down this conductivity quite noticeably whether in fine wires or larger cables. The metal must be 99.99% pure to be used in this way. To ensure this level of purity, the newly extracted copper has to be purified by electrolysis.

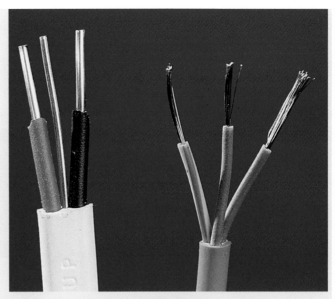

a The copper used in electrical wiring has to be very pure

b Due to the high density of copper and its cost, steel-cored aluminium cables are used for electrical transmission through national grids
Figure C5.15

The impure copper is used as the anode and is typically 1 m square, 35–50 mm thick and 330 kg in weight. The cathode is a 1 mm thick sheet and weighs about 5 kg; it is made from very pure copper. Because copper is itself involved in the electrolytic process, the copper cathode is known as an 'active' electrode. The electrolyte is a solution of copper(II) sulfate (0.3 mol/dm^3) acidified with a 2 mol/dm^3 solution of sulfuric acid to help the solution conduct electricity (Figure C5.16 on the next page).

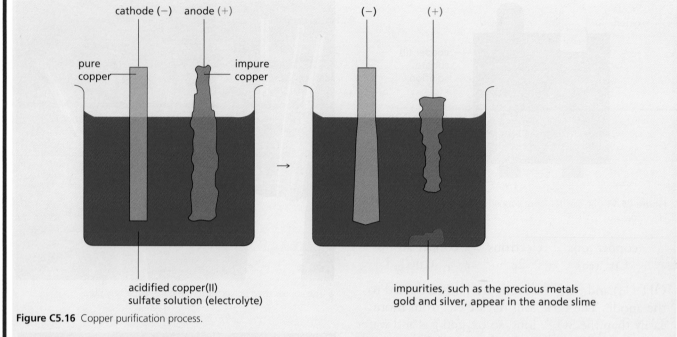

Figure C5.16 Copper purification process.

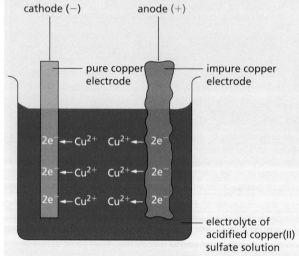

Figure C5.17 The movement of ions in the purification of copper by electrolysis.

When the current flows, the copper moves from the impure anode to the pure cathode. Any impurities fall to the bottom of the cell and collect below the anode in the form of a slime. This slime is rich in precious metals and the recovery of these metals is an important aspect of the economics of the process. The electrolysis proceeds for about three weeks until the anodes are reduced to about 10% of their original size and the cathodes weigh between

100 and 120 kg. A potential of 0.25 V and a current density of 200 A/m² are usually used.

The ions present in the solution are:

from the water: H^+(aq) OH^-(aq)
from the copper(II) sulfate: Cu^{2+}(aq) SO_4^{2-}(aq)

During the process the impure anode loses mass because the copper atoms lose electrons and become copper ions, Cu^{2+}(aq) (Figure C5.17).

copper atoms → copper ions + electrons
$Cu(s)$ → $Cu^{2+}(aq)$ + $2e^-$

The electrons released at the anode travel around the external circuit to the cathode. There the electrons are passed on to the copper ions, Cu^{2+}(aq), from the copper(II) sulfate solution and the copper is deposited or copper plated on to the cathode.

copper ions + electrons → copper atoms
$Cu^{2+}(aq)$ + $2e^-$ → $Cu(s)$

The annual production of copper worldwide is in excess of 16 million tonnes. However, a large amount of the copper we need is obtained by recycling. This way of obtaining copper is increasing in importance as it becomes more difficult and expensive to locate and extract the copper ore.

● Electrolysis guidelines

The following points may help you work out the products of electrolysis in unfamiliar situations. They will also help you remember what happens at each electrode.

- Non-metals are produced at the anode whereas metals and hydrogen gas are produced at the cathode.
- At the inert anode, chlorine, bromine and iodine (the halogens) are produced in preference to oxygen.
- At the inert cathode, hydrogen is produced in preference to metals unless unreactive metals such as copper and nickel are present.

● Electroplating

Electroplating is the process involving electrolysis to plate, or coat, one metal with another or a plastic with a metal. Often the purpose of electroplating is to give a protective coating to the metal beneath. For example, bath taps are chromium plated to prevent corrosion, and at the same time are given a shiny, more attractive finish (Figure C5.18).

Figure C5.18 This tap has been chromium plated.

Questions

8. Why do you think it is advantageous to use inert electrodes in the electrolysis processes?
9. Predict the products of electrolysis of a solution of copper(II) sulfate if carbon electrodes are used instead of those made from copper as referred to in the purification of copper section.
10. Predict the products of the electrolysis of concentrated hydrochloric acid using platinum electrodes.
11. Using your knowledge of electrolysis, predict the likely products of the electrolysis of copper(II) chloride solution, using platinum electrodes. Write electrode equations for the formation of these products.

The electroplating process is carried out in a cell such as the one shown in Figure C5.19. This is often known as the 'plating bath' and it contains a suitable electrolyte, usually a solution of a metal salt.

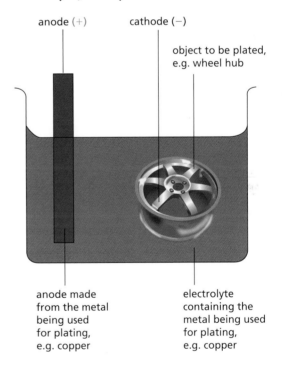

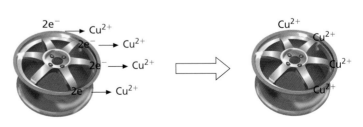

the Cu^{2+} ions are attracted to the cathode, where they gain electrons

a coating of copper forms on the wheel hub at the cathode

Figure C5.19

241

In some cases a base metal, such as nickel, is applied to the article before it is electroplated so that the plating metal will stick. For copper plating, the electrolyte is a solution of a copper salt. The article to be plated is made the cathode in the cell so that the metal ions move to it when the current is switched on. The cathode reaction in this process is:

copper ions + electrons → copper atoms

$Cu^{2+}(aq)$ $+ e^-$ $→ Cu(s)$

Questions

12 Leaves from trees can now be copper plated. Suggest a suitable method for copper plating a leaf.
13 Explain why copper(II) chloride solution would not be used as an electrolyte in the electrolyte cell used for copper plating.
14 Electroplating is an important industrial process.
   a Explain what electroplating is.
   b Why are certain metals electroplated?
   c Give two examples of the use of electroplating.

15 Write equations which represent the discharge at the cathode of the following ions:
   a K^+
   b Pb^{2+}
   c Al^{3+}

Checklist

After studying Chapter C5 you should know and understand the following.

- Anions are negative ions; attracted to the anode.
- Anode is the positive electrode. It is positively charged because electrons are drawn away from it.
- Cathode is the negative electrode. It is negatively charged because an excess of electrons move towards it.
- Cations are positive ions; attracted to the cathode.
- Electrode is a point where the electric current enters and leaves the electrolytic cell. An inert electrode is usually made of platinum or carbon and does not react with the electrolyte or the substances produced at the electrodes themselves.
- Electrolysis is a process in which a chemical reaction is caused by the passage of an electric current.
- Electrolyte is a substance which will carry electric current only when it is molten or dissolved.
- Electroplating is the process of depositing metals from solution in the form of a layer on other surfaces such as metal or plastic.
- Hall–Héroult cell is the electrolysis cell in which aluminium is extracted from purified bauxite dissolved in molten cryolite at 900 °C. This cell has both a graphite anode and a graphite cathode.
- Inert electrode is an electrode that does not react with the products of electrolysis, e.g. carbon, platinum.
- Membrane cell is an electrolytic cell used for the production of sodium hydroxide, hydrogen and chlorine from brine in which the anode and cathode are separated by a membrane.
- Oxidation takes place at the anode and involves a negative ion losing electrons.
- Reduction takes place at the cathode and involves a positive ion gaining electrons.

C6 Energy changes in chemical reactions

Combined	Co-ordinated
● Describe the meaning of *exothermic* and *endothermic* reactions	● Describe the meaning of *exothermic* and *endothermic* reactions
● Describe bond breaking as endothermic process and bond forming as exothermic process	● Describe bond breaking as endothermic process and bond forming as exothermic process
● Draw and label energy level diagrams for exothermic and endothermic reactions using data provided	● Draw and label energy level diagrams for exothermic and endothermic reactions using data provided
● Interpret energy level diagrams showing exothermic and endothermic reactions and the activation energy of a reaction	● Interpret energy level diagrams showing exothermic and endothermic reactions and the activation energy of a reaction

● Exothermic and endothermic reactions

When any chemical reaction occurs, energy is either given out to the surroundings or taken in from the surroundings.

An exothermic reaction is one which gives out energy to the surroundings when it occurs. When an exothermic reaction occurs, the temperature goes up as heat energy is lost to the surroundings. Exothermic reactions are very important to us. They keep us alive through the combustion of food in our bodies, and they keep us warm on cold days through the combustion of fossil fuels such as oil and natural gas.

An endothermic reaction is one which takes in energy from the surroundings. The temperature of the surroundings decreases when an endothermic reaction occurs. A common endothermic reaction is that of photosynthesis in plants which converts carbon dioxide gas into oxygen gas. Decomposition reactions of metal carbonates are also examples of endothermic reactions (see Chapter C13, p.314).

Question

1 State whether each of the following examples shows that an endothermic or exothermic reaction is taking place:
  a the use of hand-warming packs
  b the use of a cooling pack to minimise bruising
  c self-heating cans
  d an explosion.

Combustion

When natural gas burns in a plentiful supply of air it produces a large amount of energy.

methane + oxygen → carbon + water + heat
              dioxide   energy

$CH_4(g) + 2O_2(g) \rightarrow CO_2(g) + 2H_2O(l) + $ heat energy

During this process, the **complete combustion** of methane, heat is given out. It is an **exothermic** reaction.

The energy changes that take place during a chemical reaction can be shown by an **energy level diagram**. Figure C6.1 shows the energy level diagram for the complete combustion of methane.

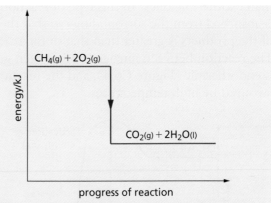

Figure C6.1 Energy level diagram for the complete combustion of methane.

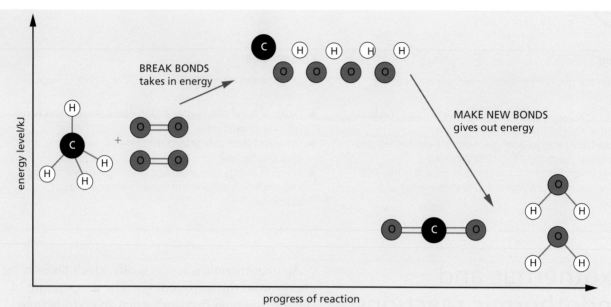

Figure C6.2 Breaking and forming bonds during the combustion of methane.

When any reaction occurs, the chemical bonds in the reactants have to be broken – this requires energy. This is an endothermic process. When the new bonds in the products are formed, energy is given out (Figure C6.2). This is an exothermic process.

When fuels, such as methane, are burned they require energy to start the chemical reaction. This is known as the **activation energy**, E_A (Figure C6.3).

In the case of methane reacting with oxygen, it is some of the energy involved in the initial bond breaking (Figure C6.3). The value of the activation energy will vary from fuel to fuel.

Endothermic reactions are much less common than exothermic ones. In this type of reaction energy is absorbed from the surroundings so that the energy of the products is greater than that of the reactants. The reaction between nitrogen and oxygen gases is endothermic (Figure C6.4), and the reaction is favoured by high temperatures.

nitrogen → oxygen → nitrogen(II) oxide
$$N_2(g) + O_2(g) \rightarrow 2NO(g) + \Delta H$$

Dissolving is often an endothermic process. For example, when ammonium nitrate dissolves in water the temperature of the water falls, indicating that energy is being taken from the surroundings. Photosynthesis and thermal decomposition are other examples of endothermic processes.

In equations it is usual to express the ΔH value in units of kJ/mol. For example:

$$CH_4(g) + 2O_2(g) \rightarrow CO_2(g) + 2H_2O(l)$$
$$\Delta H = -728\,kJ/mol$$

This ΔH value tells us that when 1 mole of methane is burned in oxygen, 728 kJ of energy are released. This value is called the **enthalpy of combustion** (or **molar heat of combustion**) of methane.

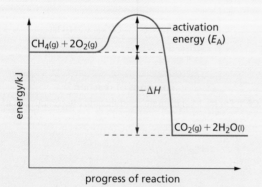

Figure C6.3 Energy level diagram for methane/oxygen.

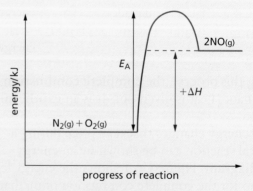

Figure C6.4 Energy level diagram for nitrogen/oxygen.

Questions

2 Explain the meaning of the terms:
   a endothermic reaction
   b exothermic reaction
   c activation energy.
3 Draw energy level diagrams for the reactions given below:
   a $NaOH(aq) + HCl(aq) \rightarrow NaCl(aq) + H_2O(l)$
      $\Delta H = -57\,kJ/mol$
   b $2H_2O(l) \rightarrow 2H_2(g) + O_2(g)$
      $\Delta H = +575\,kJ/mol$
4 State which of the following processes is endothermic and which is exothermic.
   a The breaking of a chemical bond.
   b The forming of a chemical bond.
5 How much energy is released if:
   a 0.5 mole of methane is burned?
   b 5 moles of methane are burned?
   c 4 g of methane are burned?

Checklist

After studying Chapter C6 you should know and understand the following.

● Bond energy is an amount of energy associated with a particular bond in a molecular element or compound.
● Combustion is a chemical reaction in which a substance reacts rapidly with oxygen with the production of heat and light.

● Endothermic reaction is a chemical reaction which absorbs heat energy from its surroundings.
● Exothermic reaction is a chemical reaction that releases heat energy into its surroundings.

Chemical reactions

Combined

- Describe practical methods for investigating the rate of a reaction which produces a gas
- Interpret data obtained from experiments concerned with rate of reaction
- Suggest suitable apparatus, given information, for experiments, including collection of gases and measurement of rates of reaction
- Describe the effect of concentration, particle size, catalysts and temperature on the rate of reactions
- Describe and explain the effect of changing concentration in terms of frequency of collisions between reacting particles
- Describe and explain the effect of changing temperature in terms of the frequency of collisions between reacting particles and more colliding particles possessing the minimum energy (activation energy) to react
- Describe *oxidation* and *reduction* in chemical reactions in terms of oxygen loss/gain. (Oxidation state limited to its use to name ions, e.g. iron(II), iron(III), copper(II).)
- Define and identify an *oxidising agent* as a substance which oxidises another substance during a *redox* reaction and a *reducing agent* as a substance which reduces another substance during a *redox* reaction

Co-ordinated

- Describe practical methods for investigating the rate of a reaction that produces a gas
- Interpret data obtained from experiments concerned with rate of reaction
- Suggest suitable apparatus, given information, for experiments, including collection of gases and measurement of rates of reaction
- Describe the effect of concentration, particle size, catalysts and temperature on the rate of reactions
- Describe how concentration, temperature and surface area create a danger of explosive combustion with fine powders (e.g. flour mills) and gases (e.g. methane in mines)
- Describe and explain the effect of concentration in terms of frequency of collisions between reacting particles
- Describe and explain the effect of changing temperature in terms of the frequency of collisions between reacting particles and more colliding particles possessing the minimum energy (activation energy) to react
- Describe *oxidation* and *reduction* in chemical reactions in terms of oxygen loss/gain. (Oxidation state limited to its use to name ions, e.g. iron(II), iron(III), copper(II).)
- Define *redox* in terms of electron transfer, and identify such reactions from given information, which could include simple equations
- Define and identify an *oxidising agent* as a substance which oxidises another substance during a *redox* reaction and a *reducing agent* as a substance which reduces another substance during a *redox* reaction

Figure C7.1 shows some slow and fast reactions. The two photographs on the left show examples of slow reactions. The ripening of apples takes place over a number of weeks, and the making and maturing of cheese may take months. The burning of solid fuels, such as coal, can be said to involve chemical reactions taking place at a medium speed or rate. The other example shows a fast reaction. The chemicals inside explosives, such as TNT, react very rapidly in reactions which are over in seconds or fractions of seconds.

As new techniques have been developed, the processes used within the chemical industry have become more complex. Therefore, chemists and chemical engineers have increasingly looked for ways to control the rates at which chemical reactions take place. In doing so, they have discovered that there are five main ways in which you can alter the rate of a chemical reaction. These ideas are not only incredibly useful to industry but can also be applied to reactions which occur in the school laboratory. Note that it is better to use the term *rate* rather than *speed* to describe a reaction.

Figure C7.1 Some slow (ripening fruit and cheese making), medium (coal fire) and fast (explosion) reactions.

Factors that affect the rate of a reaction

- Surface area of the reactants.
- Concentration of the reactants and gas pressure.
- Temperature at which the reaction is carried out.
- Light.
- Use of a catalyst.

Collision theory

For a chemical reaction to occur, reactant particles need to collide with one another. Not every collision results in the formation of products. For products to be formed, the collision has to have a certain minimum amount of energy associated with it. This minimum amount of energy is known as the **activation energy**, E_a (Figure C7.2). Collisions which result in the formation of products are known as successful collisions.

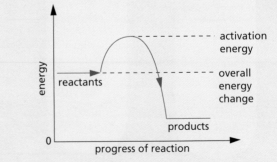

Figure C7.2 Energy level diagram showing activation energy.

Surface area

In Chapter C13, we shall see that limestone (calcium carbonate) is a substance which can be used to neutralise soil acidity. Powdered limestone is used as it neutralises the acidity faster than if lumps of limestone are used. Why do you think this is the case?

In the laboratory, the reaction between acid and limestone in the form of lumps or powder can be observed in a simple test-tube experiment. Figure C7.3 shows the reaction between dilute hydrochloric acid and limestone in lump and powdered form.

hydrochloric + calcium → calcium + carbon + water
acid   carbonate   chloride   dioxide
$2HCl(aq)$ + $CaCO_3(s)$ → $CaCl_2(aq)$ + $CO_2(g)$ + $H_2O(l)$

The rates at which the two reactions occur can be found by measuring either:

- the volume of the carbon dioxide gas which is produced
- the loss in mass of the reaction mixture with time.

These two methods are generally used for measuring the rate of reaction for processes involving the formation of a gas as one of the products.

Figure C7.3 The powdered limestone (left) reacts faster with the acid than the limestone in the form of lumps.

The apparatus shown in Figure C7.4 is used to measure the loss in mass of the reaction mixture. The mass of the conical flask plus the reaction mixture is measured at regular intervals. The total loss in mass is calculated for each reading of the balance, and this is plotted against time. Some sample results from experiments of this kind have been plotted in Figure C7.5.

Figure C7.4 After 60 seconds the mass has fallen by 1.24 g.

The reaction is generally at its fastest in the first minute. This is indicated by the slopes of the curves during this time. The steeper the slope, the faster the rate of reaction. You can see from the two traces in Figure C7.5 that the rate of reaction is greater with the powdered limestone than the lump form.

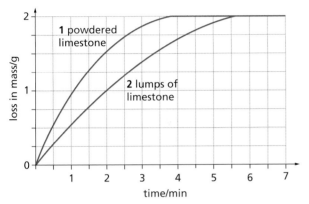

Figure C7.5 Sample results for the limestone/acid experiment.

Another way of following the rate of this reaction between calcium carbonate and hydrochloric acid would have been to have recorded the volume of carbon dioxide gas collected against time. The gas can be collected in various pieces of apparatus but using it is collected either in a gas syringe or a upturned measuring cylinder or burette.

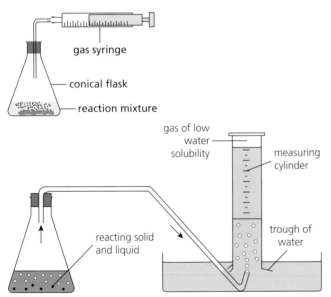

Figure C7.6 Apparatus for collecting gas.

Depending on the rate of reaction the volume of gas collected would be recorded at certain time intervals. The data obtained would then be used to plot a graph of the volume of gas collected against time (Figure C7.7).

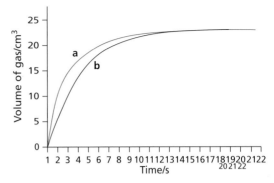

Figure C7.7 Plot of volume of gas collected against time.

Once again, the slope of the graph indicates the rate of reaction with line **a**, the reaction with fastest rate, representing the reaction with powdered limestone and line **b** with lumps of limestone.

The surface area has been increased by powdering the limestone (Figure C7.8). The acid particles now have an increased amount of surface of limestone with which to collide. The products of a reaction are formed when collisions occur between reactant particles. An increase in the surface area of a solid reactant results in an increase in the number of collisions, and this results in an increase in the number of successful collisions. Therefore, the increase in surface area of the limestone increases the rate of reaction.

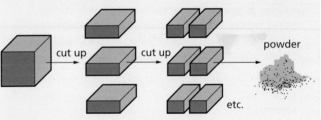

Figure C7.8 A powder has a larger surface area.

In certain industries the large surface area of fine powders and dusts can be a problem. For example, there is a risk of explosion in flourmills and mines, where the large surface area of the flour or coal dust can – and has – resulted in explosions through a reaction with oxygen gas in the air when a spark has been created by machinery or the workforce (Figure C7.9 on the next page). On 26 September 1988, two silos containing wheat exploded at the Jamaica Flour Mills Plant in Kingston, Jamaica, killing three workers, as a result of fine dust exploding.

Figure C7.9 The dust created by this cement plant in India is a potential hazard.

Methane gas, CH_4, is formed as part of the natural process of coal formation. When coal is mined, methane is released from the coal seam and the surrounding rock. The methane content in coal seams generally increases the deeper the seam and the greater the pressure, and with age. Underground mining can therefore produce substantially greater levels of methane than surface mining. Methane gas is very flammable – its release can have serious implications for the safety of mine operations. It is also a greenhouse gas.

Questions

1 What apparatus would you use to measure the rate of reaction of limestone with dilute hydrochloric acid by measuring the volume of carbon dioxide produced?
2 The following results were obtained from an experiment of the type you were asked to design in question **1**.

Time/min	0	0.5	1.0	1.5	2.0	2.5	3.0	3.5	4.0	4.5	5.0
Total volume of CO_2 gas/cm³	0	15	24	28	31	33	35	35	35	35	35

a Plot a graph of the total volume of CO_2 against time.
b At which point is the rate of reaction fastest?
c What volume of CO_2 was produced after 1 minute 15 seconds?
d How long did it take to produce 30 cm³ of CO_2?

Concentration

A yellow precipitate is produced in the reaction between sodium thiosulfate and hydrochloric acid.

sodium thiosulfate	+ hydrochloric acid	→	sodium chloride	+ sulfur	+ sulfur dioxide	+ water
$Na_2S_2O_3(aq)$	+ $2HCl(aq)$	→	$2NaCl(aq)$	+ $S(s)$	+ $SO_2(g)$	+ $H_2O(l)$

The rate of this reaction can be followed by recording the time taken for a given amount of sulfur to be

precipitated. This can be done by placing a conical flask containing the reaction mixture on to a cross on a piece of paper (Figure C7.10). As the precipitate of sulfur forms, the cross is obscured and finally disappears from view. The time taken for this to occur is a measure of the rate of this reaction. To obtain sufficient information about the effect of changing the concentration of the reactants, several experiments of this type must be carried out, using different concentrations of sodium thiosulfate or hydrochloric acid.

Figure C7.10 The precipitate of sulfur hides the cross.

Some sample results of experiments of this kind have been plotted in Figure C7.11. You will note from the graph that when the most concentrated sodium thiosulfate solution was used, the reaction was at its fastest. This is shown by the shortest time taken for the cross to be obscured.

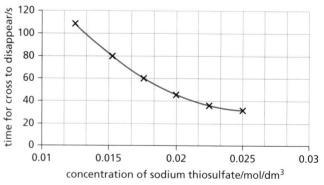

Figure C7.11 Sample data for the sodium thiosulfate/acid experiment at different concentrations of sodium thiosulfate.

From the data shown in Figure C7.11 it is possible to produce a different graph which directly shows the rate of the reaction against concentration rather than the time taken for the reaction to occur against concentration. To do this, the times can be converted to a rate using:

$$\text{rate } (/s) = \frac{1}{\text{reaction time (s)}}$$

This would give the graph shown in Figure C7.12.

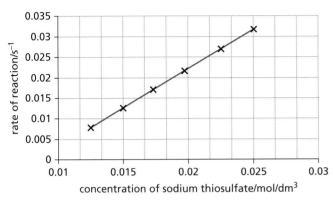

Figure C7.12 Graph to show the rate of reaction against concentration.

As discussed earlier, the products of the reaction are formed as a result of the collisions between reactant particles. There are more particles in a more concentrated solution and the collision rate between reactant particles is higher. The more often the particles collide, the greater the chance they have of having sufficient energy to overcome the activation energy of the reaction, and of a successful collision occurring. This means that the rate of a chemical reaction will increase if the concentration of reactants is increased, because there are more particles per unit volume.

In reactions involving only gases, for example the Haber process (Chapter C11, p.304), an increase in the overall pressure at which the reaction is carried out increases the rate of the reaction. The increase in pressure results in the gas particles being pushed closer together. This means that they collide more often and so react faster.

Question

3 Devise an experiment to show the effect of changing the concentration of dilute acid on the rate of reaction between magnesium and hydrochloric acid.

Temperature

Why do you think food is stored in a refrigerator? The reason is that the rate of decay is slower at lower temperatures. This is a general feature of the majority of chemical processes.

The reaction between sodium thiosulfate and hydrochloric acid can also be used to study the effect of temperature on the rate of a reaction. Figure C7.13 shows some sample results of experiments with sodium thiosulfate and hydrochloric acid (at fixed concentrations) carried out at different temperatures. You can see from the graph that the rate of the reaction is fastest at high temperatures.

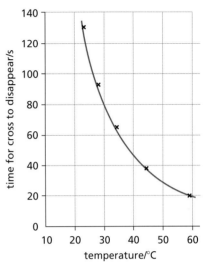

Figure C7.13 Sample data for the sodium thiosulfate/acid experiment at different temperatures.

As the temperature increases, the reactant particles increase their kinetic energy and they move faster. The faster movement results in more collisions between the particles. Some of these extra collisions, which result from the temperature increase, will be successful collisions. This causes the reaction rate to increase.

Catalysts

Over 90% of industrial processes use **catalysts**. A catalyst is a substance which can alter the rate of a reaction without being chemically changed itself. In the laboratory, the effect of a catalyst can be observed using the decomposition of hydrogen peroxide as an example.

$$\text{hydrogen peroxide} \rightarrow \text{water} + \text{oxygen}$$
$$2H_2O_2(aq) \rightarrow 2H_2O(l) + O_2(g)$$

The rate of decomposition at room temperature is very slow. There are substances, however, which will speed up this reaction, one being manganese(IV) oxide. When black manganese(IV) oxide powder is added to hydrogen peroxide solution, oxygen is produced rapidly. The rate at which this occurs can be followed by measuring the volume of oxygen gas produced with time.

Some sample results from experiments of this type have been plotted in Figure C7.14. At the end of the reaction, the manganese(IV) oxide can be filtered off and used again. The reaction can proceed even faster by increasing the amount and surface area of the catalyst. This is because the activity of a catalyst involves its surface. Note that, in gaseous reactions, if dirt or impurities are present on the surface of the catalyst, it will not act as efficiently; it is said to have been 'poisoned'. Therefore, the gaseous reactants must be pure.

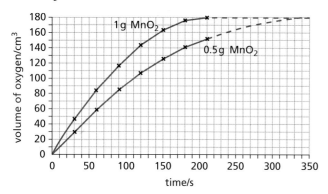

Figure C7.14 Sample data for differing amounts of MnO_2 catalyst.

Chemists have found that:

- a small amount of catalyst will produce a large amount of chemical change
- catalysts remain unchanged chemically after a reaction has taken place, but they can change physically. For example, a finer manganese(IV) oxide powder is left behind after the decomposition of hydrogen peroxide
- catalysts are specific to a particular chemical reaction.

Some examples of chemical processes and the catalysts used are shown in Table C7.1.

Table C7.1 Examples of catalysts.

Process	Catalyst
Haber process – for the manufacture of ammonia	Iron
Contact process – for the manufacture of sulfuric acid	Vanadium(V) oxide
Oxidation of ammonia to give nitric acid	Platinum
Hydrogenation of unsaturated oils to form fats in the manufacture of margarines	Nickel

Questions

4 Using a catalysed reaction of your choice, devise an experiment to follow the progress of the reaction and determine how effective the catalyst is.

5 A student performed two experiments to establish how effective manganese(IV) oxide was as a catalyst for the decomposition of hydrogen peroxide. The results below were obtained by carrying out these experiments with two different quantities of manganese(IV) oxide. The volume of the gas produced was recorded against time.

Time/s	0	30	60	90	120	150	180	210
Volume for 0.3 g/cm³	0	29	55	79	98	118	133	146
Volume for 0.5 g/cm³	0	45	84	118	145	162	174	182

  a Draw a diagram of the apparatus you could use to carry out these experiments.
  b Plot a graph of the results.
  c Is the manganese(IV) oxide acting as a catalyst in this reaction? Explain your answer.
  d i At which stage does the reaction proceed most quickly?
    ii How can you tell this from your graph?
    iii In terms of particles, explain why the reaction is quickest at the point you have chosen in **i**.
  e Why does the slope of the graph become less steep as the reaction proceeds?
  f What volume of gas has been produced when using 0.3 g of manganese(IV) oxide after 50 s?
  g How long did it take for 60 cm³ of gas to be produced when the experiment was carried out using 0.5 g of the manganese(IV) oxide?
  h Write a balanced equation for the decomposition of hydrogen peroxide.

● Oxidation and reduction

When magnesium metal reacts with oxygen gas a white solid, magnesium oxide is formed. The chemical equation for the reaction is

$$2Mg(s) + O_2(g) \rightarrow 2MgO(s)$$

When substances such as hydrogen and magnesium combine with oxygen in this way they are said to have been **oxidised**. The process is known as **oxidation**.

Reduction is the opposite of oxidation. In this process oxygen is removed instead of being added.

A **redox** reaction is one which involves the two processes of reduction and oxidation. For example, the oxygen has to be removed in the extraction of iron from iron(III) oxide. This can be done in a blast furnace with carbon monoxide. The iron(III) oxide loses oxygen to the carbon monoxide and is reduced to iron. Carbon monoxide is the **reducing agent**. A reducing agent is a substance that reduces another substance during a redox reaction. Carbon monoxide is oxidised to carbon dioxide by the iron(III) oxide. The iron(III) oxide is the **oxidising agent**. An oxidising agent is a substance which oxidises another substance during a redox reaction.

| iron(III) oxide | + | carbon monoxide | → | iron | + | carbon dioxide |

For a further discussion of oxidation and reduction see Chapter C5 and Chapter C7.

Both **reduction** and **oxidation** have taken place in this chemical process, and so this is known as a **redox** reaction.

Each atom in an element or compound is assigned an oxidation state to show how much it is reduced or oxidised. The following points should be remembered when using oxidation states.

- The oxidation state of the free element is always 0, for example in metals such as zinc and copper.

- In simple ions, the oxidation state is the same as the charge on the ion. So iodine has an oxidation state of 0 in I_2 but an oxidation state of -1 in I^-.

- Compounds have no charge overall. Hence the oxidation states of all the individual elements in a compound must add up to 0. The oxidation states of elements in compounds can vary, as seen in Table C4.3, p.219. It is possible to recognise which of the different oxidation states a metal element is in by the colour of its compounds (Figure C7.15).

- An increase in the oxidation state, for example from +2 to +3 as in the case of Fe^{2+} to Fe^{3+}, is oxidation.

Figure C7.15 Iron(II) sulfate is pale green, whilst iron(III) sulfate is yellow.

- However, a reduction in the oxidation state, for example from +6 to +3 as in the case of Cr (in CrO_4^{2-}) to Cr^{3+}, is reduction.

During a redox reaction, the substance that brings about oxidation is called an **oxidising agent** and is itself reduced during the process. A substance that brings about reduction is a **reducing agent** and is itself oxidised during the process.

For example, if a dilute solution of acidified potassium manganate(VII) (pale purple) is added to a solution of iron(II) sulfate, a colour change takes place as the reaction occurs (Figure C7.16). The iron(II) sulfate (pale green) changes to pale yellow, showing the presence of iron(III) ions.

Figure C7.16 Manganate(VII) ions (oxidising agent) and iron(II) ions (reducing agent) are involved in a redox reaction when mixed.

In this reaction the iron(II) ions have been oxidised to iron(III) ions (increase in oxidation state) and the manganate(VII) ions have been reduced to manganese(II) ions (decrease in oxidation state) which are very pale pink. Hence the manganate(VII) ions are the oxidising agent and the iron(II) ions are the reducing agent.

It is possible to recognise redox processes by looking at the oxidation states on the two sides of the chemical equation for a reaction. For example, in the reaction between magnesium and dilute sulfuric acid, the magnesium dissolves and hydrogen gas is produced. Both magnesium metal and hydrogen gas are free elements and so have an oxidation state of 0. In sulfuric acid, hydrogen has an oxidation state of +1 since the overall charge on the sulfate ion is -2. Similarly, the oxidation state of magnesium in magnesium sulfate is +2.

magnesium + sulfuric acid	→ magnesium sulfate + hydrogen

$$Mg(s) + H_2SO_4(aq) \rightarrow MgSO_4(aq) + H_2(g)$$

Oxidation states: 0   +1   +2   0

The sulfate ions are unchanged by the reaction and so can be ignored.

As you can see, the oxidation state of magnesium has increased from 0 to +2. Therefore the magnesium has been oxidised by the sulfuric acid and so sulfuric acid is the oxidising agent. The oxidation state of hydrogen has decreased from +1 in the sulfuric acid to 0 in the free element. Therefore the hydrogen has been reduced by the magnesium and so magnesium is the reducing agent.

When sodium metal reacts with chlorine gas a white ionic solid, sodium chloride, is formed. The chemical equation for this is

$$2Na(s) + Cl_2(g) \rightarrow 2NaCl(s)$$

This reaction is another example of a redox reaction. In this reaction, the sodium atoms have lost electrons to form sodium ions

$$Na(s) \rightarrow Na^+(s) + e^-$$

Sodium has been oxidised because it has lost electrons.

The chlorine has gained electrons to form chloride ions:

$$Cl_2(g) + 2e^- \rightarrow 2Cl^-(s)$$

Chlorine has been reduced because it has gained electrons.

Questions

6 Identify the oxidising and reducing agents in the following reactions:
   a copper(II) oxide + hydrogen → copper + water
   b tin(II) oxide + carbon → tin + carbon dioxide
   c $PbO(s) + H_2(g) \rightarrow Pb(s) + H_2O(l)$

7 Identify the oxidising and reducing agents in the following reactions.
   a $Zn(s) + H_2SO_4(aq) \rightarrow ZnSO_4(aq) + H_2(g)$
   b $Cu^{2+}(aq) + Zn(s) \rightarrow Cu(s) + Zn^{2+}(aq)$
   c $Mg(s) + Cu(NO_3)_2(aq) \rightarrow Mg(NO_3)_2(aq) + Cu(s)$
   d $Fe(s) + H_2SO_4(aq) \rightarrow FeSO_4(aq) + H_2(g)$

Checklist

After studying Chapter C7 you should know and understand the following.

- Activation energy is the excess energy that the reactants must acquire to permit the reaction to occur.
- Catalyst is a substance which alters the rate of a chemical reaction without itself being chemically changed.
- Oxidising agent is a substance that causes an increase in oxidation number.
- Oxidation is the process of removing an electron or electrons from an atom to create a positive ion. Gives an increase in oxidation number.

- Reaction rate is a measure of the change which happens during a reaction in a single unit of time. It may be affected by the following factors:
  - surface area of the reactants
  - concentration of the reactants
  - the temperature at which the reaction is carried out
  - light
  - use of a catalyst.
- Reducing agent is a substance that causes a decrease in oxidation number.
- Reduction is the process of adding an electron or electrons to an atom to create a negative ion. It gives a decrease in oxidation number.

Acids, bases and salts

● Acids and alkalis

All the substances shown in Figure C8.1 (on the next page) contain an **acid** of one sort or another. Acids are certainly all around us. What properties do these substances have which make you think that they are acids or contain acids?

The word acid means 'sour' and all acids possess this property. They are also:

● soluble in water
● corrosive.

Alkalis are very different from acids. They are the chemical 'opposite' of acids.

● They will remove the sharp taste from an acid.
● They have a soapy feel.

Some common alkaline substances are shown in Figure C8.2 on the next page.

Figure C8.1 What do all these foods have in common?

Figure C8.2 Some common alkaline substances.

It would be too dangerous to taste a liquid to find out if it was acidic. Chemists use substances called **indicators** which change colour when they are added to acids or alkalis. Many indicators are dyes which have been extracted from natural sources, for example litmus.

Some other indicators are shown in Table C8.1, along with the colours they turn in acids and alkalis.

Table C8.1 Indicators and their colours in acid and alkaline solution

Indicator	Colour in acid solution	Colour in alkaline solution
Blue litmus	Red	Blue
Red litmus	Red	Blue

These indicators tell chemists whether a substance is acid or alkaline (Figure C8.3). To obtain an idea of how acidic or alkaline a substance is, we use another indicator known as a **universal indicator**. This indicator is a mixture of many other indicators. The colour shown by this indicator can be matched against a **pH scale**. The pH scale was developed by a Scandinavian chemist called Søren Sørenson. The pH scale runs from below 0 to 14. A substance with a pH of less than 7 is an acid. One with a pH of greater than 7 is alkaline. One with a pH of 7 is said to be neither acid nor alkaline, that is neutral. Water is the most common example of a neutral substance. Figure C8.4 shows the universal indicator colour range along with everyday substances with their particular pH values.

Another way in which the pH of a substance can be measured is by using a pH meter (Figure C8.5). The pH electrode is placed into the solution and a pH reading is given on the digital display.

Figure C8.3 Indicators tell you if a substance is acid or alkaline.

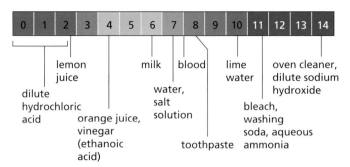

a the pH scale

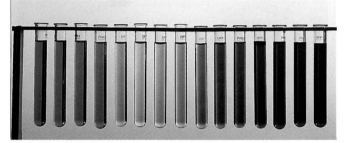

b universal indicator in solution, showing the colour range
Figure C8.4

Figure C8.5 A digital pH meter.

hydrochloric	+	sodium	→	sodium	+	water
acid		hydroxide		chloride		
$HCl(aq)$	+	$NaOH(aq)$	→	$NaCl(aq)$	+	$H_2O(l)$

As we have shown, when both hydrochloric acid and sodium hydroxide dissolve in water the ions separate completely. We may therefore write:

$$H^+(aq) + Cl^-(aq) + Na^+(aq) + OH^-(aq) \rightarrow Na^+(aq)Cl^-(aq) + H_2O(l)$$

You will notice that certain ions are unchanged on either side of the equation. They are called **spectator ions** and are usually taken out of the equation. The equation now becomes:

$$H^+(aq) + OH^-(aq) \rightarrow H_2O(l)$$

This type of equation is known as an **ionic equation**. The reaction between any acid and alkali in aqueous solution can be summarised by this ionic equation. It shows the ion which causes acidity ($H^+(aq)$) reacting with the ion which causes alkalinity ($OH^-(aq)$) to produce neutral water ($H_2O(l)$).

Controlling acidity in soils

The pH of soil varies and from place to place. Ideally the pH of soil should be kept above 5.5. Lower pH values result in a significant decrease in crop growth and yield, which could be a major problem in our goal to feed a growing world population. Several different methods are used to maintain the pH of soil at an acceptable level for the crops to be grown. Limestone, $CaCO_3$, in the form of a powder can be applied to acidic soil; this is a cheap method to use. A slightly more expensive method would be to use lime, CaO.

Neutralising an acid

A common situation involving neutralisation of an acid is when you suffer from indigestion. This is caused by a build-up of acid in your stomach. Normally you treat it by taking an indigestion remedy containing a substance which will react with and neutralise the acid.

In the laboratory, if you wish to neutralise a common acid such as hydrochloric acid you can use an alkali such as sodium hydroxide. If the pH of the acid is measured as some sodium hydroxide solution is added to it, the pH increases. If equal volumes of the same concentration of hydrochloric acid and sodium hydroxide are added to one another, the resulting solution is found to have a pH of 7. The acid has been neutralised and a neutral solution has been formed.

> ## Questions
>
> 1 Complete the following equations:
>   a $CH_3COOH + NaOH \rightarrow$
>   b $H_2SO_4 + KOH \rightarrow$
>   c $NH_3 + HBr \rightarrow$
>   In each case name the acid and the base. Also in parts **a** and **b** write the ionic equation for the reactions.
> 2 Alongside the names of various chemicals below are shown their respective pH values in aqueous solution.
> | | |
> |---|---|
> | potassium hydroxide | pH 13 |
> | hydrogen bromide | pH 2 |
> | calcium hydroxide | pH 11 |
> | sodium chloride | pH 7 |
> | hydrogen chloride | pH 2 |
> | magnesium hydroxide | pH 10 |
> | citric acid | pH 4 |

Which of the substances is/are:
a a strong acid?
b a weak acid?
c a strong alkali?
d a weak alkali?
e a neutral substance?
In each case write a chemical equation to show the molecules/ions present in solution.

3 Write a chemical equation to represent the neutralisation of sulfuric acid by sodium hydroxide.

Methods of preparing soluble salts

There are four general methods of preparing soluble salts:

Acid + metal

This method can only be used with the less reactive metals. It would be very dangerous to use a reactive metal such as sodium in this type of reaction. The metals usually used in this method of salt preparation are the **MAZIT** metals, that is, **m**agnesium, **a**luminium, **z**inc, **i**ron and **t**in. A typical experimental method is given below.

Excess magnesium ribbon is added to dilute nitric acid. During this addition an effervescence is observed due to the production of hydrogen gas.

In this reaction the hydrogen ions from the nitric acid gain electrons from the metal atoms as the reaction proceeds.

hydrogen ions + electrons → hydrogen gas
                 (from metal)
$$2H^+ \quad + \quad 2e^- \quad \rightarrow \quad H_2(g)$$

How would you test the gas to show that it was hydrogen? What would be the name and formula of the compound produced during the test you suggested?

magnesium +   nitric   → magnesium + hydrogen
                acid   nitrate
$$Mg(s) \quad + 2HNO_3(aq) \rightarrow Mg(NO_3)_2(aq) + \quad H_2(g)$$

The excess magnesium is removed by filtration (Figure C8.6).

The magnesium nitrate solution is evaporated slowly to form a saturated solution of the salt (Figure C8.7).

The hot concentrated magnesium nitrate solution produced is tested by dipping a cold glass rod into it.

If salt crystals form at the end of the rod the solution is ready to crystallise and is left to cool. Any crystals produced on cooling are filtered and dried between clean tissues.

Figure C8.6 The excess magnesium is filtered in this way.

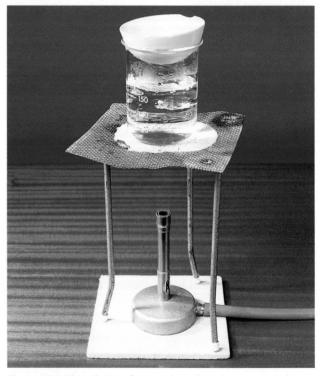

Figure C8.7 The solution of magnesium nitrate is concentrated by slow evaporation.

Acid + carbonate

This method can be used with any metal carbonate and any acid, providing the salt produced is soluble. The typical experimental procedure is similar to that carried out for an acid and a metal. For example, copper(II) carbonate would be added in excess to dilute nitric acid. Effervescence would be observed due to the production of carbon dioxide.

How would you test the gas to show it was carbon dioxide? Write an equation to help you explain what is happening during the test you have chosen.

copper(II)	+	nitric	→	copper(II)	+	carbon	+	water
carbonate		acid		nitrate		dioxide		

$CuCO_3(s) + 2HNO_3(aq) \rightarrow Cu(NO_3)_2(aq) + CO_2(g) + H_2O(l)$

Metal carbonates contain carbonate ions, CO_3^{2-}. In this reaction the carbonate ions react with the hydrogen ions in the acid.

carbonate	+	hydrogen	→	carbon	+	water
ions		ions		dioxide		

$CO_3^{2-}(aq) + 2H^+(aq) \rightarrow CO_2(g) + H_2O(l)$

Acid + alkali (soluble base)

This method is generally used for preparing the salts of very reactive metals, such as potassium or sodium. It would certainly be too dangerous to add the metal directly to the acid. In this case, we solve the problem indirectly and use an alkali which contains the particular reactive metal whose salt we wish to prepare.

Metal oxides are **basic**. Metal oxides and hydroxides that dissolve in water to produce $OH^-(aq)$ ions are known as **alkalis**, or **soluble bases**. If the metal oxide or hydroxide does not dissolve in water it is known as an **insoluble base**.

A **base** is a substance which neutralises an acid, producing a salt and water as the only products. If the base is soluble the term alkali can be used, but there are several bases which are insoluble. It is also a substance which accepts a hydrogen ion. In general, most metal oxides and hydroxides (as well as ammonia solution) are bases. Some examples of soluble and insoluble bases are shown in Table C8.2. Salts can be formed by this method only if the base is soluble.

Table C8.2 Examples of soluble and insoluble bases

Soluble bases (alkalis)	Insoluble bases
Sodium hydroxide (NaOH)	Iron(III) oxide (Fe_2O_3)
Potassium hydroxide (KOH)	Copper(II) oxide (CuO)
Calcium hydroxide ($Ca(OH)_2$)	Lead(II) oxide (PbO)
Ammonia solution ($NH_{3(aq)}$)	Magnesium oxide (MgO)

Because in this neutralisation reaction both reactants are in solution, a special technique called **titration** is required. Acid is slowly and carefully added to a measured volume of alkali using a burette (Figure C8.8) until the indicator changes colour.

An indicator is used to show when the alkali has been neutralised completely by the acid. This is called the **end-point**. Once you know where the end-point is, you can add the same volume of acid to the measured volume of alkali but this time without the indicator.

The solution which is produced can then be evaporated slowly to obtain the salt. For example,

hydrochloric	+	sodium	→	sodium	+	water
acid		hydroxide		chloride		

$HCl(aq) + NaOH(aq) \rightarrow NaCl(aq) + H_2O(l)$

Figure C8.8 The acid is added to the alkali until the indicator just changes colour.

As previously discussed on p.257, this reaction can best be described by the ionic equation:

$$H^+(aq) + OH^-(aq) \rightarrow H_2O(l)$$

Acid + insoluble base

This method can be used to prepare a salt of an unreactive metal, such as lead or copper. In these cases it is not possible to use a direct reaction of the metal with an acid so the acid is neutralised using the particular metal oxide (Figure C8.9).

The method is generally the same as that for a metal carbonate and an acid, though some warming of the reactants may be necessary. An example of such a reaction is the neutralisation of sulfuric acid by copper(II) oxide to produce copper(II) sulfate (Figure C8.10).

sulfuric acid	+	copper(II) oxide	→	copper(II) sulfate	+	water
$H_2SO_4(aq)$	+	$CuO(s)$	→	$CuSO_4(aq)$	+	$H_2O(l)$

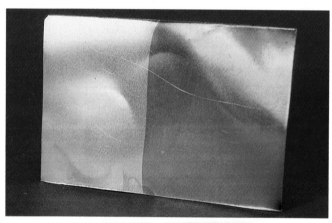

Figure C8.9 Citric acid has been used on the right-hand side of this piece of copper metal to remove the oxide coating on its surface, giving it a shinier appearance.

Figure C8.10 After slow evaporation to concentrate the solution, the solution is left to crystallise. Crystals of copper(II) sulfate are produced.

Metal oxides contain the oxide ion, O^{2-}. The ionic equation for this reaction is therefore:

$$2H^+(aq) + O^{2-}(s) \rightarrow H_2O(l)$$

or

$$CuO(s) + 2H^+(aq) \rightarrow Cu^{2+}(aq) + H_2O(l)$$

Methods of preparing insoluble salts

The methods described above can be used to make a soluble salt, one that is soluble in water. If a salt that is insoluble in water needs to be prepared, a different technique is needed. Before we describe the technique, it is first necessary to learn which salts are soluble and which are insoluble. This can be done using the following rules of solubility:

- All nitrates are soluble in water.
- All chlorides, bromides and iodides are soluble in water, except those of silver.
- All sulfates are soluble in water except barium, calcium and lead sulfates.
- All potassium, ammonium and sodium salts are soluble in water.
- All carbonates are insoluble, except those of potassium, ammonium and sodium.

An insoluble salt, such as barium sulfate, can be made by precipitation. In this case, solutions of the two chosen soluble salts are mixed (Figure C8.11). To produce barium sulfate, barium chloride and sodium sulfate can be used. The barium sulfate precipitate can be filtered off, washed with distilled water and dried. The reaction that has occurred is:

barium chloride	+	sodium sulfate	→	barium sulfate	+	sodium chloride
$BaCl_2(aq)$	+	$Na_2SO_4(aq)$	→	$BaSO_4(s)$	+	$2NaCl(aq)$

The ionic equation for this reaction is:

$$Ba^{2+}(aq) + SO_4^{2-}(aq) \rightarrow BaSO_4(s)$$

This method is sometimes known as **double decomposition** and may be summarised as follows:

soluble salt	+	soluble salt	→	insoluble salt	+	soluble salt
(AX)		(BY)		(BX)		(AY)

Figure C8.11 When barium chloride solution is added to sodium sulfate a white precipitate of barium sulfate forms.

It should be noted that even salts like barium sulfate dissolve to a very small extent. For example, 1 litre of water will dissolve 2.2×10^{-3} g of barium sulfate at 25 °C. This substance and substances like it are said to be **sparingly soluble**.

Questions

4 Complete the word equations and write balanced chemical equations for the following soluble salt preparations:
   a magnesium + sulfuric acid →
   b calcium carbonate + hydrochloric acid →
   c zinc oxide + hydrochloric acid →
   d potassium hydroxide + nitric acid →
5 Lead carbonate and lead iodide are insoluble. Which two soluble salts could you use in the preparation of each substance? Write
   a a word equation
   b a symbol equation
   c an ionic equation
   to represent the reactions taking place.

● Types of oxides

Oxides are compounds formed when elements react with oxygen. Metal oxides, for example magnesium oxide, are described as being bases, they react with acids to form salt and water. Non-metal oxides, for example, sulfur dioxide, are acidic oxides and they react with bases.

There are, however, oxides known as amphoteric oxides which react with both acids and bases.

Aluminium oxide and zinc oxide will react with both acids and alkalis.

zinc oxide	+	hydrochloric acid	→	zinc chloride	+	water

$$ZnO(s) + 2HCl(aq) \rightarrow ZnCl_2(aq) + H_2O(l)$$

zinc oxide	+	sodium hydroxide	+	water	→	sodium zincate

$$ZnO(s) + 2NaOH(aq) + H_2O(l) \rightarrow Na_2Zn(OH)_4(aq)$$

Certain non-metal oxides are classified as neutral. These oxides do not react with acids or bases. Examples include carbon monoxide (CO), nitrogen(II) oxide (nitrogen monoxide, NO), and nitrogen(I) oxide (nitrous oxide or dinitrogen oxide, N_2O).

Identification of ions and gases

This section looks at simple chemical tests which can be carried out to determine the presence of certain ions in solution and gases. Chemists often need to find out which ions are in a solution to confirm their work or to identify unknown solutions and gases.

● Identifying metal ions

When an alkali dissolves in water, it produces hydroxide ions. It is known that most metal hydroxides are insoluble. So if hydroxide ions from a solution of an alkali are added to a solution of a metal salt, an insoluble, often coloured, metal hydroxide is precipitated from solution (Figure C8.12 on the next page).

Let's take the example of iron(III) chloride with sodium hydroxide solution:

iron(III) chloride	+	sodium hydroxide	→	iron(III) hydroxide	+	sodium chloride

$$FeCl_3(aq) + 3NaOH(aq) \rightarrow Fe(OH)_3(s) + 3NaCl(aq)$$

The ionic equation for this reaction is:

iron(III) ions	+	hydroxide ions	→	iron(III) hydroxide

$$Fe^{3+}(aq) + 3OH^-(aq) \rightarrow Fe(OH)_3(s)$$

Table C8.3 on the next page shows the effects of adding a few drops of sodium hydroxide solution to solutions containing on the next page various metal ions, and of adding an excess. The colours of the insoluble metal hydroxides can be used to identify the metal cations present in solution. In some cases the precipitate dissolves in excess hydroxide, owing to

a iron(III) hydroxide is precipitated   b copper(II) hydroxide is precipitated
Figure C8.12

the amphoteric nature of the metal hydroxide. This amphoteric nature can also be used to help identify metals such as aluminium and zinc.

Aqueous ammonia can be used to identify salts of Cu^{2+}, Fe^{2+}, Fe^{3+}, Al^{3+}, Zn^{2+}, Cr^{3+} and Ca^{2+} ions. The colour of the precipitate or solution formed identifies the metal present (Table C8.4).

Table C8.3 The effect of adding sodium hydroxide solution to solutions containing various metal ions

Metal ion present in solution	Effect of adding sodium hydroxide solution	
	A few drops	An excess
Calcium	White precipitate of calcium hydroxide	Precipitate does not dissolve
Copper(II)	Blue precipitate of copper(II) hydroxide	Precipitate does not dissolve
Iron(II)	Green precipitate of iron(II) hydroxide	Precipitate does not dissolve
Iron(III)	Brown precipitate of iron(III) hydroxide	Precipitate does not dissolve
Zinc	White precipitate of zinc hydroxide	Precipitate dissolves

Table C8.4 Identifying metal ions using aqueous ammonia

Metal ion	With a few drops of ammonia solution	With excess ammonia solution
Cu^{2+}(aq)	Gelatinous blue precipitate	Precipitate dissolves to give a deep blue solution
Fe^{2+}(aq)	Dirty green precipitate	Dirty green precipitate remains
Fe^{3+}(aq)	Rust brown precipitate	Rust brown precipitate remains
Zn^{2+}(aq)	White precipitate	White precipitate dissolves to give a colourless solution
Ca^{2+}(aq)	Faint white precipitate	Faint white precipitate remains

Tests for aqueous cations

Effect of adding dilute sodium hydroxide solution

Aqueous sodium hydroxide can be used to identify salts of Al^{3+}, Ca^{2+}, Cr^{3+}, Cu^{2+}, Fe^{2+}, Fe^{3+}, Pb^{2+} and Zn^{2+} when present in aqueous solutions. All metal cations form insoluble hydroxides when sodium hydroxide solution is added to them. The colour of the precipitate and its behaviour in excess sodium hydroxide solution will help identify the metal present (Table C8.5).

Table C8.5 Effect of adding sodium hydroxide solution to solutions containing various metal ions

Added dropwise	To excess	Likely cation
White precipitate	Precipitate dissolves	Zn^{2+}
White precipitate	Precipitate does not dissolve	Ca^{2+}
Blue precipitate	Precipitate does not dissolve	Cu^{2+}
Green precipitate	Precipitate does not dissolve	Fe^{2+}
Brown precipitate	Precipitate does not dissolve	Fe^{3+}

(In the case of ammonium salts, ammonia gas is produced on warming. The ammonium cation does not form an insoluble hydroxide. However, it forms ammonia and water upon heating.)

Effect of adding dilute ammonia solution

Ammonia gas dissolved in water is usually known as aqueous ammonia. The solution is only weakly alkaline, which results in a relatively low concentration of hydroxide ions. Aqueous ammonia can be used to identify salts of Al^{3+}, Ca^{2+}, Cr^{3+}, Cu^{2+}, Fe^{2+}, Fe^{3+}, Pb^{2+} and Zn^{2+} ions. The colour of the precipitate or solution formed identifies the metal present (Table C8.6).

Table C8.6 Effect of adding aqueous ammonia to solutions containing various metal ions

Added dropwise	To excess	Cation present
Gelatinous blue precipitate	Precipitate dissolves to give a deep blue clear solution	Cu^{2+}
Dirty green precipitate	Precipitate does not dissolve	Fe^{2+}
Rust brown precipitate	Precipitate does not dissolve	Fe^{3+}
White precipitate	Precipitate dissolves	Zn^{2+}
No precipitate	No precipitate	Ca^{2+}

Flame colours

If a clean nichrome wire is dipped into a metal compound and then held in the hot part of a Bunsen flame, the flame can become coloured (Figure C8.13). Certain metal ions may be detected in their compounds by observing their flame colours (Table C8.7).

Figure C8.13 The green colour is characteristic of copper.

Table C8.7 Characteristic flame colours of some metal ions

	Metal	Flame colour
Group I	Lithium	Crimson
	Sodium	Golden yellow
	Potassium	Lilac
Others	Copper (as Cu(ɪɪ))	Green

A flame colour is obtained as a result of the electrons in the particular ions being excited when they absorb energy from the flame which is then emitted as visible light. The different electronic structures of the different ions, therefore, give rise to the different colours.

Question
6 Describe how you could use aqueous ammonia to distinguish between three unlabelled bottles containing solutions of Al^{3+}(aq), Ca^{2+}(aq) and Cu^{2+}(aq).

Testing for different salts
Sometimes we want to analyse a salt and find out what is in it. There are simple chemical tests which allow us to identify the anion part of the salt. These are often called **spot tests**.

Testing for a sulfate (SO_4^{2-})
You have seen that barium sulfate is an insoluble salt (p.261). Therefore, if you take a solution of a suspected sulfate and add it to a solution of a soluble

barium salt (such as barium chloride) then a white precipitate of barium sulfate will be produced.

$$barium\ ion\ +\ sulfate\ ion\ \rightarrow\ barium\ sulfate$$
$$Ba^{2+}(aq)\ +\ SO_4^{2-}(aq)\ \rightarrow\ BaSO_4(s)$$

A few drops of dilute hydrochloric acid are also added to this mixture. If the precipitate does not dissolve, then it is barium sulfate and the unknown salt was in fact a sulfate. If the precipitate does dissolve, then the unknown salt may have been a sulfite (containing the SO_3^{2-} ion).

Testing for a chloride (Cl⁻) and a bromide (Br⁻)
Earlier in this chapter you saw that silver chloride is an insoluble salt (p.260). Therefore, if you take a solution of a suspected chloride and add to it a small volume of dilute nitric acid, to make an **aqueous acidic solution**, followed by a small amount of a solution of a soluble silver salt (such as silver nitrate), a white precipitate of silver chloride will be produced.

$$chloride\ ion\ +\ silver\ ion\ \rightarrow\ silver\ chloride$$
$$Cl^-(aq)\ +\ Ag^+(aq)\ \rightarrow\ AgCl(s)$$

If left to stand, the precipitate goes grey (Figure C8.14).

In a similar way, a bromide will react to produce a cream precipitate of silver bromide (AgBr) (Figure C8.15 on the next page).

Figure C8.14 If left to stand the white precipitate of silver chloride goes grey. This photochemical change plays an essential part in black and white photography.

Figure C8.15 AgCl, a white precipitate and AgBr, a cream precipitate.

Testing for a carbonate

If a small amount of an acid is added to some of the suspected carbonate (either solid or in solution) then effervescence occurs. If it is a carbonate then carbon dioxide gas is produced, which will turn limewater 'milky' (a cloudy white precipitate of calcium carbonate forms).

$$\begin{array}{c}\text{carbonate} + \text{hydrogen} \rightarrow \text{carbon} + \text{water}\\ \text{ions} \quad\quad \text{ions} \quad\quad \text{dioxide}\\ CO_3^{2-}(aq) + 2H^+(aq) \rightarrow CO_2(g) + H_2O(l)\end{array}$$

Testing for a nitrate

By using Devarda's alloy (45% Al, 5% Zn, 50% Cu) in alkaline solution, nitrates are reduced to ammonia. The ammonia can be identified using damp indicator paper, which turns blue.

$$3NO_3^-(aq) + 8Al(s) + 5OH^-(aq) + 18H_2O(l) \rightarrow 3NH_3(g) + 8[Al(OH)_4]^-(aq)$$

In the reaction the nitrate ion is reduced, as oxygen is removed from the nitrogen atom, and it gains hydrogen to form ammonia, NH_3. The gain of hydrogen is also a definition of reduction.

Table C8.8 Tests for aqueous anions

Anion	Test	Test result
Carbonate (CO_3^{2-})	Add dilute acid	Effervescence, carbon dioxide produced
Chloride (Cl^-) [in solution]	Acidify with dilute nitric acid, then add aqueous silver nitrate	White ppt.
Bromide (Br^-) [in solution]	Acidify with dilute nitric acid, then add aqueous silver nitrate	Cream ppt.
Nitrate (NO_3^-) [in solution]	Add aqueous sodium hydroxide, then aluminium foil; warm carefully	Ammonia produced
Sulfate (SO_4^{2-}) [in solution]	Acidify, then add aqueous barium nitrate or barium chloride	White ppt.

Questions

7 An analytical chemist working for an environmental health organisation has been given a sample of water which is thought to have been contaminated by a sulfate, a carbonate and a chloride.
   a Describe how she could confirm the presence of these three types of salt by simple chemical tests.
   b Write ionic equations to help you explain what is happening during the testing process.
8 For each of the following pairs of substances, describe a chemical test you would carry out to distinguish between them.
   a Ammonium chloride and aluminium chloride.
   b Zinc nitrate and calcium nitrate.
   c Sodium chloride and sodium iodide.
   d Iron(ɪɪ) sulfate and copper(ɪɪ) sulfate.
9 Sodium carbonate hydrate contains water of crystallisation. When it is heated strongly it gives off the water of crystallisation, which can be collected. The substance left behind is anhydrous sodium sulfate. Describe a chemical test to show that this substance contains sodium (cation) and carbonate (anion).

Tests for gases

Table C8.9 shows the common gases which may be produced during qualitative analysis and tests which can be used to identify them. These tests are used in conjunction with the tests shown above.

Table C8.9 Tests for gases

Gas	Colour (odour)	Effect of moist indicator paper	Test
Hydrogen (H_2)	Colourless (odourless)	No effect – neutral	'Pops' in the presence of a lighted splint
Oxygen (O_2)	Colourless (odourless)	No effect – neutral	Relights a glowing splint
Carbon dioxide (CO_2)	Colourless (odourless)	Pink – weakly acidic	Turns limewater a cloudy white
Ammonia (NH_3)	Colourless (very pungent smell)	Blue – alkaline	Turns moist indicator paper blue – it is the only alkaline gas
Chlorine (Cl_2)	Yellow-green (very choking smell)	Bleaches moist indicator paper after it initially turns pale pink	Bleaches moist indicator paper
Water (H_2O)	Colourless (odourless)	No effect – neutral	• Turns blue cobalt chloride paper pink • Turns anhydrous copper(ɪɪ) sulfate from white to blue

Questions

10 Describe how you would use a combination of sodium hydroxide solution and flame tests to distinguish between different solutions containing the following ions. Explain which tests you would use, in which order you would use them, and what results you would expect to see in each case.
  a Fe^{2+}
  b Cu^{2+}
  c Li^+
  d Ca^{2+}
  e Fe^{3+}
  f Al^{3+}
  g Mg^{2+}

11 Name the substances A to E shown in the flow diagram:

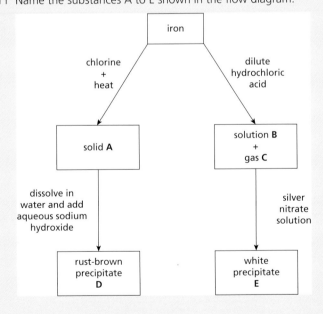

  a Solid A
  b Solution B
  c Gas C
  d Rust-brown precipitate D
  e White precipitate E

12 Describe how you would use simple test-tube reactions to distinguish between the following pairs of irons. In each case describe the test and its result.
  a Fe^{2+} and Fe^{3+}
  b CO_3^{2-} and Cl^-
  c Ca^{2+} and Zn^{2+}
  d Fe^{3+} and Al^{3+}
  e Mg^{2+} and NH_4^+

Checklist

After studying Chapter C8 you should know and understand the following.

- Acid is a substance which dissolves in water, producing $H^+(aq)$ ions as the only positive ions. An acid is a hydrogen ion (H^+) donor.
- Alkali is a soluble base which produces $OH^-(aq)$ ions in water.
- Base is a substance which neutralises an acid, producing a salt and water as the only products. A base is a hydrogen ion (H^+) accepter.

- Double decomposition is the process by which an insoluble≈salt is prepared from solutions of two suitable soluble salts.

- Indicator is a substance used to show whether a substance is acidic or alkaline (basic), for example phenolphthalein.

- Ionic equation is the simplified equation of a reaction which we can write if the chemicals involved are ionic substances.
- Metal ion precipitation is the reaction in which certain metal cations form insoluble hydroxides. The colours of these insoluble hydroxides can be used to identify the metal cations which are present; for example, copper(II) hydroxide is a blue precipitate.

- Neutralisation is the process in which the acidity or alkalinity of a substance is destroyed. Destroying acidity means removing $H^+(aq)$ by reaction with a base, carbonate or metal. Destroying alkalinity means removing the $OH^-(aq)$ by reaction with an acid.

$$H^+(aq) + OH^-(aq) \rightarrow H_2O(l)$$

- pH scale is a scale running from 0 to 14, used for expressing the acidity or alkalinity of a solution.
- Testing for a carbonate is performed by seeing if effervescence occurs when an acid is added to the suspected carbonate and the gas produced tests positively for carbon dioxide. If so, the substance is a carbonate.
- Testing for a halide is performed by seeing if a white, cream or yellow precipitate is produced when dilute nitric acid and silver nitrate solution are added to the suspected chloride. If white, the solution is a chloride; if cream, the solution is a bromide.
- Testing for a sulfate is performed by seeing if a white precipitate is produced when dilute hydrochloric acid and barium chloride solution are added to the suspected sulfate. If so, the solution contains a sulfate.

Combined

- Describe the Periodic Table as a method of classifying elements and its use to predict properties of elements
- Describe the change from metallic to non-metallic character across a period
- Describe the relationship between group number, number of outer shell electrons and metallic/non-metallic character
- Describe lithium, sodium and potassium in Group I as a collection of relatively soft metals showing a trend in melting point, density and reaction with water
- Predict the properties of other elements in Group I, given data where appropriate
- Describe the halogens, chlorine, bromine and iodine in Group VII, as a collection of diatomic non-metals showing a trend in colour and physical state
- State the reaction of chlorine, bromine and iodine with other halide ions
- Predict the properties of other elements in Group VII, given data where appropriate
- Identify trends in other groups, given data about the elements concerned
- Describe the transition elements as a collection of metals having high densities, high melting points and forming coloured compounds, and which, as elements and compounds, often act as catalysts
- Describe the noble gases, in Group VIII or 0, as being unreactive, monoatomic gases and explain this in terms of electronic structure
- State the uses of the noble gases in providing an inert atmosphere, i.e. argon in lamps, helium for filling balloons

Co-ordinated

- Describe the Periodic Table as a method of classifying elements and its use to predict properties of elements
- Describe the change from metallic to non-metallic character across a period
- Describe the relationship between group number, number of outer shell electrons and metallic/non-metallic character
- Describe lithium, sodium and potassium in Group I as a collection of relatively soft metals showing a trend in melting point, density and reaction with water
- Predict the properties of other elements in Group I, given data where appropriate
- Describe the halogens, chlorine, bromine and iodine in Group VII, as a collection of diatomic non-metals showing a trend in colour and physical state
- State the reaction of chlorine, bromine and iodine with other halide ions
- Predict the properties of other elements in Group VII, given data where appropriate
- Identify trends in other groups, given data about the elements concerned
- Describe the transition elements as a collection of metals having high densities, high melting points and forming coloured compounds, and which, as elements and compounds, often act as catalysts
- Describe the noble gases, in Group VIII or 0, as being unreactive, monoatomic gases and explain this in terms of electronic structure
- State the uses of the noble gases in providing an inert atmosphere, i.e. argon in lamps, helium for filling balloons

● Development of the Periodic Table

The Periodic Table is a vital tool used by chemists to predict the way in which elements react during chemical reactions. It is a method of categorising elements according to their properties. Scientists started to look for a way in which to categorise the known elements around 200 years ago.

The Periodic Table was devised in 1869 by the Russian Dmitri Mendeleev, who was the Professor of Chemistry at St Petersburg University (Figure C9.1). His periodic table was based on the chemical and physical properties of the 63 elements that had been discovered at that time.

Figure C9.1 Dmitri Mendeleev (1834–1907).

Other scientists had also attempted to categorise the known elements, but Mendeleev's classification proved to be the most successful. Mendeleev arranged all the 63 known elements in order of increasing atomic weight but in such a way that elements with similar properties were in the same vertical column. He called the vertical columns **groups** and the horizontal rows **periods** (Figure C9.2). If necessary he left gaps in the table.

As a scientific idea, Mendeleev's periodic table was tested by making predictions about elements that were unknown at that time but could possibly fill the gaps. Three of these gaps are shown by the symbols * and † in Figure C9.2. As new elements were discovered, they were found to fit easily into the classification. For example, Mendeleev predicted the properties of the missing element 'eka-silicon' (†). He predicted the colour, density and melting point as well as its atomic weight.

In 1886 the element we now know as germanium was discovered in Germany by Clemens Winkler; its properties were almost exactly those Mendeleev had predicted. In all, Mendeleev predicted the atomic weight of ten new elements, of which seven were eventually discovered – the other three, atomic weights 45, 146 and 175, do not exist!

Period	Group							
	1	2	3	4	5	6	7	8
1	H							
2	Li	Be	B	C	N	O	F	
3	Na	Mg	Al	Si	P	S	Cl	
4	K	Ca	*	Ti	V	Cr	Mn	Fe Co Ni
	Cu	Zn	*	†	As	Se	Br	

Figure C9.2 Mendeleev's periodic table. He left gaps for undiscovered elements.

The success of Mendeleev's predictions showed that his ideas were probably correct. His periodic table was quickly accepted by scientists as an important summary of the properties of the elements.

Mendeleev's periodic table has been modified in the light of work carried out by Rutherford and Moseley. Discoveries about sub-atomic particles led them to realise that the elements should be arranged by proton number. In the modern Periodic Table the 118 known elements are arranged in order of increasing proton number (Figure C9.3). Those

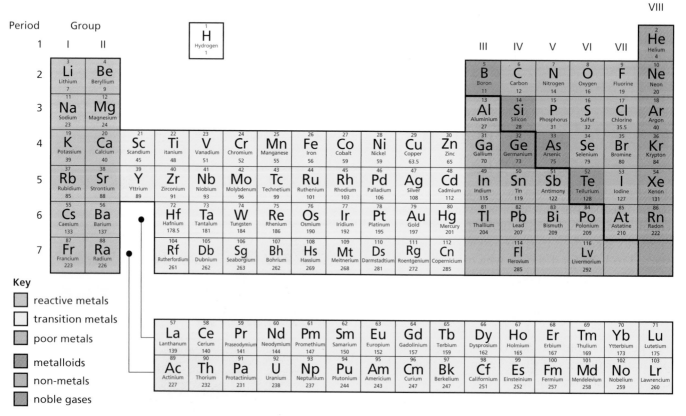

Figure C9.3 The modern Periodic Table.

Figure C9.4 Transition elements have a wide range of uses, both as elements and as alloys.

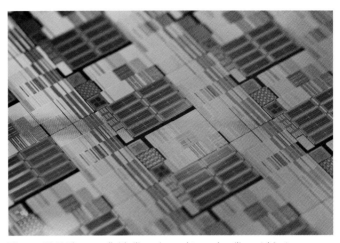

Figure C9.5 The metalloid silicon is used to make silicon 'chips'.

elements with similar chemical properties are found in the same columns or **groups**. There are eight groups of elements. The first column is called Group I; the second Group II; and so on up to Group VII. The final column in the Periodic Table is called Group VIII (or Group 0). Some of the groups have been given names.

Group I: The alkali metals
Group II: The alkaline earth metals
Group VII: The halogens
Group VIII: Inert gases or noble gases

The horizontal rows are called **periods** and these are numbered 1–7 going down the Periodic Table.

Between Groups II and III is the block of elements known as the transition elements (Figure C9.4).

The Periodic Table can be divided into two as shown by the bold line that starts beneath boron, in Figure C9.3. The elements to the left of this line are metals (fewer than three-quarters) and those on the right are non-metals (fewer than one-quarter). The elements which lie on this dividing line are known as metalloids (Figure C9.5). These elements behave in some ways as metals and in others as non-metals.

● Periodic trends

If you look at the properties of the elements across a period of the Periodic Table you will notice certain trends. For example, there is:

● a gradual change from metal to non-metal
● an increase in the number of electrons in the outer energy level of the element

- a change in the structure of the element, from giant metallic in the case of metals (e.g. magnesium), through giant covalent (e.g. diamond, p.214, Figure C3.43), to simple molecular (e.g. chlorine, p.207, Figure C3.29).

● Electronic structure and the Periodic Table

The number of electrons in the outer energy level is discussed in Chapter C3 (p.202). It can be seen that it corresponds with the number of the group in the Periodic Table in which the element is found. For example, the elements shown in Table C9.1 have one electron in their outer energy level and they are all found in Group I. The elements in Group 0, however, are an exception to this rule, as they have two or eight electrons in their outer energy level. The outer electrons are mainly responsible for the chemical properties of any element, and, therefore, elements in the same group have similar chemical properties (Tables C9.2 and C9.3).

Table C9.1 Electronic structure of the first three elements of Group I

Element	Symbol	Proton number	Electronic structure
Lithium	Li	3	2,1
Sodium	Na	11	2,8,1
Potassium	K	19	2,8,8,1

Table C9.2 Electronic structure of the first three elements of Group II

Element	Symbol	Proton number	Electronic structure
Beryllium	Be	4	2,2
Magnesium	Mg	12	2,8,2
Calcium	Ca	20	2,8,8,2

Table C9.3 Electronic structure of the first three elements in Group VII

Element	Symbol	Proton number	Electronic structure
Fluorine	F	9	2,7
Chlorine	Cl	17	2,8,7
Bromine	Br	35	2,8,18,7

The metallic character of the elements in a group increases as you move down the group. This is because electrons become easier to lose as the outer shell electrons become further from the nucleus. There is less attraction between the nucleus and the outer shell electrons because of the increased distance between them.

● Group I – the alkali metals

Group I consists of the five metals lithium, sodium, potassium, rubidium and caesium, and the radioactive element francium. Lithium, sodium and potassium are commonly available for use in school. They are all very reactive metals and they are stored under oil to prevent them coming into contact with water or air. These three metals have the following properties.

- They are good conductors of electricity and heat.
- They are soft metals. Lithium is the hardest and potassium the softest.
- They are metals with low densities. For example, lithium has a density of $0.53\,g/cm^3$ and potassium has a density of $0.86\,g/cm^3$.
- They have shiny surfaces when freshly cut with a knife (Figure C9.6).
- They have low melting points. For example, lithium has a melting point of $181\,°C$ and potassium has a melting point of $64\,°C$.
- They burn in oxygen or air, with characteristic flame.
- They react vigorously with water to give an alkaline solution of the metal hydroxide as well as producing hydrogen gas.
- Of these three metals, potassium is the most reactive towards water (Figure C9.7), followed by sodium and then lithium. Such gradual changes we call **trends**. Trends are useful to chemists as they allow predictions to be made about elements we have not observed in action.

Figure C9.6 Freshly cut sodium.

Considering the group as a whole, the further down the group you go the more reactive the metals become. Francium is, therefore, the most reactive Group I metal.

a potassium reacts very vigorously with cold water

b an alkaline solution is produced when potassium reacts with water

Figure C9.7

> **Question**
>
> 1 Using the information on pp.268 and 269, predict the properties of the element francium related to its melting point, density and softness. Predict how francium would react with water and write a balanced equation for the reaction.

● Group VII – the halogens

Group VII consists of the four elements fluorine, chlorine, bromine and iodine, and the radioactive element astatine. Of these five elements, chlorine, bromine and iodine are generally available for use in school.

Table C9.4 Colours of some halogens

Halogen	Colour
Chlorine	Pale green
Bromine	Red–brown
Iodine	Purple–black

- These elements are coloured and darken going down the group (Table C9.4).
- They exist as diatomic molecules, for example Cl_2, Br_2 and I_2.
- They show a gradual change from a gas (Cl_2), through a liquid (Br_2), to a solid (I_2) (Figure C9.8a) as the density increases.

a chlorine, bromine and iodine

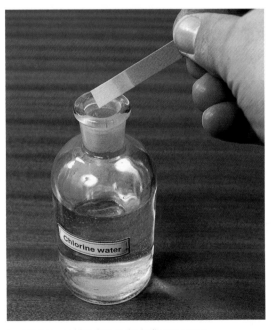

b chlorine gas bleaches moist indicator paper

Figure C9.8

Displacement reactions

If chlorine is bubbled into a solution of potassium iodide, the less reactive halogen, iodine, is **displaced** by the more reactive halogen, chlorine, as you can see from Figure C9.9:

potassium + chlorine → potassium + iodine
iodide   chloride
$2KI(aq) + Cl_2(g) → 2KCl(aq) + I_2(aq)$

Figure C9.9 Iodine being displaced from potassium iodide solution as chlorine is bubbled through.

The observed order of reactivity of the halogens, confirmed by similar displacement reactions, is:

Decreasing reactivity

chlorine   bromine   iodine

You will notice that, in contrast to the elements of Groups I and II, the order of reactivity decreases on going down the group.

Table C9.5 shows the electronic structure for chlorine and bromine. In each case the outer energy level contains seven electrons. When these elements react they gain one electron per atom to gain the stable electron configuration of a noble gas. You will learn more about the stable nature of these gases in the next section. For example, when chlorine reacts it gains a single electron and forms a negative ion (Figure C9.10).

Table C9.5 Electronic structure of chlorine and bromine

Element	Symbol	Proton number	Electronic structure
Chlorine	Cl	17	2,8,7
Bromine	Br	35	2,8,18,7

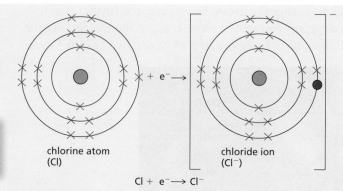

chlorine atom (Cl)   chloride ion (Cl⁻)

$Cl + e^- → Cl^-$

Figure C9.10 A chlorine atom gains an electron to form a chloride ion.

Chlorine is more reactive than bromine because the incoming electron is being more strongly attracted into the outer energy level of the smaller atom. The attractive force on it will be greater than in the case of bromine, since the outer energy level of chlorine is closer to the nucleus. As you go down the group this outermost extra electron is further from the nucleus. It will, therefore, be held less securely, and the resulting reactivity of the elements in Group VII will decrease down the group.

Questions

2 Write word and balanced chemical equations for the reactions between:
   a bromine and potassium iodide solution
   b bromine and potassium chloride solution.
      If no reaction will take place, write 'no reaction' and explain why.
   c Using the information on pp.271–272, predict the properties of the element astatine related to its melting point, density and physical state at room temperature. Predict how astatine would react with sodium bromide solution.

3 a Consider the chemical properties and physical properties of the halogens chlorine, bromine and iodine. Using these properties, predict the following about the other two halogens, fluorine and astatine.

Property	Fluorine	Astatine
State at room temperature and pressure		
Colour		
Reactivity with sodium metal		

   b i   Write a word equation for the reaction of fluorine gas with sodium chloride solution.
      ii Write a balanced chemical equation for the reaction, with state symbols.
      iii Write an ionic equation for the reaction, with state symbols.

● Transition elements

This block of metals includes many you will be familiar with, for example copper, iron, nickel, zinc and chromium (Figure C9.11).

- They are harder and stronger than the metals in Groups I and II.
- They have much higher densities than the metals in Groups I and II.
- They have high melting points (except for mercury, which is a liquid at room temperature).
- They are less reactive metals.
- They form a range of brightly coloured compounds.
- They are good conductors of heat and electricity.
- They show catalytic activity (Chapter C7, p.252) as elements and compounds. For example, iron is used in the industrial production of ammonia gas (Haber process, Chapter C11, p.304).
- They do not react (corrode) so quickly with oxygen and/or water.

c monel is an alloy of nickel and copper, it is extremely resistant to corrosion, even that caused by sea water

a copper is used in many situations which involve good heat and electrical conduction, it is also used in medallions and bracelets

d this bucket has been coated with zinc to prevent the steel of the bucket corroding

b these gates are made of iron, iron can easily be moulded into different shapes

e the alloy stainless steel contains a high proportion of chromium, which makes it corrosion resistant

Figure C9.11 Everyday uses of transition elements and their compounds. They are often known as the 'everyday metals'.

Table C9.6 Electronic structure of helium, neon and argon

Element	Symbol	Proton number	Electronic structure
Helium	He	2	2
Neon	Ne	10	2,8
Argon	Ar	18	2,8,8

Although unreactive, they have many uses. Argon, for example, is the gas used to fill light bulbs to prevent the tungsten filament reacting with air. Neon is used extensively in advertising signs and in lasers.

Helium is separated from natural gas by the liquefaction of the other gases. The other noble gases are obtained in large quantities by the fractional distillation of liquid air.

a Sir William Ramsay (1852–1916)

Group VIII – the noble gases

Helium, neon, argon, krypton, xenon and the radioactive element radon make up a most unusual group of non-metals, called the noble gases. They were all discovered after Mendeleev had published his periodic table. They were discovered between 1894 and 1900, mainly through the work of the British scientists Sir William Ramsay (Figure C9.12a) and Lord John William Strutt Rayleigh (Figure C9.12b).

- They are colourless gases.
- They are monatomic gases – they exist as individual atoms, for example He, Ne and Ar.
- They are very unreactive.
- An alternative name for Group 0 is Group VIII

No compounds of helium, neon or argon have ever been found. However, more recently a number of compounds of xenon and krypton with fluorine and oxygen have been produced, for example XeF_6.

These gases are chemically unreactive because they have electronic structures which are stable and very difficult to change (Table C9.6). They are so stable that other elements attempt to attain these electron configurations during chemical reactions (Chapter C3, pp.203 and 207). You have probably seen this in your study of the elements of Groups I, II and VII.

b Lord Rayleigh (1842–1919)

Figure C9.12 Both helped to discover the noble gases and won the Nobel Prize in Chemistry in 1904 for their work.

Questions

7 Why are the Group VIII gases so unreactive?

8 All of the Group VIII gases are found as monatomic molecules. What are monatomic molecules?

Checklist

After studying Chapter C9 you should know and understand the following.

- Alkali metals are the six metallic elements found in Group I of the Periodic Table.
- Alkaline earth metals are the six metallic elements found in Group II of the Periodic Table.
- Displacement reaction is a reaction in which a more reactive element displaces a less reactive element from solution.
- Group is a vertical column of the Periodic Table containing elements with similar properties with the same number of electrons in their outer energy levels. They have an increasing number of inner energy levels as you descend the group.
- Halogens are the elements found in Group VII of the Periodic Table.

- Metalloid (semi-metal) is any of the class of chemical elements intermediate in properties between metals and non-metals, for example boron and silicon.
- Noble gases are the unreactive gases found in Group 0 of the Periodic Table.
- Periodic Table is a table of elements arranged in order of increasing proton number to show the similarities of the chemical elements with related electronic structures.
- Periods are the horizontal rows of the Periodic Table. Within a period the atoms of all the elements have the same number of occupied energy levels but have an increasing number of electrons in the outer energy level.
- Transition elements are the elements found in the centre of the Periodic Table, between Groups II and III.

C10 Metals

Combined	Co-ordinated
<ul><li>Describe the general physical properties of metals as solids with high melting and boiling points, malleable and good conductors of heat and electricity</li><li>Describe alloys, such as brass, as mixtures of a metal with other elements</li><li>Explain in terms of their properties why alloys are used instead of pure metals</li><li>Identify representations of alloys from diagrams of structure</li><li>Place in order of reactivity: potassium, sodium, calcium, magnesium, aluminium, (carbon), zinc, iron, (hydrogen) and copper, by reference to the reactions, if any, of the elements with: water or steam; dilute hydrochloric acid; reduction of their oxides with carbon</li><li>Describe the reactivity series in terms of the tendency of a metal to form its positive ion, illustrated by its reaction, if any, with the aqueous ions of other listed metals</li><li>Deduce an order of reactivity from a given set of experimental results</li><li>Describe the use of carbon in the extraction of copper from copper oxide</li><li>Describe and explain the essential reactions in the extraction of iron from hematite in the blast furnace $C + O_2 \rightarrow CO_2$ $C + CO_2 \rightarrow 2CO$ $Fe_2O_3 + 3CO \rightarrow 2Fe + 3CO_2$</li><li>Know that aluminium is extracted from the ore bauxite by electrolysis</li><li>Relate the method of extraction of a metal from its ore to its position in the reactivity series for the metals listed above and for other metals, given information</li><li>Describe metal ores as a finite resource and hence the need to recycle metals</li></ul>	<ul><li>Describe the general physical properties of metals as solids with high melting and boiling points, malleable and good conductors of heat and electricity</li><li>Describe metallic bonding as a lattice of positive ions in a 'sea of electrons' and use this to describe the electrical conductivity and malleability of metals</li><li>Describe alloys, such as brass, as mixtures of a metal with other elements</li><li>Explain in terms of their properties why alloys are used instead of pure metals</li><li>Describe how the properties of iron are changed by the controlled use of additives to form steel alloys, such as mild steel and stainless steel</li><li>Identify representations of alloys from diagrams of structure</li><li>Place in order of reactivity: potassium, sodium, calcium, magnesium, aluminium, (carbon), zinc, iron, (hydrogen) and copper, by reference to the reactions, if any, of the elements with: water or steam; dilute hydrochloric acid; reduction of their oxides with carbon</li><li>Describe the reactivity series in terms of the tendency of a metal to form its positive ion, illustrated by its reaction, if any, with: aqueous ions of other listed metals; the oxides of the other listed metals</li><li>Deduce an order of reactivity from a given set of experimental results</li><li>Describe the use of carbon in the extraction of some metals from their ores</li><li>Describe and explain the essential reactions in the extraction of iron from hematite in the blast furnace, including the removal of acidic impurities as slag $C + O_2 \rightarrow CO_2$ $C + CO_2 \rightarrow 2CO$ $Fe_2O_3 + 3CO \rightarrow 2Fe + 3CO_2$ $CaCO_3 \rightarrow CaO + CO_2$ $CaO + SiO_2 \rightarrow CaSiO_3$</li><li>Know that aluminium is extracted from the ore bauxite by electrolysis</li><li>Relate the method of extraction of a metal from its ore to its position in the reactivity series for the metals listed in section C10.2 and for other metals, given information</li><li>Describe metal ores as a finite resource and hence the need to recycle metals</li><li>Describe the uses of aluminium: in aircraft parts because of its strength and low density; in food containers because of its resistance to corrosion</li><li>Describe and explain the apparent unreactivity of aluminium in terms of the oxide layer which adheres to the metal</li><li>State the uses of mild steel (car bodies and machinery) and stainless steel (chemical plant and cutlery)</li><li>Explain the uses of zinc for galvanising steel and for making brass</li></ul>

a sodium burning in air/oxygen

Figure C10.1

b iron rusts when left unprotected

c gold is used in leaf form on this giant Buddha as it is unreactive

As you can see from the Periodic Table, metals make up the majority of the elements. All metals have similar physical properties but they do differ in many other ways. Look closely at the photographs in Figure C10.1.

Sodium is a very reactive metal which reacts so violently with oxygen in the air that it must be stored under oil. Iron reacts with oxygen much more slowly and in the presence of water it will rust. Gold is a very unreactive metal and will not react with oxygen even after many hundreds of years. Sodium is said to be more reactive than iron and gold and iron is more reactive than gold. These three metals all differ in their reactivity but they still share similar physical properties.

All the elements on the Periodic Table can be classified according to their various properties. A simple way to do this is to classify them as metals or non-metals. Table C10.1 shows a comparison of various properties of metals and non-metals.

Table C10.1 How the properties of metals and non-metals compare

Property	Metal	Non-metal
Physical state at room temperature	Usually solid (occasionally liquid)	Solid, liquid or gas
Malleability	Good	Poor – usually soft or brittle
Ductility	Good	
Appearance (solids)	Shiny (lustrous)	Dull
Melting point	Usually high	Usually low
Boiling point	Usually high	Usually low
Density	Usually high	Usually low
Conductivity (thermal and electrical)	Good	Very poor

● Metallic bonding

Another way in which atoms obtain a more stable electron structure is found in metals. The electrons in the outer energy level of the atom of a metal move freely throughout the structure (they are **delocalised** forming a mobile 'sea' of electrons, (Figure C10.2). When the metal atoms lose these electrons, they form a lattice of positive ions. Therefore, metals consist of positive ions embedded in moving clouds of electrons. The negatively charged electrons attract all the positive metal ions and bond them together with strong electrostatic forces of attraction as a single unit. This is the **metallic bond**.

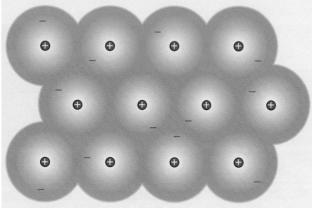

Figure C10.2 Metals consist of positive ions surrounded by a 'sea' of electrons.

Properties of metals

Metals have the following properties.

- They usually have high melting and boiling points due to the strong attraction between the positive metal ions and the mobile 'sea' of electrons.
- They conduct electricity due to the mobile electrons within the metal structure. When a metal is connected in a circuit, the electrons move towards the positive terminal while at the same time electrons are fed into the other end of the metal from the negative terminal. Metals conduct

heat by the mobile electrons colliding with the metal ions and other mobile electrons in the metal structure.
- They are malleable and ductile. Unlike the fixed bonds in diamond, metallic bonds are not rigid but are still strong. If a force is applied to a metal, rows of ions can slide over one another. They reposition themselves and the strong bonds re-form as shown in Figure C10.3. Malleable means that metals can be hammered into different shapes. Ductile means that the metals can be pulled out into thin wires.

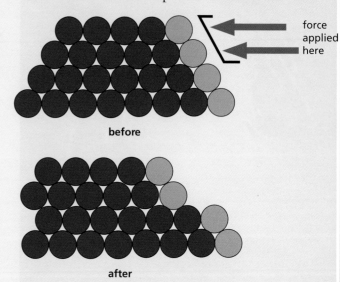

before

after

Figure C10.3 The positions of the positive ions in a metal before and after a force has been applied.

- They have high densities because the atoms are very closely packed in a regular manner as can be seen in Figure C10.4.

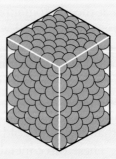

Figure C10.4 Arrangement of ions in the crystal lattice of a metal.

● Metal reactions

By carrying out reactions in the laboratory with other metals and with air, water and dilute acid, it is possible to produce an order of reactivity of the metals.

With acid

Look closely at the photograph in Figure C10.5 showing magnesium metal reacting with dilute hydrochloric acid. You will notice effervescence, which is caused by bubbles of hydrogen gas being formed as the reaction between the two substances proceeds. The other product of this reaction is the salt, magnesium chloride.

magnesium + hydrochloric → magnesium + hydrogen
acid   chloride

$$Mg(s) + 2HCl(aq) → MgCl_2(aq) + H_2(g)$$

If a metal reacts with dilute hydrochloric acid then hydrogen and the metal chloride are produced.

If similar reactions are carried out using other metals with acid, an order of reactivity can be produced by measuring the rate of evolution of hydrogen. This is known as a **reactivity series**. An order of reactivity, giving the most reactive metal first, using results from experiments with dilute acid, is shown in Table C10.2. The table also shows how the metals react with air/oxygen and water/steam, and, in addition, the ease of extraction of the metal.

Figure C10.5 Effervescence occurs when magnesium is put into acid.

In all these reactions the most reactive metal is the one that has the highest tendency to lose outer electrons to form a positive metal ion.

Table C10.2 Order of reactivity

Reactivity series	Reaction with dilute acid	Reaction with air/oxygen	Reaction with water	Ease of extraction	
Potassium (K) Sodium (Na)	Produce H_2 with decreasing vigour	Burn very brightly and vigorously	Produce H_2 with decreasing vigour with cold water	Difficult to extract	
Calcium (Ca) Magnesium (Mg)		Burn to form an oxide with decreasing vigour	React with steam with decreasing vigour	Easier to extract	Increasing reactivity of metal
Aluminium (Al*)					
[Carbon (C)]					
Zinc (Zn)					
Iron (Fe)					
Lead (Pb) [Hydrogen (H)]		React slowly to form the oxide	Do not react with cold water or steam		
Copper (Cu)	Do not react with dilute acids				
Silver (Ag)		Do not react		Found as the element (native)	
Gold (Au)					
Platinum (Pt)					

* Because aluminium reacts so readily with the oxygen in the air, a protective oxide layer is formed on its surface. This often prevents any further reaction and disguises aluminium's true reactivity. This gives us the use of a light and strong metal.

With air/oxygen

Many metals react directly with oxygen to form oxides. For example, magnesium burns brightly in oxygen to form the white powder magnesium oxide.

$$\text{magnesium} + \text{oxygen} \rightarrow \text{magnesium oxide}$$
$$2\text{Mg(s)} + \text{O}_2\text{(g)} \rightarrow 2\text{MgO(s)}$$

With water/steam

Reactive metals such as potassium, sodium and calcium react with cold water to produce the metal hydroxide and hydrogen gas. For example, the reaction of sodium with water produces sodium hydroxide and hydrogen.

$$\text{sodium} + \text{water} \rightarrow \text{sodium hydroxide} + \text{hydrogen}$$
$$2\text{Na(s)} + 2\text{H}_2\text{O(l)} \rightarrow 2\text{NaOH(aq)} + \text{H}_2\text{(g)}$$

The moderately reactive metals, magnesium, zinc and iron, react slowly with water. They will, however, react more rapidly with steam (Figure C10.6). In their reaction with steam, the metal oxide and hydrogen are formed. For example, magnesium produces magnesium oxide and hydrogen gas.

$$\text{magnesium} + \text{steam} \rightarrow \text{magnesium oxide} + \text{hydrogen}$$
$$\text{Mg(s)} + \text{H}_2\text{O(g)} \rightarrow \text{MgO(s)} + \text{H}_2\text{(g)}$$

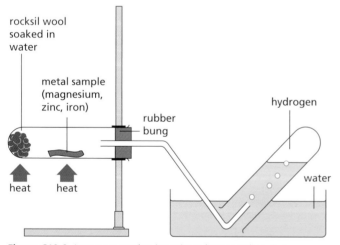

rocksil wool soaked in water

metal sample (magnesium, zinc, iron)

rubber bung

hydrogen

water

heat   heat

Figure C10.6 Apparatus used to investigate how metals such as magnesium react with steam.

Generally, it is the unreactive metals that we find the most uses for; for example, the metals iron and copper can be found in many everyday objects (Figure C10.7). However, magnesium is one of the metals used in the construction of the Airbus A380 (Figure C10.8).

a this wood-burning stove is made of iron

b copper pots and pans
Figure C10.7

Figure C10.8 Planes are made of an alloy which contains magnesium and aluminium.

Both sodium and potassium are so reactive that they have to be stored under oil to prevent them from coming into contact with water or air. However, because they have low melting points and are good conductors of heat, they are used as coolants for nuclear reactors.

● Using the reactivity series

The reactivity series is useful for predicting how metals will react. It can also be used to predict the reactions of some metal compounds.

You can see that metal compounds from a similar part of the series behave in a similar manner.

Competition reactions in the solid state

A more reactive metal has a greater tendency to form a metal ion by losing electrons than a less reactive metal does. Therefore, if a more reactive metal is heated with the oxide of a less reactive metal, then it will remove the oxygen from it (as the oxide anion). You can see from the reactivity series that iron is less reactive than aluminium (p.279). If iron(III) oxide is mixed with aluminium and the mixture is heated using a magnesium fuse (Figure C10.9), a very violent reaction occurs as the competition between the aluminium and the iron for the oxygen takes place.

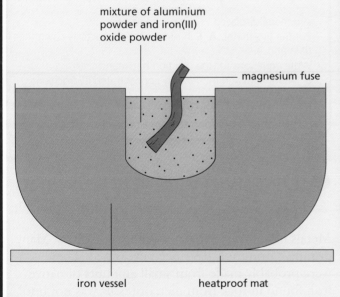

Figure C10.9 Thermit reaction mixture apparatus.

The aluminium, being the more reactive metal, takes the oxygen from the less reactive iron. It is a very exothermic reaction. When the reaction is over, a solid lump of iron is left along with a lot of white aluminium oxide powder.

$$\text{iron(III) oxide} + \text{aluminium} \xrightarrow{\text{heat}} \text{aluminium oxide} + \text{iron}$$
$$Fe_2O_3(s) + 2Al(s) \longrightarrow Al_2O_3(s) + 2Fe(s)$$

or

$$2Fe^{3+}(s) + 2Al(s) \longrightarrow 2Al^{3+}(s) + 2Fe(s)$$

This is a **redox reaction** (see Chapter C5, p.232, and Chapter C7, p.252) for a discussion of this type of reaction).

This particular reaction is known as the **Thermit reaction** (Figure C10.10). Since large amounts of heat are given out and the iron is formed in a molten state, this reaction is used to weld together damaged railway lines. It is also used in incendiary bombs.

Figure C10.10 The Thermit reaction in a laboratory. The same reaction is used to weld damaged railway lines.

Some metals, such as the transition metals chromium and titanium, are prepared from their oxides using this type of competition reaction.

Carbon, a non-metal, is included in Table C10.2 (p.279) just below aluminium. It is able to reduce metal oxides below it in the series.

Competition reactions in aqueous solutions

In another reaction, metals compete with each other for other anions. This type of reaction is known as a **displacement reaction**. As in the previous type of competitive reaction, the reactivity series can be used to predict which of the metals will 'win'.

In a displacement reaction, a more reactive metal will displace a less reactive metal from a solution of its salt. Zinc is above copper in the reactivity series. Figure C10.11 shows what happens when a piece of zinc metal is left to stand in a solution of copper(II) nitrate. The copper(II) nitrate slowly loses its blue colour as the zinc continues to displace the copper from the solution and eventually becomes colourless zinc nitrate.

zinc + copper(II) → zinc nitrate + copper
nitrate

$$Zn(s) + Cu(NO_3)_2(aq) \rightarrow Zn(NO_3)_2(aq) + Cu(s)$$

Figure C10.11 Zinc displaces copper.

The ionic equation for this reaction is:

zinc + copper ions → zinc ions + copper

$$Zn(s) + Cu^{2+}(aq) \rightarrow Zn^{2+}(aq) + Cu(s)$$

This is also a redox reaction involving the transfer of two electrons from the zinc metal to the copper ions. The zinc is oxidised to zinc ions in aqueous solution, while the copper ions are reduced. (See Chapter C5, p.232, for a discussion of oxidation and reduction in terms of electron transfer.) It is possible to confirm the reactivity series for metals using competition reactions of the types discussed in this section.

Questions

1 The data below was obtained by carrying out displacement reactions of five metals with the nitrates of the same five metals. Strips of each metal were placed in solutions of the other four metals' nitrate solutions.

	Nitrates				
	A	B	C	D	E
A	—	✓	✓	✓	✗
B	✗	—	✗	✗	✗
C	✗	✓	—	✓	✗
D	✗	✓	✗	—	✗
E	✓	✓	✓	✓	—

✓ = metal displaced   ✗ = no reaction

Put the five metals **A–E** in order of their reactivity using the data above.

2 Write equations for the reaction between:
  a aluminium and moderately concentrated hydrochloric acid
  b aluminium and moderately concentrated sodium hydroxide (producing sodium aluminate, NaAl(OH)4).

● Discovery of metals and their extraction

Metals have been used since prehistoric times. Many primitive iron tools have been excavated. These were probably made from small amounts of native iron found in rock from meteorites. It was not until about 2500 BC that iron became more widely used. This date marks the dawn of the iron age, when people learned how to get iron from its ores in larger quantities by reduction using charcoal. An ore is a naturally occurring mineral from which a metal can be extracted.

Over the centuries other metals, which like iron are also relatively low in the reactivity series, were isolated in a similar manner. These included copper, lead, tin and zinc. However, due to the relatively low abundance of the ores containing these metals, they were not extracted and used in large amounts.

Metals high in the reactivity series have proved very difficult to isolate. It was not until more recent times, through Sir Humphry Davy's work on electrolysis, that potassium (1807), sodium (1807), calcium (1808) and magnesium (1808) were isolated. Aluminium, the most plentiful reactive metal in the Earth's crust, was not extracted from its ore until 1827, by Friedrich Wöhler, and the extremely reactive metal rubidium was not isolated until 1861 by Robert Bunsen and Gustav Kirchhoff.

The majority of metals are too reactive to exist on their own in the Earth's crust, and they occur naturally in rocks as compounds in ores (Figure C10.12). These ores are usually carbonates, oxides or sulfides of the metal, mixed with impurities.

Some metals, such as gold and silver, occur in a native form as the free metal (Figure C10.13). They are very unreactive and have withstood the action of water and the atmosphere for many thousands of years without reacting to become compounds.

Some of the common ores are shown in Table C10.3. Large lumps of the ore are first crushed and ground up by very heavy machinery. Some ores are already fairly concentrated when mined. For example, in some parts of the world, haematite contains over 80% Fe_2O_3. However, other ores, such as copper pyrites, are often found to be less concentrated, with only 1% or less of the copper compound, and so they have to be concentrated before the metal can be extracted. The method used to extract the metal from its ore depends on the position of the metal in the reactivity series.

Reactive metals such as sodium and aluminium are usually extracted from their compounds found in ores using electrolysis, an expensive method to use. Less and moderately reactive metals can be extracted using carbon. Copper can be obtained from copper(II) oxide by reduction with carbon.

Figure C10.12 Metal ores – chalcopyrite (top) and galena.

Figure C10.13 Gold crystals.

Table C10.3 Some common ores

Metal	Name of ore	Chemical name of compound in ore	Formula	Usual method of extraction
Aluminium	Bauxite	Aluminium oxide	$Al_2O_3.2H_2O$	Electrolysis of oxide dissolved in molten cryolite
Copper	Copper pyrites	Copper iron sulfide	$CuFeS_2$	The sulfide ore is roasted in air
Iron	Haematite	Iron(III) oxide	Fe_2O_3	Heat oxide with carbon
Sodium	Rock salt	Sodium chloride	NaCl	Electrolysis of molten sodium chloride
Zinc	Zinc blende	Zinc sulfide	ZnS	Sulfide is roasted in air and the oxide produced is heated with carbon

Extraction of reactive metals

Because reactive metals, such as sodium, hold on to the element(s) they have combined with, they are usually difficult to extract. For example, sodium chloride (as rock salt) is an ionic compound with the Na^+ and Cl^- ions strongly bonded to one another. The separation of these ions and the subsequent isolation of the sodium metal is therefore difficult.

Electrolysis of the molten, purified ore is the method used in these cases. During this process, the metal is produced at the cathode while a non-metal is produced at the anode. As you might expect, extraction of metal by electrolysis is expensive. In order to keep costs low, many metal smelters using electrolysis are situated in regions where there is hydroelectric power (Chapter P2, p.367).

For further discussion of the extraction of aluminium, see Chapter C5, pp.232–234.

Aluminium is the most abundant metallic element in Earth's crust, found in the ore bauxite as aluminium oxide, Al_2O_3. Aluminium makes up 8% of the crust. Reactive metals such as aluminium are extracted from their ores by electrolysis because these metals hold on tightly to the element(s) they have combined with. During the electrolysis molten aluminium oxide, the aluminium metal is obtained as one product and oxygen as the other. The aluminium produced has many uses such as electrical power cables, in the aircraft and car manufacturing industries.

Extraction of fairly reactive metals

Metals towards the middle of the reactivity series, such as iron and zinc, may be extracted by reducing the metal oxide with the non-metal carbon.

Iron

Iron is extracted mainly from its oxides, haematite (Fe_2O_3) and magnetite (Fe_3O_4), in a blast furnace (Figures C10.14 and C10.15). These ores contain at least 60% iron. The iron ores used are a blend of those extracted in Australia, Canada, Sweden, Venezuela and Brazil. The blast furnace is a steel tower approximately 50 m high lined with heat-resistant bricks. It

is loaded with the 'charge' of iron ore (usually haematite), coke (made by heating coal) and limestone (calcium carbonate).

A blast of hot air is sent in near the bottom of the furnace through holes (tuyères) which makes the 'charge' glow, as the coke burns in the preheated air.

$$\text{carbon} + \text{oxygen} \rightarrow \text{carbon dioxide}$$
$$C(s) + O_2(g) \rightarrow CO_2(g)$$

Figure C10.14 A blast furnace.

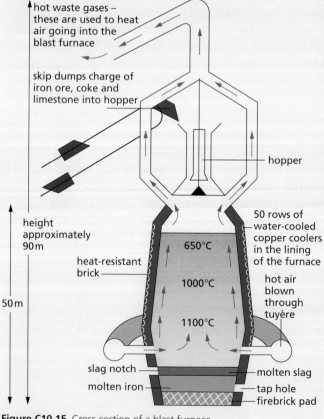

hot waste gases – these are used to heat air going into the blast furnace

skip dumps charge of iron ore, coke and limestone into hopper

hopper

height approximately 90 m

50 m

heat-resistant brick

650°C

1000°C

1100°C

50 rows of water-cooled copper coolers in the lining of the furnace

hot air blown through tuyère

slag notch

molten iron

molten slag

tap hole

firebrick pad

Figure C10.15 Cross-section of a blast furnace.

A number of chemical reactions then follow.

- The limestone begins to decompose:

$$\text{calcium carbonate} \rightarrow \text{calcium oxide} + \text{carbon dioxide}$$
$$CaCO_3(s) \rightarrow CaO(s) + CO_2(g)$$

- The carbon dioxide gas produced reacts with more hot coke higher up in the furnace, producing carbon monoxide in an endothermic reaction.

$$\text{carbon dioxide} + \text{coke} \rightarrow \text{carbon monoxide}$$
$$CO_2(g) + C(s) \rightarrow 2CO(g)$$

- Carbon monoxide is a reducing agent (Chapter C7, p.253). It rises up the furnace and reduces the iron(III) oxide ore. This takes place at a temperature of around 700 °C:

$$\text{iron(III) oxide} + \text{carbon monoxide} \rightarrow \text{iron} + \text{carbon dioxide}$$
$$Fe_2O_3(s) + 3CO(g) \rightarrow 2Fe(l) + 3CO_2(g)$$

The molten iron trickles to the bottom.

- Calcium oxide is a base and this reacts with acidic impurities such as silicon(IV) oxide in the iron, to form a slag which is mainly calcium silicate.

$$\text{calcium oxide} + \text{silicon(IV) oxide} \rightarrow \text{calcium silicate}$$
$$CaO(s) + SiO_2(s) \rightarrow CaSiO_3(l)$$

The slag trickles to the bottom of the furnace, but because it is less dense than the molten iron, it floats on top of it.

Generally, metallic oxides, such as calcium oxide (CaO), are basic and non-metallic oxides, such as silicon(IV) oxide (SiO_2), are acidic.

Certain oxides, such as carbon monoxide (CO), are neutral and others, such as zinc oxide (ZnO), are amphoteric.

The molten iron, as well as the molten slag, may be **tapped off** (run off) at regular intervals.

Figure C10.16 Slag is used in road foundations.

The waste gases, mainly nitrogen and oxides of carbon, escape from the top of the furnace. They are used in a heat exchange process to heat incoming air and so help to reduce the energy costs of the process. Slag is the other waste material. It is used by builders and road makers (Figure C10.16) for foundations.

The extraction of iron is a continuous process and is much cheaper to run than an electrolytic method.

The iron obtained by this process is known as 'pig' or cast iron and contains about 4% carbon (as well as some other impurities). The name pig iron arises from the fact that if it is not subsequently converted into steel it is poured into moulds called pigs. Because of its brittle and hard nature, the iron produced by this process has limited use. Gas cylinders are sometimes made of cast iron, since they are unlikely to get deformed during their use.

The majority of the iron produced in the blast furnace is converted into different steel alloys such as manganese and tungsten steels as well as the well-known example of stainless steel (p.288).

The annual production of iron worldwide is 1536 million tonnes. The larger blast furnaces are capable of producing 10 000 tonnes of iron per day (Figure C10.17 on the next page).

Figure C10.17 Redcar steelworks at Teesside, UK.

Figure C10.18 These people are panning for gold.

Questions

3 How does the method used for extracting a metal from its ore depend on the metal's position in the reactivity series?

4 'It is true to say that almost all the reactions by which a metal is extracted from its ore are reduction reactions.'

Discuss this statement with respect to the extraction of iron, aluminium and zinc.

5 Titanium is extracted from rutile (TiO_2). Use your research skills, including the Internet, to suggest the detail of the extraction process.

Extraction of unreactive metals

Silver and gold

These are very unreactive metals. Silver exists mainly as silver sulfide, Ag_2S (silver glance). The extraction involves treatment of the pulverised ore with sodium cyanide. Zinc is then added to displace the silver from solution. The pure metal is obtained by electrolysis. Silver also exists to a small extent native in the Earth's crust. Gold is nearly always found in its native form (Figure C10.18). It is also obtained in significant amounts during both the electrolytic refining of copper and the extraction of lead.

Silver and gold, because of their resistance to corrosion, are used to make jewellery. Both of these metals are also used in the electronics industry because of their high electrical conductivity.

● Metal waste

Recycling has become commonplace in recent years (Figure C10.19). Why should we really want to recycle metals? Certainly, if we extract fewer metals from the Earth then the existing reserves will last that much longer. Also, recycling metals prevents the creation of a huge environmental problem (Figure C10.20). However, one of the main considerations is that it saves money.

The main metals which are recycled include aluminium and iron. Aluminium is saved by many households as drinks cans and milk bottle tops, to be melted down and recast. Iron is collected at community tips in the form of discarded household goods and it also forms a large part of the materials collected by scrap metal dealers. Iron is recycled to steel. Many steel-making furnaces run mainly on scrap iron.

Figure C10.19 Aluminium can recycling.

Figure C10.20 If we did not recycle metals, then this sight would be commonplace.

Aluminium is especially easy to recycle at low cost. Recycling uses only 5% of the energy needed to extract the metal by electrolysis from bauxite. Approximately 60% of the European need for aluminium is obtained by recycling.

Questions

6 Many local authorities collect used cans from households. The cans collected can be made from different metals such as aluminium and iron. How could cans made of iron be separated easily from aluminium can?

7 As well as saving money in terms of energy costs, what other reasons could be given to promote recycling of aluminium cans?

● Alloys

The majority of the metallic substances used today are **alloys**. Alloys are mixtures of two or more metals and are formed by mixing molten metals thoroughly. It is generally found that alloying produces a metallic substance that has more useful properties than the original pure metals it was made from. For example, the alloy brass is made from copper and zinc. The alloy is harder and more corrosion resistant than either of the metals it is made from.

Steel, which is a mixture of the metal iron and the non-metal carbon, is also considered to be an alloy. Of all the alloys we use, steel is perhaps the most important. Many steels have been produced; they contain not only iron but also carbon and other metals. For example, nickel and chromium are the added metals when stainless steel is produced (Figure C10.21). The chromium prevents the steel from rusting while the nickel makes it harder.

Figure C10.21 A stainless steel exhaust system. Why do you think more people are buying these exhaust systems?

Production of steel

The 'pig iron' obtained from the blast furnace contains between 3% and 5% of carbon and other impurities, such as sulfur, silicon and phosphorus. These impurities make the iron hard and brittle. In order to improve the quality of the metal, most of the impurities must be removed and in doing this, steel is produced.

The impurities are removed in the **basic oxygen process**, which is the most important of the steel-making processes. In this process:

- Molten pig iron from the blast furnace is poured into the basic oxygen furnace (Figure C10.22).
- A water-cooled 'lance' is introduced into the furnace and oxygen at 5–15 atm pressure is blown onto the surface of the molten metal.
- Carbon is oxidised to carbon monoxide and carbon dioxide, while sulfur is oxidised to sulfur dioxide. These escape as gases.
- Silicon and phosphorus are oxidised to silicon(IV) oxide and phosphorus pentoxide, which are solid oxides.
- Some calcium oxide (lime) is added to remove these solid oxides as slag. The slag may be skimmed or poured off the surface.
- Samples are continuously taken and checked for carbon content. When the required amount of carbon has been reached, the blast of oxygen is turned off.

The basic oxygen furnace can convert up to 300 tonnes of pig iron to steel per hour. Worldwide production by this process is 430 million tonnes.

There are various types of steel that differ only in their carbon content. The differing amounts of carbon present confer different properties on the steel and they are used for different purposes (Table C10.4). If other types of steel are required then up to 30% scrap steel is added, along with other metals (such as tungsten), and the carbon is burned off.

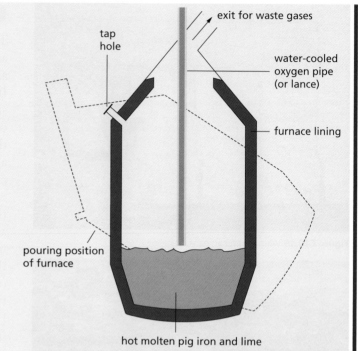

a a section through the basic oxygen furnace

b basic oxygen furnace

Figure C10.22

Table C10.4 Different types of steel

Steel	Typical composition	Properties	Uses
Mild steel	99.5% iron, 0.5% carbon	Easily worked Lost most of brittleness	Car bodies, large structures, machinery
Hard steel	99% iron, 1% carbon	Tough and brittle	Cutting tools, chisels, razor blades
Manganese steel	87% iron, 13% manganese	Tough, springy	Drill bits, springs
Stainless steel	74% iron, 18% chromium, 8% nickel	Tough, does not corrode	Cutlery, kitchen sinks, surgical instruments, chemical plant reaction vessels
Tungsten steel	95% iron, 5% tungsten	Tough, hard, even at high temperatures	Edges of high-speed cutting tools

Steel recycling

The recycling of scrap steel contributes 310 million tonnes to the world supply of the alloy – 750 million tonnes. It has been calculated that the energy savings are equivalent to 160 million tonnes of coal. Also, it has been calculated that the raw materials conserved are equivalent to 200 million tonnes of iron ore.

Alloys to order

Just as the properties of iron can be changed by alloying, so the same can be done with other useful metals. Metallurgists have designed alloys to suit a wide variety of different uses. Many thousands of alloys are now made, with the majority being 'tailor-made' to do a particular job (Figure C10.23).

Table C10.5 shows some of the more common alloys, together with some of their uses.

a Bronze is often used in sculptures

Table C10.5 Uses of common alloys

Alloy	Composition	Use
Brass	65% copper, 35% zinc	Jewellery, machine bearings, electrical connections, door furniture
Bronze	90% copper, 10% tin	Castings, machine parts
Cupro-nickel	30% copper, 70% nickel	Turbine blades
	75% copper, 25% nickel	Coinage metal
Duralumin	95% aluminium, 4% copper, 1% magnesium, manganese and iron	Aircraft construction, bicycle parts
Magnalium	70% aluminium, 30% magnesium	Aircraft construction
Pewter	30% lead, 70% tin, a small amount of antimony	Plates, ornaments and drinking mugs
Solder	70% lead, 30% tin	Connecting electrical wiring

By mixing together different metals, or carbon, to form alloys the properties of the individual metals used are changed. One reason for the different properties is that the atoms of the metals which have been mixed together have different sizes, which distorts the way in which they can pack together. This makes it more difficult for the layers to slide over one another and causes the alloy to be harder than the individual metals used.

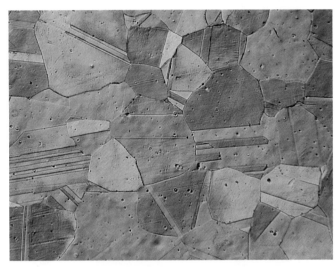

b A polarised light micrograph of brass showing the distinct grain structure of this alloy

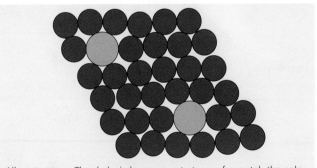

c Alloy structure. The dark circles represent atoms of a metal; the pale circles are the larger atoms of a different metal added to make the alloy. The different size of these atoms gives the alloy different physical properties from those of the pure metal.

Figure C10.23

Questions

8 Calcium oxide is a base. It combines with solid, acidic oxides in the basic oxygen furnace.
Write a chemical equation for one of these oxides reacting with the added lime.

9 'Many metals are more useful to us when mixed with some other elements.' Discuss this statement with respect to stainless steel.

Uses of metals

Using cheap electrical energy has allowed aluminium to be produced in such large quantities that it is the second most widely used metal after iron. It is used in the manufacture of electrical cables because of its low density, chemical inertness and good electrical conductivity. Owing to the first two of these properties, it is also used for making cars, bikes, cooking foil and food containers as well as in alloys (Table C10.5) such as duralumin, which is used in the manufacture of aeroplane bodies (Figure C10.24). Worldwide production of aluminium now exceeds 40 million tonnes each year.

Figure C10.24 Aluminium is used in the manufacture of aeroplane bodies.

Zinc and copper are used in the manufacture of the alloy brass. Brass has a gold-like appearance and has many uses in plumbing in the manufacture of door knobs and musical instruments. It is an unreactive alloy so does not react with water or oxygen, making it corrosion resistant. It is also hard.

Another use of zinc is in galvanising. In the process a thin layer of zinc is coated onto the steel or iron object to prevent the object from rusting. Zinc is more reactive than the iron in the object so it corrodes in preference to the iron in a process known as sacrificial protection. The object will be protected as long as some zinc is coated on it. Galvanising is used to protect steel frameworks used in buildings, in the manufacture of cars and metal roofing.

Question

10 Name the metals used in the production of these alloys:
a brass
b zinc amalgam
c bronze
d solder

Checklist

After studying Chapter C10 you should know and understand the following.

- An alloy is generally, a mixture of two or more metals (for example, brass is an alloy of zinc and copper) or of a metal and a non-metal (for example, steel is an alloy of iron and carbon, sometimes with other metals included). Alloys are formed by mixing the molten substances thoroughly. Generally, it is found that alloying produces a metallic substance which has more useful properties than the original pure metals it was made from.

- A blast furnace is used for smelting iron ores such as haematite (Fe_2O_3) and magnetite (Fe_3O_4) to produce pig (or cast) iron. In a modified form it can be used to extract metals such as zinc.
- Competition reactions are reactions in which metals compete for oxygen or anions. The more reactive metal:
  - takes the oxygen from the oxide of a less reactive metal
  - displaces the less reactive metal from a solution of that metal salt – this type of competition reaction is known as a displacement reaction.

- Corrosion is the process that takes place when metals and alloys are chemically attacked by oxygen, water or any other substances found in their immediate environment.

- Metal extraction refers to the method used to extract a metal from its ore. The method used depends on the position of the metal in the reactivity series.

  - Reactive metals are usually difficult to extract. The preferred method is by electrolysis of the molten ore (electrolytic reduction); for example, sodium from molten sodium chloride.
  - Moderately reactive metals (those near the middle of the reactivity series) are extracted using a chemical reducing agent (for example carbon) in a furnace; for example, iron from haematite in the blast furnace.
  - Unreactive metals, for example gold and silver, occur in an uncombined (native) state as the free metal.

- Metal ion precipitations are reactions in which certain metal cations form insoluble hydroxides. The colours of these insoluble hydroxides can be used to identify the metal cations which are present; for example, copper(II) hydroxide is a blue precipitate.

- Ores are naturally occurring minerals from which a metal can be extracted.

- The reactivity series of metals is an order of reactivity, giving the most reactive metal first, based on results from experiments with oxygen, water and dilute hydrochloric acid.

- Metal drink cans such as those made of aluminium are collected in large 'banks' for the sole purpose of recycling them. Reusing the metal in this way saves money.

C11 Air and water

Combined

- Describe a chemical test for water using copper(II) sulfate and cobalt(II) chloride
- Describe, in outline the treatment of the water supply in terms of filtration and chlorination
- State the composition of clean air as being a mixture of 78% nitrogen, 21% oxygen and small quantities of noble gases, water vapour and carbon dioxide
- Name the common pollutants in air as being carbon monoxide, sulfur dioxide and oxides of nitrogen
- State the adverse effect of these common air pollutants on buildings and on health
- State the conditions required for the rusting of iron (presence of oxygen and water)
- Describe and explain barrier methods of rust prevention, including paint and other coatings
- State the formation of carbon dioxide: as a product of complete combustion of carbon-containing substances; as a product of respiration; as a product of the reaction between an acid and a carbonate; as a product of thermal decomposition of calcium carbonate
- State that carbon dioxide and methane are greenhouse gases
- State that increased concentrations of greenhouse gases cause an enhanced greenhouse effect, which may contribute to climate change

Co-ordinated

- Describe a chemical test for water using copper(II) sulfate and cobalt(II) chloride
- Describe, in outline the treatment of the water supply in terms of filtration and chlorination
- State the composition of clean air as being a mixture of 78% nitrogen, 21% oxygen and small quantities of noble gases, water vapour and carbon dioxide
- Name the common pollutants in air as being carbon monoxide, sulfur dioxide and oxides of nitrogen
- State the adverse effect of these common air pollutants on buildings and on health
- State the source of each of these pollutants: carbon monoxide from the incomplete combustion of carbon-containing substances; sulfur dioxide from the combustion of fossil fuels which contain sulfur compounds (leading to acid rain); oxides of nitrogen from car engines
- Describe some approaches to reducing emissions of sulfur dioxide, including the use of low sulfur petrol and flue gas desulfurisation by calcium oxide
- Describe, in outline, how a catalytic converter removes nitrogen monoxide and carbon monoxide from exhaust emissions by reaction over a hot catalyst
$$2CO + O_2 \rightarrow 2CO_2$$
$$2NO + 2CO \rightarrow N_2 + 2CO$$
$$2NO \rightarrow N_2 + O_2$$
- State the conditions required for the rusting of iron (presence of oxygen and water)
- Describe and explain barrier methods of rust prevention, including paint and other coatings
- Describe and explain sacrificial protection in terms of the reactivity series of metals and galvanising as a method of rust prevention
- State the formation of carbon dioxide: as a product of complete combustion of carbon-containing substances; as a product of respiration; as a product of the reaction between an acid and a carbonate; as a product of thermal decomposition of calcium carbonate
- State that carbon dioxide and methane are greenhouse gases
- State that increased concentrations of greenhouse gases cause an enhanced greenhouse effect, which may contribute to climate change
- Describe the need for nitrogen-, phosphorus- and potassium-containing fertilisers
- Describe the displacement of ammonia from its salts
- Describe and explain the essential conditions for the manufacture of ammonia by the Haber process including the sources of the hydrogen (reaction of methane/natural gas with steam) and nitrogen (from the air)

In this chapter we will study the gaseous mixture we know as the **air** (or atmosphere) and the most important and plentiful liquid on this planet, **water**. The importance of air and water is not in doubt. Without either of these, life would not be possible on Earth!

● Water

Water is the commonest compound on this planet. More than 70% of the Earth's surface is covered with sea, and the land masses are dotted with rivers and lakes (Figure C11.1a). It is vital to our existence and survival because it is one of the main constituents in all living organisms. For example, your bones contain 72% water, your kidneys are about 82% water and your blood is about 90% water (Figure C11.1b).

Water is a neutral, colourless liquid which (at 1 atmosphere pressure) boils at 100 °C and freezes at 0 °C (Figure C11.2).

a millions of tonnes of water pass over this waterfall every day

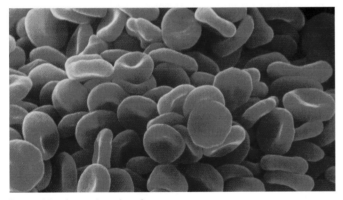

b your blood contains a lot of water

Figure C11.1

Figure C11.2 Liquid water turns to steam at 100 °C and to ice at 0 °C.

You can find out whether a colourless liquid contains water by adding the unknown liquid to anhydrous copper(II) sulfate. If this changes from white to blue, then the liquid contains water (Figure C11.3a on the next page).

Another test is to dip blue cobalt chloride paper into the liquid. If the paper turns pink, then the liquid contains water (Figure C11.3b).

You have already seen in Chapter C5 that water may be electrolysed (when acidified with a little dilute sulfuric acid). When this is done, the ratio of the volume of the gas produced at the cathode to that produced at the anode is 2 : 1. This is what you might expect, since the formula of water is H_2O!

a anhydrous copper(II) sulfate goes blue when water is added to it

b cobalt chloride paper turns pink when water is dropped on to it

Figure C11.3 Tests for the presence of water.

● Water pollution and treatment

An adequate supply of water is essential to the health and well-being of the world's population. Across the planet, biological and chemical pollutants are affecting the quality of our water. Lack of availability of fresh water leads to waterborne diseases, such as cholera and typhoid, and to diarrhoea, which is one of the biggest killers across the world.

Water is very good at dissolving substances. Thus, it is very unusual to find really pure water on this planet. As water falls through the atmosphere, on to and then through the surface of the Earth, it dissolves a tremendous variety of substances. Chemical fertilisers washed off surrounding land will add nitrate ions (NO_3^-) and phosphate ions (PO_4^{3-}) to the water, owing to the use of artificial fertilisers such as ammonium nitrate and ammonium phosphate.

All these artificial, as well as natural, impurities must be removed from the water before it can be used. Regulations in many countries impose strict guidelines on the amounts of various substances allowed in drinking water.

Figure C11.4 This lake is used as a source of drinking water.

A lot of drinking water is obtained from lakes and rivers where the pollution levels are low (Figure C11.4). Undesirable materials removed from water include:

● colloidal clay (clay particles in the water)
● bacteria
● chemicals which cause the water to be coloured and foul tasting
● acids, which are neutralised.

Making water fit to drink

The treatment needed to make water fit to drink depends on the source of the water. Some sources, for example mountain streams, may be almost pure and boiling may be enough to kill any micro-organisms present. However, others, such as slow-flowing rivers, may be contaminated. The object of treating contaminated water is to remove all micro-organisms that may cause disease.

The process of water treatment involves both filtration and chlorination and is summarised in Figure C11.5.

1 Impure water is passed through screens to filter out floating debris.
2 Aluminium sulfate is added to make the small particles of clay stick together so that they form larger clumps, which settle more rapidly.
3 Filtration through coarse sand traps larger, insoluble particles. The sand also contains specially grown microbes which remove some of the bacteria.
4 A sedimentation tank has chemicals added to it to make the smaller particles stick together and sink to the bottom of the tank.
5 These particles are removed by further filtration through fine sand. Sometimes a carbon slurry is used to remove unwanted tastes and odours, and a lime slurry is used to adjust the acidity.
6 Finally, a little chlorine gas is added, which sterilises the water and kills any remaining bacteria.

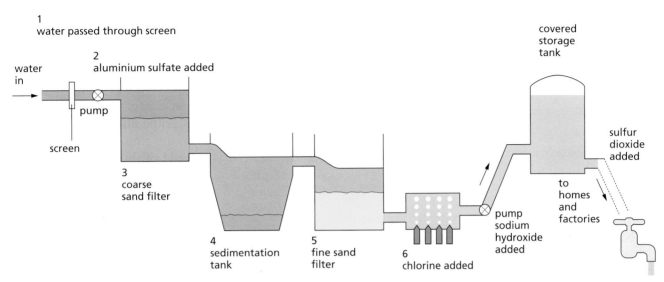

Figure C11.5 The processes involved in water treatment.

Questions

1 Make a list of four major water pollutants and explain where they come from. What damage can these pollutants do?
2 In the treatment of water for public use, state the purpose of the addition of:
   a aluminium sulfate
   b chlorine
   c sodium hydroxide
   d sulfur dioxide.
3 Many industries use water as a coolant. Suggest the sorts of problems that may be created by this 'thermal pollution'.

● The air

The composition of the atmosphere

If a sample of dry, unpolluted air was taken from any location in the troposphere and analysed, the composition by volume of the sample would be similar to that shown in Table C11.1.

Table C11.1 Composition of the atmosphere

Component	%
Nitrogen	78.08
Oxygen	20.95
Argon	0.93
Carbon dioxide	0.04
Neon	0.002
Helium	0.0005
Krypton	0.0001
Xenon plus minute amounts of other gases	0.00001

● Atmospheric pollution

The two major resources considered in this chapter, water and air, are essential to our way of life and our very existence. Water and air make up the environment of a living organism. The environment is everything in the surroundings of an organism that could possibly influence it. Humans continually pollute these resources. We now look at the effects of the various sources of pollution of the air and at the methods used to control or eliminate them.

Air pollution is all around us. Concentrations of gases in the atmosphere such as carbon monoxide, sulfur dioxide and nitrogen oxides are increasing with the increasing population. As the population rises there is a consequent increase in the need for energy, industries and motor vehicles. These gases are produced primarily from the combustion of the fossil fuels coal, oil and gas, but they are also produced by the smoking of cigarettes.

Motor vehicles are responsible for much of the air pollution in large towns and cities. They produce four particularly harmful pollutants:

● carbon monoxide – toxic gas
● sulfur dioxide – major irritant and constituent of acid rain
● hydrocarbons – carcinogenic
● oxides of nitrogen – major irritant, acid rain and photochemical smog
● lead compounds – toxic.

Carbon monoxide is formed when carbon-containing substances, for example methane, burn in a limited supply of oxygen.

methane + oxygen → carbon + water + heat
monoxide energy

$$2CH_4(g) + 3O_2(g) \rightarrow 2CO(g) + 4H_2O(l) + \text{heat energy}$$

This is the incomplete combustion of methane.

Nitrogen monoxide is formed by the reaction of nitrogen and oxygen inside the internal combustion engine at high temperatures.

nitrogen + oxygen → nitrogen monoxide

$$N_2(g) + O_2(g) \rightarrow 2NO(g)$$

The nitrogen monoxide, emitted as an exhaust gas, reacts with oxygen from the air to form the The nitrogen monoxide, emitted as an exhaust gas, reacts with oxygen from the air to form the brown acidic gas nitrogen(IV) oxide (nitrogen dioxide).

nitrogen monoxide + oxygen → nitrogen(IV) oxide

$$2NO(g) + O_2(g) \rightarrow 2NO_2(g)$$

Heavy industry (Figure C11.6) and power stations are major sources of sulfur dioxide, formed by the combustion of coal, oil and gas, which contain small amounts of sulfur.

sulfur + oxygen → sulfur dioxide

$$S(s) + O_2(g) \rightarrow SO_2(g)$$

This sulfur dioxide gas dissolves in rainwater to form the weak acid, sulfurous acid (H_2SO_3).

sulfur dioxide + water ⇌ sulfurous acid

$$SO_2(g) + H_2O(l) \rightleftharpoons H_2SO_3(aq)$$

A further reaction occurs in which the sulfurous acid is oxidised to sulfuric acid. Solutions of these acids are the principal contributors to acid rain.

The amount of sulfur dioxide in the atmosphere has increased dramatically over recent years. There has always been some sulfur dioxide in the atmosphere, from natural processes such as volcanoes and rotting vegetation. Over many countries, however, around 80% of the sulfur dioxide in the atmosphere is formed from the combustion of fuels containing sulfur (Figure C11.6) such as coal, fuel oil, diesel and petrol. After dissolving in rain to produce sulfurous acid, it reacts further with oxygen to form sulfuric acid. This is the main constituent of acid rain.

Rainwater is naturally acidic since it dissolves carbon dioxide gas from the atmosphere as it falls. Natural rainwater has a pH of about 5.7. In recent years the pH of rainwater in many countries has fallen to between pH 3 and pH 4.8.

This increase in acidity has led to extensive damage to forests (Figure C11.7a), lakes and marine life. In addition it has led to the increased corrosion of exposed metals and to damage to buildings and statues made from limestone or marble (Figure C11.7b). The sulfurous acid in rainwater oxidises to sulfuric acid. The sulfuric acid reacts with the limestone, which is eaten away by the chemical process.

limestone + sulfuric acid → calcium sulfate + water + carbon dioxide

$$CaCO_3(s) + H_2SO_4(aq) \rightarrow CaSO_4(s) + H_2O(l) + CO_2(g)$$

Figure C11.6 Sulfur dioxide is a major pollutant produced by industry.

Low sulfur petrol

As you saw earlier the amount of sulfur dioxide has increased because of the combustion of fuels that contain some sulfur. In the case of fuels for vehicles sulfur can be removed from these fuels at the oil refinery. However, this makes the fuel more expensive to produce, but it prevents sulfur dioxide being produced by combustion of fuels such as petrol and diesel. You may have noticed 'low sulfur' petrol and diesel on sale at filling stations in your area.

a this forest has been devastated by acid rain

b acid rain is responsible for much of the damage to this temple on the Acropolis in Athens

Figure C11.7

Flue gas desulfurisation

Units called flue gas desulfurisation (FGD) units are being fitted to some power stations throughout the world to prevent the emission of sulfur dioxide gas. Here, the sulfur dioxide gas is removed from the waste gases by passing them through calcium hydroxide slurry. This not only removes the sulfur dioxide but also creates calcium sulfate, which can be sold to produce plasterboard (Figure C11.8). The FGD units are very expensive and therefore the sale of the calcium sulfate is an important economic part of the process.

Figure C11.8 This plasterboard is made using calcium sulfate from an FGD plant.

Questions

4 a Explain what is meant by the term 'pollution' with reference to air.
  b i Name an air pollutant produced by the burning of coal.
    ii Name a different air pollutant produced by the combustion of petrol in a car engine.
  c Write a balanced chemical equation to represent the reaction which takes place between sulfur dioxide and calcium hydroxide slurry in the FGD unit of a power station.
5 Explain why power stations are thought to be a major cause of acid rain.

Catalytic converters

Usually a country's regulations state that all new cars have to be fitted with catalytic converters as part of their exhaust system (Figure C11.9). Car exhaust fumes contain pollutant gases such as carbon monoxide (CO) formed from the incomplete combustion of hydrocarbons in the fuel, and nitrogen(II) oxide (NO) formed by the reaction of nitrogen gas and oxygen gas from the air. The following reactions proceed of their own accord but very slowly under the conditions inside an exhaust.

carbon monoxide + oxygen → carbon dioxide
$$2CO(g) \quad + \quad O_2(g) \quad \rightarrow \quad 2CO_2(g)$$

nitrogen(II) + carbon → nitrogen + carbon
oxide monoxide dioxide
$$2NO(g) \quad + \quad 2CO(g) \quad \rightarrow \quad N_2(g) \quad + \quad 2CO_2(g)$$

The catalyst in the converter speeds up these reactions considerably. In these reactions, the pollutants are converted to carbon dioxide and nitrogen, which are naturally present in the air. The removal of oxides of nitrogen is important because they cause respiratory disease. They are also involved in the production of photochemical smogs (Figure C11.10) which occur worldwide in major cities, especially in the summer. It should be noted, however, that the catalytic converter can only be used with unleaded petrol and that, due to impurities being deposited on the surface of the catalyst, it becomes poisoned and has to be replaced every five or six years.

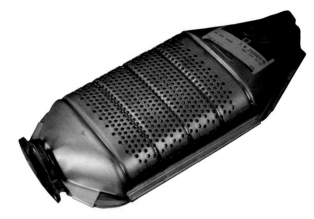
a catalytic converter

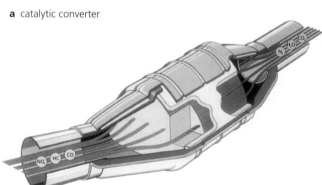
b a section through a catalytic converter
Figure C11.9

Questions

6 Why do some people consider catalytic converters not to be as environmentally friendly as suggested in their advertising material?

7 Unreacted hydrocarbons such as octane, C_8H_{18} (from petrol), also form part of the exhaust gases. These gases are oxidised in the converter to carbon dioxide and water vapour. Write an equation for the oxidation of octane.

Figure C11.10 The haze is due to pollution caused mainly by cars without catalyst exhaust systems.

● Rusting of iron

After a period of time, objects made of iron or steel will become coated with rust. The rusting of iron is a serious problem and wastes enormous amounts of money each year. Estimates are difficult to make, but it is thought that over £1 billion a year is spent worldwide on replacing iron and steel structures.

Rust is an orange–red powder consisting mainly of hydrated iron(III) oxide ($Fe_2O_3.xH_2O$). Both water and oxygen are essential for iron to rust, and if one of these two substances is not present then rusting will not take place. The rusting of iron is encouraged by salt. Figure C11.11 shows an experiment to show that oxygen (from the air) and water are needed for iron to rust.

Rust prevention

To prevent iron rusting, it is necessary to stop oxygen (from the air) and water coming into contact with it. There are several ways of doing this.

Painting

Ships, lorries, cars, bridges and many other iron and steel structures are painted to prevent rusting (Figure C11.12). However, if the paint is scratched, the iron beneath it will start to rust (Figure C11.13) and corrosion can then spread under the paintwork which is still sound. This is why it is essential that the paint is kept in good condition and checked regularly.

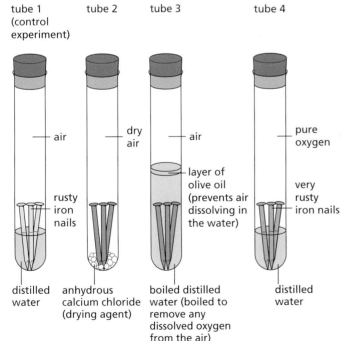

tube 1 (control experiment)   tube 2   tube 3   tube 4

air — rusty iron nails — distilled water

dry air — anhydrous calcium chloride (drying agent)

air — layer of olive oil (prevents air dissolving in the water) — boiled distilled water (boiled to remove any dissolved oxygen from the air)

pure oxygen — very rusty iron nails — distilled water

Figure C11.11 Rusting experiment with nails.

Figure C11.12 Painting keeps the air and water away from the steel used to build a ship.

Figure C11.13 A brand new car is protected against corrosion (top). However, if the paintwork is damaged, then rusting will result.

Oiling/greasing

The iron and steel in the moving parts of machinery are coated with oil to prevent them from coming into contact with air or moisture. This is the most common way of protecting moving parts of machinery, but the protective film must be renewed.

Coating with plastic

The exteriors of refrigerators, freezers and many other items are coated with plastic, such as PVC, to prevent the steel structure rusting (Figure C11.14).

c

Figure C11.14 A coating of plastic stops metal objects coming into contact with oxygen or water.

a

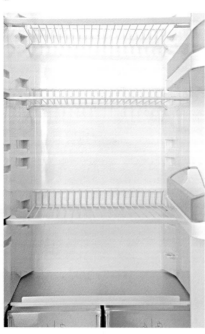

b

Plating

Cans for food can be made from steel coated with tin. The tin is deposited on to the steel used to make food cans by dipping the steel into molten tin. Some car bumpers, as well as bicycle handlebars, are electroplated with chromium to prevent rusting. The chromium gives a decorative finish as well as protecting the steel beneath.

Galvanising

Some steel girders, used in the construction of bridges and buildings, are **galvanised**. Coal bunkers and steel dustbins are also galvanised. This involves dipping the object into molten zinc (Figure C11.15). The thin layer of the more reactive zinc metal coating the steel object slowly corrodes and loses electrons to the iron, thereby protecting it. This process continues even when much of the layer of zinc has been scratched away, so the iron continues to be protected.

Sacrificial protection

Bars of zinc are attached to the hulls of ships and to oil rigs (as shown in Figure C11.16a). Zinc is above iron in the reactivity series and will react in preference to it and so is corroded. It forms positive ions more readily than the iron:

$$Zn(s) + Fe^{2+}(aq) \rightarrow Zn^{2+}(aq) + Fe(s)$$

As long as some of the zinc bars remain in contact with the iron structure, the structure will be protected from rusting. When the zinc runs out,

Figure C11.15 The Burnley Singing Ringing Tree in the UK is a sculpture made from galvanised tubes.

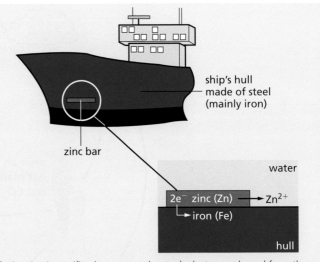

b the zinc is sacrificed to protect the steel, electrons released from the dissolving zinc cause reduction to occur at the surface of the hull

Figure C11.16 Sacrificial protection.

it must be renewed. Gas and water pipes made of iron and steel are connected by a wire to blocks of magnesium to obtain the same result. In both cases, as the more reactive metal corrodes it loses electrons to the iron and so protects it (Figure C11.16b).

a bars of zinc on the hull of a ship

Questions

8 What is rust? Explain how rust forms on structures made of iron or steel.
9 Rusting is a redox reaction. Explain the process of rusting in terms of oxidation and reduction (Chapter C5, p.230).
10 Design an experiment to help you decide whether steel rusts faster than iron.
11 Why do car exhausts rust faster than other structures made of steel?

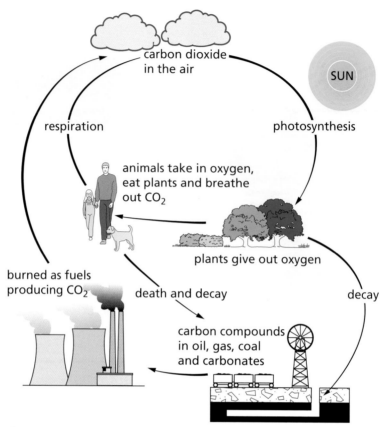

Figure C11.17 The carbon cycle.

● Carbon dioxide

Carbon forms two oxides – carbon monoxide (CO) and carbon dioxide (CO_2). Carbon dioxide is the more important of the two, and in industry large amounts of carbon dioxide are obtained from the liquefaction of air. Air contains approximately 0.03% by volume of carbon dioxide. This value has remained almost constant for a long period of time and is maintained via the **carbon cycle** (Figure C11.17). However, scientists have recently detected an increase in the amount of carbon dioxide in the atmosphere to approximately 0.04%.

Carbon dioxide is produced by burning fossil fuels. It is also produced by all living organisms through **aerobic respiration**. Animals take in oxygen and breathe out carbon dioxide.

glucose   + oxygen → carbon dioxide + water + energy
$$C_6H_{12}O_6(aq) + 6O_2(g) \rightarrow 6CO_2(g) + 6H_2O(l)$$

Carbon dioxide is taken in by plants through their leaves and used together with water, taken in through their roots, to synthesise sugars. This is the process of **photosynthesis**, and it takes place only in sunlight and only in green leaves, as they contain **chlorophyll** (the green pigment) which catalyses the process.

$$\text{carbon dioxide} + \text{water} \xrightarrow[\text{chlorophyll}]{\text{sunlight}} \text{glucose} + \text{oxygen}$$
$$6CO_2(g) + 6H_2O(l) \longrightarrow C_6H_{12}O_6(aq) + 6O_2(g)$$

The carbon cycle has continued in this manner for millions of years. However, scientists have detected an imbalance in the carbon cycle due to the increase in the amount of carbon dioxide produced through burning fossil fuels and the deforestation of large areas of tropical rain forest. The Earth's climate is affected by the levels of carbon dioxide (and water vapour) in the atmosphere. If the amount of carbon dioxide, in particular, builds up in the air, it is thought that the average temperature of the Earth will rise. This effect is known as the **enhanced greenhouse effect**. This is the 'enhanced' effect caused by the increased concentration and effect of the so-called greenhouse gases, such as carbon dioxide, methane and fluorocarbons. (Figure C11.18).

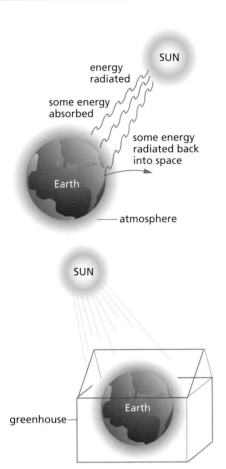

Figure C11.18 The greenhouse effect.

Some energy from the Sun is absorbed by the Earth and its atmosphere. The remainder is reflected back into space. The energy that is absorbed helps to heat up the Earth. The Earth radiates some heat energy back into space but the 'greenhouse gases', including carbon dioxide, prevent it from escaping. This effect is similar to that observed in a greenhouse where sunlight (visible/ultraviolet radiation) enters through the glass panes but heat (infrared radiation) has difficulty escaping through the glass. Other gases also contribute to the greenhouse effect. One of these is methane, which is produced from agriculture and released from landfill sites as well as rice fields.

The long-term effect of the higher temperatures of the greenhouse effect and the subsequent **global warming** will be the continued gradual melting of ice caps and consequent flooding in low-lying areas of the Earth. There will also be further changes in the weather patterns which will further affect agriculture worldwide.

These problems have been recognised by nations worldwide. Agreements under the Kyoto Protocol, and more recently the Paris Agreements between nations, mean that there will be some reduction in the amount of carbon dioxide (and other greenhouse gases) produced over the next few years. However, there is still a long way to go especially as 2016 was the hottest year on record globally!

Other sources of carbon dioxide

As well as being a product of aerobic respiration and the complete combustion of carbon-containing substances, carbon dioxide is also formed in reactions of metal carbonates.

● Most metal carbonates decompose when heated to form the metal oxide and carbon dioxide. For example, when calcium carbonate is heated in furnaces to produce calcium oxide to make products for the building industry then calcium oxide and carbon dioxide are produced:

$$\text{calcium carbonate} \rightarrow \text{calcium oxide} + \text{carbon dioxide}$$
$$CaCO_3(s) \rightarrow CaO(s) + CO_2(g)$$

This is an example of **thermal decomposition**. Thermal decomposition is the chemical breakdown of as substance under the influence of heat.

● Carbonates react with acids to form salts, carbon dioxide and water (Chapter C8, p.259). For example, calcium carbonate reacts with dilute hydrochloric acid to form calcium chloride, carbon dioxide and water.

$$\begin{aligned}\text{calcium} & + \text{hydrochloric} \rightarrow \text{calcium} + \text{carbon} + \text{water} \\ \text{carbonate} & \quad\;\; \text{acid} \qquad\quad \text{chloride} \quad \text{dioxide}\end{aligned}$$
$$CaCO_3(s) + 2HCl(aq) \rightarrow CaCl_2(aq) + CO_2(g) + H_2O(l)$$

Methane – another greenhouse gas!

Methane, occurs naturally. Cows produce it in huge quantities when digesting their food. It is also formed by growing rice. Like carbon dioxide, it is a greenhouse gas because it acts like the glass in a greenhouse – it will let in heat from the Sun but will not let all of the heat back out again. It is thought that the greenhouse effect may contribute to climate change, which could have disastrous effects for life on this planet.

Questions

12 Use your research skills to discover changes that are taking place to the ice caps and weather patterns worldwide.
13 Use your research skills to find out:
   a any other sources of methane found in nature
   b how climate change might affect your particular environment.

● Ammonia – an important nitrogen-containing chemical

Nitrogen from the air is used to manufacture ammonia, a very important **bulk chemical**. A bulk chemical is one that, because of its large usage across a range of uses, is produced in very large quantities. The major process used for making ammonia is the **Haber process**. This process was developed by the German scientist Fritz Haber in 1913 (Figure C11.19). He was awarded a Nobel Prize in 1918 for his work. The process involves reacting nitrogen and hydrogen. It was first developed to satisfy the need for explosives during World War I, as explosives can be made from ammonia. We now have many more uses for this important gas including the manufacture of nitric acid and of fertilisers such as ammonium nitrate.

Figure C11.19 Fritz Haber (1868–1934).

Ammonia (NH_3) is a gaseous compound containing the elements nitrogen and hydrogen. The raw materials needed to make it are:

- nitrogen obtained by cooling air to a point where the nitrogen liquefies followed by fractional distillation
- hydrogen obtained by the reaction between methane and steam:

methane + steam $\rightleftharpoons$ hydrogen + carbon monoxide
$$CH_4(g) + H_2O(g) \rightleftharpoons 3H_2(g) + CO(g)$$

This process is known as steam re-forming.

Nitrogen is an unreactive gas and so special conditions (very high temperature of between 350 °C and 500 °C and pressure of 200 atmospheres) are needed to make it react with hydrogen to form ammonia.

The reaction between the nitrogen and hydrogen takes place inside a steel pressurised vessel which is fitted with an iron catalyst. The catalyst speeds up the reaction between the nitrogen and hydrogen.

nitrogen + hydrogen $\rightleftharpoons$ ammonia
$$N_2(g) + 3H_2(g) \rightleftharpoons 2NH_3(g) \quad \Delta H = -92\,kJ\,mol^{-1}$$

The equation shows arrows travelling in both directions. This is because some of the ammonia which is produced immediately changes back into hydrogen and nitrogen. The reaction is reversible (see Chapter C2, p.193) – it can work in both directions. The conditions of high temperature and pressure help make sure that more ammonia is produced than is changed back into hydrogen and nitrogen. The amount of ammonia formed is called the yield. If for example the yield is 15%, the 85% of the unreacted gases are recycled – returned into the system to react again. The 15% of ammonia produced does not seem a great deal. The reason for this is the reversible nature of the reaction. Once the ammonia is made from nitrogen and hydrogen, most of it decomposes to produce nitrogen and hydrogen.

There comes a point when the rate at which the nitrogen and hydrogen react to produce ammonia is equal to the rate at which the ammonia decomposes. This situation is called a **chemical equilibrium**. Because the processes continue to happen, the

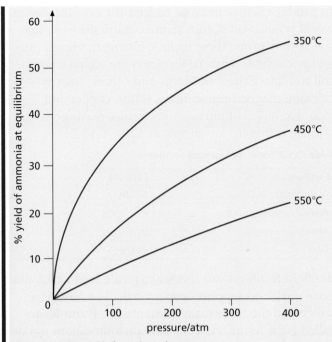

Figure C11.20 Yields from the Haber process.

ammonia at an acceptable rate. It should be noted, however, that the increased pressure used is very expensive in capital terms and so alternative, less expensive routes involving biotechnology are being sought at the present time.

Figure C11.21 Henri Le Chatelier (1850–1936).

equilibrium is said to be **dynamic**. The conditions used ensure that the ammonia is made economically. Figure C11.20 shows how the percentage of ammonia produced varies with the use of different temperatures and pressures.

You will notice that the higher the pressure and the lower the temperature used, the more ammonia is produced. Relationships such as this were initially observed by Henri Le Chatelier, a French scientist, in 1888 (Figure C11.21). He noticed that if the pressure was increased in reactions involving gases, the reaction which produced the fewest molecules of gas was favoured. If you look at the reaction for the Haber process you will see that, going from left to right, the number of molecules of gas goes from four to two. This is why the Haber process is carried out at high pressures. Le Chatelier also noticed that reactions which were exothermic produced more products if the temperature was low. Indeed, if the Haber process is carried out at room temperature you get a higher percentage of ammonia. However, in practice the rate of the reaction is lowered too much and the ammonia is not produced quickly enough for the process to be economical. An **optimum temperature** is used to produce enough

Although most of the ammonia produced is used in the manufacture of fertilisers, some is used for explosives and for making nitric acid. Worldwide, in excess of 150 million tonnes of ammonia are produced by the Haber process each year.

Questions

14 What problems do the builders of a chemical plant to produce ammonia have to consider when they start to build such a plant?
15 What problems are associated with building a plant which uses such high pressures as those required in the Haber process?

Making ammonia in the laboratory

Ammonia can be produced by *displacing it* from one of its salts. This involves the use of a strong base such as sodium hydroxide or calcium hydroxide. This process can be used to prepare ammonia in the laboratory.

Small quantities of ammonia gas can be produced by heating any ammonium salt, such as ammonium chloride, with the base calcium hydroxide.

calcium   + ammonium → calcium   + water   + ammonia
hydroxide   chloride   chloride

$$Ca(OH)_2(s) + 2NH_4Cl(s) \rightarrow CaCl_2(s) + 2H_2O(g) + 2NH_3(g)$$

Water vapour is removed from the ammonia gas by passing the gas formed through a drying tower containing calcium oxide (Figure C11.22).

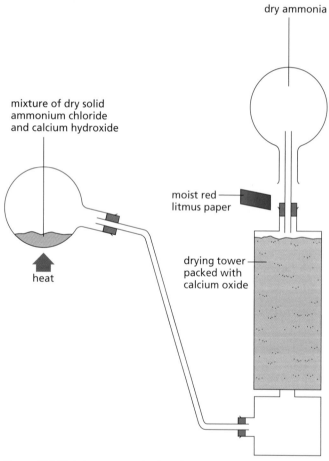

Figure C11.22 Laboratory production of ammonia gas.

● Artificial fertilisers

Some of the ammonia produced by the Haber process is used for the production of many artificial fertilisers. The use of artificial fertilisers is essential if farmers are to produce sufficient crops to feed the ever-increasing world population. Crops remove nutrients from the soil as they grow; these include nitrogen, phosphorus and potassium. Artificial fertilisers are added to the soil to replace these nutrients and others, such as calcium, magnesium, sodium, sulfur, copper and iron. Examples of nitrogenous fertilisers (those which contain nitrogen) are shown in Table C11.2.

Table C11.2 Some nitrogenous fertilisers

Fertiliser	Formula
Ammonium nitrate	NH_4NO_3
Ammonium phosphate	$(NH_4)_3PO_4$
Ammonium sulfate	$(NH_4)_2SO_4$
Urea	$CO(NH_2)_2$

Artificial fertilisers can also make fertile land which was once unable to support crop growth. The fertilisers which add the three main nutrients (N, P and K) are called NPK fertilisers. They contain ammonium nitrate (NH_4NO_3), ammonium phosphate ($(NH_4)_3PO_4$) and potassium chloride (KCl) in varying proportions (Figure C11.23). Fertilisers have an important role in the nitrogen cycle (see below)

a Different fertilisers contain differing amounts of the elements nitrogen, phosphorus and potassium

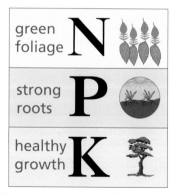

b The different NPK elements are responsible for the healthy growth of plants in different ways
Figure C11.23

Figure C11.24 Fertilisers have been used to help create some of the best fruit on sale.

Questions

16 Ammonia is prepared in the laboratory by the action of heat on a mixture of an alkali and an ammonium compound. The dry gas is collected by upward delivery into a flask.
   a Name a suitable alkali for this preparation.
   b Name a suitable ammonium compound that can be used in the preparation.
   c Name two other products of the reaction.
   d Write a word and symbol equation for the reaction.
   e What substance can be used to dry the ammonia gas?
   f Explain why dry ammonia gas has no effect on dry indicator paper but will turn damp red litmus paper blue.
17 Why do you think that commercial fertilisers have become necessary in present methods of food production?
18 Write down a method that you could carry out in a school laboratory to prepare a sample of the ammonium sulfate fertiliser which is also a salt. Include all the practical details along with a word and balanced chemical equation.

Checklist

After studying Chapter C11 you should know and understand the following.

- Acid rain is rainwater which has a pH in the range 3 to 4.8.
- Artificial fertiliser is a substance added to soil to increase the amount of elements such as nitrogen, potassium and phosphorus. This enables crops grown in the soil to grow more healthily and to produce higher yields.
- Atmosphere (air) is the mixture of gases that surrounds the Earth.
- Bulk chemicals are chemicals that, because of their large usage across a range of uses, are produced in large quantities.
- Carbon dioxide is a colourless, odourless gas, soluble in water, producing a weak acid called carbonic acid. It makes up 0.04% of air. It is produced by respiration in all living things and by the burning of fossil fuels. It is taken in by plants in photosynthesis.
- Catalyst is a substance which alters the rate of a chemical reaction without itself being chemically changed.
- Catalytic converter is a device for converting dangerous exhaust gases from cars into less harmful emissions. For example, carbon monoxide gas is converted to carbon dioxide gas.
- Chemical equilibrium is a dynamic state. The concentration of reactants and products remain constant. This is because the rate at which the forward reaction occurs is the same as that of the reverse reaction.
- Corrosion is the process that takes place when metals and alloys are chemically attacked by oxygen, water or any other substances found in their immediate environment.

- Flue gas desulfurisation (FGD) is the process by which sulfur dioxide gas is removed from the waste gases of power stations by passing them through calcium hydroxide slurry.
- Global warming is an average warming taking place due to the increasing presence of greenhouse gases such as carbon dioxide in the atmosphere.
- Greenhouse effect is the absorption of reflected infrared radiation from the Earth by gases in the atmosphere such as carbon dioxide (a greenhouse gas) leading to atmospheric or global warming.
- Haber process is the chemical process by which ammonia is made in very large quantities from nitrogen and hydrogen.
- Optimum temperature is a compromise temperature used in industry to ensure that the yield of product and the rate at which it is produced make the process as economical as possible.
- Photosynthesis is the chemical process by which green plants synthesise their carbon compounds from atmospheric carbon dioxide using light as the energy source and chlorophyll as the catalyst.
- Pollution is the modification of the environment caused by human influence. It often renders the environment harmful and unpleasant to life. Atmospheric pollution is caused by gases such as sulfur dioxide, carbon monoxide and nitrogen oxides being released into the atmosphere by a variety of industries and also by the burning of fossil fuels. Water pollution is caused by many substances, such as those found in fertilisers and in industrial effluent.
- Raw materials are basic materials from which a product is made. For example, the raw materials for the Haber process are nitrogen and hydrogen.

- Reversible reaction is a chemical reaction which can go both ways. This means that once some of the products have been formed they will undergo a chemical change once more to re-form the reactants. The reaction from left to right, as the equation for the reaction is written, is known as the forward reaction and the reaction from right to left is known as the back reaction.

- Rust is a loose, orange-brown, flaky layer of hydrated iron(III) oxide found on the surface of iron or steel. The conditions necessary for rusting to take place are the presence of oxygen and water. The rusting process is encouraged by other substances such as salt. It is an oxidation process.
- To prevent iron rusting it is necessary to stop oxygen and water coming into contact with it. The methods employed include painting, oiling/greasing, coating with plastic, plating, galvanising and sacrificial protection.

Co-ordinated

● Name the use of sulfur in the manufacture of sulfuric acid

● Describe the manufacture of sulfuric acid by the Contact process, including essential conditions and reactions

$S + O_2 \rightarrow SO_2$

$2SO_2 + O_2 \rightleftharpoons 2SO_3$

$H_2SO_4 + SO_3 \rightarrow H_2S_2O_7$

$H_2S_2O_7 + H_2O \rightarrow 2H_2SO_4$

● Sulfur – the element

Sulfur is a yellow non-metallic element. It is found in Group VI of the Periodic Table. It is a brittle, non-conducting solid with a fairly low melting point (115 °C). Sulfur will not dissolve in water but will dissolve in solvents such as carbon disulfide and methylbenzene (toluene). Like carbon, sulfur has allotropes. Its main allotropes are called rhombic sulfur and monoclinic sulfur (Figure C12.1).

Figure C12.1 Sulfur – rhombic (top) and monoclinic.

Sulfur has a very important role in the chemical industry. It is used to vulcanise rubber, a process which makes the rubber harder and increases its elasticity. Relatively small amounts are used in the manufacture of matches, fireworks and fungicides, as a sterilising agent and in medicines.

However, the vast majority of sulfur is used to produce perhaps the most important industrial chemical, sulfuric acid.

> **Question**
>
> 1 'Sulfur is a non-metallic element.' Discuss this statement, giving physical and chemical reasons to support your answer.

● Sulfuric acid

Industrial manufacture of sulfuric acid – the Contact process

The major use of sulfur is in the production of sulfuric acid. This is probably the most important industrial chemical, and the quantity of it produced by a country has been linked with the economic stability of the country. In excess of 150 million tonnes of sulfuric acid are produced worldwide each year. It is used mainly as the raw material for the production of many substances (Figure C12.2 on the next page).

The process by which sulfuric acid is produced is known as the **Contact process** (Figure C12.3 on the next page).

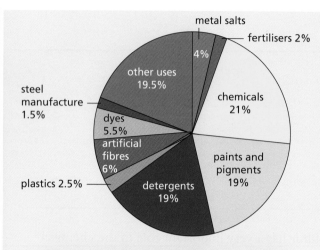

Figure C12.2 Products made from sulfuric acid include detergents, paints and pigments.

Figure C12.3 A Contact process plant used for making sulfuric acid.

The process has the following stages.

- Sulfur dioxide is first produced, primarily by the reaction of sulfur with air.

$$\text{sulfur} \; + \; \text{oxygen} \; \rightarrow \; \text{sulfur dioxide}$$
$$S(s) \; + \; O_2(g) \; \rightarrow \; SO_2(g)$$

- Any dust and impurities are removed from the sulfur dioxide produced, as well as any unreacted oxygen. These 'clean' gases are heated to a temperature of approximately 450 °C and fed into a reaction vessel, where they are passed over a catalyst of vanadium(v) oxide (V_2O_5). This catalyses the reaction between sulfur dioxide and oxygen to produce sulfur trioxide (sulfur(vi) oxide, SO_3).

$$\text{sulfur} \; + \text{oxygen} \rightleftharpoons \; \text{sulfur}$$
$$\text{dioxide} \qquad\qquad\qquad \text{trioxide}$$
$$2SO_2(g) + \; O_2(g) \; \rightleftharpoons 2SO_3(g) \; \Delta H = -197 \text{ kJ/mol}$$

This reaction is reversible, as shown by the reversible sign in the equation $\rightleftharpoons$. So the reaction can be manipulated by adjusting the conditions of temperature and pressure to produce sufficient sulfur trioxide at an economical rate. This gives rise to an optimum temperature of 450 °C and a reaction pressure of 1 atmosphere. Under these conditions, about 96% of the sulfur dioxide and oxygen are converted into sulfur trioxide. The heat produced by this reaction is used to heat the incoming gases, thereby saving money.

- If this sulfur trioxide is added directly to water, sulfuric acid is produced. This reaction, however, is very violent and a thick mist is produced.

$$\text{sulfur trioxide} + \text{water} \rightarrow \text{sulfuric acid}$$
$$SO_3(g) + H_2O(l) \rightarrow H_2SO_4(l)$$

This acid mist is very difficult to deal with and so a different route to sulfuric acid is employed. Instead, the sulfur trioxide is dissolved in concentrated sulfuric acid (98%) to give a substance called **oleum**.

$$\text{sulfuric acid} + \text{sulfur trioxide} \rightarrow \text{oleum}$$
$$H_2SO_4(aq) + SO_3(g) \rightarrow H_2S_2O_7(l)$$

The oleum formed is then added to the correct amount of water to produce sulfuric acid of the required concentration.

$$\text{oleum} + \text{water} \rightarrow \text{sulfuric acid}$$
$$H_2S_2O_7(l) + H_2O(l) \rightarrow 2H_2SO_4(l)$$

Uses of sulfuric acid

As you saw on p.310 sulfuric acid has many uses in industry. It is such an important bulk chemical that the amount of sulfuric acid which a country uses in one year can be seen as a measure of that country's economic development, that is, how modern or wealthy it is.

Figure C12.4 Concentrated sulfuric acid is very corrosive.

Questions

2 Study the following reaction scheme:

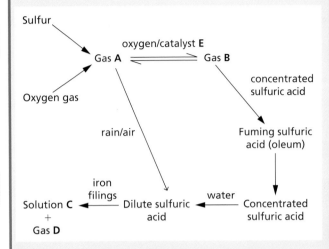

a Identify the substances **A** to **D** by giving their names and formulae.
b Write a balanced chemical equation for the formation of gas **B**.
c Describe a chemical test, and give the positive result of it, to identify gas **D**.
d How would you obtain solid **C** from the solution **C**?
e Which pathway shows the formation of acid rain?
f Where does the oxygen gas come from to form gas **A**?
3 Describe how you would prepare some crystals of hydrated copper(II) sulfate from copper(II) oxide and dilute sulfuric acid. Draw a diagram of the apparatus you would use and write a balanced chemical equation for the reaction.

Checklist

After studying Chapter C12 you should know and understand the following.
- Industrial (or bulk) chemicals are chemicals produced in large quantities by standard chemical reactions, for example ammonia and sulfuric acid.

- Contact process is the industrial manufacture of sulfuric acid using the raw materials sulfur and air.
- Dibasic acid is an acid which contains two replaceable hydrogen atoms per molecule of the acid, for example sulfuric acid, H_2SO_4.
- Oleum is very concentrated sulfuric acid (98%).

- Sulfate is a salt of sulfuric acid formed by the reaction of the acid with carbonates, bases and some metals. It is possible to test for the presence of a sulfate by the addition of dilute hydrochloric acid and some barium chloride solution. A white precipitate of barium sulfate is formed if a sulfate is present.

C13 Carbonates

Co-ordinated

- Describe the manufacture of lime (calcium oxide) from calcium carbonate (limestone) in terms of the chemical reactions involved, and its uses in treating acidic soil and neutralising acidic industrial waste products
- Describe the thermal decomposition of calcium carbonate (limestone)

● Limestone

Figure C13.1 This gorge in the Peak District National Park in the UK is made from limestone.

Limestone is composed of calcium carbonate ($CaCO_3$) in the form of the mineral calcite (Figures C13.1 and C13.2). Chalk and marble are also made of calcite which is the second most abundant mineral in the Earth's crust after the different types of silicates (which include clay, granite and sandstone).

Chalk is made of the 'shells' of marine algae (that is, plants). It is a form of limestone. Most other limestones are formed from the debris of animal structures, for example brachiopods and crinoids.

Marble is a metamorphic rock made of calcium carbonate. It is formed when limestone is subjected to high pressures or high temperatures, or sometimes both acting together, to create crystals of calcium carbonate in the rock.

In a typical year, in excess of 500 million tonnes of limestone are quarried worldwide. Although it is cheap to quarry, as it is found near the surface, there are some environmental costs in its extraction.

Figure C13.2a Chalk and calcite are forms of calcium carbonate.

Figure C13.2b Marble is also a form of calcium carbonate.

● Uses of limestone

Limestone has a variety of uses in, for example, the making of cement, road building, glass making and the extraction of iron (Figure C13.3).

Neutralisation of acid soil

Powdered limestone is most often used to neutralise acid soil (Figure C13.4 on the next page) because it is cheaper than any form of lime (calcium oxide), which has to be produced by heating limestone, and because it is slow acting and an excess does not make the soil alkaline. The reaction of limestone with acidic soil can be shown by the following ionic equation.

carbonate ion + hydrogen ion → carbon + water
(from CaCO₃)   (from acid soils)   dioxide

$$CO_3^{2-}(s) + 2H^+(aq) \rightarrow CO_2(g) + H_2O(l)$$

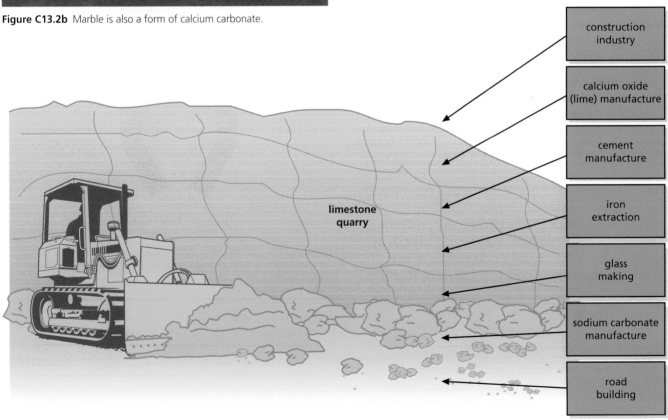

Figure C13.3 Uses of limestone.

Figure C13.4 Spreading limestone on to soil.

Lime manufacture

When calcium carbonate is heated strongly it **thermally decomposes** (Chapter C11, p.303) to form calcium oxide (lime) and carbon dioxide.

calcium carbonate	$\rightleftharpoons$	calcium oxide	+	carbon dioxide
$CaCO_3(s)$	$\rightleftharpoons$	$CaO(s)$	+	$CO_2(g)$

This reaction is an important industrial process and takes place in a lime kiln (Figure C13.5).

The calcium oxide produced from this process is known as quicklime or lime. Very large quantities of calcium oxide are produced worldwide every year because of its variety of uses. Calcium oxide (CaO) is

a base and is still used by some farmers to spread on fields to neutralise soil acidity and to improve drainage of water through soils that contain large amounts of clay. It is also used to neutralise industrial waste products, for example in flue gas desulfurisation. It also has uses as a drying agent in industry and in the manufacture of mouthwash. Soda glass is made by heating sand with soda (sodium carbonate, Na_2CO_3) and lime.

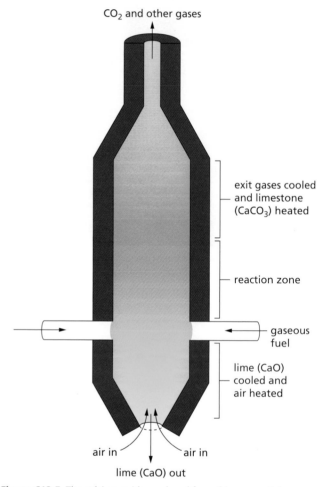

Figure C13.5 The calcium oxide produced from this process is known as quicklime or lime and is used in large quantities in the manufacture of soda glass.

Questions

1 Use the words and formulae below to complete the following passage about limestone and its uses.

CaO building CaCO₃ acids thermal CO₂ oxide acidity quarries quicklime calcium

Limestone is a very common rock. The main chemical in limestone is _____ carbonate (chemical formula, _____). Limestone is obtained from _____ .
The uses of limestone are many and varied. For example, because it is easy to cut into blocks it is useful as a _____ material. Also it will react with _____ and so it is used in the powder form to reduce soil _____ .
When limestone is heated very strongly, it breaks down into _____ (chemical name, calcium _____) and carbon dioxide (chemical formula, _____). This kind of reaction is known as _____ decomposition.

2 Lime is a very important substance. For example it is a base. It is also used in flue gas desulfurisation.
   a What do you understand by the term base?
   b Which gas is the main gas removed by flue gas desulfurisation?
   c Name a gas you have studied which can be dried using lime.

Checklist

After studying Chapter C13 you should know and understand the following.

- Carbonate is a salt of carbonic acid containing the carbonate ion, CO_3^{2-}, for example $CaCO_3$.
- Lime is a white solid known chemically as calcium oxide (CaO). It is produced by heating limestone. It is used to counteract soil acidity and to manufacture calcium hydroxide (slaked lime). It is also used as a drying agent in industry.
- Thermal decomposition is the breakdown of a substance under the influence of heat.

Organic chemistry

Combined

- State that coal, natural gas and petroleum are fossil fuels that produce carbon dioxide on combustion
- Name methane as the main constituent of natural gas
- Describe petroleum as a mixture of hydrocarbons and its separation into useful fractions by fractional distillation
- Describe the properties of molecules within a fraction
- Name the uses of the fractions as: refinery gas for bottled gas for heating and cooking; gasoline fraction for fuel (petrol) in cars; naphtha fraction as a feedstock for making chemicals; diesel oil/gas oil for fuel in diesel engines; bitumen for road surfaces
- Describe the homologous series of alkanes and alkenes as families of compounds with the same general formula and similar chemical properties
- Describe alkanes as saturated hydrocarbons whose molecules contain only single covalent bonds
- Describe the properties of alkanes (exemplified by methane) as being generally unreactive, except in terms of burning
- Describe the complete combustion of hydrocarbons to give carbon dioxide and water
- Describe alkenes as unsaturated hydrocarbons whose molecules contain one double covalent bond
- State that *cracking* is a reaction that produces alkenes
- Describe the formation of smaller alkanes, alkenes and hydrogen by the cracking of larger alkane molecules and state the conditions required for cracking
- Recognise saturated and unsaturated hydrocarbons: from molecular structures; by their reaction with aqueous bromine
- Describe the formation of poly(ethene) as an example of addition polymerisation of monomer units

Co-ordinated

- Name and draw the structures of methane, ethane, ethene and ethanol
- State the type of compound present, given a chemical name ending in -*ane*, -*ene* and -*ol*, or a molecular structure
- Name and draw the structures of the unbranched alkanes and alkenes (not *cis–trans*), containing up to four carbon atoms per molecule
- State that coal, natural gas and petroleum are fossil fuels that produce carbon dioxide on combustion
- Name methane as the main constituent of natural gas
- Describe petroleum as a mixture of hydrocarbons and its separation into useful fractions by fractional distillation
- Describe the properties of molecules within a fraction
- Name the uses of the fractions as: refinery gas for bottled gas for heating and cooking; gasoline fraction for fuel (petrol) in cars; naphtha fraction as a feedstock for making chemicals; diesel oil/gas oil for fuel in diesel engines; bitumen for road surfaces
- Describe the homologous series of alkanes and alkenes as families of compounds with the same general formula and similar chemical properties
- Describe alkanes as saturated hydrocarbons whose molecules contain only single covalent bonds
- Describe the properties of alkanes (exemplified by methane) as being generally unreactive, except in terms of burning
- Describe the complete combustion of hydrocarbons to give carbon dioxide and water
- Describe alkenes as unsaturated hydrocarbons whose molecules contain one double covalent bond
- State that *cracking* is a reaction that produces alkenes
- Describe the formation of smaller alkanes, alkenes and hydrogen by the cracking of larger alkane molecules and state the conditions required for cracking
- Recognise saturated and unsaturated hydrocarbons: from molecular structures; by their reaction with aqueous bromine
- Describe the properties of alkenes in terms of addition reactions with bromine, hydrogen and steam, exemplified by ethene
- State that ethanol may be formed by fermentation and by reaction between ethene and steam
- Describe the formation of ethanol by fermentation and the catalytic addition of steam to ethene
- Describe the complete combustion of ethanol to give carbon dioxide and water
- State the uses of ethanol as a solvent and as a fuel
- Define *polymers* as long chain molecules formed from small units (monomers)
- Understand that different polymers have different monomer units and/or different linkages
- Describe the formation of poly(ethene) as an example of addition polymerisation of monomer units

A lot of the compounds that are present in living things have been found to be compounds containing carbon (Figure C14.1). These are known as **organic compounds**. All living things are made from organic compounds based on chains of carbon atoms which are not only covalently bonded to each other but also covalently bonded to hydrogen, oxygen and/or other elements. The organic compounds are many and varied. Some scientists suggest that there are more than ten million known organic compounds.

Figure C14.1 Living things contain organic compounds.

Crude oil is made up of a complex mixture of hydrocarbon compounds. This mixture is a very important raw material in the organic chemical industry. Our world would be a very different place without these substances. Can you imagine life without the substances from oil and natural gas? There would be no oil-based fuels, such as petrol and diesel, and the chemical industry, particularly the plastics industry, would also suffer since substances extracted from oil are used as raw materials for many plastics.

● Substances from oil

What do the modes of transport shown in Figure C14.2 (below and on the next page) have in common? They all use liquids obtained from **crude oil** (petroleum) as fuels.

a

b

c

d

e

f

Figure C14.2 These modes of transport all use fuels that have been extracted from crude oil.

Figure C14.3 Crude oil is a mixture of hydrocarbons.

Crude oil is not very useful to us until it has been processed. The process, known as **refining**, is carried out at an oil refinery (Figure C14.4).

Refining involves separating crude oil into various batches or **fractions**. Chemists use a technique called **fractional distillation** to separate the different fractions. This process works in a similar way to that discussed in Chapter C2, p.190, for separating ethanol (alcohol) and water. The different components (fractions) separate because

Oil refining

Crude oil is a complex mixture of compounds known as **hydrocarbons** (Figure C14.3). Hydrocarbons are molecules which contain only the elements carbon and hydrogen bonded together covalently (Chapter C3, p.208). These carbon compounds form the basis of a group called **organic compounds**. All living things are made from organic compounds based on chains of carbon atoms similar to those found in crude oil. Crude oil is not only a major source of fuel but is also a raw material of enormous importance. It supplies a large and diverse chemical industry to make dozens of products.

Figure C14.4 An oil refinery.

a fractional distillation of crude oil in a refinery

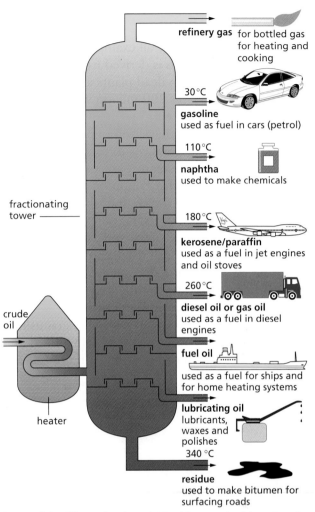

b uses of the different fractions obtained from crude oil (you do not need to know about kerosene, fuel oil and lubricating oil)

Figure C14.5

they have different boiling points. The crude oil is heated to about 400 °C to vaporise all the different parts of the mixture. The mixture of vapours passes into the fractionating column near the bottom (Figure C14.5). Each fraction is obtained by collecting hydrocarbon molecules which have a boiling point in a given range of temperatures. For example, the fraction we know as petrol contains molecules which have boiling points between 30 °C and 110 °C. The molecules in this fraction contain between five and ten carbon atoms. These smaller molecules with lower boiling points condense higher up the tower. The bigger hydrocarbon molecules which have the higher boiling points condense in the lower half of the tower.

The liquids condensing at different levels are collected on **trays**. In this way the crude oil is separated into different fractions. These fractions usually contain a number of different hydrocarbons. The individual single hydrocarbons can then be obtained, again by refining the fraction by further distillation.

Furthermore there are several different types of crude oil and the proportion of the different fractions obtained by fractional distillation will depend on the type which is fed into the process For example, crude oil from Venezuela, in South America, is dark and thick and is known as 'heavy crude'. It contains a lot of long chain hydrocarbons. However, Saudi Arabia in Asia, and Nigeria in Africa, produce a crude oil which is much paler and more runny (less viscous) because this 'light crude' contains many more smaller hydrocarbon molecules. These smaller hydrocarbon molecules are more useful as fuels as well as for making chemicals

● Fossil fuels

Coal, oil and natural gas are all examples of **fossil fuels**. The term fossil fuels is derived from the fact that they are formed from dead plants and animals which were fossilised over 200 million years ago during the carboniferous era.

Coal was produced by the action of pressure and heat on dead wood from ancient forests which once grew in the swampland in many parts of the world under the prevailing weather conditions of that time. When dead trees fell into the swamps they were buried by mud. This prevented aerobic decay (which takes place in the presence of oxygen). Over millions of years, due to movement of the Earth's crust as well as to changes in climate, the land sank and the decaying wood became covered by even more layers of mud and sand. Anaerobic decay (which takes place in the absence of oxygen) occurred, and as time passed the gradually forming coal became more and more compressed as other material was laid down above it (Figure C14.6).

Figure C14.6 Piece of coal showing a fossilised leaf.

Figure C14.7 Cutting coal today is extremely mechanised.

Over millions of years, as the layers of forming coal were pushed deeper and the pressure and temperature increased, the final conversion to coal took place (Figure C14.7). Different types of coal were formed as a result of different pressures being applied during its formation. For example, anthracite is a hard coal with a high carbon content, typical of coal produced at greater depths. Table C14.1 shows some of the different types of coal along with their carbon contents.

Table C14.1 The different coal types

Type of coal	Carbon content/%
Anthracite	90
Bituminous coal	60
Lignite	40
Peat	20

Oil and gas were formed during the same period as coal. It is believed that oil and gas were formed from the remains of plants, animals and bacteria that once lived in seas and lakes. This material sank to the bottom of these seas and lakes and became covered in mud, sand and silt which thickened with time.

Anaerobic decay took place and, as the mud layers built up, high temperatures and pressures were created which converted the material slowly into oil and gas. As rock formed, earth movements caused it to buckle and split, and the oil and gas were trapped in folds beneath layers of non-porous rock or cap-rock (Figures C14.8 and C14.9).

Figure C14.8 Oil production in the North Sea.

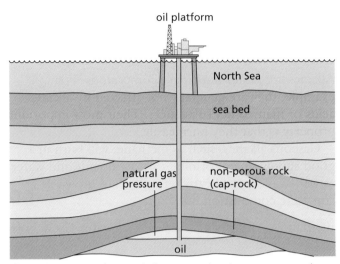

Figure C14.9 Natural gas and oil are trapped under non-porous rock.

● What is a fuel?

A fuel is a substance which can be conveniently used as a source of energy. Fossil fuels release energy in the form of heat when they undergo **combustion**.

fossil fuel + oxygen → carbon dioxide + water + energy

For example, natural gas burns readily in air (C6 p.243).

methane + oxygen → carbon + water + energy
dioxide

$$CH_4(g) + 2O_2(g) \rightarrow CO_2(g) + 2H_2O(l)$$

It should be noted that natural gas, like crude oil, is a mixture of hydrocarbons such as methane (main constituent), ethane and propane, and may also contain some sulfur. The sulfur content varies from source to source. Natural gas obtained from the North Sea is quite low in sulfur.

Questions

1 Why is the sulfur content of fuels a problem with the fuels we use?
2 The combustion of methane (natural gas) is an oxidation reaction. Explain with respect to this reaction the term oxidation.

● Alkanes

Most of the hydrocarbons in crude oil belong to the family of compounds called **alkanes**. The molecules within the alkane family contain carbon atoms covalently bonded to four other atoms by single bonds (Figure C14.10). Because these

molecules possess only single bonds they are said to be **saturated**, as no further atoms can be added. This can be seen in the bonding scheme for methane (Figure C14.11). The physical properties of the first six members of the alkane family are shown in Table C14.2.

You will notice from Figure C14.10 (below and on the next page) and Table C14.2 that the compounds have a similar structure and similar name endings. They also behave chemically in a similar way. A family with these factors in common is called a homologous series.

All the members of a homologous series can also be represented by a general formula. In the case of the alkanes the general formula is:

$$C_nH_{2n+2}$$

where n is the number of carbon atoms present.

As you go up a homologous series, in order of increasing number of carbon atoms, the physical properties of the compounds gradually change. For example, the melting and boiling points of the alkanes shown in Table C14.2 gradually increase. This is due to the fact that the intermolecular forces (van der Waals' forces) increase as the size and mass of the molecule increases.

Under normal conditions molecules with up to four carbon atoms are gases, those with between five and 16 carbon atoms are liquids, while those with more than 16 carbon atoms are solids.

methane

H
|
H—C—H
|
H

ethane

H   H
| |
H—C—C—H
| |
H   H

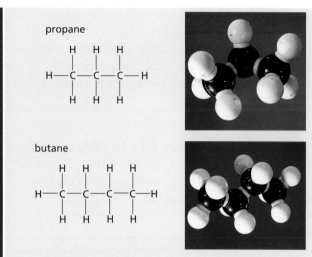

propane

butane

Figure C14.10 The fully displayed (or structural) formulae and molecular models of the first six alkanes.

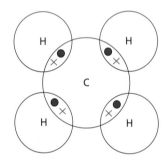

methane molecule (CH$_4$)

Figure C14.11 The covalent bonding scheme for methane.

Table C14.2 Some alkanes and their physical properties

Alkane	Formula	Melting point/°C	Boiling point/°C	Physical state at room temperature
Methane	CH$_4$	−182	−162	Gas
Ethane	C$_2$H$_6$	−183	−89	Gas
Propane	C$_3$H$_8$	−188	−42	Gas
Butane	C$_4$H$_{10}$	−138	0	Gas

Naming the alkanes

All the alkanes have names ending in -*ane*.

The rest of the name tells you the number of carbon atoms present in the molecule. For example, the compound whose name begins with:

- *meth*- has one carbon atom
- *eth*- has two carbon atoms
- *prop*- has three carbon atoms
- *but*- has four carbon atoms

and so on.

● The chemical behaviour of alkanes

Alkanes are rather unreactive compounds. For example, they are generally not affected by alkalis, acids or many other substances. Their most important property is that they burn easily.

Gaseous alkanes, such as methane, will burn in a good supply of air, forming carbon dioxide and water as well as plenty of heat energy. This is known as complete combustion.

methane + oxygen → carbon + water + energy
dioxide

$$CH_4(g) + 2O_2(g) \rightarrow CO_2(g) + 2H_2O(g)$$

The gaseous alkanes are some of the most useful fuels. Methane, better known as natural gas, is used for cooking as well as for heating offices, schools and homes (Figure C14.12a). Propane and butane burn with very hot flames and they are sold as liquefied petroleum gas (LPG). In rural areas where there is no supply of natural gas, central heating systems can be run on propane gas (Figure C14.12b). Butane, sometimes mixed with propane, is used in portable blowlamps and in gas lighters.

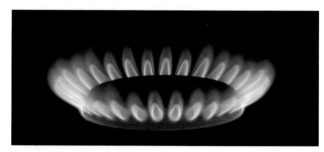

a this is burning methane

b central heating systems can be run on propane
Figure C14.12

● Alkenes

Alkenes form another homologous series of hydrocarbons of the general formula C_nH_{2n} where n is the number of carbon atoms. The alkenes are more reactive than the alkanes because they each contain a double covalent bond between the carbon atoms (Figure C14.13). Molecules that possess a double covalent bond of this kind are said to be **unsaturated**, because it is possible to break one of the two bonds to add extra atoms to the molecule.

The chemical test to show the difference between saturated and unsaturated hydrocarbons is discussed on p.324.

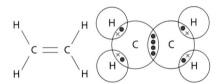

Figure C14.13 The bonding in ethene, the simplest alkene.

Naming the alkenes

All alkenes have names ending in -*ene*.

Alkenes, especially ethene, are very important industrial chemicals. They are used extensively in the plastics industry and in the production of alcohols such as ethanol and propanol. See Table C14.3 and Figure C14.14.

Table C14.3 The first three alkenes and their physical properties.

Alkene	Formula	Melting point/°C	Boiling point/°C	Physical state at room temperature
Ethene	C_2H_4	−169	−104	Gas
Propene	C_3H_6	−185	−47	Gas
Butene	C_4H_8	−184	−6	Gas

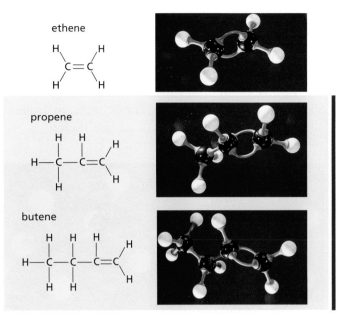

Figure C14.14 Structure and shape of the first three alkenes.

Where do we get alkenes from?

Very few alkenes are found in nature. Most of the alkenes used by the petrochemical industry are obtained by breaking up larger, less useful alkane molecules obtained from the fractional distillation of crude oil. This is usually done by a process called **catalytic cracking**.

In this process the alkane molecules to be 'cracked' (split up) are passed over a mixture of aluminium and chromium oxides heated to about 500 °C.

$$\text{dodecane} \longrightarrow \text{decane} + \text{ethene}$$
$$C_{12}H_{26}(g) \longrightarrow C_{10}H_{22}(g) + C_2H_4(g)$$
(found in kerosene)   shorter alkane   alkene

Another possibility is:

$$C_{12}H_{26}(g) \rightarrow C_8H_{18}(g) + C_4H_8(g)$$

There is a further cracking process which is more versatile, called **thermal cracking**. Thermal cracking is carried out at a higher temperature than catalytic cracking, 800–850 °C. This process is more expensive owing to the higher temperature used. However, larger alkane molecules can be more successfully cracked using this process than by the catalytic method.

Note that in these reactions hydrogen may also be formed during cracking. The amount of hydrogen produced depends on the conditions used.

● The chemical behaviour of alkenes

The double bond makes alkenes more reactive than alkanes in chemical reactions. For example, hydrogen adds across the double bond of ethene, under suitable conditions, forming ethane (Figure C14.15).

Figure C14.15 The addition of hydrogen to ethene using molecular models.

Addition reactions
Hydrogenation

This reaction is called **hydrogenation**. The conditions necessary for this reaction to take place are a temperature of 200 °C in the presence of a nickel or platinum catalyst.

$$\text{ethene} + \text{hydrogen} \longrightarrow \text{ethane}$$
$$C_2H_4(g) + H_2(g) \longrightarrow C_2H_6(g)$$

Hydrogenation reactions like the one shown with ethene are used in the manufacture of margarines from vegetable oils. Vegetable oils contain fatty acids, such as linoleic acid ($C_{18}H_{32}O_2$). These are unsaturated molecules, containing several double bonds. These double bonds make the molecule less flexible. Hydrogenation can convert these molecules into more saturated ones. Now the molecules are less rigid and can flex and twist more easily, and hence pack more closely together. This in turn causes an increase in the intermolecular forces and so raises the melting point. The now solid margarines can be spread on bread more easily than liquid oils.

There is another side to this process. Many doctors now believe that unsaturated fats are healthier than saturated ones. Because of this, many margarines are left partially unsaturated. They do not have all the C=C taken out of the fat molecules. However, the matter is far from settled and the debate continues.

Hydration

Another important **addition reaction** is the one used in the manufacture of ethanol. Ethanol has important uses as a solvent and a fuel (p.326). It is formed when water (as steam) is added across the double bond in ethene. For this reaction to take place, the reactants have to be passed over a catalyst of phosphoric(v) acid (absorbed on silica pellets) at a temperature of 300 °C and pressure of 60 atmospheres (1 atmosphere = 1×10^5 pascals).

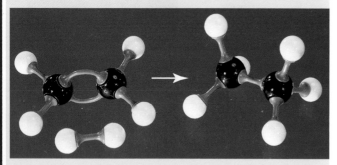

This reaction is reversible as is shown by the equilibrium ($\rightleftharpoons$) sign. The conditions have been chosen to ensure the highest possible yield of ethanol. In other words, the conditions have been chosen so that they favour the forward reaction.

For a further discussion of ethanol and alcohols generally see p.325.

Halogenation – a test for unsaturated compounds

The addition reaction between bromine dissolved in an organic solvent, or water, and alkenes is used as a chemical test for the presence of a double bond between two carbon atoms. When a few drops of this bromine solution are shaken with the hydrocarbon, if it is an alkene, such as ethene, a reaction takes place in which bromine joins to the alkene double bond. This results in the bromine solution losing its red/brown colour. If an alkane, such as hexane, is shaken with a bromine solution of this type, no colour change takes place (Figure C14.16). This is because there are no double bonds between the carbon atoms of alkanes.

ethene + bromine $\longrightarrow$ dibromoethane

$$C_2H_4(g) + Br_2 \text{ (in solution)} \longrightarrow C_2H_4Br_2\text{(in solution)}$$

$$\underset{H}{\overset{H}{\diagdown}}C=C\underset{H}{\overset{H}{\diagup}} + Br\!-\!Br \longrightarrow H-\underset{\underset{Br}{|}}{\overset{\overset{H}{|}}{C}}-\underset{\underset{Br}{|}}{\overset{\overset{H}{|}}{C}}-H$$

Questions

5 What is meant by the term 'addition reaction'?
6 Write a word and balanced chemical equation for the reaction between ethene and hydrogen chloride.
7 Write the structural formula for pentene.
8 Which of the following organic chemicals are alkanes or alkenes?
   Propene, C_3H_6
   Butanol, C_4H_9OH
   Octane, C_8H_{18}
   Nonane, C_9H_{20}
   Methanoic acid, HCOOH
   Butene, C_4H_8
   State why you have chosen your answers.

● Alcohols (R—OH)

The alcohols (alkanols) form another homologous series with the general formula $C_nH_{2n+1}OH$ (or R—OH, where R represents an alkyl group) and have names ending in -ol.

Table C14.4 shows the names and condensed formulae of the first four members along with their melting and boiling points.

Table C14.4 Some members of the alcohol family.

Alcohol	Formula	Melting point/°C	Boiling point/°C
Methanol	CH_3OH	−94	64
Ethanol	CH_3CH_2OH	−117	78
Propanol	$CH_3CH_2CH_2OH$	−126	97
Butanol	$CH_3CH_2CH_2CH_2OH$	−89	117

Many other materials, such as food flavourings, are made from ethanol. As ethanol is also a very good solvent and evaporates easily, it is used extensively as a solvent for paints, glues, aftershave and many other everyday products (Figure C14.18 on the next page).

Figure C14.17 shows the structure of ethanol alongside its molecular model.

Figure C14.16 The alkene decolourises bromine in 1,1,1-trichloroethane.

ethanol

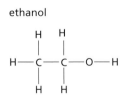

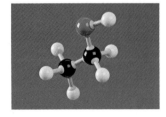

Figure C14.17 Ethanol looks like the corresponding model alongside.

Figure C14.18 This aftershave contains alcohol.

Ethanol is by far the most important of the alcohols and is often just called 'alcohol'. Ethanol can be produced by fermentation as well as by the hydration of ethene (p.324). It is a neutral, colourless, volatile liquid which does not conduct electricity. The more concentrated forms of alcoholic drinks such as the spirits whiskey and brandy contain high concentrations of ethanol. These are produced by distillation after the fermentation is complete (Chapter C2, p.190).

Combustion

Ethanol burns quite readily with a clean, hot flame.

ethanol	+ oxygen	→	carbon dioxide	+	water	+ energy

$$CH_3CH_2OH(l) + 3O_2(g) \rightarrow 2CO_2(g) + 3H_2O(g) + energy$$

As methylated spirit, it is used in spirit (camping) stoves. Methylated spirit is ethanol with small amounts of poisonous substances added to stop people drinking it. Some countries, like Brazil, already use ethanol mixed with petrol as a fuel for cars (Chapter P2, p.367) and this use is increasing worldwide.

Formation of ethanol

Industrially, ethanol is produced by the reaction between ethene and steam (p.324). It is also formed by **fermentation**, brought about by micro-organisms or enzymes.

Fermentation in the laboratory can be carried out using sugar solution. A micro-organism called yeast is added to the solution. The yeast uses the sugar for energy during **anaerobic respiration** (respiration without oxygen), and so the sugar is broken down to give carbon dioxide and ethanol. The best temperature for this process to be carried out is at 37 °C.

$$glucose \xrightarrow{yeast} ethanol + carbon\ dioxide$$
$$C_6H_{12}O_6(aq) \longrightarrow 2C_2H_5OH(l) + 2CO_2(g)$$

Figure C14.19 shows a simple apparatus for obtaining ethanol from glucose in the laboratory.

If a bottle of wine is left exposed to the atmosphere then further oxidation takes place and the ethanol is oxidised to ethanoic acid.

Figure C14.19 Fermenting glucose and yeast to produce ethanol. The bag is inflated during the experiment by CO_2.

Questions

9 Explain why alcoholic drinks go sour if left open to the atmosphere for some time.
10 The equation below represents the fermentation process:
   A → **B** + carbon dioxide
   a Identify and give the formulae of substances **A** and **B**.
   b Give a chemical test to identify carbon dioxide.
   c Which separation technique would you use to separate substance **B** from the fermentation mixture?

● A special addition reaction of alkene molecules

Polythene is a plastic that was discovered by accident. Through the careful examination of this substance, when it was accidentally discovered, the plastics industry was born. Polythene is now produced in millions of tonnes worldwide every year. It is made by heating ethene to a relatively high temperature under a high pressure in the presence of a catalyst.

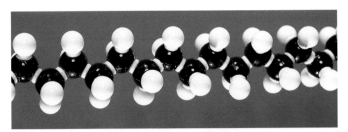

Figure C14.20 This model shows part of the poly(ethene) polymer chain.

where *n* is a very large number. In poly(ethene) the ethene molecules have joined together to form a very long hydrocarbon chain (Figure C14.20). The ethene molecules are able to form chains like this because they possess carbon–carbon double bonds.

Poly(ethene) is produced in three main forms:

- low density poly(ethene) (LDPE)
- linear low density poly(ethene) (LLDPE)
- high density poly(ethene) (HDPE).

The world production of all types of poly(ethene) is in excess of 52 million tonnes per year.

Poly(ethene) has many useful properties:

- it is easily moulded
- it is an excellent electrical insulator
- it does not corrode
- it is tough
- it is not affected by the weather
- it is durable.

It can be found as a substitute for natural materials in plastic bags, sandwich boxes, washing-up bowls, wrapping film, milk-bottle crates and washing-up liquid bottles (Figure C14.21).

Figure C14.21 These crates are made from poly(ethene).

Other alkene molecules can also produce substances like poly(ethene); for example, propene produces poly(propene), which is used to make ropes and packaging.

When small molecules like ethene join together to form long chains of atoms, called **polymers**, the process is called **polymerisation**. The small molecules, like ethene, which join together in this way are called **monomers**. A polymer chain, a very large molecule or a macromolecule, often consists of many thousands of monomer units and in any piece of plastic there will be many millions of polymer chains. Since in this polymerisation process the monomer units add together to form only one product, the polymer, the process is called **addition polymerisation**.

Other addition polymers

Many other addition polymers have been produced. Often the plastics are produced with particular properties in mind, for example PVC (polyvinyl chloride or poly(chloroethene)) and PTFE (poly(tetrafluoroethene)). Both of these plastics have monomer units similar to ethene.

PVC monomer
(vinyl chloride or
chloroethene)

PTFE monomer
(tetrafluoroethene)

If we use chloroethene (Figure C14.22a on the next page), the polymer we make is slightly stronger and harder than poly(ethene) and is particularly good for making pipes for plumbing (Figure C14.23 on the next page).

monomer

polymer chain

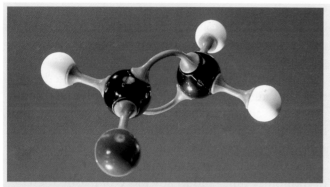

a model of chloroethene, the PVC monomer

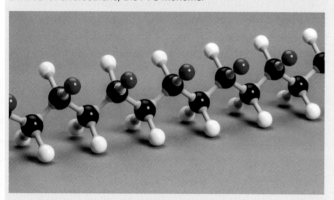

b model of part of a PVC polymer chain

Figure C14.22

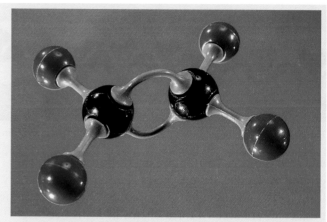

a model of tetrafluoroethene, the PTFE monomer

b model of part of the PTFE polymer chain

Figure C14.24

- it will withstand very high temperatures, of up to 260 °C
- it forms a very slippery surface
- it is hydrophobic (water repellent)
- it is highly resistant to chemical attack.

These properties make PTFE an ideal 'non-stick' coating for frying pans and saucepans. Every year more than 50 000 tonnes of PTFE are made.

Figure C14.23 These pipes are made from PVC.

PVC is the most versatile plastic and is the second most widely used, after poly(ethene). Worldwide more than 27 million tonnes are produced annually.

If we start from tetrafluoroethene (Figure C14.24a) the polymer we make, PTFE, has some slightly unusual properties:

$$n \left(\begin{array}{c} \mathrm{F} \quad\quad \mathrm{F} \\ \diagdown \quad \diagup \\ \mathrm{C}{=}\mathrm{C} \\ \diagup \quad \diagdown \\ \mathrm{F} \quad\quad \mathrm{F} \end{array} \right) \longrightarrow \left(\begin{array}{cc} \mathrm{F} & \mathrm{F} \\ | & | \\ {-}\mathrm{C}{-}\mathrm{C}{-} \\ | & | \\ \mathrm{F} & \mathrm{F} \end{array} \right)_{n}$$

monomer   polymer chain

The properties of some addition polymers along with their uses are given in Table C14.5.

Table C14.5 Some addition polymers

Plastic	Monomer	Properties	Uses
Poly(ethene)	$CH_2 = CH_2$	Tough, durable	Carrier bags, bowls buckets, packaging
Poly(propene)	$CH_3CH = CH_2$	Tough, durable	Ropes, packaging
PVC	$CH_2 = CHCl$	Strong, hard (less flexible than poly(ethene))	Pipes, electrical insulation, guttering
PTFE	$CF_2 = CF_2$	Non-stick surface, withstands high temperatures	Non-stick frying pans, soles of irons
Polystyrene	$CH_2 = CHC_6H_5$	Light, poor conductor of heat	Insulation, packaging (especially as foam)
Perspex	$CH_2 = C(CO_2CH_3)CH_3$	Transparent	Used as a glass substitute

Questions

11 Write the general equation to represent the formation of polystyrene from its monomer.
12 Draw the structure of the repeating unit of the addition polymer formed from $CH_3—CH＝CH_2$.
13 Draw the structure of the monomer from which the addition polymer below has been produced.

$$
\begin{array}{ccccccccccc}
& C_6H_5 & H & & C_6H_5 & H & & C_6H_5 & H & \\
& | & | & & | & | & & | & | & \\
-\!C\! & -\!C\! & -\!C\! & -\!C\! & -\!C\! & -\!C\!- & & & & \\
& | & | & & | & | & & | & | & \\
& H & H & & H & H & & H & H &
\end{array}
$$

● Condensation polymers

On p.326 you studied the different addition polymers produced from alkenes. Not all polymers are formed by addition reactions, though. Some are produced as a result of a different type of reaction. In 1935 Wallace Carothers discovered a different sort of plastic when he developed the thermoplastic, nylon. Nylon is made by reacting two different chemicals together, unlike poly(ethene) which is made only from monomer units of ethene. Poly(ethene), formed by addition polymerisation, can be represented by:

–A–A–A–A–A–A–A–A–A–A–

where A = monomer.

The starting molecules for nylon are more complicated than those for poly(ethene) and are called 1,6-diaminohexane and hexanedioic acid.

1,6–diaminohexane
$H_2N(CH_2)_6NH_2$
$+$
hexanedioic acid
$HOOC(CH_2)_4COOH$

$\downarrow$

$H_2N(CH_2)_6\mathbf{NHOC}(CH_2)_4COOH + H_2O$

amide link

The polymer chain is made up from the two starting molecules arranged alternately (Figure C14.25) as these molecules react and therefore link up. Each time a reaction takes place a molecule of water is lost.

Figure C14.25 A nylon polymer chain is made up from the two molecules arranged alternately just like the two different coloured poppet beads in the photo.

This sort of reaction is called **condensation polymerisation**. This differs from addition polymerisation, where there is only one product. Because an amide link is formed during the polymerisation, nylon is known as a **polyamide**. This is the same amide link as found in proteins. It is often called the **peptide link**. This type of polymerisation, in which two kinds of monomer unit react, results in a chain of the type:

–A–B–A–B–A–B–A–B–A–B–

Generally, polyamides have the structure

$$
\begin{array}{c}
\quad O \qquad\quad O \qquad\qquad\qquad O \qquad\quad O \\
\quad \| \qquad\quad \| \qquad\qquad\qquad \| \qquad\quad \| \\
-C\!-\!\blacksquare\!-\!C\!-\!N\!-\!\square\!-\!N\!-\!C\!-\!\blacksquare\!-\!C\!-\!N\!-\!\square\!-\!N- \\
\qquad\qquad\qquad | \qquad\qquad | \qquad\qquad\qquad\qquad | \qquad\qquad | \\
\qquad\qquad\qquad H \qquad\qquad H \qquad\qquad\qquad\qquad H \qquad\qquad H
\end{array}
$$

Figure C14.26 Nylon fibre is formed by forcing molten plastic through hundreds of tiny holes.

When nylon is made in industry, it forms as a solid which is melted and forced through small holes (Figure C14.26). The long filaments cool and solid nylon fibres are produced which are stretched to align the polymer molecules and then dried. The resulting yarn can be woven into fabric to make shirts, ties, sheets and parachutes or turned into ropes or racket strings for tennis and badminton rackets. The annual worldwide production of nylon is expected to reach 6 million tonnes by 2015.

We can obtain different polymers with different properties if we carry out condensation polymerisation reactions between other monomer molecules. For example, if we react ethane-1,2-diol with benzene-1,4-dicarboxylic acid, then we produce a polymer called Terylene.

ethane–1,2–diol   +   benzene–1,4–dicarboxylic acid
$HO(CH_2)_2OH$ $HOOC(C_6H_4)COOH$

$$HO(CH_2)_2\mathbf{OCO}(C_6H_4)COOH \ + \ H_2O$$

ester link

This ester link is the same linkage as in fats. Generally, polyesters have the structure

$$-\overset{\overset{\displaystyle O}{\|}}{C}-\square-\overset{\overset{\displaystyle O}{\|}}{C}-O-\square-O-\overset{\overset{\displaystyle O}{\|}}{C}-\square-\overset{\overset{\displaystyle O}{\|}}{C}-O-\square-O-$$

Like nylon, Terylene can be turned into yarn, which can then be woven. Terylene clothing is generally softer than that made from nylon but both are hard wearing. Because an ester link is formed during the polymerisation, Terylene is known as a **polyester**.

Fats possess the same sort of linkage as Terylene but have different units.

Questions

14 A piece of cheese contains protein. Proteins are natural polymers made up of amino acids. There are 20 naturally occurring amino acids. The structures of two amino acids are shown below.

          glycine   alanine

$$\begin{array}{cc} & H \\ & | \\ H_2N-C-COOH \\ & | \\ & H \end{array} \qquad \begin{array}{cc} & H \\ & | \\ H_2N-C-COOH \\ & | \\ & CH_3 \end{array}$$

  a   Name the type of polymerisation involved in protein formation.

  b   Draw a structural formula to represent the part of the protein chain formed by the reaction between the amino acids shown above.

15 a   Name the polymerisation process that is used to make nylon.

  b   Name the starting materials for:
      i   nylon
      ii   terylene.

  c   Give the name and formula of the small molecule produced during the polymerisation reactions to produce nylon.

  d   Give the name of the chemical link that holds together

  e   Give two uses for nylon

  f   Explain the difference between the type of polymerisation you have named in part **a** and addition polymerisation.

16 Explain the differences between an addition polymer and a condensation polymer.

Checklist

After studying Chapter C14 you should know and understand the following.

- Addition polymer is a polymer formed by an addition reaction. For example, poly(ethene) is formed from ethene.

- Addition reaction is a reaction in which an atom or group of atoms is added across a carbon-carbon double bond.

- Alcohols are organic compounds containing the –OH group. They have the general formula $C_nH_{2n+1}OH$. Ethanol is by far the most important of the alcohols and is often just called 'alcohol'.

- Alkanes are a family of saturated hydrocarbons with the general formula C_nH_{2n+2}. The term 'saturated', in this context, is used to describe molecules that have only single bonds. The alkanes can only undergo substitution reactions in which there is replacement of one atom in the molecule by another atom.

- Alkenes are a family of unsaturated hydrocarbons with the general formula C_nH_{2n}. The term 'unsaturated', in this context, is used to describe molecules which contain one or more carbon–carbon double bonds. Unsaturated compounds undergo addition reactions across the carbon–carbon double bonds and so produce saturated compounds. The addition of hydrogen across the carbon–carbon double bonds is used to reduce the amount of unsaturation during the production of margarines.

- Anaerobic respiration is respiration that takes place in the absence of air.

- Catalytic cracking is the decomposition of higher alkanes into alkenes and alkanes of lower relative molecular mass. The process involves passing the larger alkane molecules over a catalyst of aluminium and chromium oxides, heated to 500 °C.

- Condensation polymer is a polymer formed by a condensation reaction (one in which water is given out). For example, nylon is produced by the condensation reaction between 1,6-diaminohexane and hexanedioic acid.

- Fermentation is a series of biochemical reactions brought about by the enzymes in yeast or, more generally, by microorganisms.

- Halogenoalkanes are organic compounds in which one or more hydrogen atoms of an alkane have been substituted by halogen atoms such as chlorine.

- Homologous series is a series of compounds in which each member differs from the next by a specific number and kind of atom. These compounds have the same general formula and similar properties.

- Monomer is a simple molecule, such as ethene, which can be polymerised.

- Organic chemistry is the branch of chemistry concerned with compounds of carbon found in living organisms. These compounds are called organic compounds.

- Polyamide is a condensation polymer, such as nylon, that contains the amide(or peptide) link, –NHOC–.

- Polymer is a substance possessing very large molecules consisting of repeated units or monomers. Polymers therefore have a very large relative molecular mass.

- Polymerisation is the chemical reaction in which molecules (monomers) join together to form a polymer.

- Saturated hydrocarbon is a type of hydrocarbon molecule in which the molecule has the maximum possible number of hydrogen atoms and so has no double bonds.

- Thermal cracking refers to the decomposition of higher alkanes to alkenes of lower relative molecular mass at high temperatures, 800–850°C.

- Unsaturation can be tested by for shaking a few drops of bromine dissolved in an organic solvent with the hydrocarbon. If it is decolourised, the hydrocarbon is unsaturated.

- Unsaturated hydrocarbon is a hydrocarbon molecule which contains double or triple covalent bonds between carbon atoms.

Physics

Combined

- Use and describe the use of rules and measuring cylinders to find a length or volume
- Use and describe the use of clocks and devices, both analogue and digital, for measuring an interval of time
- Obtain an average value for a small distance and for a short interval of time by measuring multiples (including the period of a pendulum)
- Define *speed* and calculate average speed from total distance / total time
- Plot and interpret a speed–time graph and a distance–time graph
- Recognise from the shape of a speed–time graph when a body is: at rest; moving with constant speed; moving with changing speed
- Demonstrate understanding that acceleration and deceleration are related to changing speed including qualitative analysis of the gradient of a speed–time graph
- Calculate the area under a speed–time graph to work out the distance travelled for motion with constant acceleration
- Calculate acceleration from the gradient of a speed–time graph
- Recognise linear motion for which the acceleration is constant and calculate the acceleration
- Recognise motion for which the acceleration is not constant
- Distinguish between *mass* and *weight*
- Know that the Earth is the source of a gravitational field
- Recognise that *g* is the gravitational force on unit mass and is measured in N/kg
- Recall and use the equation $W = mg$
- Describe, and use the concept of, weight as the effect of a gravitational field on a mass
- Describe an experiment to determine the density of a liquid and of a regularly shaped solid and make the necessary calculation
- Recall and use the equation $\rho = m/v$
- Describe the determination of the density of an irregularly shaped solid by the method of displacement and make the necessary calculation
- Describe how forces may change the size, shape and motion of a body
- Understand friction as the force between two surfaces which impedes motion and results in heating
- Recognise air resistance as a form of friction
- Find the resultant of two or more forces acting along the same line
- Recognise that if there is no resultant force on a body it either remains at rest or continues at constant speed in a straight line
- Plot and interpret extension–load graphs and describe the associated experimental procedure
- State Hooke's Law and recall and use the expression $F = kx$ where *k* is the spring constant
- Recognise the significance of the term *limit of proportionality* for an extension–load graph

Co-ordinated

- Use and describe the use of rules and measuring cylinders to find a length or volume
- Use and describe the use of clocks and devices, both analogue and digital, for measuring an interval of time
- Obtain an average value for a small distance and for a short interval of time by measuring multiples (including the period of a pendulum)
- Understand that a micrometer screw gauge is used to measure very small distances
- Define *speed* and calculate average speed from total distance/total time
- Plot and interpret a speed–time graph and a distance–time graph
- Recognise from the shape of a speed–time graph when a body is: at rest; moving with constant speed; moving with changing speed
- Demonstrate an understanding that acceleration and deceleration are related to changing speed including qualitative analysis of the gradient of a speed–time graph
- Calculate the area under a speed–time graph to work out the distance travelled for motion with constant acceleration
- State that the acceleration of free fall *g* for a body near to the Earth is constant
- Distinguish between *speed* and *velocity*
- Define and calculate *acceleration* using $\dfrac{\text{change of velocity}}{\text{time taken}}$
- Calculate acceleration from the gradient of a speed–time graph
- Recognise linear motion for which the acceleration is constant and calculate the acceleration
- Recognise motion for which the acceleration is not constant
- Distinguish between *mass* and *weight*
- Know that the Earth is the source of a gravitational field
- Recognise that *g* is the gravitational force on unit mass and is measured in N/kg
- Recall and use the equation $W = mg$
- Demonstrate understanding that weights (and hence masses) may be compared using a balance
- Describe, and use the concept of, weight as the effect of a gravitational field on a mass
- Describe an experiment to determine the density of a liquid and of a regularly shaped solid and make the necessary calculation
- Recall and use the equation $\rho = m/v$
- Describe the determination of the density of an irregularly shaped solid by the method of displacement and make the necessary calculation
- Describe how forces may change the size, shape and motion of a body
- Understand friction as the force between two surfaces which impedes motion and results in heating

- Recognise air resistance as a form of friction
- Find the resultant of two or more forces acting along the same line
- Recognise that if there is no resultant force on a body it either remains at rest or continues at constant speed in a straight line
- Plot and interpret extension–load graphs and describe the associated experimental procedure
- State Hooke's Law and recall and use the expression $F = kx$ where k is the spring constant
- Recognise the significance of the term *limit of proportionality* for an extension–load graph
- Recall and use the relationship between resultant force, mass and acceleration, $F = ma$
- Describe the moment of a force as a measure of its turning effect, and give everyday examples

- Calculate moment using the product force × perpendicular distance from the pivot
- Recognise that, when there is no resultant force and no resultant turning effect, a system is in equilibrium

- Apply the principle of moments to the balancing of a weightless beam about a pivot
- Apply the principle of moments to different situations
- Perform and describe an experiment to determine the position of the centre of mass of a plane lamina
- Describe qualitatively the effect of the position of the centre of mass on the stability of simple objects
- Relate qualitatively pressure to force and area, using appropriate examples

- Recall and use the equation $p = F/A$

Units and basic quantities

Before a measurement can be made, a standard or **unit** must be chosen. The size of the quantity to be measured is then found with an instrument having a scale marked in the unit.

Three basic quantities we measure in physics are **length**, **mass** and **time**. Units for other quantities are based on them. The SI (Système International d'Unités) system is a set of metric units now used in many countries. It is a decimal system in which units are divided or multiplied by 10 to give smaller or larger units.

Figure P1.1 Measuring instruments on the flight deck of a passenger jet provide the crew with information about the performance of the aircraft.

Length

The unit of **length** is the **metre** (m) and is the distance travelled by light in a vacuum during a specific time interval. At one time it was the distance between two marks on a certain metal bar. Submultiples are:

$$1 \text{ decimetre (dm)} = 10^{-1}\,\text{m}$$
$$1 \text{ centimetre (cm)} = 10^{-2}\,\text{m}$$
$$1 \text{ millimetre (mm)} = 10^{-3}\,\text{m}$$

A multiple for large distances is

$$1 \text{ kilometre (km)} = 10^3\,\text{m} \left(\tfrac{5}{8} \text{ mile approx.}\right)$$

Many length measurements are made with rulers; the correct way to read one is shown in Figure P1.2. The reading is 76 mm or 7.6 cm. Your eye must be directly over the mark on the scale or the thickness of the ruler causes a parallax error.

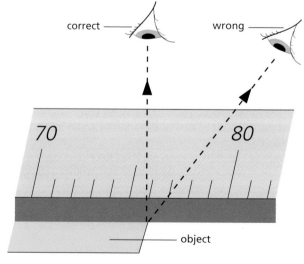

Figure P1.2 The correct way to measure with a ruler.

To obtain an average value for a small distance, multiples can be measured. For example, in ripple tank experiments (Chapter P4) measure the distance occupied by five waves, then divide by 5 to obtain the average wavelength.

● Area

The **area** of the square in Figure P1.3a with sides 1 cm long is 1 square centimetre (1 cm²). In Figure P1.3b the rectangle measures 4 cm by 3 cm and has an area of 4 × 3 = 12 cm² since it has the same area as twelve squares each of area 1 cm². The area of a square or rectangle is given by

area = length × breadth

The SI unit of area is the square metre (m²) which is the area of a square with sides 1 m long. Note that

$$1\,cm^2 = \frac{1}{100}\,m \times \frac{1}{100}\,m = \frac{1}{10\,000}\,m^2 = 10^{-4}\,m^2$$

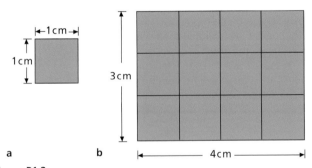

a   b

Figure P1.3

● Volume

Volume is the amount of space occupied. The unit of volume is the **cubic metre** (m³) but as this is rather large, for most purposes the **cubic centimetre** (cm³) is used. The volume of a cube with 1 cm edges is 1 cm³. Note that:

$$1\,cm^3 = \frac{1}{100}\,m \times \frac{1}{100}\,m \times \frac{1}{100}\,m$$

$$= \frac{1}{1\,000\,000}\,m^3 = 10^{-6}\,m^3$$

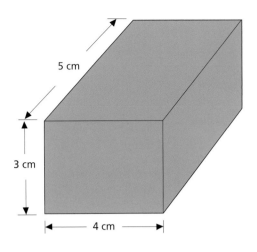

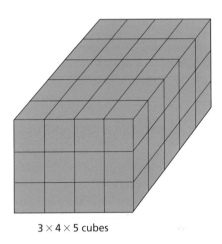

3 × 4 × 5 cubes

Figure P1.4

For a regularly shaped object such as a rectangular block, Figure P1.4 shows that:

volume = length × breadth × height

The volume of a sphere of radius r is $\frac{4}{3}\pi r^3$ and that of a cylinder of radius r and height h is $\pi r^2 h$.

The volume of a liquid may be obtained by pouring it into a measuring cylinder, Figure P1.5 on the next page. When making a reading the cylinder must be upright and your eye must be level with the bottom of the curved liquid surface, i.e. the **meniscus**. The meniscus formed by mercury is curved oppositely to that of other liquids and the top is read.

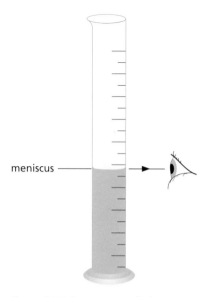

Figure P1.5 A measuring cylinder.

Liquid volumes are also expressed in litres (l); 1 litre $= 1000\,cm^3 = 1\,dm^3$. One millilitre ($1\,ml$) $= 1\,cm^3$.

● Time

The unit of **time** is the **second** (s) which used to be based on the length of a day, this being the time for the Earth to revolve once on its axis. However, days are not all of exactly the same duration and the second is now defined as the time interval for a certain number of energy changes to occur in the caesium atom.

Time-measuring devices rely on some kind of constantly repeating oscillation. In traditional clocks and watches a small wheel (the balance wheel) oscillates to and fro; in digital clocks and watches the oscillations are produced by a tiny quartz crystal. A swinging pendulum controls a pendulum clock.

To measure an interval of time in an experiment, first choose a timer that is accurate enough for the task. A stopwatch is adequate for finding the period in seconds of a pendulum, see Figure P1.6, but to measure the speed of sound (p.405), a clock that can time in milliseconds is needed. To measure very short time intervals, a digital clock that can be triggered to start and stop by an electronic signal from a microphone, photogate or mechanical switch is useful. Tickertape timers or dataloggers are

often used to record short time intervals in motion experiments (pp.341 and 350).

Accuracy can be improved by measuring longer time intervals. Several oscillations (rather than just one) are timed to find the average period of a pendulum. 'Tenticks' (rather than 'ticks') are used in tickertape timers.

Practical work

Period of a simple pendulum

In this investigation you have to make time measurements using a stopwatch or clock.

Attach a small metal ball (called a bob) to a piece of string, and suspend it as shown in Figure P1.6. Pull the bob a small distance to one side, and then release it so that it oscillates to and fro through a small angle.

Find the time for the bob to make several complete oscillations; one oscillation is from A to O to B to O to A (Figure P1.6). Repeat the timing a few times for the same number of oscillations and work out the average. The time for one oscillation is the **period** T. What is it for your system? The **frequency** f of the oscillations is the number of complete oscillations per second and equals $1/T$. Calculate f.

How does the amplitude of the oscillations change with time?

Investigate the effect on T of **(i)** a longer string, **(ii)** a heavier bob. A motion sensor connected to a datalogger and computer (pp.341 and 350) could be used instead of a stopwatch for these investigations.

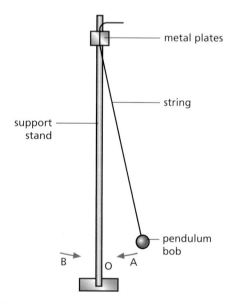

Figure P1.6

Vernier scales and micrometers

Lengths can be measured with a ruler to an accuracy of about 1 mm. Some investigations may need a more accurate measurement of length, which can be achieved by using **vernier calipers** (Figure P1.7) or **a micrometer screw gauge**.

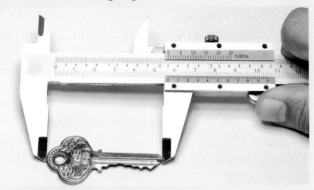

Figure P1.7 Vernier calipers in use.

Micrometer screw gauge

This measures very small objects to 0.001 cm. One revolution of the drum opens the accurately flat, parallel jaws by one division on the scale on the shaft of the gauge; this is usually $\frac{1}{2}$ mm, i.e. 0.05 cm. If the drum has a scale of 50 divisions round it, then rotation of the drum by one division opens the jaws by $0.05/50 = 0.001$ cm (Figure P1.8). A friction clutch ensures that the jaws exert the same force when the object is gripped.

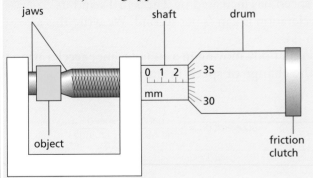

Figure P1.8 Micrometer screw gauge.

The object shown in Figure P1.8 has a length of

$$2.5 \text{ mm on the shaft scale } +$$
$$33 \text{ divisions on the drum scale}$$
$$= 0.25 \text{ cm} + 33(0.001) \text{ cm}$$
$$= 0.283 \text{ cm}$$

Before making a measurement, check to ensure that the reading is zero when the jaws are closed. Otherwise the zero error must be allowed for when the reading is taken.

Questions

1. How many millimetres are there in
   - a 1 cm
   - b 4 cm
   - c 0.5 cm
   - d 6.7 cm
   - e 1 m?
2. What are these lengths in metres?
   - a 300 cm
   - b 550 cm
   - c 870 cm
   - d 43 cm
   - e 100 mm
3. a Write the following as powers of ten with one figure before the decimal point:
      100 000   3500   428 000 000   504   27 056
   b Write out the following in full:
      10^3 2×10^6 6.92×10^4 1.34×10^2 10^9
4. The pages of a book are numbered 1 to 200 and each leaf is 0.10 mm thick. If each cover is 0.20 mm thick, what is the thickness of the book?
5. A rectangular block measures 4.1 cm by 2.8 cm by 2.1 cm. Calculate its volume giving your answer to an appropriate number of significant figures.
6. How many blocks of ice cream each 10 cm × 10 cm × 4 cm can be stored in the compartment of a freezer measuring 40 cm × 40 cm × 20 cm?
7. What are the readings on the micrometer screw gauges in Figures 1.9a and b?

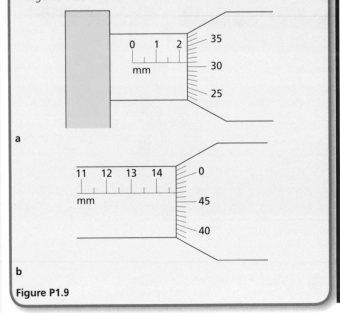

a

b

Figure P1.9

Speed

If a car travels 300 km from Liverpool to London in five hours, its **average speed** is 300 km/5 h = 60 km/h. The speedometer would certainly not read 60 km/h for the whole journey but might vary considerably from this value. That is why we state the average speed. If a car could travel at a constant speed of 60 km/h for five hours, the distance covered would still be 300 km. It is *always* true that:

$$\text{average speed} = \frac{\text{distance moved}}{\text{time taken}}$$

To find the actual speed at any instant we would need to know the distance moved in a very short interval of time. This can be done by multiflash photography. In Figure P1.10 the golfer is photographed while a flashing lamp illuminates him 100 times a second. The speed of the club-head as it hits the ball is about 200 km/h.

Figure P1.10 Multiflash photograph of a golf swing.

Velocity

Speed is the distance travelled in unit time; **velocity is the distance travelled in unit time in a stated direction**. If two trains travel due north at 20 m/s, they have the same speed of 20 m/s and the same velocity of 20 m/s *due north*. If one travels north and the other south, their speeds are the same but not their velocities since their directions of motion are different.

$$\text{velocity} = \frac{\text{distance moved in a stated direction}}{\text{time taken}}$$

The velocity of a body is uniform or constant if it moves with a steady speed in a straight line. It is not uniform if it moves in a curved path. Why?

The units of speed and velocity are the same, km/h, m/s.

$$60\,\text{km/h} = \frac{60000\,\text{m}}{3600\,\text{s}} = 17\,\text{m/s}$$

Distance moved in a stated direction is called the **displacement**. It is a vector, unlike distance which is a scalar. Velocity may also be defined as:

$$\text{velocity} = \frac{\text{displacement}}{\text{time taken}}$$

Acceleration

When the speed of a body moving in a straight line changes we say the body **accelerates**. If a car starts from rest and has speed 2 m/s after 1 second, its speed has increased by 2 m/s in 1 s and its acceleration is 2 m/s per second. We write this as 2 m/s^2.

For a body moving in a straight line, **acceleration is the change of speed in unit time**, or:

$$\text{acceleration} = \frac{\text{change of speed}}{\text{time taken for change}}$$

For a steady increase of speed from 20 m/s to 50 m/s in 5 s

$$\text{acceleration} = \frac{(50-20)\,\text{m/s}}{5\,\text{s}} = 6\,\text{m/s}^2$$

Acceleration is also a vector and both its magnitude and direction should be stated. However, at present we will consider only motion in a straight line and so the magnitude of the velocity will equal the speed, and the magnitude of the acceleration will equal the change of speed in unit time.

The speeds of a car accelerating on a straight road are shown below.

Time/s	0	1	2	3	4	5	6
Speed/m/s	0	5	10	15	20	25	30

The speed increases by 5 m/s every second and the acceleration of 5 m/s² is said to be **uniform**.

An acceleration is positive if the velocity increases and negative if it decreases. A negative acceleration is also called a **deceleration** or **retardation**.

● Speed–time graphs

If the speed of a body is plotted against the time, the graph obtained is a **speed–time graph**. It provides a way of solving motion problems.

The area under a speed–time graph measures the distance travelled.

In Figure P1.11, AB is the speed–time graph for a body moving with a **uniform speed** of 20 m/s. Since distance = average speed × time, after 5 s it will have moved 20 m/s × 5 s = 100 m. This is the shaded area under the graph, i.e. rectangle OABC.

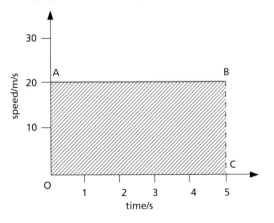

Figure P1.11 Uniform speed.

In Figure P1.12a, PQ is the speed–time graph for a body moving with **uniform acceleration**. At

the start of the timing the speed is 20 m/s but it increases steadily to 40 m/s after 5 s. If the distance covered equals the area under PQ, i.e. the shaded area OPQS, then

distance = area of rectangle OPRS
+ area of triangle PQR

$= OP \times OS + \frac{1}{2} \times PR \times QR$
(area of a triangle = $\frac{1}{2}$base × height)

$= 20\,m/s \times 5\,s + \frac{1}{2} \times 5\,s \times 20\,m/s$

$= 100\,m + 50\,m = 150\,m$

The linear shape (PQ) of the speed-time graph shown in Figure P1.12a, means that the slope, and hence the acceleration of the body, are constant over the time period OS.

Figure P1.12b shows a speed-time graph for non-uniform acceleration. The curved shape, OX, means that the slope of the graph, and hence the acceleration of the body, change over the time period OY – the acceleration is not constant.

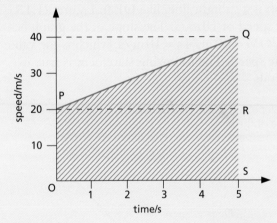

a uniform acceleration.

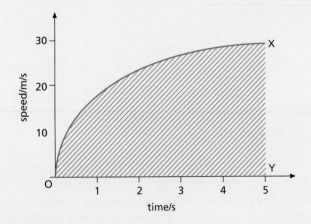

b non-uniform acceleration.
Figure P1.12

Notes

1 When calculating the area from the graph, the unit of time must be the same on both axes.
2 This rule for finding distances travelled is true even if the acceleration is not uniform. In Figure P1.12b, the distance travelled equals the shaded area OXY.

The slope or gradient of a speed–time graph represents the acceleration of the body.

In Figure P1.11, the slope of AB is zero, as is the acceleration. In Figure P1.12a, the slope of PQ is QR/PR = 20/5 = 4: the acceleration is a constant $4 \, \text{m/s}^2$. In Figure P1.12b, when the slope along OX changes, so does the acceleration.

● Distance–time graphs

A body travelling with uniform speed covers equal distances in equal times. Its **distance–time graph** is a straight line, like OL in Figure P1.13 for a speed of 10 m/s. The slope of the graph is LM/OM = 40 m/4 s = 10 m/s, which is the value of the speed. The following statement is true in general:

The slope or gradient of a distance–time graph represents the speed of the body.

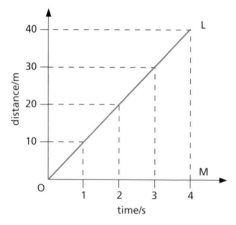

Figure P1.13 Uniform speed.

When the speed of the body is changing, the slope of the distance–time graph varies, as in Figure P1.14, and at any point equals the slope of the tangent. For example, the slope of the tangent at T is AB/BC = 40 m/2 s = 20 m/s. The speed at the instant corresponding to T is therefore 20 m/s.

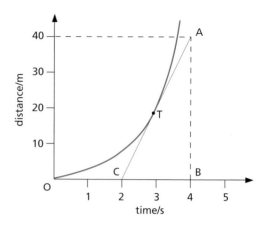

Figure P1.14 Non-uniform speed.

● An equation for uniform acceleration

Problems involving bodies moving with **uniform acceleration in a straight line** can often be solved quickly using the **equations of motion**.

If a body is moving with uniform acceleration a in a straight line and its speed increases from u to v in time t, then:

$$a = \frac{\text{change of speed}}{\text{time taken}} = \frac{v - u}{t}$$

$$\therefore \quad at = v - u$$

or:

$$v = u + at \qquad (1)$$

Note that the initial speed u and the final speed v refer to the start and the finish of the *timing* and do not necessarily mean the start and finish of the motion.

● Falling objects

In air, a coin falls faster than a small piece of paper. In a vacuum they fall at the same rate, as may be shown with the apparatus of Figure P1.15 on the next page. The difference in air is due to **air resistance** having a greater effect on light bodies than on heavy bodies. The air resistance to a light body is large when compared with the body's weight. With a dense piece of metal the resistance is negligible at low speeds.

There is a story, untrue we now think, that in the 16th century the Italian scientist Galileo dropped a small iron ball and a large cannonball ten times heavier from the top of the Leaning Tower of Pisa (Figure P1.16 on the next page). And we are told that, to the surprise of onlookers who expected the cannonball to arrive first, they reached the ground almost simultaneously. You will learn more about air resistance on p.349.

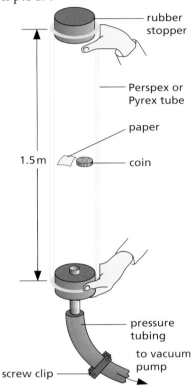

Figure P1.15 A coin and a piece of paper fall at the same rate in a vacuum.

Figure P1.16 The Leaning Tower of Pisa, where Galileo is said to have experimented with falling objects.

Practical work

Motion of a falling body

Arrange things as shown in Figure P1.17 and investigate the motion of a 100 g mass falling from a height of about 2 m.

A tickertape timer has a marker that vibrates at 50 times a second and makes dots at 1/50s intervals on a paper tape being pulled through it. What does the spacing of the dots on the tape tell you about the motion of the falling mass? Ignore the start of the tape where the dots are too close. Repeat the experiment with a 200 g mass; what do you notice?

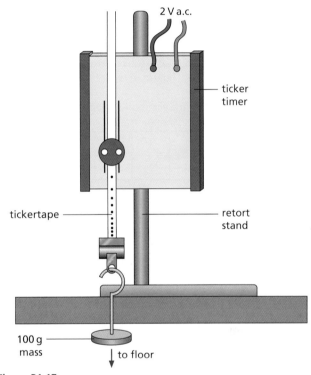

Figure P1.17

● Acceleration of free fall

All bodies falling freely under the force of gravity do so with uniform acceleration if air resistance is negligible (i.e. the 'steps' in the tape chart from the practical work should all be equal).

This acceleration, called the **acceleration of free fall,** is denoted by the italic letter g. Its value varies slightly over the Earth but is constant in each place; in India for example, it is about $9.8\,\text{m/s}^2$ or near enough $10\,\text{m/s}^2$. The speed of a free-falling body therefore increases by $10\,\text{m/s}$ every second. A ball shot straight upwards with a speed of $30\,\text{m/s}$ decelerates by $10\,\text{m/s}$ every second and reaches its highest point after $3\,\text{s}$.

In calculations using the equations of motion, g replaces a. It is given a positive sign for falling bodies (i.e. $a = g = +10\,\text{m/s}^2$) and a negative sign for rising bodies since they are decelerating (i.e. $a = -g = -10\,\text{m/s}^2$).

341

Questions

8 A motorcyclist starts from rest and reaches a speed of 6 m/s after travelling with uniform acceleration for 3 s. What is his acceleration?

9 An aircraft travelling at 600 km/h accelerates steadily at 10 km/h per second. Taking the speed of sound as 1100 km/h at the aircraft's altitude, how long will it take to reach the 'sound barrier'?

10 A vehicle moving with a uniform acceleration of 2 m/s² has a velocity of 4 m/s at a certain time. What will its velocity be
   a 1 s later,
   b 5 s later?

11 If a bus travelling at 20 m/s is subject to a steady deceleration of 5 m/s², how long will it take to come to rest?

12 The speeds of a car travelling on a straight road are given below at successive intervals of 1 second.

Time/s	0	1	2	3	4
Speed/m/s	0	2	4	6	8

The car travels
1 with an average velocity of 4 m/s
2 16 m in 4 s
3 with a uniform acceleration of 2 m/s².
Which statement(s) is (are) correct?
A 1, 2, 3 B 1, 2 C 2, 3 D 1 E 3

13 The distance–time graph for a girl on a cycle ride is shown in Figure P1.18.
   a How far did she travel?
   b How long did she take?
   c What was her average speed in km/h?
   d How many stops did she make?
   e How long did she stop for altogether?
   f What was her average speed *excluding* stops?
   g How can you tell from the shape of the graph when she travelled fastest? Over which stage did this happen?

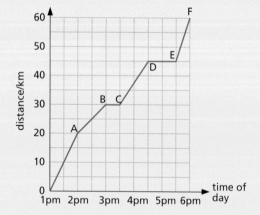

Figure P1.18

14 The graph in Figure P1.19 represents the distance travelled by a car plotted against time.
   a How far has the car travelled at the end of 5 seconds?
   b What is the speed of the car during the first 5 seconds?
   c What has happened to the car after A?
   d Draw a graph showing the speed of the car plotted against time during the first 5 seconds.

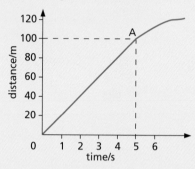

Figure P1.19

15 Figure P1.20 shows an incomplete speed–time graph for a boy running a distance of 100 m.
   a What is his acceleration during the first 4 seconds?
   b How far does the boy travel during i the first 4 seconds, ii the next 9 seconds?
   c Copy and complete the graph showing clearly at what time he has covered the distance of 100 m. Assume his speed remains constant at the value shown by the horizontal portion of the graph.

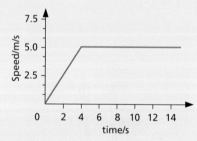

Figure P1.20

16 The approximate speed–time graph for a car on a 5-hour journey is shown in Figure P1.21. (There is a very quick driver change midway to prevent driving fatigue!)
   a State in which of the regions OA, AB, BC, CD, DE the car is i accelerating, ii decelerating, iii travelling with uniform speed.
   b Calculate the value of the acceleration, deceleration or constant speed in each region.
   c What is the distance travelled over each region?
   d What is the total distance travelled?
   e Calculate the average speed for the whole journey.

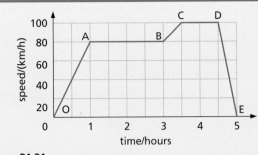

Figure P1.21

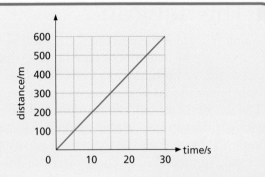

Figure P1.22

17 The distance–time graph for a motorcyclist riding off from rest is shown in Figure P1.22.
 a Describe the motion.
 b How far does the motorbike move in 30 seconds?
 c Calculate the speed.

● Mass

The **mass** of an object is the measure of the amount of matter in it. The unit of mass is the kilogram (kg) and is the mass of a piece of platinum–iridium alloy at the Office of Weights and Measures in Paris. The gram (g) is one-thousandth of a kilogram.

$$1\,g = \frac{1}{1000}\,kg = 10^{-3}\,kg = 0.001\,kg$$

The term **weight** is often used when mass is really meant. In science the two ideas are distinct and have different units, as we shall see later.

The confusion between mass and weight is not helped by the fact that mass is found on a balance by a process we unfortunately call 'weighing'!

There are several kinds of balance. In the **beam balance** the unknown mass in one pan is balanced against known masses in the other pan. In the **lever balance** a system of levers acts against the mass when it is placed in the pan. A direct reading is obtained from the position on a scale of a pointer joined to the lever system. A digital **top-pan balance** is shown in Figure P1.23.

● Weight

We all constantly experience the force of **gravity**, in other words. the pull of the Earth. It causes an unsupported body to fall from rest to the ground.

> The weight of a body is the force of gravity on it.

For a body above or on the Earth's surface, the nearer it is to the centre of the Earth, the more the Earth attracts it. Since the Earth is not a perfect sphere but is flatter at the poles, the weight of a body varies over the Earth's surface. It is greater at the poles than at the equator.

Gravity is a force that can act through space, i.e. there does not need to be contact between the Earth and the object on which it acts as there does when we push or pull something. Other action-at-a-distance forces which, like gravity, decrease with distance are:

● **magnetic** forces between magnets, and
● **electric** forces between electric charges.

When a body experiences a gravitational force we say it is in a gravitational field (see next page). Weight is the result of a gravitational field acting on a mass.

Figure P1.23 A digital top-pan balance.

The newton

The unit of force is the **newton** (N). It will be defined later (p.350); the definition is based on the change of speed a force can produce in a body. Weight is a force and therefore should be measured in newtons.

The weight of a body can be measured by hanging it on a spring balance marked in newtons (Figure P1.24) and letting the pull of gravity stretch the spring in the balance. The greater the pull, the more the spring stretches.

On most of the Earth's surface:

> The weight of a body of mass 1 kg is 9.8 N.

Often this is taken as 10 N. A mass of 2 kg has a weight of 20 N, and so on. The mass of a body is the same wherever it is and, unlike weight, does not depend on the presence of the Earth.

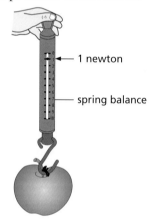

← 1 newton

— spring balance

Figure P1.24 The weight of an average-sized apple is about 1 newton.

Weight and gravity

The weight W of a body is the force of gravity acting on it which gives it an acceleration g when it is falling freely near the Earth's surface. If the body has mass m, then W can be calculated from $F = ma$. We put $F = W$ and $a = g$ to give

$$W = mg$$

Taking $g = 9.8\,\text{m/s}^2$ and $m = 1\,\text{kg}$, this gives $W = 9.8\,\text{N}$, i.e. a body of mass 1 kg has weight 9.8 N, or near enough 10 N. Similarly a body of mass 2 kg has weight of about 20 N, and so on. While the mass of a body is always the same, its weight varies depending on the value of g. On the Moon the acceleration of free fall is only about $1.6\,\text{m/s}^2$, and so a mass of 1 kg has a weight of just 1.6 N there.

The weight of a body is directly proportional to its mass, which explains why g is the same for all bodies. The greater the mass of a body, the greater is the force of gravity on it but it does not accelerate faster when falling because of its greater inertia (i.e. its greater resistance to acceleration).

Gravitational field

The force of gravity acts through space and can cause a body, not in contact with the Earth, to fall to the ground. It is an invisible, action-at-a-distance force. We try to 'explain' its existence by saying that the Earth is surrounded by a **gravitational field** which exerts a force on any body in the field.

> The strength of a gravitational field is defined as the force acting on unit mass in the field.

Measurement shows that on the Earth's surface a mass of 1 kg experiences a force of 9.8 N, i.e. its weight is 9.8 N. The strength of the Earth's field is therefore 9.8 N/kg (near enough 10 N/kg). It is denoted by g, the letter also used to denote the acceleration of free fall. Hence

> $$g = 9.8\,\text{N/kg} = 9.8\,\text{m/s}^2$$

We now have two ways of regarding g. When considering bodies *falling freely*, we can think of it as an acceleration of $9.8\,\text{m/s}^2$. When a body of known mass is *at rest* and we wish to know the force of gravity (in N) acting on it we think of g as the Earth's gravitational field strength of 9.8 N/kg.

Questions

18 A body of mass 1 kg has weight 10 N at a certain place. What is the weight of
   a 100 g
   b 5 kg
   c 50 g?

19 What does an astronaut of mass 100 kg weigh
   a on Earth where the gravitational field strength is 10 N/kg
   b on the Moon where the gravitational field strength is 1.6 N/kg?

● Density

In everyday language, lead is said to be 'heavier' than wood. By this it is meant that a certain volume of lead is heavier than the same volume of wood. In science such comparisons are made by using the term **density**. This is the **mass per unit volume** of a substance and is calculated from

$$\text{density} = \frac{\text{mass}}{\text{volume}}$$

The density of lead is 11 grams per cubic centimetre ($11\,\text{g/cm}^3$) and this means that a piece of lead of volume $1\,\text{cm}^3$ has mass $11\,\text{g}$. A volume of $5\,\text{cm}^3$ of lead would have mass $55\,\text{g}$. If the density of a substance is known, the mass of *any* volume of it can be calculated. This enables engineers to work out the weight of a structure if they know from the plans the volumes of the materials to be used and their densities. Strong enough foundations can then be made.

The SI unit of density is the **kilogram per cubic metre**. To convert a density from g/cm^3, normally the most suitable unit for the size of sample we use, to kg/m^3, we multiply by 10^3. For example the density of water is $1.0\,\text{g/cm}^3$ or $1.0 \times 10^3\,\text{kg/m}^3$.

The approximate densities of some common substances are given in Table P1.1.

Table P1.1 Densities of some common substances

Solids	Density/g/cm³	Liquids	Density/g/cm³
aluminium	2.7	paraffin	0.80
copper	8.9	petrol	0.80
iron	7.9	pure water	1.0
gold	19.3	mercury	13.6
glass	2.5	**Gases**	**Density/kg/m³**
wood (teak)	0.80	air	1.3
ice	0.92	hydrogen	0.09
polythene	0.90	carbon dioxide	2.0

● Calculations

Using the symbols ρ (rho) for density, m for mass and V for volume, the expression for density is

$$\rho = \frac{m}{V}$$

Rearranging the expression gives

$$m = V \times \rho \qquad \text{and} \qquad V = \frac{m}{\rho}$$

These are useful if ρ is known and m or V have to be calculated. The triangle in Figure P1.25 is an aid to remembering them. If you cover the quantity you want to know with a finger, such as m, it equals what you can still see, i.e. $\rho \times V$. To find V, cover V and you get $V = m/\rho$.

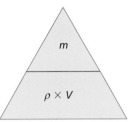

Figure P1.25

● Worked example

Taking the density of copper as $9\,\text{g/cm}^3$, find a the mass of $5\,\text{cm}^3$ and b the volume of $63\,\text{g}$.

a $\rho = 9\,\text{g/cm}^3$, $V = 5\,\text{cm}^3$ and m is to be found.
$$m = V \times \rho = 5\,\text{cm}^3 \times 9\,\text{g/cm}^3 = 45\,\text{g}$$
b $\rho = 9\,\text{g/cm}^3$, $m = 63\,\text{g}$ and V is to be found.

$$\therefore \qquad V = \frac{m}{\rho} = \frac{63\,\text{g}}{9\,\text{g/cm}^3} = 7\,\text{cm}^3$$

● Simple density measurements

If the mass m and volume V of a substance are known, its density can be found from $\rho = m/V$.

Regularly shaped solid

The mass is found on a balance and the volume by measuring its dimensions with a ruler.

Liquid

The mass of an empty beaker is found on a balance. A known volume of the liquid is transferred from a burette or a measuring cylinder into the beaker. The mass of the beaker plus liquid is found and the mass of liquid is obtained by subtraction.

Irregularly shaped solid, such as a pebble or glass stopper

The mass of the solid is found on a balance. Its volume is measured by one of the methods shown in Figures P1.26a and b. In Figure P1.26a the volume is the difference between the first and second readings. In Figure P1.26b it is the volume of water collected in the measuring cylinder.

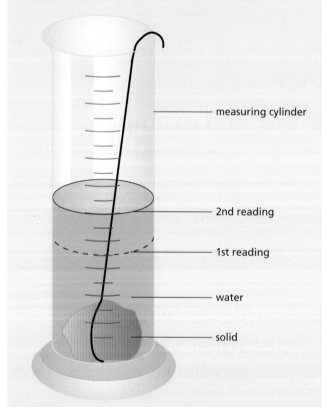

a measuring the volume of an irregular solid: method 1.
Figure P1.26

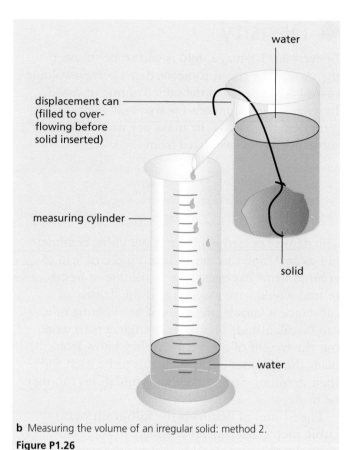

b Measuring the volume of an irregular solid: method 2.
Figure P1.26

Questions

20 a If the density of wood is 0.5 g/cm³ what is the mass of
    i   1 cm³
    ii 2 cm³
    iii 10 cm³?
   b What is the density of a substance of
    i   mass 100 g and volume 10 cm³
    ii volume 3 m³ and mass 9 kg?
   c The density of gold is 19 g/cm³. Find the volume of
    i   38 g
    ii 95 g of gold.
21 A piece of steel has a volume of 12 cm³ and a mass of 96 g. What is its density in
   a g/cm³
   b kg/m³?
22 What is the mass of 5 m³ of cement of density 3000 kg/m³?
23 What is the mass of air in a room measuring 10 m × 5.0 m × 2.0 m if the density of air is 1.3 kg/m³?
24 When a golf ball is lowered into a measuring cylinder of water, the water level rises by 30 cm³ when the ball is completely submerged. If the ball weighs 33 g in air, find its density.

● Force

A **force** is a push or a pull. It can cause a body at rest to move, or if the body is already moving it can change its speed or direction of motion. A force can also change a body's shape or size; for example a spring (or wire) will stretch when loaded with a weight (Figure P1.27).

Practical work

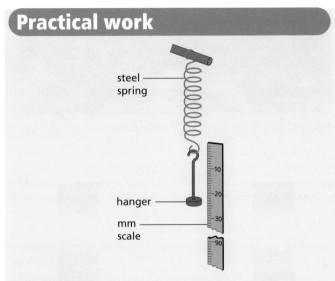

steel spring

hanger

mm scale

Figure P1.27

Stretching a spring

Arrange a steel spring as in Figure P1.27. Read the scale opposite the bottom of the hanger. Add 100 g loads one at a time (thereby increasing the stretching force by steps of 1 N) and take the readings after each one. Enter the readings in a table for loads up to 500 g.

Note that at the head of columns (or rows) in data tables it is usual to give the name of the quantity or its symbol followed by **/** and the unit.

Stretching force/N	Scale reading/mm	Total extension/mm

Do the results suggest any rule about how the spring behaves when it is stretched?

Sometimes it is easier to discover laws by displaying the results on a graph. Do this on graph paper by plotting stretching force readings along the *x*-axis (horizontal axis) and total extension readings along the *y*-axis (vertical axis). Every pair of readings will give a point; mark them by small crosses and draw a smooth line through them. What is its shape?

● Hooke's law

Springs were investigated by Robert Hooke nearly 350 years ago. He found that the extension was proportional to the stretching force provided the spring was not permanently stretched. This means that doubling the force doubles the extension, trebling the force trebles the extension, and so on. Using the sign for proportionality, ∝, we can write **Hooke's law** as

> extension ∝ stretching force

It is true only if the **elastic limit** or 'limit of proportionality' of the spring is not exceeded. In other words, the spring returns to its original length when the force is removed.

The graph of Figure P1.28 on the next page is for a spring stretched beyond its elastic limit, E. OE is a straight line passing through the origin O and is graphical proof that Hooke's law holds over this range. If the force for point A on the graph is applied to the spring, the proportionality limit is passed and on removing the force some of the extension (OS) remains. Over which part of the graph does a spring balance work?

The **force constant**, k, of a spring is the force needed to cause unit extension, i.e. 1 m. If a force F produces extension x then

$$k = \frac{F}{x}$$

Rearranging the equation gives

$$F = kx$$

This is the usual way of writing Hooke's law in symbols.

Hooke's law also holds when a force is applied to a straight metal wire or an elastic band, provided they are not permanently stretched. Force–extension graphs similar to Figure P1.28 are obtained. You should label each axis of your graph with the name of the quantity or its symbol followed by / and the unit, as shown in Figure P1.28.

For a rubber band, a small force causes a large extension.

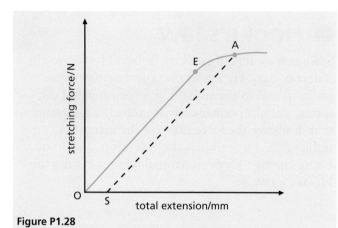

Figure P1.28

● Worked example

A spring is stretched 10 mm (0.01 m) by a weight of 2.0 N. Calculate: **a** the force constant k, and **b** the weight W of an object that causes an extension of 80 mm (0.08 m).

a $k = \dfrac{F}{x} = \dfrac{2.0\ \text{N}}{0.01\ \text{m}} = 200\ \text{N/m}$

b W = stretching force F
$= k \times x$
$= 200\ \text{N/m} \times 0.08\ \text{m}$
$= 16\ \text{N}$

● Forces and resultants

Force has both magnitude (size) and direction. It is represented in diagrams by a straight line with an arrow to show its direction of action.

Usually more than one force acts on an object. As a simple example, an object resting on a table is pulled downwards by its weight W and pushed upwards by a force R due to the table supporting it (Figure P1.29). Since the object is at rest, the forces must balance, i.e. $R = W$.

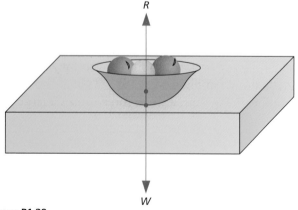

Figure P1.29

Figure P1.30 The design of an offshore oil platform requires an understanding of the combination of many forces.

Figure P1.31 The resultant of forces acting in the same straight line is found by addition or subtraction.

In structures such as a giant oil platform (Figure P1.30), two or more forces may act at the same point. It is then often useful for the design engineer to know the value of the single force, i.e. the **resultant**, which has exactly the same effect as these forces. If the forces act in the same straight line, the resultant is found by simple addition or subtraction as shown in Figure P1.31.

● Friction

Friction is the force that opposes one surface moving, or trying to move, over another. It can be a help or a hindrance. We could not walk if there was no friction between the soles of our shoes and the ground. Our feet would slip backwards, as they tend to if we walk on ice. On the other hand, engineers try to reduce friction to a minimum in the moving parts of machinery by using lubricating oils and ball-bearings.

When a gradually increasing force P is applied through a spring balance to a block on a table (Figure P1.32), the block does not move at first. This is because an equally increasing but opposing frictional force F acts where the block and table touch. At any instant P and F are equal and opposite.

If P is increased further, the block eventually moves; as it does so F has its maximum value, called **starting** or **static friction**. When the block is moving at a steady speed, the balance reading is slightly less than that for starting friction. **Sliding** or **dynamic friction** is therefore less than starting or static friction.

Placing a mass on the block increases the force pressing the surfaces together and increases friction.

When work is done against friction, the temperatures of the bodies in contact rise (as you can test by rubbing your hands together); mechanical energy is being changed into heat energy (see Chapter P2).

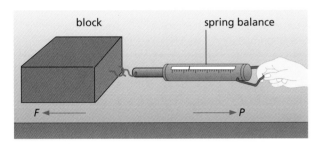

Figure P1.32 Friction opposes motion between surfaces in contact.

Air resistance

For a moving body, air resistance is a frictional force which opposes the motion of the body. The force increases as the speed of the body increases, and acts to reduce acceleration and slow the body down. The lighter the object, and the larger its surface area, the greater the effect of air resistance; the speed of fall of a sky diver is quickly reduced when his parachute opens.

● Newton's first law

Friction and air resistance cause a car to come to rest when the engine is switched off. If these forces were absent we believe that a body, once set in motion, would go on moving forever with a constant speed in a straight line. That is, force is not needed to keep a body moving with uniform velocity provided that no opposing forces act on it.

This idea was proposed by Galileo and is summed up in **Newton's first law of motion**:

> A body stays at rest, or if moving it continues to move with uniform velocity, unless an external force makes it behave differently.

It seems that the question we should ask about a moving body is not 'what keeps it moving' but 'what changes or stops its motion'.

The smaller the external forces opposing a moving body, the smaller is the force needed to keep it moving with uniform velocity. An 'airboard', which is supported by a cushion of air (Figure P1.33), can skim across the ground with little frictional opposition, so that relatively little power is needed to maintain motion.

Figure P1.33 Friction is much reduced for an airboard.

Practical work

Effect of force and mass on acceleration

The apparatus consists of a trolley to which a force is applied by a stretched length of elastic (Figure P1.34 on the next page). The velocity of the trolley is found from a tickertape timer or a motion sensor, datalogger and computer.

A tickertape timer has a marker that vibrates 50 times a second and makes dots at $\frac{1}{50}$ s intervals on a paper tape being pulled through it; 1/50 s is called a tick and a tentick = $10 \times \frac{1}{50}$ s = $\frac{1}{5}$ s. Speed and acceleration can be calculated from the tape as follows:

$$\text{Average speed} = \frac{\text{distance moved}}{\text{time taken}}$$

$$= \frac{\text{length of tape occupied by 10 ticks}}{1/5\,\text{s}}$$

$$\text{Acceleration} = \frac{\text{change of speed}}{\text{time taken}}$$

$$= \frac{\text{(change in average speed between adjacent tenticks)}}{1/5\,\text{s}}$$

First compensate the runway for friction: raise one end until the trolley runs down with uniform velocity when given a push. The dots on the tickertape should be equally spaced, or a horizontal trace obtained on a velocity–time graph. There is now no resultant force on the trolley and any acceleration produced later will be due only to the force caused by the stretched elastic.

a) Force and acceleration (mass constant)

Fix one end of a short length of elastic to the rod at the back of the trolley and stretch it until the other end is level with the front of the trolley. Practise pulling the trolley down the runway, keeping the same stretch on the elastic. After a few trials you should be able to produce a steady accelerating force.

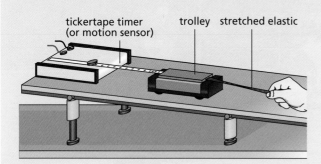

tickertape timer (or motion sensor)   trolley   stretched elastic

Figure P1.34

Repeat using first two and then three *identical* pieces of elastic, stretched side by side by the same amount, to give two and three units of force.

If you are using tickertape, calculate the acceleration produced by each force over a tentick time period. Ignore the start of the tape (where the dots are too close) and the end (where the force may not be steady). If you use a motion sensor and computer to plot a velocity–time graph, the acceleration can be obtained in m/s^2 from the slope of the graph.

Does a steady force cause a steady acceleration? Put the results in a table. Do they suggest any relationship between acceleration, a, and force F?

Force (F)/(no. of pieces of elastic)	1	2	3
Acceleration (a)/cm/tentick² or m/s²			

b) Mass and acceleration (force constant)

Do the experiment as in **a)** using two pieces of elastic (i.e. constant F) to accelerate first one trolley, then two (stacked one above the other) and finally three. Check the friction compensation of the runway each time.

Find the accelerations from the ticker tapes or computer plots and tabulate the results. Do they suggest any relationship between a and m?

Mass (m)/(no. of trolleys)	1	2	3
Acceleration (a)/cm/tentick² or m/s²			

● Newton's second law

The previous experiment should show roughly that the acceleration a is

(i) directly proportional to the applied force F for a fixed mass, i.e., $a \propto F$, and

(ii) inversely proportional to the mass m for a fixed force, i.e., $a \propto 1/m$.

Combining the results into one equation, we get

$$a \propto \frac{F}{m} \quad \text{or} \quad F \propto ma$$

Therefore
$$F = kma$$

where k is the constant of proportionality.

> One newton is defined as the force which gives a mass of 1 kg an acceleration of 1 m/s², i.e., $1\,N = 1\,kg\,m/s^2$.

So if $m = 1\,kg$ and $a = 1\,m/s^2$, then $F = 1\,N$. Substituting in $F = kma$, we get $k = 1$ and so we can write

$$F = ma$$

This is **Newton's second law of motion**. When using it two points should be noted. First, F is the resultant (or unbalanced) force causing the acceleration a. Second, F must be in newtons, m in kilograms and a in metres per second squared, otherwise k is not 1. The law shows that a will be largest when F is large and m small.

You should now appreciate that when the forces acting on a body do not balance there is a net (resultant) force which causes a change of motion, i.e. the body accelerates or decelerates. If the forces balance, there is no change in the motion of the body. However, there may be a change of shape, in which case internal forces in the body (i.e. forces between neighbouring atoms) balance the external forces.

Questions

25 What is the force constant of a spring which is stretched
   a 2 mm by a force of 4 N
   b 4 cm by a mass of 200 g?

26 The spring in Figure P1.35 stretches from 10 cm to 22 cm when a force of 4 N is applied. If it obeys Hooke's law, its total length in cm when a force of 6 N is applied is
   A 28 B 42 C 50 D 56 E 100

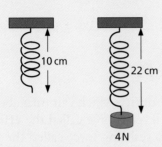

Figure P1.35

27 Jo, Daniel and Helen are pulling a metal ring. Jo pulls with a force of 100 N in one direction and Daniel with a force of 140 N in the opposite direction. If the ring does not move, what force does Helen exert if she pulls in the same direction as Jo?

28 A boy drags a suitcase along the ground with a force of 100 N. If the frictional force opposing the motion of the suitcase is 50 N, what is the resultant forward force on the suitcase?

29 a What resultant force produces an acceleration of 5 m/s² in a car of mass 1000 kg?
   b What acceleration is produced in a mass of 2 kg by a resultant force of 30 N?

30 A rocket has a mass of 500 kg.
   a What is its weight on Earth where g = 10 N/kg?
   b At lift-off the rocket engine exerts an upward force of 25 000 N. What is the resultant force on the rocket? What is its initial acceleration?

31 Explain the following using $F = ma$.
   a A racing car has a powerful engine and is made of strong but lightweight material.
   b A car with a small engine can still accelerate rapidly.

● Moment of a force

The handle on a door is at the outside edge so that it opens and closes easily. A much larger force would be needed if the handle were near the hinge. Similarly it is easier to loosen a nut with a long spanner than with a short one.

The **turning effect of a force** is called the **moment of the force**. It depends on both the size of the force and how far it is applied from the pivot or **fulcrum**. It is measured by multiplying the force by the perpendicular distance of the line of action of the force from the fulcrum. The unit is the **newton metre** (N m).

> moment of a force = force × perpendicular distance of the line of action of the force from fulcrum

In Figure P1.36a, a force F acts on a gate at its edge, and in Figure P1.36b it acts at the centre.
In Figure P1.36a:

   moment of F about O = 5 N × 3 m = 15 N m

In Figure P1.36b:

   moment of F about O = 5 N × 1.5 m = 7.5 N m

The turning effect of F is greater in the first case; this agrees with the fact that a gate opens most easily when pushed or pulled at the edge furthest from the hinge.

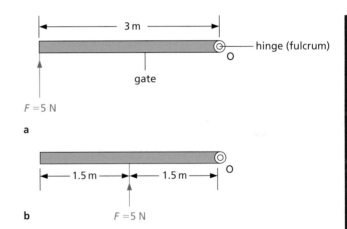

Figure P1.36

● Balancing a beam

To balance a beam about a pivot, like the ruler in Figure P1.37 on the next page, the weights must be moved so that the clockwise turning effect equals the anticlockwise turning effect and the net moment on the beam becomes zero. If the beam tends to swing clockwise, m_1 can be moved further from the pivot to increase its turning effect; alternatively m_2 can be moved nearer to the pivot to reduce its turning effect. What adjustment would you make to the position of m_2 to balance the beam if it is tending to swing anticlockwise?

Practical work

Law of moments

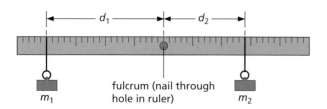

Figure P1.37

Balance a half-metre ruler at its centre, adding Plasticine to one side or the other until it is horizontal.

Hang unequal loads m_1 and m_2 from either side of the fulcrum and alter their distances d_1 and d_2 from the centre until the ruler is again balanced (Figure P1.37). Forces F_1 and F_2 are exerted by gravity on m_1 and m_2 and so on the ruler; the force on 100 g is 1 N. Record the results in a table and repeat for other loads and distances.

m_1/g	F_1/N	d_1/cm	$F_1 \times d_1$ /N cm	m_2/g	F_2/N	d_2/cm	$F_2 \times d_2$ / N cm

F_1 is trying to turn the ruler anticlockwise and $F_1 \times d_1$ is its moment. F_2 is trying to cause clockwise turning and its moment is $F_2 \times d_2$. When the ruler is balanced or, as we say, **in equilibrium**, the results should show that the anticlockwise moment $F_1 \times d_1$ equals the clockwise moment $F_2 \times d_2$.

The **law of moments** (also called the **law of the lever**) is stated as follows.

> When a body is in equilibrium the sum of the clockwise moments about any point equals the sum of the anticlockwise moments about the same point. There is no *net* moment on a body which is in equilibrium.

● Worked example

The see-saw in Figure P1.38 balances when Shani of weight 320 N is at A, Tom of weight 540 N is at B and Harry of weight W is at C. Find W.

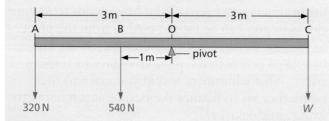

Figure P1.38

Taking moments about the fulcrum, O:

$$\text{anticlockwise moment} = (320\,N \times 3\,m) + (540\,N \times 1\,m)$$
$$= 960\,N\,m + 540\,N\,m$$
$$= 1500\,N\,m$$

$$\text{clockwise moment} = W \times 3\,m$$

By the law of moments,

clockwise moments = anticlockwise moments

$$\therefore \quad W \times 3\,m = 1500\,N\,m$$

$$\therefore \quad W = \frac{1500\,N\,m}{3\,m} = 500\,N$$

● Levers

A **lever** is any device which can turn about a pivot. In a working lever a force called the **effort** is used to overcome a resisting force called the **load**. The pivotal point is called the fulcrum.

If we use a crowbar to move a heavy boulder (Figure P1.39), our hands apply the effort at one end of the bar and the load is the force exerted by the boulder on the other end. If distances from the fulcrum O are as shown and the load is 1000 N (i.e. the part of the weight of the boulder supported by the crowbar), the effort can be calculated from the law of moments. As the boulder just begins to move we can say, taking moments about O, that

clockwise moment = anticlockwise moment

$$\text{effort} \times 200\,cm = 1000\,N \times 10\,cm$$

$$\text{effort} = \frac{10000\,N\,cm}{200\,cm} = 50\,N$$

Examples of other levers are shown in Figure P1.40. How does the effort compare with the load for scissors and a spanner in Figures P1.40c and d?

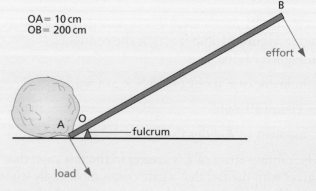

OA = 10 cm
OB = 200 cm

Figure P1.39 Crowbar.

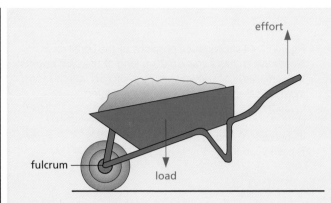

a wheelbarrow

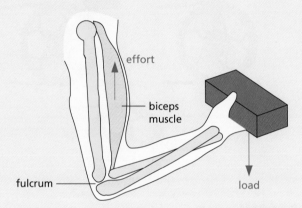

b forearm

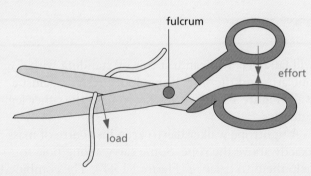

c scissors

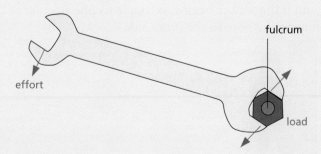

d spanner

Figure P1.40

● Conditions for equilibrium

Sometimes a number of parallel forces act on a body so that it is in equilibrium. We can then say:

> (i) The sum of the forces in one direction equals the sum of the forces in the opposite direction.
> (ii) The law of moments must apply.

A body is in equilibrium when there is no resultant force and no resultant turning effect acting on it.

As an example consider a heavy plank resting on two trestles, as in Figure P1.41. In the next section we will see that the whole weight of the plank (400 N) may be taken to act vertically downwards at its centre, O. If P and Q are the upward forces exerted by the trestles on the plank (called reactions) then we have from **(i)** above:

$$P + Q = 400 \, \text{N} \qquad (1)$$

Moments can be taken about any point but if we take them about C, the moment due to force Q is zero.

$$\text{clockwise moment} = P \times 5 \, \text{m}$$

$$\begin{aligned} \text{anticlockwise moment} &= 400 \, \text{N} \times 2 \, \text{m} \\ &= 800 \, \text{N m} \end{aligned}$$

Since the plank is in equilibrium we have from **(ii)** above:

$$P \times 5 \, \text{m} = 800 \, \text{N m}$$

$$\therefore \quad P = \frac{800 \, \text{N m}}{5 \, \text{m}} = 160 \, \text{N}$$

From equation (1)

$$Q = 240 \, \text{N}$$

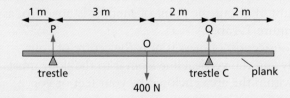

Figure P1.41

Questions

32 The weight of the uniform bar in Figure P1.42 is 10 N. Does it balance, tip to the right or tip to the left?

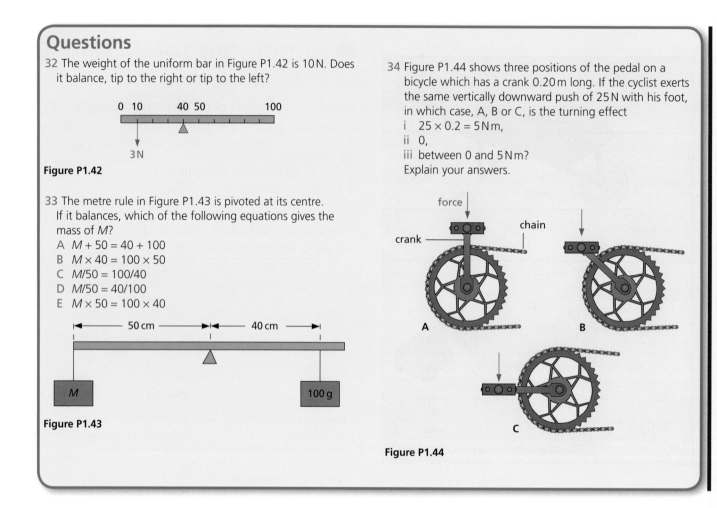

Figure P1.42

33 The metre rule in Figure P1.43 is pivoted at its centre. If it balances, which of the following equations gives the mass of *M*?
A $M + 50 = 40 + 100$
B $M \times 40 = 100 \times 50$
C $M/50 = 100/40$
D $M/50 = 40/100$
E $M \times 50 = 100 \times 40$

Figure P1.43

34 Figure P1.44 shows three positions of the pedal on a bicycle which has a crank 0.20 m long. If the cyclist exerts the same vertically downward push of 25 N with his foot, in which case, A, B or C, is the turning effect
i $25 \times 0.2 = 5 \, \text{N m}$,
ii 0,
iii between 0 and 5 N m?
Explain your answers.

Figure P1.44

● Centres of mass

A body behaves as if its whole mass were concentrated at one point, called its **centre of mass** or **centre of gravity**, even though the Earth attracts every part of it. The body's weight can be considered to act at this point. The centre of mass of a uniform ruler is at its centre and when supported there it can be balanced, as in Figure P1.45a. If it is supported at any other point it topples because the moment of its weight *W* about the point of support is not zero, as in Figure 1.45b.

Your centre of mass is near the centre of your body and the vertical line from it to the floor must be within the area enclosed by your feet or you will fall over. You can test this by standing with one arm and the side of one foot pressed against a wall (Figure P1.46). Now try to raise the other leg sideways.

A tightrope walker has to keep his centre of mass exactly above the rope. Some carry a long pole to help them to balance (Figure P1.47). The combined weight of the walker and pole is then spread out more and if the walker begins to topple to one side, he moves the pole to the other side.

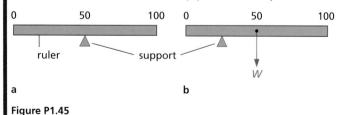

a   b

Figure P1.45

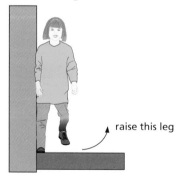

Figure P1.46 Can you do this without falling over?

Figure P1.47 A tightrope walker using a long pole.

The centre of mass of a regularly shaped body that has the same density throughout is at its centre. In other cases it can be found by experiment.

Practical work

Centre of mass using a plumb line

Suppose we have to find the centre of mass of an irregularly shaped lamina (a thin sheet) of cardboard.

Make a hole A in the lamina and hang it so that it can *swing freely* on a nail clamped in a stand. It will come to rest with its centre of mass vertically below A. To locate the vertical line through A, tie a plumb line (a thread and a weight) to the nail (Figure P1.48), and mark its position AB on the lamina. The centre of mass lies somewhere on AB.

Hang the lamina from another position, C, and mark the plumb line position CD. The centre of mass lies on CD and must be at the point of intersection of AB and CD. Check this by hanging the lamina from a third hole. Also try balancing it at its centre of mass on the tip of your forefinger.

Devise a method using a plumb line for finding the centre of mass of a tripod.

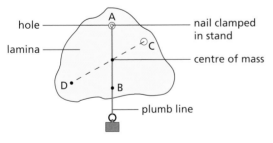

Figure P1.48

Toppling

The position of the centre of mass of a body affects whether or not it **topples** over easily. This is important in the design of such things as tall vehicles (which tend to overturn when rounding a corner), racing cars, reading lamps and even drinking glasses.

A body topples when the vertical line through its centre of mass falls outside its base, as in Figure P1.49a. Otherwise it remains stable, as in Figure P1.49b, where the body will not topple.

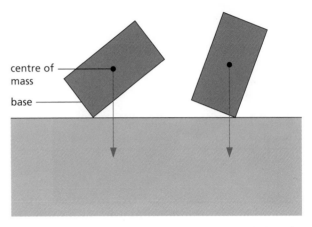

a topples   **b** will not topple (stable)

Figure P1.49

Toppling can be investigated by placing an empty can on a plank (with a rough surface to prevent slipping) which is slowly tilted. The angle of tilt is noted when the can falls over. This is repeated with a mass of 1 kg in the can. How does this affect the position of the centre of mass? The same procedure is followed with a second can of the same height as the first but of greater width. It will be found that the second can with the mass in it can be tilted through the greater angle.

The stability of a body is therefore increased by

- lowering its centre of mass, and
- increasing the area of its base.

In Figure P1.50a on the next page, the centre of mass of a tractor is being found. It is necessary to do this when testing a new design since tractors are often driven over sloping surfaces and any tendency to overturn must be discovered.

The stability of double-decker buses is being tested in Figure P1.50b. When the top deck only is fully laden with passengers (represented by sand bags in the test), it must not topple if tilted through an angle of 28°.

Racing cars have a low centre of mass and a wide wheelbase for maximum stability.

a a tractor under test to find its centre of mass

b a double-decker bus being tilted to test its stability

Figure P1.50

● Pressure

To make sense of some effects in which a force acts on a body we have to consider not only the force but also the area on which it acts. For example, wearing skis or riding a snowboard (Figure P1.51) prevents you sinking into soft snow because your weight is spread over a greater area. We say the **pressure** is less.

Figure P1.51

The greater the area over which a force acts, the less the pressure. Figure P1.52 shows the pressure exerted on the floor by the same box standing on end (Figure P1.52a) and lying flat (Figure P1.52b). This is why a tractor with wide wheels can move over soft ground. The pressure is large when the area is small and this is why nails are made with sharp points and stilleto heels may scratch a wooden floor. Walnuts can be broken in the hand by squeezing two together but not one. Why?

> **Pressure is the force** (or thrust) **acting on unit area** (i.e. 1 m²) and is calculated from
>
> $$\text{pressure} = \frac{\text{force}}{\text{area}}$$

The unit of pressure is the **pascal** (Pa); it equals 1 newton per square metre (N/m²) and is quite a small pressure. An apple in your hand exerts about 1000 Pa.

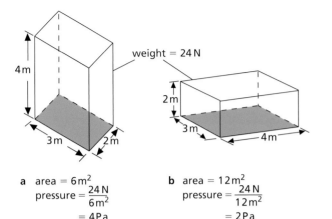

a area = 6 m²
pressure = $\frac{24\,N}{6\,m^2}$
= 4 Pa

b area = 12 m²
pressure = $\frac{24\,N}{12\,m^2}$
= 2 Pa

Figure P1.52

Questions

35 Which of the following will damage a wood-block floor that can withstand a pressure of 2000 kPa (2000 kN/m²)?
1   A block weighing 2000 kN standing on an area of 2 m².
2   An elephant weighing 200 kN standing on an area of 0.2 m².
3   A girl of weight 0.5 kN wearing stiletto-heeled shoes standing on an area of 0.0002 m².
Use the answer code:
A   1, 2, 3
B   1, 2
C   2, 3
D   1
E   3

36 a What is the pressure on a surface when a force of 50 N acts on an area of
   i   2.0 m²,
   ii   100 m²,
   iii 0.50 m²?
   b A pressure of 10 Pa acts on an area of 3.0 m². What is the force acting on the area?

37   A girl plans to take a walk across a muddy field. Which type of footwear should she wear if she does not wish to sink into the mud?
   A   stiletto heels
   B   wellington boots
   C   ice skates.

Checklist

After studying Chapter P1 you should know and understand the following.

● Recall three basic quantities in physics.
● Write a number in powers of ten (standard notation).
● Recall the unit of length and the meaning of the prefixes kilo, deci, centi and milli.
● Use a ruler to measure length so as to minimise errors.
● Measure the volume of regular solids and of liquids.
● Recall the unit of time and how time is measured.
● Describe the use of clocks and devices, both analogue and digital, for measuring an interval of time.
● Use multiples to obtain an average value of a small measurement.
● Describe an experiment to find the period of a pendulum.

● Take measurements with a micrometer screw gauge.

● Define speed and acceleration.

● Distinguish between speed and velocity.

● Draw and interpret speed–time and distance–time graphs.
● Recognise the shape of a speed-time graph for a body at rest, moving with constant speed or moving with changing speed.
● Recognise from the slope of a speed-time graph when a body is accelerating.

● Use the area under a speed–time graph to calculate the distance travelled.

● Use the slope of distance–time graphs to calculate speed.
● Describe the motion of an object falling in air.

● Recognise linear motion where the acceleration is not constant.
● Recognise and calculate the acceleration for linear motion where the acceleration is constant.

● State that the acceleration of free fall for a body near the Earth is constant.
● Recall the unit of mass and how mass is measured.
● Distinguish between mass and weight.

● Recall that the weight of a body is the force of gravity on it.

● Recall and use the equation $W = mg$.
● Define the strength of the Earth's gravitational field.
● Define density and perform calculations using $\rho = m/V$.
● Describe experiments to measure the density of solids and liquids.

● Determine the density of an irregularly shaped solid by the method of displacement.

● Recall that a force can cause a change in the motion, size or shape of a body.
● Recall the unit of force and how force is measured.

- Describe an experiment to study the relation between force and extension for springs.
- Draw conclusions from force–extension graphs.
- Recall Hooke's law and solve problems using it.
- Recognise the significance of the term limit of proportionality.

- Combine forces acting along the same straight line to find their resultant.
- Understand friction as the force between two surfaces that impedes motion and results in heating.
- Recognise air resistance is a form of friction.
- Recall Newton's first law of motion.

- Describe an experiment to investigate the relationship between force, mass and acceleration.
- State Newton's second law of motion and use it to solve problems.

- Define the moment of a force about a point.
- Describe qualitatively the balancing of a beam about a pivot.

- Describe an experiment to verify that there is no net moment on a body in equilibrium.
- State the law of moments and use it to solve problems.
- Explain the action of common tools and devices as levers.

- State the conditions for equilibrium when parallel forces act on a body.
- Recall that an object behaves as if its whole mass were concentrated at its centre of mass.
- Recall that an object's weight acts through the centre of mass (or centre of gravity).
- Describe an experiment to find the centre of mass of an object,
- Connect the stability of an object to the position of its centre of mass.
- Relate pressure to force and area and give examples.
- Define pressure and recall its unit.

Work, energy and power

Combined

- Relate (without calculation) work done to the magnitude of a force and distance moved in the direction of the force
- Recall and use $W = F{\times}d = \Delta E$
- Demonstrate an understanding that work done = energy transferred
- Demonstrate understanding that an object may have energy due to its motion (kinetic energy, K.E.) or its position (potential energy, P.E.) and that energy may be transferred and stored
- Give and identify examples of changes in kinetic, gravitational potential, chemical potential, elastic potential (strain), thermal, sound and electrical potential energy that have occurred as a result of an event or process
- Recognise that energy is transferred during events and processes, including examples of transfer by forces (mechanical working), by electric currents (electrical working), by heating and by waves
- Apply the principle of conservation of energy to simple examples
- Recall and use the expressions K.E. = $\frac{1}{2}mv^2$ and gravitational potential energy (G.P.E.) = mgh or change in G.P.E. = $mg\Delta h$
- Relate (without calculation) power to work done and time taken, using appropriate examples
- Recall and use the equation $P = \Delta E/t$ in simple systems, including electrical circuits
- Distinguish between renewable and non-renewable sources of energy
- Describe how electricity or other useful forms of energy may be obtained from: chemical energy stored in fuel; water, including the energy stored in waves, in tides, and in water behind hydroelectric dams; geothermal resources; nuclear fission; heat and light from the Sun (solar cells and panels); wind energy
- Give advantages and disadvantages of each method in terms of renewability, cost, reliability, scale and environmental impact
- Understand that the Sun is the source of energy for all our energy resources except geothermal, nuclear and tidal
- Understand that the source of tidal energy is mainly the moon
- Show an understanding that energy is released by nuclear fusion in the Sun

Co-ordinated

- Relate (without calculation) work done to the magnitude of a force and distance moved in the direction of the force
- Recall and use $W = F{\times}d = \Delta E$
- Demonstrate an understanding that work done = energy transferred
- Demonstrate understanding that an object may have energy due to its motion (kinetic energy, K.E.) or its position (potential energy, P.E.) and that energy may be transferred and stored
- Give and identify examples of changes in kinetic, gravitational potential, chemical potential, elastic potential (strain), nuclear, thermal, light, sound and electrical energy that have occurred as a result of an event or process
- Recognise that energy is transferred during events and processes, including examples of transfer by forces (mechanical working), by electric currents (electrical working), by heating and by waves
- Apply the principle of conservation of energy to simple examples
- Show a qualitative understanding of efficiency
- Recall and use the expressions K.E. = $\frac{1}{2}mv^2$ and gravitational potential energy (G.P.E.) = mgh or change in G.P.E. = $mg\Delta h$
- Relate (without calculation) power to work done and time taken, using appropriate examples
- Recall and use the equation $P = \Delta E/t$ in simple systems, including electrical circuits
- Distinguish between renewable and non-renewable sources of energy
- Describe how electricity or other useful forms of energy may be obtained from: chemical energy stored in fuel; water, including the energy stored in waves, in tides, and in water behind hydroelectric dams; geothermal resources; nuclear fission; heat and light from the Sun (solar cells and panels); wind energy
- Give advantages and disadvantages of each method in terms of renewability, cost, reliability, scale and environmental impact
- Understand that the Sun is the source of energy for all our energy resources except geothermal, nuclear and tidal
- Understand that the source of tidal energy is mainly the moon
- Show an understanding that energy is released by nuclear fusion in the Sun
- Recall and use the equation:

$$\text{efficiency} = \frac{\text{useful energy output}}{\text{energy input}} \times 100\%$$

$$\text{efficiency} = \frac{\text{useful power output}}{\text{power input}} \times 100\%$$

Energy is a theme that pervades all branches of science. It links a wide range of phenomena and enables us to explain them. It exists in different forms and when something happens, it is likely to be due to energy being transferred from one form to another. Energy transfer is needed to enable people, computers, machines and other devices to work and to enable processes and changes to occur. For example, in Figure P2.1, the water skier can only be pulled along by the boat if there is energy transfer in its engine from the burning petrol to its rotating propeller.

Figure P2.1 Energy transfer in action.

● Work

In science the word **work** has a different meaning from its everyday use. **Work is done when a force moves.** No work is done in the scientific sense by someone standing still holding a heavy pile of books: an upward force is exerted, but no motion results.

If a building worker carries ten bricks up to the first floor of a building, he does more work than if he carries only one brick because he has to exert a larger force. Even more work is required if he carries the ten bricks to the second floor. The amount of work done depends on the size of the force applied and the distance it moves.

We measure work by:

> work = force × distance moved in direction of force

The unit of work is the **joule** (J); it is the work done when a force of 1 newton (N) moves through 1 metre (m). For example, if you have to pull with a force of 50 N to move a crate steadily 3 m in the direction of the force (Figure P2.2a), the work done is 50 N × 3 m = 150 N m = 150 J. That is:

> joules = newtons × metres

If you lift a mass of 3 kg vertically through 2 m (Figure P2.2b), you have to exert a vertically upward force equal to the weight of the body, i.e. 30 N (approximately) and the work done is 30 N × 2 m = 60 N m = 60 J.

Note that we must always take the distance in the direction in which the force acts.

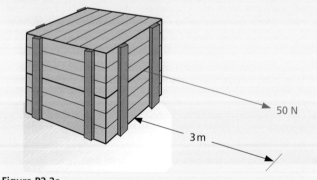

Figure P2.2a

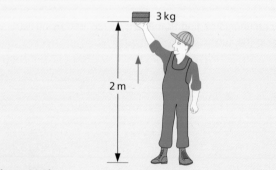

Figure P2.2b

Questions

1 How much work is done when a mass of 3 kg (weighing 30 N) is lifted vertically through 6 m?
2 A hiker climbs a hill 300 m high. If she has a mass of 50 kg calculate the work she does in lifting her body to the top of the hill.
3 In loading a lorry a man lifts boxes each of weight 100 N through a height of 1.5 m.
   a How much work does he do in lifting one box?
   b How much energy is transferred when one box is lifted?

● Forms of energy

Chemical energy

Food and fuels, like oil, gas, coal and wood, are concentrated stores of **chemical energy** (see p.365). The energy of food is released by chemical reactions in our bodies, and during the transfer to other forms we are able to do useful jobs. Fuels cause energy transfers when they are burnt in an engine or a boiler. Batteries are compact sources of chemical energy, which in use is transferred to electrical energy.

Potential energy (P.E.)

This is the energy a body has because of its position or condition. A body above the Earth's surface, like water in a mountain reservoir, has **potential energy** (P.E.) stored in the form of **gravitational potential energy**.

Work has to be done to compress or stretch a spring or elastic material and energy is transferred to potential energy; the P.E. is stored in the form of **strain energy** (or **elastic potential energy**). If the catapult in Figure P2.4c on the next page were released, the strain energy would be transferred to the projectile.

Kinetic energy (K.E.)

Any moving body has **kinetic energy** (K.E.) and the faster it moves, the more K.E. it has. As a hammer drives a nail into a piece of wood, there is a transfer of energy from the K.E. of the moving hammer to other forms of energy.

Electrical energy

Electrical energy is produced by energy transfers at power stations and in batteries. It is the commonest form of energy used in homes and industry because of the ease of transmission and transfer to other forms.

Heat energy

This is also called **thermal** or **internal energy** and is the final fate of other forms of energy. It is transferred by conduction, convection or radiation.

Other forms

These include **light energy** and other forms of **electromagnetic radiation**, **sound** and **nuclear energy**.

● Energy transfers

Demonstration

The apparatus in Figure P2.3 can be used to show a battery changing **chemical energy** to **electrical energy** which becomes **kinetic energy** in the electric motor. The motor raises a weight, giving it **potential energy**. If the changeover switch is joined to the lamp and the weight allowed to fall, the motor acts as a generator in which there is an energy transfer from **kinetic energy** to **electrical energy**. When this is supplied to the lamp, it produces a transfer to **heat** and **light energy**.

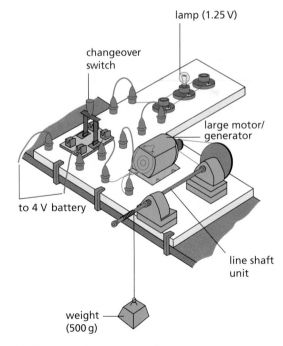

Figure P2.3 Demonstrating energy transfers.

Other examples

Study the energy transfers shown in Figures P2.4a to d. Some devices have been invented to cause particular energy transfers. For example, a **microphone** changes sound energy into electrical energy; a **loudspeaker** does the reverse. Belts, chains or gears are used to transfer energy between moving parts, such as those in a bicycle.

a potential energy to kinetic energy

b electrical energy to heat and light energy

c chemical energy (from muscles in the arm) to p.e. (strain energy of catapult)

d potential energy of water to kinetic energy of turbine to electrical energy from generator

Figure P2.4 Some energy transfers.

● Measuring energy transfers

The unit of work is the **joule** (J), which is the work done when a force of 1 newton (N) moves through 1 metre (m). In an energy transfer, work is done. **The work done is a measure of the amount of energy transferred.** For example, if you have to exert an upward force of 10 N to raise a stone steadily through a vertical distance of 1.5 m, the work done is 15 J. This is also the amount of chemical energy transferred from your muscles to potential energy of the stone. All forms of energy, as well as work, are measured in joules.

● Energy conservation

Principle of conservation of energy

This is one of the basic laws of physics and is stated as follows.

Energy cannot be created or destroyed; it is always conserved.

However, energy is continually being transferred from one form to another. Some forms, such as electrical and chemical energy, are more easily transferred than others, such as heat, for which it is hard to arrange a useful transfer.

Ultimately all energy transfers result in the surroundings being heated (as a result of doing work against friction) and the energy is wasted, i.e. spread out and increasingly more difficult to use. For example, when a brick falls its potential energy becomes kinetic energy; as it hits the ground, its temperature rises and heat and sound are produced. If it seems in a transfer that some energy has disappeared, the 'lost' energy is often converted into non-useful heat. This appears to be the fate of all energy in the Universe and is one reason why new sources of useful energy have to be developed (p.366).

Efficiency of energy transfers

The **efficiency** of a device is the percentage of the energy supplied to it that is usefully transferred.

It is calculated from the expression:

$$\text{efficiency} = \frac{\text{useful energy output}}{\text{total energy input}} \times 100\%$$

For example, for a lever (see p.352)

$$\text{efficiency} = \frac{\text{work done on load}}{\text{work done by effort}} \times 100\%$$

This will be less than 100% if there is friction in the fulcrum.

Table P2.1 lists the efficiencies of some devices and the energy transfers involved.

Table P2.1

Device	% Efficiency	Energy transfer
large electric motor	90	electrical to K.E.
large electric generator	90	K.E. to electrical
domestic gas boiler	75	chemical to heat
compact fluorescent lamp	50	electrical to light
steam turbine	45	heat to K.E.
car engine	25	chemical to K.E.
filament lamp	10	electrical to light

A device is efficient if it transfers energy mainly to useful forms and the 'lost' energy is small.

Kinetic energy (K.E.)

Kinetic energy is the energy a body has because of its motion.

For a body of mass m travelling with velocity v,

$$\text{kinetic energy} = E_k = \frac{1}{2}mv^2$$

If m is in kg and v in m/s, then kinetic energy is in J. For example, a football of mass 0.4 kg (400 g) moving with velocity 20 m/s has

$$\text{k.e.} = \frac{1}{2}mv^2 = \frac{1}{2} \times 0.4\,\text{kg} \times (20)^2\,\text{m}^2/\text{s}^2$$

$$= 0.2 \times 400\,\text{kg m/s}^2 \times \text{m}$$

$$= 80\,\text{Nm} = 80\,\text{J}$$

Since K.E. depends on v^2, a high-speed vehicle travelling at 1000 km/h (Figure P2.5 on the next page), has one hundred times the k.e. it has at 100 km/h.

Potential energy (P.E.)

Potential energy is the energy a body has because of its position or condition.

A body above the Earth's surface is considered to have an amount of gravitational potential energy equal to the work that has been done against gravity by the force used to raise it. To lift a body of mass m through a vertical height h at a place where the Earth's gravitational field strength is g, needs a force equal and opposite to the weight mg of the body. Hence

$$\text{work done by force} = \text{force} \times \text{vertical height}$$
$$= mg \times h$$

$$\therefore \text{potential energy} = E_p = mgh$$

When m is in kg, g in N/kg (or m/s^2) and h in m, the potential energy is in J. For example, if $g = 10$ N/kg, the potential energy gained by a 0.1 kg (100 g) mass raised vertically by 1 m is

$$0.1\,\text{kg} \times 10\,\text{N/kg} \times 1\,\text{m} = 1\,\text{Nm} = 1\,\text{J}$$

Note Strictly speaking we are concerned with *changes* in potential energy from that which a body has at the Earth's surface, rather than with actual values. The expression for potential energy is therefore more correctly written

$$\Delta E_p = mgh$$

where Δ (pronounced 'delta') stands for 'change in'.

Figure P2.5 Kinetic energy depends on the square of the velocity.

Practical work

Change of P.E. to K.E.

Friction-compensate a runway and arrange the apparatus as in Figure P2.6 with the bottom of the 0.1 kg (100 g) mass 0.5 m from the floor.

Start the timer and release the trolley. It will accelerate until the falling mass reaches the floor; after that it moves with *constant* velocity v.

From your results calculate v in m/s (on the tickertape 50 ticks = 1 s). Find the mass of the trolley in kg. Work out:

K.E. gained by trolley and 0.1 kg mass = ___ J
P.E. lost by 0.1 kg mass = ___ J

Compare and comment on the results.

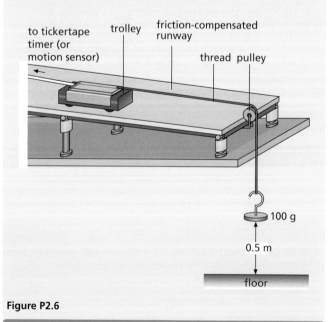

Figure P2.6

Questions

4 Name the energy transfers which occur when
 a an electric bell rings
 b someone speaks into a microphone
 c a ball is thrown upwards
 d there is a picture on a television screen
 e a torch is on.
5 Name the forms of energy represented by the letters A, B, C and D in the following statement.
 In a coal-fired power station, the (A) energy of coal becomes (B) energy which changes water into steam. The steam drives a turbine which drives a generator. A generator transfers (C) energy into (D) energy.
6 State what energy transfers occur in
 a a hairdryer
 b a refrigerator
 c an audio system.

7 a When the energy input to a gas-fired power station is 1000 MJ, the electrical energy output is 300 MJ. What is the efficiency of the power station in changing the energy in gas into electrical energy?
 b What form does the 700 MJ of 'lost' energy take?
 c What is the fate of the 'lost' energy?

8 Calculate the K.E. of
 a a 1 kg trolley travelling at 2 m/s
 b a 2 h (o.002 kg) bullet travelling at 400 m/s
 c a 500 kg car travelling at 72 km/h.
9 a What is the velocity of an object of mass 1 kg which has 200 J of K.E.?
 b Calculate the P.E. of a 5 kg mass when it is
  i   3 m
  ii 6 m
  above the ground. (g = 10 N/kg)

● Power

The more powerful a car is, the faster it can accelerate or climb a hill, i.e. the more rapidly it does work. The **power** of a device is the work it does per second, i.e. the rate at which it does work. This is **the same as the rate at which it transfers energy from one form to another.**

$$\text{power} = \frac{\text{work done}}{\text{time taken}} = \frac{\text{energy transfer}}{\text{time taken}}$$

The unit of power is the **watt** (W) and is **a rate of working of 1 joule per second**, i.e. $1\,W = 1\,J/s$. Larger units are the **kilowatt** (kW) and the **megawatt** (MW):

$1\,kW = 1000\,W = 10^3\,W$

$1\,MW = 1\,000\,000\,W = 10^6\,W$

If a machine does $500\,J$ of work in $10\,s$, its power is $500\,J/10\,s = 50\,J/s = 50\,W$. A small car develops a maximum power of about $25\,kW$.

Practical work

Measuring power

a) Your own power

Get someone with a stopwatch to time you running up a flight of stairs, the more steps the better. Find your weight (in newtons). Calculate the total vertical height (in metres) you have climbed by measuring the height of one step and counting the number of steps.

   The work you do (in joules) in lifting your weight to the top of the stairs is (your weight) × (vertical height of stairs). Calculate your power (in watts). About 0.5 kW is good.

b) Electric motor

This experiment is described on p.436.

Questions

10 A boy whose weight is 600 N runs up a flight of stairs 10 m high in 12 s. What is his average power?
11 An escalator carries 60 people of average mass 70 kg to a height of 5 m in one minute. Find the power needed to do this.

Energy is needed to heat buildings, to make cars move, to provide artificial light, to make computers work, and so on. The list is endless. This 'useful' energy needs to be produced in controllable energy transfers pp.361 and 362. For example, in power stations a supply of useful energy in the form of electricity is produced. The 'raw materials' for energy production are **energy sources**. These may be **non-renewable** or **renewable**.

Apart from nuclear, geothermal, hydroelectric or tidal energy, the Sun is the source for all our energy resources.

● Non-renewable energy sources

Once used up these cannot be replaced.

Fossil fuels

These include coal, oil and natural gas, formed from the remains of plants and animals which lived millions of years ago and obtained energy originally from the Sun. At present they are our main energy source. Predictions vary as to how long they will last since this depends on what reserves are recoverable and on the future demands of a world population expected to increase from about 7000 million in 2011 to at least 7600 million by the year 2050. Some estimates say oil and gas will run low early in the present century but coal should last for 200 years or so.

   Burning fossil fuels in power stations and in cars pollutes the atmosphere with harmful gases such as carbon dioxide and sulfur dioxide.

Carbon dioxide emission aggravates the greenhouse effect (p.303) and increases global warming. It is not immediately feasible to prevent large amounts of carbon dioxide entering the atmosphere, but less is produced by burning natural gas than by burning oil or coal; burning coal produces most carbon dioxide for each unit of energy produced. When coal and oil are burnt they also produce sulfur dioxide which causes acid rain. The sulfur dioxide can be extracted from the waste gases so it does not enter the atmosphere or the sulfur can be removed from the fuel before combustion, but these are both costly processes which increase the price of electricity produced using these measures.

Nuclear fuels

The energy released in a nuclear reactor from **uranium**, found as an ore in the ground, can be used to produce electricity.

Nuclear fuels do not pollute the atmosphere with carbon dioxide or sulfur dioxide but they do generate radioactive waste materials with very long half-lives (p.449); safe ways of storing this waste for perhaps thousands of years must be found. As long as a reactor is operating normally it does not pose a radiation risk, but if an accident occurs, dangerous radioactive material can leak from the reactor and spread over a large area.

Two advantages of all non-renewable fuels are

(i) their high **energy density** (i.e. they are concentrated sources) and the relatively small size of the energy transfer device (e.g. a furnace) which releases their energy

(ii) their ready **availability** when energy demand increases suddenly or fluctuates seasonally.

● Renewable energy sources

These cannot be exhausted and are generally non-polluting.

Solar energy

The energy falling on the Earth from the Sun is mostly in the form of light and in an hour equals the total energy used by the world in a year. Unfortunately its low energy density requires large collecting devices and its availability varies. Its greatest potential use is as an energy source for low-temperature water heating. This uses **solar panels** as the energy transfer devices, which convert light into heat energy. They are used increasingly to produce domestic hot water at about 70 °C and to heat swimming pools.

The source of the Sun's energy is nuclear fusion. The temperature in the Sun is high enough for the conversion of hydrogen into helium to occur, in a process in which mass is lost and energy is released.

Each of these fusion reactions results in a loss of mass and a release of energy. Overall, tremendous amounts of energy are created that help to maintain the very high temperature of the Sun.

Figure P2.7 Solar cells on a house provide electricity.

Solar energy can also be used to produce high-temperature heating, up to 3000 °C or so, if a large curved mirror (a **solar furnace**) focuses the Sun's rays on to a small area. The energy can then be used to turn water to steam for driving the turbine of an electric generator in a power station.

Solar cells, made from semiconducting materials, convert sunlight into electricity directly. A number of cells connected together can be used to supply electricity to homes (Figure P2.7) and to the electronic equipment in communication and other satellites. They are also used for small-scale power generation in remote areas of developing countries where there is no electricity supply. Recent developments have made large-scale generation more cost effective and there is now a large solar power plant in California. There are many designs for prototype light vehicles run on solar power (Figure P2.8).

Figure P2.8 Solar-powered car.

Wind energy

Giant windmills called **wind turbines** with two or three blades each up to 30 m long drive electrical generators. 'Wind farms' of 20 to 100 turbines spaced about 400 m apart, supply about 400 MW (enough electricity for 250 000 homes) in the UK and provide a useful 'top-up' to the National Grid.

Wind turbines can be noisy and may be considered unsightly so there is some environmental objection to wind farms, especially as the best sites are often in coastal or upland areas of great natural beauty.

Wave energy

The rise and fall of sea waves has to be transferred by some kind of wave-energy converter into the rotary motion required to drive a generator. It is a difficult problem and the large-scale production of electricity by this means is unlikely in the near future, but small systems are being developed to supply island communities with power.

Tidal and hydroelectric energy

The gravitational field of the Moon exerts a pull on the water in the oceans on Earth. Water bulges outwards at places which are closest to, and furthest from, the Moon (where the pull is greatest and least), which results in a high tide at each place. As the Earth rotates, the position of the high tides move over its surface, giving two high and two low tides a day at most places.

The flow of water from a higher to a lower level from behind a **tidal barrage** (barrier) or the dam of a **hydroelectric scheme** is used to drive a water turbine (water wheel) connected to a generator.

One of the largest working tidal schemes is the La Grande I project in Canada (Figure P2.9). Feasibility studies have shown that a 10-mile-long barrage across the Severn Estuary could produce about 7% of today's electrical energy consumption in England and Wales. Such schemes have significant implications for the environment, as they may destroy wildlife habitats of wading birds for example, and also for shipping routes.

In the UK, hydroelectric power stations generate about 2% of the electricity supply. Most are located in Scotland and Wales where the average rainfall is higher than in other areas. With good management hydroelectric energy is a reliable energy source, but there are risks connected with the construction of dams, and a variety of problems may result from the impact of a dam on the environment. Land previously used for forestry or farming may have to be flooded.

Figure P2.9 Tidal barrage in Canada.

Geothermal energy

If cold water is pumped down a shaft into hot rocks below the Earth's surface, it may be forced up another shaft as steam. This can be used to drive a turbine and generate electricity or to heat buildings. The energy that heats the rocks is constantly being released by radioactive elements deep in the Earth as they decay (p.448).

Geothermal power stations are in operation in the USA, New Zealand and Iceland.

Biomass (vegetable fuels)

These include cultivated crops (e.g. oilseed rape), crop residues (e.g. cereal straw), natural vegetation (e.g. gorse), trees (e.g. spruce) grown for their wood, animal dung and sewage. **Biofuels** such as alcohol (ethanol) and methane gas are obtained from them by fermentation using enzymes or by decomposition by bacterial action in the absence of air. Liquid biofuels can replace petrol (Figure P2.10 on the next page); although they have up to 50% less energy per litre, they are lead- and sulfur-free and so cleaner. **Biogas** is a mix of methane and carbon dioxide with an energy content about two-thirds that of natural gas. In developing countries it is produced from animal and human waste in 'digesters' (Figure P2.11) and used for heating and cooking.

Figure P2.10 Filling up with biofuel in Brazil.

Figure P2.11 Feeding a biogas digester in rural India.

● Power stations

The processes involved in the production of electricity at **power stations** depend on the energy source being used.

Non-renewable sources

These are used in **thermal** power stations to produce heat energy that turns water into steam. The steam drives turbines which in turn drive the generators that produce electrical energy as described on p.439. If fossil fuels are the energy source (usually coal but natural gas is favoured in new stations), the steam is obtained from a boiler. If nuclear fuel is used, such as

uranium or plutonium, the steam is produced in a heat exchanger.

Renewable sources

In most cases the renewable energy source is used to drive turbines directly, as explained earlier in the cases of hydroelectric, wind, wave, tidal and geothermal schemes.

The block diagram and energy-transfer diagram for a hydroelectric scheme like that in Figure P2.4d (p.362) are shown in Figure P2.12. The efficiency of a large installation can be as high as 85–90% since many of the causes of loss in thermal power stations (e.g. water cooling towers) are absent. In some cases the generating costs are half those of thermal stations.

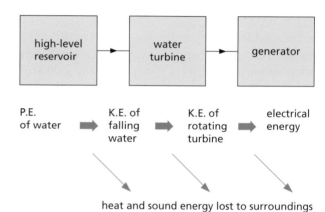

Figure P2.12 Energy transfers in a hydroelectric power station.

● Economic, environmental and social issues

When considering the large-scale generation of electricity, the economic and environmental costs of using various energy sources have to be weighed against the benefits that electricity brings to society as a 'clean', convenient and fairly 'cheap' energy supply.

Environmental problems such as polluting emissions that arise with different energy sources were outlined when each was discussed previously. Apart from people using less energy, how far pollution can be reduced by, for example, installing desulfurisation processes in coal-fired power stations, is often a matter of cost.

Although there are no fuel costs associated with electricity generation from renewable energy sources such as wind power, the energy is so 'dilute' that the capital costs of setting up the generating installation are high. Similarly, although fuel costs for nuclear power stations are relatively low, the costs of building the stations and of dismantling them at the end of their useful lives is higher than for gas- or coal-fired stations.

It has been estimated that currently it costs between 6p and 15p to produce a unit of electricity in a gas- or coal-fired power station in the UK. The cost for a nuclear power station is in excess of 8p per unit. Wind energy costs vary, depending upon location, but are in the range 8p to 21p per unit. In the most favourable locations wind competes with coal and gas generation.

The reliability of a source has also to be considered, as well as how easily production can be started up and shut down as demand for electricity varies. Natural gas power stations have a short start-up time, while coal and then oil power stations take successively longer to start up; nuclear power stations take longest. They are all reliable in that they can produce electricity at any time of day and in any season of the year as long as fuel is available. Hydroelectric power stations are also very reliable and have a very short start-up time which means they can be switched on when the demand for electricity peaks. The electricity output of a tidal power station, although predictable, is not as reliable because it depends on the height of the tide which varies over daily, monthly and seasonal time scales. The wind and the Sun are even less reliable sources of energy since the output of a wind turbine changes with the strength of the wind and that of a solar cell with the intensity of light falling on it; the output may not be able to match the demand for electricity at a particular time.

Renewable sources are still only being used on a small scale globally. The contribution of the main energy sources to the world's total energy consumption at present is given in Table P2.2. (The use of biofuels is not well documented.) The pattern in the UK is similar but France generates nearly three-quarters of its electricity from nuclear plants; for Japan and Taiwan the proportion is one-third, and it is in the developing economies of East Asia where interest in nuclear energy is growing most dramatically. However, the great dependence on fossil fuels worldwide is evident. It is clear the world has an energy problem.

Table P2.2 World use of energy sources

Oil	Coal	Gas	Nuclear	Hydroelectric
36%	29%	23%	6%	6%

Consumption varies from one country to another; North America and Europe are responsible for about 42% of the world's energy consumption each year. Table P2.3 shows approximate values for the annual consumption per head of population for different areas. These figures include the 'hidden' consumption in the manufacturing and transporting of goods. The world average consumption is 69×10^9 J per head per year.

Table P2.3 Energy consumption per head per year/J $\times 10^9$

N. America	UK	Japan	S. America	China	Africa
335	156	172	60	55	20

Questions

12 The pie chart in Figure P2.13 shows the percentages of the main energy sources used by a certain country.
  a What percentage is supplied by water power?
  b Which of the sources is/are renewable?
  c What is meant by 'renewable'?
  d Name two other renewable sources.
  e Why, if energy is always conserved, is it important to develop renewable sources?

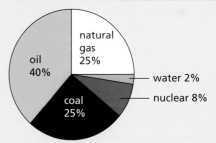

Figure P2.13

13 List six properties which you think the ideal energy source should have for generating electricity in a power station.

Checklist

After studying Chapter P2 you should know and understand the following.

- Relate work done to the magnitude of a force and the distance moved.

- Use the relation work done = force × distance moved to calculate energy transfer.
- Define the unit of work.
- Recall the different forms of energy.
- Describe energy transfers in given examples.
- State the principle of conservation of energy.
- Understand qualitatively the meaning of efficiency.

- Recall and use the equation

$$\text{efficiency} = \frac{\text{useful energy output}}{\text{energy input}} \times 100\%$$

- Define kinetic energy (K.E.).

- Perform calculations using the equation K.E. = $\frac{1}{2}mv^2$.

- Define gravitational potential energy (G.P.E.).

- Calculate changes in G.P.E. using the equation G.P.E. = mgh.

- Apply the principle of conservation of energy to simple mechanical systems, such as a pendulum.
- Relate power to work done and time taken, and give examples.

- Recall that power is the rate of energy transfer, give its unit and solve problems using the equation
P = energy transfer/time taken.
- Describe an experiment to measure your own power.
- Distinguish between renewable and non-renewable energy sources.
- Give some advantages and some disadvantages of using non-renewable fuels.
- Describe the different ways of harnessing solar, wind, wave, tidal, hydroelectric, geothermal and biomass energy.
- Describe the energy transfer processes in a thermal and a hydroelectric power station.

- Recognise that the Sun is the source of energy for all our energy resources except geothermal, nuclear and tidal.
- Recall that the source of the Sun's energy is nuclear fusion.
- Recognise that the moon is the main source of tidal energy.
- Compare and contrast the advantages and disadvantages of using different energy sources to generate electricity.
- Discuss the environmental and economic issues of electricity production and consumption.

Thermal physics

Combined

- State the distinguishing properties of solids, liquids and gases
- Describe qualitatively the molecular structure of solids, liquids and gases in terms of the arrangement, separation and motion of the molecules
- Describe qualitatively the pressure of a gas and the temperature of a gas, liquid or solid in terms of the motion of its particles
- Use and describe the use of thermometers to measure temperature on the Celsius scale
- State the meaning of *melting point* and *boiling point*, and recall the melting and boiling points for water
- Describe evaporation in terms of the escape of more-energetic molecules from the surface of a liquid
- Relate evaporation to the consequent cooling of the liquid
- Relate the properties of solids, liquids and gases to the forces and distances between the molecules and to the motion of the molecules
- Demonstrate an understanding of how temperature, surface area and draught over a surface influence evaporation
- Describe qualitatively the thermal expansion of solids, liquids and gases at constant pressure
- Identify and explain some of the everyday applications and consequences of thermal expansion
- Recognise and name typical good and bad thermal conductors
- Describe experiments to demonstrate the properties of good and bad thermal conductors
- Explain conduction in solids in terms of molecular vibrations and transfer by electrons
- Recognise convection as the main method of energy transfer in fluids
- Interpret and describe experiments designed to illustrate convection in liquids and gases (fluids)
- Relate convection in fluids to density changes
- Recognise radiation as the method of energy transfer that does not require a medium to travel through
- Identify infrared radiation as the part of the electromagnetic spectrum often involved in energy transfer by radiation
- Describe the effect of surface colour (black or white) and texture (dull or shiny) on the emission, absorption and reflection of radiation
- Interpret and describe experiments to investigate the properties of good and bad emitters and good and bad absorbers of infrared radiation
- Identify and explain some of the everyday applications and consequences of conduction, convection and radiation

Co-ordinated

- State the distinguishing properties of solids, liquids and gases
- Describe qualitatively the molecular structure of solids, liquids and gases in terms of the arrangement, separation and motion of the molecules
- Describe qualitatively the pressure of a gas and the temperature of a gas, liquid or solid in terms of the motion of its particles
- Show an understanding of Brownian motion (the random motion of particles in a suspension) as evidence for the kinetic molecular model of matter
- Use and describe the use of thermometers to measure temperature on the Celsius scale
- Describe *melting* and *boiling* in terms of energy input without a change in temperature
- State the meaning of *melting point* and *boiling point*, and recall the melting and boiling points for water
- Describe condensation and solidification
- Explain evaporation in terms of the escape of more-energetic molecules from the surface of a liquid
- Relate evaporation to the consequent cooling of the liquid
- Relate the properties of solids, liquids and gases to the forces and distances between molecules and to the motion of the molecules
- Describe qualitatively the pressure of a gas in terms of the motion of its molecules and their colliding with the walls creating a force
- Show an appreciation that massive particles may be moved by light, fast-moving molecules
- Distinguish between *boiling* and *evaporation*
- Demonstrate an understanding of how temperature, surface area and draught over a surface influence evaporation
- Describe qualitatively, in terms of molecules, the effect on the pressure of a gas of: a change of temperature at constant volume; a change of volume at constant temperature
- Describe qualitatively the thermal expansion of solids, liquids and gases at constant pressure
- Identify and explain some of the everyday applications and consequences of thermal expansion
- Explain in terms of the motion and arrangement of molecules, the relative order of the magnitude of the expansion of solids, liquids and gases
- Describe how a physical property that varies with temperature may be used for the measurement of temperature, and state examples of such properties
- Recognise the need for and identify fixed points
- Describe and explain the structure and action of liquid-in-glass thermometers

Matter is made up of tiny particles or **molecules** which are too small for us to see directly. But they can be 'seen' by scientific 'eyes'. One of these is the **electron microscope**. Figure P3.1 is a photograph taken with such an instrument showing molecules of a protein. Molecules consist of even smaller particles called **atoms** and are in continuous motion.

Figure P3.1 Protein molecules.

Practical work

Brownian motion

The apparatus is shown in Figure P3.2a. First fill the glass cell with smoke using a match (Figure P3.2b). Replace the lid on the apparatus and set it on the microscope platform. Connect the lamp to a 12 V supply; the glass rod acts as a lens and focuses light on the smoke.

Carefully adjust the microscope until you see bright specks dancing around haphazardly (Figure P3.2c). The specks are smoke particles seen by reflected light; their random motion is called **Brownian motion**. It is due to collisions with fast-moving air molecules in the cell.

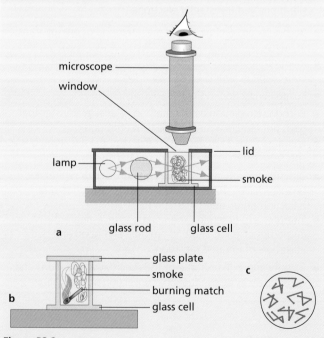

Figure P3.2

A smoke particle is massive compared with an air molecule but if there are more high-speed molecules striking one side of it than the other at a given instant, the particle will move in the direction in which there is a net force. The imbalance, and hence the direction of the net force, changes rapidly in a random manner.

Kinetic theory of matter

As well as being in continuous motion, molecules also exert strong electrical forces on one another when they are close together. The forces are both attractive and repulsive. (The former hold molecules together and the latter cause matter to resist compression.) The **kinetic theory** (see also pp.179, 180 and 181) can explain the existence of the three **states** or **phases** of matter.

In solids the atoms or molecules are close together and the attractive and repulsive forces between neighbouring molecules balance. Each molecule vibrates to and fro about one position. Solids therefore usually have a regular, repeating molecular pattern, i.e. are crystalline; they have a definite shape and volume, and they resist compression.

In liquids the molecules are usually slightly further apart than in solids and, as well as vibrating, they can at the same time move rapidly over short distances. However they are never near each other long enough to get trapped in a regular pattern, and a liquid can flow. Liquids have a definite volume, but when poured into a differently shaped container, their shape will change; they resist compression.

In gases the molecules are much farther apart than in solids or liquids (about ten times). They dash around at very high speed ($500\,ms^{-1}$ for air molecules) in all the space available. It is only during the brief spells when they collide with other molecules or with walls of the container that the molecular forces act. Gases can be readily compressed and have no definite shape or volume as these depend on the dimensions of the container.

A model illustrating the states of matter is shown in Figure P3.3. The tray is moved to and fro on the bench and the motion of the marbles (molecules) observed. Figure P3.3b is a model of a gas; the faster the vibrator works, the more often the ball bearings have collisions with the lid, the tube and each other, representing a gas at a higher temperature. Adding more ball bearings is like pumping more air into a tyre; it increases the pressure. If a polystyrene ball (1 cm diameter) is dropped into the tube its irregular motion demonstrates Brownian motion on a large scale.

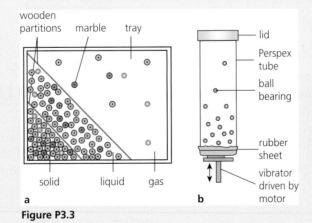

Figure P3.3

● Melting and freezing

When a solid is heated, it may melt and **change its state** from solid to liquid. If ice is heated it becomes water. The opposite process, freezing, occurs when a liquid solidifies.

The **melting point** of a pure solid is the **temperature** at which it changes from solid to liquid when it is heated. The temperature of the solid remains constant during the melting process, the energy supplied being used to overcome the attractive forces between the molecules so that they gain a greater freedom of movement. During melting, the potential energy of the molecules increases, but their average kinetic energy remains constant. For pure ice, the melting point is $0\,°C$.

The reverse process of solidification, or freezing, occurs at the same temperature.

● Evaporation and boiling

Evaporation

A few energetic molecules close to the surface of a liquid may escape and become gas molecules. This process occurs at all temperatures and is called **evaporation**. Evaporation happens more rapidly when

- the **temperature is higher**, since then more molecules in the liquid are moving fast enough to escape from the surface
- the **surface area of the liquid is large**, so giving more molecules a chance to escape because more are near the surface
- a **wind** or **draught** is blowing over the surface carrying vapour molecules away from the surface, thus stopping them from returning to the liquid and making it easier for more liquid molecules to break free. (Evaporation into a vacuum occurs much more rapidly than into a region where there are gas molecules.)

Cooling by evaporation

Evaporation occurs when faster-moving molecules escape from the surface of the liquid. The average speed and therefore the average kinetic energy of the molecules left behind decreases, i.e. the temperature of the liquid falls. Any body in contact with an evaporating liquid will be cooled by the evaporation.

Boiling

The **boiling point** of a pure liquid is the **temperature** at which it changes from a liquid to a gas when it is heated. The temperature of the liquid remains constant during the boiling process, the energy supplied being used to overcome the attractive forces between the molecules, enabling them to move over larger distances, as in a gas. For pure water (at normal atmospheric pressure) the boiling point is $100\,°C$.

The difference between evaporation and boiling

Boiling occurs at a definite temperature and is accompanied by bubbles of gas forming throughout the liquid. By contrast, in **evaporation,** a liquid changes to a vapour without ever reaching its boiling point. Evaporation can occur at any temperature, but only at the surface of the liquid, from where the more energetic molecules can escape to the gas phase. Evaporation results in a cooling of the liquid.

● Condensation and solidification

In **condensation**, a gas changes to a liquid state and latent heat of vaporisation is released. In **solidification**, a liquid changes to a solid and latent heat of fusion is given out. In each case the potential energy of the molecules decreases. Condensation of steam is easily achieved by contact with a cold surface, for example a cold windowpane.

Questions

1 Which one of the following statements is *not* true?
   A The molecules in a solid vibrate about a fixed position.
   B The molecules in a liquid are arranged in a regular pattern.
   C The molecules in a gas exert negligibly small forces on each other, except during collisions.
   D The densities of most liquids are about 1000 times greater than those of gases because liquid molecules are much closer together than gas molecules.
   E The molecules of a gas occupy all the space available.
2 Using what you know about the compressibility (squeezability) of the different states of matter, explain why
   a air is used to inflate tyres
   b steel is used to make railway lines.
3 Some water is stored in a bag of porous material, such as canvas, which is hung where it is exposed to a draught of air. Explain why the temperature of the water is lower than that of the air.
4 Explain why a bottle of milk keeps better when it stands in water in a porous pot in a draught.

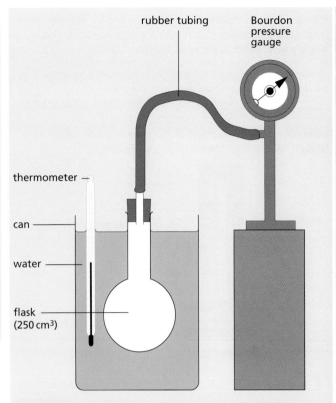

Figure P3.4

● Pressure of a gas

Practical work

Effect on pressure of temperature (volume constant) – the Pressure law

The apparatus is shown in Figure P3.4. The rubber tubing from the flask to the pressure gauge should be as short as possible. The flask must be in water almost to the top of its neck and be securely clamped to keep it off the bottom of the can.

Record the pressure over a wide range of temperatures, but before taking a reading, stop heating, stir and allow time for the gauge reading to become steady; the air in the flask will then be at the temperature of the water. Tabulate the results.

Plot a graph of pressure on the *y*-axis and temperature on the *x*-axis.

Practical work

Effect on volume of pressure (temperature constant) – Boyle's law

Changes in the volume of a gas due to pressure changes can be studied using the apparatus in Figure P3.5. The volume *V* of air trapped in the glass tube is read off on the scale behind. The pressure is altered by pumping air from a foot pump into the space above the oil reservoir. This forces more oil into the glass tube and increases the pressure *p* on the air in it; *p* is measured by the Bourdon gauge.

If a graph of pressure against volume is plotted using the results, a curve like that in Figure P3.6a, on the next page, is obtained. Close examination of the graph shows that if *p* is doubled, *V* is halved. That is, **p is inversely proportional to V**. In symbols

$$p \propto \frac{1}{V} \quad \text{or} \quad p = \text{constant} \times \frac{1}{V}$$

$$\therefore \quad pV = \text{constant}$$

If several pairs of readings, p_1 and V_1, p_2 and V_2, etc. are taken, then it can be confirmed that $p_1V_1 = p_2V_2 = $ constant. This is **Boyle's law**, which is stated as follows:

> The pressure of a fixed mass of gas is inversely proportional to its volume if its temperature is kept constant.

Since p is inversely proportional to V, then p is directly proportional to $1/V$. A graph of p against $1/V$ is therefore a straight line through the origin (Figure P3.6b).

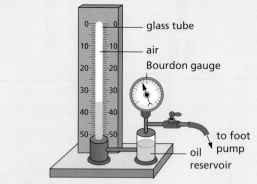

glass tube
air
Bourdon gauge
to foot pump
oil reservoir

Figure P3.5

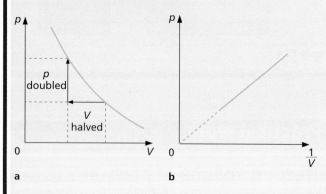

a

b

Figure P3.6

Gases and the kinetic theory

The kinetic theory can explain the behaviour of gases.

Cause of gas pressure

All the molecules in a gas are in rapid random motion, with a wide range of speeds, and repeatedly hit and rebound from the walls of the container in huge numbers per second. Each collision of a gas molecule with a wall of the container produces a force on the wall. The average force and hence the pressure exerted on the walls is constant since pressure is force on unit area.

Boyle's law

If the volume of a fixed mass of gas is halved by halving the volume of the container (Figure P3.7), the number of molecules per cm^3 will be doubled. There will be twice as many collisions per second with the walls, i.e. the pressure is doubled. This is Boyle's law.

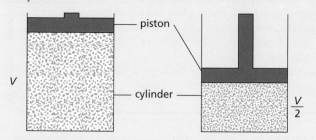

piston
cylinder

Figure P3.7 Halving the volume doubles the pressure.

Temperature

When a gas is heated and its temperature rises, the average speed of its molecules increases. If the volume of the gas stays constant, its pressure increases because there are more frequent and more violent collisions of the molecules with the walls. If the pressure of the gas is to remain constant, the volume must increase so that the frequency of collisions does not go up.

Questions

5 If the temperature of a fixed mass of gas rises, and its volume remains constant, does the pressure:
   a increase
   b stay the same
   c decrease?
6 If the volume of a fixed mass of gas is doubled, and the temperature remains constant, is the pressure:
   a doubled
   b unchanged
   c halved?

● Expansion of solids, liquids and gases

In general, when matter is heated it expands and when cooled it contracts. If the changes are resisted large forces are created which are sometimes useful but at other times are a nuisance.

> According to the kinetic theory (pp.179 and 373) the molecules of solids and liquids are in constant vibration. When heated they vibrate faster and force each other a little further apart. Expansion results, and this is greater for liquids than for solids; gases expand even more. The linear (length) expansion of solids is small and for the effect to be noticed, the solid must be long and/or the temperature change must be large.

● Uses of expansion

In Figure P3.8 the axles have been shrunk by cooling in liquid nitrogen at −196 °C until the gear wheels can be slipped on to them. On regaining normal temperature the axles expand to give a very tight fit.

In the kitchen, a tight metal lid can be removed from a glass jar by immersing the lid in hot water so that it expands.

Figure P3.8 'Shrink-fitting' of axles into gear wheels.

● Precautions against expansion

Gaps used to be left between lengths of railway lines to allow for expansion in summer. They caused a familiar 'clickety-click' sound as the train passed over them. These days rails are welded into lengths of about 1 km and are held by concrete 'sleepers' that can withstand the large forces created without buckling. Also, at the joints the ends are tapered and overlap (Figure P3.9a). This gives a smoother journey and allows some expansion near the ends of each length of rail.

For similar reasons slight gaps are left between lengths of aluminium guttering. In central heating pipes 'expansion joints' are used to join lengths of pipe (Figure P3.9b); these allow the copper pipes to expand in length inside the joints when carrying very hot water.

a tapered overlap of rails

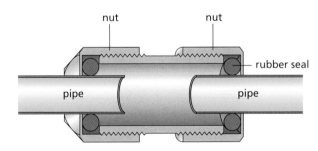

b expansion joint

Figure P3.9

● Bimetallic strip

If equal lengths of two different metals, such as copper and iron, are riveted together so that they cannot move separately, they form a **bimetallic strip** (Figure P3.10a). When heated, copper expands more than iron and to allow this the strip bends with copper on the outside (Figure P3.10b). If they had expanded equally, the strip would have stayed straight.

Bimetallic strips have many uses.

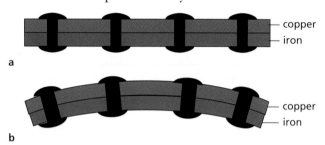

a

b

Figure P3.10 A bimetallic strip: **a** before heating; **b** after heating.

Fire alarm

Heat from the fire makes the bimetallic strip bend and complete the electrical circuit, so ringing the alarm bell (Figure P3.11a).

A bimetallic strip is also used in this way to work the flashing direction indicator lamps in a car, being warmed by an electric heating coil wound round it.

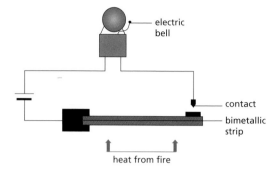

a

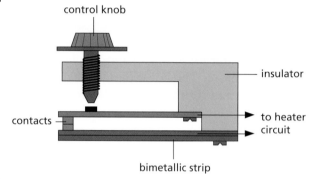

b

Figure P3.11 Uses of a bimetallic strip: **a** fire alarm; **b** a thermostat in an iron.

Thermostat

A **thermostat** keeps the temperature of a room or an appliance constant. The one in Figure P3.11b uses a bimetallic strip in the electrical heating circuit of, for example, an iron.

When the iron reaches the required temperature the strip bends down, breaks the circuit at the contacts and switches off the heater. After cooling a little the strip remakes contact and turns the heater on again. A near-steady temperature results.

If the control knob is screwed down, the strip has to bend more to break the heating circuit and this needs a higher temperature.

Questions

7 Explain why
  a the metal lid on a glass jam jar can be unscrewed easily if the jar is inverted for a few seconds with the *lid* in very hot water
  b furniture may creak at night after a warm day
  c concrete roads are laid in sections with pitch between them.
8 A bimetallic strip is made from aluminium and copper. When heated it bends in the direction shown in Figure P3.12. Which metal expands more for the same rise in temperature, aluminium or copper?
  Draw a diagram to show how the bimetallic strip would appear if it were cooled to below room temperature.

Figure P3.12

Measurement of temperature

The **temperature** of a object tells us how hot the object is. It is measured using a thermometer and usually in **degrees Celsius** (°C).

The kinetic theory (pp.179 and 373) regards temperature as a measure of the average kinetic energy (K.E.) of the molecules of the body. The greater this is, the faster the molecules move and the higher the temperature of the body.

There are different kinds of thermometer, each type being more suitable than another for a certain job. In each type the physical property used must vary continuously over a wide range of temperature. It must be accurately measurable with simple apparatus and vary in a similar way to other physical properties.

Properties used include:

- the change in volume of a liquid such as mercury (see liquid-in-glass thermometer below)
- the change in volume of a gas, for example air
- the change in electrical resistance of a metal such as platinum
- the generation of a voltage (e.m.f.) by a thermocouple (see thermocouple thermometer below).

Liquid-in-glass thermometer

In this type the liquid in a glass bulb expands up a capillary tube when the bulb is heated. The liquid must be easily seen and must expand (or contract) rapidly and by a large amount over a wide range of temperature. It must not stick to the inside of the tube or the reading will be too high when the temperature is falling.

Mercury and coloured alcohol are in common use. Mercury freezes at −39 °C and boils at 357 °C. Alcohol freezes at −115 °C and boils at 78 °C and is therefore more suitable for low temperatures.

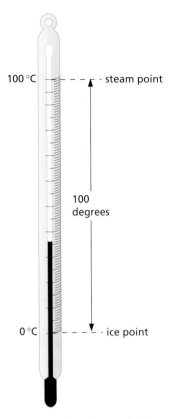

Figure P3.13 A temperature scale in degrees Celsius.

Scale of temperature

A **scale** and unit of temperature are obtained by choosing two temperatures, called the **fixed points**, and dividing the range between them into a number of equal divisions or **degrees**.

On the Celsius scale (named after the Swedish scientist who suggested it), **the lower fixed point is the temperature of pure melting ice** and is taken as 0 °C. **The upper fixed point is the temperature of the steam above water boiling at normal atmospheric pressure**, 10^5 Pa (or N/m²), and is taken as 100 °C.

When the fixed points have been marked on the thermometer, the distance between them is divided into 100 equal degrees (Figure P3.13). The thermometer now has a **linear** scale, in other words it has been **calibrated** or **graduated**.

Linearity implies that a change in the property being measured (for example the length of a column of mercury) is proportional to the change in temperature.

● Clinical thermometer

A **clinical thermometer** is a special type of mercury-in-glass thermometer used by doctors and nurses. Its scale only extends over a few degrees on either side of the normal body temperature of 37 °C (Figure P3.14), i.e. it has a small **range**. Because of the very narrow capillary tube, temperatures can be measured very accurately, in other words, the thermometer has a high **sensitivity**.

The tube has a constriction (a narrower part) just beyond the bulb. When the thermometer is placed under the tongue the mercury expands, forcing its way past the constriction. When the thermometer is removed (after 1 minute) from the mouth, the mercury in the bulb cools and contracts, breaking the mercury thread at the constriction. The mercury beyond the constriction stays in the tube and shows the body temperature. After use the mercury is returned to the bulb by a flick of the wrist. Since mercury is a toxic material, digital thermometers are now replacing mercury thermometers for clinical use.

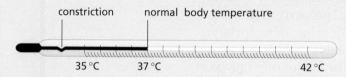

Figure P3.14 A clinical thermometer.

● Thermocouple thermometer

A **thermocouple** consists of wires of two different materials, such as copper and iron, joined together (Figures P3.15 and P3.16). When one junction is at a higher temperature than the other, an electric current flows and produces a reading on a sensitive meter which depends on the temperature difference.

Thermocouples are used in industry to measure a wide range of temperatures from −250 °C up to about 1500 °C, especially rapidly changing temperatures and those of small objects.

Figure P3.15 Use of a thermocouple probe thermometer to measure a temperature of about 1160 °C in lava.

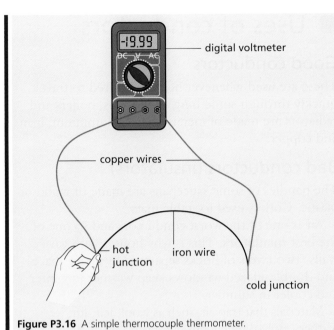

Figure P3.16 A simple thermocouple thermometer.

Other thermometers

One type of **resistance thermometer** uses the fact that the electrical resistance (p.426) of a platinum wire increases with temperature.

A resistance thermometer can measure temperatures accurately in the range −200 °C to 1200 °C but it is bulky and best used for steady temperatures. A **thermistor** can also be used but over a small range, such as −5 °C to 70 °C; its resistance decreases with temperature.

The **constant-volume gas thermometer** uses the change in pressure of a gas to measure temperatures over a wide range. It is an accurate but bulky instrument, basically similar to the apparatus of Figure P3.4 (p.375).

Thermochromic liquids which change colour with temperature have a limited range around room temperatures.

Questions

9 1530°C 120°C 55°C 37°C 19°C 0°C −12°C −50°C
From the above list of temperatures choose the most likely value for *each* of the following:
a the melting point of iron
b the temperature of a room that is comfortably warm
c the melting point of pure ice at normal pressure
d the lowest outdoor temperature recorded in London in winter
e the normal body temperature of a healthy person.

10 a How must a property behave to measure temperature?
b Name three properties that qualify.
c Name a suitable thermometer for measuring
   i a steady temperature of 1000°C
   ii the changing temperature of a small object
   iii a winter temperature at the North Pole.

11 In order to make a mercury thermometer that will measure small changes in temperature accurately, would you
A decrease the volume of the mercury bulb
B put the degree markings further apart
C decrease the diameter of the capillary tube
D put the degree markings closer together
E leave the capillary tube open to the air?

12 Describe the main features of a clinical thermometer.

Conduction is the flow of thermal energy (heat) through matter from places of higher temperature to places of lower temperature without movement of the matter as a whole.

A simple demonstration of the different conducting powers of various metals is shown in Figure P3.17. A match is fixed to one end of each rod using a little melted wax. The other ends of the rods are heated by a burner. When the temperatures of the far ends reach the melting point of wax, the matches drop off. The match on copper falls first, showing it is the best **conductor**, followed by aluminium, brass and then iron.

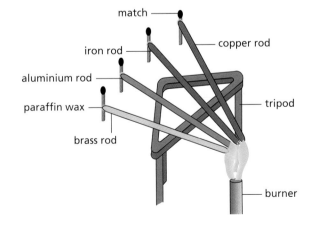

Figure P3.17 Comparing conducting powers.

Conduction

The handle of a metal spoon held in a hot drink soon gets warm. Heat passes along the spoon by **conduction**.

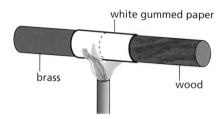

white gummed paper

brass

wood

Figure P3.18 The paper over the brass does not burn.

Heat is conducted faster through a rod if it has a large cross-sectional area, is short and has a large temperature difference between its ends.

Most metals are good conductors of heat; materials such as wood, glass, cork, plastics and fabrics are bad conductors. The arrangement in Figure P3.18 can be used to show the difference between brass and wood. If the rod is passed through a flame several times, the paper over the wood scorches but not the paper over the brass. The brass conducts the heat away from the paper quickly, preventing the paper from reaching the temperature at which it burns. The wood conducts the heat away only very slowly.

Metal objects below body temperature *feel* colder than those made of bad conductors – even if all the objects are at exactly the same temperature – because they carry heat away faster from the hand.

Liquids and gases also conduct heat but only very slowly. Water is a very poor conductor, as shown in Figure P3.19. The water at the top of the tube can be boiled before the ice at the bottom melts.

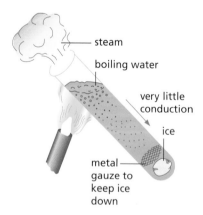

steam

boiling water

very little conduction

ice

metal gauze to keep ice down

Figure P3.19 Water is a poor conductor of heat.

● Uses of conductors

Good conductors

These are used whenever heat is required to travel quickly through something. Saucepans, boilers and radiators are made of metals such as aluminium, iron and copper.

Bad conductors (insulators)

The handles of some saucepans are made of wood or plastic. Cork is used for table mats.

Air is one of the worst conductors and so one of the best **insulators**. This is why houses with cavity walls (two layers of bricks separated by an air space) and double-glazed windows keep warmer in winter and cooler in summer.

Materials that trap air, such as wool, felt, fur, feathers, polystyrene foam, fibreglass, are also very bad conductors. Some of these materials are used as 'lagging' to insulate water pipes, hot water cylinders, ovens, refrigerators and the walls and roofs of houses (Figures P3.20a and P3.20b). Others are used to make warm winter clothes like 'fleece' jackets (Figure P3.20c).

a lagging in a cavity wall provides extra insulation

b laying lagging in a house loft

c fleece jackets help you to retain your body warmth

Figure P3.20

'Wet suits' are worn by divers and water skiers to keep them warm. The suit gets wet and a layer of water gathers between the person's body and the suit. The water is warmed by body heat and stays warm because the suit is made of an insulating fabric, such as neoprene, a synthetic rubber.

● Convection in liquids

Convection is the usual method by which thermal energy (heat) travels through fluids such as liquids and gases. It can be shown in water by dropping a few crystals of potassium permanganate down a tube to the bottom of a beaker or flask of water. When the tube is removed and the beaker heated just below the crystals by a *small* flame (Figure P3.21a), purple streaks of water rise upwards and fan outwards.

a convection currents shown by potassium permanganate in water

● Conduction and the kinetic theory

Two processes occur in metals. Metals have a large number of 'free' electrons (p.415) which wander about inside them. When one part of a metal is heated, the electrons there move faster (their kinetic energy increases) and further. As a result they 'jostle' atoms in cooler parts, so passing on their energy and raising the temperature of these parts. This process occurs quickly.

The second process is much slower. The atoms themselves at the hot part make 'colder' neighbouring atoms vibrate more vigorously. This is less important in metals but is the only way conduction occurs in non-metals since these do not have 'free' electrons; hence non-metals are poor conductors of heat.

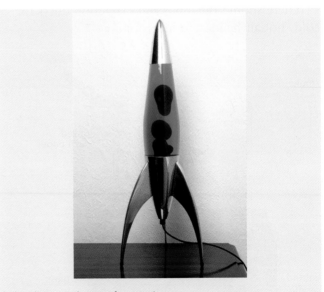

b lava lamps make use of convection

Figure P3.21

Convection is the flow of heat through a fluid from places of higher temperature to places of lower temperature by movement of the fluid itself.

Streams of warm moving fluids are called **convection currents**. They arise when a fluid is heated because it expands, becomes less dense and is forced upwards by surrounding cooler, denser fluid which moves under it. We say 'hot water (or hot air) rises'. Warm fluid behaves like a cork released under water: being less dense it bobs up. Lava lamps (Figure P3.21b) use this principle.

● Convection in air

Black marks often appear on the wall or ceiling above a lamp or a radiator. They are caused by dust being carried upwards in air convection currents produced by the hot lamp or radiator.

A laboratory demonstration of convection currents in air can be given using the apparatus of Figure P3.22. The direction of the convection current created by the candle is made visible by the smoke from the touch paper (made by soaking brown paper in strong potassium nitrate solution and drying it).

Convection currents set up by electric, gas and oil heaters help to warm our homes. Many so-called 'radiators' are really convector heaters.

Where should the input and extraction ducts for cold/hot air be located in a room?

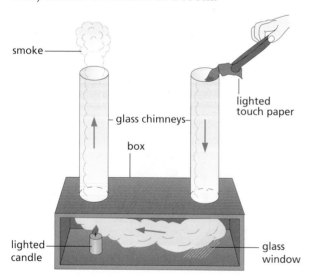

Figure P3.22 Demonstrating convection in air.

● Natural convection currents

Coastal breezes

During the day the temperature of the land increases more quickly than that of the sea. The hot air above the land rises and is replaced by colder air from the sea. A breeze from the sea results (Figure P3.23a).

At night the opposite happens. The sea has more heat to lose and cools more slowly. The air above the sea is warmer than that over the land and a breeze blows from the land (Figure P3.23b).

Gliding

Gliders, including 'hang-gliders' (Figure P3.24), depend on hot air currents, called **thermals**.

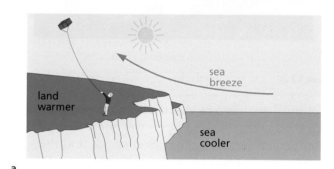

a

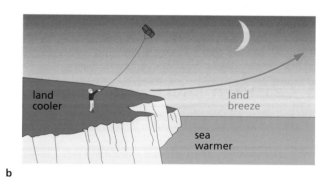

b

Figure P3.23 Coastal breezes are due to convection: **a** day; **b** night.

Figure P3.24 Once airborne, a hang-glider pilot can stay aloft for several hours by flying from one thermal to another.

Figure P3.25 Why are buildings in hot countries often painted white?

● Radiation

Radiation is a third way in which heat can travel, but whereas conduction and convection both need matter to be present, radiation can occur in a vacuum; particles of matter are not involved. Radiation is the way heat reaches us from the Sun.

Radiation has all the properties of electromagnetic waves (p.402), such as it travels at the speed of radio waves and gives interference effects. When it falls on an object, it is partly reflected, partly transmitted and partly absorbed; the absorbed part raises the temperature of the object.

> Radiation is the flow of heat from one place to another by means of electromagnetic waves.

Radiation is emitted by all bodies above absolute zero and consists mostly of **infrared radiation** (p.403) but light and **ultraviolet** are also present if the body is very hot (e.g. the Sun).

● Good and bad absorbers

Some surfaces absorb radiation better than others, as may be shown using the apparatus in Figure P3.26. The inside surface of one lid is shiny and of the other dull black. The coins are stuck on the outside of each lid with candle wax. If the heater is midway between the lids they each receive the same amount of radiation. After a few minutes the wax on the black lid melts and the coin falls off. The shiny lid stays cool and the wax unmelted.

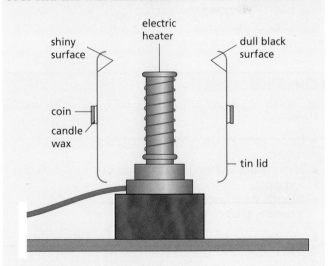

Figure P3.26 Comparing absorbers of radiation.

Dull black surfaces are better absorbers of radiation than white shiny surfaces – the latter are good **reflectors** of radiation. Reflectors on electric fires are made of polished metal because of its good reflecting properties.

385

● Good and bad emitters

Some surfaces also emit radiation better than others when they are hot. If you hold the backs of your hands on either side of a hot copper sheet that has one side polished and the other side blackened (Figure P3.27), it will be found that the **dull black surface is a better emitter of radiation than the shiny one**.

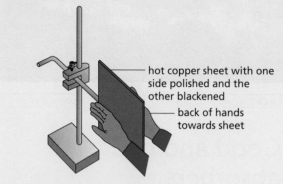

hot copper sheet with one side polished and the other blackened

back of hands towards sheet

Figure P3.27 Comparing emitters of radiation.

The cooling fins on the heat exchangers at the back of a refrigerator are painted black so that they lose heat more quickly. By contrast, saucepans that are polished are poor emitters and keep their heat longer.

In general, surfaces that are good absorbers of radiation are good emitters when hot.

Questions

13 Explain why
   a newspaper wrapping keeps hot things hot, e.g. fish and chips, and cold things cold, e.g. ice cream
   b fur coats would keep their owners warmer if they were worn inside out
   c a string vest helps to keep a person warm even though it is a collection of holes bounded by string.

14 What is the advantage of placing an electric immersion heater
   a near the top
   b near the bottom
       of a tank of water?

15 Explain why on a cold day the metal handlebars of a bicycle feel colder than the rubber grips.

16 The door canopy in Figure P3.28 shows in a striking way the difference between white and black surfaces when radiation falls on them. Explain why.

Figure P3.28

Checklist

After studying Chapter P3 you should know and understand the following.

- Describe and explain an experiment to show Brownian motion.
- State the distinguishing physical properties of solids, liquids and gases.
- Describe the arrangement, separation and motion of molecules in solids, liquids and gases.
- Use the kinetic theory to explain the physical properties of solids, liquids and gases.
- Describe pressure and temperature in terms of the motion of molecules.
- Recognise that during a change of state the temperature stays constant.
- State the meaning of melting point and boiling point and recall the temperatures for water.
- Explain what is meant by evaporation and boiling.

- State the factors that affect evaporation.
- Explain cooling by evaporation using the kinetic theory.
- Recall the differences between evaporation and boiling.
- Describe condensation and solidification.
- Describe experiments to study the relationships between the pressure, volume and temperature of a gas.
- Explain the behaviour of gases using the kinetic theory.
- Explain qualitatively the thermal expansion of solids, liquids and gases.
- Recall and explain in terms of the motion and arrangement of molecules, the relative order of magnitude of the expansion of solids, liquids and gases.
- Describe some uses of expansion in solids,
- Describe precautions taken against expansion.
- Explain the action of a bimetallic strip and its use in a thermostat and fire alarm.
- Describe and use thermometers to measure temperature.

- Recall the properties of mercury and alcohol which make them suitable for use in thermometers.
- Define the fixed points on the Celsius scale.
- Explain the action of liquid in glass thermometers.
- Describe the structure and use of clinical and thermocouple thermometers.
- Understand the meaning of range, sensitivity and linearity in relation to thermometers.
- Recall some other types of thermometer and the physical properties on which they depend.

- Recall that conduction is the flow of thermal energy (heat) through matter, from places of higher temperature to places of lower temperature, without the movement of the matter as a whole.
- Describe experiments to show the different conducting powers of various substances.
- Name good and bad conductors and state uses for each.
- Explain the importance of insulating a building.
- Explain conduction using the kinetic theory.

- Recall that convection is the flow of heat through a fluid, by the movement of the fluid itself.

- Recognise that the density of a fluid is usually lower in regions where the temperature is higher (due to expansion of the fluid) causing it to rise and enabling convection to occur.
- Describe experiments to show convection in fluids (liquids and gases).
- Relate convection to phenomena such as land and sea breezes.
- Recall that radiation is the flow of heat from one place to another by means of electromagnetic waves, mainly in the form of infrared radiation.
- Describe the effect of surface colour and texture on the emission, absorption and reflection of radiation.
- Describe experiments to study factors affecting the absorption and emission of radiation.
- Recall that good absorbers are also good emitters.

- Recognise and explain some everyday examples of conduction, convection and radiation.

Combined

- Demonstrate understanding that waves transfer energy without transferring matter
- Describe what is meant by *wave motion* as illustrated by vibration in ropes and springs and by experiments using water waves
- State the meaning of *speed*, *frequency*, *wavelength* and *amplitude*
- Describe how waves can undergo: reflection at a plane surface; refraction due to a change of speed
- Distinguish between *transverse* and *longitudinal* waves and give suitable examples
- Understand that refraction is caused by a change in speed as a wave moves from one medium to another
- Recall and use the equation $v = f\lambda$
- Describe the formation of an optical image by a plane mirror and give its characteristics
- Recall and use the law
  angle of incidence i = angle of reflection r
  recognising these angles are measured to the normal
- Perform simple constructions, measurements and calculations for reflection by plane mirrors
- Interpret and describe an experimental demonstration of the refraction of light
- Describe the action of a thin converging lens on a beam of light
- Use the terms *principal focus* and *focal length*
- Draw ray diagrams for the formation of a real image by a single lens
- Use and describe the use of a single lens as a magnifying glass
- Describe the main features of the electromagnetic spectrum in order of frequency, from radio waves to gamma radiation (γ)
- State that all electromagnetic waves travel with the same high speed in a vacuum and approximately the same in air
- Describe typical properties and uses of radiations in all the different regions of the electromagnetic spectrum including: radio and television communications (radio waves); satellite television and telephones (microwaves); electrical appliances, remote controllers for televisions and intruder alarms (infra-red); medicine and security (X-rays)
- Demonstrate an understanding of safety issues regarding the use of microwaves and X-rays
- State the dangers of ultraviolet radiation, from the Sun or from tanning lamps
- State that the speed of electromagnetic waves in a vacuum is 3.0×10^8 m/s
- Describe the production of sound by vibrating sources
- State that the approximate range of audible frequencies for a healthy human ear is 20 Hz to 20 000 Hz
- Show an understanding that a medium is needed to transmit sound waves

Co-ordinated

- Demonstrate understanding that waves transfer energy without transferring matter
- Describe what is meant by *wave motion* as illustrated by vibration in ropes and springs and by experiments using water waves
- Use the term *wavefront*
- State the meaning of *speed*, *frequency*, *wavelength* and *amplitude*
- Describe how waves can undergo: reflection at a plane surface; refraction due to a change of speed
- Distinguish between *transverse* and *longitudinal waves* and give suitable examples
- Understand that refraction is caused by a change in speed as a wave moves from one medium to another
- Recall and use the equation $v = f\lambda$
- Describe how waves can undergo diffraction through a narrow gap
- Describe the use of water waves to demonstrate diffraction
- Describe the formation of an optical image by a plane mirror and give its characteristics
- Recall and use the law
  angle of incidence i = angle of reflection r
  recognising these angles are measured to the normal
- Perform simple constructions, measurements and calculations for reflection by plane mirrors
- Interpret and describe an experimental demonstration of the refraction of light
- Use the terminology for the angle of incidence i and angle of refraction r and describe the passage of light through parallel-sided transparent material
- Recall and use the definition of refractive index n in terms of speed
- Recall and use the equation for refractive index, $n = \sin i / \sin r$
- Describe internal and total internal reflection using ray diagrams
- Give the meaning of *critical angle*
- Describe and explain the action of optical fibres particularly in medicine and communications technology
- Describe the action of a thin converging lens on a beam of light
- Use the terms *principal focus* and *focal length*
- Draw ray diagrams for the formation of a real image by a single lens
- Describe the nature of an image using the terms enlarged/same size/diminished and upright/inverted
- Describe the difference between a real image and a virtual image
- Use and describe the use of a single lens as a magnifying glass

Combined (continued...)

- Describe and interpret an experiment to determine the speed of sound in air, including calculation
- Relate the loudness and pitch of sound waves to amplitude and frequency
- Describe how the reflection of sound may produce an echo

- Describe the longitudinal nature of sound waves
- Describe the transmission of sound waves in air in terms of compressions and rarefactions
- Recognise that sound travels faster in liquids than gases and faster in solids than in liquids

Co-ordinated (continued...)

- Describe the main features of the electromagnetic spectrum in order of frequency, from radio waves to gamma radiation (γ)
- State that all electromagnetic waves travel with the same high speed in a vacuum and approximately the same in air
- State that the speed of electromagnetic waves in a vacuum is 3.0×10^8 m/s

- Describe typical properties and uses of radiations in all the different regions of the electromagnetic spectrum including: radio and television communications (radio waves); satellite television and telephones (microwaves); electrical appliances, remote controllers for televisions and intruder alarms (infrared); medicine and security (X-rays)
- Demonstrate an understanding of safety issues regarding the use of microwaves and X-rays
- State the dangers of ultraviolet radiation, from the Sun or from tanning lamps
- Describe the production of sound by vibrating sources
- State that the approximate range of audible frequencies for a healthy human ear is 20 Hz to 20 000 Hz
- Show an understanding that a medium is needed to transmit sound waves
- Describe and interpret an experiment to determine the speed of sound in air, including calculation
- Relate the loudness and pitch of sound waves to amplitude and frequency
- Describe how the reflection of sound may produce an echo
- Describe the longitudinal nature of sound waves
- Describe the transmission of sound waves in air in terms of compressions and rarefactions
- Recognise that sound travels faster in liquids than gases and faster in solids than in liquids

● Types of wave

Several kinds of wave occur in physics. **Mechanical waves** are produced by a disturbance, such as a vibrating object, in a material medium and are transmitted by the particles of the medium vibrating to and fro. Such waves can be seen or felt and include waves on a rope or spring, water waves and sound waves in air or in other materials.

A **progressive** or travelling wave is a disturbance which carries energy from one place to another without transferring matter.

There are two types of progressive wave, **transverse** and **longitudinal**.

Transverse waves

In a transverse wave, the direction of the disturbance is at **right angles** to the direction of travel of the

wave. A transverse wave can be sent along a rope (or a spring) by fixing one end and moving the other rapidly up and down (Figure P4.1). The disturbance generated by the hand is passed on from one part of the rope to the next which performs the same motion but slightly later. The humps and hollows of the wave travel along the rope as each part of the rope vibrates transversely about its undisturbed position.

Water waves are transverse waves.

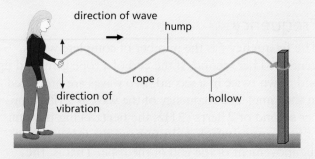

Figure P4.1 A transverse wave.

Longitudinal waves

In a progressive longitudinal wave the particles of the transmitting medium vibrate to and fro along the same line as that in which the wave is travelling and not at right angles to it as in a transverse wave. A longitudinal wave can be sent along a spring, stretched out on the bench and fixed at one end, if the free end is repeatedly pushed and pulled sharply, as shown in Figure P4.2.

Sound waves are longitudinal waves.

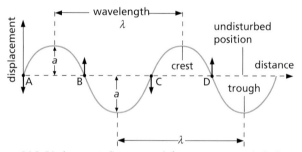

Figure P4.2 A longitudinal wave.

● Describing waves

Terms used to describe waves can be explained with the aid of a **displacement–distance graph** (Figure P4.3). It shows, at a certain instant of time, the distance moved (sideways from their undisturbed positions) by the parts of the medium vibrating at different distances from the cause of the wave.

Wavelength

The **wavelength** of a wave, represented by the Greek letter λ ('lambda'), is the distance between successive crests.

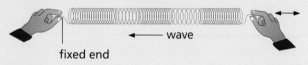

Figure P4.3 Displacement–distance graph for a wave at a particular instant.

Frequency

The **frequency** f is the number of complete waves generated per second. If the end of a rope is moved up and down twice in a second, two waves are produced in this time. The frequency of the wave is 2 vibrations per second or 2 hertz (2 Hz; the **hertz** being the unit of frequency), which is the same as the frequency of the movement of the end of the rope. That is, the frequencies of the wave and its source are equal.

The frequency of a wave is also the number of crests passing a chosen point per second.

Speed

The **speed** v of the wave is the distance moved in the direction of travel of the wave by a crest or any point on the wave in 1 second.

Amplitude

The **amplitude** a is the height of a crest or the depth of a trough measured from the undisturbed position of what is carrying the wave, such as a rope.

● The wave equation

The faster the end of a rope is vibrated, the shorter the wavelength of the wave produced. That is, the higher the frequency of a wave, the smaller its wavelength. There is a useful connection between f, λ and v, which is true for all types of wave.

Suppose waves of wavelength $\lambda = 20\,\text{cm}$ travel on a long rope and three crests pass a certain point every second. The frequency $f = 3\,\text{Hz}$. If Figure P4.4 represents this wave motion then, if crest A is at P at a particular time, 1 second later it will be at Q, a distance from P of three wavelengths, i.e. $3 \times 20 = 60\,\text{cm}$. The speed of the wave is $v = 60\,\text{cm}$ per second (60 cm/s), obtained by multiplying f by λ. Hence:

speed of wave = frequency × wavelength

or

$$v = f\lambda$$

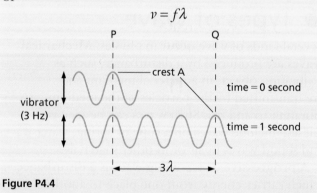

Figure P4.4

Practical work

The ripple tank

The behaviour of water waves can be studied in a ripple tank. It consists of a transparent tray containing water, having a light source above and a white screen below to receive the wave images (Figure P4.5).

Pulses (i.e. short bursts) of ripples are obtained by dipping a finger in the water for circular ripples and a ruler for straight ripples. **Continuous ripples** are generated using an electric motor and a bar. The bar gives straight ripples if it just touches the water or circular ripples if it is raised and has a small ball fitted to it.

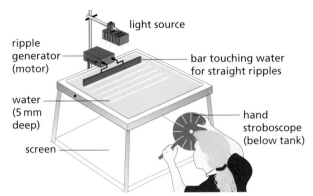

Figure P4.5 A ripple tank.

Continuous ripples are studied more easily if they are *apparently* stopped ('frozen') by viewing the screen through a disc with equally spaced slits, which can be spun by hand, i.e. a **stroboscope**. If the disc speed is such that the waves have advanced one wavelength each time a slit passes your eye, they appear at rest.

Wavefronts

In two dimensions, a **wavefront** is a line on which the disturbance has the same phase at all points; the **crests of waves** in a ripple tank can be thought of as wavefronts. A vibrating source produces a succession of wavefronts, all of the same shape. In a ripple tank, straight wavefronts are produced by a vibrating bar (a line source) and circular wavefronts are produced by a vibrating ball (a point source).

Reflection

In Figure P4.6 **straight** water waves are falling on a metal strip placed in a ripple tank at an angle i to the normal. The wavefronts are represented by straight lines and can be thought of as the crests of the waves. They are at right angles to the direction of travel. The waves are reflected at the metal plate and it is found that the angle of reflection, r, is always equal to the angle of incidence, i.

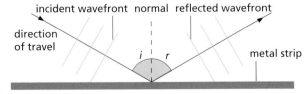

Figure P4.6 Reflection of waves.

Refraction

If a glass plate is placed in a ripple tank so that the water over the glass plate is about 1 mm deep but is 5 mm deep elsewhere, continuous straight waves in the shallow region are found to have a shorter wavelength than those in the deeper parts, i.e. the wavefronts are closer together (Figure P4.7). Both sets of waves have the frequency of the vibrating bar and, since $v = f\lambda$, if λ has decreased so has v, since f is fixed. Hence **waves travel more slowly in shallow water.**

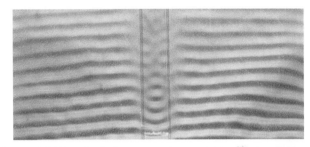

Figure P4.7 Waves in shallower water have a shorter wavelength.

When the plate is at an angle to the waves (Figure P4.8a), their direction of travel in the shallow region is bent towards the normal (Figure P4.8b). The change in the direction of travel of the waves, which occurs when their speed and hence wavelength changes, is termed **refraction**.

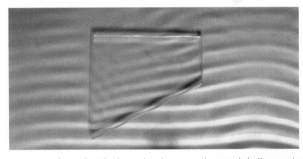

a waves are refracted at the boundary between deep and shallow regions

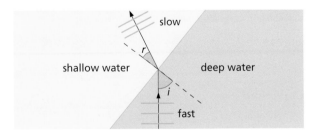

b the direction of travel is bent towards the normal in the shallow region

Figure P4.8

The speed of waves also changes, and refraction occurs, when waves move from one medium to another. For example, light waves are refracted when they move from air to glass.

● Diffraction

In Figures P4.9a and P4.9b, straight water waves in a ripple tank are meeting gaps formed by obstacles. In Figure P4.9a the gap width is about the same as the wavelength of the waves (1 cm); the wavefronts that pass through become circular and spread out in all directions. In Figure P4.9b the gap is wide (10 cm) compared with the wavelength and the waves continue straight on; some spreading occurs but it is less obvious.

Figure P4.10 Model of a harbour used to study wave behaviour.

The spreading of waves at the edges of obstacles is called **diffraction**; when designing harbours, engineers use models like that in Figure P4.10 to study it.

a spreading of waves after passing through a narrow gap

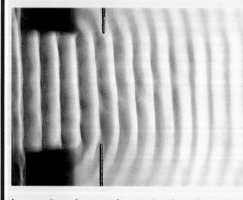

b spreading of waves after passing through a wide gap

Figure P4.9

Questions

1 The lines in Figure P4.11 are crests of straight ripples.
   a What is the wavelength of the ripples?
   b If 5 seconds ago ripple A occupied the position now occupied by ripple F, what is the frequency of the ripples?
   c What is the speed of the ripples?

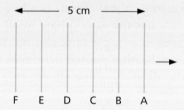

Figure P4.11

2 During the refraction of a wave which two of the following properties change?
   A The speed.
   B The frequency.
   C The wavelength.
3 One side of a ripple tank ABCD is raised slightly (Figure P4.12), and a ripple started at P by a finger. After 1 second the shape of the ripple is as shown.
   a Why is it not circular?
   b Which side of the tank has been raised?

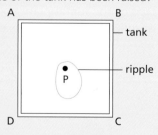

Figure P4.12

4 Copy Figure P4.13 and show on it what happens to the waves as they pass through the gap, if the water is much shallower on the right-hand side than on the left.

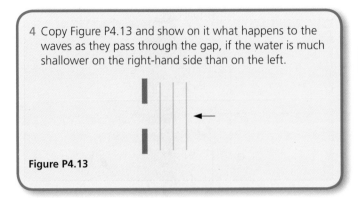

Figure P4.13

● Reflection of light

If we know how light behaves when it is reflected, we can use a mirror to change the direction in which the light is travelling. This happens when a mirror is placed at the entrance of a concealed drive to give warning of approaching traffic.

An ordinary mirror is made by depositing a thin layer of silver on one side of a piece of glass and protecting it with paint. The silver – at the *back* of the glass – acts as the reflecting surface.

● Law of reflection

Terms used in connection with reflection are shown in Figure P4.14. The perpendicular to the mirror at the point where the incident ray strikes it is called the **normal**. Note that the **angle of incidence** i is the angle between the incident ray and the normal; similarly the **angle of reflection** r is the angle between the reflected ray and the normal.

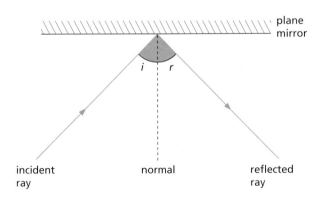

Figure P4.14 Reflection of light by a plane mirror.

The law of reflection states:

The angle of incidence equals the angle of reflection.

The incident ray, the reflected ray and the normal all lie in the same plane. (This means that they could all be drawn on a flat sheet of paper.)

Practical work

Reflection by a plane mirror

Draw a line AOB on a sheet of paper and using a protractor mark angles on it. Measure them from the perpendicular ON, which is at right angles to AOB. Set up a plane (flat) mirror with its reflecting surface on AOB.

Shine a narrow ray of light along, say, the 30° line onto the mirror (Figure P4.15).

Mark the position of the reflected ray, remove the mirror and measure the angle between the reflected ray and ON. Repeat for rays at other angles. What can you conclude?

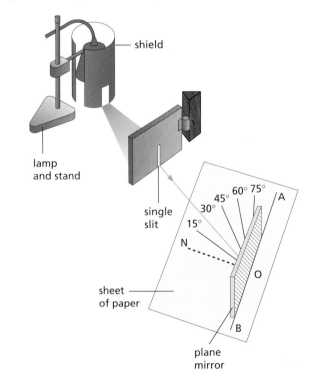

Figure P4.15

● Plane mirrors

When you look into a plane mirror on the wall of a room you see an image of the room behind the mirror; it is as if there were another room. Restaurants sometimes have a large mirror on one wall just to make them look larger. You may be able to say how much larger after the next experiment.

The position of the image formed by a mirror depends on the position of the object.

Practical work

Position of the image

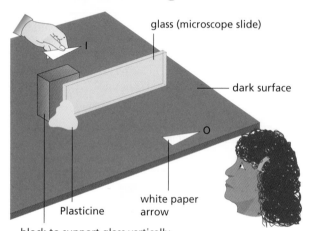

Figure P4.16

Support a piece of thin glass on the bench, as in Figure P4.16. It must be *vertical* (at 90° to the bench). Place a small paper arrow, O, about 10 cm from the glass. The glass acts as a poor mirror and an image of O will be seen in it; the darker the bench top, the brighter the image will be.

Lay another identical arrow, I, on the bench behind the glass; move it until it coincides with the image of O. How do the sizes of O and its image compare? Imagine a line joining them. What can you say about it? Measure the distances of the points of O and I from the glass along the line joining them. How do they compare? Try placing O at other distances.

● Real and virtual images

A **real image** is one which can be produced on a screen (as in a pinhole camera) and is formed by rays that actually pass through it.

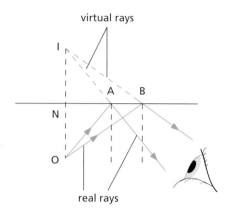

Figure P4.17 A plane mirror forms a virtual image.

A **virtual image** cannot be formed on a screen and is produced by rays which seem to come from it but do not pass through it. The image in a plane mirror is virtual. Rays from a point on an object are reflected at the mirror and appear to our eyes to come from a point behind the mirror where the rays would intersect when produced backwards (Figure P4.17). IA and IB are construction lines and are shown as broken lines.

● Lateral inversion

If you close your left eye, your image in a plane mirror seems to close the right eye. In a mirror image, left and right are interchanged and the image appears to be **laterally inverted**. The effect occurs whenever an image is formed by one reflection and is very evident if print is viewed in a mirror (Figure P4.18). What happens if two reflections occur, as in a periscope?

Figure P4.18 The image in a plane mirror is laterally inverted.

● Properties of the image

The image in a plane mirror is

(i) as far behind the mirror as the object is in front, with the line joining the object and image being perpendicular to the mirror
(ii) the same size as the object
(iii) virtual
(iv) laterally inverted.

● Refraction of light

If you place a coin in an empty dish and move back until you *just* cannot see it, the result is surprising if someone *gently* pours in water. Try it.

Although light travels in straight lines in a transparent material, such as air, if it passes into a different material, such as water, it changes direction at the boundary between the two, i.e. it is bent. The **bending of light** when it passes from one material (called a medium) to another is called **refraction**. It causes effects such as the coin trick.

● Facts about refraction

(i) A ray of light is bent **towards** the normal when it enters an optically denser medium at an angle, for example from air to glass as in Figure P4.19a. The angle of refraction *r* is less than the angle of incidence *i*.
(ii) A ray of light is bent **away from** the normal when it enters an optically less dense medium, for example from glass to air.
(iii) A ray emerging from a parallel-sided block is **parallel** to the ray entering, but is **displaced sideways**, like the ray in Figure P4.19a.
(iv) A ray travelling along the normal direction at a boundary is **not refracted** (Figure P4.19b).

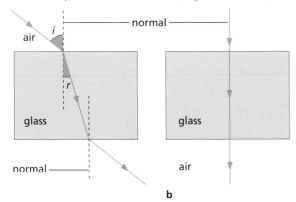

a
b
Figure P4.19 Refraction of light in glass.

Note 'Optically denser' means having a greater refraction effect; the actual density may or may not be greater.

Practical work

Refraction in glass

Shine a ray of light at an angle on to a glass block (which has its lower face painted white or frosted), as in Figure P4.20. Draw the outline ABCD of the block on the sheet of paper under it. Mark the positions of the various rays in air and in glass.

Remove the block and draw the normals on the paper at the points where the ray enters side AB (see Figure P4.20) and where it leaves side CD.

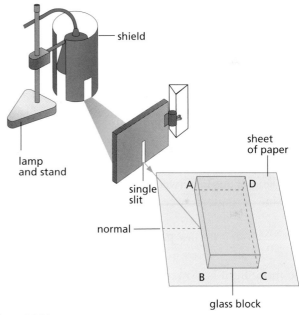

Figure P4.20

Questions

1 What *two* things happen to the light falling on AB?
2 a When the ray enters the glass at AB, is it bent towards or away from the part of the normal in the block?
  b How is it bent at CD?
3 What can you say about the direction of the ray falling on AB and the direction of the ray leaving CD?
4 What happens if the ray hits AB at right angles?

● Refractive index

Light is refracted because its speed changes when it enters another medium. An analogy helps to explain why.

Suppose three people A, B, C are marching in line, with hands linked, on a good road surface. If they approach marshy ground at an angle (Figure P4.21a), person A is slowed down first, followed by B and then C. This causes the whole line to swing round and change its direction of motion.

In air (and a vacuum) light travels at 300 000 km/s (3×10^8 m/s); in glass its speed falls to 200 000 km/s (2×10^8 m/s) (Figure P4.21b). The **refractive index**, n, of a medium, in this case glass, is defined by the equation

refractive index, $n = \dfrac{\text{speed of light in air (or a vacuum)}}{\text{speed of light in medium}}$

for glass, $\quad n = \dfrac{300\,000 \text{ km/s}}{200\,000 \text{ km/s}} = \dfrac{3}{2}$

Experiments also show that:

$n = \dfrac{\text{sine of angle between ray in air and normal}}{\text{sine of angle between ray in glass and normal}}$

$= \dfrac{\sin i}{\sin r} \quad$ (see Figure P4.19a)

The more light is slowed down when it enters a medium from air, the greater is the refractive index of the medium and the more the light is bent.

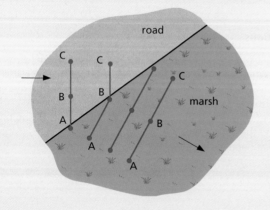

a

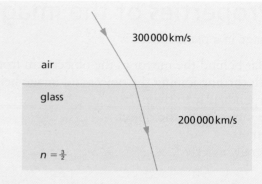

b

Figure P4.21

We saw earlier (p.391) that water waves are refracted when their speed changes. The change in the direction of travel of a light ray when its speed changes on entering another medium suggests that light may also be a type of wave motion.

● Critical angle

When light passes at small angles of incidence from an optically dense to a less dense medium, such as from glass to air, there is a strong refracted ray and a weak ray reflected back into the denser medium (Figure P4.22a). Increasing the angle of incidence increases the angle of refraction.

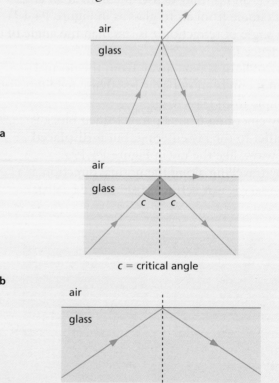

a

b

c = critical angle

c

Figure P4.22

At a certain angle of incidence, called the **critical angle**, *c*, the angle of refraction is 90° (Figure P4.22b). For angles of incidence greater than *c*, the refracted ray disappears and all the incident light is reflected inside the denser medium (Figure P4.22c). The light does not cross the boundary and is said to undergo **total internal reflection**.

Practical work

Critical angle of glass

Place a semicircular glass block on a sheet of paper (Figure P4.23), and draw the outline LOMN where O is the centre and ON the normal at O to LOM. Direct a narrow ray (at an angle of about 30° to the normal ON) along a radius towards O. The ray is not refracted at the curved surface. Why? Note the refracted ray emerging from LOM into the air and also the weak internally reflected ray in the glass.

Slowly rotate the paper so that the angle of incidence on LOM increases until total internal reflection *just* occurs. Mark the incident ray. Measure the angle of incidence; this is the critical angle.

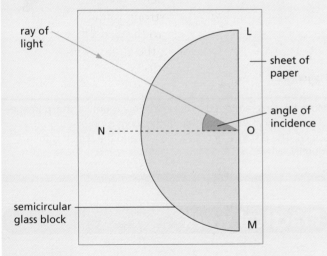

ray of light

L

sheet of paper

angle of incidence

N - - - - - - - - O

semicircular glass block

M

Figure P4.23

● Light pipes and optical fibres

Light can be trapped by total internal reflection inside a bent glass rod and 'piped' along a curved path (Figure P4.24). A single, very thin glass fibre behaves in the same way.

Figure P4.24 Light travels through a curved glass rod or fibre by total internal reflection.

If several thousand such fibres are taped together, a flexible light pipe is obtained that can be used, for example, by doctors as an 'endoscope' (Figure P4.25a), to obtain an image from inside the body (Figure P4.25b), or by engineers to light up some awkward spot for inspection. The latest telephone 'cables' are optical (very pure glass) fibres carrying information as pulses of laser light.

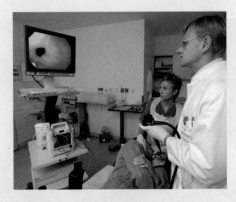

a endoscope in use

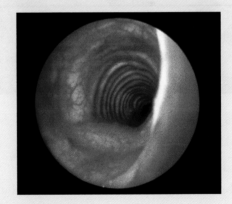

b trachea (windpipe) viewed by an endoscope

Figure P4.25

Converging lenses

Lenses are used in optical instruments such as cameras, spectacles, microscopes and telescopes; they often have spherical surfaces and there are two types. A **converging** (or convex) lens is thickest in the centre and bends light inwards (Figure P4.26a). You may have used one as a magnifying glass (Figure P4.26b) or as a burning glass.

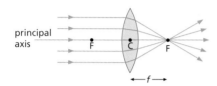

a

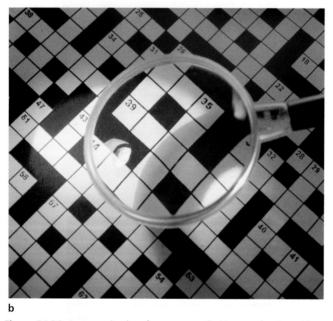

b

Figure P4.26 A converging lens forms a magnified image of a close object.

Principal focus

When a beam of light parallel to the principal axis passes through a converging lens it is refracted so as to converge to a point on the axis called the **principal focus**, F. It is a real focus. A diverging lens has a virtual principal focus behind the lens, from which the refracted beam seems to diverge.

Since light can fall on both faces of a lens it has two principal foci, one on each side, equidistant from C. The distance CF is the **focal length** f of the lens (see Figure P4.26a); it is an important property of a lens. The more curved the lens faces are, the smaller is f and the more powerful is the lens.

Practical work

Focal length, *f*, of a converging lens

We use the fact that rays from a point on a very distant object, i.e. at infinity, are nearly parallel (Figure P4.27a).

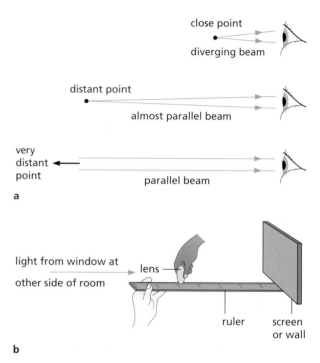

a

b

Figure P4.27

Move the lens, arranged as in Figure P4.27, until a **sharp** image of a window at the other side of the room is obtained on the screen. The distance between the lens and the screen is then *f*, roughly. Why?

Practical work

Images formed by a converging lens

In the formation of images by lenses, two important points on the principal axis are F and 2F; 2F is at a distance of twice the focal length from C.

First find the focal length of the lens by the 'distant object method' just described, then fix the lens upright with Plasticine at the centre of a metre rule. Place small pieces of Plasticine at the points F and 2F on both sides of the lens, as in Figure P4.28.

Place a small light source, such as a torch bulb, as the object supported on the rule beyond 2F and move a white card, on the other side of the lens from the light, until a sharp image is obtained on the card.

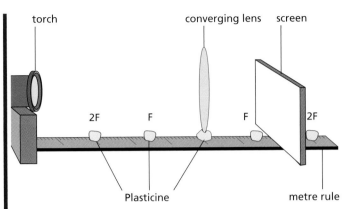

Figure P4.28

Note and record, in a table like the one below, the image position as 'beyond 2F', 'between 2F and F' or 'between F and lens'. Also note whether the image is 'larger' or 'smaller' than the actual bulb or 'same size' and if it is 'upright' or 'inverted'. Now repeat with the light at 2F, then between 2F and F.

Object position	Image position	Larger, smaller or same size?	Upright or inverted?
beyond 2F			
at 2F			
between 2F and F			
between F and lens			

So far all the images have been real since they can be obtained on a screen. When the light is between F and the lens, the image is **virtual** and is seen by *looking through the lens* at the light. Do this. Is the virtual image larger or smaller than the object? Is it upright or inverted? Record your findings in your table.

● Ray diagrams

Information about the images formed by a lens can be obtained by drawing two of the following rays.

1 A ray parallel to the principal axis which is refracted through the principal focus, F.
2 A ray through the optical centre, C, which is undeviated for a thin lens.
3 A ray through the principal focus, F, which is refracted parallel to the principal axis.

In diagrams a thin lens is represented by a straight line at which all the refraction is considered to occur.

In each ray diagram in Figure P4.29, two rays are drawn from the top A of an object OA. Where these rays intersect after refraction gives the top B of the

image IB. The foot I of each image is on the axis since ray OC passes through the lens undeviated. In Figure P4.29, the broken rays, and the image, are virtual. In all parts of Figure P4.29, the lens is a converging lens.

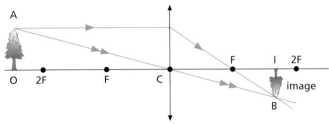

Image is between F and 2F, real, inverted, smaller

a object beyond 2F

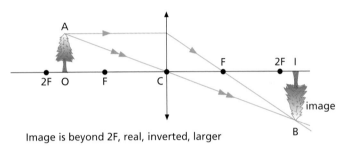

Image is beyond 2F, real, inverted, larger

b object at 2F

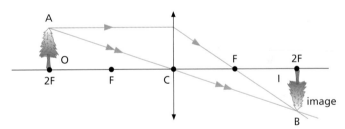

Image is at 2F, real, inverted, same size

c object between 2F and F

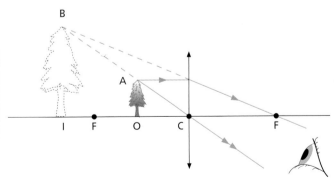

Image is behind object, virtual, erect, larger

d object between F and C

Figure P4.29

● Magnifying glass

The apparent size of an object depends on its actual size and on its distance from the eye. The sleepers on a railway track are all the same length but those nearby seem longer. This is because they enclose a larger angle at your eye than more distant ones: their image on the retina is larger, so making them appear bigger.

A converging lens gives an enlarged, upright virtual image of an object placed between the lens and its principal focus F (Figure P4.30a). It acts as a magnifying glass since the angle β made at the eye by the image is greater than the angle α made by the object when it is viewed directly without the magnifying glass (Figure P4.30b).

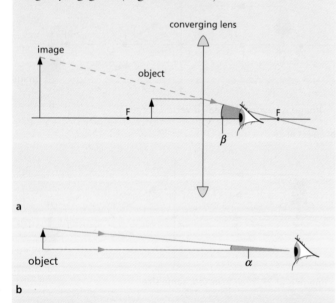

a

object

α

b

Figure P4.30 Magnification by a converging lens: angle β is larger than angle α.

The fatter (more curved) a converging lens is, the shorter its focal length and the more it magnifies. Too much curvature, however, distorts the image.

Questions

5 Figure P4.31 shows a ray of light PQ striking a mirror AB. The mirror AB and the mirror CD are at right angles to each other. QN is a normal to the mirror AB.

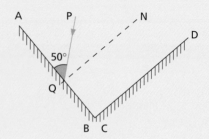

Figure P4.31

a What is the value of the angle of incidence of the ray PQ on the mirror AB?
b Copy the diagram, and continue the ray PQ to show the path it takes after reflection at both mirrors.
c What are the values of the angle of reflection at AB, the angle of incidence at CD and the angle of reflection at CD?
d What do you notice about the path of the ray PQ and the final reflected ray?

6 A ray of light strikes a plane mirror at an angle of incidence of 60°, is reflected from the mirror and then strikes a second plane mirror placed so that the angle between the mirrors is 45°. The angle of reflection at the second mirror, in degrees, is
A 15   B 25   C 45   D 65   E 75

7 In Figure P4.32 at which of the points A to E will the observer see the image in the plane mirror of the object?

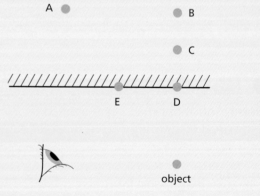

Figure P4.32

8 Figure P4.33 shows the image in a plane mirror of a clock. The correct time is
   A 2.25   B 2.35   C 6.45   D 9.25

Figure P4.33

9 A girl stands 5 m away from a large plane mirror. How far must she walk to be 2 m away from her image?
10 The image in a plane mirror is
   A upright, real and larger
   B upright, virtual and the same size
   C inverted, real and smaller
   D inverted, virtual and the same size
   E inverted, real and larger.
11 Figure P4.34 shows a ray of light entering a rectangular block of glass.
   a Copy the diagram and draw the normal at the point of entry.
   b Sketch the approximate path of the ray through the block and out of the other side.

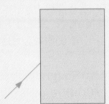

Figure P4.34

12 Which diagram in Figure P4.35 shows the ray of light refracted correctly?

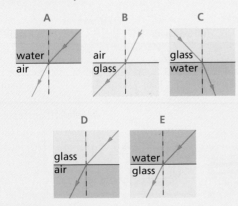

Figure P4.35

13 What is the speed of light in a medium of refractive index 6/5 if its speed in air is 300 000 km/s?
14 Figure P4.36 shows rays of light in a semicircular glass block.

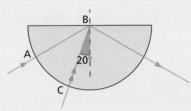

Figure P4.36
   a Explain why the ray entering the glass at A is not bent as it enters.
   b Explain why the ray AB is reflected at B and not refracted.
   c Ray CB does not stop at B. Copy the diagram and draw its approximate path after it leaves B.
15 Light travels up through a pond of water of critical angle 49°. What happens at the surface if the angle of incidence is: **a** 30°; **b** 60°?

16 A small torch bulb is placed at the focal point of a converging lens. When the bulb is switched on, does the lens produce a convergent, divergent or parallel beam of light?
17 a What kind of lens is shown in Figure P4.37?

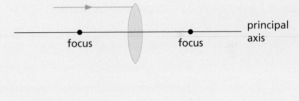

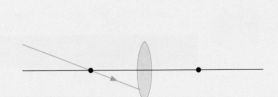

Figure P4.37

   b Copy the diagrams and complete them to show the path of the light after passing through the lens.
   c Figure P4.38 shows an object AB 6 cm high placed 18 cm in front of a lens of focal length 6 cm. Draw the diagram to scale and, by tracing the paths of rays from A, find the position and size of the image formed.

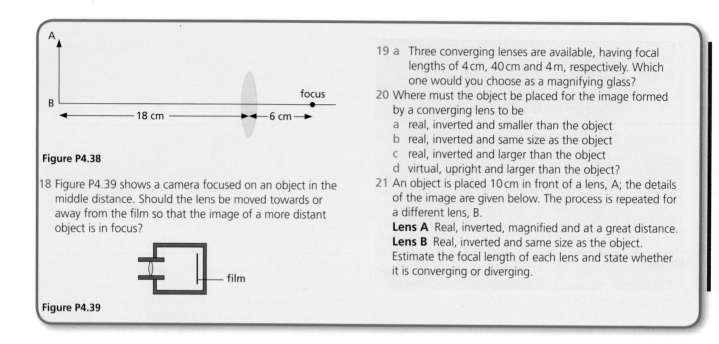

Figure P4.38

18 Figure P4.39 shows a camera focused on an object in the middle distance. Should the lens be moved towards or away from the film so that the image of a more distant object is in focus?

Figure P4.39

19 a Three converging lenses are available, having focal lengths of 4 cm, 40 cm and 4 m, respectively. Which one would you choose as a magnifying glass?
20 Where must the object be placed for the image formed by a converging lens to be
   a real, inverted and smaller than the object
   b real, inverted and same size as the object
   c real, inverted and larger than the object
   d virtual, upright and larger than the object?
21 An object is placed 10 cm in front of a lens, A; the details of the image are given below. The process is repeated for a different lens, B.
   Lens A Real, inverted, magnified and at a great distance.
   Lens B Real, inverted and same size as the object.
   Estimate the focal length of each lens and state whether it is converging or diverging.

● Electromagnetic spectrum

Light is one member of the family of electromagnetic radiation which forms a continuous spectrum beyond both ends of the visible (light) spectrum (Figure P4.40). While each type of radiation has a different source, all result from electrons in atoms undergoing an energy change and all have certain properties in common.

● In a vacuum, all types of electromagnetic radiation travel at the same high speed as light does, i.e. with the speed of light.

● In air, they all travel at approximately the speed of light.
● They all carry energy form place to place and can be absorbed by matter to cause heating and other effects.

● They obey the wave equation, $v = f\lambda$, where v is the speed of light, f is the frequency of the waves and λ is the wavelength. Since v is constant for a particular medium, it follows that large f means small λ.
● The speed of electromagnetic waves in a vacuum is 3×10^8 m/s (300 000 m/s).

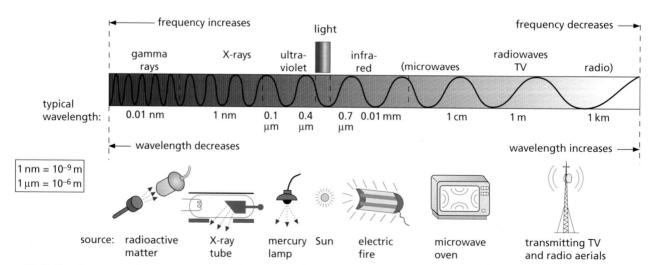

Figure P4.40 The electromagnetic spectrum and sources of each type of radiation.

Types of electromagnetic radiation

Light waves

Red light has the longest wavelength, which is about 0.0007 mm (7×10^{-7} m = 0.7 μm), while violet light has the shortest wavelength of about 0.0004 mm (4×10^{-7} m = 0.4 μm). Colours between these in the spectrum of white light have intermediate values. Light of one colour and so of one wavelength is called **monochromatic** light.

Infrared radiation

Our bodies detect **infrared** radiation (IR) by its heating effect on the skin.

Anything which is hot but not glowing, i.e. below 500 °C, emits IR alone. At about 500 °C a body becomes red hot and emits red light as well as IR – the heating element of an electric fire, a toaster or a grill are examples. At about 1500 °C, things such as lamp filaments are white hot and radiate IR and white light, i.e. all the colours of the visible spectrum.

Infrared is also detected by special temperature-sensitive photographic films which allow pictures to be taken in the dark. Infrared sensors are used on satellites and aircraft for weather forecasting, monitoring of land use (Figure P4.41), assessing heat loss from buildings, intruder alarms and locating victims of earthquakes.

Figure P4.41 Infrared aerial photograph of Washington DC.

Infrared lamps are used to dry the paint on cars during manufacture and in the treatment of muscular complaints. The remote control for an electronic device contains a small infrared transmitter to send signals to the device, such as a television or DVD player.

Ultraviolet radiation

Ultraviolet (UV) rays have shorter wavelengths than light. They cause sun tan and produce vitamins in the skin but can penetrate deeper, causing skin cancer. Dark skin is able to absorb more UV, so reducing the amount reaching deeper tissues. Exposure to the harmful UV rays present in sunlight can be reduced by wearing protective clothing such as a hat or by using sunscreen lotion.

Ultraviolet causes fluorescent paints and clothes washed in some detergents to fluoresce (Figure P4.42). They glow by re-radiating as light the energy they absorb as UV. This effect may be used to verify 'invisible' signatures on bank documents.

Figure P4.42 White clothes fluorescing in a club.

Radio waves

Radio waves have the longest wavelengths in the electromagnetic spectrum. They are radiated from aerials and used to 'carry' sound, pictures and other information over long distances.

Microwaves

These are used for international telecommunications and television relay via geostationary satellites and for mobile phone networks via microwave aerial towers and low-orbit satellites. The microwave signals are transmitted through the ionosphere by dish aerials, amplified by the satellite and sent back to a dish aerial in another part of the world.

Microwaves are also used for **radar** detection of ships and aircraft, and in police speed traps.

Microwaves can be used for cooking since they cause water molecules in the moisture of the food to vibrate vigorously at the frequency of the microwaves. As a result, heating occurs inside the food which cooks itself.

Living cells can be damaged or killed by the heat produced when microwaves are absorbed by water in the cells. There is some debate at present as to whether their use in mobile phones is harmful; 'hands-free' mode, where separate earphones are used, may be safer.

X-rays

These are produced when high-speed electrons are stopped by a metal target in an X-ray tube. **X-rays** have smaller wavelengths than UV.

They are absorbed to some extent by living cells but can penetrate some solid objects and affect a photographic film. With materials like bones, teeth and metals which they do not pass through easily, shadow pictures can be taken, like that in Figure P4.43 of a hand on an alarm clock. They are widely used in dentistry and in medicine, for example to detect broken bones. X-rays are also used in security machines at airports for scanning luggage; some body scanners, now being introduced to screen passengers, use very low doses of X-rays. In industry X-ray photography is used to inspect welded joints.

X-ray machines need to be shielded with lead since normal body cells can be killed by high doses and made cancerous by lower doses.

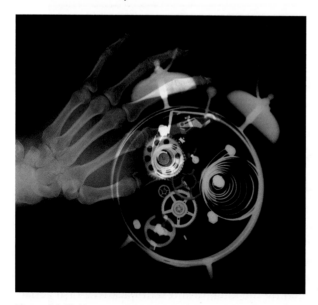

Figure P4.43 X-rays cannot penetrate bone and metal.

> ## Question
> 22 Name one type of electromagnetic radiation which
>   a causes sun tan
>   b is used for satellite communication
>   c is used in a TV remote control
>   d is used to cook food
>   e is used to detect a break in a bone.

● Origin and transmission of sound

Sources of sound all have some part that **vibrates**. A guitar has strings (Figure P4.44), a drum has a stretched skin and the human voice has vocal cords. The sound travels through the air to our ears and we hear it. That the air is necessary may be shown by pumping the air out of a glass jar containing a ringing electric bell (Figure P4.45); the sound disappears though the striker can still be seen hitting the gong. Evidently sound cannot travel in a vacuum as light can. Other materials, including solids and liquids, transmit sound.

Figure P4.44 A guitar string vibrating. The sound waves produced are amplified when they pass through the circular hole into the guitar's sound box.

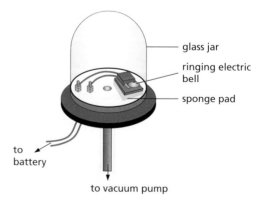

Figure P4.45 Sound cannot travel through a vacuum.

Sound waves

Sound gives **interference** and **diffraction** effects. Because of this and its other properties, we believe it is a form of energy (as the damage from supersonic booms shows) which travels as a progressive wave, but of a type called **longitudinal**.

A sound wave, produced for example by a loudspeaker, consists of a train of compressions ('squashes') and rarefactions ('stretches') in the air (Figure P4.46).

The speaker has a cone which is made to vibrate in and out by an electric current. When the cone moves out, the air in front is compressed; when it moves in, the air is rarefied (goes 'thinner'). The wave progresses through the air but the air as a whole does not move. The air particles (molecules) vibrate backwards and forwards a little as the wave passes. When the wave enters your ear the compressions and rarefactions cause small, rapid pressure changes on the eardrum and you experience the sensation of sound.

The number of compressions produced per second is the frequency f of the sound wave (and equals the frequency of the vibrating loudspeaker cone); the distance between successive compressions is the wavelength λ. As with transverse waves, the speed, v, $= f\lambda$.

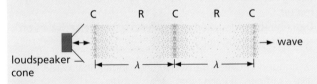

Figure P4.46 Sound travels as a longitudinal wave.

Reflection and echoes

Sound waves are reflected well from hard, flat surfaces such as walls or cliffs and obey the same laws of reflection as light. The reflected sound forms an **echo**.

If the reflecting surface is nearer than 15 m from the source of sound, the echo joins up with the original sound which then seems to be prolonged. This is called **reverberation**. Some is desirable in a concert hall to stop it sounding 'dead', but too much causes 'confusion'. Modern concert halls are designed for the optimal amount of reverberation. Seats and some wall surfaces are covered with sound-absorbing material.

Speed of sound

The **speed of sound** depends on the material through which it is passing. It is greater in solids than in liquids or gases because the molecules in a solid are closer together than in a liquid or a gas. Some values are given in Table P4.1.

Table P4.1 Speed of sound in different materials

Material	air (0 °C)	water	concrete	steel
Speed/m/s	330	1400	5000	6000

In air the speed **increases with temperature** and at high altitudes, where the temperature is lower, it is less than at sea level. Changes of atmospheric pressure do not affect it.

An estimate of the speed of sound can be made directly if you stand about 100 metres from a high wall or building and clap your hands. Echoes are produced. When the clapping rate is such that each clap coincides with the echo of the previous one, the sound has travelled to the wall and back in the time between two claps, i.e. one interval. By timing 30 intervals with a stopwatch, the time t for one interval can be found. Also, knowing the distance d to the wall, a rough value is obtained from:

$$\text{speed of sound in air} = \frac{2d}{t}$$

The speed of sound in air can be found directly by measuring the time t taken for a sound to travel past two microphones separated by a distance d:

$$\text{speed of sound in air} = \frac{\text{distance travelled by the sound}}{\text{time taken}}$$

$$= \frac{d}{t}$$

Limits of audibility

Humans hear only sounds with frequencies from about 20 Hz to 20 000 Hz. These are the limits of audibility; the upper limit decreases with age.

Practical work

Speed of sound in air

Set two microphones about a metre apart, and attach one to the 'start' terminal and the other to the 'stop' terminal of a digital timer, as shown in Figure P4.47 on the next page. The timer should have millisecond accuracy. Measure and record the distance *d* between the centres of the microphones with a metre ruler. With the small hammer and metal plate to one side of the 'start' microphone, produce a sharp sound. When the sound reaches the 'start' microphone, the timer should start; when it reaches the 'stop' microphone, the timer should stop. The time displayed is then the time taken for the sound to travel the distance *d*. Record the time and then reset the timer; repeat the experiment a few times and work out an *average* value for *t*.

Calculate the speed of sound in air from *d/t*. How does your value compare with that given in Table P4.1?

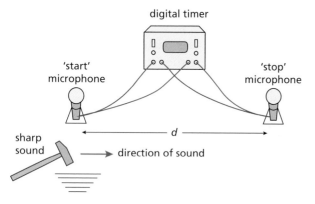

Figure P4.47 Measuring the speed of sound.

Musical notes

Irregular vibrations such as those of motor engines cause **noise**; regular vibrations, such as occur in an orchestra, produce musical notes. The frequency and amplitude of a musical note determine the pitch and loudness of the sound produced.

Pitch

The pitch of a note depends on the frequency of the sound wave reaching the ear, i.e. on the frequency of the source of sound. A high-pitched note has a high frequency and a short wavelength. The frequency of middle C is 256 vibrations per second or 256 Hz and that of upper C is 512 Hz. Notes are an **octave** apart if the frequency of one is twice that of the other. Pitch is like colour in light; both depend on the frequency.

Loudness

A note becomes louder when more sound energy enters our ears per second than before. This will happen when the source is vibrating with a larger amplitude. If a violin string is bowed more strongly, its amplitude of vibration increases as does that of the resulting sound wave and the note heard is louder because more energy has been used to produce it.

Questions

23 If 5 seconds elapse between a lightning flash and the clap of thunder, how far away is the storm? (Speed of sound = 330 m/s.)

24 a A girl stands 160 m away from a high wall and claps her hands at a steady rate so that each clap coincides with the echo of the one before. If her clapping rate is 60 per minute, what value does this give for the speed of sound?
  b If she moves 40 m closer to the wall she finds the clapping rate has to be 80 per minute. What value do these measurements give for the speed of sound?
  c If she moves again and finds the clapping rate becomes 30 per minute, how far is she from the wall if the speed of sound is the value you found in **a**?

25 a What properties of sound suggest it is a wave motion?
  b How does a progressive transverse wave differ from a longitudinal one? Which type of wave is a sound wave?

26 a Draw the waveform of
    i a loud, low-pitched note
    ii a soft, high-pitched note.
  b If the speed of sound is 340 m/s what is the wavelength of a note of frequency
    i 340 Hz
    ii 170 Hz?

Checklist

After studying Chapter P4 you should know and understand the following.

• Recognise that waves transfer energy without transferring matter.
• Describe the production of progressive transverse waves on ropes, springs and ripple tanks.

• Distinguish between transverse and longitudinal waves and give examples of each type.

• Recall the meaning of wavelength, frequency, speed and amplitude.
• Represent a transverse wave on a displacement–distance graph and extract information from it.

• Recall the wave equation $v = f\lambda$ and use it to solve problems.

• Use the term wavefront.
• Describe experiments to show reflection and refraction of waves.
• Recall that refraction at a straight boundary is due to change of wave speed but not of frequency.

• Explain the term diffraction.
• Describe experiments to show diffraction of waves.
• Draw diagrams for the diffraction of straight wavefronts at single slits of different widths.

- State the law of reflection and use it to solve problems.
- Describe an experiment to show that the angle of incidence equals the angle of reflection.
- Describe an experiment to show that the image in a plane mirror is as far behind the mirror as the object is in front, and that the line joining the object and image is at right angles to the mirror.
- Draw a diagram to explain the formation of a virtual image by a plane mirror.
- Explain the apparent lateral inversion of an image in a plane mirror.
- State what the term refraction means.
- Give examples of effects that show light can be refracted.
- Describe an experiment to study refraction.
- Draw diagrams of the passage of light rays through rectangular blocks and recall that lateral displacement occurs for a parallel-sided block.
- Recall that light is refracted because it changes speed when it enters another medium.

- Recall the definition of refractive index as n = speed in air/ speed in medium.
- Recall and use the equation $n = \sin i / \sin r$.
- Explain with the aid of diagrams what is meant by critical angle and total internal reflection.
- Describe an experiment to find the critical angle of glass or Perspex.
- Explain the action of optical fibres.

- Draw a diagram showing the effect of a converging lens on a beam of parallel rays.
- Recall the meaning of optical centre, principal axis, principal focus and focal length.
- Describe an experiment to measure the focal length of a converging lens.
- Draw ray diagrams to show formation of a real image by a converging lens.
- Describe the image formed by a lens in terms of its size, and whether it is upright or inverted (relative to the object).

- State the difference between a real image and a virtual image.
- Draw a ray diagram to show the formation of a virtual image by a single lens.
- Describe how a single lens is used as a magnifying glass.

- Recall the different types of electromagnetic radiation.
- Recall that all electromagnetic waves have the same high speed in space and are progressive transverse waves.
- Recall that in air, electromagnetic waves travel at approximately the speed of light in a vacuum.

- Recall that the speed of all electromagnetic waves in a vacuum is 3×10^8 m/s.
- Use the term monochromatic.

- Recall that the colour of light depends on its frequency, and that red light has a lower frequency (but longer wavelength) than blue light.
- Distinguish between microwaves, infrared radiation, ultraviolet radiation, radio waves and X-rays in terms of their wavelengths, properties and uses.
- Be aware of the harmful effects of different types of electromagnetic radiation and of how exposure to them can be reduced.
- Recall that sound is produced by vibrations.
- Describe an experiment to show that sound is not transmitted through a vacuum.

- Describe how sound travels in a medium as progressive longitudinal waves.

- Recall the limits of audibility (i.e. the range of frequencies) for the normal human ear.
- Explain echoes and reverberation.
- Describe an experiment to measure the speed of sound in air.

- State the order of magnitude of the speed of sound in air, liquids and solids.

- Relate the loudness and pitch of sound waves to amplitude and frequency.

Electrical quantities, electricity and magnetism

P5

Combined

- State that there are positive and negative charges
- State that unlike charges attract and that like charges repel
- Describe and interpret simple experiments to show the production and detection of electrostatic charges by friction
- State that charging a body involves the addition or removal of electrons
- Distinguish between electrical conductors and insulators and give typical examples
- Demonstrate understanding of *current, potential difference, e.m.f.* and *resistance*.
- State that current is related to the flow of charge
- State that current in metals is due to a flow of electrons
- State that the potential difference (p.d.) across a circuit component is measured in volts
- Use and describe the use of an ammeter and a voltmeter, both analogue and digital
- State that the electromotive force (e.m.f.) of an electrical source of energy is measured in volts
- Know and use the formula $Q = I\,t$
- Show understanding that a current is a rate of flow of charge and recall and use the equation $I = Q/t$
- State that resistance = p.d./current and understand qualitatively how changes in p.d. or resistance affect current
- Recall and use the equation $R = V/I$
- Recall and use quantitatively the proportionality between resistance and length, and the inverse proportionality between resistance and cross-sectional area of a wire

Co-ordinated

- Describe the forces between magnets, and between magnets and magnetic materials
- Draw and describe the pattern and direction of magnetic field lines around a bar magnet
- Distinguish between the magnetic properties of soft iron and steel
- Distinguish between the design and use of permanent magnets and electromagnets
- Describe methods of magnetisation to include stroking with a magnet, use of direct current (d.c.) in a coil and hammering in a magnetic field
- Give an account of induced magnetism
- State that there are positive and negative charges
- State that unlike charges attract and that like charges repel
- Describe and interpret simple experiments to show the production and detection of electrostatic charges by friction
- State that charging a body involves the addition or removal of electrons
- Distinguish between electrical conductors and insulators and give typical examples
- Describe an electric field as a region in which an electric charge experiences a force
- Demonstrate understanding of current, potential difference, e.m.f. and resistance
- State that current is related to the flow of charge
- State that current in metals is due to a flow of electrons
- State that the potential difference (p.d.) across a circuit component is measured in volts
- Use and describe the use of an ammeter and a voltmeter, both analogue and digital
- State that the electromotive force (e.m.f.) of an electrical source of energy is measured in volts
- Show understanding that a current is a rate of flow of charge and recall and use the equation $I = Q/t$
- Show understanding that e.m.f. is defined in terms of energy supplied by a source in driving charge around a complete circuit
- State that resistance = p.d./current and understand qualitatively how changes in p.d. or resistance affect current
- Recall and use the equation $R = V/I$
- Sketch and explain the current–voltage characteristic of an ohmic resistor and a filament lamp
- Recall and use quantitatively the proportionality between resistance and length, and the inverse proportionality between resistance and cross-sectional area of a wire

● Properties of magnets

Magnetic materials

Magnets attract strongly only certain materials such as iron, steel, nickel and cobalt, which are called **ferro-magnetics**.

Magnetic poles

The **poles** are the places in a magnet to which magnetic materials, such as iron filings, are attracted. They are near the ends of a bar magnet and occur in pairs of equal strength.

North and south poles

If a magnet is supported so that it can swing in a horizontal plane it comes to rest with one pole, the **north-seeking** or N pole, always pointing roughly towards the Earth's north pole. A magnet can therefore be used as a **compass**.

Law of magnetic poles

If the N pole of a magnet is brought near the N pole of another magnet, repulsion occurs. Two S (south-seeking) poles also repel. By contrast, N and S poles always attract. The law of magnetic poles summarises these facts and states:

Like poles repel, unlike poles attract.
The force between magnetic poles decreases as their separation increases.

● Magnetisation of iron and steel

Chains of small iron nails and steel paper clips can be hung from a magnet (Figure P5.1). Each nail or clip magnetises the one below it and the unlike poles so formed attract.

If the iron chain is removed by pulling the top nail away from the magnet, the chain collapses, showing that **magnetism induced in iron is temporary**. When the same is done with the steel chain, it does not collapse; **magnetism induced in steel is permanent**.

Magnetic materials such as iron that magnetise easily but readily lose their magnetism (are easily demagnetised) are said to be **soft**. Those such as steel that are harder to magnetise than iron but stay magnetised are **hard**. Both types have their uses; very hard ones are used to make permanent magnets. Solenoids can be used to magnetise and demagnetise magnetic materials (see below); dropping or heating a magnet also causes demagnetisation. Hammering a magnetic material in a magnetic field causes magnetisation but in the absence of a field it causes demagnetisation. 'Stroking' a magnetic material several times in the same direction with one pole of a magnet will also cause it to become magnetised.

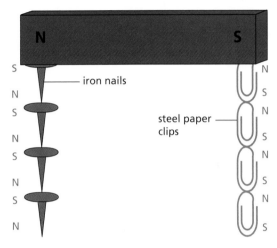

Figure P5.1 Investigating the magnetisation of iron and steel.

● Magnetic fields

The space surrounding a magnet where it produces a magnetic force is called a **magnetic field**. The force around a bar magnet can be detected and shown to vary in direction, using the apparatus in Figure P5.2. If the floating magnet is released near the N pole of the bar magnet, it is repelled to the S pole and moves along a curved path known as a **line of force** or a **field line**. It moves in the opposite direction if its south pole is uppermost.

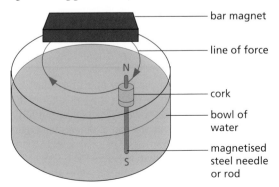

Figure P5.2 Detecting magnetic force.

It is useful to consider that a magnetic field has a direction and to represent the field by lines of force. It has been decided that the **direction of the field at any point should be the direction of the force on a N pole**. To show the direction, arrows are put on the lines of force and point away from a N pole towards a S pole. The magnetic field is stronger in regions where the field lines are close together than where they are further apart.

The force between two magnets is a result of the interaction of their magnetic fields.

Practical work

Plotting lines of force

a) Plotting compass method

A plotting compass is a small pivoted magnet in a glass case with non-magnetic metal walls (Figure P5.3a).

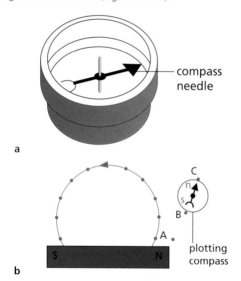

Figure P5.3

Lay a bar magnet on a sheet of paper. Place the plotting compass at a point such as A (Figure P5.3b), near one pole of the magnet. In Figure P5.3b it is the N pole. Mark the position of the poles (n, s) of the compass by pencil dots B, A. Move the compass so that pole s is exactly over B, mark the new position of N by dot C.

Continue this process until the other pole of the bar magnet is reached (in Figure P5.3b it is the S pole). Join the dots to give one line of force and show its direction by putting an arrow on it. Plot other lines by starting at different points round the magnet.

A typical field pattern is shown in Figure P5.4.

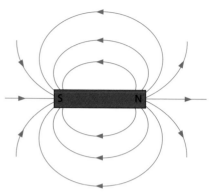

Figure P5.4 Magnetic field lines around a bar magnet.

b) Iron filings method

Place a sheet of paper *on top of* a bar magnet and sprinkle iron filings *thinly and evenly* on to the paper from a 'pepper pot'.

Tap the paper gently with a pencil and the filings should form patterns showing the lines of force. Each filing turns in the direction of the field when the paper is tapped.

This method is quick but no use for weak fields. Figures P5.5a and b show typical patterns with two magnets. Why are they different? What combination of poles would give the observed patterns?

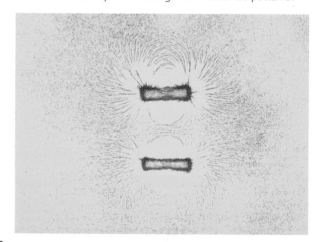

a

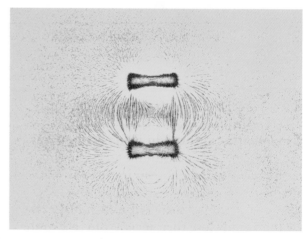

b

Figure P5.5 Field lines round two bar magnets shown by iron filings.

Magnetisation and demagnetisation

A ferromagnetic material can be magnetised by placing it inside a solenoid and gradually increasing the current. This increases the magnetic field strength in the solenoid (the density of the field lines increases), and the material becomes magnetised. Reversing the direction of current flow reverses the direction of the magnetic field and reverses the polarity of the magnetisation. A magnet can be demagnetised by placing it inside a solenoid through which the current is repeatedly reversed and reduced.

Practical work

Simple electromagnet

An **electromagnet** is a coil of wire wound on a soft iron core. A 5 cm iron nail and 3 m of PVC-covered copper wire (SWG 26) are needed.

(a) Leave about 25 cm at one end of the wire (for connecting to the circuit) and then wind about 50 cm as a single layer on the nail. **Keep the turns close together and always wind in the same direction.** Connect the circuit of Figure P5.6, setting the rheostat at its maximum resistance. Find the number of paper clips the electromagnet can support when the current is varied between 0.2 A and 2.0 A. Record the results in a table. How does the 'strength' of the electromagnet depend on the current?

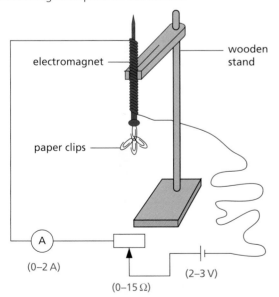

(b) Add another two layers of wire to the nail, winding in the *same direction* as the first layer. Repeat the experiment. What can you say about the 'strength' of an electromagnet and the number of turns of wire?

(c) Place the electromagnet on the bench and under a sheet of paper. Sprinkle iron filings on the paper, tap it gently and observe the field pattern. How does it compare with that given by a bar magnet?

(d) Use the right-hand screw (or grip) rule (see p.434) to predict which end of the electromagnet is a N pole. Check with a plotting compass.

Electromagnets

The magnetism of an electromagnet is *temporary* and can be switched on and off, unlike that of a permanent magnet. It has a core of soft iron which is magnetised only when there is current in the surrounding coil.

The strength of an electromagnet increases if:

(i) the **current** in the coil increases
(ii) the **number of turns** on the coil increases
(iii) the poles are moved **closer together**.

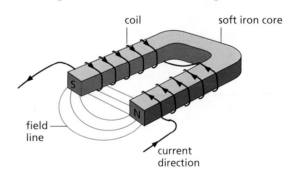

Figure P5.7 C-core or horseshoe electromagnet.

In C-core (or horseshoe) electromagnets condition (iii) is achieved (Figure P5.7). Note that the coil on each limb of the core is wound in *opposite* directions.

As well as being used in cranes to lift iron objects, scrap iron, etc. (Figure P5.8 on the next page), electromagnets are an essential part of many electrical devices.

Figure P5.6

Figure P5.8 Electromagnet being used to lift scrap metal.

● Induced magnetism

When a piece of unmagnetised magnetic material touches or is brought near to the pole of a permanent magnet, it becomes a magnet itself. The material is said to have magnetism induced in it. Figure P5.9 shows that a N pole induces a N pole in the far end.

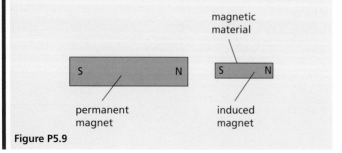

Figure P5.9

This can be checked by hanging two iron nails from the N pole of a magnet. Their lower ends repel each other (Figure P5.10a) and both are repelled by the N pole of another magnet (Figure P5.10b).

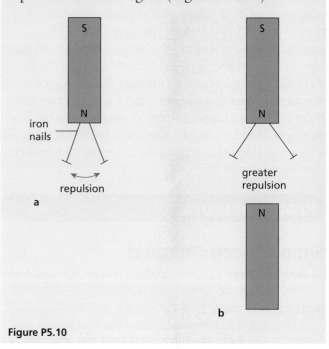

Figure P5.10

Questions

1 Which one of these statements is true?
   A magnet attracts
   A plastics   B any metal   C iron and steel
   D aluminium   E carbon
2 Copy Figure P5.11 which shows a plotting compass and a magnet. Label the N pole of the magnet and draw the field line on which the compass lies.

Figure P5.11

Static electricity

Figure P5.12 A flash of lightning is nature's most spectacular static electricity effect.

Clothes containing nylon often crackle when they are taken off. We say they are 'charged with static electricity'; the crackles are caused by tiny electric sparks which can be seen in the dark. Pens and combs made of certain plastics become charged when rubbed on your sleeve and can then attract scraps of paper.

The production of charges by rubbing can be explained by supposing that electrons are transferred from one material to the other. For example, when cellulose acetate is rubbed with a cloth, electrons go from the acetate to the cloth, leaving the acetate short of electrons, i.e. positively charged. The cloth now has more electrons than protons and becomes negatively charged. Note that it is only electrons which move; the protons remain fixed in the nucleus.

How does polythene become charged when rubbed?

Positive and negative charges

When a strip of polythene is rubbed with a cloth it becomes charged. If it is hung up and another rubbed polythene strip is brought near, repulsion occurs (Figure P5.13). Attraction occurs when a rubbed strip of cellulose acetate is brought near.

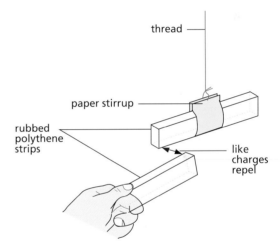

Figure P5.13 Investigating charges.

This shows there are two kinds of electric charge. That on cellulose acetate is taken as **positive** (+) and that on polythene is **negative** (−). It also shows that:

> Like charges (+ and +, or − and −) repel, while unlike charges (+ and −) attract.

The force between electric charges decreases as their separation increases.

Practical work

Gold-leaf electroscope

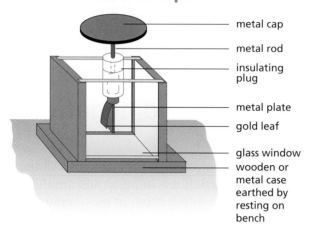

- metal cap
- metal rod
- insulating plug
- metal plate
- gold leaf
- glass window
- wooden or metal case earthed by resting on bench

Figure P5.14 Gold-leaf electroscope.

A gold-leaf electroscope consists of a metal cap on a metal rod at the foot of which is a metal plate with a leaf of gold foil attached (Figure P5.14). The rod is held by an insulating plastic plug in a case with glass sides to protect the leaf from draughts.

Detecting a charge

Bring a charged polythene strip towards the cap: the leaf rises away from the plate. When you remove the charged strip, the leaf falls again. Repeat with a charged acetate strip.

Charging by contact

Draw a charged polythene strip *firmly across the edge of the cap*. The leaf should rise and stay up when the strip is removed. If it does not, repeat the process but press harder. The electroscope has now become negatively charged by contact with the polythene strip, from which electrons have been transferred.

Insulators and conductors

Touch the cap of the charged electroscope with different things, such as a piece of paper, a wire, your finger, a comb, a cotton handkerchief, a piece of wood, a glass rod, a plastic pen, rubber tubing. Record your results.

When the leaf falls, charge is passing to or from the ground through you and the material touching the cap. If the fall is rapid the material is a **good conductor**; if the leaf falls slowly, the material is a poor conductor. If the leaf does not alter, the material is a **good insulator**.

● Electrons, insulators and conductors

In an insulator all electrons are bound firmly to their atoms; in a conductor some electrons can move freely from atom to atom. An insulator can be charged by rubbing because the charge produced cannot move from where the rubbing occurs, i.e. the electric charge is **static**. A conductor will become charged only if it is held with an insulating handle; otherwise electrons are transferred between the conductor and the ground via the person's body.

Good insulators include plastics such as polythene, cellulose acetate, Perspex and nylon. All metals and carbon are good conductors. In between are materials that are both poor conductors and (because they conduct to some extent) poor insulators. Examples are wood, paper, cotton, the human body and the Earth. Water conducts and if it were not present in materials like wood and on the surface of, for example, glass, these would be good insulators. Dry air insulates well.

● Electric fields

When an electric charge is placed near to another electric charge it experiences a force. The electric force does not require contact between the two charges so we call it an 'action-at-a-distance force' – it acts through space. The region of space where an electric charge experiences a force due to other charges is called an **electric field**. If the electric force felt by a charge is the same everywhere in a region, the field is uniform; a uniform electric field is produced between two oppositely charged parallel metal plates (Figure P5.15). It can be represented by evenly spaced parallel lines drawn perpendicular to the metal surfaces. The direction of the field, denoted by arrows, is the direction of the force on a small positive charge placed in the field (negative charges experience a force in the opposite direction to the field).

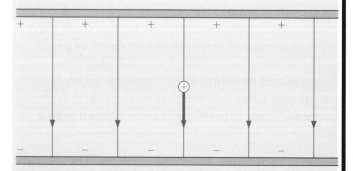

Figure P5.15 Uniform electric field.

Questions

3 Two identical conducting balls, suspended on nylon threads, come to rest with the threads making equal angles with the vertical, as shown in Figure P5.16.
Which of these statements is true?
This shows that:
A the balls are equally and oppositely charged
B the balls are oppositely charged but not necessarily equally charged
C one ball is charged and the other is uncharged
D the balls both carry the same type of charge
E one is charged and the other may or may not be charged.

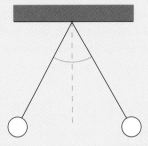

Figure P5.16

4 Explain in terms of electron movement what happens when a polythene rod becomes charged negatively by being rubbed with a cloth.

5 Which of statements A to E is true?
In the process of electrostatic induction
A a conductor is rubbed with an insulator
B a charge is produced by friction
C negative and positive charges are separated
D a positive charge induces a positive charge
E electrons are 'sprayed' into an object.

● Electric current

An **electric current** consists of moving electric charges. In Figure P5.17, when the van de Graaff machine is working, the table-tennis ball shuttles rapidly to and fro between the plates and the meter records a small current. As the ball touches each plate it becomes charged and is repelled to the other plate. In this way charge is carried across the gap. This also shows that 'static' charges, produced by friction, cause a deflection on a meter just as current electricity produced by a battery does.

In a metal, each atom has one or more loosely held electrons that are free to move. When a van de Graaff or a battery is connected across the ends of such a conductor, the free electrons drift slowly along it in the direction from the negative to the positive terminal of a battery. There is then a current of negative charge.

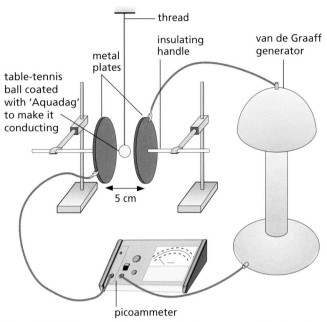

Figure P5.17 Demonstrating that an electric current consists of moving charges.

● The ampere and the coulomb

The unit of current is the **ampere** (A) which is defined using the magnetic effect. One milliampere (mA) is one-thousandth of an ampere. Current is measured by an **ammeter**. The unit of charge, the **coulomb** (C), is defined in terms of the ampere.

> One coulomb is the charge passing any point in a circuit when a steady current of 1 ampere flows for 1 second. That is, $1\,C = 1\,A\,s$.

A charge of $3\,C$ would pass each point in $1\,s$ if the current were $3\,A$. In $2\,s$, $3\,A \times 2\,s = 6\,A\,s = 6\,C$ would pass. In general, if a steady current I (amperes) flows for time t (seconds) the charge Q (coulombs) passing any point is given by

$$Q = I \times t$$

This is a useful expression connecting charge and current. It can be rearranged to give an expression for the current I, which is the rate of flow of charge:

$$I = \frac{Q}{t}$$

Note: Current must have a complete path (a circuit) of conductors if it is to flow. When drawing circuit diagrams, components are represented by symbols. Some commonly used symbols are shown in Figure P6.1 (p.423).

Practical work

Measuring current

(a) Connect the circuit of Figure P5.18a (on a circuit board if possible) ensuring that the + of the cell (the metal stud) goes to the + of the ammeter (marked red). Note the current.

(b) Connect the circuit of Figure P5.18b. The cells are **in series** (+ of one to – of the other), as are the lamps. Record the current. Measure the current at B, C and D by disconnecting the circuit at each point in turn and inserting the ammeter. What do you find?

(c) Connect the circuit of Figure P5.18c. The lamps are **in parallel**. Read the ammeter. Also measure the currents at P, Q and R. What is your conclusion?

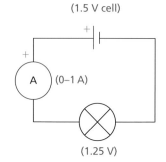

a

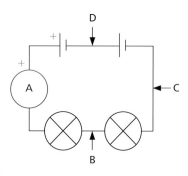

b

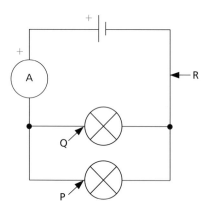

c

Figure P5.18

● Potential difference

A battery transforms chemical energy to electrical energy. Because of the chemical action going on inside it, it builds up a surplus of electrons at one of its terminals (the negative) and creates a shortage at the other (the positive). It is then able to maintain a **flow of electrons**, i.e. an **electric current**, in any circuit connected across its terminals for as long as the chemical action lasts.

The battery is said to have a **potential difference** (**p.d.** for short) at its terminals. Potential difference is measured in **volts** (V) and the term **voltage** is sometimes used instead of p.d. The p.d. of a car battery is 12 V and the domestic mains supply in the UK is 230 V.

● Energy transfers and p.d.

In an electric circuit electrical energy is supplied from a source such as a battery and is transferred to other forms of energy by devices in the circuit. A lamp produces heat and light.

When each one of the circuits of Figure P5.19 is connected up, it will be found from the ammeter readings that the current is about the same (0.4 A) in each lamp. However, the mains lamp with a potential difference of 230 V applied to it gives much more light and heat than the car lamp with 12 V across it. In terms of energy, the mains lamp transfers a great deal more electrical energy in a second than the car lamp.

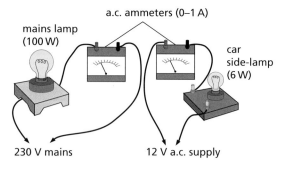

Figure P5.19 Investigating the effect of p.d. (potential difference) on energy transfer.

Evidently the p.d. across a device affects the rate at which it transfers electrical energy. This gives us a way of defining the unit of potential difference: the volt.

Model of a circuit

It may help you to understand the definition of the volt, i.e. what a volt is, if you *imagine* that the current in a circuit is formed by 'drops' of electricity, each having a charge of 1 coulomb and carrying equal-sized 'bundles' of electrical energy. In Figure P5.20, Mr Coulomb represents one such 'drop'. As a 'drop' moves around the circuit it gives up all its energy which is changed to other forms of energy. Note that **electrical energy, not charge or current, is 'used up'**.

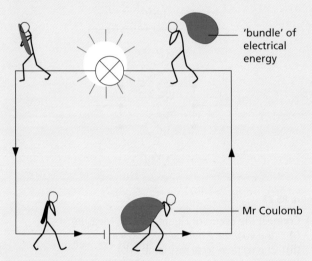

Figure P5.20 Model of a circuit.

In our imaginary representation, Mr Coulomb travels round the circuit and unloads energy as he goes, most of it in the lamp. We think of him receiving a fresh 'bundle' every time he passes through the battery, which suggests he must be travelling very fast. In fact, as we found earlier (p.415), the electrons drift along quite slowly. As soon as the circuit is complete, energy is delivered at once to the lamp, not by electrons directly from the battery but from electrons that were in the connecting wires. The model is helpful but is not an exact representation.

The volt

The demonstrations of Figure P5.19 show that the greater the voltage at the terminals of a supply, the larger is the 'bundle' of electrical energy given to each coulomb and the greater is the rate at which light and heat are produced in a lamp.

> The p.d. between two points in a circuit is 1 volt if 1 joule of electrical energy is transferred to other forms of energy when 1 coulomb passes from one point to the other.

That is, 1 volt = 1 joule per coulomb ($1 \text{ V} = 1 \text{ J/C}$).

If 2 J are given up by each coulomb, the p.d. is 2 V. If 6 J are transferred when 2 C pass, the p.d. is $6 \text{ J}/2 \text{ C} = 3 \text{ V}$.

In general if E (joules) is the energy transferred (i.e. the work done) when charge Q (coulombs) passes between two points, the p.d. V (volts) between the points is given by:

$$V = E/Q \text{ or } E = Q V$$

If Q is in the form of a steady current I (amperes) flowing for time t (seconds) then $Q = It$ and:

$$E = ItV$$

Cells, batteries and e.m.f.

A 'battery' (Figure P5.21) consists of two or more **electric cells**. Greater voltages are obtained when cells are joined in series, i.e. + of one to − of next. In Figure P5.22a on the next page, the two 1.5 V cells give a voltage of 3 V at the terminals A, B. Every coulomb in a circuit connected to this battery will have 3 J of electrical energy.

The cells in Figure P5.22b are in opposition and the voltage at X, Y is zero. If two 1.5 V cells are connected in parallel, as in Figure P5.22c, the voltage at terminals P, Q is still 1.5 V but the arrangement behaves like a larger cell and will last longer.

Figure P5.21 Compact batteries.

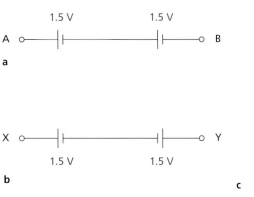

Figure P5.22

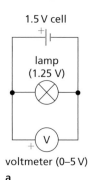

(a) Connect the circuit of Figure P5.23a. The voltmeter gives the voltage across the lamp. Read it.

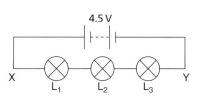

voltmeter (0–5 V)

a

b

> When no current is drawn from a battery it is said to be an 'open circuit' and its terminal p.d. is a maximum. This maximum voltage is termed the **electromotive force (e.m.f.)** of the battery. Like potential difference, e.m.f. is measured in volts.
>
> In energy terms, the e.m.f. is defined as the number of joules of chemical energy transferred to electrical energy and heat when one coulomb of charge passes through the battery (or cell).

Figure P5.23

Practical work

Measuring voltage

A **voltmeter** is an instrument for measuring voltage or p.d. It looks like an ammeter but has a scale marked in volts. Whereas an ammeter is inserted **in series** in a circuit to measure the current, a voltmeter is connected across that part of the circuit where the voltage is required, i.e. **in parallel**. (So that they do not affect the values they are measuring a voltmeter should have a high resistance and an ammeter a low resistance.)

To prevent damage the + terminal (marked red) must be connected to the point nearest the + of the battery.

(b) Connect the circuit of Figure P5.21b. Measure:
   (i)   the voltage V between X and Y
   (ii) the voltage V_1 across lamp L_1
   (iii) the voltage V_2 across lamp L_2
   (iv) the voltage V_3 across lamp L_3.
   How does the value of V compare with $V_1 + V_2 + V_3$?
(c) Connect the circuit of Figure P5.21c, so that two lamps L_1 and L_2 are in parallel across one 1.5 V cell. Measure the voltages, V_1 and V_2, across each lamp in turn. How do V_1 and V_2 compare?

Questions

6 If the current in a floodlamp is 5 A, what charge passes in
   a 1 s
   b 10 s
   c 5 minutes?
7 What is the current in a circuit if the charge passing each point is
   a 10 C in 2 s
   b 20 C in 40 s
   c 240 C in 2 minutes?
8 The p.d. across the lamp in Figure P5.24 is 12 V. How many joules of electrical energy are changed into light and heat when

a a charge of 1 C passes through it
b a charge of 5 C passes through it
c a current of 2 A flows in it for 10 s?

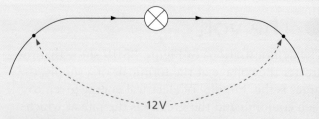

Figure P5.24

● Resistance

Electrons move more easily through some conductors than others when a p.d. is applied. The opposition of a conductor to current is called its **resistance**. A good conductor has a low resistance and a poor conductor has a high resistance. The resistance of a wire of a certain material

- increases as its length increases
- increases as its cross-sectional area decreases
- depends on the material.

A long thin wire has more resistance than a short thick one of the same material. Silver is the best conductor, but copper, the next best, is cheaper and is used for connecting wires and for domestic electric cables.

> Experiments show that the resistance R of a wire of a given material is:
>
> - directly proportional to its length l, i.e. $R \propto l$
> - inversely proportional to its cross-sectional area A, i.e. $R \propto 1/A$. Combining these two statements we get
> $$R \propto l/A$$
>   This means that if A is doubled, R is halved; or if l is doubled, R is doubled.

● The ohm

If the current in a conductor is I when the voltage across it is V, as shown in Figure P5.25a, its resistance R is defined by

$$R = \frac{V}{I}$$

This is a reasonable way to measure resistance since the smaller I is for a given V, the greater is R. If V is in volts and I in amperes, then R is in **ohms** (symbol Ω, the Greek letter omega). For example, if $I = 2\,\text{A}$ when $V = 12\,\text{V}$, then $R = 12\,\text{V}/2\,\text{A}$, that is, $R = 6\,\Omega$.

> The ohm is the resistance of a conductor in which the current is 1 ampere when a voltage of 1 volt is applied across it.

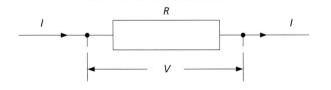

a

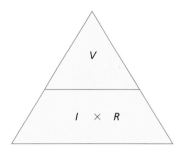

b

Figure P5.25

Alternatively, if R and I are known, V can be found from

$$V = IR$$

Also, when V and R are known, I can be calculated from

$$I = \frac{V}{R}$$

The triangle in Figure P5.25b is an aid to remembering the three equations. It is used like the 'density triangle' on p.345.

● Resistors

Conductors intended to have resistance are called **resistors** and are made either from wires of special alloys or from carbon. Those used in radio and television sets have values from a few ohms up to millions of ohms (Figure P5.26a).

a resistor

b variable resistor (potentiometer)

Figure P5.26

Variable resistors are used in electronics (and are then called **potentiometers**) as volume and other controls (Figure P5.26b). Variable resistors that take larger currents, like the one shown in Figure P5.27 on the next page, are useful in laboratory experiments. These consist of a coil of constantan wire (an alloy of 60% copper, 40% nickel) wound on a tube with a sliding contact on a metal bar above the tube.

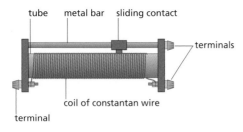

Figure P5.27 Large variable resistor.

Practical work

Measuring resistance

The resistance *R* of a conductor can be found by measuring the current *I* in it when a p.d. *V* is applied across it and then using $R = V/I$. This is called the **ammeter–voltmeter** method.

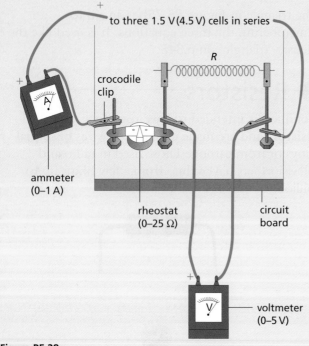

Figure P5.28

Set up the circuit of Figure P5.28 in which the unknown resistance *R* is 1 metre of SWG 34 constantan wire. Altering the rheostat changes both the p.d. *V* and the current *I*. Record in a table, with three columns, five values of *I* (e.g. 0.10, 0.15, 0.20, 0.25 and 0.3 A) and the corresponding values of *V*. Work out *R* for each pair of readings.

Repeat the experiment, but instead of the wire use
(i) a lamp (e.g. 2.5 V, 0.3 A), **(ii)** a semiconductor diode (e.g. 1 N4001) connected first one way then the other way round, **(iii)** a thermistor (e.g. TH 7).

● *I–V* graphs: Ohm's law

The results of the previous experiment allow graphs of *I* against *V* to be plotted for different conductors.

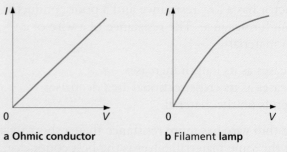

Figure P5.29 *I–V* graphs.

Metallic conductors

Metals and some alloys give *I–V* graphs that are a straight line through the origin, as in Figure P5.29a, provided that their temperature is constant. *I* is directly proportional to *V*, i.e. $I \propto V$. Doubling *V* doubles *I*, etc. Such conductors obey **Ohm's law**, stated as follows.

> The current in a metallic conductor is directly proportional to the p.d. across its ends if the temperature and other conditions are constant.

They are called **ohmic** or **linear conductors** and since $I \propto V$, it follows that V/I = a constant (obtained from the slope of the *I–V* graph). The resistance of an ohmic conductor therefore does not change when the p.d. does.

Filament lamp

A filament lamp is a non-ohmic conductor at high temperatures. For a filament lamp the *I–V* graph bends over as *V* and *I* increase (Figure P5.29b). That is, the resistance (V/I) increases as *I* increases and makes the filament hotter.

Questions

9 What is the resistance of a lamp when a voltage of 12 V across it causes a current of 4 A?

10 Calculate the p.d. across a 10 Ω resistor carrying a current of 2 A.

11 The p.d. across a 3 Ω resistor is 6 V. What is the current flowing (in ampere)?

   A $\frac{1}{2}$ B 1   C 2   D 6   E 8

12 a The graph in Figure P5.28 illustrates how the p.d. across the ends of a conductor is related to the current in it.
   i What law may be deduced from the graph?
   ii What is the resistance of the conductor?

b Draw diagrams to show how six 2 V lamps could be lit to normal brightness when using a
   i   2 V supply
   ii 6 V supply
   iii 12 V supply.

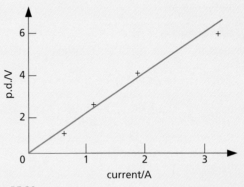

Figure P5.30

Checklist

After studying Chapter P5 you should know and understand the following.

● State the properties of magnets.
● Explain what is meant by soft and hard magnetic materials.
● Recall that a magnetic field is the region round a magnet where a magnetic force is exerted and is represented by lines of force whose direction at any point is the direction of the force on a N pole.
● Map magnetic fields (by the plotting compass and iron filings methods).
● Describe methods of magnetisation and demagnetisation.
● Distinguish between the design and use of permanent magnets and electromagnets.

● Explain what is meant by induced magnetism.

● Describe how positive and negative charges are produced by rubbing.
● Recall that like charges repel and unlike charges attract.
● Explain the charging of objects in terms of the motion of negatively charged electrons.
● Describe simple experiments which can be used to produce and detect electrostatic charges.
● Distinguish between insulators and conductors and give typical examples of each.

● Explain what is meant by an electric field.

● State that an electric current is a flow of charge.
● Recall that an electric current in a metal is a flow of electrons from the negative to the positive terminal of the battery round a circuit.

● State the unit of electric current and recall that current is measured by an ammeter.

● Define the unit of charge in terms of the unit of current.
● Recall the relation $Q = It$ and use it to solve problems.

● Recall that current is a rate of flow of charge and use the relation $I = Q/t$.
● Recall the definition of the unit of p.d. and that p.d. (also called 'voltage') is measured by a voltmeter.
● Use, and describe the use of, ammeters and voltmeters in circuits.
● Describe simple experiments to show the transfer of electrical energy to other forms (e.g. in a lamp).
● Work out the voltages of cells connected in series and parallel.
● Explain the meaning of the term electromotive force (e.m.f.) and recall it is measured in volts.
● Define resistance and state the factors on which it depends.

● Relate the resistance of a wire to its length and cross-sectional area.

● Recall the unit of resistance.
● Solve simple problems using $R = V/I$.

● Describe experiments using the ammeter–voltmeter method to measure resistance, and to study the relationship between current and p.d. for an ohmic resistor and a filament lamp.
● Plot *I–V* graphs from the results of such experiments and draw appropriate conclusions from them.

Combined	Co-ordinated
• Draw and interpret circuit diagrams containing sources, switches, resistors (fixed and variable), lamps, ammeters, voltmeters and fuses Symbols for other common circuit components will be provided in questions.	• Draw and interpret circuit diagrams containing sources, switches, resistors (fixed and variable), lamps, ammeters, voltmeters and fuses Symbols for other common circuit components will be provided in questions.
• Understand that the current at every point in a series circuit is the same	• Understand that the current at every point in a series circuit is the same
• Calculate the combined resistance of two or more resistors in series	• Calculate the combined resistance of two or more resistors in series
• State that, for a parallel circuit, the current from the source is larger than the current in each branch	• State that, for a parallel circuit, the current from the source is larger than the current in each branch
• State that the combined resistance of two resistors in parallel is less than that of either resistor by itself	• State that the combined resistance of two resistors in parallel is less than that of either resistor by itself
• State the advantages of connecting lamps in parallel in a circuit	• State the advantages of connecting lamps in parallel in a circuit
• Recall and use the fact that the sum of the p.d.s across the components in a series circuit is equal to the total p.d. across the supply	• Recall and use the fact that the sum of the p.d.s across the components in a series circuit is equal to the total p.d. across the supply
• Recall and use the fact that the current from the source is the sum of the currents in the separate branches of a parallel circuit	• Recall and use the fact that the current from the source is the sum of the currents in the separate branches of a parallel circuit
• Calculate the combined resistance of two resistors in parallel	• Calculate the combined resistance of two resistors in parallel
• Recall and use the equations $P = IV$ and $E = IVt$	• Draw and interpret circuit diagrams containing NTC thermistors and light-dependent resistors (LDRs)
• Identify electrical hazards including: damaged insulation; overheating of cables; damp conditions	• Describe the action of NTC thermistors and LDRs and show understanding of their use as input transducers
• State that a fuse protects a circuit	• Recall and use the equations $P = IV$ and $E = IVt$
• Explain the use of fuses and choose appropriate fuse ratings	• Identify electrical hazards including: damaged insulation; overheating of cables; damp conditions
	• State that a fuse protects a circuit
	• Explain the use of fuses and choose appropriate fuse ratings

● Circuit diagrams

Current must have a complete path (a circuit) of conductors if it is to flow. Wires of copper are used to connect batteries, lamps, etc. in a circuit since copper is a good electrical conductor. If the wires are covered with insulation, such as plastic, the ends are bared for connecting up.

The signs or symbols used for various parts of an electric circuit are shown in Figure P6.1.

Note that by convention, arrows in circuit diagrams show the direction in which positive charges would flow, i.e. from the positive to negative terminals of a battery. Negatively charged electrons flow in the opposite direction to the conventional current.

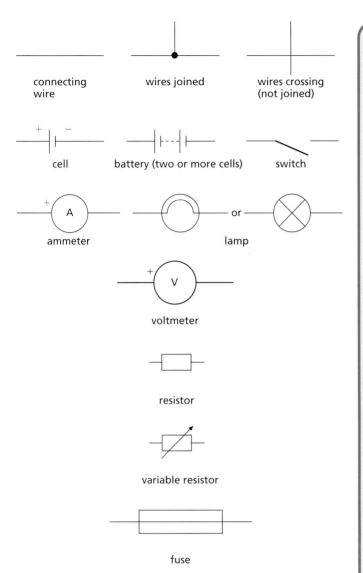

connecting wire   wires joined   wires crossing (not joined)

cell   battery (two or more cells)   switch

ammeter   lamp

voltmeter

resistor

variable resistor

fuse

Figure P6.1 Circuit symbols.

Questions

1 Study the circuits in Figure P6.2. The switch S is open (there is a break in the circuit at this point). In which circuit would lamps Q and R light but not lamp P?

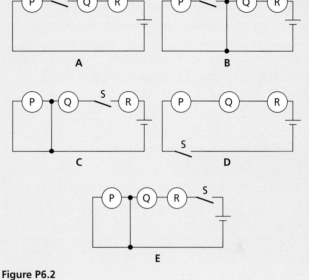

Figure P6.2

2 Using the circuit in Figure P6.3, which of the following statements is correct?
  A When S_1 and S_2 are closed, lamps A and B are lit.
  B With S_1 open and S_2 closed, A is lit and B is not lit.
  C With S_2 open and S_1 closed, A and B are lit.

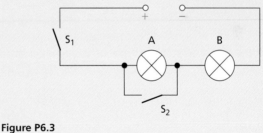

Figure P6.3

● Series and parallel circuits

Series

In a **series circuit**, such as the one shown in Figure P6.4, the different parts follow one after the other and there is just one path for the current to follow. The reading on the ammeter when in the position shown in the diagram is also obtained at B, C and D. That is, current is not used up as it goes round the circuit.

The current is the same at all points in a series circuit.

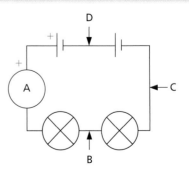

Figure P6.4

Parallel

In a **parallel circuit**, as in Figure P6.5, the lamps are side by side and there are alternative paths for the current. The current splits: some goes through one lamp and the rest through the other. The current from the source is larger than the current in each branch. For example, if the ammeter reading was 0.4 A in the position shown, then if the lamps are identical, the reading at P would be 0.2 A, and so would the reading at Q, giving a total of 0.4 A. Whether the current splits equally or not depends on the lamps (as we will see later); for example, it might divide so that 0.3 A goes one way and 0.1 A by the other branch.

The sum of the currents in the branches of a parallel circuit equals the current entering or leaving the parallel section.

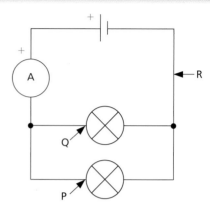

Figure P6.5

● Voltages round a circuit

Series

In the circuit of Figure P6.6

$$V = V_1 + V_2 + V_3$$

For example, if $V_1 = 1.4$ V, $V_2 = 1.5$ V and $V_3 = 1.6$ V, then V will be $(1.4 + 1.5 + 1.6)$ V = 4.5 V.

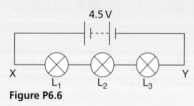

Figure P6.6

The p.d. at the terminals of a battery equals the sum of the p.d.s across the devices in the external circuit from one battery terminal to the other.

Parallel

In the circuit of Figure P6.6

$$V_1 = V_2$$

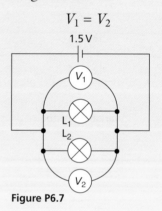

Figure P6.7

The p.d.s across devices in parallel in a circuit are equal.

● Resistors in series

The resistors in Figure P6.8 are in series. The same current I flows through each and the total voltage V across all three is the sum of the separate voltages across them, i.e.

$$V = V_1 + V_2 + V_3$$

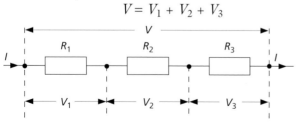

Figure P6.8 Resistors in series.

But $V_1 = IR_1$, $V_2 = IR_2$ and $V_3 = IR_3$. Also, if R is the combined resistance, $V = IR$, and so

$$IR = IR_1 + IR_2 + IR_3$$

Dividing both sides by I,

$$R = R_1 + R_2 + R_3$$

● Resistors in parallel

The resistors in Figure P6.9 are in parallel. The **voltage V between the ends of each is the same** and the total current I equals the sum of the currents in the separate branches, i.e.

$$I = I_1 + I_2 + I_3$$

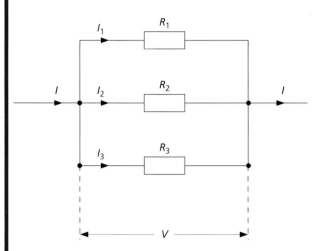

Figure P6.9 Resistors in parallel.

But $I_1 = V/R_1$, $I_2 = V/R_2$ and $I_3 = V/R_3$. Also, if R is the combined resistance, $I = V/R$,

$$\frac{V}{R} = \frac{V}{R_1} + \frac{V}{R_2} + \frac{V}{R_3}$$

Dividing both sides by V,

$$\frac{1}{R} = \frac{1}{R_1} + \frac{1}{R_2} + \frac{1}{R_3}$$

For the simpler case of *two* resistors in parallel

$$\frac{1}{R} = \frac{1}{R_1} + \frac{1}{R_2} = \frac{R_2}{R_1 R_2} + \frac{R_1}{R_1 R_2}$$

$$\therefore \quad \frac{1}{R} = \frac{R_2 + R_1}{R_1 R_2}$$

Inverting both sides,

$$R = \frac{R_1 R_2}{R_1 + R_2} = \frac{\text{product of resistances}}{\text{sum of resistances}}$$

The combined resistance of two resistors in parallel is less than the value of either resistor alone. Check this is true in the following Worked example.

Lamps are connected in parallel rather than in series in a lighting circuit. This ensures (i) the p.d. across each lamp is fixed, so that the lamp shines with the same brightness, irrespective of how many other lights are switched on, and (ii) each lamp can be turned on and off independently; if one lamp fails the others can still be operated.

● Worked example

A p.d. of 24 V from a battery is applied to the network of resistors in Figure P6.10a.

a What is the combined resistance of the $6\,\Omega$ and $12\,\Omega$ resistors in parallel?

b What is the current in the $8\,\Omega$ resistor?

c What is the voltage across the parallel network?

d What is the current in the $6\,\Omega$ resistor?

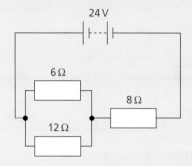

a

b

Figure P6.10

e Let R_1 = resistance of $6\,\Omega$ and $12\,\Omega$ in parallel. Then

$$\frac{1}{R_1} = \frac{1}{6} + \frac{1}{12} = \frac{2}{12} + \frac{1}{12} = \frac{3}{12}$$

$$\therefore \quad R_1 = \frac{12}{3} = 4\,\Omega$$

f Let R = total resistance of circuit = $4 + 8$, that is, $R = 12\,\Omega$. The equivalent circuit is shown in Figure P6.10b, and if I is the current in it then, since $V = 24\,V$

$$I = \frac{V}{R} = \frac{24\ V}{12\ \Omega} = 2\ A$$

$\therefore$ current in $8\,\Omega$ resistor = $2\,A$

425

g Let V_1 = voltage across parallel network in Figure P6.10a. Then

$$V_1 = I \times R_1 = 2\,\text{A} \times 4\,\Omega = 8\,\text{V}$$

h Let I_1 = current in $6\,\Omega$ resistor, then since $V_1 = 8\,\text{V}$

$$I_1 = \frac{V_1}{6\,\Omega} = \frac{8\,\text{V}}{6\,\Omega} = \frac{4}{3}\,\text{A}$$

● Electronic systems

Figure P6.11 Electronic system.

Any electronic system can be considered to consist of the three parts shown in the block diagram of Figure P6.11, i.e.

(i) an **input sensor** or **input transducer**
(ii) a **processor**
(iii) an **output transducer**.

A 'transducer' is a device for converting a non-electrical input into an electrical signal or vice versa.

The **input sensor** detects changes in the environment and converts them from their present form of energy into electrical energy. Input sensors or transducers include LDRs (light-dependent resistors), thermistors, microphones and switches that respond, for instance, to pressure changes.

The **processor** decides on what action to take on the electrical signal it receives from the input sensor. It may involve an operation such as counting, amplifying, timing or storing.

The **output transducer** converts the electrical energy supplied by the processor into another form. Output transducers include lamps, LEDs (light-emitting diodes), loudspeakers, motors, heaters, relays and cathode ray tubes.

In a radio, the input sensor is the aerial that sends an electrical signal to processors in the radio. These processors, among other things, amplify the signal so that it can enable the output transducer, in this case a loudspeaker, to produce sound.

● Input transducers

Thermistor

An NTC (Negative Temperature Coefficient) thermistor contains semiconducting metallic oxides whose resistance decreases markedly when the temperature rises. The temperature may rise either because the thermistor is directly heated or because a current is in it.

Figure P6.12a shows one type of thermistor. Figure P6.12b shows the symbol for a thermistor in a circuit to demonstrate how the thermistor works. When the thermistor is heated with a match, the lamp lights.

A thermistor in series with a meter marked in °C can measure temperatures (p.381). Used in series with a resistor it can provide an input signal to a transistor or other switching circuit.

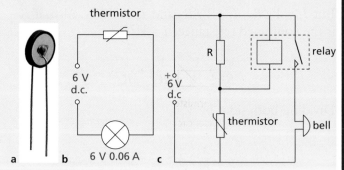

Figure P6.12 a Thermistor; **b** thermistor demonstration circuit; **c** high-temperature alarm.

Figure P6.12c shows how a thermistor can be used to switch a relay. The thermistor forms part of a potential divider across the d.c. source. When the temperature rises, the resistance of the thermistor falls, and so does the p.d. across it. The voltage across resistor R and the relay increases. When the voltage across the relay reaches its operating p.d. the normally open contacts close, so that the circuit to the bell is completed and it rings. If a variable resistor is used in the circuit, the temperature at which the alarm sounds can be varied.

Variation of resistance with temperature

In general, an increase of temperature increases the resistance of metals, as for the filament lamp in Figure P5.29b (p.420), but it decreases the resistance of semiconductors. The resistance of semiconductor **thermistors** decreases if their temperature rises, i.e. their I–V graph bends upwards, as in Figure P6.13.

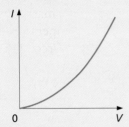

Figure P6.13 Thermistor.

If a resistor and a thermistor are connected as a potential divider (Figure P6.14), the p.d. across the resistor increases as the temperature of the thermistor increases; the circuit can be used to monitor temperature, for example in a car radiator.

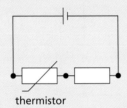

Figure P6.14 Potential divider circuit for monitoring temperature.

Light-dependent resistor (LDR)

The action of an LDR depends on the fact that the resistance of the semiconductor cadmium sulfide decreases as the intensity of the light falling on it increases.

An LDR and a circuit showing its action are shown in Figures P6.15a and b. Note the circuit symbol for an LDR, sometimes seen without a circle. When light from a lamp falls on the 'window' of the LDR, its resistance decreases and the increased current lights the lamp.

LDRs are used in photographic exposure meters and in series with a resistor to provide an input signal for a switching circuit.

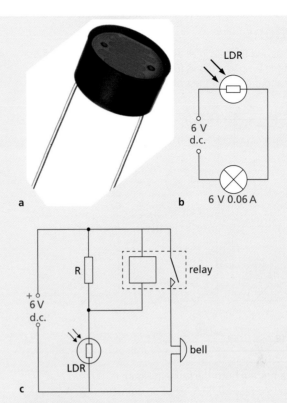

Figure P6.15 a LDR; **b** LDR demonstration circuit; **c** light-operated intruder alarm.

Figure P6.15c shows how an LDR can be used to switch a 'relay'. The LDR forms part of a potential divider across the 6 V supply. When light falls on the LDR, the resistance of the LDR, and hence the voltage across it, decreases. There is a corresponding increase in the voltage across resistor R and the relay; when the voltage across the relay coil reaches a high enough p.d. (its operating p.d.) it acts as a switch and the normally open contacts close, allowing current to flow to the bell, which rings. If the light is removed, the p.d. across resistor R and the relay drops below the operating p.d. of the relay so that the relay contacts open again; power to the bell is cut and it stops ringing.

Variation of resistance with light intensity

The resistance of some semiconducting materials decreases when the intensity of light falling on them increases. This property is made use of in LDRs. The I–V graph for an LDR is similar to that shown in Figure P6.13 for a thermistor. Both thermistors and LDRs are non-ohmic conductors.

Questions

3 The lamps and the cells in all the circuits of Figure P6.16 are the same. If the lamp in **a** has its full, normal brightness, what can you say about the brightness of the lamps in **b, c, d, e** and **f**?

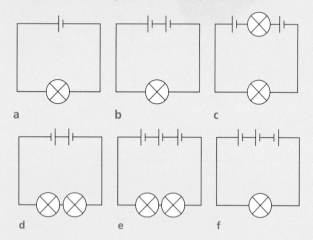

Figure P6.16

4 If the lamps are both the same in Figure P6.17 and if ammeter A_1 reads 0.50 A, what do ammeters A_2, A_3, A_4 and A_5 read?

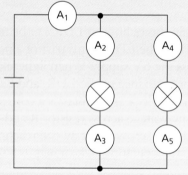

Figure P6.17

5 Three 2 V cells are connected in series and used as the supply for a circuit.
  a What is the p.d. at the terminals of the supply?
  b How many joules of electrical energy does 1 C gain on passing through
    (i) one cell,   (ii) all three cells?

6 Three voltmeters V, V_1 and V_2 are connected as in Figure P6.18.
  a If V reads 18 V and V_1 reads 12 V, what does V_2 read?
  b If the ammeter A reads 0.5 A, how much electrical energy is changed to heat and light in lamp L_1 in one minute?

c Copy Figure P6.18 and mark with a + the positive terminals of the ammeter and voltmeters for correct connection.

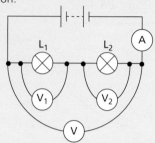

Figure P6.18

7 Three voltmeters are connected as in Figure P6.19.

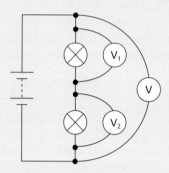

Figure P6.19

What are the voltmeter readings x, y and z in the table below (which were obtained with three different batteries)?

V/V	V_1/V	V_2/V
x	12	6
6	4	y
12	z	4

8 Calculate the effective resistance between A and B in Figure P6.20.

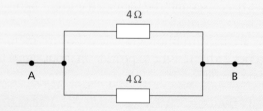

Figure P6.20

9 What is the effective resistance in Figure P6.21 between
   a   A and B
   b   C and D?

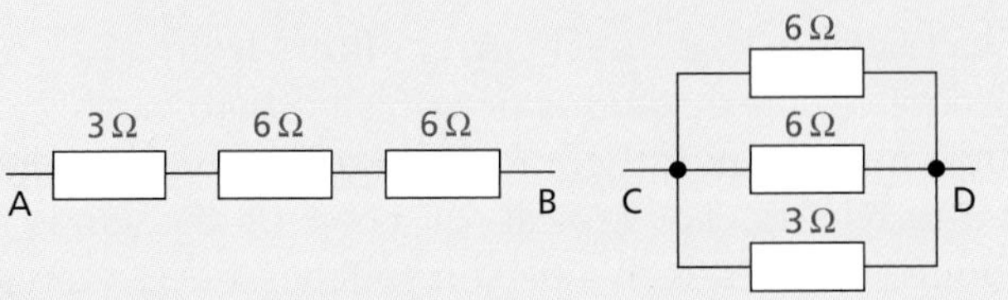

Figure P6.21

10 Figure P6.22 shows three resistors. Their combined resistance in ohms is

A $1\frac{5}{7}$ B 14   C $1\frac{1}{5}$ D $7\frac{1}{2}$ E $6\frac{2}{3}$

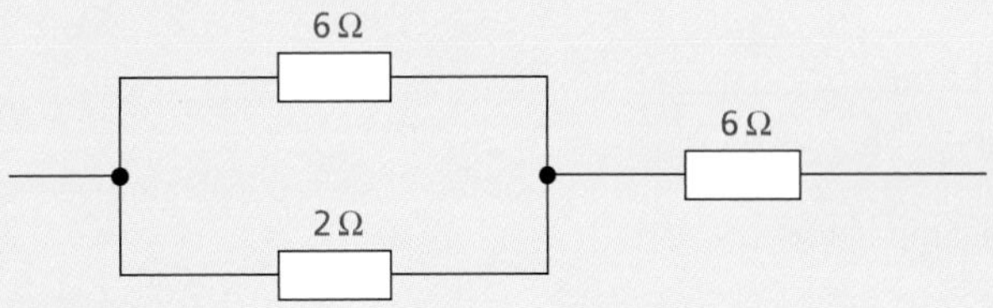

Figure P6.22

● Power in electric circuits

In many circuits it is important to know the rate at which electrical energy is transferred into other forms of energy. Earlier (Chapter P2) we said that **energy transfers were measured by the work done** and power was defined by the equation

$$\text{power} = \frac{\text{work done}}{\text{time taken}} = \frac{\text{energy transfer}}{\text{time taken}}$$

In symbols

$$P = \frac{E}{t}$$

where if E is in joules (J) and t in seconds (s) then P is in J/s or watts (W).

From the definition of p.d. (Chapter P5) we saw that if E is the electrical energy transferred when there is a steady current I (in amperes) for time t (in seconds) in a device (e.g. a lamp) with a p.d. V (in volts) across it, as in Figure P6.23, then

$$E = ItV \qquad (2)$$

Substituting for E in (1) we get

$$P = \frac{E}{t} = \frac{ItV}{t}$$

or

$$P = IV$$

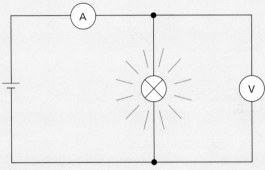

Figure P6.23

Therefore to calculate the power P of an electrical appliance we multiply the current I in it by the p.d. V across it. For example if a lamp on a 240 V supply has a current of 0.25 A in it, its power is 240 V × 0.25 A = 60 W. The lamp is transferring 60 J of electrical energy into heat and light each second. Larger units of power are the **kilowatt** (kW) and the **megawatt** (MW) where

1 kW = 1000 W   and   1 MW = 1 000 000 W

In units

$$\text{watts} = \text{amperes} \times \text{volts} \qquad (3)$$

It follows from (3) that since

$$\text{volts} = \frac{\text{watts}}{\text{amperes}} \qquad (4)$$

the volt can be defined as a **watt per ampere** and p.d. calculated from (4).

If all the energy is transferred to heat in a resistor of resistance R, then $V = IR$ and the rate of production of heat is given by

$$P = V \times I = IR \times I = I^2R$$

That is, if the current is doubled, four times as much heat is produced per second. Also, $P = V^2/R$.

Practical work

Measuring electric power

a) Lamp

Connect the circuit of Figure P6.24. Note the ammeter and voltmeter readings and work out the electric power supplied to the lamp in watts.

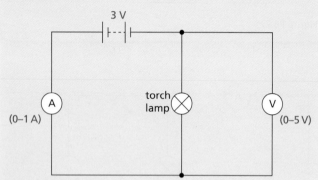

Figure P6.24

b) Motor

Replace the lamp in Figure P6.24 by a small electric motor. Attach a known mass m (in kg) to the axle of the motor with a length of thin string and find the time t (in s) required to raise the mass through a known height h (in m) at a steady speed. Then the power output P_o (in W) of the motor is given by

$$P_o = \frac{\text{work done in raising mass}}{\text{time taken}} = \frac{mgh}{t}$$

If the ammeter and voltmeter readings I and V are noted while the mass is being raised, the power input P_i (in W) can be found from

$$P_i = IV$$

The efficiency of the motor is given by

$$\text{efficiency} = \frac{P_o}{P_i} \times 100\%$$

Also investigate the effect of a greater mass on: (i) the speed, (ii) the power output and (iii) the efficiency of the motor at its rated p.d.

● Dangers of electricity

Electric shock

Electric shock occurs if current flows from an electric circuit through a person's body to earth. This can happen if there is **damaged insulation** or **faulty wiring**. The typical resistance of dry skin is about $10\,000\,\Omega$, so if a person touches a wire carrying electricity at $240\,V$, an estimate of the current flowing through them to earth would be $I = V/R = 240/10\,000 = 0.024\,A = 24\,mA$. For wet skin, the resistance is lowered to about $1000\,\Omega$ (since water is a good conductor of electricity) so the current would increase to around $240\,mA$.

It is the **size of the current** (not the voltage) and the **length of time** for which it acts which determine the strength of an electric shock. The path the current takes influences the effect of the shock; some parts of the body are more vulnerable than others. A current of $100\,mA$ through the heart is likely to be fatal.

Damp conditions increase the severity of an electric shock because water lowers the resistance of the path to earth; wearing shoes with insulating rubber soles or standing on a dry insulating floor increases the resistance between a person and earth and will reduce the severity of an electric shock.

Fire risks

If flammable material is placed too close to a hot appliance such as an electric heater, it may catch fire. Similarly if the electrical wiring in the walls of a house becomes overheated, a fire may start. Wires become hot when they carry electrical currents – the larger the current carried, the hotter a particular wire will become, since the rate of production of heat equals I^2R (see p.429).

To reduce the risk of fire through **overheated cables**, the maximum current in a circuit should be limited by taking these precautions:

- Use plugs that have the correct fuse.
- Do not attach too many appliances to a circuit.
- Don't overload circuits by using too many adapters.
- Appliances such as heaters use large amounts of power (and hence current), so do not connect them to a lighting circuit designed for low current use. (Thick wires have a lower resistance than thin wires so are used in circuits expected to carry high currents.)

Damaged insulation or faulty wiring which leads to a large current flowing to earth through flammable material can also start a fire.

The factors leading to fire or electric shock can be summarised as follows:

damaged insulation	→ electric shock and fire risk
overheated cables	→ fire risk
damp conditions	→ increased severity of electric shocks

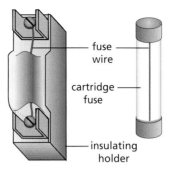

Figure P6.25 Two types of fuse.

Fuses

A **fuse** protects a circuit. It is a short length of wire of material with a low melting point, often 'tinned copper', which melts and breaks the circuit when the current in it exceeds a certain value. Two reasons for excessive currents are 'short circuits' due to worn insulation on connecting wires and overloaded circuits. Without a fuse the wiring would become hot in these cases and could cause a fire. **A fuse should ensure that the current-carrying capacity of the wiring is not exceeded.** In general the thicker a cable is, the more current it can carry, but each size has a limit.

Two types of fuse are shown in Figure P6.25. **Always switch off before replacing a fuse,** and always replace with one of the same value as recommended by the manufacturer of the appliance.

Questions

11 What steps should be taken before replacing a blown fuse in a plug?
12 What size fuse (3 A or 13 A) should be used in a plug connected to
   a a 150 W television,
   b a 900 W iron,
   c a 2 kW kettle,
   if the supply is 230 V?

13 How much electrical energy in joules does a 100 watt lamp transfer in
   a 1 second
   b 5 seconds
   c 1 minute?
14 a What is the power of a lamp rated at 12 V 2 A?
   b How many joules of electrical energy are transferred per second by a 6 V 0.5 A lamp?
15 The largest number of 100 W lamps connected in parallel which can safely be run from a 230 V supply with a 5 A fuse is
   A 2   B 5   C 11   D 12   E 0
16 What is the maximum power in kilowatts of the appliance(s) that can be connected safely to a 13 A 230 V mains socket?
17 a Below is a list of wattages of various appliances. State which is most likely to be the correct one for each of the appliances named.
   60 W   250 W   850 W   2 kW   3.5 kW
   i   kettle
   ii table lamp
   iii iron
   b What will be the current in a 920 W appliance if the supply voltage is 230 V?

Checklist

After studying Chapter P6 you should know and understand the following.

- Use circuit symbols for wires, cells, switches, ammeters, voltmeters, resistors, lamps and fuses.
- Distinguish between electron flow and conventional current.
- Draw and connect simple series and parallel circuits, observing correct polarities for meters.
- Recall that the current in a series circuit is the same everywhere in the circuit.
- State that for a parallel circuit, the current from the source is larger than the current in each branch.

- Recall that the sum of the currents in the branches of a parallel circuit equals the current entering or leaving the parallel section.
- Demonstrate that the sum of the p.d.'s across any number of components in series equals the p.d. across all of those components.

- Use the formulae for resistors in series.

- Demonstrate that the p.d.'s across any number of components connected in parallel are the same.

- Recall that the combined resistance of two resistors in parallel is less than that of either resistor alone.
- State the advantages of connecting lamps in parallel in a lighting circuit.

- Calculate the effective resistance of two resistors in parallel.

- Recall the functions of the input sensor, processor and output transducer in an electronic system and give some examples.
- Draw and interpret circuit diagrams containing LDR's and thermistors.
- Describe the action of an LDR and a thermistor and show an understanding of their use as input transducers.

- Recall the relations $E = ItV$ and $P = IV$ and use them to solve simple problems on energy transfers.

- Recall the hazards of damaged insulation, damp conditions and overheating of cables and the associated risks.
- Understand the function of a fuse.
- Choose the appropriate fuse rating for an appliance.

Electromagnetic effects

Co-ordinated

- Describe the pattern of the magnetic field (including direction) due to currents in straight wires and in solenoids
- Describe the effect on the magnetic field of changing the magnitude and direction of the current
- Describe an experiment to show that a force acts on a current-carrying conductor in a magnetic field, including the effect of reversing: the current; the direction of the field
- State and use the relative directions of force, field and current
- State that a current-carrying coil in a magnetic field experiences a turning effect and that the effect is increased by: increasing the number of turns on the coil; increasing the current; increasing the strength of the magnetic field
- Relate this turning effect to the action of an electric motor including the action of a split-ring commutator
- Show understanding that a conductor moving across a magnetic field or a changing magnetic field linking with a conductor can induce an e.m.f. in the conductor
- State the factors affecting the magnitude of an induced e.m.f.
- Distinguish between direct current (d.c.) and alternating current (a.c.)
- Describe and explain the operation of a rotating-coil generator and the use of slip rings
- Sketch a graph of voltage output against time for a simple a.c. generator
- Describe the construction of a basic transformer with a soft-iron core, as used for voltage transformations
- Describe the principle of operation of a transformer
- Use the terms step-up and step-down
- Recall and use the equation $(V_p/V_s) = (N_p/N_s)$ (for 100% efficiency)
- Describe the use of the transformer in high-voltage transmission of electricity
- Recall and use the equation $I_pV_p = I_sV_s$ (for 100% efficiency)
- Explain why power losses in cables are lower when the voltage is high

● Oersted's discovery

In 1819 Oersted accidentally discovered the magnetic effect of an electric current. His experiment can be repeated by holding a wire over and parallel to a compass needle that is pointing N and S (Figure 17.1). The needle moves when the current is switched on. Reversing the current causes the needle to move in the opposite direction.

Evidently around a wire carrying a current there is a magnetic field. As with the field due to a permanent magnet, we represent the field due to a current by **field lines** or **lines of force**. Arrows on the lines show the direction of the field, i.e. the direction in which a N pole points.

Different field patterns are given by differently shaped conductors.

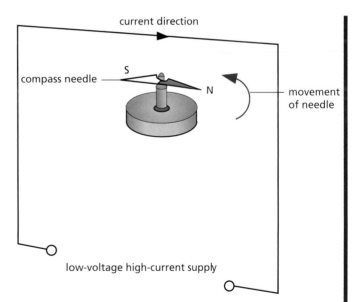

Figure P7.1 An electric current produces a magnetic effect.

● Field due to a straight wire

If a straight vertical wire passes through the centre of a piece of card held horizontally and there is a current

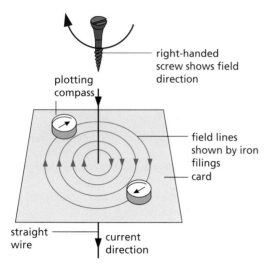

Figure P7.2 Field due to a straight wire.

in the wire (Figure P7.2), iron filings sprinkled on the card settle in concentric circles when the card is gently tapped.

Plotting compasses placed on the card settle along the field lines and show the direction of the field at different points.

When the current direction is reversed, the compasses point in the opposite direction showing that the direction of the field reverses when the current reverses.

If the current direction is known, the direction of the field can be predicted by the **right-hand screw rule**:

> If a right-handed screw moves forwards in the direction of the current (conventional), the direction of rotation of the screw gives the direction of the field.

When the current through the wire is increased, the strength of the magnetic field around the wire increases and the field lines become closer together.

● Field due to a circular coil

The field pattern is shown in Figure P7.3. At the centre of the coil the field lines are straight and at right angles to the plane of the coil. The right-hand screw rule again gives the direction of the field at any point.

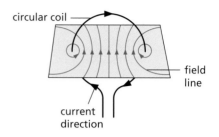

Figure P7.3 Field due to a circular coil.

● Field due to a solenoid

A **solenoid** is a long cylindrical coil. It produces a field similar to that of a bar magnet; in Figure P7.4a, end A behaves like a N pole and end B like a S pole.

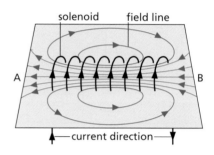

a field due to a solenoid

The polarity can be found as before by applying the right-hand screw rule to a short length of one turn of the solenoid. Alternatively the **right-hand grip rule** can be used. This states that if the fingers of the right hand grip the solenoid in the direction of the current (conventional), the thumb points to the N pole (Figure P7.4b). Figure P7.4c shows how to link the end-on view of the current direction in the solenoid to the polarity.

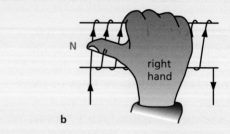

b the right right-hand grip rule

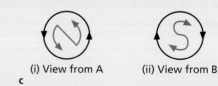

c end-on views

Figure P7.4

Inside the solenoid in Figure P7.4a, the field lines are closer together than they are outside the solenoid. This indicates that the magnetic field is stronger inside a solenoid than outside it.

The field inside a solenoid can be made very strong if it has a large number of turns or a large current. Permanent magnets can be made by allowing molten ferromagnetic metal to solidify in such fields.

Questions

1 The vertical wire in Figure P7.5 is at right angles to the card. In what direction will a plotting compass at A point when
  a there is no current in the wire,
  b the current direction is upwards?

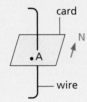

Figure P7.5

2 Figure P7.6 shows a solenoid wound on a core of soft iron. Will the end A be a N pole or S pole when the current is in the direction shown?

Figure P7.6

● The motor effect

A wire carrying a current in a magnetic field experiences a force. If the wire can move, it does so.

Demonstration

In Figure P7.7 the flexible wire is loosely supported in the strong magnetic field of a C-shaped magnet (permanent or electromagnet). When the switch is closed, current flows in the wire which jumps upwards as shown. If either the direction of the current or the direction of the field is reversed, the

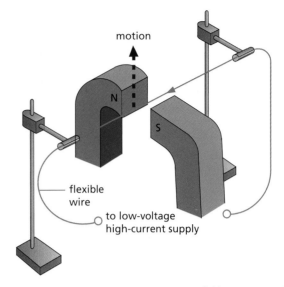

Figure P7.7 A wire carrying a current in a magnetic field experiences a force.

wire moves downwards. **The force increases if the strength of the field increases and if the current increases.**

Explanation

Figure P7.8a is a side view of the magnetic field lines due to the wire and the magnet. Those due to the wire are circles and we will assume their direction is as shown. The dotted lines represent the field lines of the magnet and their direction is towards the right.

The resultant field obtained by combining both fields is shown in Figure P7.8b. There are more lines below than above the wire since both fields act in the same direction below but they are in opposition above. If we *suppose* the lines are like stretched elastic, those below will try to straighten out and in so doing will exert an upward force on the wire.

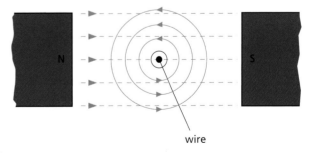

wire

a

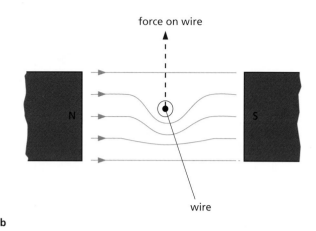

force on wire

N   S

wire

b

Figure P7.8

● Fleming's left-hand rule

The direction of the force or thrust on the wire can be found by this rule which is also called the **motor rule** (Figure P7.9).

Hold the thumb and first two fingers of the left hand at right angles to each other with the **F**irst finger pointing in the direction of the **F**ield and the se**C**ond finger in the direction of the **C**urrent, then the **Th**umb points in the direction of the **Th**rust.

If the wire is not at right angles to the field, the force is smaller and is zero if the wire is parallel to the field.

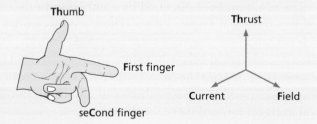

Thumb

First finger

seCond finger

Thrust

Current   Field

Figure P7.9 Fleming's left-hand (motor) rule.

● Simple d.c. electric motor

When a rectangular coil of wire is mounted in a magnetic field, as shown in Figure P7.10, it experiences a turning effect, or couple, when current flows in the coil. The couple is greater if:

● the number of turns on the coil is increased
● the current is increased
● the strength of the magnetic field is increased.

A simple motor to work from direct current (d.c.) consists of a rectangular coil of wire mounted on

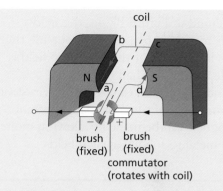

coil

b   c

N   S

a   d

brush (fixed)   brush (fixed)
commutator
(rotates with coil)

Figure P7.10 Simple d.c. motor.

an axle which can rotate between the poles of a C-shaped magnet (Figure P7.10). Each end of the coil is connected to half of a split ring of copper, called a **commutator**, which rotates with the coil. Two carbon blocks, the **brushes**, are pressed lightly against the commutator by springs. The brushes are connected to an electrical supply.

If Fleming's left-hand rule is applied to the coil in the position shown, we find that side **ab** experiences an upward force and side **cd** a downward force. (No forces act on **ad** and **bc** since they are parallel to the field.) These two forces form a **couple** which rotates the coil in a clockwise direction until it is vertical.

The brushes are then in line with the gaps in the commutator and the current stops. However, because of its inertia, the coil overshoots the vertical and the commutator halves change contact from one brush to the other. This reverses the current through the coil and so also the directions of the forces on its sides. Side **ab** is on the right now, acted on by a downward force, while **cd** is on the left with an upward force. The coil thus carries on rotating clockwise.

The more turns there are on the coil, or the larger the current through it, the greater is the couple on the coil and the faster it turns. The coil will also turn faster if the strength of the magnetic field is increased.

● Practical motors

Practical motors have:

● **a coil of many turns wound on a soft iron cylinder or core** which rotates with the coil. This makes it more powerful. The coil and core together are called the **armature**.
● **several coils** each in a slot in the core and each having a pair of commutator segments. This gives increased

power and smoother running. The motor of an electric drill is shown in Figure P7.11.

- **an electromagnet** (usually) to produce the field in which the armature rotates.

Most electric motors used in industry are **induction motors**. They work off a.c. (alternating current) on a different principle from the d.c. motor.

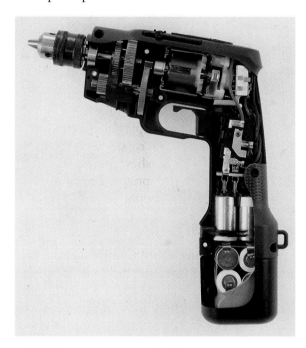

Figure P7.11 Motor inside an electric drill.

Practical work

A model motor

The motor shown in Figure P7.12 is made from a kit.

1. Wrap Sellotape round one end of the metal tube which passes through the wooden block.
2. Cut two rings off a piece of narrow rubber tubing; slip them on to the Sellotaped end of the metal tube.
3. Remove the insulation from one end of a 1.5-metre length of SWG 26 PVC-covered copper wire and fix it under both rubber rings so that it is held tight against the Sellotape. This forms one end of the coil.
4. Wind 10 turns of the wire in the slot in the wooden block and finish off the second end of the coil by removing the PVC and fixing this too under the rings but on the opposite side of the tube from the first end. The bare ends act as the **commutator**.
5. Push the axle through the metal tube of the wooden base so that the block spins freely.
6. Arrange two 0.5-metre lengths of wire to act as **brushes** and leads to the supply, as shown. Adjust the brushes so that they are vertical and each touches one bare end of the coil when the plane of the coil is horizontal. **The motor will not work if this is not so**.
7. Slide the base into the magnet with *opposite poles facing*. Connect to a 3 V battery (or other low-voltage d.c. supply) and a slight push of the coil should set it spinning at high speed.

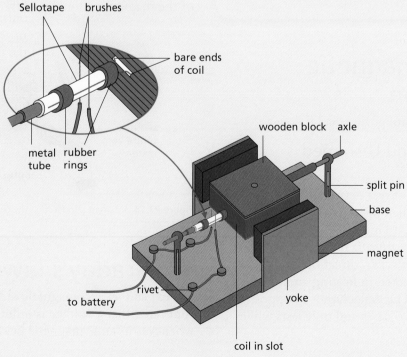

Figure P7.12 A model motor.

Questions

3 In the simple electric motor of Figure P7.13, the coil rotates anticlockwise as seen by the eye from the position X when current flows in the coil. Is the current flowing clockwise or anticlockwise around the coil when viewed from above?

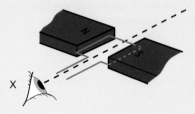

Figure P7.13

4 An electric motor is a device which transfers
 A mechanical energy to electrical energy
 B heat energy to electrical energy
 C electrical energy to heat only
 D heat to mechanical energy
 E electrical energy to mechanical energy and heat.

5 a Draw a labelled diagram of the essential components of a simple motor. Explain how continuous rotation is produced and show how the direction of rotation is related to the direction of the current.
 b State what would happen to the direction of rotation of the motor you have described if
  i the current was reversed
  ii the magnetic field was reversed
  iii both current and field were reversed simultaneously.

● Electromagnetic induction

Two ways of investigating the effect follow.

Straight wire and U-shaped magnet

First the wire is held at rest between the poles of the magnet. It is then moved in each of the six directions shown in Figure P7.14 and the meter observed. Only *when it is moving upwards* (direction 1) or *downwards* (direction 2) is there a deflection on the meter, indicating an induced current in the wire. The deflection is in opposite directions in these two cases and only lasts while the wire is in motion.

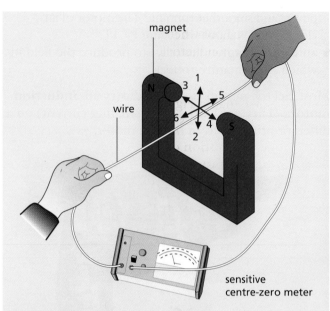

Figure P7.14 A current is induced in the wire when it is moved up or down between the magnet poles.

Bar magnet and coil

The magnet is pushed into the coil, one pole first (Figure P7.15), then held still inside it. It is then withdrawn. The meter shows that current is induced in the coil in one direction as the magnet is *moved in* and in the opposite direction as it is *moved out*. There is no deflection when the magnet is at rest. The results are the same if the coil is moved instead of the magnet, i.e. only *relative motion* is needed.

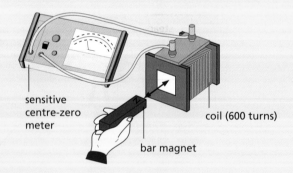

Figure P7.15 A current is induced in the coil when the magnet is moved in or out.

● Faraday's law

To 'explain' electromagnetic induction Faraday suggested that a voltage is induced in a conductor whenever it 'cuts' magnetic field lines, i.e. moves *across* them, but not when it moves along them or is at rest. If the conductor forms part of a complete circuit, an induced current is also produced.

Faraday found, and it can be shown with apparatus like that in Figure P7.15, that the induced p.d. or voltage increases with increases of:

- the **speed of motion** of the magnet or coil,
- the **number of turns** on the coil,
- the **strength of the magnet**.

These facts led him to state a law:

> The size of the induced p.d. is directly proportional to the rate at which the conductor cuts magnetic field lines.

Direct and alternating current

In a **direct current (d.c.)** the electrons flow in one direction only. Graphs for steady and varying d.c. are shown in Figure P7.16.

In an **alternating current (a.c.)** the direction of flow reverses regularly, as shown in the graph in Figure P7.17. The circuit sign for a.c. is given in Figure P7.18.

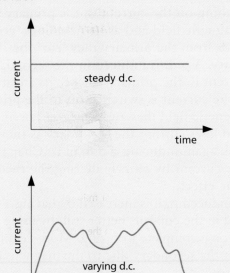

Figure P7.16 Direct current (d.c.).

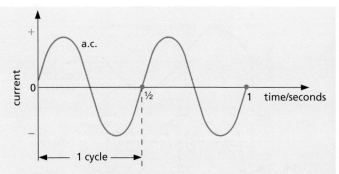

Figure P7.17 Alternating current (a.c.).

Figure P7.18 Symbol for alternating current.

The pointer of an ammeter for measuring d.c. is deflected one way by the direct current. Alternating current makes the pointer move to and fro about the zero if the changes are slow enough; otherwise no deflection can be seen.

Batteries give d.c.; generators can produce either d.c. or a.c.

Simple a.c. generator (alternator)

The simplest alternating current (a.c.) generator consists of a rectangular coil between the poles of a C-shaped magnet (Figure P7.19a). The ends of the coil are joined to two **slip rings** on the axle and against which **carbon brushes** press.

When the coil is rotated it cuts the field lines and a voltage is induced in it. Figure P7.19b shows how the voltage varies over one complete rotation.

As the coil moves through the vertical position with **ab** uppermost, **ab** and **cd** are moving along the lines (**bc** and **da** do so always) and no cutting occurs. The induced voltage is zero.

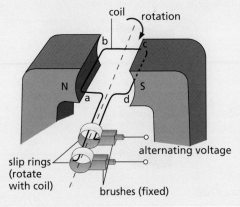

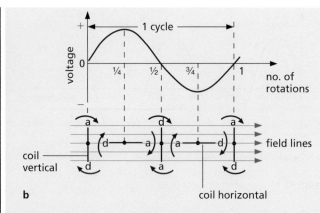

Figure P7.19 A simple a.c. generator and its output.

During the first quarter rotation the p.d. increases to a maximum when the coil is horizontal. Sides **ab** and **dc** are then cutting the lines at the greatest rate.

In the second quarter rotation the p.d. decreases again and is zero when the coil is vertical with **dc** uppermost. After this, the direction of the p.d. reverses because, during the next half rotation, the motion of **ab** is directed upwards and **dc** downwards.

An alternating voltage is generated which acts first in one direction and then the other; it causes alternating current (a.c.) to flow in a circuit connected to the brushes. The **frequency** of an a.c. is the number of complete cycles it makes each second and is measured in **hertz** (Hz), i.e. 1 cycle per second = 1 Hz. If the coil rotates twice per second, the a.c. has frequency 2 Hz. The mains supply is a.c. of frequency 50 Hz.

Questions

6 a The south pole of a bar magnet is moved steadily into a coil of wire which is connected to a centre-zero ammeter. What happens to the pointer on the meter?

  b The magnet is then withdrawn quickly from the coil. What happens to the pointer on the meter now?

7 A simple generator is shown in Figure P7.20.

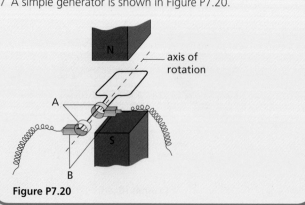

Figure P7.20

a What are A and B called and what is their purpose?

b What changes can be made to increase the p.d. generated?

8 Describe the deflections observed on the sensitive, centre-zero galvanometer G (Figure P7.21) when the copper rod XY is connected to its terminals and is made to vibrate up and down (as shown by the arrows), between the poles of a U-shaped magnet, at right angles to the magnetic field. Explain what is happening.

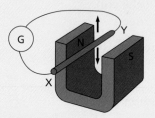

Figure P7.21

● Mutual induction

When the current in a coil is switched on or off or changed, a voltage is induced in a neighbouring coil. The effect, called **mutual induction**, is an example of electromagnetic induction and can be shown with the arrangement of Figure P7.22. Coil A is the **primary** and coil B the **secondary**.

Switching on the current in the primary sets up a magnetic field and as its field lines 'grow' outwards from the primary they 'cut' the secondary. A p.d. is induced in the secondary until the current in the primary reaches its steady value. When the current is switched off in the primary, the magnetic field dies away and we can imagine the field lines cutting the secondary as they collapse, again inducing a p.d. in it. Changing the primary current by *quickly* altering the rheostat has the same effect.

The induced p.d. is increased by having a soft iron rod in the coils or, better still, by using coils wound on a complete iron ring. More field lines then cut the secondary due to the magnetisation of the iron.

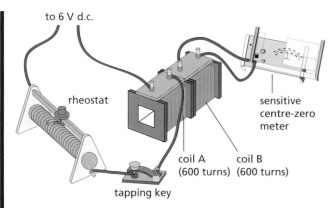

Figure P7.22 A changing current in a primary coil (A) induces a current in a secondary coil (B).

Practical work

Mutual induction with a.c.

An alternating current is changing all the time and if it flows in a primary coil, an alternating voltage and current are induced in a secondary coil.

Connect the circuit of Figure P7.23. The 1 V high current power unit supplies a.c. to the primary and the lamp detects the secondary current.

Find the effect on the brightness of the lamp of:

(i) pulling the C-cores apart slightly
(ii) increasing the secondary turns to 15
(iii) decreasing the secondary turns to 5.

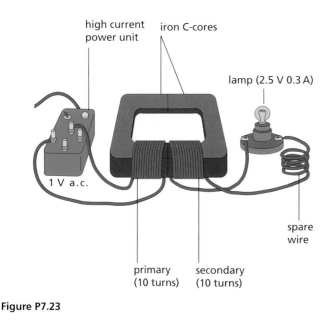

Figure P7.23

● Transformer equation

A **transformer** transforms (changes) an *alternating* voltage from one value to another of greater or smaller value. It has a primary coil and a secondary coil wound on a complete soft iron core, either one on top of the other (Figure P7.24a) or on separate limbs of the core (Figure P7.24b).

An alternating voltage applied to the primary induces an alternating voltage in the secondary. The value of the secondary voltage can be shown, for a transformer in which all the field lines cut the secondary, to be given by:

$$\frac{\text{secondary voltage}}{\text{primary voltage}} = \frac{\text{secondary turns}}{\text{primary turns}}$$

In symbols

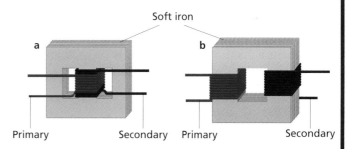

Figure P7.24 Primary and secondary coils of a transformer.

$$\frac{V_s}{V_p} = \frac{N_s}{N_p}$$

A **step-up transformer** has more turns on the secondary than the primary and V_s is greater than V_p (Figure P7.25a). For example, if the secondary has twice as many turns as the primary, V_s is about twice V_p. In a **step-down transformer** there are fewer turns on the secondary than the primary and V_s is less than V_p (Figure P7.25b).

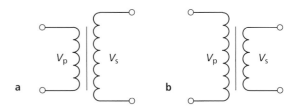

Figure P7.25 Symbols for a transformer: **a** step-up ($V_s > V_p$); **b** step-down ($V_p > V_s$).

Energy losses in a transformer

If the p.d. is stepped up in a transformer, the current is stepped down in proportion. This must be so if we assume that all the electrical energy given to the primary appears in the secondary, i.e. that energy is conserved and the transformer is 100% efficient or 'ideal' (many approach this efficiency). Then

> power in primary = power in secondary
>
> $V_p \times I_p = V_s \times I_s$

where I_p and I_s are the primary and secondary currents, respectively.

$$\therefore \qquad \frac{I_s}{I_p} = \frac{V_p}{V_s}$$

So, for the ideal transformer, if the p.d. is doubled the current is halved. In practice, it is more than halved, because of small energy losses in the transformer.

Worked example

A transformer steps down the mains supply from 230 V to 10 V to operate an answering machine.

a What is the turns ratio of the transformer windings?
b How many turns are on the primary if the secondary has 100 turns?
c What is the current in the primary if the transformer is 100% efficient and the current in the answering machine is 2 A?
a Primary voltage, $V_p = 230$ V
  Secondary voltage, $V_s = 10$ V

$$\text{Turns ratio} = \frac{N_s}{N_p} = \frac{V_s}{V_p} = \frac{10 \text{ V}}{230 \text{ V}} = \frac{1}{23}$$

b Secondary turns, $N_s = 100$
  From a,

$$\frac{N_s}{N_p} = \frac{1}{23}$$

$$\therefore \qquad N_p = 23 \times N_s = 23 \times 100$$

$$= 2300 \text{ turns}$$

c Efficiency = 100%

$\therefore$ power in primary = power in secondary

$$V_p \times I_p = V_s \times I_s$$

$$\therefore \quad I_p = \frac{V_s \times I_s}{V_p} = \frac{10 \text{ V} \times 2 \text{ A}}{230 \text{ V}} = \frac{2}{23} \text{A} = 0.09 \text{ A}$$

Note In this ideal transformer the current is stepped up in the same ratio as the voltage is stepped down.

Power losses in transmission cables

The efficiency with which transformers step alternating p.d.s up and down accounts for the use of a.c. rather than d.c. in power transmission. High voltages are used in the transmission of electric power to reduce the amount of energy 'lost' as heat.

Power cables have resistance, and so electrical energy is transferred to heat during the transmission of electricity from the power station to the user. The power 'lost' as heat in cables of resistance R is I^2R, so I should be kept low to reduce energy loss. Since power = IV, if 400 000 W of electrical power has to be sent through cables, it might be done, for example, either as 1 A at 400 000 V or as 1000 A at 400 V. Less energy will be transferred to heat if the power is transmitted at the lower current and higher voltage, i.e. 1 A at 400 000 V. High p.d.s require good insulation but are readily produced by a.c. generators.

Questions

9 The main function of a step-down transformer is to
 A decrease current
 B decrease voltage
 C change a.c. to d.c.
 D change d.c. to a.c.
 E decrease the resistance of a circuit.
10 a Calculate the number of turns on the secondary of a step-down transformer which would enable a 12 V lamp to be used with a 230 V a.c. mains power, if there are 460 turns on the primary.
 b What current will flow in the secondary when the primary current is 0.10 A? Assume there are no energy losses.
11 A transformer has 1000 turns on the primary coil. The voltage applied to the primary coil is 230 V a.c. How many turns are on the secondary coil if the output voltage is 46 V a.c.?
 A 20 B 200 C 2000 D 4000 E 8000

Checklist

After studying Chapter P7 you should know and understand the following.

- Describe and draw sketches of the magnetic fields round current-carrying, straight and circular conductors and solenoids.
- Identify regions of different magnetic field strength around a solenoid.

- Recall the right-hand screw and right-hand grip rules for relating current direction and magnetic field direction.
- Describe the effect on the magnetic field of changing the magnitude and direction of the current in a solenoid.

- Describe a demonstration to show that a force acts on a current-carrying conductor in a magnetic field, and recall that it increases with the strength of the field and the size of the current.
- Draw the resultant field pattern for a current-carrying conductor which is at right angles to a uniform magnetic field.
- Recall that a rectangular current-carrying coil experiences a couple in a uniform magnetic field.

- Recall that the size of the couple increases when the number of turns on the coil, the strength of the magnetic field or the current increases.

- Explain how a simple d.c. electric motor works.
- Describe experiments to show electromagnetic induction.
- Recall Faraday's explanation of electromagnetic induction, and state the factors affecting the magnitude of an induced e.m.f.
- Distinguish between d.c. and a.c,
- Draw a diagram of a simple a.c. generator and sketch a graph of its output.
- Describe the construction, and explain the principle of the transformer.
- Recall the transformer equation $Vs/Vp = Ns/Np$ and use it to solve problems,
- State that for an ideal transformer $Vp \times Ip = Vs \times Is$ and use the relation to solve problems.
- Explain why high voltage a.c. is used for transmitting electrical power.

P8 Atomic physics

Charges, atoms and electrons

There is evidence that we can picture an atom as being made up of a small central nucleus containing positively charged particles called **protons**, surrounded by an equal number of negatively charged **electrons**. The charges on a proton and an electron are equal and opposite so an atom as a whole is normally electrically neutral, i.e. has no net charge.

Hydrogen is the simplest atom with one proton and one electron (Figure P8.1). A copper atom has 29 protons in the nucleus and 29 surrounding electrons. Every nucleus except hydrogen also contains uncharged particles called **neutrons**.

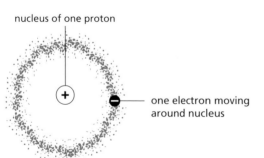

Figure P8.1 Hydrogen atom.

nucleus of one proton

one electron moving around nucleus

Protons and neutrons

We now believe as a result of other experiments, in some of which α particles and other high-speed particles were used as 'atomic probes', that atoms contain three basic particles – protons, neutrons and electrons.

A **proton** is a hydrogen atom minus an electron, i.e. a positive hydrogen ion. Its charge is equal in size but opposite in sign to that of an electron but its mass is about 2000 times greater.

A **neutron** is uncharged with almost the same mass as a proton.

Protons and neutrons are in the nucleus and are called **nucleons**. Together they account for the mass of the nucleus (and most of that of the atom); the protons account for its positive charge. These facts are summarised in Table P8.1.

In a neutral atom the number of protons equals the number of electrons surrounding the nucleus. Table P8.2 shows the particles in some atoms. Hydrogen is simplest with one proton and one

Table P8.1

Particle	Relative mass	Charge	Location
proton	1836	+e	in nucleus
neutron	1839	+0	in nucleus
electron	1	−e	outside nucleus

Table P8.2

	Hydrogen	Helium	Lithium	Oxygen	Copper
protons	1	2	3	8	29
neutrons	0	2	4	8	34
electrons	1	2	3	8	29

electron. Next is the inert gas helium with two protons, two neutrons and two electrons. The soft white metal lithium has three protons and four neutrons.

> The atomic or proton number Z of an atom is the number of protons in the nucleus.

The **atomic number** is also the number of electrons in the atom. The electrons determine the chemical properties of an atom and when the elements are arranged in order of atomic number in the Periodic Table, they fall into chemical families.

In general, $A = Z + N$, where N is the **neutron number** of the element.

Atomic **nuclei** are represented by symbols. Hydrogen is written as ^1_1H, helium as ^4_2He and lithium a ^7_3Li. In general atom X is written in nuclide notation as ^A_ZX, where A is the nucleon number and Z the proton number.

> The mass or nucleon number A of an atom is the number of nucleons (protons and neutrons) in the nucleus.

● Isotopes and nuclides

Isotopes of an element are atoms that have the same number of protons but different numbers of neutrons. That is, their proton numbers are the same but not their nucleon numbers.

Isotopes have identical chemical properties since they have the same number of electrons and occupy the same place in the Periodic Table. (In Greek, *isos* means same and *topos* means place.)

Few elements consist of identical atoms; most are mixtures of isotopes. Chlorine has two isotopes; one has 17 protons and 18 neutrons (i.e. $Z = 17$, $A = 35$) and is written $^{35}_{17}Cl$, the other has 17 protons and 20 neutrons (i.e. $Z = 17$, $A = 37$) and is written $^{37}_{17}Cl$. They are present in ordinary chlorine in the ratio of three atoms of $^{35}_{17}Cl$ to one atom of $^{37}_{17}Cl$, giving chlorine an average atomic mass of 35.5.

Hydrogen has three isotopes: ^1_1H with one proton, **deuterium** ^2_1D with one proton and one neutron and **tritium** ^3_1T with one proton and two neutrons. Ordinary hydrogen consists 99.99 per cent of ^1_1H atoms. Water made from deuterium is called 'heavy water' (D_2O); it has a density of $1.108\,g/cm^3$, it freezes at $3.8\,°C$ and boils at $101.4\,°C$.

Each form of an element is called a **nuclide**. Nuclides with the same Z number but different A numbers are isotopes. Radioactive isotopes are termed **radioisotopes** or **radionuclides**; their nuclei are unstable.

Rutherford–Bohr model

Shortly after Rutherford proposed his nuclear model of the atom, Bohr, a Danish physicist, developed it to explain how an atom emits light. He suggested that the electrons circled the nucleus at high speed, being kept in certain orbits by the electrostatic attraction of the nucleus for them. He pictured atoms as miniature solar systems. Figure P8.2 shows the model for three elements.

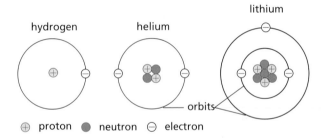

⊕ proton   ● neutron   ⊖ electron

Figure P8.2 Electron orbits.

Questions

1 Which one of the following statements is *not* true?
   A An atom consists of a tiny nucleus surrounded by orbiting electrons.
   B The nucleus always contains protons and neutrons, called nucleons, in equal numbers.
   C A proton has a positive charge, a neutron is uncharged and their mass is about the same.
   D An electron has a negative charge of the same size as the charge on a proton but it has a much smaller mass.
   E The number of electrons equals the number of protons in a normal atom.
2 A lithium atom has a nucleon (mass) number of 7 and a proton (atomic) number of 3.
   1 Its symbol is ^7_4Li.
   2 It contains three protons, four neutrons and three electrons.
   3 An atom containing three protons, three neutrons and three electrons is an isotope of lithium.
   Which statement(s) is (are) correct?
   A 1, 2, 3   B 1, 2   C 2, 3   D 1   E 3

● Radioactivity

The discovery of radioactivity in 1896 by the French scientist Becquerel was accidental. He found that uranium compounds emitted radiation that: **(i)** affected a photographic plate even when it was wrapped in black paper, and **(ii)** ionised a gas. Soon afterwards Marie Curie discovered the radioactive element radium. We now know that radioactivity arises from unstable nuclei which may occur naturally or be produced in reactors. Radioactive materials are widely used in industry, medicine and research.

We are all exposed to natural **background radiation** caused partly by radioactive materials in rocks, the air and our bodies, and partly by cosmic rays from outer space (see p.451).

● Ionising effect of radiation

A charged electroscope discharges when a lighted match or a radium source (**held in forceps**) is brought near the cap (Figures P8.3a and b).

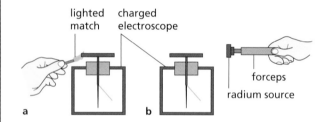

Figure P8.3

In the first case the flame knocks electrons out of surrounding air molecules leaving them as positively charged **ions**, i.e. air molecules which have lost one or more electrons (Figure P8.4); in the second case radiation causes the same effect, called **ionisation**. The positive ions are attracted to the cap if it is negatively charged; if it is positively charged the electrons are attracted. As a result in either case the charge on the electroscope is neutralised, i.e. it loses its charge.

Figure P8.4 Ionisation.

● Geiger–Müller (GM) tube

The ionising effect is used to detect radiation.

When radiation enters a **GM tube** (Figure P8.5), either through a thin end-window made of mica, or, if the radiation is very penetrating, through the wall, it creates argon ions and electrons. These are accelerated towards the electrodes and cause more ionisation by colliding with other argon atoms.

On reaching the electrodes, the ions produce a current pulse which is amplified and fed either to a **scaler** or a **ratemeter**. A scaler counts the pulses and shows the total received in a certain time. A ratemeter gives the counts per second (or minute), or **count-rate**, directly. It usually has a loudspeaker which gives a 'click' for each pulse.

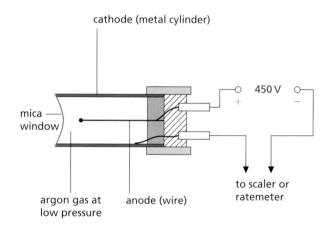

Figure P8.5 Geiger–Müller (GM) tube.

● Alpha, beta and gamma radiation

Experiments to study the penetrating power, ionising ability and behaviour of radiation in magnetic and electric fields show that a radioactive substance emits one or more of three types of radiation – called **alpha** (α), **beta** (β^- or β^+) and **gamma** (γ) rays.

Penetrating power can be investigated as in Figure P8.6 by observing the effect on the count-rate of placing one of the following in turn between the GM tube and the lead sheet:

- a sheet of thick paper (the radium source, lead and tube must be close together for this part)
- a sheet of aluminium 2 mm thick
- a further sheet of lead 2 cm thick.

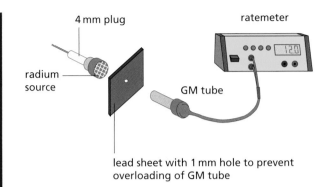

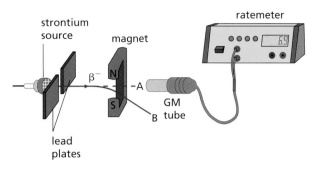

Figure P8.6 Investigating the penetrating power of radiation.

Radium (Ra-226) emits α-particles, β-particles and γ-rays. Other sources can be tried, such as americium, strontium and cobalt.

Alpha particles

These are stopped by a thick sheet of paper and have a range in air of only a few centimetres since they cause intense ionisation in a gas due to frequent collisions with gas molecules. They are deflected by electric and strong magnetic fields in a direction and by an amount which suggests they are helium atoms minus two electrons, i.e. helium ions with a double positive charge. From a particular substance, they are all emitted with the same speed (about 1/20th of that of light).

Americium (Am-241) is a pure α source.

Beta particles

These are stopped by a few millimetres of aluminium and some have a range in air of several metres. Their ionising power is much less than that of α-particles. As well as being deflected by electric fields, they are more easily deflected by magnetic fields. Measurements show that β⁻-particles are streams of **high-energy electrons**, like cathode rays, emitted with a range of speeds up to that of light. Strontium (Sr-90) emits β⁻-particles only.

The magnetic deflection of β⁻-particles can be shown as in Figure P8.7. With the GM tube at A and without the magnet, the count-rate is noted. Inserting the magnet reduces the count-rate but it increases again when the GM tube is moved sideways to B.

Figure P8.7 Demonstrating magnetic deflection of β⁻-particles.

Gamma rays

These are the most penetrating and are stopped only by many centimetres of lead. They ionise a gas even less than β-particles and are not deflected by electric and magnetic fields. They give interference and diffraction effects and are electromagnetic radiation travelling at the speed of light. Their wavelengths are those of very short X-rays, from which they differ only because they arise in atomic nuclei whereas X-rays come from energy changes in the electrons outside the nucleus.

Cobalt (Co-60) emits γ-rays and β⁻-particles but can be covered with aluminium to provide pure γ-rays.

Comparing alpha, beta and gamma radiation

In a collision, α-particles, with their relatively large mass and charge, have more of a chance of knocking an electron from an atom and causing ionisation than the lighter β-particles; γ-rays, which have no charge, are even less likely than β-particles to produce ionisation.

A GM tube detects β-particles and γ-rays and energetic α-particles; a charged electroscope detects only α-particles. All three types of radiation cause fluorescence.

The behaviour of the three kinds of radiation in a magnetic field is summarised in Figure P8.8a on the next page. The deflections (not to scale) are found from Fleming's left-hand rule, taking negative charge moving to the right as equivalent to positive (conventional) current to the left.

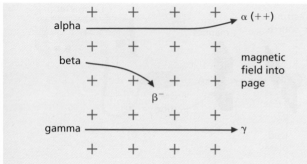

a deflection of α-, β- and γ-radiation in a magnetic field.

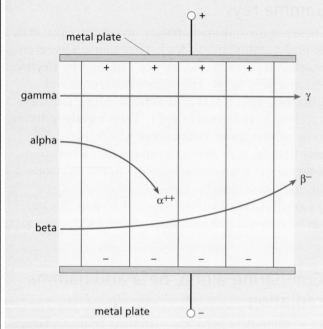

b deflection of α-, β- and γ-radiation in a uniform electric field.

Figure P8.8

Figure P8.8b shows the behaviour of α-particles, β⁻-radiation and γ-rays in a uniform electric field: α-particles are attracted towards the negatively charged metal plate, β⁻-particles are attracted towards the positively charged plate and γ-rays pass through undeflected.

● Radioactive decay

Radioactive atoms have unstable nuclei and, when they emit α-particles or β-particles, they **decay** into atoms of different elements that have more stable nuclei. These changes are spontaneous and cannot be controlled; also, it does not matter whether the material is pure or combined chemically with something else.

Alpha decay

An α-particle is a helium nucleus, having two protons and two neutrons, and when an atom decays by emission of an α-particle, its nucleon number decreases by four and its proton number by two. For example, when radium of nucleon number 226 and proton number 88 emits an α-particle, it decays to radon of nucleon number 222 and proton number 86. We can write:

the word equation:

radium → radon + α-particle

or in nuclide notation

$$^{226}_{88}\text{Ra} \rightarrow {}^{222}_{86}\text{Rn} + {}^{4}_{2}\text{He}$$

The values of A and Z must balance on both sides of the equation since nucleons and charge are conserved.

Beta decay

In β⁻ decay a neutron changes to a proton and an electron. The proton remains in the nucleus and the electron is emitted as a β⁻-particle. The new nucleus has the same nucleon number, but its proton number increases by one since it has one more proton.

We can write the word equation for the process occurring in the nucleus as:

neutron → proton + β⁻-particle'

Radioactive carbon, called carbon-14, decays by β⁻ emission to nitrogen:

The word equation for the change is:

carbon → nitrogen + β⁻-particle

or in nuclide notation:

$$^{14}_{6}\text{C} \rightarrow {}^{14}_{7}\text{N} + {}^{0}_{-1}\text{e}$$

Gamma emission

After emitting an α-particle, or β⁻- or β⁺-particles, some nuclei are left in an 'excited' state. Rearrangement of the protons and neutrons occurs and a burst of γ-rays is released.

We can write the word equation as:

excited nucleus → stable nucleus + gamma rays

Half-life

The **rate of decay** is unaffected by temperature but every radioactive element has its own definite decay rate, expressed by its **half-life**. This is the **average time for half the atoms in a given sample to decay**. It is difficult to know when a substance has lost all its radioactivity, but the time for its activity to fall to half its value can be found more easily.

Decay curve

The average number of disintegrations (i.e. decaying atoms) per second of a sample is its **activity**. If it is measured at different times (e.g. by finding the count-rate using a GM tube and ratemeter), a decay curve of activity against time can be plotted. The ideal curve for one element (Figure P8.9) shows that the activity decreases by the same fraction in successive equal time intervals. It falls from 80 to 40 disintegrations per second in 10 minutes, from 40 to 20 in the next 10 minutes, from 20 to 10 in the third 10 minutes and so on. The half-life is 10 minutes.

Half-lives vary from millionths of a second to millions of years. For radium it is 1600 years.

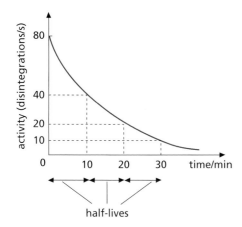

Figure P8.9 Decay curve.

Experiment to find the half-life of thoron

The half-life of the α-emitting gas **thoron** can be found as shown in Figure P8.10. The thoron bottle is squeezed three or four times to transfer some thoron to the flask (Figure P8.10a). The clips are then closed, the bottle removed and the stopper replaced by a GM tube so that it seals the top (Figure P8.10b).

When the ratemeter reading has reached its maximum and started to fall, the count-rate is noted every 15 s for 2 minutes and then every 60 s for

the next few minutes. (The GM tube is left in the flask for at least 1 hour until the radioactivity has decayed.)

A measure of the background radiation is obtained by recording the counts for a period (say 10 minutes) at a position well away from the thoron equipment. The count-rates in the thoron decay experiment are then corrected by subtracting the average background count-rate from each reading. A graph of the corrected count-rate against time is plotted and the half-life (52 s) estimated from it.

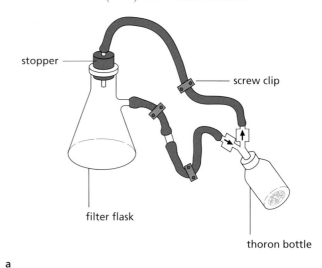

a

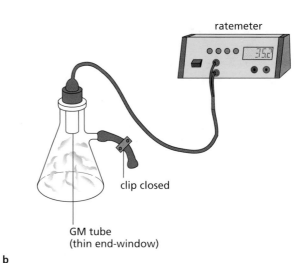

b

Figure P8.10

Random nature of decay

During the previous experiment it becomes evident that the count-rate varies irregularly: the loudspeaker of the ratemeter 'clicks' erratically, not at a steady rate. This is because radioactive decay is a **random** process, in that it is a matter of pure chance whether or not a particular atom will decay during a certain period of time. All we can say is that about half the atoms in a sample will decay during the half-life. We cannot say which atoms these will be, nor can we influence the process in any way. Radioactive emissions occur randomly over space and time.

● Uses of radioactivity

Radioactive substances, called **radioisotopes**, are now made in nuclear reactors and have many uses.

Thickness gauge

If a radioisotope is placed on one side of a moving sheet of material and a GM tube on the other, the count-rate decreases if the thickness increases. This technique is used to control automatically the thickness of paper, plastic and metal sheets during manufacture (Figure P8.11). Because of their range, β-emitters are suitable sources for monitoring the thickness of thin sheets but γ-emitters would be needed for thicker materials.

Flaws in a material can be detected in a similar way; the count-rate will increase where a flaw is present.

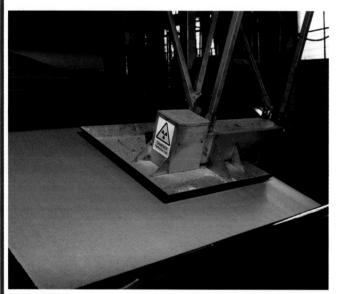

Figure P8.11 Quality control in the manufacture of paper using a radioactive gauge.

Tracers

The progress of a small amount of a weak radioisotope injected into a system can be 'traced' by a GM tube or other detector. The method is used in medicine to detect brain tumours and internal bleeding, in agriculture to study the uptake of fertilisers by plants, and in industry to measure fluid flow in pipes.

A tracer should be chosen whose half-life matches the time needed for the experiment; the activity of the source is then low after it has been used and so will not pose an ongoing radiation threat. For medical purposes, where short exposures are preferable, the time needed to transfer the source from the production site to the patient also needs to be considered.

Radiotherapy

Gamma rays from strong cobalt radioisotopes are used in the treatment of cancer.

Sterilisation

Gamma rays are used to sterilise medical instruments by killing bacteria. They are also used to 'irradiate' certain foods, again killing bacteria to preserve the food for longer. They are safe to use as no radioactive material goes into the food.

Archaeology

A radioisotope of carbon present in the air, carbon-14, is taken in by living plants and trees along with non-radioactive carbon-12. When a tree dies no fresh carbon is taken in. So as the carbon-14 continues to decay, with a half-life of 5700 years, the amount of carbon-14 compared with the amount of carbon-12 becomes smaller. By measuring the residual radioactivity of carbon-containing material such as wood, linen or charcoal, the age of archaeological remains can be estimated within the range 1000 to 50 000 years (Figure P8.12). See Worked example 2, on p.452.

The ages of rocks have been estimated in a similar way by measuring the ratio of the number of atoms of a radioactive element to those of its decay product in a sample. See Worked example 3, on p.452.

Figure P8.12 The year of construction of this Viking ship has been estimated by radiocarbon techniques to be AD 800.

● Dangers and safety

We are continually exposed to radiation from a range of sources, both natural ('background') and artificial, as indicated in Figure P8.13.

- Cosmic rays (high-energy particles from outer space) are mostly absorbed by the atmosphere and produce radioactivity in the air we breathe, but some reach the Earth's surface.
- Numerous homes, particularly in Scotland, are built from granite rocks that emit radioactive radon gas; this can collect in basements or well-insulated rooms if the ventilation is poor.
- Radioactive potassium-40 is present in food and is absorbed by our bodies.
- Various radioisotopes are used in certain medical procedures.
- Radiation is produced in the emissions from nuclear power stations and in fall-out from the testing of nuclear bombs; the latter produce strontium isotopes with long half-lives which are absorbed by bone.

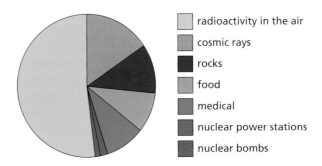

radioactivity in the air
cosmic rays
rocks
food
medical
nuclear power stations
nuclear bombs

Figure P8.13 Radiation sources.

We cannot avoid exposure to radiation in small doses but large doses can be dangerous to our health. The ionising effect produced by radiation causes damage to cells and tissues in our bodies and can also lead to the mutation of genes. The danger from α-particles is small, unless the source enters the body, but β- and γ-radiation can cause radiation burns (i.e. redness and sores on the skin) and delayed effects such as eye cataracts and cancer. Large exposures may lead to radiation sickness and death. The symbol used to warn of the presence of radioactive material is shown in Figure P8.14.

Figure P8.14 Radiation hazard sign.

The increasing use of radioisotopes in medicine and industry has made it important to find ways of disposing of radioactive waste safely. One method is to enclose the waste in steel containers which are then buried in concrete bunkers; possible leakage is a cause of public concern, as water supplies could be contaminated allowing radioactive material to enter the food chain.

The weak sources used at school should always be:

- **lifted with forceps**
- **held away from the eyes**
- **kept in their boxes when not in use**.

In industry, sources are handled by long tongs and transported in thick lead containers. Workers are protected by lead and concrete walls, and wear radiation dose badges that keep a check on the amount of radiation they have been exposed to over a period (usually one month). The badge contains several windows which allow different types of radiation to fall onto a photographic film; when the film is developed it is darkest where the exposure to radiation was greatest.

● Worked examples

1 A radioactive source has a half-life of 20 minutes. What fraction is left after 1 hour?

After 20 minutes, fraction left = 1/2
After 40 minutes, fraction left = 1/2 × 1/2 = 1/4
After 60 minutes, fraction left = 1/2 × 1/4 = 1/8

2 Carbon-14 has a half-life of 5700 years. A 10 g sample of wood cut recently from a living tree has an activity of 160 counts/minute. A piece of charcoal taken from a prehistoric campsite also weighs 10 g but has an activity of 40 counts/minute. Estimate the age of the charcoal.

After 1 × 5700 years the activity will be 160/2 = 80 counts per minute
After 2 × 5700 years the activity will be 80/2 = 40 counts per minute
The age of the charcoal is 2 × 5700 = 11 400 years

3 The ratio of the number of atoms of argon-40 to potassium-40 in a sample of radioactive rock is analysed to be 1 : 3. Assuming that there was no potassium in the rock originally and that argon-40 decays to potassium-40 with a half-life of 1500 million years, estimate the age of the rock. Assume there were N atoms of argon-40 in the rock when it was formed.

After 1×1500 million years there will be $N/2$ atoms of argon left and $N-(N/2)=N/2$ atoms of potassium formed, giving an Ar : K ratio of 1 : 1.

After $2 \times 1500 = 3000$ million years, there would be $(N/2)/2 = N/4$ argon atoms left and $N-(N/4)=3N/4$ potassium atoms formed, giving an Ar : K ratio of 1 : 3 as measured.
The rock must be about 3000 million years old.

Questions

3 Which type of radiation from radioactive materials
  a has a positive charge?
  b is the most penetrating?
  c consists of waves?
  d causes the most intense ionisation?
  e has the shortest range in air?
  f has a negative charge?

  g is easily deflected by a magnetic field?
  h is not deflected by an electric field?

4 In an experiment to find the half-life of radioactive iodine, the count-rate falls from 200 counts per second to 25 counts per second in 75 minutes. What is its half-life?

5 If the half-life of a radioactive gas is 2 minutes, then after 8 minutes the activity will have fallen to a fraction of its initial value. This fraction is
  A 1/4   B 1/6   C 1/8   D 1/16   E 1/32

Checklist

After studying Chapter P8 you should know and understand the following.

- Recall the charge, relative mass and location in the atom of protons, neutrons and electrons.
- Define the terms proton number (Z), neutron number (N) and nucleon number (A), and use the equation $A = Z + N$.
- Explain the terms isotope and nuclide and use symbols to represent them, e.g. $^{35}_{17}Cl$.
- Recall that the radiation emitted by a radioactive substance can be detected by its ionising effect.
- Recall the nature of α, β and γ radiation.
- Describe experiments to compare the range and penetrating power of α, β and γ radiation in different materials.
- Recall the ionising abilities of α, β and γ radiation and relate them to their ranges.

- Predict how α, β and γ radiation will be deflected in magnetic and electric fields.

- Recall that radioactivity is (a) a random process, (b) due to nuclear instability, (c) independent of external conditions.
- Understand the meaning of background radiation.
- Write word equations for radioactive decay and interpret them.

- Use nuclide notation in equations to show α and β decay.

- Define the term half-life.
- Describe an experiment from which a radioactive decay curve can be obtained.
- Show from a graph that radioactive decay processes have a constant half-life.
- Solve simple problems on half-life.

- Recall some uses of radioactivity.

- Discuss the dangers of radioactivity and safety precautions necessary.

The Periodic Table

Group

Key

atomic number
atomic symbol
name
relative atomic mass

I	II	III	IV	V	VI	VII	VIII
							2 **He** Helium 4
3 **Li** Lithium 7	4 **Be** Beryllium 9	5 **B** Boron 11	6 **C** Carbon 12	7 **N** Nitrogen 14	8 **O** Oxygen 16	9 **F** Fluorine 19	10 **Ne** Neon 20
11 **Na** Sodium 23	12 **Mg** Magnesium 24	13 **Al** Aluminium 27	14 **Si** Silicon 28	15 **P** Phosphorus 31	16 **S** Sulfur 32	17 **Cl** Chlorine 35.5	18 **Ar** Argon 40

1 **H** Hydrogen 1

19 **K** Potassium 39	20 **Ca** Calcium 40	21 **Sc** Scandium 45	22 **Ti** Titanium 48	23 **V** Vanadium 51	24 **Cr** Chromium 52	25 **Mn** Manganese 55	26 **Fe** Iron 56	27 **Co** Cobalt 59	28 **Ni** Nickel 59	29 **Cu** Copper 64	30 **Zn** Zinc 65	31 **Ga** Gallium 70	32 **Ge** Germanium 73	33 **As** Arsenic 75	34 **Se** Selenium 79	35 **Br** Bromine 80	36 **Kr** Krypton 84
37 **Rb** Rubidium 85	38 **Sr** Strontium 88	39 **Y** Yttrium 89	40 **Zr** Zirconium 91	41 **Nb** Niobium 93	42 **Mo** Molybdenum 96	43 **Tc** Technetium –	44 **Ru** Ruthenium 101	45 **Rh** Rhodium 103	46 **Pd** Palladium 106	47 **Ag** Silver 108	48 **Cd** Cadmium 112	49 **In** Indium 115	50 **Sn** Tin 119	51 **Sb** Antimony 122	52 **Te** Tellurium 128	53 **I** Iodine 127	54 **Xe** Xenon 131
55 **Cs** Caesium 133	56 **Ba** Barium 137	57-71 Lanthanoids	72 **Hf** Hafnium 178	73 **Ta** Tantalum 181	74 **W** Tungsten 184	75 **Re** Rhenium 186	76 **Os** Osmium 190	77 **Ir** Iridium 192	78 **Pt** Platinum 195	79 **Au** Gold 197	80 **Hg** Mercury 201	81 **Tl** Thallium 204	82 **Pb** Lead 207	83 **Bi** Bismuth 209	84 **Po** Polonium –	85 **At** Astatine –	86 **Rn** Radon –
87 **Fr** Francium –	88 **Ra** Radium –	89-103 Actinoids	104 **Rf** Rutherfordium –	105 **Db** Dubnium –	106 **Sg** Seaborgium –	107 **Bh** Bohrium –	108 **Hs** Hassium –	109 **Mt** Meitnerium –	110 **Ds** Darmstadtium –	111 **Rg** Roentgenium –	112 **Cn** Copernicium –		114 **Fl** Flerovium –		116 **Lv** livermorium –		

Lanthanoids

57 **La** lanthanum 139	58 **Ce** Cerium 140	59 **Pr** Praseodymium 141	60 **Nd** Neodymium 144	61 **Pm** Promethium –	62 **Sm** Samarium 150	63 **Eu** Europium 152	64 **Gd** Gadolinium 157	65 **Tb** Terbium 159	66 **Dy** Dysprosium 163	67 **Ho** Holmium 165	68 **Er** Erbium 167	69 **Tm** Thulium 169	70 **Yb** Ytterbium 173	71 **Lu** Lutetium 175

Actinoids

89 **Ac** actinium –	90 **Th** Thorium 232	91 **Pa** Protactinium 231	92 **U** Uranium 238	93 **Np** Neptunium –	94 **Pu** Plutonium –	95 **Am** Americium –	96 **Cm** Curium –	97 **Bk** Berkelium –	98 **Cf** Californium –	99 **Es** Einsteinium –	100 **Fm** Fermium –	101 **Md** Mendelevium –	102 **No** Nobelium –	103 **Lr** Lawrecium –

The volume of one mole of any gas is 24 dm^3 at room temperature and pressure (r.t.p.).

International hazard warning symbols

You will need to be familiar with these symbols when undertaking practical experiments in the laboratory.

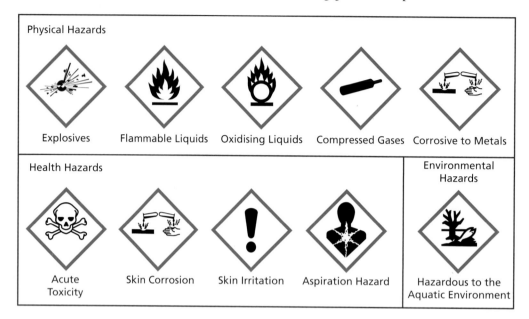

Additional experimental chemistry and qualitative analysis

● Objectives for experimental skills and investigations

The Cambridge IGCSE Combined Science and Co-ordinated Sciences syllabuses suggest that you should be able to:

1 know how to safely use techniques, apparatus and materials (including following a sequence of instructions where appropriate)
2 plan experiments and investigations
3 make and record observations, measurements and estimates
4 interpret and evaluate experimental observations and data
5 evaluate methods and suggest possible improvements.

You must take one of the following papers based on the criteria above:

● Paper 5 – Practical Test, or
● Paper 6 – Alternative to Practical (written paper).

The practical assessment is 20% of the available marks.

● Suggestions for practical work and assessment

The following list shows additional practical exercises that your teacher may either demonstrate or will supervise closely, both to support the assessment objectives given above and to enrich your study of chemistry. In addition, it should suggest plenty of opportunities for the enhancement and assessment of your practical skills.

The suggested list is neither exhaustive nor prescriptive: the actual selection of practical work, whether from this list or from elsewhere, has to be governed by local factors such as the facilities that you have available and safety considerations.

Safety

In the suggested additional practical exercises, materials are used which, although familiar in many cases, are of a potentially hazardous nature. To keep you safe you must:

● follow the instructions given to you by your teacher
● wear eye protection at all times
● wear disposable gloves in certain cases when requested to do so
● work tidily at all times
● check the hazard labels of any of the substances you are using and then take appropriate care and precautions.

Redox: The concept of redox, either in its elementary form (that is, as the loss or gain of oxygen) or as electron transfer, is a constant theme throughout the syllabus and the associated practical work. The list below suggests plenty of varied examples, designated by **R,** to reinforce the theory.

C1 The particulate nature of matter

Solids, liquids and gases

● A simple demonstration to illustrate the three states of matter and their interconversions – ice, water and steam.
● A demonstration of the compressibility of gases and the incompressibility of liquids by using a syringe to show that the volume of a gas (e.g. air) decreases with pressure whereas that of a liquid (e.g. water) does not.

Changes of state

● Measure the melting points of both a pure sample and an impure sample of a solid; this demonstrates that melting point is a means of assessing purity.
● Measure the temperature of melting ice, then repeat after adding salt to the ice.
● Measure the melting point of octadecanoic acid using a water bath, then repeat using a sample that is contaminated with a trace of salol (phenyl 2-hydroxybenzoate).
● Use a liquid paraffin bath or electrical heating apparatus to measure the melting point of an unknown compound and decide whether it is a pure sample.
● Boiling point as a criterion of purity. Use a test tube and thermometer to measure the boiling point of a suitable liquid. A simple example would involve heating calcium chloride solution in a test tube with a few anti-bumping granules. Note that the bulb of the thermometer must be in the liquid

itself to measure its boiling point (typically 102 °C in this case) and not in the vapour above the liquid (where it would register 100 °C).

Heating and cooling curves

- You should already be familiar with melting and boiling; your teacher may provide you with data so that you can construct and interpret these curves.

Diffusion

- Brownian motion can be demonstrated using pollen or smoke.
- An additional demonstration of gaseous diffusion is similar, but uses a gas-jar of hydrogen *above* a gas jar of carbon dioxide. Both gas-jars can be tested for the presence of carbon dioxide. It is preferable to set up this experiment twice, then, using the second set, hydrogen can be shown to be in both jars.
- Demonstrate the ammonia and hydrochloric acid experiment described in the text (Figure C1.9, p.182). This also illustrates the dependence of the rate of diffusion on the relative molecular mass of a gas, M_r.
- An alternative is an arrangement of manometer and porous pot which effectively compares the rate of diffusion of a gas with that of air. This can be used to show that carbon dioxide diffuses slower than air and hydrogen diffuses faster.

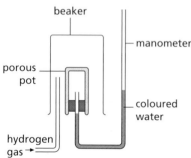

a The pressure inside the porous pot rises because hydrogen diffuses in faster than air diffuses out.

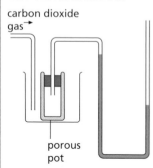

b The pressure inside the porous pot falls because air diffuses out faster than carbon dioxide diffuse in.

Figure A.1 Comparing the rate of diffusion of gases with that of air.

- Diffusion of a coloured solute in water. A large crystal of copper(II) sulfate is added to a measuring cylinder of water and is observed over several days.

C2 Experimental technique

Separating mixtures

- Illustrate the use of chromatography as a test of purity and an analytical tool. Suitable examples include coloured inks, food colouring, pigments from flowers or grass, metallic cations and identification of sugars.

At least one exercise should involve developing a chromatogram and at least one should involve the measurement of R_f values (p.188).

- Filtration used to separate a solid from a liquid (p.189).
- Crystallisation of impure benzoic acid. Benzoic acid is contaminated with a trace of a blue dye and then dissolved in the minimum amount of boiling water. Allow to cool and separate crystals by filtration. The blue colour will have disappeared or become fainter, showing that crystallisation has removed the impurity.
- Demonstrate simple distillation to separate a solvent from a solution (p.189).

C3 Atoms, elements, compounds

Reversible reactions

- Acid/base indicators colour changes on addition of dilute acid and dilute alkali.
- Action of heat on copper(II) sulfate-5-water followed by the careful addition of water to the solid product (p.193).
- Add dilute sodium hydroxide solution to a solution of a zinc, an aluminium salt. The hydroxide addition of dilute nitric acid the hydroxide will reappear, only to dissolve with the addition of more nitric acid.

$$\text{metallic cation} \underset{H^+}{\overset{OH^-}{\rightleftharpoons}} \text{metal hydroxide} \underset{H^+}{\overset{OH^-}{\rightleftharpoons}} \text{metallic anion}$$

Elements

- Display samples of as many elements as possible, either on information cards or on a copy of the Periodic Table. This is an effective observation exercise.
- Set up a circus of activities which includes both collecting data from computers or data books (e.g. melting and boiling points and density) and practical exercises on comparing electrical conductivities. These activities will illustrate the physical differences between metals and non-metals.

Compounds and mixtures

- Demonstrate the combination of elements to form compounds (chemical changes), for example magnesium and oxygen, iron and chlorine, hydrogen and oxygen, zinc and sulfur, carbon and oxygen, and aluminium and iodine.
- Demonstrate the iron and sulfur experiment described in the text (p.196).

Atoms

- Make up models of atoms to show the electron structure using pipe cleaners/wire and modelling clay (p.200).

Ionic bonding

- Look up the melting and boiling points of ionic compounds in data books.
- Show that most ionic compounds dissolve in water.
- Demonstrate that an ionic compound, potassium iodide or lithium chloride, conducts electricity in the molten state but not as a solid.

Covalent bonding

- Look up the melting and boiling points of simple covalent compounds in data books.
- Show that they are not good conductors of electricity in the liquid phase – demonstrate this with hexane, ethanol or phosphorus(III) chloride.
- Show that graphite is both soft and a good conductor of electricity (p.213).
- Use a glass cutter to illustrate the hardness of diamond (p.213).

C4 Stoichiometry

Moles and gases

- Measure the molar volume at rtp for hydrogen. Use a flask with a delivery tube and collect the gas over water in an inverted measuring cylinder or burette (Figure A.2). Put an excess of dilute hydrochloric acid, say $100\,cm^3$ of $20\,mol/dm^3$ acid, in the flask and add a piece of magnesium ribbon whose mass is known accurately and is about $0.10\,g$.
  (It is useful to measure the mass of a $10\,m$ length of ribbon and then the mass of a smaller length can be calculated.) Measure the volume of hydrogen collected in the measuring cylinder or burette.

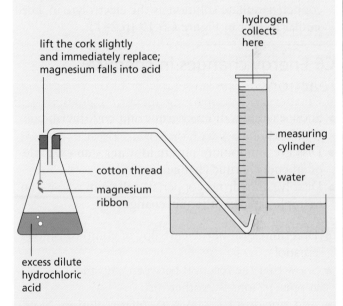

Figure A.2 Measuring the molar volume of a gas at rtp.

- Measure the molar volume at rtp for carbon dioxide. Repeat the experiment above, using a known mass of a carbonate and collecting the carbon dioxide in a syringe.

C5 Electricity and chemistry

- Introductory practical. Electrolytes only conduct in the liquid phase, either molten or in aqueous solution. Experiments can be carried out to illustrate the differences between strong, weak and non-electrolytes. Use a circuit similar to that in Figure C5.2 (p.231), but with an ammeter in preference to the lamp, and measure the

conductivity of a selection of liquids, for example sodium chloride solution, hydrochloric acid, sodium hydroxide solution, water, dilute ethanoic acid, aqueous ammonia, paraffin and ethanol.
- Electrolysis as decomposition, for example of copper chloride solution, zinc bromide solution, hydrochloric acid and acidified water. Include tests for chlorine, oxygen and hydrogen. **R**
- Electrolysis of aqueous solutions of the following using inert electrodes: sodium chloride, copper(II) sulfate, sodium sulfate and sodium hydroxide.

- Electrolysis of aqueous copper(II) sulfate using copper electrodes.

- Examples of electroplating, such as copper plating. Use an iron strip anode, a copper cathode and copper(II) sulfate solution as the electrolyte in a cell similar to that in Figure C5.19 (p.241).

C6 Energy changes in chemical reactions

- Show examples of exothermic and endothermic reactions.
- Dissolve ammonium nitrate in water – an example of an endothermic change.
- Dissolve anhydrous copper(II) sulfate in water – an example of an exothermic change.

- Determination of the enthalpy of combustion of ethanol.
- Show that the reaction between zinc and copper(II) ions is exothermic.
- Add zinc dust to copper(II) sulfate solution. Note the temperature of the solution before and after the addition of the zinc. Here chemical energy is transformed into heat energy.

C7 Chemical reactions

- Reaction of calcium carbonate and acid (Figure C7.4, p.248) – the effect of concentration and surface area.
- Reaction of sodium thiosulfate and acid (Figure C7.10, p.250) – the effect of concentration.
- Decomposition of hydrogen peroxide, catalysed by manganese(IV) oxide – the effect of concentration and mass of catalyst on the rate and on the volume of product.

First use a mixture of 2 cm³ of 20 vol hydrogen peroxide and 48 cm³ of water, with 0.2 g of manganese(IV) oxide. Then use a mixture of 4 cm³ of 20 vol hydrogen peroxide and 46 cm³ of water with 0.2 g of manganese dioxide. Finally use a mixture of 2 cm³ of 20 vol hydrogen peroxide and 48 cm³ of water with 0.4 g of manganese dioxide. Collect the oxygen over water in an inverted measuring cylinder or burette and obtain sets of readings of volume against time.
- Add a 2 cm length of magnesium ribbon to an excess of 2 mol/dm³ hydrochloric acid and measure the time taken for the metal to react. Repeat, with the same sized piece of magnesium but a different concentration of acid. (Another version of this experiment is to make temperature the variable and use hydrochloric acid at different temperatures.)
- Add a 2 cm length of magnesium ribbon to an excess of 2 mol/dm³ ethanoic acid. Measure the time taken for the metal to react and compare this result with the one above.
- Reaction of metal and acid – the effect of concentration and surface area on the reaction rate and on the volume of product. Collect the hydrogen and obtain data on the volume evolved against time. The apparatus used could be a flask with delivery tube and a gas syringe or burette.
A length of magnesium ribbon is suspended above excess acid and is allowed to fall into the acid as the timing starts.
The experiment could be repeated using different lengths of ribbon and different concentrations of acid. Also, a mass of magnesium powder equal to that of the ribbon could be suspended above the acid in a small tube.
- Identical mixtures of sodium thiosulfate solution and hydrochloric acid are used at different temperatures in the experiment described on p.250. The results illustrate how rate depends on temperature when the concentrations are kept constant.
- Add a few drops of washing-up liquid to 20 vol hydrogen peroxide. Divide this mixture into two portions and add manganese(IV) oxide to one portion. Compare the rate of decomposition of hydrogen peroxide in the two samples.

C8 Acids, bases and salts

Acids and alkalis

- With simple indicators, find the acid colour, the alkaline colour and the neutral colour. Hold the acid tube and the alkaline tube up to a light together and look through both to see the neutral colour.
- Dilution experiments using universal indicator and 0.1 mol/dm³ solutions of hydrochloric acid, sodium hydroxide, ethanoic acid and ammonia.
- These will establish the pH scale and promote an understanding of the distinction between strong and weak electrolytes.

Formation of salts

- Reactions of a typical acid with metals. Use hydrochloric and/or sulfuric acid with magnesium, aluminium, zinc, iron and copper. **R**
- Reactions of typical acids with bases and carbonates. Use a selection of alkalis, insoluble bases and carbonates with hydrochloric, sulfuric and nitric acids.
- Small-scale preparation of a salt from a metal – magnesium sulfate-7-water (p.258).
- Preparation of a salt by titration – sodium chloride or sodium sulfate-10-water (p.259).
- Preparation of a salt from an acid and an insoluble base – copper(II) sulfate-5-water (p.260).

- Preparation of a number of insoluble salts by precipitation on a test-tube scale – an exercise in practical skills, observation, recording and writing equations.
- One formal preparation of an insoluble salt, such as lead iodide, to include filtering, washing and drying (p.260).

Amphoteric hydroxides and oxides

- Hydroxides are classified as basic or amphoteric. The qualitative exercises above will provide a practical basis for the underpinning theory. A useful extension exercise is to provide unknown cations in solution and for the students to ascertain if their hydroxides are basic or amphoteric.

- Another informative practical involves adding dilute acid dropwise to an aluminate or zincate and observing the changes in reverse.

$$Al^{3+} \underset{H^+}{\overset{OH^-}{\rightleftharpoons}} Al(OH)_3 \underset{H^+}{\overset{OH^-}{\rightleftharpoons}} Al(OH)_4^-$$

- Oxides are classified as basic, acidic, neutral or amphoteric. An exercise with unknown oxides is conducted using the following tests:
  - Does the oxide dissolve in water? If so, measure the pH.
  - Do the insoluble oxides react with 4 mol/dm³ nitric acid?
  - Do the insoluble oxides react with 4 mol/dm³ sodium hydroxide?

Identifying metal ions

- Reactions of cations in aqueous solution with sodium hydroxide – Fe^{2+}, Fe^{3+}, Cu^{2+}, Ca^{2+}, Zn^{2+}. An excess of sodium hydroxide solution is added slowly to a small volume of the solution containing the cation. This is an exercise in observation, organisational and recording skills and in the ability to write chemical equations – word, molecular and ionic (p.261).
- Reactions of the same cations with aqueous ammonia. This is essentially a repeat of the exercise above but with less emphasis on equation writing (p.261).
- Identification of unknown cations using sodium hydroxide solution and aqueous ammonia (p.261).

C9 The Periodic Table

Group I – the alkali metals

- Lithium, sodium and potassium are soft metals and good conductors of electricity. Find the densities and melting points of these metals using data books.
- The metals are burnt in air or oxygen and then it is shown that their oxides are alkaline. Using a deflagrating spoon, the hot metal is placed into a gas jar of oxygen, the colour of the flame is noted and the pH of the white powder formed is measured.
- The reactions of lithium, sodium and potassium with cold water can be demonstrated to show that alkaline solutions are formed and to illustrate the difference in their reactivities.
- Sodium is burnt in chlorine to demonstrate the formation of sodium chloride.

Group VII – the halogens

- Investigate their physical properties by inspection and using data books.

- Demonstrate their displacement reactions. **R**
  Add chlorine water to potassium bromide solution.
  Add chlorine water to potassium iodide solution.
  Add bromine water to potassium iodide solution.

- Demonstrate the formation of halides. Use small quantities in all of these reactions, which must be performed in an efficient fume cupboard.

Metals

- Most metals react with dilute acids. Add a small piece of a metal to dilute hydrochloric acid and test for hydrogen. Use magnesium, aluminium, zinc, iron and copper.
- Differences in the physical properties of the transition elements, such as melting points and densities, can be established from data books.
- Transition metals react with oxygen to form insoluble oxides that are not alkaline. The reactions of these metals with acids will illustrate their lower reactivity.

C10 – Metals

Typical reactions of metals

- Reaction of metals with dilute acids (p.279). **R**
- Reaction of metals with air and oxygen (p.280). **R**
- Reaction of metals with cold water or steam (p.280). **R**

Competition reactions

- Reduction of metal oxides by other metals. Demonstrate the Thermit reaction and the reactions between the metals magnesium, zinc, iron and copper and their oxides. This will establish an order of reactivity for these metals. Some of these reactions are very violent so the use of small quantities and a rehearsal before the class demonstration are essential. **R**
- Reduction of metal oxides by methane/hydrogen. It is safer to use methane, which is passed over heated copper oxide. **R**
- Metal/metal displacement reactions in aqueous solution. Clean pieces of a metal are added to the aqueous nitrate of another metal. The students

look for evidence of displacement and so establish an order of reactivity. Suitable metals are magnesium, zinc, lead, copper and silver. **R**

C11 Air and water

Water

- Tests to show the presence of water using cobalt chloride paper and anhydrous copper(II) sulfate.
- Tests to show that water is pure: it melts at $0\,^{\circ}C$ or boils at $100\,^{\circ}C$.

Air

- Demonstrate how to find the percentage of oxygen in the air using large gas syringes and passing air over heated copper powder.

Rusting of iron

- Experiment on rusting as described in the text (Figure C11.11, p.299). **R**

- Set up a demonstration cell with two iron electrodes connected through a voltmeter and bubble oxygen onto one electrode. From the polarity of the cell, students can deduce the direction of the electron flow and analyse the cell reactions in terms of electron transfer. **R**
- Set up a zinc/iron cell to demonstrate sacrificial protection. Analyse the cell reactions that are taking place as above. **R**

Carbon dioxide

- Demonstrate that carbon and carbon-containing compounds form carbon dioxide on combustion. Burn a variety of materials and test for carbon dioxide with limewater. Suitable materials include a candle, wood shavings, charcoal, paraffin.
- Reactions of typical dilute acids with carbonates. Use a selection of different carbonates, e.g. sodium, calcium and copper with hydrochloric and sulfuric acid.

Ammonia gas

- Demonstrate laboratory preparation of ammonia (Figure C11.22, p.306).
- Show that ammonia is a base. Neutralise dilute acids by adding dilute aqueous ammonia to dilute acids in the presence of universal indicator.

- Precipitation of metal hydroxides – see Chapter C8 (p.261).
- Test for the ammonium ion (p.262).

- **Reversible reactions** such as those shown for Chapter C3 (p.293).

C12 Sulfur

- Demonstrate the burning of a small amount of sulfur in air or oxygen. Show that an acidic gas is formed.

- Demonstration of the preparation of sulfur trioxide. Pass dry oxygen and sulfur dioxide over heated platinised mineral wool. Collect sulfur trioxide as a solid in a cooled receiver.
- Demonstration of the reaction of sulfur trioxide with water – great care is needed. Test the solution to show that it is acidic (using both universal indicator and magnesium powder), and that it contains sulfate ions (by adding acidified barium chloride solution).

C13 Carbonates

- Heat a piece of calcium carbonate strongly. Allow it to cool and carefully add water dropwise. Then add excess water and filter. Keep the filtrate, a solution of calcium hydroxide. Make carbon dioxide by adding an acid to calcium carbonate. Bubble this gas through the previously prepared calcium hydroxide solution until no further change is observed. Boil the resulting solution of calcium hydrogencarbonate.
- Reaction of dilute acids with a selection of carbonates (see Chapter C8 p.259).

C14 Organic chemistry

- Demonstrate combustion of some alkanes. Use a Bunsen burner to show complete and incomplete combustion of methane. Burn a range of alkanes to show the variation in ease of ignition – pentane and hexane are highly flammable but liquid paraffin and paraffin wax need pre-heating and/or a wick.

- Demonstrate thermal cracking of liquid paraffin by passing over heated broken porcelain.

- Demonstrate the reaction of alkenes with bromine water– test for unsaturation (p.325).

Alcohols

- Add ethanol to water to show that the two liquids are miscible.
- Combustion of ethanol in a small spirit lamp to demonstrate that it burns with a small blue flame.
- Show examples of ethanol as a solvent, e.g. perfume.

- Making ethanol by fermentation (Figure C14.19, p.326).

Condensation polymers

- Demonstrate the 'nylon rope trick'. The diamine, 1,6-diaminohexane, is dissolved in water to which some sodium carbonate has been added. A solution of a diacid chloride, adipoyl chloride, in cyclohexane is added and a nylon thread can be pulled from the interface between the two phases.

● Notes on qualitative analysis

The branch of chemistry that deals with the identification of elements or grouping of elements present in a sample is called **qualitative chemical analysis**, or **qualitative analysis** for short. It does not deal with anything to do with quantities.

The techniques employed in qualitative analysis vary in their complexity, depending on the nature of the sample under investigation. In some cases it is only necessary to confirm the presence of certain elements or groups for which specific chemical tests, or 'spot' tests, applicable directly to the sample, may be available. More often, the sample is a complex mixture, and a systematic analysis must be made in order that all the component parts may be identified. Often, the first simple stages of qualitative analysis require no apparatus at all. Things like colour and smell can be observed without any need for apparatus.

The following summary collects together information from throughout the book which would allow you to carry out qualitative analysis.

A preliminary examination of the substance will give you a start. The appearance or smell of a substance can often indicate what it might contain (see Table A1).

Table A1 Deductions that can be made from a substance's appearance or smell

Observation on substance	Indication
black powder	carbon, or contains O^{2-} ions (as in CuO), or S^{2-} ions (as in CuS)
pale green crystals	contains Fe^{2+} ions (as in iron(II) salts)
blue or blue-green crystals	contains Cu^{2+} ions (as in copper(II) salts)
yellow-brown crystals	contains Fe^{3+} ions (as in iron(III) salts)
smell of ammonia	contains NH_4^+ ions (as in ammonium salts)

Flame colours

If a clean nichrome wire is dipped into a metal compound and then held in the hot part of a Bunsen flame, the flame can become coloured (Figure A3). Certain metal ions may be detected in their compounds by observing their flame colours (Table A2).

Table A2 Characteristic flame colours for some metal ions

Metal ion	Flame colour
lithium (Li^+)	red
sodium (Na^+)	yellow
potassium (K^+)	lilac
copper(II) (Cu^{2+})	blue-green

Figure A3 The green colour is characteristic of copper.

Tests for anions and cations

It is possible to identify various anions and cations by the use of a variety of chemical reagents you have studied in the text. Tables A3 and A4 show the particular tests and the results of these tests with particular anions and cations.

Table A3 Tests for anions

Anion	Test	Test result
carbonate (CO_3^{2-})	add dilute acid	effervescence, carbon dioxide produced
chloride (Cl^-) [in solution]	acidify with dilute nitric acid, then add aqueous silver nitrate	white ppt.
bromide (Br^-) [in solution]	acidify with dilute nitric acid, then add aqueous silver nitrate	cream ppt.
nitrate (NO_3^-) [in solution]	add aqueous sodium hydroxide, then aluminium foil; warm carefully	ammonia produced
sulfate (SO_4^{2-}) [in solution]	acidify, then add aqueous barium nitrate	white ppt.

Table A4 Tests for aqueous cations

Cation	Effect of aqueous sodium hydroxide	Effect of aquous ammonia
ammonium (NH_4^+)	ammonia produced on warming	
calcium (Ca^{2+})	white ppt., insoluble in excess	no ppt. or very slight white ppt.
copper (Cu^{2+})	light blue ppt., insoluble in excess	light blue ppt., soluble in excess, giving a dark blue solution
iron(II) (Fe^{2+})	green ppt., insoluble in excess	green ppt., insoluble in excess
iron (III) (Fe^{3+})	red-brown ppt., insoluble in excess	red-brown ppt., insoluble in excess
excess zinc (Zn^{2+})	white ppt., soluble in excess, giving a colourless solution	white ppt., soluble in excess, giving a colourless solution

Tests for gases

Table A5 shows the common gases which may be produced during qualitative analysis and tests which can be used to identify them. These tests are used in conjunction with the tests shown above.

Table A5 Tests for gases

Gas	Test and test result
ammonia (NH_3)	turns damp, red litmus paper blue
carbon dioxide (CO_2)	turns limewater milky
chlorine (Cl_2)	bleaches damp litmus paper
hydrogen (H_2)	'pops' with a lighted splint
oxygen (O_2)	relights a glowing splint

● Questions to help your understanding

1 For each of the following pairs of substances, describe a possible test you would carry out to distinguish between them.
   a Sodium chloride and sodium bromide
   b Iron(II) sulfate and copper(II) sulfate
   c Potassium chloride and sodium chloride
   d Zinc chloride and calcium chloride

Revision and exam-style questions

● Combined Science

Biology

1 a Figure 1.1 shows what happens when a plant is placed near a window where bright light is coming from one side.

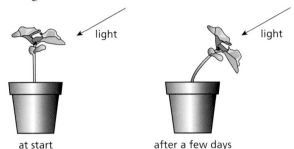

Figure 1.1

  i Name the response shown by the plant. [1]

  ii Explain why the response shown in Figure 1.1 is an advantage to the plant. [2]

  iii Using the information in Figure 1.1 name **two** characteristics of living things shown by this plant. [2]

b A student carries out an experiment to find out more about plant responses. He uses simple shoots and light coming from one side. The results are shown in Figure 1.2.

at the start	after a few days
light shoot **X**	light shoot **X**
foil light shoot **Y**	foil light shoot **Y**
tip removed light shoot **Z**	tip removed light shoot **Z**

Figure 1.2

  i Describe the results shown in Figure 1.2. [2]

  ii Suggest a possible conclusion about the control of plant responses in the shoots. Explain your answer. [2]

c Animals are able to respond to situations by secreting the hormone adrenaline. Adrenaline is secreted into the blood when an athlete starts to run a race. Suggest how this helps the athlete to run fast. [2]

(Cambridge IGCSE Combined Science 0653 Paper 22 Q7 Nov 2014)

2 a A student is looking at a sample of blood using a microscope. Blood has four main components. These are labelled **A** to **D** in Figure 2.1.

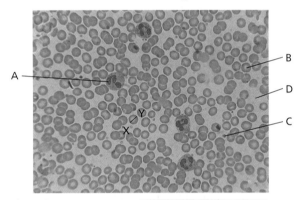

Figure 2.1

  i Name the components **A** to **D** in Figure 2.1. [4]

  ii Measure the length of the line **X–Y** in Fig. 2.1 in millimetres.
actual diameter_____ mm [1]

  iii The magnification of the photograph in Figure 2.1 is ×1000. Use this information and your measurement in **a ii** to calculate the actual diameter in millimetres of the component with the line **X–Y** in Figure 2.1. Show your working.
actual diameter = _____ mm [2]

b Some students investigate the effect of physical activity on pulse rate.
  • They record their pulse as the number of beats in 15 seconds.
  • They each jog on a treadmill for 5 minutes and immediately record their pulse again as the number of beats for 15 seconds.

The students' results are shown in Table 2.1.

Table 2.1

recording	average number of beats in 15 seconds	average heart rate in beats per minutes
before jogging	17	
after jogging	35	

    i Complete Table 2.1 calculating the average pulse rate in beats per minute. [1]

    ii Suggest why the pulse rate changes after jogging. [1]

    ii Explain why this method is more reliable than just one student using their own pulse rate. [1]

(Cambridge IGCSE Combined Science 0653 Paper 61 Q4 May 2015)

3 a Most of the chemicals in living things are compounds made from two or more elements chemically joined together. Choose words from the list of elements below to complete the sentences. Each word may be used once, more than once or not at all.

    carbon   **hydrogen**   **magnesium**
    nitrogen   **oxygen**   **potassium**
    phosphorus   **sulfur**

    i The elements contained in carbohydrates are _____ , _____ and _____ . [1]

    ii The elements in fats are _____ , _____ and _____ . [1]

b Figure 3.1 shows an animal cell.

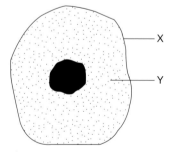

    Figure 3.1

    i Name the parts of the cell shown by **X** and **Y** on Figure 3.1. [2]

    ii One function of a cell is to carry out respiration, which needs a constant supply of oxygen. Outline how oxygen gets from the alveoli of the lungs to a muscle cell. [2]

c Energy is released by respiration in cells. Explain why the rate of respiration increases in some cells during exercise. [1]

d Food stores in the body are broken down by respiration to release energy during exercise. Some people exercise when they are trying to lose weight.

Table 3.1 shows the approximate energy needed for a person of body mass 70 kg to do 30 minutes of different types of exercise.

Table 3.1

type of exercise	energy needed for 30 minutes of exercise/kJ
cycling	850
golf	670
jogging	1260
swimming	830
walking	580

Sarbjit and Anna each have a body mass of 70 kg. They both exercise for 90 minutes. During this time they do 30 minutes each of three different exercises. Calculate the total energy needed for each girl's exercise, as follows.

    i Sarbjit did jogging, swimming and golf.
    Total energy needed = _____ kJ
    Anna did cycling, walking and swimming
    Total energy needed = _____ kJ [1]

    ii State and explain which girl's exercises were more effective for losing weight. [2]

    iii Suggest **one** reason why the energy values given in Table 3.1 cannot be exactly the same for everyone doing the exercises. [1]

(Cambridge IGCSE Combined Science 0653 Paper 21 Q2 May 2015)

4 Milk is a liquid produced by cows and other mammals, on which they feed their young.
Table 4.1 shows the mass of some of the substances in 100 g samples of milk from two mammals.

Table 4.1

substance	cow's milk	water-buffalo's milk
protein/g	3.2	4.5
fat/g	3.9	8.0
carbohydrate/g	4.8	4.9
calcium/mg	120	195

a Which substance in Table 4.1 is present in the samples of milk in the smallest quantity? [1]

b Suggest which substance, **not** shown in Table 4.1, is present in the samples of milk in the largest quantity. [1]

c Explain why both cow's milk and water-buffalo's milk produce a violet colour when tested with biuret solution. [1]
d Predict the colour you would see if you added iodine solution to cow's milk. Explain your answer. [2]
e List the components of milk, shown in Table 4.1, that provide energy. [1]
f Explain **one** way in which drinking water-buffalo's milk might be better for a person's health than drinking cow's milk. [2]
(Cambridge IGCSE Combined Science 0653 Paper 21 Q5 May 2013)

5 a Figure 5.1 shows how the emission gases from a power station can lead to the formation of acid rain.

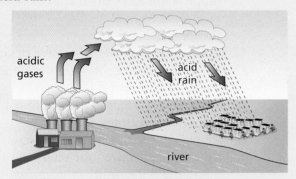

Figure 5.1

i State how the acidic gases are produced in the power station. [1]
ii The water in the river becomes acidic. Describe how this could have resulted from the power station's activities. [2]
b A scientist is concerned about the acidity of the river and the effect it might have on living organisms. The scientist found ten species of animal that live in local rivers. He looked up how many of these species were able to live in water of different pH values. The results are shown in Figure 5.2.

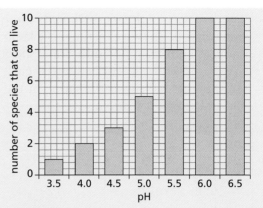

Figure 5.2

The pH of the river near the factory varies between pH 4.5 and 6.0.
i Suggest **two** reasons why the pH of the river varies. [2]
ii Use the information in Figure 5.2 to find how many of the species studied would be able to survive the changes in pH of the river. Explain your answer. [2]
iii The acid in the water may enter the cells of the animals living in the river. Suggest how this may affect the enzymes in their cells. Explain your answer. [2]
(Cambridge IGCSE Combined Science 0653 Paper 32 Q9 Nov 2014)

6 Figure 6.1 shows what happens when a plant is placed near a window where bright light is coming from one side.

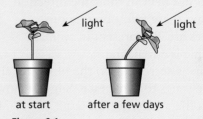

Figure 6.1

a Name the response shown by the plant. [1]
b The response shown in Figure 6.1 is caused by plant hormones called auxins which are produced at the tip of the shoot of the plant.

A student sets up three experiments using young shoots. In two experiments a lamp produces light from one side. Some shoots have pieces of plastic inserted into their stems. Figure 6.2 shows the shoots at the start and after a few days.

at the start	after a few days
light ← shoot X	light ← shoot X
light ← plastic shoot Y	light ← plastic shoot Y
in the dark plastic shoot Z	in the dark plastic shoot Z

Figure 6.2

i) Explain fully what causes the response shown by shoot **X**. [3]

ii) Explain why there is no response shown by shoot **Y**. [1]

iii) Shoot **Z** has grown less than shoot **X** but has bent in the same direction. Explain these **two** observations. [2]

c Hormones are also present in animals. An example is adrenaline. Adrenaline is secreted into the blood when an athlete starts to run a race. Suggest how this helps the athlete to run fast. [2]

(Cambridge IGCSE Combined Science 0653 Paper 32 Q7 Nov 2014)

7 a Vitamins are needed in small quantities as part of a balanced diet. One vitamin is vitamin C.

i State what is meant by the term *balanced diet*. [1]

ii Explain why we need vitamin C in our diet. [1]

iii Suggest why vitamin C does **not** need to be digested. [2]

b Table 7.1 gives details about the vitamin C content of some fruits.

Table 7.1

fruit	mass of vitamin C in 100 g fruit/mg	mass of vitamin C in an average portion/mg
Apple	6	8
Kiwifruit	98	74
Mango	28	57
Orange	53	70
Watermelon	10	27

The recommended daily allowance (RDA) of vitamin C for humans is 60 mg.

i State which of the fruits listed in Table 7.1 provide the RDA of vitamin C in just one portion. Explain your answer. [2]

ii Calculate the mass of mango needed to supply a full RDA of vitamin C. Show your working.

answer = _____ g [2]

c Citrus fruits provide a good source of vitamin C. However, many of them are weakly acidic.

i Explain why the acid in the citrus fruits could be harmful for teeth if a lot of fruit is eaten. [1]

ii Describe what a person can do to reduce the effects on the teeth of eating the acidic fruit. [1]

(Cambridge IGCSE Combined Science 0653 Paper 23 Q4 Nov 2015)

8 Figure 8.1 shows part of a section across a root from a radish plant, photographed through a microscope.

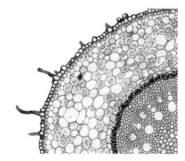

Figure 8.1

a On Figure 8.1, use a label line to label a root hair cell. [1]

b Root hair cells absorb substances from the soil. Name **two** substances that root hair cells absorb from the soil. [2]

c A complete radish plant was placed with the lower part of the root standing in water. A soluble red dye was added to the water. After a while, the veins in the leaves of the radish plant became red.

i Name the tissue in the radish plant through which the coloured water was transported from the roots to the leaves. [1]

ii On Figure 8.1, write the letter **A** to show the position of this tissue in the root. [1]

d i The cells in the radish root are plant cells. Complete Table 8.1 to show which structures are present in plant cells and which are present in animal cells.
Use a tick (✓) to show that the structure is present. Use a cross (✗) to show that the structure is not present.
You should place either a tick or a cross in every space in the table. [4]

Table 8.1

structure	plant cells	animal cells
cell membrane		
cell wall		
nucleus		
vacuole containing sap		

ii Would you expect the cells in the radish root to contain chloroplasts? Explain your answer. [1]

(Cambridge IGCSE Combined Science 0653 Paper 21 Q6 May 2012)

9 A student investigates plant transport systems using a celery stalk and coloured water. He cuts a piece of celery stalk and places it into some coloured water for five minutes with the freshly cut end downwards as shown in Figure 9.1.

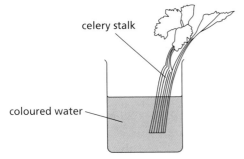

Figure 9.1

After five minutes he removes the stalk from the coloured water and cuts a slice from the end. Figure 9.2 shows what the cross section looks like.

Figure 9.2

a i Make a pencil drawing of the piece of celery stalk in Figure 9.2 to show the shape of the outline. Label **two** of the stained areas.

ii Name the tissue that has become coloured and state what can be concluded about its function. [2]

b The student crushes a piece of the celery with distilled water using a pestle and mortar.
- He divides the mixtures between three test-tubes.
- To one test-tube he adds an equal amount of Benedict's solution and then places it in a hot water-bath for about five minutes.
- To a second test-tube he adds biuret solution.
- To the third test-tube he adds iodine solution. His observations are shown in Table 9.1. Complete Table 9.1 by writing a conclusion for each of the three tests. [3]

Table 9.1

test	observation	conclusion
Benedict's solution	orange	
biuret solution	blue	
iodine solution	orange	

c Plan an experiment based on the method described above, to investigate the effect of temperature on the speed of movement of the coloured water in pieces of celery stalk. [3]

(Cambridge ICGSE Combined Science 0653 Paper 61 Q1 May 2015)

10 a Figure 10.1 shows the human gas exchange system.

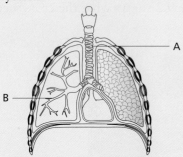

Figure 10.1

Name structures **A** and **B**. [2]

b Figure 10.2 shows an alveolus where exchange takes place in the lungs. Describe **two** features of the alveolus visible in Figure 10.2 that adapt it for gaseous exchange. [2]

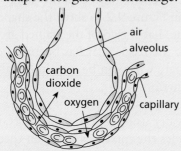

Figure 10.2

c A student investigates his breathing before and after exercise. He measures the number of breaths taken during one minutes. He also measures the average volume of one breath during this minute. His results are shown in Table 10.1.

Table 10.1

	number of breaths per minute	average volume of one breath/ dm³	total volume of air breathed per minute/dm³
at rest	20		10
immediately after exercise	35	1.2	

i Calculate:
the average volume of one breath at rest
volume= _____ dm³
the total volume of air breathed per minute immediately after exercise.
volume = _____ dm³ [2]

ii Explain fully why the changes in breathing rate and volume (depth) are needed by the body during exercise. [3]

(Cambridge IGCSE Combined Science 0653 Paper 32 Q3 Nov 2014)

11 Figure 11.1 shows the human gas exchange system.

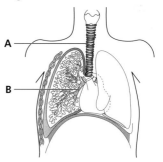

Figure 11.1

a Name structures **A** and **B**. [2]

b Table 11.1 shows the differences in the composition of inspired and expired air.

Table 11.1

gas	percentage in inspired air	percentage in expired air
nitrogen	78	
oxygen	21	17
carbon dioxide	0.04	4
noble gases	1	

i Complete Table 11.1. [1]
ii Name **one** noble gas that is present in air. [1]

(Cambridge IGCSE Combined Science 0653 Paper 21 Q8 a and b (i) & (ii) May 2013)

12 a Figure 12.1 shows the human gas exchange system.

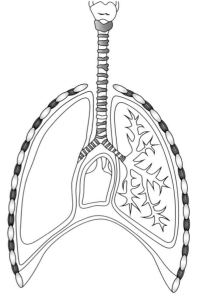

Figure 12.1

On Figure 12.1, draw label lines with names to show:
the larynx,
the trachea,
a bronchus. [3]

b Some people suffer from asthma which affects the bronchioles of the gas system. Figure 12.2 shows cross-sections of a normal bronchiole and a bronchiole of a person who has asthma. The airflow towards the alveoli is reduced if a person has asthma. Describe **two** features visible in Figure 12.2 which could reduce the airflow in the bronchiole of the person suffering from asthma. [2]

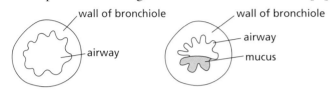

normal bronchiole   bronchiole of a person with asthma

Figure 12.2

c A study is carried out to compare the breathing of people with asthma with the breathing of healthy people. The volumes of air inhaled in one minute are measured and an average is calculated for both groups. Both groups of people are tested while resting.

Results
average volume inhaled by a healthy person
= 5.8 dm³ minute
average volume inhaled by a person with asthma = 12.5 dm³ minute.

i Calculate the average percentage of **extra** air the person with asthma inhales per minute compared with a healthy person. Show your working. answer = _____% [2]

ii Suggest two ways in which the breathing of an asthmatic person is likely to be different from a normal person's breathing in order to inhale a greater volume of air. [2]

(Cambridge IGCSE Combined Science 0653 Paper 23 Q1 Nov 2015)

13 a Figure 13.1 shows part of a food web in a forest ecosystem.

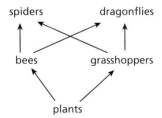

Figure 13.1

i Plants are the producers in this food web. Define the term *producer*. [2]

ii Name **one** organism in the food web that is a carnivore. [1]

iii What do the arrows in the food web represent? [1]

b The food web shows that bees depend on plants. Some flowering plants also depend on bees and other insects to help them to reproduce.

i Complete the sentences, using words from the list.

anthers   asexual   diploid   haploid
ovary   petals   sexual   stigma

Flowers are organs in which _____ reproduction takes place.
Pollen grains are made in the _____.
During pollination, insects carry pollen grains from one flower to another. The pollen grains are transferred to the _____. [3]

ii After they have been pollinated, flowers produce seeds. List **two** environmental conditions that all seeds need for germination. [2]

(Cambridge IGCSE Combined Science 0653 Paper 22 Q4 Nov 2012)

14 Figure 14.1 is a photograph of a flower in section.

Figure 14.1

a i Make a pencil drawing of this flower to show the male and female parts and the petals. [2]

ii On your drawing, **label** a carpel and a stamen. [2]

b i Measure the line **X–Y** on Figure 14.1 in mm. [1]

ii Measure the length of the same part on your drawing in mm. [1]

c Use these two measurements to calculate the magnification of your drawing. Show your working. [1]

d On your drawing, mark with a **Z** the structure that receives pollen during pollination. [1]

e Describe the procedure you would use if you wanted to examine a sample of pollen from this flower. [2]

(Cambridge IGCSE Combined Science 0653 Paper 63 Q1 May 2014)

15 a Figure 15.1 shows a plant cell.

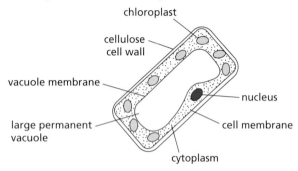

Figure 15.1

i Describe the function of the cell membrane. [1]

ii Name **two** structures labelled on Figure 15.1 that are **not** found in animal cells. [2]

iii Describe how photosynthesis is carried out in the cell shown in Figure 15.1. [3]

b About one tenth of the Earth's surface is covered by forests in which much photosynthesis takes place. List **three** ways in which extensive deforestation could harm the environment. [3]

(Cambridge IGCSE Combined Science 0653 Paper 21 Q9 Nov 2013)

16 a In some areas of the world large areas of forest are cleared to use the land for agriculture. However, sometimes not all of the trees are cleared from the area. Some of the largest trees are left standing and the areas in between them are cleared. This is called partial deforestation.

i Describe and explain why partial deforestation is better than complete deforestation for the soil in the forest. [2]

ii Describe **two** advantages of partial deforestation compared with complete deforestation for the animal life in the forest. [2]

b In some areas of the world raw sewage is discharged into rivers or lakes. This can cause problems for plants and animals that live in the water.

i Explain why the sewage reduces the amount of dissolved oxygen in the water. [2]

ii When sewage is added to water it can affect the transparency of the water by making it cloudy. Explain why this reduces the growth of aquatic plants. [2]

(Cambridge IGCSE Combined Science 0653 Paper 23 Q7 Nov 2015)

17 Figure 17.1 shows some organisms that live in and around a pond.

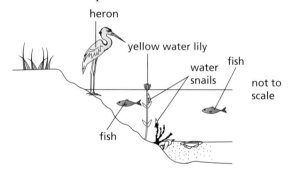

Figure 17.1

a Herons eat fish. Water snails eat water plants, such as yellow water lilies. Tick **all** the boxes that correctly describe each organism.

	producer	consumer	carnivore	herbivore
heron				
water snail				
yellow water lily				

[3]

b The addition of a harmful substance to the environment is called pollution. Two examples of pollution caused by human activities are:
• untreated sewage entering a pond
• the release of methane into the atmosphere.

i Explain why untreated sewage entering a pond may cause fish to die. [2]

ii Methane is produced by bacteria and other decomposers breaking down organic waste material in rubbish dumps. Describe how air pollution by methane can harm the environment. [2]

(Cambridge IGCSE Combined Science 0653 Paper 21 Q3 May 2013)

Chemistry

1 a Table 1.1 shows the number of protons, neutrons and electrons in four atoms, **A**, **B**, **C** and **D**.

Table 1.1

atom	protons	neutrons	electrons
A	1	0	1
B	8	8	8
C	1	1	1
D	15	16	15

  i Name the central part of an atom that contains protons and neutrons [1]
  ii Explain which of the atoms, **A**, **B**, **C** or **D**, has a nucleon number (mass number) of 16. [2]
  iii Use the information of Table 1.1 to explain why atoms do **not** have an overall electrical charge. [2]
b Figure 1.1 shows containers of hydrogen and helium.

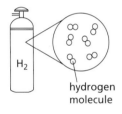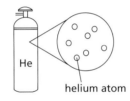

hydrogen molecule   helium atom

Figure 1.1

  i Hydrogen is usually described as a non-metal. Name the type of chemical bond joining the atoms in a hydrogen molecule. [1]
  ii Suggest why helium exists as uncombined atoms. [1]
c Hydrogen is often included in the reactivity series of metals. Use the idea of reactivity to explain the observations in Figure 1.2. [2]

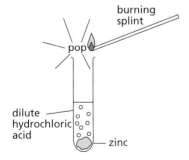

Figure 1.2

(Cambridge IGCSE Combined Science 0653 Paper 21 Q1 May 2013)

2 a Table 2.1 shows some of the properties of the halogens in Group VII of the Periodic Table.

Table 2.1

period	halogen	colour	physical state at room temperature
3	chlorine	pale yellow-green	gas
4	bromine	dark red-brown	liquid
5	iodine	blue-black	solid

  Describe **one** trend in the physical properties of chlorine, bromine and iodine. [1]
b i A dilute solution of chlorine is added to a colourless solution of potassium bromide. Describe what is seen. [1]
  ii Write a **word** equation for this reaction.
  _____ + _____ → _____ + _____ [2]
c Figure 2.1 shows the arrangement of the outer electrons of the atoms in a chlorine molecule, Cl_2. State the name of this type of bonding. [1]

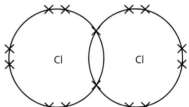

Figure 2.1

d Chlorine is used in the purification of the public water supply. Explain why chlorine is added to water supplied to homes. [2]

(Cambridge IGCSE Combined Science 0653 Paper 23 Q7 May 2014)

3 a Petroleum (crude oil) is a fossil fuel consisting of a mixture of different hydrocarbons. Figure 3.1 shows the industrial apparatus used to separate useful products from petroleum. Petroleum is vaporised and passed up a tower. Useful products from petroleum condense at different positions in the tower.

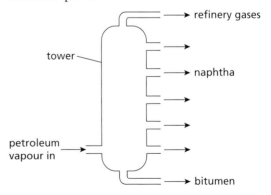

Figure 3.1

  i State the name of the process shown in Figure 3.1. [1]

ii Different products for this process have different boiling point ranges. State how the boiling point of a product affects the position in the tower where a product wil condense. [1]

iii Three of the useful products obtained from petroleum are shown in Figure 3.1. State the name of **another** useful product that is separated from petroleum. State **one** use of this product. [2]

b Table 3.1 contains some information about gases in the Earth's atmosphere.

Table 3.1

gases in the Earth's atmosphere	percentage
carbon dioxide	very small
nitrogen	
oxygen	
other gases	about 1%
water vapour	variable

Complete Table 3.1 to show the percentages of nitrogen and oxygen in the atmosphere. [2]

c Natural gas is a fossil fuel consisting mostly of methane. It is used as a fuel to heat a greenhouse for growing vegetables.

i Describe the changes to the atmosphere in a greenhouse that will occur. [2]

ii Burning methane is an exothermic chemical change. State the meaning of:
exothermic
chemical change [2]

(Cambridge IGCSE Combined Science 0653 Paper 23 Q4 May 2014)

4 Some sulfur has become contaminated with a small amount of aluminium powder.

a A liquid is added to the mixture which dissolves the sulfur. Figure 4.1 shows how sulfur is separated from the mixture of aluminium and sulfur. Suggest how the processes of filtration and crystallisation could be used to obtain pure sulfur from the sulfur solution and aluminium. You could draw diagrams to show your arrangement of apparatus. [3]

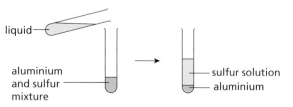

Figure 4.1

b Aluminium sulfide is a compound made by heating a mixture of aluminium and sulfur. Aluminium sulfide is a compound of the elements aluminium and sulfur. The left hand column in Figure 4.2 gives four descriptions of materials. The right hand column shows three different types of materials.
Draw a line from each description on the left hand side to the correct material on the right.[4]

cannot be broken down into simpler substances	
	compound
contains different atoms chemically bonded together	
	element
contains more than one type of atom which are not bonded together	
	mixture
contains one type of atom	

Figure 4.2

c i When aluminium and sulfur atoms react together, positive aluminium ions and negative sulfide ions are formed. Describe, in terms of electrons, how these ions are formed from atoms. [2]

ii Aluminium sulfide consists of two aluminium ions to every three sulfide ions. State the chemical formula of aluminium sulfide. [1]

(Cambridge IGCSE Combined Science 0653 Paper 22 Q8 Nov 2014)

5 a Figure 5.1 shows an early type of airship filled with hydrogen gas. A hydrogen molecule consists of two hydrogen atoms bonded together. Each hydrogen atom contains a small number of subatomic particles.

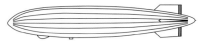

Figure 5.1

i State the names and numbers of the subatomic particles in most hydrogen atoms. [2]

ii State the type of bonding involved in a hydrogen molecule. [1]

iii The use of hydrogen for airships declined following a disaster in which an airship caught fire. Write a word equation for the combustion of hydrogen.

_____ + _____ → _____ [2]

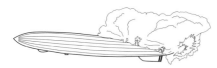

Figure 5.2

iv The combustion of hydrogen is an exothermic reaction. State the meaning of the term *exothermic*. [1]

v Hydrogen can be displaced from an acid by reaction with another substance. Name a substance that could be used to displace hydrogen safely from an acid. Explain your answer in terms of the reactivity series. [2]

b Figure 5.3 shows a modern weather balloon containing hydrogen or helium gas. Explain why helium is safer to use than hydrogen. [1]

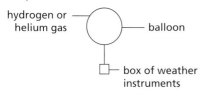

Figure 5.3

c Modern hot air balloons burn propane gas to heat air which inflates the balloon. Propane is a hydrocarbon.

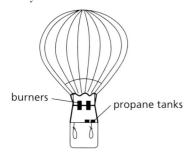

Figure 5.4

Figure 5.5 shows a model of a propane molecule.

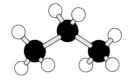

 hydrogen atom

● carbon atom

Figure 5.5

State the molecular formula of propane. [1]
(Cambridge IGCSE Combined Science 0653 Paper 21 Q1 May 2015)

Physics

1 Figure 1.1 shows a method that uses solar energy to purify drinking water. The method is used in hot desert countries.
The impure water is heated by the Sun and distilled. The pure water is collected separately, while the impurities are left behind.

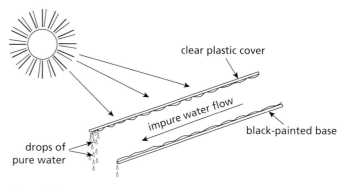

Figure 1.1

a State the part of the Sun's electromagnetic spectrum that heats the water. [1]

b Solar energy produces water vapour from the impure water. Explain why water molecules are able to escape more easily from warm water than from cold water. [2]

c Explain why thermal energy transfer from the Sun only occurs by radiation and not by conduction or convection. [1]

d Figure 1.2 shows a ray of sunlight about to pass through the plastic cover. Draw the path of the ray from the point where it enters the plastic to show what happens at the lower face of the plastic. Indicate the angles of incidence and refraction at the upper face. [3]

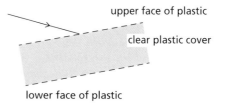

Figure 1.2

(Cambridge IGCSE Combined Science 0653 Paper 22 Q6 Nov 2014)

2 A student is testing the Law of Reflection which says that the angle of reflection is equal to the angle of incidence. He is using a mirror made of polished stainless steel and a light source that creates a narrow beam. This is shown in Figure 2.1.

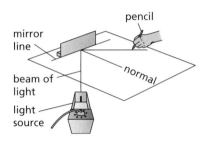

Figure 2.1

Procedure

- The student draws a straight line on a piece of paper and labels it *mirror line*.
- He draws another line and labels it *normal*.
- He places the stainless steel mirror on the mirror line.
- He switches on the light source and arranges it so that the beam hits the mirror line at the point where the normal meets the mirror line.
- Using a pencil, the student marks the incident and reflected beams of light.
- He removes the mirror and light source and then draws the incident and reflected rays. See Figure 2.2.

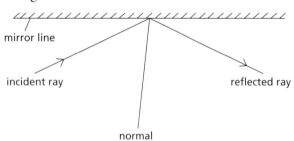

Figure 2.2

- He measures two angles on the diagram.
a The student has measured two angles. He has written the following two statements.
   A "*The angle between the incident ray and the mirror line is equal to the angle between the reflected ray and the mirror line.*"
   B "*This proves that the Law of Reflection is obeyed.*"
   i Use a protractor to measure the angle of incidence and the angle of reflection.
   angle of incidence = _____ degrees
   angle of reflection = _____ degrees [2]
   ii Describe the student's mistake in drawing the diagram. [1]
   iii State and explain whether or not your measurements prove that the Law of Reflection is obeyed. [1]
b The student decides to test the same Law of Reflection using a mirror made from polished

aluminium. He uses the same procedure as before, but he draws the normal line correctly. Figure 2.3 shows the results of this experiment. The student has used a pencil to mark the incident and reflected beams.

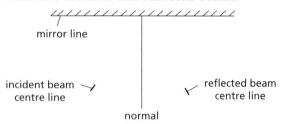

Figure 2.3

   i Complete Figure 2.3 to show an incident ray and a reflected ray. [1]
   ii Use a protractor to measure the angle of incidence and the angle of reflection.
   angle of incidence = _____ degrees
   angle of reflection = _____ degrees [2]
   iii The teacher tells the student that he has made mistakes in this experiment. As a result, the two angles are not equal. Suggest a mistake that the student may have made when he:
   placed the mirror on the paper,
   drew the incident beam and reflected beam lines on the paper. [2]
c The experiments use a solid metal and a solid metal alloy as reflective surfaces. The student states that solid metals reflect light because of the free movement of particles within them. Suggest the name of these particles. [1]
(Cambridge IGCSE Combined Science 0653 Paper 62 Q6 Nov 2014)

3 Figure 3.1 shows the circuit symbols for an electric bell and a push-switch.

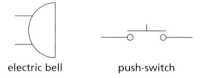

Figure 3.1

a i Complete the circuit diagram in Figure 3.2 for a circuit for a door-bell with a push-switch, powered by a battery with four cells, for the front door of a house. [2]

Figure 3.2

ii Add a voltmeter to the completed circuit diagram in Figure 3.2 to measure the voltage across the battery. [1]

b The ringing bell emits a sound of frequency 400 Hz.

  i State the meaning of the term *frequency*. [1]

  ii The house owner makes the sound of the bell louder by adding another cell to the battery, but the pitch of the sound from the bell remains unchanged. State the effect this change has on the amplitude and frequency of the sound emitted. [2]

c i The voltage provided by the battery is 6 V. When the bell is rung, a current of 2 A flows through the bell.

  Use the formula $R = \dfrac{V}{I}$

  to calculate the resistance of the bell. Show your working and state the unit of your answer.

  resistance = _____ unit _____ [2]

  ii The house owner adds a second identical bell in the circuit in parallel to the first bell. When the switch is pushed, both bells ring. Suggest the effect the second bell will have on the current taken from the battery when the bells are rung. Give a reason for your answer. [2]

(Cambridge IGCSE Combined Science 0653 Paper 22 Q4 Nov 2014)

4 Figure 4.1 shows a man on a snowboard moving down a hill.

Figure 4.1

Figure 4.2 shows a graph of the man's speed as he goes down the hill.

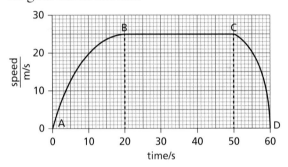

Figure 4.2

a State the force that causes the man to move downhill. [1]

b Describe the motion of the man between points.
  A and **B**
  B and **C** [2]

c Calculate the distance travelled by the man between points **B** and **C**. State the formula you use and show your working.
  distance = _____ m [2]

d The man on the snowboard wants to go faster down the hill. Explain in terms of the forces acting on the man and his snowboard why

  i he covers the underside of the snowboard with wax to make it smooth [1]

  ii he bends down low on the snowboard while going down the hill. [1]

e Snow is made of solid ice crystals. Copy the box below and draw a diagram to show the arrangement in a solid. One particle has been drawn for you. You need to draw at least 11 more. [2]

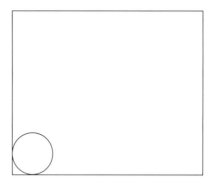

*(Cambridge IGCSE Combined Science 0653
Paper 21 Q3 May 2015)*

5   Figure 5.1 shows a van being driven along a
     flat road at a constant speed. The arrows on the
     diagram represent the four main forces acting
     on the van.

Figure 5.1

a i   On Figure 5.1, use the words from the
           list to complete the boxes next to the
           arrows to label the three missing forces.
           Each word from the list can be used
           once, more than once or not at all.   [2]

**driving   friction   gravity
mass   pressure   weight**

ii   The reaction force is 30 000 N. State
         the value of the downward force. Give a
         reason for your answer.
         downward force = _____ N   [2]
iii Explain where the downward force
         in **a ii** comes from.   [1]

b Figure 5.2 shows a speed/time graph for the
     van for a short journey.

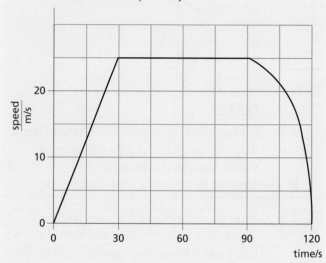

Figure 5.2

i   Describe the motion of the van between
         30 s and 120 s.   [2]
ii   Use the speed/time graph in Figure
         5.2 to calculate the distance travelled in
         kilometres in the first 90 s of the journey.
         Show your working.
         Distance travelled = _____ km   [3]

*(Cambridge IGCSE Combined Science 0653
Paper 32 Q1 Nov 2015)*

● Co-ordinated Sciences

Biology

1 a Figure 1.1 shows what happens when a plant
        is placed near a window where bright light is
        coming from one side.

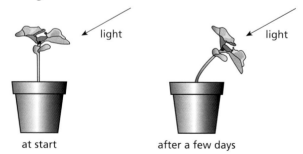

at start   after a few days

Figure 1.1

i   Name the response shown by the plant. [1]
ii   Explain why the response shown in
         Figure 1.1 is an advantage to the plant. [2]

iii Using the information in Figure 1.1 name **two** characteristics of living things shown by this plant. [2]

b A student carries out an experiment to find out more about plant responses. He uses simple shoots and light coming from one side. The results are shown in Figure 1.2.

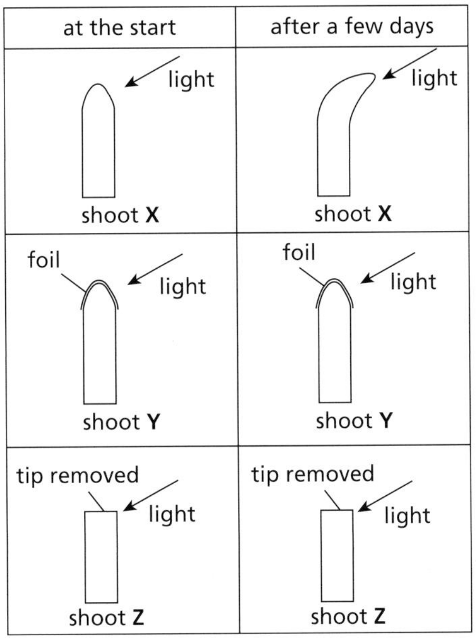

at the start	after a few days
light shoot **X**	light shoot **X**
foil light shoot **Y**	foil light shoot **Y**
tip removed light shoot **Z**	tip removed light shoot **Z**

Figure 1.2

i Describe the results shown in Figure 1.2. [2]
ii Suggest a possible conclusion about the control of plant responses in the shoots. Explain your answer. [2]

c Animals are able to respond to situations by secreting the hormone adrenaline. Adrenaline is secreted into the blood when an athlete starts to run a race. Suggest how this helps the athlete to run fast. [2]

(Cambridge IGCSE Combined Science 0653 Paper 22 Q7 Nov 2014)

2 Soya beans are an important crop in Brazil. Soya beans contain a lot of protein, plus smaller quantities of starch and fat.

a Describe how you could test a sample of soya beans to find out if they contain fat. [3]
b Explain why protein is an important part of a balanced diet. [2]
c When a person eats soya beans, the beans are chewed in the mouth. Explain why this makes it easier for enzymes in the digestive system to digest the beans. [2]

d Raw soya beans contain substances that stop protease enzymes from working. Cooking destroys these substances. Suggest how eating uncooked soya beans could prevent the absorption of some of the nutrients from them. [2]

e Large areas of rainforest have been cleared in Brazil to provide more land for growing soya beans. Explain how cutting down the rainforest can harm the environment. [4]

(Cambridge IGCSE Co-ordinated Sciences 0654 Paper 23 Q4 Nov 13)

3 Figure 3.1 shows a root hair cell.

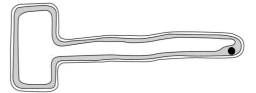

Figure 3.1

a Use the letters **A**, **B** and **C** to label these parts of the root hair cell in Figure 3.1.
A The cell membrane.
B The part that contains chromosomes.
C A structure that is **not** present in animal cells. [3]
b Name **two** substances that are absorbed by root hair cells. [2]
c Figure 3.2 shows part of a plant stem from which the outer layer, including the phloem, has been removed.

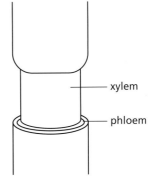

— xylem

— phloem

Figure 3.2

i State the function of the phloem. [2]
ii Suggest why this treatment would cause the roots of the plant to die. [2]

(Cambridge IGCSE Co-ordinated Sciences 0654 Paper 23 Q1 Nov 13)

4 Figure 4.1 shows two liver cells, as seen under a light microscope.

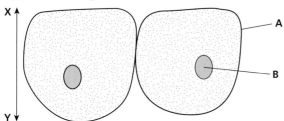

Figure 4.1

a Name the structures labelled **A** and **B**. [2]
b State **two** functions of liver cells. [2]
c Give **three** ways in which a plant palisade cells differs from a liver cell. [3]
d In Figure 4.1, the actual height of the cell along the line **X–Y** is 0.03 mm. Calculate the magnification of the drawing. [2]
e Name **two** of the blood vessels that are associated with the liver, and outline their function. [2]

(Cambridge IGCSE Co-ordinated Sciences 0654 Paper 21 Q11 Nov 14)

5 Figure 5.1 shows a cell from a plant. The cell absorbs water from the soil.

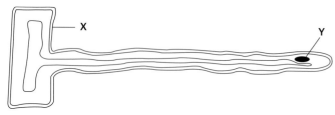

Figure 5.1

a i Name this type of cell. [1]
ii Name the structures labelled **X** and **Y**. [2]
b State **one** other function of the cell, apart from water absorption. [1]
c Most of the water absorbed by this cell evaporates from the plant.
i Name the process by which water evaporates from a plant. [1]
ii State where most of this evaporation occurs. [1]
d Not all of the water absorbed by a plant is lost by evaporation. Suggest **one** way in which a plant might make use of the absorbed water. [1]

(Cambridge IGCSE Co-ordinated Sciences 0654 Paper 22 Q10 May 15)

6 Two experiments were set up as in Figure 6.1. The apparatus is a model of the digestion and absorption of starch in the alimentary canal. The piece of 'visking tubing' represents the alimentary canal. The visking tubing is a selectively permeable membrane, which allows smaller molecules to pass through it but not larger molecules.

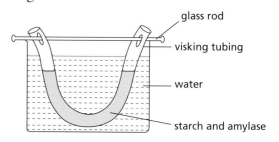

Figure 6.1

In **experiment 1,** the liquid inside the visking tubing was starch solution.
In **experiment 2,** this liquid was a mixture of starch and amylase solution.
Both experiments were left for one hour. After this time, the liquid inside the visking tubing and the water in the beaker were each tested with iodine solution and with Benedict's solution. The results are shown in Table 6.1.

Table 6.1

experiment	liquid tested	test	colour obtained	conclusion
1	inside visking tubing	iodine test		
		Benedict's test	blue	
	water in the beaker	iodine test	brown	
		Benedict's test	blue	
2	inside visking tubing	iodine test	brown	
		Benedict's test	red	
	water in the beaker	iodine test	brown	
		Benedict's test	red	

a i Fill in the colour that was obtained for the top row of Table 6.1. [1]
ii In the top row of the last column of the table, state what can be concluded from this result. [1]
iii Fill in the remainder of the last column of Table 6.1, stating in each case whether starch or sugar is present or absent. [2]

b i Explain what the results from **experiment 2** tell you about the effect of amylase on starch molecules. [1]

ii What do the results from **experiment 2** tell you about the ability of sugar molecules to pass through the visking tubing? Explain your answer. [2]

c For the experiment shown in Figure 6.1,

i state which part of the alimentary canal is represented by the visking tubing [1]

ii state what the beaker of water represents. [1]

d Using the results of these experiments, explain why starch needs to be digested in the alimentary canal. [1]

(Cambridge IGCSE Co-ordinated Sciences 0654 Paper 61 Q1 Nov 13)

7 A student carries out some tests to determine the food groups present in rice and milk.

a i Complete the top row of Table 7.1 to show which food group each test is able to identify. [3]

b Milk gives a positive result with Benedict's reagent and biuret reagent. Rice gives a positive result with biuret reagent and iodine solution. Complete Table 7.1 to show the colours observed for these positive results. [3]

Table 7.1

reagent	benedict's	biuret	iodine
food group identified			
colour with milk at end of test			orange
colour with rice at end of test	blue		

c i Describe how you could carry out the test for the presence of fats in a food. [2]

ii State what is observed if the result of the test in **ci** is positive. [1]

iii Suggest why the test you have described in **ci** may be difficult to carry out on the milk. [1]

(Cambridge IGCSE Co-ordinated Sciences 0654 Paper 62 Q1 Nov 15)

8 **a** Explain what is meant by the term *enzyme*. [2]

b Figure 8.1 shows the effect of pH on the activity of an enzyme. Describe the effect of pH on the activity of this enzyme. [2]

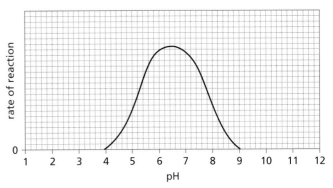

Figure 8.1

c A protease enzyme works in the human stomach, where hydrochloric acid is secreted. This enzyme is adapted to work best in these conditions.

i On Figure 8.1, sketch a curve to show how pH affects the activity on this protease enzyme. [1]

ii After the food has been in the stomach for a while, it passes into the duodenum. Pancreatic juice, which contains sodium hydrogen carbonate, is mixed with the food in the duodenum. Explain why the protease enzyme stops working when it enters the duodenum. [2]

iii Name the substrate and product of a protease enzyme. [2]

iv Explain how the activity of this enzyme makes it possible for body cells to obtain nutrients from the food inside the digestive system.

(Cambridge IGCSE Co-ordinated Sciences 0654 Paper 22 Q3 May 2012)

9 The enzyme pectinase is used in the production of fruit juices. It speeds the breakdown of the walls of plant cells. This helps to release juice from the cells. A student did an experiment in which she investigated the action of pectinase on apples. She wanted to find the optimum pH for the enzyme. This value would produce the greatest volume of fruit juice.

• The student made up solutions of enzyme at different pH values.

• She prepared small cubes of apples, all the same size, and placed equal masses of cubes into five dishes.

• She added 1 cm³ pectinase solution to the dishes of apple so that each dish contained pectinase at a different pH.

• She thoroughly mixed the enzyme and apple in each dish.

- After 10 minutes the contents of each dish were filtered.
  The filtrate was the juice from the apples. It dripped into the measuring cylinder. The volume of juice produced was a measure of how reactive the enzyme was.

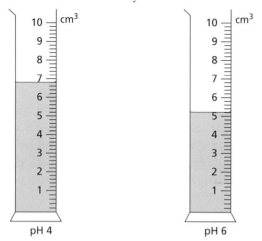

Figure 9.1

a i Read the scales of the measuring cylinders in Figure 9.1 and enter the missing volumes of juice for pH values 4 and 6 in Table 9.1. [2]

Table 9.1

pH of enzyme solution	volume of juice produced/cm³
3	4.6
4	
5	9.6
6	
7	2.2

ii Plot a graph of volume of juice produced/cm³ against pH of enzyme solution. Draw the best curve. [3]

iii Suggest the optimum pH for the enzyme.
optimum pH = _____ [1]

iv Explain why you cannot be sure of the exact optimum pH value. [1]

b Describe a control experiment the student could do to prove that the enzyme was responsible for the production of fruit juice. [1]

c Use your knowledge of the activity of enzymes to suggest **one** different method of increasing the activity of the enzyme. Explain why it would work. [2]

(Cambridge IGCSE Co-ordinated Sciences 0654 Paper 61 Q4 May 13)

10 A student is investigating the relationship between yeast activity and temperature. Active yeast produces a gas which may appear as a foam.

- The student stirs a yeast and sugar suspension and immediately measures out 20 cm³ into each of two large test-tubes.
- He places one test-tube into beaker **A** containing some water which he maintains at about 20 °C.
- He places the other test-tube into beaker **B** containing some water which he maintains at about 40 °C.

The apparatus is shown in Figure 10.1.

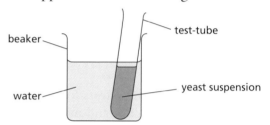

Figure 10.1

He measures the temperature of the water in each beaker.

The temperature of beaker A is 190.0 °C.

a The thermometer in Figure 10.2 shows the temperature in beaker **B**. Read and record this temperature.

beaker B = _____ °C [1]

°C

40
39
38
37

Figure 10.2

He uses a ruler to measure the height *h* of the liquid (including any foam) in each test-tube at regular intervals. The arrangement is shown in Figure 10.3.

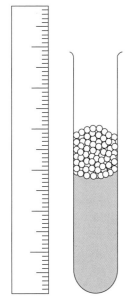

Figure 10.3

b On Figure 10.3, draw a labelled arrow to show the height *h*. Mark clearly the top of the measurement. [1]

The student measures the height *h* in each test-tube at 2 minute intervals for ten minutes. During this time he maintains the temperatures of the beakers. He records his measurements in Table 10.1.

Table 10.1

time/min	beaker **A** height *h*/mm	beaker **B** height *h*/mm
0	40	40
2	40	62
4	40	75
6	41	90
8	42	98
10	44	105

c On the grid provided, plot graphs of height *h* for each beaker against time. Draw best-fit lines and label them **A** and **B**. [4]

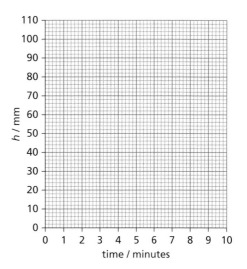

d A teacher says that yeast activity stops when the temperature of the yeast is too high. Plan and describe an investigation based on the equipment the student carried out to find out the minimum temperature at which yeast activity stops due to temperature being too high. [4]

(Cambridge IGCSE Co-ordinated Sciences 0654 Paper 61 Q1 Nov 14)

11 A student carries out an experiment to investigate the effect of temperature on the activity of the enzyme pepsin. Pepsin breaks down protein in the stomach. The activity of pepsin can be measured by timing how long it takes to break down a cloudy protein solution into a clear solution.

- The study places $5.0\,cm^3$ of the protein solution into a test-tube and adds $1.0\,cm^3$ hydrochloric acid.
- He places $1.0\,cm^3$ of pepsin solution into another test-tube.
- He places both test-tubes into a water-bath for 35 °C for five minutes.
- He then pours the pepsin solution into the protein solution and times how long it takes for the contents of the tube to go clear.
- He records this time in Table 11.1.
- He repeats this procedure for the different temperatures as shown in Table 11.1.
- The thermometer reading for the last temperature used is shown in Figure 11.1.

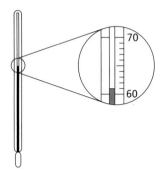

Figure 11.1

a i Read the thermometer in Figure 11.1 and record the value in the last row of Table 11.1. [1]

The stopwatch reading for the final temperature used is shown in Figure 11.2.

Figure 11.2

Table 11.1

temperature/°C	time taken for solution to go clear/2	rate of reaction in 1/s
35	400	0.0025
41	175	0.0057
46	80	0.0125
52	30	0.0333
56	120	0.0083

ii Read the stopwatch and record in Table 11.1 the time shown **in seconds**.[1]
iii Complete Table 11.1 by calculating the rate of reaction, $\frac{1}{s}$, for the final temperature. [1]

b i On the grid provided, plot a graph of rate of reaction against temperature. Draw the best-fit **curve**. [2]

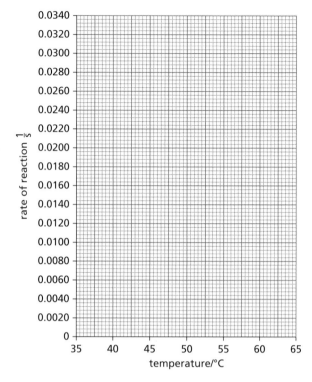

ii Use the graph to estimate the optimum temperature for the activity of pepsin.
Optimum temperature = _____ °C [1]
iii Explain why you cannot be sure that this is an accurate optimum temperature. [1]
c Describe an experiment to show that acid is required for pepsin to break down protein. [3]
(Cambridge IGCSE Co-ordinated Sciences 0654 Paper 63 Q4 May 15)

12 a Figure 12.1 shows the effects of pH on the activity of an enzyme.

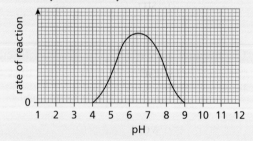

Figure 12.1

i Describe the effect of pH on the activity of this enzyme. [2]
ii Explain why pH affects the enzyme in this way. [2]

iii A protease enzyme works in the human stomach, where hydrochloric acid is secreted. This enzyme is adapted to work best in these conditions. On **Figure 12.1** sketch a curve to show how pH affects the activity of this protease enzyme. [1]

iv After the food has been in the stomach a while, it passes into the duodenum. Pancreatic juice, which contains sodium hydrogencarbonate, is mixed with the food in the duodenum. Explain why the protease enzyme stops working when it enters the duodenum. [2]

b Explain how the protease enzyme enables body cells to obtain nutrients. [3]

c Figure 12.2 shows the structure of a villus.

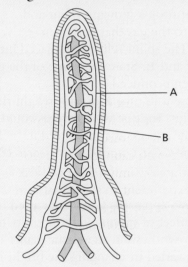

Figure 12.2

i Name the structures labelled **A** and **B**. [2]

ii Describe the role of villi in the human alimentary canal. [3]
Cambridge IGCSE Co-ordinated Sciences 0654 Paper 32 Q3 May 12)

13 a Complete the word equation for photosynthesis.
water + _____ → _____ + _____ [2]

b Figure 13.1 is a photograph of a cross-section of a leaf, taken through a microscope.

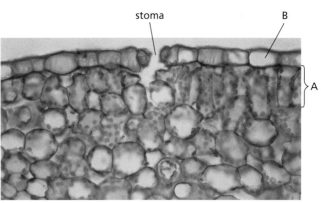

Figure 13.1

Name the parts of the leaf labelled **A** and **B**. [2]

c There are small gaps in the lower surface of the leaf, called stomata. Explain the role of stomata in photosynthesis. [2]

d Stomata allow water vapour to diffuse out of the leaf. State the correct term for the loss of water vapour from a leaf. [1]

e Plants that live in hot, dry deserts often have fewer stomata than plants that live in places where there is plenty of water. Suggest how this helps the desert plants to survive. [1]

f Most leaves have stomata on their lower surfaces. Plants that live in water, with leaves that float on the water, often have stomata on the upper surfaces of the leaves. Suggest how this helps the water plants to survive. [2]

g Plants must have a good supply of magnesium ions, in order to grow well. State why they need magnesium ions. [1]
(Cambridge IGCSE Co-ordinated Sciences 0654 Paper 22 Q9 May 2012)

14 A student investigated the effect of light on the chemical composition of leaves. Two plants of the same species were used. Leaf **A** had been removed from a plant that had been in strong light for a period of 24 hours. Leaf **B** had been removed from a plant that had been kept in the dark for 48 hours.

• The student picked up leaf **A** with a pair of tweezers and carefully held it in very hot water for 15 seconds. He carried out the same procedure on leaf **B**.

• He placed the leaves separately into the bottom of two large tubes labelled **A** and **B**.

- The leaves were covered with alcohol (ethanol) and the tubes placed into a very hot water bath for 5 minutes.
- He removed the tubes from the water bath and poured off the alcohol into a beaker.

a He noted that the colour of the alcohol that had been poured off had turned green in colour. The leaves are now white in colour.

   i Suggest what substance from the leaf has dissolved in the alcohol. [1]

- He placed leaves A and B into separate Petri dishes, laid them flat and covered them in iodine solution for two minutes.
- He removed the excess iodine solution by washing the leaves with cold water.

   ii Suggest, and record in Table 14.1, the colour of the leaves after they had been tested with iodine solution. For each leaf, what conclusion may be made from your suggested colours?
   Record your conclusion for each leaf in Table 14.1.

Table 14.1

	leaf **A**	leaf **B**
colour of leaf after testing with iodine solution		
conclusion		

[4]

b The student carried out a second experiment.
- He took four pieces of pond weed and placed them into separate beakers labelled **C, D, E** and **F**.
- He placed a funnel over each piece of pond weed.
- He placed measuring cylinders full of water over the funnels to collect any gases produced, as in Figure 14.1.
- Beakers **C, D** and **E** were placed in strong light for 48 hours.
- Beaker **F** was kept in the dark for 48 hours.

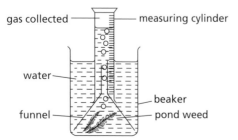

Figure 14.1

Figure 14.2 shows the measuring cylinders after the experiment.

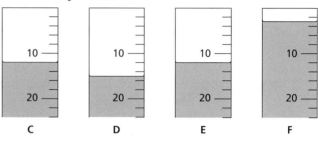

Figure 14.2

   i Record the volumes of gas in all four measuring cylinders in Table 14.2. [2]

Table 14.2

measuring cylinder	C	D	E	F
volume of gas/cm³				

   ii The student took a glowing splint and placed it into the gas that had been collected. The splint relit when placed into tubes **C, D** and **E**. State the name of the gas that has been produced. [1]

   iii The gas present in tube **F** did not relight the glowing splint. Suggest what this gas could be and name the process that produced it. [2]

   (Cambridge IGCSE Co-ordinated Sciences 0654 Paper 61 Q1 May 2012)

15 Figure 15.1 shows apparatus that can be used to investigate the effect of varying light intensity on the rate of photosynthesis in an aquatic plant. The light intensity is varied by changing the brightness of the lamp. The rate of photosynthesis is determined by measuring the rate at which the water level moves down in the capillary tube. This happens because the gas produced in photosynthesis forces the water down the tube.

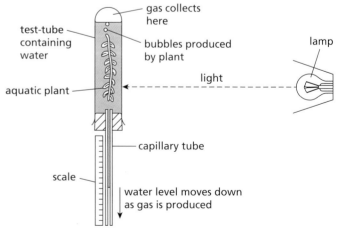

Figure 15.1

a State why light is necessary for photosynthesis. [1]

b Name the gas that collects at the top of the test-tube in Figure 15.1. [1]

c Write a balanced chemical equation for photosynthesis. [2]

d i Using the axes in Figure 15.2, sketch a graph to show how the rate of photosynthesis of the plant will change as the light intensity varies from very low to very high. [2]

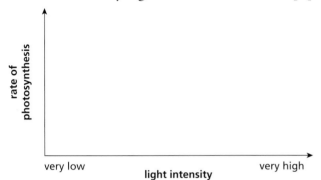

Figure 15.2

   ii Suggest reasons for the shape of your graph:
- at low light intensities
- at very high light intensities. [2]

e Name **two** environmental conditions other than light intensity that affect the rate of photosynthesis. [2]

f Only the green parts of a plant can photosynthesise.

   i Name the green substance present in plants. [1]

   ii State why this green substance is needed for photosynthesis. [1]

(Cambridge IGCSE Co-ordinated Sciences 0654 Paper 33 Q5 Nov 14)

16 For healthy growth, plants must absorb magnesium ions from the soil. If a plant cannot absorb enough magnesium, its leaves lose their green colour. Later, the plant grows more slowly.

a i Explain why a lack of magnesium causes plants to lose their green colour. [1]

   ii Explain why, later, the plant grows more slowly. [2]

b Two groups of wheat plants of the same variety were grown in two different fields, field **A** and field **B**. The two fields were next to each other, and with the same conditions except for the amount of fertiliser added to the soil.

- Field **A** had regularly been treated with a nitrogen-containing fertiliser over the previous five years.
- Field **B** had not been treated with any fertiliser during this time.

In each field, the height of the wheat plants was measured over a period of 120 days, and the final wheat yield was also measured. Figure 16.1 shows the results.

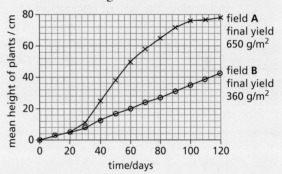

Figure 16.1

   i Compare the change in heights of the wheat plants in field **B** and in those in field **A** for the
- first 20 days
- next 100 days. [3]

   ii Suggest why adding fertiliser to field **A** resulted in a higher final yield. [2]

   iii Describe how fertiliser from farms can damage the environment in nearby rivers or lakes. [3]

(Cambridge IGCSE Co-ordinated Sciences 0654 Paper 31 Q6 May 15)

17 Seeds need oxygen for respiration when they are germinating.

a i Write the **word** equation for aerobic respiration. [2]

   ii List **two** environmental conditions, other than a supply of oxygen, that all seeds require germination. [2]

b An investigation was carried out to find the effect of temperature on the rate of respiration of germinating seeds. Four experiments, **A**, **B**, **C** and **D** were set up. Each experiment used either germinating or dead seeds. The results are shown in Table 17.1.

Table 17.1

experiment	seeds	temperature/°C	relative rate of respiration
A	germinating seeds	0	1
B	germinating seeds	10	2
C	germinating seeds	20	4
D	dead seeds	20	0

  i   Explain why it was important to include set **D** in the experiment. [1]

  ii With reference to Table 17.1, describe the effect of temperature on the rates of respiration of germinating seeds. [2]

  iii Respiration is controlled by enzymes. Predict and explain the rate of respiration of germinating seeds at a temperature of 60 °C. [2]

(Cambridge IGCSE Co-ordinated Sciences 0654 Paper 21 Q5 Nov12)

18 Figure 18.1 shows the human skull, seen from the side.

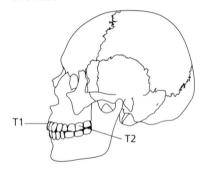

Figure 18.1

a Name the type of tooth labelled **T1**. [1]

b Describe how tooth **T2** is different from tooth **T1** in its structure and in its function. [2]

c Explain why it is important to chew food that we eat. [2]

d Explain how regular brushing of the teeth helps to prevent tooth decay. [2]

e Apart from brushing the teeth, state **two** other ways in which tooth decay can be prevented. [2]

(Cambridge IGCSE Co-ordinated Sciences 0654 Paper 22 Q12 May 15)

19 Table 19.1 shows the composition of 100 cm³ cow's milk and goat's milk.

Table 19.1

amount per 100 cm³	cow's milk	goat's milk
energy (kJ)	290	320
fat (g)	3.4	3.9
protein (g)	3.4	3.5
carbohydrate (g)	4.9	4.7
calcium (mg)	110	120
iron (mg)	0.020	0.010
vitamin C (mg)	1.50	1.48
vitamin D (mg)	0.001	0.001

a Using the information in Table 19.1,

  i   name **two** substances that are present in goat's milk at higher concentrations than in cow's milk [2]

  ii name **one** mineral ion that is present in cow's milk at higher concentration than in goat's milk [1]

  iii suggest why goat's milk provides more energy per 100 cm³ than cow's milk. [1]

b i A healthy adult has to consume 90 mg of vitamin C per day to meet their dietary vitamin C requirement. An adult could get all their daily vitamin C requirement from drinking cow's milk. Use the information in Table 19.1 to calculate how much cow's milk would be needed.

    _____ mg vitamin C is present in 100 cm³ cow's milk so, _____ mg vitamin C is present in 1 litre (1000 cm³) milk, so 90 mg vitamin C is present in _____ litres of milk.

    milk required = _____ litres per day [2]

  ii Use your answer to state whether cow's milk is a good dietary source of vitamin C. Explain your answer. [1]

  iii State the deficiency symptoms that result from a diet that does not contain enough vitamin C. [2]

c i Milk contains no dietary fibre (roughage). State the importance of fibre in the diet. [1]

  ii Name a food that is a good source of dietary fibre. [1]

(Cambridge IGCSE Co-ordinated Sciences 0654 Paper 23 Q1 Nov 15)

20 A student used the apparatus shown in Figure 20.1 to study the transpiration rate in a leafy shoot. As water vapour is transpired from the leaves, water is drawn through the apparatus. The rate of movement of the small bubble along the tube is used as an indication of the rate of transpiration. The student wanted to find which surface of the leaves lost the greater amount of water vapour. The student did two experiments, the first with the leaves untreated and a second with grease applied to the upper surface of the leaves.

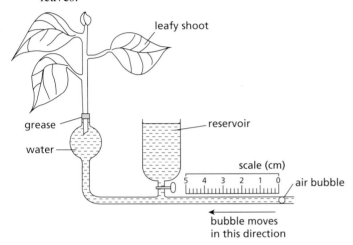

Figure 20.1

a The student prepared the shoot by cutting the stem under water.
- He placed the shoot in the rubber tubing at the top of the apparatus as shown in Figure 20.1.
- He added water from the reservoir to move the bubble to the zero mark.
- He then started timing.
- He read the position of the bubble every minute for three minutes and recording the readings in Table 20.1.

Table 20.1

condition of leaves	time/ minutes	reading on scale/ cm	distance moved by bubble per minute/cm	average distance moved by bubble per minute/cm
untreated	1			
	2			
	3			

  i Take the readings from the scales illustrated in Figure 20.2 and record them in Table 20.1. Read the value from the left side of the bubble. [1]
  ii Calculate the distance moved by the bubble during each minute and enter the values in column 4 of Table 20.1. [1]

iii Using the three values found in **aii**, calculate the average distance moved by the bubble per minute and enter this value in column 5 of Table 20.1. [1]

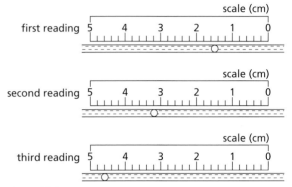

Figure 20.2

b The student then applied grease to all of the upper surfaces of the leaves to prevent loss of water vapour.
- He added water from the reservoir to return the bubble to zero.
- He repeated the procedure as in part **a** and calculated a new average distance moved by the bubble per minute. This new value was 1.2 cm.
  i Use the average value from **aiii** and the average value given in **b** to calculate the percentage of water vapour loss that took place from the lower surface of the leaf. [2]
  ii The student concluded that the rest of the water vapour was lost from the upper surface of the leaf. Describe what the student could do to confirm this. [1]
c Study column 4 of the Table 20.1. The three values for the distance the bubble moved per minute are not identical to each other. Suggest **two** environmental conditions that could cause the differences. [2]
d i Explain why the student cut the stem of the leafy shoot under water before putting it into the apparatus. [1]
  ii Suggest a possible reason why the amount of water taken up by the plant shoot may **not** be exactly the same as the amount lost by transpiration. [1]

(Cambridge IGCSE Co-ordinated Sciences 0654 Paper 61 Q4 Nov12)

21 Figure 21.1 shows a selection through a blood capillary.

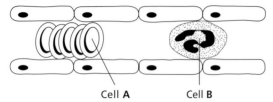

Figure 21.1

a Describe how cell **A** transports oxygen. [2]
b Describe the function of cell **B**. [2]
c Outline the functions of a blood capillary. [2]

(Cambridge IGCSE Co-ordinated Sciences 0654 Paper 22 Q6 May 13)

22 a Define the term *transpiration*. [2]
b Figure 22.1 shows xylem vessels from the stem of a plant as seen in longitudinal section.

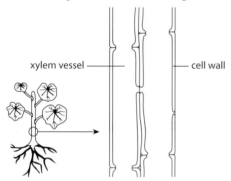

Figure 22.1

   i On Figure 22.1 draw an arrow to show the direction in which water flows through the xylem vessel. [1]
   ii Name **one** other substance, apart from water, that is transported through xylem vessels. [1]
c Figure 22.2 shows a stem and a root in transverse section. On the stem, the positions of the xylem and the phloem tissues have been labelled.

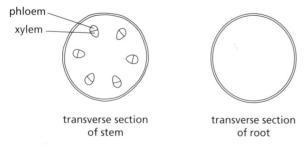

Figure 22.2

   i Complete the diagram of the root by drawing in the positions of the xylem and the phloem tissues and labelling them. [3]
   ii State the function of the phloem. [1]
d Plants absorb water from the soil. Name the plant cells that take up most of this water. [1]

(Cambridge IGCSE Co-ordinated Sciences 0654 Paper 21 Q4 Nov 14)

23 Part of a plant shoot was cut, and then placed in a beaker of coloured water, as shown in Figure 23.1.

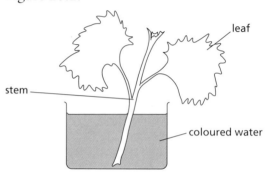

Figure 23.1

After two hours, the shoot was removed. Figure 23.2 shows what the shoot looked like.

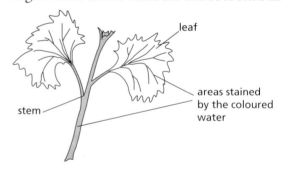

Figure 23.2

a Name the main tissue that has been stained by the coloured water. [1]
b The movement of the coloured water is caused by transpiration. Describe the process of transpiration. You should use these terms in your explanation.

evaporation   mesophyll   stomata   vapour [3]

c Suggest how the result shown in Figure 23.2, would have been different if the cut shoot had been left for two hours in more humid conditions. [1]

(Cambridge IGCSE Co-ordinated Sciences 0654 Paper 23 Q7 Nov 15)

24 Figure 24.1 shows the contents of the human thorax (chest).

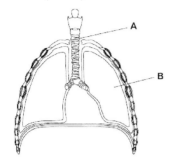

Figure 24.1

a On Figure 24.1, name structures **A** and **B**. [2]

b Oxygen diffuses into the blood from the alveoli inside the lungs. Carbon dioxide diffuses into the alveoli from the blood.

 i Define the term *diffusion*. [2]

 ii Name the component of blood that transports dissolved carbon dioxide. [1]

 iii When a person is doing vigorous exercise, the concentration of carbon dioxide in the blood increases. Explain why this happens. [2]

 iv Suggest how this will affect the rate of diffusion of carbon dioxide from the blood to the alveoli. Explain your answer. [2]

(Cambridge IGCSE Co-ordinated Sciences 0654 Paper 23 Q10 Nov 13)

25 Figure 25.1 shows the concentration of carbon dioxide in a muscle cell of an athlete before, during and after a period of exercise.

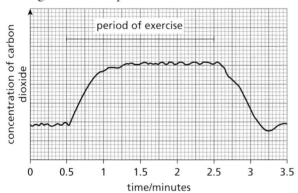

Figure 25.1

a i Name the process that produces carbon dioxide in cells. [1]

 ii Complete the word equation for this process.

 ———— + ———— → ———— + carbon dioxide [2]

b State the time in Figure 25.1 at which the carbon dioxide concentration is lowest. [1]

c During exercise, the blood flow to the muscles increases. Explain why this increased blood flow is important during exercise. [2]

d Training increases the number of red blood cells in an athlete's body. Suggest how this affects the amount of lactic acid produced when an athlete is sprinting. Explain your answer. [2]

(Cambridge IGCSE Co-ordinated Sciences 0654 Paper 21 Q7 Nov 14)

26 a A student wants to find out the largest volume of air that he can breathe out in one breath. This is called the vital capacity. Describe how he could use the apparatus in Figure 26.1 to do this. [3]

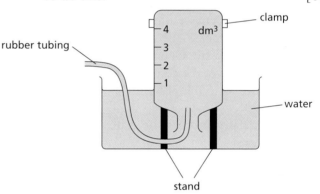

Figure 26.1

b Suggest how he could check the reliability of his results. [2]

c i The teacher suggests that there is a relationship between a person's height and vital capacity. Plan an experiment to test this hypothesis. [2]

 ii Describe how you would present your results to show any relationship. You may wish to draw a suitable table. [1]

d Another student has two gas jars. One jar contains exhaled air and the other jar contains inhaled air. She places a lighted candle inside each jar. Suggest and explain the difference in results from the two samples of air. [2]

(Cambridge IGCSE Co-ordinated Sciences 0654 Paper 61 Q4 Nov 14)

27 A student is investigating respiration in yeast cells. She uses the indicator methylene blue to measure the rate of respiration. A solution of methylene blue is decolourised when oxygen is removed by respiration. She sets up three test-tubes labelled **A**, **B** and **C** as shown in Figure 27.1.

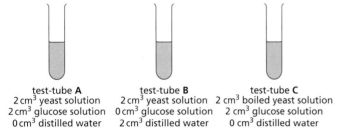

test-tube **A**
2 cm³ yeast solution
2 cm³ glucose solution
0 cm³ distilled water

test-tube **B**
2 cm³ yeast solution
0 cm³ glucose solution
2 cm³ distilled water

test-tube **C**
2 cm³ boiled yeast solution
2 cm³ glucose solution
0 cm³ distilled water

Figure 27.1

- She places the three test-tubes in a water bath at 35 °C for 5 minutes.
- She adds 2 cm³ methylene blue indicator to each test-tube.
- She starts a stopclock.
- She observes the colour of each test-tube each minute for 6 minutes.

Results

The indicator in test-tube **A** decolourised at 2 minutes.

The indicator in test-tube **B** decolourised at 5 minutes.

There is no change in test-tube **C**.

a Explain why there is no change in test-tube **C**. [1]

b Use all the information given above to complete the heading for column 1 and the observations in Table 27.1.

Table 27.1

	colour in test-tube **A**	colour in test-tube **B**	colour in test-tube **C**
1	blue	blue	blue
2			
3			
4			
5			
6			

c i Explain why distilled water is added to test-tube **B**. [1]

ii Describe and explain the difference in results for test-tubes **A** and **B**. [2]

d She removes test-tube **A** from the water bath and shakes it vigorously until it froths. Describe and explain what you would expect to observe. [2]

(Cambridge IGCSE Co-ordinated Sciences 0654 Paper 63 Q1 May 15)

28 Figure 28.1 shows apparatus that can be used to compare the composition of inspired and expired air.

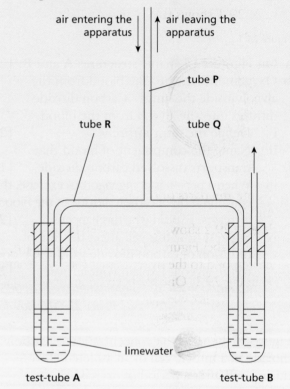

air entering the apparatus

air leaving the apparatus

tube **P**

tube **R**

tube **Q**

limewater

test-tube **A**

test-tube **B**

Figure 28.1

a A person breathes slowly in and out of the apparatus at tube **P** for half a minute, as shown in Figure 28.1.

i On Figure 28.1, draw two arrows to show the directions of air flow in tubes **Q** and **R** while the person is breathing in and out through the apparatus. [1]

ii As the person breathes in and out, the composition of the air flowing **into the apparatus** tube **P** is different from the air **leaving the apparatus** through tube **P**. State **two** of these differences for the air leaving the apparatus. [2]

iii Describe what you would expect to observe in the limewater in test-tube **A** and in test-tube **B** after half a minute. [2]

iv Assume that the change that you predicted in **aiii** occurs. State what could then be concluded from this experiment. [1]

b Suggest and explain how the results of this experiment would be different if the person breathing through the apparatus had just finished some vigorous exercise. [2]

(Cambridge IGCSE Co-ordinated Sciences 0654 Paper 31 Q3 May 15)

29 Figure 29.1 shows the structure of the human eye as seen in horizontal section.

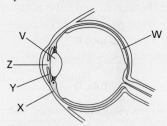

Figure 29.1

a Name the parts of the eye labelled **V** and **W**. [2]

b Figure 29.2 shows an eye as seen from the front. Label Figure 29.2 to show which parts correspond to the structures labelled, **X**, **Y** and **Z** in Fig 29.1. One has been done for you. [2]

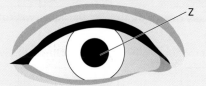

Figure 29.2

c Complete Table 29.1 to show what happens when the eye changes its focus from a distant object to a near object.

Table 29.1

structure	change when starting to focus on a near object
ciliary muscles	
suspensory ligaments	
lens – shape	
lens – focal length	decreased

d Older people often find it difficult to focus on near objects, although they are still able to focus well on distant objects. Suggest and explain a reason for this. [2]

(Cambridge IGCSE Co-ordinated Sciences 0654 Paper 31 Q10 May 15)

30 a Each time a human child is born, there is an equal chance that it will be a boy or a girl. Complete the genetic diagram to explain why. [3]

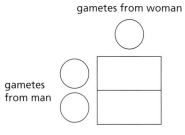

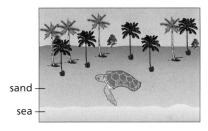

b Hawksbill turtles are an endangered species. They lay their eggs in nests in the sand on a beach.

The sex of hawksbill turtles is determined by the temperature of the sand in which the eggs develop.
• At 29 °C, equal numbers of males and females develop.
• Higher temperatures produce more females.
• Lower temperatures produce more males.
  i Researchers measured the temperature, at a depth of 30 cm, in two different parts of a beach, on Antigua, where hawksbill turtles lay their eggs. The results are shown in Figure 30.1. The tops of the bars represent the mean temperature.

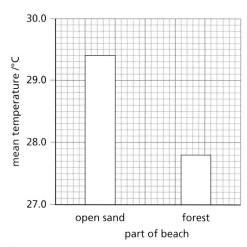

Figure 30.1

With reference to Figure 30.1, describe the effect of the presence of trees on the temperature of the sand. [2]

ii The researchers counted the proportion of male and female turtles hatching from nests in the two different parts of the beach. The results are shown in Table 30.1.

Table 30.1

part of beach	nests producing more males than females	nests producing more females than males	nests producing equal number of females and males
open sand	0	16	0
in forest	36	0	0

Use information in Figure 30.1 to explain the results for nests in open sand and in forest, shown in Table 30.1. [2]

iii Suggest why hawksbill turtles might become extinct if all the forest by the beaches are cut down. [2]

c State **two** harmful effects to the environment, other than extinction of the species, that can result from deforestation. [2]

(Cambridge IGCSE Co-ordinated Sciences 0654 Paper 22 Q6 May 2012)

31 Figure 31.1 shows the male reproductive system.

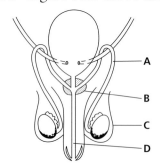

Figure 31.1

a i Name parts **C** and **D**. [2]
  ii State the functions of parts **A** and **B**. [1]
  iii On Figure 31.1, use a label line and the letter **S** to indicate where the male gametes are made. [1]

b The sex of a baby is determined by the X and Y chromosomes.
  i Name the part of a cell in which the X and Y chromosomes are found. [1]
  ii Describe how the sex of a human baby is inherited. [2]

c The human immunodeficiency virus (HIV) can be transmitted during sexual intercourse. Outline **two** other ways in which HIV can be transmitted. [2]

(Cambridge IGCSE Co-ordinated Sciences 0654 Paper 21 Q8 Nov 12)

32 In an experiment to investigate some of the conditions needed for seed germination, four Petri dishes were set up as shown in Figure 32.1. Each Petri dish contains some pea seeds. The seeds were soaked in water for 24 hours before being placed in the dishes. The four Petri dishes were treated as follows.

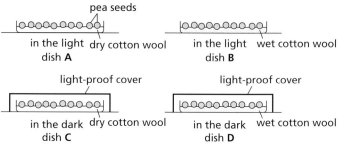

Figure 32.1

- Dish **A** was left in the light, with the seeds on dry cotton wool.
- Dish **B** was left in the light, with the seeds on wet cotton wool.
- Dish **C** was left in the dark, with the seeds on dry cotton wool.
- Dish **D** was left in the dark, with the seeds on wet cotton wool.

The dishes were then left for 10 days. After 10 days, when the covers were removed, the results were as shown in Figure 32.2.

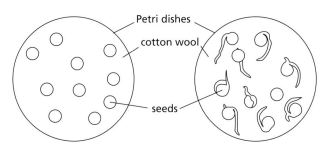

in the light, dry cotton wool
dish **A**

in the light, wet cotton wool
dish **B**

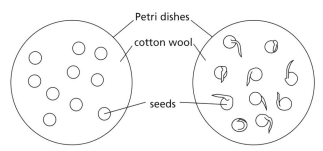

in the dark, dry cotton wool
dish **C**

in the dark, wet cotton wool
dish **D**

Figure 32.2

a Examine Figure 32.2 and make a note of
  i the total number of seeds in each dish
  ii the number of seeds that have begun to
     germinate as indicated by the clear emergence
     of a radicle (young root) from any seed.
     Record these numbers in Table 32.1.   [2]

Table 32.1

petri dish	A	B	C	D
total number of seeds in the dish				
number of germinating seeds in the dish				

b Use the results to write conclusions about
  whether light and water are needed for the
  germination of pea seeds.   [2]
c Explain why several seeds were placed in each
  dish, rather than just one seed.   [1]
d Suggest **two** other environmental conditions,
  apart from light and water, that could be
  important for the germination of pea seeds.   [2]

  *(Cambridge IGCSE Co-ordinated Sciences 0654
  Paper 61 Q1 a,b,c & d Nov 12)*

33 **a** The ovary of a flower contains one or more
     ovules. The ovules contain female gametes.
     After fertilisation, an ovule becomes a seed
     containing an embryo plant. Figure 33.1
     shows a pea seed developing inside a pod.

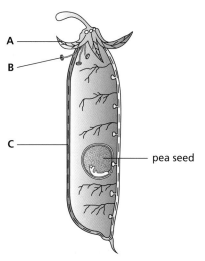

pea seed

Figure 33.1

  i Explain the meaning of each of the
    following terms:
    gamete
    fertilisation   [2]
  ii Parts **A** and **B** in Figure 33.1 remain
     from the flower.
     State the name of part **A** and function
     of part **B** of these parts in the flower.   [2]
  iii Suggest the part of the flower from
     which structure **C** developed.   [1]
b Four sets of pea seeds were placed in Petri
  dishes containing either damp soil or damp filter
  paper. They were left in different conditions,
  shown in Table 33.1. Predict which sets of seeds
  will germinate. Explain your answer.   [3]

Table 33.1

set	conditions		
A	damp soil	cold	dark
B	damp filter paper	warm	light
C	damp filter paper	warm	dark
D	damp soil	cold	light

c A pea seed was planted in a pot. When the
  seed had grown into a young plant, the pot
  was placed on its side, in a room where light
  was coming in from all sides. Figure 33.2
  shows the young pea plant three days after the
  pot had been placed on its side.

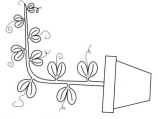

Figure 33.2

i   Name the response shown by the pea
    plant in Figure 33.2.   [2]
ii Suggest how this response will help
    the plant to reproduce sexually.   [3]
(Cambridge IGCSE Co-ordinated Sciences 0654
Paper 22 Q8 May 13)

34 a Figure 34.1 shows a flower seen in
longitudinal section.

Figure 34.1

i   Make a large, clear pencil drawing of
    this flower.   [2]
ii On your drawing, label a stamen and the
    carpel. Next to each of these labels, state
    (in brackets) whether the part is male
    or female.   [2]
b A student took a petal of a different flower
and tested it for the presence of reducing
sugar, using Benedict's test. Figure 34.2
shows the appearance of the petal before and
after carrying out the Benedict's test.

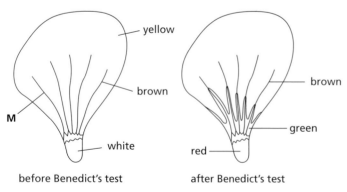

before Benedict's test   after Benedict's test

Figure 34.2

i   Describe how you would carry out the
     Benedict's test.   [1]
ii   State the function of the petals of
     this flower.   [1]
iii Suggest how the following features help
     the function of the flower:
     • the colour of the petal, before carrying
       out the Benedict's test,
     • the lines and markings, labelled **M**. [2]
iv   State your conclusion from the results
     of the Benedict's test. Explain the
     significance of this in relation to your
     answers to **ii** and **iii**.   [2]
(Cambridge IGCSE Co-ordinated Sciences 0654
Paper 61 Q1 May 13)

35   A student was investigating the structure of
plants. The student had a bean seedling. It is
shown in Figure 35.1.

Figure 35.1

a i   Make a large drawing of the seedling. [2]
ii   Measure to the nearest millimetre the
          complete length of the seedling in the
          photograph in Figure 35.1.
          length = _____ mm   [1]
iii   Measure to the nearest millimetre the
          complete length of the seedling in your
          drawing.
          length of drawing = _____ mm   [1]
iv   Calculate the magnification of your
          drawing.
          magnification = _____   [1]
b The student then prepared a slide of a transverse
section of the root of the bean seedling.

Figure 35.2 shows the distribution of the different tissues in this root using a microscope.

Figure 35.2

   i Draw a clear straight line on **your** diagram in **ai** to represent the transverse section that the student made. [1]

   ii Label the xylem tissue on Figure 35.2. [1]

c Outline a method the student could use to find where the xylem tissue is distributed in the stem of the bean seedling. [3]

(Cambridge IGCSE Co-ordinated Sciences 0654 Paper 61 Q4 Nov 13)

36 Figure 36.1 shows some of the stages in human reproduction.

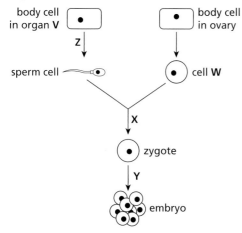

Figure 36.1

a Name organ **V** and cell **W**. [2]

b Name the process that is occurring at **X**. [1]

c State what type of nuclear division is occurring when the cells divide at **Y** and **Z**. [2]

d The nucleus of the cell in the ovary contains 46 chromosomes. State the number of chromosomes present in the nuclei of:

   • cell **W**

   • a cell from the embryo. [2]

(Cambridge IGCSE Co-ordinated Sciences 0654 Paper 33 Q7 Nov 2014)

37 Figure 37.1 shows the female reproductive system.

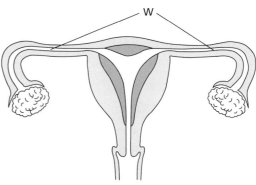

Figure 37.1

a Name the part of the female reproductive system in which the female gametes are produced. [1]

b i Name the tubes labelled **W**. [1]

   ii Infertility in women can sometimes be caused by the tubes **W** becoming blocked. Explain why this would lead to infertility. [1]

c The female reproductive system produces hormones.

   i Define a *hormone*. [3]

   ii On Figure 37.1, use a label line to name and identify the part that produces hormones. [1]

(Cambridge IGCSE Co-ordinated Sciences 0654 Paper 22 Q7 May 15)

38 Figure 38.1 shows a strawberry plant.

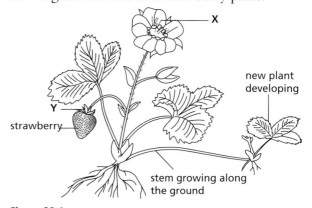

Figure 38.1

a A stem of the strawberry plant is growing along the ground, with a new plant developing at the end of this stem.

   i Name the type of reproduction shown by this process. [1]

ii Explain why the new plant will produce exactly the same type of strawberries as the parent plant. [1]
b The strawberry plant has leaves and flowers. State the main function of
  i   the leaves [1]
  ii the flowers. [1]
c Using Figure 38.1, name
  i   the part of the flower labelled **X** [1]
  ii the leaf-like structure above the strawberry, labelled **Y**. [1]
d Figure 38.2 shows an insect called a strawberry blossom weevil. The strawberry blossom weevil destroys some of the strawberry flowers. Explain why these blossom weevils will reduce the amount of fruit produced by a strawberry plant. [1]

Figure 38.2

(Cambridge IGCSE Co-ordinated Sciences 0654 Paper 23 Q5 Nov 15)

39 In a flower, ripe stigmas produce a fluid containing sugar. The sugar stimulates pollen grains that land on a stigma to grow pollen tubes. These pollen tubes allow the nucleus from the pollen to travel to the egg (ovum) in the ovary so that fertilisation can take place. Pollen tubes can be observed using a light microscope. Figure 39.1 shows a photograph of some of these pollen tubes.

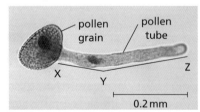

Figure 39.1

a Measure and record the total length of the pollen tube as indicated by the line **X–Y–Z** on

Figure 39.1. With the help of the scale bar on the slide of Figure 39.1, calculate the actual length of the pollen tube. Show your working.
Total length of pollen tube on image
(**X–Y–Z**) = _____ mm [2]
Actual length of **X–Y–Z** = _____ mm [2]
b A student investigates the effect of different strength sugar solutions on the growth of pollen tubes.
  • He places a drop of sugar solution on a microscope slide and adds pollen grains to it.
  • He leaves the slide in a warm place for an hour and then looks at the slide using the microscope.
  • He counts the number of pollen grains that he can see and then calculates the percentage that have pollen tubes.
  His results are shown in Table 39.1.

Table 39.1

concentration of sugar solution (mol/dm³)	% of pollen grains with pollen tubes			
	experiment 1	experiment 2	experiment 3	average
0	0	0	0	0
0.25	36	28	32	
0.50	72	68	76	
0.75	49	41	45	
1	10	7	13	

Complete the last column of Table 39.1. [1]
c i   Use Table 39.1 to plot a graph of average percentage of pollen grains with tubes (vertical axis) against sugar concentration. Draw a best-fit curve. [4]
  ii Use your graph to suggest the best concentration of sugar for pollen tube growth. [1]
(Cambridge IGCSE Co-ordinated Sciences 0654 Paper 62 Q4 Nov 15)

40 Figure 40.1 shows an animal cell, just before it divides.

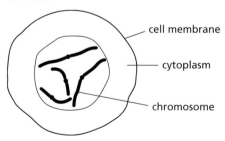

Figure 40.1

a Define the term *chromosome.* [2]

b Some cattle have horns, but other cattle do not. This is determined by a gene. The allele of the gene that produces horns, **h**, is recessive.

   i Complete Table 40.1 to show the phenotypes of cattle with each of the possible genotypes for this gene.

Table 40.1

genotype	phenotype
HH	no horns
Hh	
hh	

   ii A farmer has a bull with no horns. He wants to make sure that the bull does not have the recessive allele, **h**, for horns. He breeds the bull with a cow that has horns. Complete the genetic diagram to show the possible offspring if the bull does have the allele for horns. [3]

parents   bull with no horns   cow with no horns

genotype of parents   **Hh**   **hh**

gametes ◯ and ◯ ◯

gametes from cow

gametes from bull

   iii Explain how the results of the cross can help the farmer to decide whether the bull has the allele **h** or not. [2]

   iv Cows usually give birth to one or two calves each time. Explain why the farmer needs to cross the bull with the cow several times before he can be sure whether the bull has the allele **h** or not. [2]

(Cambridge IGCSE Co-ordinated Sciences 0654 Paper 22 Q3 May 13)

41 Ball pythons (royal pythons) are snakes that are kept as pets in many parts of the world. The colour of a ball python is determined by its genes. Some ball pythons are albino (white). This is caused by a recessive allele, **a**. The dominant allele, **A**, gives normal colouring.

a Complete Table 41.1 to show the possible genotypes and colours arising from this gene. [2]

Table 41.1

genotype	colour
AA	
Aa	normal
	albino

b State the correct biological term of the visible appearance produced by the genotype, in this case the colour of the snake. [1]

c i Complete the genetic diagram to explain the results of crossing two snakes that are heterozygous for these alleles. [3]

genotype of parents Aa and ....

gametes ◯ and ◯ ◯ and ◯

gametes from one parent

gametes from the other parent

   ii State the ratio of offspring that you would expect from this cross. Ratio of normal : albino offspring = _____ : _____ [1]

d A breeder has several snakes with normal colouring. Suggest how she can find out whether a particular snake is homozygous or heterozygous. [2]

(Cambridge IGCSE Co-ordinated Sciences 0654 Paper 23 Q7 Nov 13)

42 a Use the words in the list to complete the sentences, which are about evolution. You may use each word once, more than once or not at all.

adaptation   reproduction   respond
selection   survive   variation

Organisms show _____ , which means that no two individuals are exactly alike. Some individuals show better _____ to their environment, and these individuals are more likely to _____ and reproduce. This may lead to evolution as a result of the process of natural _____ .   [4]

b Table 42.1 shows, for a species of bacterium, the percentage of bacteria that were resistant to the antibiotic penicillin. The data are for samples of bacteria taken in two different countries in the years 1980 and 2010.

Table 42.1

	country **A**	country **B**
percentage of antibiotic-resistant bacteria in 1980	3	4
percentage of antibiotic-resistant bacteria in 2010	54	12

    i   Compare the incidence of antibiotic-resistance in the two countries
        • in 1980
        • in 2010.   [2]

   ii   In both countries, antibiotic-resistance increased between 1980 and 2010. Use the idea of evolution to explain how this may have happened.   [3]

  iii Suggest a reason why resistance to antibiotics increased faster in country **A** than in country **B**.   [1]

(Cambridge IGCSE Co-ordinated Sciences 0654 Paper 33 Q1 Nov 14)

43 On a farm, the wheat yield from one field was recorded over a period of sixty years. Figure 43.1 shows the results.

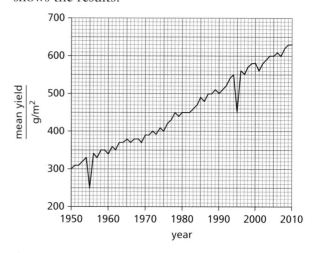

Figure 43.1

a i   State in which year the yield from this field was lowest.   [1]
   ii   Calculate how much the mean yield increased between 1950 and 2010.
        yield increase _____ g/m²   [1]

b i   It is suggested that the increase in yield shown in Figure 43.1 was caused by artificial selection. Describe how artificial selection would have been carried out.   [2]
   ii   Suggest **two** other possible explanations of the increase in yield that do **not** involve artificial selection.   [2]

c Suggest a possible reason for the results that were obtained in 1955 and 1995.   [1]

d In addition to yield, give **one** other characteristic of wheat plants that farmers might try to improve through artificial selection.   [1]

(Cambridge IGCSE Co-ordinated Sciences 0654 Paper 22 Q5 May 15)

44 Figure 44.1 shows an okapi. Okapis are rare animals. Their habitat is in the forests of central Africa.

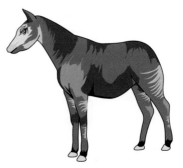

Figure 44.1

Okapis are threatened with extinction. The two main causes of this are hunting and the cutting down of trees by humans.

a i State the term for the cutting down of large numbers of trees by humans. [1]

ii Suggest **two** reasons why humans cut down large numbers of trees in the forests of central Africa. [2]

b Suggest **two** ways in which the extinction of the okapi could be prevented. [2]

c Figure 44.2 shows a food chain that includes the okapi.

| tree leaves | → | okapi | → | leopard |

Figure 44.2

If the okapi became extinct, explain how this would affect

i the trees in the forest [1]

ii the leopards. [1]

(Cambridge IGCSE Co-ordinated Sciences 0654 Paper 23 Q10 Nov 15)

45 a Figure 45.1 shows part of the carbon cycle.

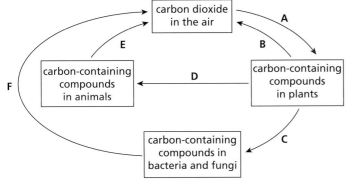

Figure 45.1

i State the letter or letters **A, B, C, D, E** or **F** that represent
• photosynthesis
• respiration [2]

ii Name **one** carbon-containing compound in plants. [1]

iii State the approximate percentage of carbon dioxide in the air. [1]

b Earthworms play an important part in the carbon cycle. They eat dead leaves, and egest material containing plant nutrients in the soil. Explain the meaning of the term *egest*. [2]

c In Florida, USA, some people collect earthworms by vibrating the soil. Earthworms respond to vibrations in the ground by crawling out of their burrows onto the soil surface.

A student investigated the effect of different frequencies of vibrations on the numbers of earthworms that emerged from the soil. Figure 45.2 shows this result.

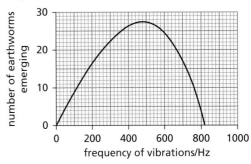

Figure 45.2

i Describe the effect of different frequencies of vibrations on the numbers of earthworms emerging. [2]

ii Fishermen catch large numbers of earthworms to use as bait. There are concerns that too many worms are being collected in some parts of Florida, USA. Suggest why it is important to conserve earthworms. [2]

iii Moles are predators that live underground and eat earthworms. When moles burrow through the ground, they produce vibrations of around 500 Hz. Explain why the genes of earthworms that respond to vibrations of this frequency have a strong chance of being passed on to the next generation. [2]

(Cambridge IGCSE Co-ordinated Sciences 0654 Paper 21 Q2 Nov12)

46 Figure 46.1 shows a food chain. The arrows show how energy flows from one organism to another, along the chain.

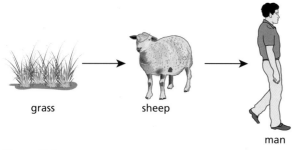

grass   sheep   man

Figure 46.1

a Energy enters the food chain as sunlight. Plant leaves use this energy to make food.

   i   Name the substance in the leaves of a plant that absorbs this energy.   [1]

   ii Name the **two** raw materials that the plant uses to make food.   [2]

   iii Name the gas released from plant leaves during this process.   [1]

b A sheep is a herbivore. Define the term *herbivore*.   [2]

c Meat from the sheep contains protein. Describe the importance of protein in the diet.   [2]

d In the cells of the plant, sheep and man, useful energy is released from the food by respiration. Some of the energy is released as heat. Explain why the following changes occur when the man's body temperature rises too high.

   • The arterioles near the surface of his skin dilate.

   • His sweat glands produce more sweat.   [4]

(Cambridge IGCSE Co-ordinated Sciences 0654 Paper 22 Q11 May13)

47 Figure 47.1 shows part of the carbon cycle.

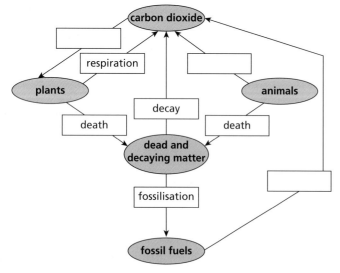

Figure 47.1

a Fill in the empty boxes in Figure 47.1, naming the processes involved in the carbon cycle. Chose words from the list. You may use each word once, more than once, or not at all.

breathing   combustion   decomposition
photosynthesis   respiration   transpiration [3]

b Add an arrow to Figure 47.1 to show how animals obtain their carbon.   [1]

c Use the ideas of the carbon cycle to explain why, in a deciduous (temperate) forest, the carbon dioxide concentration in the atmosphere:

   • falls slightly in spring and summer

   • rises again in the autumn.   [2]

d In many parts of the world, large areas of forest are being cut down. With reference to Figure 47.1 explain why the carbon dioxide concentration of the atmosphere might be affected by this.   [2]

(Cambridge IGCSE Co-ordinated Sciences 0654 Paper 22 Q3 May 15)

48 a Figure 48.1 shows part of a food web in the forest ecosystem around Chernobyl, in Ukraine.

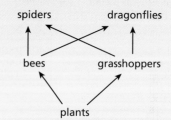

Figure 48.1

   i   Define the term *ecosystem*.   [2]

   ii What do the arrows in the food web represent?   [1]

   iii State the trophic level at which spiders feed.   [1]

   iv The food web shows that bees depend on plants. Some species of flowering plants also depend on bees and other insects. Explain how bees help flowering plant species to survive.   [3]

b In 1986, major errors by operators resulted in a huge explosion of the Chernobyl nuclear reactor. Radioactive substances were released into the environment. One of the main radioactive substances released was caesium-137. When caesium-137 decays, it forms barium-137. Table 48.1 shows information about the radioactive decay of caesium-137 and barium-137.

Table 48.1

	caesium-137	barium-137
radiation emitted	β (beta)	γ (gamma)
half-life	30 years	2.5 minutes

i Explain why the area around Chernobyl still has high levels of both β and γ radiation today, more than 26 years after the explosion. [3]

ii Complete the equation to show how caesium-137 decays to form barium-137. [2]

$$^{137}_{55}Cs \longrightarrow \underline{\hspace{2cm}} + ^{0}_{-1}e$$

iii In 2009, scientists counted the number of spiders at different distances from the Chernobyl reactor. They also measured the radiation levels. The number of spiders counted with different radiation levels are shown in Figure 48.2. Suggest reasons for the pattern of results shown in Figure 48.2. You should use your knowledge of the effects of ionising radiation on living organisms, and the information in the food web in Figure 48.1. [3]

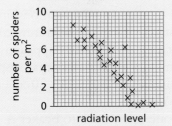

Figure 48.2

(Cambridge IGCSE Co-ordinated Sciences 0654 Paper 32 Q4 Nov 12)

Chemistry

1 A student is investigating how the concentration of a reactant affects the rate of a reaction. In this reaction potassium iodate reacts with a reducing agent to produce iodine. The reaction can be followed using starch solution as an indicator; it turns blue-black when iodine is present.

- She places $10 \, cm^3$ potassium iodate solution into a conical flask.
- She adds $5 \, cm^3$ starch solution to the conical flask.
- She starts the timer as she adds $5 \, cm^3$ of the reducing agent to the conical flask.
- She stops the timer when the mixture goes blue-black.
- She records the time taken, to the nearest second, for the mixture to go blue-black in Table 1.1.
- She repeats the experiment four times varying the volumes of potassium iodate solution and water as shown in Table 1.1.

Table 1.1

volume potassium	volume water/cm^3	time/s	$\frac{1}{time}$
10	0	10	0.100
8	2	13	0.077
6	4		
4	6	30	0.033
2	8		

a Read the stop clocks in Figure 1.1 and record the times to the nearest second in Table 1.1. [2]

6 cm³ potassium iodate solution   2 cm³ potassium iodate solution

Figure 1.1

b i Calculate $\frac{1}{time}$ (rate) for the missing values and enter the results in the last column of Table 1.1. [1]

ii Plot a graph of $\frac{1}{time}$ (vertical axis) against the volume of potassium iodate solution/cm^3, drawing the best straight line through the origin. [4]

c i State what your graph tells you about how the rate of the reaction depends upon the volume of potassium iodate solution present. [1]

ii When the potassium iodate is reduced iodine is formed. What observation made by the student confirms this? [1]

iii Why are different volumes of water used in each experiment? [1]

(Cambridge IGCSE Co-ordinated Sciences 0654 Paper 61 Q3 May 13)

2 The science class is making a display to show the elements in Period 3 of the Periodic Table, as in Figure 2.1. A sample of each element is placed next to a card giving its symbol and atomic number.

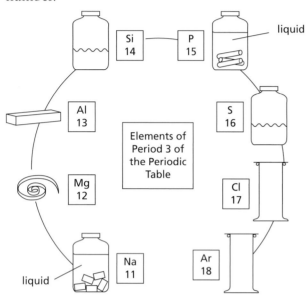

Figure 2.1

a Write the names of element number 12 and element number 14. [2]

b Elements 11 and 15 are contained in bottles and covered with a liquid to prevent the element reacting with air. One element is covered by water and the other one by oil. Complete the sentences.
The name of the element covered by water is _____ .
The name of the element covered by oil is _____ . [1]

c The two gas-jars holding samples of elements 17 and 18 have lost their labels. How can a student tell from the appearance of the gases which gas-jar contains element number 17? [1]

d Describe an experiment that a student can do to show that element number 13 is a metal. State the observation that the student will make. You may draw a diagram to help you. [2]

Another student is doing an experiment to show the burning of element number 16 in oxygen. This is shown in Figure 2.2.

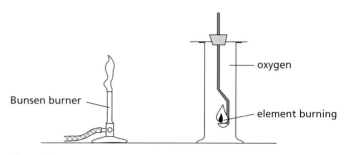

Figure 2.2

He places some of the powder in a spoon and heats it in a Bunsen flame. When the element ignites, he holds the spoon in the gas-jar of oxygen. After the powder finishes burning, he adds water to the gas-jar, places the lid on and shakes the jar. Then he adds Universal Indicator (full-range indicator) solution.

e i State the flame colour of the burning element number 16. [1]
ii Suggest why the student adds water to the gas-jar. [1]
iii State the colour of the Universal Indicator (full-rage indicator) in the gas-jar. [1]
iv The student does the same experiment with a piece of element number 12. Suggest the colour of the Universal Indicator in this gas-jar. [1]
(Cambridge IGCSE Co-ordinated Sciences 0654 Paper 61 Q5 Nov 13)

3 A student is investigating the relationship between yeast activity and temperature. Active yeast produces a gas which may appear as a foam.
• The student stirs a yeast and sugar suspension and immediately measures out $20\,cm^3$ into each of two large test-tubes.
• He places one test-tube into beaker **A** containing some water which he maintains at about 20 °C.
• He places the other test-tube into beaker **B** containing some water which he maintains at about 40 °C.
The apparatus is shown in Figure 3.1.

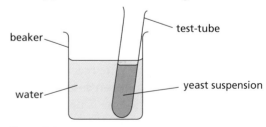

Figure 3.1

He measures the temperature of the water in each beaker.

The temperature of beaker **A** is 190.0 °C.

a The thermometer in Figure 3.2 shows the temperature in beaker **B**. Read and record this temperature.

beaker B = _____ °C [1]

°C

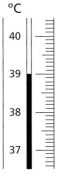

Figure 3.2

He uses a ruler to measure the height *h* of the liquid (including any foam) in each test-tube at regular intervals. The arrangement is shown in Figure 3.3.

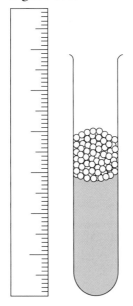

Figure 3.3

b On Figure 3.3, draw a labelled arrow to show the height *h*. Mark clearly the top and bottom of the measurement. [1]

The student measures the height *h* in each test-tube at 2 minute intervals for ten minutes. During this time he maintains the temperatures of the beakers. He records his measurements in Table 3.1.

Table 3.1

time/min	beaker **A** height *h*/mm	beaker **B** height *h*/mm
0	40	40
2	40	62
4	40	75
6	41	90
8	42	98
10	44	105

c On the grid provided, plot graphs of height *h* for each beaker against time. Draw best-fit lines and label them **A** and **B**. [4]

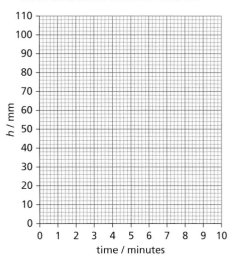

d A teacher says that yeast activity stops when the temperature of the yeast is too high. Plan and describe an investigation based on the experiment the student carried out to find out the minimum temperature at which yeast activity stops due to temperature being too high. [4]

(Cambridge IGCSE Co-ordinated Sciences 0654 Paper 61 Q1 Nov 14)

4 a Water is a compound which contains the elements hydrogen and oxygen. Describe **one** difference, other than physical state, between the **compound** water and a mixture of the elements hydrogen and oxygen. [2]

b Table 4.1 shows information about water and three compounds that form mixtures with water.

Table 4.1

compound	melting point/°C	boiling point/°C	solubility in water
water	0	100	-
sodium chloride	801	1413	soluble
silicon dioxide	1650	2230	insoluble
hexane	−95	69	insoluble

  i State which compound in Table 4.1 could be separated from a mixture with water by filtration. [1]

  ii Explain why the other two compounds **cannot** be separated from a mixture with water by filtration. [2]

  iii A student looked at a magnified image of some sodium chloride crystals through a microscope. Figure 4.1 shows what she observed through the microscope. Draw a simple diagram of the structure of sodium chloride. Your diagram should clearly show the nature and arrangement of the particles involved and should show why the crystals have the shape shown in Figure 4.1. [3]

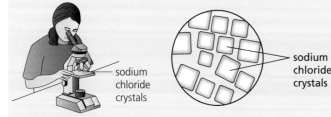

sodium chloride crystals

sodium chloride crystals

Figure 4.1

c The student is asked to use the reaction between the insoluble compound copper carbonate and dilute sulfuric acid to make some crystals of copper sulfate. Describe the main steps of a method the student should carry out this task. You may draw labelled diagrams if it helps you to answer this question. [4]

(Cambridge IGCSE Co-ordinated Sciences 0654 Paper 32 Q8 May 12)

5 Figure 5.1 shows apparatus a student used to investigate temperature changes that occurred during chemical reactions. The student added reactants to the insulated beaker and stirred the mixture. She recorded the final temperature of each mixture. At the start of each experiment, the temperature of the reactants was 22 °C. Table 5.1 contains the results the student obtained.

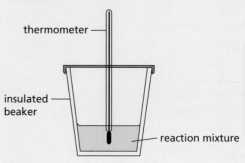

thermometer

insulated beaker

reaction mixture

Figure 5.1

Table 5.1

experiment	reactant A	reactant B	final temperature /°C
1	dilute hydrochloric acid	sodium hydrogencarbonate	16
2	dilute hydrochloric acid	potassium hydroxide solution	26
3	magnesium	copper sulfate solution	43
4	copper	magnesium sulfate solution	22

a i Explain which experiment **1, 2, 3** or **4** was a reaction involving an alkali.
- experiment _____
- explanation _____ [1]

  ii State and explain which experiment **1, 2, 3** or **4** was an endothermic reaction.
- experiment _____
- explanation _____ [1]

  iii Suggest and explain a reason for the result obtained in experiment **4**. [2]

b The student carried out two further experiments, **5** and **6**, to investigate the reaction between zinc and copper sulfate solution. In experiment **5** the student used 3.25 g of zinc powder, and in experiment **6** she used a single piece of zinc which also had a mass of 3.25 g. The student observed the readings on the thermometer over five minutes during each experiment. Predict and explain any difference in the way that the temperature would change between experiments **5** and **6**. [3]

c In the reaction in **b**, zinc atoms react with copper ions. This chemical change may be represented by the symbolic equation below.
$$Zn(s) + Cu^{2+}(aq) \rightarrow Zn^{2+}(aq) + Cu(s)$$
Explain, in terms of the transfer of electrons, why this reaction is an example of oxidation and reduction (redox). [1]

(Cambridge IGCSE Co-ordinated Sciences 0654 Paper 32 Q11 a,b,c May 12)

6 Large amounts of chemical energy are stored in the world's reserves of fossil fuels such as natural gas and petroleum (crude oil).

a i Name the main compound in natural gas. Write the **word** chemical equation for the complete combustion of this compound. [3]

ii Before it is refined, petroleum contains sulfur compounds. Describe and explain how water in rivers and lakes could become polluted if sulfur compounds are **not** removed from fossil fuels before they are used. [4]

b i Sulfur is removed from petroleum by combining it with hydrogen to form the gaseous compound hydrogen sulfide, H_2S. Complete the bonding diagram of one molecule of hydrogen sulfide below to show:
- the chemical symbols of the elements
- how the outer electrons in each element are arranged. [2]

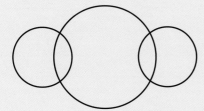

ii Each year, millions of tonnes of sulfur are removed from petroleum, and used as a raw material in the Contact Process. Name the final product of the Contact Process. [1]

(Cambridge IGCSE Co-ordinated Sciences 0654 Paper 32 Q8 Nov 12)

7 a When sodium is burned in air a mixture of solid products, which contains the ionic compound sodium oxide, is produced. Figure 7.1 shows diagrams of a sodium atom and an oxygen atom as they exist just before sodium oxide starts to form.

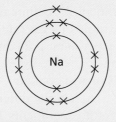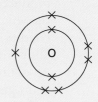

Figure 7.1

i Describe how sodium and oxygen atoms become bonded together. Your answer should explain why the formula of sodium oxide is Na_2O. [3]

ii Describe **two** differences in the properties of a typical ionic compound and a typical covalent compound. [2]

b Figure 7.2 shows apparatus a student used to investigate the electrolysis of dilute sulfuric acid. The variable resistor was included in the electrolysis circuit so that the student could alter the current.

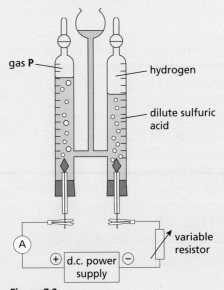

Figure 7.2

Table 7.1 shows some of the measurements the student made in his investigation.

Table 7.1

experiment number	current /A	time current was passed/seconds	volume of hydrogen collected/cm³
1	0.48	400	24
2	0.24	400	12

i Name gas **P**. [1]

ii Calculate the rate at which hydrogen was produced in experiment **1**. Show your working and state the units. [2]

iii Calculate the number of moles of hydrogen produced in experiment **2**. Assume that the volume of one mole of a gas under the conditions of the experiment is 24 dm³. Show your working. [2]

iv All dilute solutions of acid contain hydrogen ions, H^+. Explain the difference between the results for experiments **1** and **2** in terms of electrons, ions, atoms and electric current. [3]

(Cambridge IGCSE Co-ordinated Sciences 0654 Paper 32 Q5 May 13)

8 Most of the elements in the Periodic Table can be classified as either metals or non-metals. Table 8.1 shows the elements in Group 4 of the Periodic Table.

Table 8.1

C
Si
Ge
Sn
Pb

a Use the classification of metal or non-metal to describe how the Group 4 elements differ from both Group 1 (alkali metals) and Group 7 (halogens). [2]

b Carbon occurs naturally in the Earth's crust as the uncombined element. Diamond and graphite are different forms of carbon (carbon allotropes) that have very different physical properties. A small section of the structure of one of the carbon allotropes is shown in Figure 8.1.
State and explain **one** use of the carbon allotrope shown in Figure 8.1. [2]

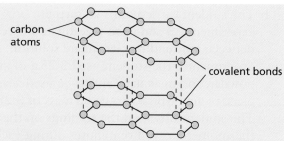

Figure 8.1

c Figure 8.2 shows apparatus used to extract lead from lead oxide, PbO.

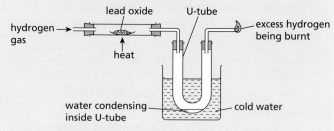

Figure 8.2

i Construct a balanced symbol equation for the reaction between hydrogen and lead oxide. [2]

ii Suggest why the method shown in Figure 8.2 could **not** be used to extract calcium from calcium oxide. [2]

(Cambridge IGCSE Co-ordinated Sciences 0654 Paper 32 Q1 May 13)

9 a Dutch metal is an alloy of copper and zinc that has been formed into very thin sheets. When a small piece of Dutch metal is dropped into a container filled with chlorine, it bursts into flame and two compounds are produced as shown in Figure 9.1.

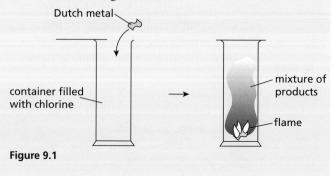

Figure 9.1

i State the meaning of the term *alloy*. [1]

ii State the physical property of metals that allows them to be formed into very thin sheets. [1]

iii Suggest the names of the **two** compounds formed when Dutch metal reacts with chlorine. [1]

b Sodium burns in oxygen gas to produce a white solid that contains the ionic compound sodium oxide. Figure 9.2 shows a sodium atom and an oxygen atom.

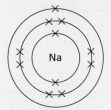

Figure 9.2

Predict and explain, in terms of changes and electronic structure, the chemical formula of sodium oxide. You may wish to draw diagrams to help you to answer this question. [3]

c Phosphorus is a non-metallic element containing molecules that have the formula P_4. The chemical formula of phosphorus oxide shows four phosphorus atoms bonded with ten oxygen atoms. Construct a balanced symbolic equation for the reaction between phosphorus and oxygen gas to form phosphorus oxide. [3]

(Cambridge IGCSE Co-ordinated Sciences 0654 Paper 33 Q3 May 14)

10 a A colourless gas contained in a flask is either propane or propene.

i The gas is shaken with bromine solution. Describe the observation, if any, that would be made if the gas is
- propane,
- propene. [2]

ii Describe **one** difference between the structures of propane and propene molecules. [1]

b Ethanol, C_2H_6O, is produced from glucose, $C_6H_{12}O_6$, in a fermentation reaction.

The balanced equation below shows the conversion of glucose to ethanol.

$$C_6H_{12}O_6(aq) \rightarrow 2C_2H_6O(aq) + 2CO_2(g)$$

The fermentation reaction starts when yeast is added to the aqueous solution of glucose. Figure 10.1 shows apparatus that can be used for the reaction.

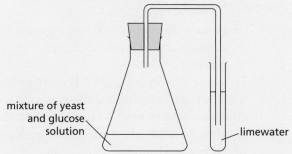

mixture of yeast and glucose solution

limewater

Figure 10.1

i Describe how and explain why the appearance of the limewater changes during the fermentation reaction. [2]

ii Calculate the relative molecular mass of glucose $C_6H_{12}O_6$. Show your working.
relative molecular mass = _____ [1]

iii Calculate the mass of glucose that has to be dissolved in $5.0\,dm^3$ of water to produce a solution whose concentration is $3.5\,mol/dm^3$. Show your working
mass of glucose = _____ g [2]

c i Name the element present in **all** amino acids but **not** in ethanol. [1]

ii Many different amino acids exist in nature. Name the compound that is formed when amino acids link together in a condensation polymerisation reaction. [1]

(Cambridge IGCSE Co-ordinated Sciences 0654 Paper 31 Q5 Nov 15)

11 a In the Periodic Table the elements are organised into groups and periods.

i State the total number of elements in the **period** that includes nitrogen, N. [1]

ii Figure 11.1 shows the electron arrangement and the numbers of protons in one atom of nitrogen. Name the other type of sub-atomic particle contained in this nucleus. [1]

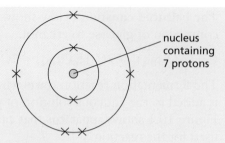

Figure 11.1

iii Draw a diagram, similar to Figure 11.1, to show an atom of the element phosphorus, P. [2]

b Hydrogen, proton number 1, combines with nitrogen to produce the covalent compound ammonia, NH_3. Complete the covalent bonding diagram of one molecule of ammonia to show:
 • the chemical symbols of each atom.
 • how the outer electrons of each atom are arranged. [2]

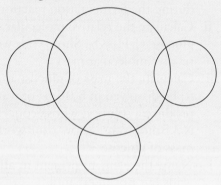

c Ammonia is made in industry by reacting nitrogen and hydrogen together on the surface of a solid material containing iron. A simplified diagram of the process is shown in Figure 11.2.

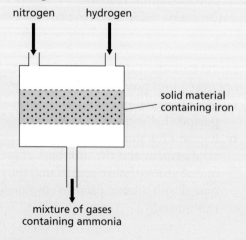

Figure 11.2

i State the name of the industrial process shown in Figure 11.2. [1]

ii Hydrogen gas for the process is produced by reacting methane, CH_4, with steam, H_2O. In this reaction each methane reacts with **one** of the molecules in steam. The reaction produces **three** molecules of hydrogen. Deduce the balanced symbol equation for this reaction. [3]

iii State the purpose of the solid material containing iron that is used in the process shown in Figure 11.2. [1]

(Cambridge IGCSE Co-ordinated Sciences 0654 Paper 31 Q1 Nov 15)

12 Salts are produced when acids are neutralised.

a Using only substances chosen from the list, complete the word equations for the reactions that produce the two salts, magnesium sulfate and zinc sulfate. Each substance may be used once, more than once or not at all.

hydrochloric acid	**hydrogen**
magnesium	**magnesium carbonate**
magnesium oxide	**sulfuric acid**
water	**zinc**
zinc carbonate	**zinc oxide**

_____ + _____ → magnesium + hydrogen
sulfate

_____ + _____ → zinc + carbon + _____
sulfate dioxide [2]

b Figure 12.1 shows what happens to the temperature when sodium hydrogencarbonate solution reacts with dilute hydrochloric acid.

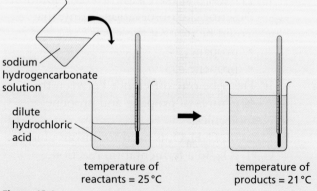

Figure 12.1

i   Complete the equation to show the type of energy transformation that occurs in this reaction.
_____ energy → _____ energy   [1]
ii   Explain your answer to **bi**.   [1]
c   Figure 12.2 shows the apparatus a student uses to investigate the rate of reaction between calcium carbonate and excess dilute hydrochloric acid.

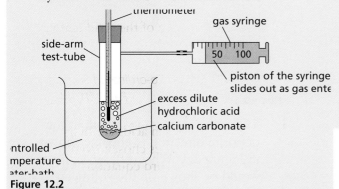

Figure 12.2

The student obtains data using the following method.
- She pushes the piston completely into the gas syringe.
- She adds a known amount of dilute hydrochloric acid to the side-arm test-tube and checks that the temperature is steady.
- She adds a known mass of calcium carbonate to the side-arm test-tube, places the bung in position and starts her stopwatch.
- She records the volume of gas in the gas syringe every 10 seconds for 90 seconds.

Figure 12.3 shows a graph of her results.

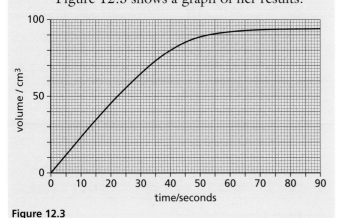

Figure 12.3

i   Explain the shape of the graph between 75 and 90 seconds.   [2]
ii   The student repeated her experiment but this time she uses **half** of the mass of calcium carbonate used in the first experiment. She made sure that all the other variables have the same values as in the first experiment. On Figure 12.3 sketch the graph of her results from the second experiment.   [3]
iii   Explain in terms of collisions why the rate of the reaction increases when the temperature of the acid is increased.   [2]

(Cambridge IGCSE Co-ordinated Sciences 0654 Paper 31 Q12 Nov 15)

Physics

1 a   A student is finding the value of an unknown mass, M, of a fixed load by balancing it against a range of known masses on a metre rule. The apparatus is set up as shown in Figure 1.1.

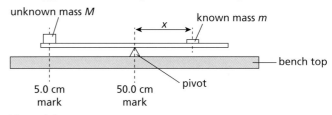

Figure 1.1

The unknown load of mass M, is fixed at the 5.0 cm position. The student places a 60 g mass, m, on the ruler. He adjusts the position of mass m, until the ruler is balanced. He records the distance, x cm, from the 50.0 cm balance point in Table 1.1.

Table 1.1

mass m/g	distance x/cm	$\frac{1}{x}$
60	37.4	
70	31.9	
80		
90		
100	22.7	

i   Use Figure 1.2 to find the distance, x, for masses equal to 80 g and 90 g and complete column 2 of Table 1.1. Measure to the centre of the mass.   [2]

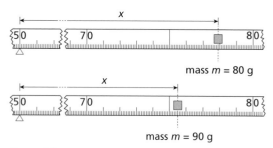

mass m = 80 g

mass m = 90 g

Figure 1.2

ii Calculate $\frac{1}{x}$ for each value of x and record your answers to 3 decimal places in Table 1.1.

b i On the grid provided, plot a graph of mass, m, (vertical axis) against $\frac{1}{x}$. Draw the best straight line. [2]

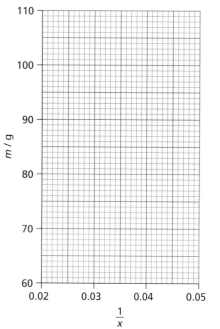

Figure 1.3

ii Calculate the gradient of the line. Show clearly, on the graph, how you did this. [2]

c Calculate the value of the unknown load of mass M, using the equation.

$$M = \frac{\text{gradient}}{45}$$

$$M = \text{_____ g} \qquad [1]$$

d This method of finding unknown masses is unsuitable for very small or very large masses. Suggest a reason for either of these. [1]

(Cambridge IGCSE Co-ordinated Sciences 0654 Paper 61 Q6 May 13)

2 a Figure 2.1 shows a diagram of a small electrical a.c. generator producing an alternating voltage.

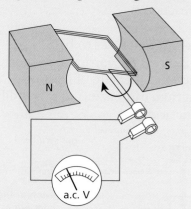

Figure 2.1

i The coil is now made to spin in the opposite direction to the one shown in Figure 2.1. What difference, if any, would be shown on the voltmeter reading? [1]

ii State **two** ways in which the size of the induced voltage can be increased. [2]

b In a power station there are several large generators. Explain why transformers are needed between the power transmission cables from the power station and the cables supplying homes. [2]

(Cambridge IGCSE Co-ordinated Sciences 0654 Paper 32 Q6 Nov 12)

3 Figure 3.1 shows four swimmers at the start of a race.

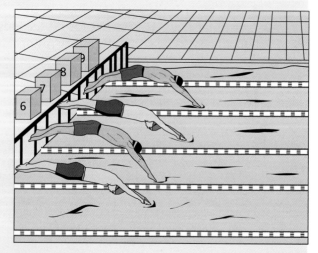

Figure 3.1

a The swimmers start their race when they hear a loud, high-pitched sound from a loudspeaker.

   i Describe how the loudspeaker causes the sound to travel through the air. Use the idea of compressions and rarefactions in your answer. You may draw a diagram if it helps your answer. [2]

   ii Explain why sound travels at a different speed through water than through air. [2]

b Figure 3.2 shows the trace of a sound wave as it appears on an oscilloscope screen. On Figure 3.2 draw another trace of a sound wave from a sound that is louder than the one shown, but has the same pitch. [2]

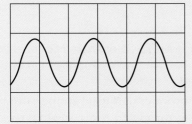

Figure 3.2

c Sound travels at 330 m/s in air. The loudspeaker produces a sound with a frequency of 200 Hz. Calculate the wavelength of this sound. State the formula that you use and show your working. [2]

(Cambridge IGCSE Co-ordinated Sciences 0654 Paper 32 Q3 a,b,c Nov 12)

4 a A resistor of 1200 Ω is connected in parallel with another resister of 2400 Ω. Calculate the combined resistance of these two resisters. State the formula that you use and show your working. [3]

b Torches (flashlights) are usually powered by electrical cells. They can also be powered by energy from the Sun (solar energy). Solar energy is a renewable energy resource.

   i Write the energy resources below into the table to show which are renewable and which are non-renewable. [1]

     coal   **geothermal**   **hydroelectric**
     natural gas   **oil**   **tidal**
     wave   **wind**

renewable resource	non-renewable resource

   ii Name the process that releases energy within the Sun. [1]

   iii Energy is transferred from the Sun to the Earth by radiation. Explain why energy cannot be transferred from the Sun to the Earth by conduction. [1]

c Figure 4.1 shows a torch that works without electrical cells. To use the torch it is first shaken for 40 seconds. This moves the magnet backwards and forwards inside the torch. The magnet can move between points **X** and **Y**. Explain why shaking the torch produces an electric current. [4]

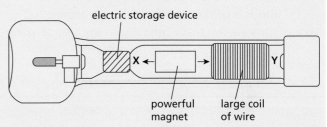

Figure 4.1

(Cambridge IGCSE Co-ordinated Sciences 0654 Paper 32 Q7 May 13)

5 a An elephant of mass 5000 kg exerts a constant force of 1400 N to push a tree trunk along at a steady speed of 1.5 m/s.

   i Calculate the work done by the elephant when the tree trunk moves 10 m. State the formula that you use and show your working. [2]

   ii Calculate the kinetic energy of the elephant when it is moving at 1.5 m/s. State the formula that you use and show your working. [2]

b The elephant has a weight of 50 000 N and stands with all four feet in contact with the ground. Each foot of the elephant has an area of 0.2 m². Calculate the pressure exerted by the elephant on the ground. State the formula that you use and show your working. [2]

c The volume of the elephant is 5 m³. Its mass is 5000 kg. Calculate the density of the elephant. State the formula that you use and show your working. [2]

(Cambridge IGCSE Co-ordinated Sciences 0654 Paper 32 Q2 May 13)

6 Figure 6.1 shows a solar-powered golf cart used to carry golfers around a golf course.

Figure 6.1

a As the cart moves around the course, the motion of the cart is measured. Figure 6.2 shows a distance/time graph for a small part of the journey lasting 60 minutes.

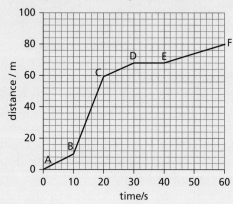

Figure 6.2

i Show that the speed of the cart between **B** and **C** is 5 m/s. Show your working. [1]

ii The mass of the cart is 400 kg. Calculate the kinetic energy of the cart between **B** and **C**. State the formula that you use, show your working and state the unit of your answer. [2]

iii Describe the motion of the cart between **D** and **E**. [1]

iv Later in the journey, the cart accelerates from 1 m/s to 3 m/s in 5 seconds. Calculate the acceleration of the cart. State the formula that you use, show your working and state the unit of your answer. [2]

b i During the cart's journey, the temperature of the air in the tyres increases by 15 °C. The volume of the air in the tyre remains the same. Explain in terms of particles why the **pressure** of the air in the tyre increases when this happens. [1]

ii Sometimes the golfer's hands begin to sweat. Explain in terms of particles how sweating cools his hands by evaporation. [2]

iii During the evaporation, water changes state from liquid to gas. Complete the diagrams to show the arrangement of particles in a liquid and in a gas. [2]

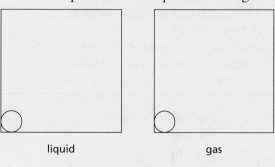

liquid   gas

(Cambridge IGCSE Co-ordinated Sciences 0654 Paper 33 Q9 Nov 13)

7 a Figure 7.1 shows a circuit used to measure the current passing through a resistor when the voltage across it is changed.

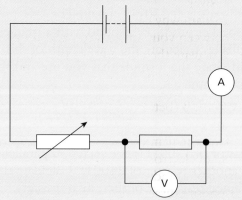

Figure 7.1

Complete the sentences below using suitable words.
When the voltage across the resistor is reduced, the current through the resistor

_____

When the voltage of the supply is reduced, the voltage across the resistor _____ [1]

b The resistance of a piece of wire depends on a number of variables such as the temperature of the wire and the material from which it is made. State **two other** factors which affect the resistance of a piece of wire. [2]

c Figure 7.2 shows a circuit used to power a small motor. The voltage across the motor is 3 V. The current through the motor is 0.6 A.

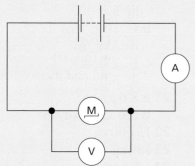

Figure 7.2

i Calculate the power input to the motor. State the formula that you use, show your working and state the unit of your answer. [2]

ii The motor is able to lift a load of 40 N through 1.2 m in 36 seconds. Calculate the power output of the motor. State the formula that you use, show your working and state the unit of your answer. [3]

iii Explain why there is a difference between your answers to **i** and **ii**. [1]

iv Calculate the efficiency of the motor. Show your working. [2]

d An electric current in a wire is a flow of electrons. β (beta)-radiation also consists of electrons.

i State the name of the sign of the charge on an electron. [1]

ii α (alpha)-radiation moves in the opposite direction to β-radiation in an electrical field. γ (gamma)-radiation passes through an electrical field without deviation. Explain these two statements. [2]

(Cambridge IGCSE Co-ordinated Sciences 0654 Paper 33 Q3 Nov 13)

8 a Two bar magnets **A** and **B** are shown in Figure 8.1. Magnet **A** is moved towards magnet **B**.

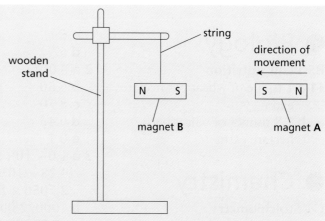

Figure 8.1

i Describe and explain what happens to magnet **B** as magnet **A** is moved towards it. [1]

ii Magnet **A** is replaced by a piece of unmagnetised iron **C**. Predict what happens as the unmagnetised iron **C** is moved towards **B**. Explain your prediction. [2]

b Figure 8.2 shows two plastic balls hanging from threads. Both balls are electrically charged. Ball **Y** is negatively charged.

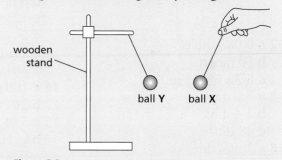

Figure 8.2

i State the charge on ball **X**. Give a reason for your answer. [1]

ii Describe and explain how ball **Y** has been given a negative charge. [2]

iii There is an electric field between ball **X** and ball **Y**. State what happens to an electrical charge placed in this field. [1]

c The mass of ball **X** is 3.97 g (3.97 × 10⁻³ kg). The volume of ball **X** is 4.17 cm³ (4.17 × 10⁻⁶ m³). Calculate the density of the plastic used to make ball **X**. State the formula that you use and show your working. State the units of your answer. [3]

(Cambridge IGCSE Co-ordinated Sciences 0654 Paper 33 Q5 May 14)

Answers to numerical questions

● Biology

B5 Plant nutrition

11 a 1 tonne of wheat per hectare extra

  b 1.8 tonnes of wheat per hectare extra

● Chemistry

C4 Stoichiometry

 6 4.4 g

 7 128×10^6 g or 128 tonnes

 8 a 0.1 moles

  b 0.167 moles

  c 2 moles

 9 a 3.2 g

  b 160 g

  c 5.75 g

10 a 0.1 moles

  b 1 mole

  c 10 moles

11 a 162 g

  b 8.5 g

  c 55.825 g

12 a 0.083 moles

  b 10 moles

  c 8.33×10^{-4} moles

13 a 7.2 dm³

  b 2.4 dm³

  c 48 dm³

14 a 2 mol dm⁻³

  b 0.2 mol dm⁻³

15 a 7.975 g

  b 40.4 g

16 0.309 g

C7 Chemical reactions

 2 c 26 cm³ (± 0.5 cm³)

  d 1 minute and 51 seconds (± 3 seconds)

 5 f 46 cm³

  g 43 seconds (± 1 second)

● Physics

P1 Motion

 1 a 10

  b 40

 c 5

 d 67

 2 a 3.00

  b 5.50

  c 8.70

  d 0.43

  e 0.1

 3 a 1.0×10^5; 3.5×10^3; 4.28×10^8; 5.04×10^2; 2.7056×10^4

  b 1000; 2 000 000; 69 200; 134; 1 000 000 000

 4 10 mm

 5 24 cm²

 6 80

 7 a 2.31 mm

  b 14.97 mm

 8 2 m/s²

 9 50 s

10 a 6 m/s

  b 14 m/s

11 4 s

13 a 60 km

  b 5 hours

  c 12 km/h

  d 2

  e 1½ hours

  f 60 km/3½ h = 17 km/h

14 a 100 m

  b 20 m/s

15 a 5/4 m/s²

  b i 10 m

   ii 45 m

16 b OA: a = +80 km/h²
   AB: v = 80 km/h
   BC: a = +40 km/h²
   CD: v = 100 km/h
   DE: a = –200 km/h²

  c OA 40 km; AB 160 km; BC (5 + 40) = 45 km; CD 100 km; DE 25 km

  d 370 km

  e 74 km/h

17 b 600 m

  c 20 m/s

18 a 1 N

  b 50 N

  c 0.50 N

19 a 1000 N

  b 160 N

20 a i 0.5 g

   ii 1 g

   iii 5 g

  b i 10 g/cm³

   ii 3 kg/m³

  c i 2.0 cm³

   ii 5.0 cm³

21 a 8.0 g/cm³

  b 8.0×10^3 kg/m³

22 15 000 kg

23 130 kg

24 1.1 g/cm³

25 a 2000 N/m

  b 50 N/m

27 40 N

28 50 N

29 a 5000 N

  b 15 m/s²

30 a 5000 N

  b 20 000 N; 40 m/s²

35 a 2 J

  b 160 J

  c 100 000 = 10^5 J

36 a 20 m/s

  b i 150 J

   ii 300 J

38 a i 25 Pa

   ii 0.50 Pa

   iii 100 Pa

  b 30 N

P2 Work, energy and power

 1 180 J

 2 1.5×10^5 J

 3 a 150 J

  b 150 J

  c 10 W

 7 a (300/1000) × 100 = 30%

 8 a 2 J

  b 160 J

  c 100 000 = 10^5 J

 9 a 20 m/s

  b i 150 J

   ii 300 J

10 500 W

11 3.5 kW

12 a 2%

P4 Properties of waves
  1 a 1 cm
     b 1 hz
     c 1 cm/s
  5 a 40°
     c 40°, 50°, 50°
  9 4 m towards mirror
  13 250 000 km/s
  20 Distance from lens
     a beyond 2F
     b 2F
     c between F and 2F
     d nearer than F
  21 A: converging f = 10 cm
      B: converging f = 5 cm
  23 1650 m (about 1 mile)
  24 a 2 × 160 = 320 m/s
      b 240/(3/4) = 320 m/s
      c 320 m
  26 b i 1.0 m
        ii 2.0 m

P5 Electrical quantities, electricity and magnetism
  6 a 5 C
     b 50 C
     c 1500 C
  7 a 5 A
     b 0.5 A
     c 2 A
  8 a 12 J
     b 60 J
     c 240 J

P6 Electric circuits
  4 All read 0.25 A
  5 a 6 V
     b i 2 J
       ii 6 J
  6 a 6 V
     b 360 J
  7 x = 18, y = 2, z = 8
  8 2 Ω

  9 a 15 Ω
     b 1.5 Ω
  13 a 100 J
      b 500 J
      c 6000 J
  14 a 24 W
      b 31 J/s
  16 2.99 kW
  17 a i 2 kW
        ii 60 W
        iii 850 W
      b 4 A

P7 Electromagnetic effects
  10 a 24
      b 1.9 A

P8 Atomic physics
  4 25 minutes

Acknowledgements

The Publishers would like to thank the following for permission to reproduce copyright material. Every effort has been made to trace all copyright holders, but if any have been inadvertently overlooked the Publishers will be pleased to make the necessary arrangements at the first opportunity.
p.1 © Biophoto Associates/Science Photo Library; **p.2** © David McGill/Alamy Stock Photo; **p.3** © Moshbidon/Shutterstock.com; **p.4** © Foto Factory/Alamy Stock Photo; **p.6** © Biophoto Associates/Science Photo Library; **p.8** ©Last Refuge/Robert Harding Picture Library Ltd/Alamy Stock Photo; **p.9** *both* © Biophoto Associates/Science Photo Library; **p.17** © Nigel Cattlin/Alamy; **p.19** © inga spence/Alamy; **p.20** *tl* © London News Pictures/Rex Features, *tr* © Mark Extance/REX, *br* © Science Photo Library/Alamy; **p.21** © Gonzalo Arroyo Moreno/Getty Images; **p.22** *tr* © D.G. Mackean, *b both* © J.C. Revy, ISM/Science Photo Library; **p.41** © Natural Visions/Alamy; **p.46** *t* © Sidney Moulds/Science Photo Library, *b* © Dr Geoff Holroyd/Lancaster University; **p.49** © Gene Cox; **p.50** © Dilston Physic Garden/Colin Cuthbert/Science Photo Library; **p.56** © Mediscan/Alamy Stock Photo; **p.60** © Jeff Rotman/Alamy; **p.61** © Okea – Fotolia; **p.69** © David Scharf/Science Photo Library; **p.76** *both* © Biophoto Associates/Science Photo Library; **p.77** *l* © Biophoto Associates/Science Photo Library, *r* © D.G. Mackean; **p.79** © Rolf Langohr – Fotolia; **p.82** © imageBROKER/Alamy; **p.85** © Biophoto Associates/Science Photo Library; **p.88** © Biophoto Associates/Science Photo Library; **p.91** © Andrew Syred/Science Photo Library; **p.95** © Biophoto Associates/Science Photo Library; **p.99** © Philip Harris Education/www.findel-education.co.uk; **p.100** © Steve Gschmeissner/Science Photo Library/SuperStock; **p.105** © Jason Oxenham/Getty Images; **p.114** *t* © Biophoto Associates/Science Photo Library, *b* © milphoto – Fotolia; **p.116** © D.G. Mackean; **p.117** © D.G. Mackean; **p.119** © D.G. Mackean; **p.123** © adrian davies/Alamy Stock Photo; **p.125** © Science Pictures Limited/Science Photo Library; **p.128** © D.G. Mackean; **p.129** *l* © Ami Images/Science Photo Library, *r* © Power And Syred/Science Photo Library; **p.130** © blickwinkel/Alamy; **p.136** © London Fertility Centre; **p.142** © SMC Images/Oxford Scientific/Getty Images; **p.144** © Manfred Kage/Science Photo Library; **p.148** © Philip Harris Education/www.findel-education.co.uk; **p.151** With permission from East Malling Research; **p.154** © Biophoto Associates/Science Photo Library; **p.155** *l* © Bill Coster IN/Alamy, *r* © Michael W. Tweedie/Science Photo Library; **p.156** © Valery Shanin – Fotolia; **p.157** © outdoorsman – Fotolia, *r* © Wolfgang Kruck – Fotolia, *bl* © Kim Taylor/Warren Photographic; **p.160** *l* © Karandaev – Fotolia, *r* © Joachim Opelka – Fotolia; **p.161** © Sir Ralph Riley; **p.165** *l* © D.P. Wilson/Flpa/Minden Pictures/Getty Images, *r* © Wim van Egmond/Visuals Unlimited, Inc./Science Photo Library; **p.166** *both* © Colin Green; **p.171** © buFka – Fotolia; **p.172** *l* © Biophoto Associates/Science Photo Library, *r* © Simon Fraser/Science Photo Library; **p.174** *l* © J Svedberg/Ardea.com, *r* © Photoshot Holdings Ltd/Alamy; **p.175** *t* © Roy Pedersen – Fotolia, *b* © Mike Goldwater/Alamy; **p.177** © National Motor Museum/Motoring Picture Library/Alamy Stock Photo; **p.178** *tr* © Keith Pritchard/ARGO Images/Alamy Stock Photo, *l* © Helo-Pilote – Fotolia, *br* © Adam Booth – Fotolia; **p.179** *l* © Donald L Fackler Jr/Alamy, *c* © Andrew Lambert Photography/Science Photo Library, *r* © Geoscience Features Picture Library/Dr.B.Booth; **p.182** *all* © Andrew Lambert Photography/Science Photo Library; **p.183** *l* © Andrew Lambert Photography/Science Photo Library, *r* © Mary Evans Picture Library; **p.184** © Andrew Lambert Photography/Science Photo Library; **p.185** *t* © burnel11 – Fotolia, *b* © Martyn F Chillmaid; **p.186** *both* © Martyn F Chillmaid; **p.187** *l* © Science Photo Library/Geoff Tompkinson, *tr* © Niall McDiarmid/Alamy, *br* © Galyna Andrushko – Fotolia; **p.188** © Andrew Lambert Photography/Science Photo Library; **p.189** *l* © Andrew Lambert Photography/Science Photo Library, *r* © Ricardo Funari/Brazilphotos/Alamy; **p.190** *l* © Andrew Lambert Photography/Science Photo Library, *r* © Sipa Press/Rex Features; **p.191** © Science Photo Library; **p.193** *l* © Andrew Lambert Photography/Science Photo Library, *r* © Amelia Fox/Shutterstock.com; **p.194** *l* © Robert Harding/Getty Images, *tr* © FlemishDreams – Fotolia, *br* © Mihaela Bof – Fotolia; **p.195** *r* © BL Images Ltd/Alamy, *tl* © BAY ISMOYO/AFP/Getty Images, *bl* © Christie's Images/The Bridgeman Art Library; **p.196** *l* © Andrew Lambert Photography/Science Photo Library, *b* © Andrew Lambert Photography/Science Photo Library; **p.197** *l* © Deyan Georgiev/Shutterstock.com, *tr* © Andrew Lambert Photography/Science Photo Library, *c* © Dmitriy Sladkov/123RF, *r* © Sonny Meddle/Shutterstock/Rex Features; **p.198** © Digital Instruments/Veeco/Science Photo Library; **p.200** © Henry Westheim Photography/Alamy; **p.203** *tl and r* © Andrew Lambert Photography/Science Photo Library, *c* © midosemsem – Fotolia; **p.207** © Andrew Lambert Photography/ Science Photo Library; **pp.208-11** © Andrew Lambert Photography/ Science Photo Library; **p.212** © Science Photo Library/Getty image; **p.213** *tl* © Science Photo Library/Ricjard Megna/Fundamental, *bl* © Michael Pettigrew – Fotolia, *tr* © Science Photo Library/Sheila Terry, *br* © Science Photo Library/Manfred Kage; **p.214** *l* © Science Photo Library/Philippe Plailly, *r* © Robert Harding Photo Library; **p.215** © Science Photo Library/E R Degginger; **p.218** *t* © Martyn F. Chillmaid/Science Photo Library, *l* © molekuul_be/Shutterstock.com, *r* © lculig/123RF; **p.222** © Science Photo Library/Rosenfeld Images Ltd; **p.223** *both* © Andrew Lambert Photography / Science Photo Library; **p.224** © Andrew Lambert Photography/ Science Photo Library; **p.227** © Dirk Wiersma/Science Photo Library; **p.231** *tl* © Alexander Maksimenko – Fotolia, *bl* © Last Resort Picture Library/Dick Makin, *r* © Robert Harding Photo Library; **p.233** © Howard Davies/Getty Images; **p.234** © Brent Lewin/Bloomberg via Getty Images; **p.235** © Trevor Clifford Photography/Science Photo Library; **p.236** *tl* © Jimmy Yan/Shutterstock.com, *bl* © Nigel Cattlin/Alamy Stock Photo, *r* © Ted Foxx/Alamy Stock Photo; **p.239** *t* © Andrew Lambert Photography/Science Photo Library, *b* © Clynt Garnham Renewable Energy/Alamy; **p.241** © Science Photo Library/Adam Hart Davis; **p.247** *tl* © OutdoorPhotos – Fotolia, *bl* © Virginia Sherwood/Bravo/NBCU Photo Bank via Getty Images, *tr* © Arnaud SantiniI – Fotolia, *br* © National Motor Museum/Motoring Picture Library/Alamy Stock Photo; **p.248** *all* © Andrew Lambert Photography/Science Photo Library; **p.250** *all* © Andrew Lambert Photography/Science Photo Library; **p.253** © Martyn F. Chillmaid; **p.256** *tl* © Last Resort Picture Library/Dick Makin 07-01-1, *bl* © Last Resort Picture Library/Dick Makin 07-02, *r* © Andrew Lambert Photography/Science Photo Library; **pp.257-264** *all* © Andrew Lambert Photography/Science Photo Library; **p.267** © Science Photo Library; **p.269** *tl* © Windsor – Fotolia, *ctl* © jon11 – Fotolia, *cbl* © Debby Moxon, *bl* © Mihaela Bof – Fotolia, *r* © Maurice Tsai/Bloomberg via Getty Images; **p.270** © Andrew Lambert Photography/Science Photo Library; **p.271** *all* © Andrew Lambert Photography/Science Photo Library; **p.272** © Martyn F Chillmaid; **p.273** *tl* © Last Resort Picture Library/Dick Makin, *bl* © Helene Rogers/Art Directors & TRIP/Alamy Stock Photo, *tr* © Koichi Kamoshida/Getty Images, *cr* © Last Resort Picture Library/Dick Makin, *br* © Last Resort Picture Library/Dick Makin; **p274** *t* © Science Photo Library, *b* © Science Photo Library; **p.277** *l* © Andrew Lambert Photography/Science Photo Library, *tr* © Digital Vision/Getty Images, *br* © Robert Harding Picture Library Ltd/Alamy; **p.279** © Andrew Lambert Photography/Science Photo Library; **p.280** *t* © govicinity – Fotalia.com, *c* © Owen Franken/Getty Images, *b* © Antony Nettle/Alamy; **p.281** © Andrew Lambert Photography/Science Photo Library; **p.282** © Andrew Lambert Photography/Science Photo Library; **p.283** *t* © GeoScience Features Picture Library, *c* © GeoScience Features Picture Library, *b* © GeoScience Features Picture Library; **p.284** © Tata Steel; **p.285** © Brent Lewin/Bloomberg via Getty Images; **p.286** *l* © Science Photo Library/Martin Bond, *r* © The Travel Library/Rex Features; **p.287** *tl* © Science Photo Library/Hank Morgan, *bl* © Digital Vision/Getty Images, *r* © Rex Features; **p.288** © Science Photo Library/Maximillian Stock Ltd; **p.289** *t* © Robert Harding Photo Library, *b* © Science Photo Library/Manfred Kage; **p.290** © dpa picture alliance archive/Alamy; **p.293** *tl* © Patricia Elfreth – Fotolia, *bl* © BSIP SA/Alamy, *tr* © Can Balcioglu – Fotolia, *br* © Galina Barskaya – Fotolia; **p.294** *tl* © sciencephotos/Alamy, *bl* © Andrew Lambert Photography/Science Photo Library, *r* © AoshiVN/iStock/Thinkstock; **p.296** © Photodisc/Getty Images; **p.297** *tl* © Anticiclo/Shutterstock.com, *bl* © Heracles Kritikos/Shutterstock.com, *r* © Falko Matte – Fotolia; **p.298** *t* © Astrid & Hanns-Frieder Michler/Science Photo Library, *b* © VisualHongKong/Alamy; **p.299** *t* ©Helene Rogers Art/Directors & TRIP/Alamy Stock Photo, *c* ©Visual China Group/Getty Images, *b* © Last Resort Picture Library/Dick Makin; **p.300** *t* © Last Resort Picture Library/Dick Makin, *c* © g215 – Fotolia, *b* © Gravicapa – Fotolia, *tr* © steven gillis hd9 imaging/Alamy, *b* © Leslie Garland Picture Library/Alamy; **p.304** © SSPL/Getty Images, **p.305** Photograph of Henri Le Chatelier (French scientist, 1850–1936); **p.306** © Andrew Lambert Photography/Science Photo Library; **p.307** © Dudarev Mikhail – Fotolia; **p.309** *t* © GeoScience Features Picture Library, *b* © Andrew Lambert Photography/Science Photo Library; **p.310** *tl* © whiteboxmedia limited/Alamy, *bl* © Andrew Lambert Photography/Science Photo Library, *r* © ICI Chemicals & Polymers; **p.312** *l* © Ronald Evans/Alamy, *tr* © Africa Studio – Fotolia, *br* © Science Photo Library/Martin Land; **p.313** © yang yu - Fotolia.com; **p.314** © romaneau – Fotolia; **p.317** *l* © Centaur – Fotolia, *tr* © Dinodia Photos/Alamy, *br* © Oleg Zhukov – Fotolia, *cr* © Matt K –

Fotolia; **p.318** *tl* © Dmitry Sitin – Fotolia, *cl* © iofoto – Fotolia, *bl* © yang yu – Fotolia, *tr* © Andrew Lambert Photography/Science Photo Library, *br* © Science Photo Library; **p.319** © Science Photo Library/Stevie Grand; **p.320** *tl* © GeoScience Features Picture Library, *bl* © Dadang Tri/Bloomberg via Getty Images, *r* © Science Photo Library/Richard Folwell; **p.321** *both* © Andrew Lambert Photography/Science Photo Library; **p.322** *tl* © Andrew Lambert Photography/Science Photo Library, *bl* © Andrew Lambert Photography/Science Photo Library, *tr* © nikkytok – Fotolia, *br* © Keith Morris/age fotostock/SuperStock; **p.323-324** © Andrew Lambert Photography/Science Photo Library; **p.325** *l* © Andrew Lambert Photography / Science Photo Library, *r* © Martyn F Chillmaid. Thanks to Molymod.com for providing the model; **p.326** *l* © Ian Dagnall/Alamy, *r* © Andrew Lambert Photography/Science Photo Library; **p.327** *t* © Andrew Lambert Photography/Science Photo Library, *b* © Josie Elias/Alamy; **p.328** *tl* © Josie Elias/Alamy, *cl* © Martyn f. Chillmaid. Thanks to Molymod.com for providing the model, *bl* © Steve Cukrov – Fotolia, *r* © Andrew Lambert Photography/Science Photo Library; **p.329** © Andrew Lambert Photography/Science Photo Library; **p.330** © Leonid Shcheglov – Fotolia; **p.332** © Richard Cummins/Getty Images; **p.334** © Chris Ratcliffe/Bloomberg via Getty Images; **p.337** © nirutft – Fotolia; **p.338** © Images-USA/Alamy; **p.341** © Images&Stories/Alamy; **p.343** © David J. Green - studio/Alamy; **p.348** © Arnulf Husmo/Getty Images; **p.349** Photo of Arbortech Airboard © Arbortech Pty Ltd; **p.355** © Kerstgens/SIPA Press/Rex Features; **p.356** *tl* © BBSRC/Silsoe Research Institute, *bl* © BBSRC/Silsoe Research Institute, *r* © Dennis van de Water/Shutterstock.com; **p.360** © Ray Fairall/Photoreporters/Rex Features; **p.362** *t-b* © Richard Cummins/ Getty Images, © GDC Group Ltd, © Alt-6/Alamy, © Scottish & Southern energy plc; **p.364** © Charles Ommanney/Rex Features; **p.366** *t* © Alex Bartel/Science Photo Library, *b* © Courtney Black - The Aurora Solar Car Team; **p.367** © Hemis/Alamy; **p.368** *t* © Mark Edwards/Still Pictures/ Robert Harding, *b* © Mark Edwards/Still Pictures/Robert Harding; **p.372** © Dr Linda Stannard, UCT/Science Photo Library; **p.377** *l* © The Linde Group, *r* © Chris Mattison/Alamy; **p.380** © Pete Mouginis-Mark; **p.382** *t* © Zoonar RF/Thinkstock, *b* © Glenn Bo/IStockphoto/Thinkstock; **p.383** *l* © Fogstock LLC/SuperStock, *tr* © sciencephotos/Alamy, *br* © sciencephotos/Alamy; **p.385** *l* © Don B. Stevenson/Alamy, *r* © Sandor Jackal - Fotolia.com; **p.386** © James R. Sheppard; **p.391** © Andrew Lambert/Science Photo Library; **p.392** *l* © Andrew Lambert /Science Photo Library, *r* © HR Wallingford Ltd; **p.394** © Colin Underhill/Alamy; **p.397** *t* © vario images GmbH & Co.KG/Alamy, *b* © CNRI/Science Photo Library; **p.398** © S.T. Yiap Selection/Alamy; **p.403** *l* © US Geological Survey/Science Photo Library, *r* © Mohamad Zaid/Rex Features; **p.404** *l* © Image Source White/Image Source/Thinkstock, *r* © Jonathan Watts/Science Photo Library; **p.410** Andrew Lambert/Science Photo Library; **p.412** Alex Bartel/ Science Photo Library; **p.413** © Keith Kent/Science Photo Library; **p.417** © Andrew Lambert/Science Photo Library; **p.419 and 428** Courtesy and © RS Components Ltd; **p.437** © Elu Power Tools; **p.450** © Martin Bond/Science Photo Library; **p.451** © University Museum of Cultural Heritage – University of Oslo, Norway (photo Eirik Irgens Johnsen); **p.462** © Andrew Lambert Photography/Science Photo Library **p.467** © John Boud/Alamy Stock Photo; **p.462** © Andrew Lambert Photography/Science Photo Library; p.463 © Chamaiporn Naprom/Shutterstock; **p.467** © John Boud/Alamy Stock Photo; **p.471** © D.G. Mackean; **p.485** © Jubal Harshaw/Shutterstock.com; **p.495** © D.G. Mackean; **p.496** © Richard Griffin/Shutterstock; **p.498** © Carolina Biological Supply Co, Visuals Unlimited/Science Photo Library

t = top, *b* = bottom, *l* = left, *r* = right, *c* = centre

Index